The United States
at War

A Da Capo Press Reprint Series

FRANKLIN D. ROOSEVELT
AND THE ERA OF THE NEW DEAL

GENERAL EDITOR: FRANK FREIDEL

Harvard University

UNITED STATES BUREAU OF THE BUDGET

COMMITTEE ON RECORDS OF WAR ADMINISTRATION
WAR RECORDS SECTION

The United States
at War

DEVELOPMENT AND ADMINISTRATION OF
THE WAR PROGRAM
BY THE FEDERAL GOVERNMENT

DA CAPO PRESS • NEW YORK • 1972

Library of Congress Cataloging in Publication Data

U.S. Bureau of the Budget.
 The United States at war.

 (Franklin D. Roosevelt and the era of the New Deal)
 At head of title: United States Bureau of the Budget, Committee on Records of War Administration, War Records Section.
 Reprint of the 1946 ed., originally published as no. 1 in the Bureau of the Budget series, Historical reports on war administration.
 1. World War, 1939-1945 — U.S. 2. U.S. — Defenses. 3. U.S. — Politics and government — 1933-1945.
 I. Title. II. Series. III. Series: United States. United States Government historical reports on war administration no. 1.
 D769.A55   1972   940.5373   79-169909
 ISBN 0-306-70330-0

940.5373
U 581 u

M

This Da Capo Press edition of *The United States at War* is an unabridged republication of the first edition published in Washington, D. C., in 1946 as No. 1 in the Bureau of the Budget series, *Historical Reports on War Administration*

Published by Da Capo Press, Inc.
A Subsidiary of Plenum Publishing Corporation
227 West 17th Street, New York, New York 10011

The United States
at War

DEVELOPMENT AND ADMINISTRATION OF
THE WAR PROGRAM
BY THE FEDERAL GOVERNMENT

PREPARED UNDER THE AUSPICES OF THE COMMITTEE

OF RECORDS OF WAR ADMINISTRATION

BY THE

WAR RECORDS SECTION

Bureau of the Budget

HISTORICAL REPORTS ON WAR ADMINISTRATION

BUREAU OF THE BUDGET

No. 1

Foreword

One of the things that make a democracy work is critical appraisal of the objectives of the Government and the methods used. During my years in the public service I have been impressed many times by the value of objective and intelligent criticism in improving governmental administration.

Within a short period of time, the war brought a wealth of experiences in government, experiences which, in variety and importance could be matched only by decades of peacetime conditions. Clearly these experiences should be recorded and appraised and the lessons from them be made, as quickly as possible, a part of our general knowledge of government.

In this volume a small group of trained professional men, working under the guidance of scholars of high professional repute, have attempted to supply an objective report of what this Government sought to do during the war, how it went about the task, and what success it achieved.

This study will, I am sure, serve to increase public knowledge of our wartime problems. It should also make all of us more conscious of the usefulness of continued, careful, and intelligent appraisal. I hope it will be read widely and thoughtfully.

HARRY S. TRUMAN

III

Letter to the President of the United States from the Director of the Bureau of the Budget

JUNE 19, 1946.

My DEAR MR. PRESIDENT: I am sending you herewith a volume entitled "The United States at War." It has been submitted to me by the Committee on Records of War Administration. This study, along with accounts being prepared by many of the executive agencies' and establishments, has grown out of the suggestion made by President Roosevelt in March 1942, that I appoint a committee to help in the task of "preserving for those who come after us an accurate and objective account of our present experience."

This account has been prepared, for the Committee and under its guidance, by the War Records Section of the Bureau of the Budget. It is an account of the Federal Government's role in the mobilization of the nation for World War II that pays particular attention to major problems of administration and their solution. It impresses me, as it impressed the Committee, as an objective and useful treatment of many important parts of our war experience.

Fortunately, this war will leave behind it much more systematic reports on its administration than did World War I. Most of the executive agencies have prepared or are preparing final accounts that are designed to tell what problems they faced and how they handled them. The purpose of these documents is to tell the story of the war impartially and analytically; the total product should be a valuable contribution.

In my opinion, this volume will add substantially to public understanding of the war effort, but it will do more than this. It will help to show the magnitude and the complexity of the problems that Government faces and how Government in a great democracy can deal with major problems within the framework of the democratic traditions that we cherish. Finally, its analysis of the way in which we rose administratively to meet crisis after crisis may hold some useful lessons for those of us, within and without Government, who are striving for better public administration in peace as well as in war.

Sincerely yours

HAROLD D. SMITH
Director.

The PRESIDENT,
The White House

IV

Letter to the Director of the Bureau of the Budget from the Chairman of the Committee on Records of War Administration

JUNE 17, 1946.

MY DEAR MR. SMITH: On behalf of the Committee on Records of War Administration, I am transmitting to you an account of how our Government mobilized the Nation's human and material resources for the winning of the war.

The war posed the most stupendous set of problems in the management of public activities that the country has ever faced. We fought that war on a greater scale than anyone could have dreamed: the Government regulated production, censored mail, drafted men, controlled prices, rationed food and commodities; we had to move, rapidly and purposefully, in spite of manifold differences of interests and opinions. We had to conquer the world's most powerful dictatorships—and urgency required us to do many seemingly dictatorial things in the process—yet we had to do this within the framework of those processes and principles of democracy on which our Nation has been built.

This is a study of how the job was done, with emphasis on the civilian rather than the military aspects of the effort. It deals with the growth of war production and certain allied problems such as stabilization, transportation, manpower, and food. Certain other fields, important but a little farther from the main theme, have been left for others to report on; these fields include civilian defense, field operations of the various agencies, special administrative problems like personnel and budgeting, much of the rationing program, and the notable contribution of volunteer war workers. The principal emphasis is upon the period when the Nation's machinery for war was being put into operation; and less attention is given to the preceding period that led up to war and the later period of high level but relatively stable production.

This study tries to throw light on how the Government's complex and difficult administrative problems were tackled. The story of all of the substantive things that were done will require many volumes by other students. Details about many of the subjects that this account touches upon will have to be filled in; many of them will be covered in the reports that other Government agencies are preparing. One major goal throughout has been to make the report objective; to carry the analysis only as far as the available facts justify; and to show our difficulties, our growing pains, and our mistakes along with our successes.

The volume was prepared, under the guidance of the Committee on Records of War Administration, by the War Records Section of the

Bureau of the Budget.   Although each chapter was drafted initially by one man who turned his specialized attention to the subject over a considerable period of time, the project has been from the beginning a joint effort that has embodied the collective thinking of the Committee and the staff.

The Committee feels that this volume is a useful contribution to the task of capturing, recording, and analyzing the Nation's experience in the administration of its war effort.   We are obviously too close to the war to evaluate what has happened.   We hope, however, that we have presented enough of the story so that the basis for later evaluation is in the book.   We hope finally that this material will be a contribution to general public knowledge and to the literature of public administration.

Sincerely,

PENDLETON HERRING
Chairman, Committee on
Records of War Administration.

Hon. HAROLD D. SMITH,
Director, Bureau of the Budget,
Washington, D. C.

Preface

By the Committee on Records of War Administration

In March 1942 the Director of the Bureau of the Budget, at the suggestion of the President, appointed a Committee on Records of War Administration to provide guidance and support in the assembly and analysis of material on the administration of the Nation's war effort. This Committee was asked to advise with staff members of the Bureau of the Budget assigned to this field and to encourage the various Government agencies to prepare accounts of their own administrative experiences.

There were several reasons for recognizing, at an early date and in the midst of other preoccupations, the importance of capturing and recording the story of our administrative response to the crisis of war. The contemporary reporting on World War I was neither systematic nor analytical. Later attempts to find adequate analyses of our methods of meeting problems in World War I were largely futile. At the outset of World War II, people with foresight realized that a relatively small investment of effort would avoid a repetition of this neglect and would provide a store of information that might be of incalculable value in any future period of national emergency. Such observers also foresaw that the war period would concentrate into a short span of years a lifetime of administrative experimentation and experience just as it had in medicine, and science. They saw the importance of recording these things, whether they proved to be valuable administrative inventions or merely instructive essays in trial and error, for whatever purpose they might serve in improving quality of peacetime administration.

President Roosevelt showed his interest in the problem and took the step that led to the creation of the Committee in his letter to the Director of the Bureau of the Budget on March 4, 1942:

> MY DEAR MR. SMITH: I am very much interested in the steps that you have been taking to keep a current record of war administration. I suggest that you carry this program further by covering the field more intensively, drawing on whatever scholarly talent may be necessary.
>
> I wonder if it wouldn't be desirable to appoint a committee on records of war administration, to be composed of representatives

of appropriate learned societies and perhaps two or three agencies of the Government which might be interested in such a program.

The present program strengthened in this manner might be helpful to the work of the Bureau of the Budget in planning current improvements in administration in addition. to its main objective of preserving for those who come after us an accurate and objective account of our present experience. I hope that officials in war agencies will bear in mind the importance of systematic records, and to the extent commensurate with their heavy duties, cooperate in this undertaking.

Very truly yours,

Hon. HAROLD D. SMITH,
Director, Bureau of the Budget.

The Committee originally consisted of seven leaders in those areas of social sciences most directly related to the problem of recording our wartime administrative experiences. These seven members were:

Waldo Leland, director, American Council of Learned Societies, chairman of the Committee

William Anderson, chairman, Committee on Public Administration, Social Science Research Council

Louis Brownlow, director, Public Administration Clearing House

Solon J. Buck, Archivist of the United States

Archibald MacLeish, Librarian of Congress

Arthur Schlesinger, professor of history, Harvard University

Donald Young, research secretary, Social Science Research Council

Pendleton Herring, Bureau of the Budget, executive secretary of the Committee

In the 4 years of its existence, the Committee increased in numbers and certain changes were made as some of the members had to withdraw because of the pressure of other commitments and the following were appointed members of the Committee:

Luther H. Evans, Librarian of Congress

Guy Stanton Ford, secretary, American Historical Association and Editor of American Historical Review

George A. Graham, professor of politics, Princeton University

Luther Gulick, president, American Society for Public Administration

Harold W. Stoke, president, University of New Hampshire.

Leonard D. White, professor of political science, University of Chicago

Patterson H. French, Bureau of the Budget, executive secretary of the Committee

Of the original membership, Messrs. Leland, Buck, Schlesinger, and Young continued to serve. In 1945 Dr. Herring succeeded Dr. Leland as Chairman.

Even before the creation of the Committee, a small staff of the Administrative Management Division of the Bureau of the Budget had begun to do two things: to stimulate the Federal agencies in the maintenance of adequate records of war administration; and to carry on independent studies of the war program on a Government-wide basis. After the Committee's appointment, this staff was organized as the War Records Section of the Division of Administrative Management and has continued its work to the present time.

On January 25, 1944, President Roosevelt expressed his continuing interest in this project in a letter to the Director of the Bureau of the Budget.

MY DEAR MR. SMITH: I'm glad to have your memorandum telling of the progress being made in recording the administrative story of this war. We need both for current use and for future reference a full and objective account of the way the Federal Government is carrying out its wartime duties. The Committee on Records of War Administration is doing a useful job and I am much pleased to know that 30 of our Federal agencies are actively cooperating in their program.

I am personally very much interested in this study of administration and I hope that each department and agency head will see to it that the story of his agency in wartime is systematically developed. The best way to advance our knowledge of administration is through the study of actual experience. Those agencies which have not yet established units to deal with the recording of their administrative experience should do so.

It is a well established practice for officials to make a public accounting of their stewardship. Soon after the war each agency should have ready a good final report that will sum up both what was accomplished and how the job was done. If organizational changes make this impossible the Bureau of the Budget should see that the report is completed. We should also remember that full records must be preserved for deposit with the National Archives.

There is much to be gained from our wartime experience for improving administration in the future. I feel sure that a careful recording of this experience not only will help to win the war but also will serve the needs of the postwar era.

Very truly yours,

Franklin D Roosevelt

Hon. HAROLD D. SMITH,
Director, Bureau of the Budget.

President Truman also expressed his interest in this matter of analyzing and reporting on wartime experiences in a letter to the Director of the Bureau of the Budget on July 6, 1945. The President said:

MY DEAR MR. SMITH: I am pleased to learn of the efforts which the agencies and departments are making to record the administrative history of this war and I wish that you would express to the members of the Advisory Committee on Records of War Administration my appreciation of their continued interest and assistance.

The heads of the departments and agencies should have the program brought as nearly as practicable to a current basis during 1945. I would like to see completed soon after the war is over an objective account of how problems of administration were handled. Both failures and successes should be analyzed. The development of governmental administration can be greatly aided by such investigations.

This information will probably be most useful within the government, but a final report to the American people of wartime administration also seems highly appropriate. I hope that you will give particular attention to the ways in which our administrative experience during World War II can be turned to practical use in the future. Experience is a stern teacher; we must not forget the lessons so dearly bought.

Very truly yours,

Harry Truman

Hon. HAROLD D. SMITH,
Director, Bureau of the Budget.

Cooperation between the Bureau of the Budget and the executive agencies has resulted in the development of historical activities in some 40 agencies. A number of agencies hope to publish general histories of their operations in one or more volumes. Many agencies will publish either in addition to a general volume or instead of this kind of treatment, special studies covering subjects or problems of particular importance. These accounts, which are already beginning to appear and which will be available in increasing numbers over the next year or two, will form a permanent and instructive legacy for those who want to translate our wartime experience into a body of useful data for postwar administration.

The other interest of the Committee and the War Records Section has been in the broad analysis of wartime administration as a whole. The Committee believed that the preparation of a general study in this field could provide a broad and reliable perspective on our entire war administration and background for the more specialized studies being prepared by other Government agencies.

This volume is the result of this interest on the part of the Committee and the support given by the Bureau. The Committee has provided general stimulus and has concerned itself particularly to the end that the study be of a professional and objective nature. Important contributions to the planning of the study and in the supervision of its preparation were made by George A. Graham and Patterson H. French, who were successively in charge of the work of the War Records Section during the time the study was under way. Phillips D. Carleton assisted in the final editing.

The primary responsibility for research, interpretation and the actual writing of the text has rested on the staff members of the War Records Section. As Dr. Herring's letter points out, the volume is the product of a staff working in close collaboration and enjoying the benefits of the suggestions and criticism of numerous qualified individuals not only among their associates within the Bureau but also in other Government agencies. The book, however, is basically the work of the authors who prepared the various chapters:

Ethan P. Allen	Elias Huzar
Clarence H. Danhof	V. O. Key, Jr.
Harold F. Gosnell	Donald H. Morrison
Luther Gulick	Lloyd G Reynolds

In their work on this book these men have participated in an experiment in a new type of public reporting. They, of necessity, have written before all the evidence became available. On the other hand, they wrote before the data existing in the temper of the times and in the working environment of wartime administration were lost with the passage of years. Working so soon after the event, they could not have the perspective which comes with time, but they had the advantage of current impressions created by the events with which they dealt, and they were able to capture some phases of wartime administration which would otherwise be lost. Torn between their interests in the technical aspects of administration and their mandate to produce an analysis of general interest, they have combined their efforts to turn out a volume which might have been designed differently had any single one of them been charged with sole responsibility.

The Committee's sincere appreciation is due to Mr. Harold D. Smith, Director of the Bureau of the Budget, and to Mr. Donald C. Stone, Assistant Director in Charge of Administrative Management, for their support from the beginning of this enterprise. Acknowledgment needs to be made also to some 20 persons in the Bureau and elsewhere who read part or all of the manuscript and gave the staff the benefit of their suggestions.

Contents

XIII

Contents

PART 4. POSTLUDE TO WAR

PRELUDE TO WAR

Prelude to War

IN World War II the United States faced the greatest administrative test since its founding. The Government took millions of men from their homes for the armed services, prescribed how much food the housewife might buy, determined how much and what kinds of goods were to be produced by its mightiest corporations, and went far toward deciding just where a man might work and what he might receive for his labor. Yet it managed to do these dictatorial things within the framework of the democratic system, and even in the forms and changes of its administrative machinery it preserved the methods of democracy so that the resolutions of tensions proceeded, if not always smoothly, yet directly and firmly.

Modern war is not merely a battle or succession of battles between groups of fighting men. A fighting army is only the cutting edge of a militarized industrial system. A nation's fighting strength depends on how well and to what extent its entire resources have been mobilized and managed toward the ends of war. To accomplish this mobilization and management a government adapted to the needs of peace must be enlarged and reorganized so that it can assume enormous tasks foreign to its traditions. New departments, new agencies, new offices must be organized and staffed. Policies must be hammered out in unaccustomed areas. In the process the most complex and delicate problems in government and public administration have to be solved.

Problems of wartime administration are not simply problems of the mechanics and procedures of government. The objectives of government, even in time of war, are often in warm dispute and the building of administrative mechanisms must proceed with great urgency in an atmosphere of conflict about what the objectives should be. The evaluation and leadership of public opinion occupies a position of no less significance than administrative expertness. In the American democracy, a government, no matter how wise its judgment may be, cannot for long execute its will arbitrarily against the opposition of substantial blocs of opinion. It must educate, placate, temporize, and act boldly as conditions require. Governmental action on questions of administration, like action on other questions, must proceed within a changing context of public opinion which limits and influences what may be done and may govern the timing of decision.

The full story of the Nation's wartime experience, must **begin**

3

well before December 7, 1941, with the first of the Axis challenges to the democratic system and with the first halting actions taken in the face of strong democratic opposition which stemmed from a general disbelief in the possibility of war. When the Japanese entered Manchuria, we were indifferent; when the Germans marched into the Rhineland, we were startled—but our first attempts at action were negative; we were still trying to stay out of war. Finally, in the two years of 1939 and 1940, we made up our national mind in a great period of national debate. We made up our mind and recast our thinking about national protection with all the creaks and groans, charges and countercharges, exaggerations and vitriol characteristic of discussion under the democratic process. Hindsight makes it clear that we could have done better to act more promptly. On the other hand, the Government pursued firmly a course toward strengthening the national defense, and it moved about as rapidly as national consent was obtainable. Each great issue was discussed until it became clear that the proposed line of action was in accord with the wishes and the judgment of a majority of the people. In all these issues we had to deal with unprecedented situations and it took time to make up our minds. It took time to grasp the fact that nations could and would attack ruthlessly and suddenly, without warning and in violation of the traditional rules of war and our notions of fair play. It took some reflection to see that a war on the other side of the world affected us.

That we were able to settle these questions without serious internal dissension was not a surprise to those with faith in the democratic tradition, but it could not have been done without intelligent leadership nor did the Axis strategists believe that we could do it at all. Their miscalculation was that they believed that internal conflict— between capital and labor, between farmer and city dweller, between white and black—would paralyze the United States, especially if the conflicts were encouraged by deftly managed propaganda under Nazi guidance. Authoritarian nations were unable to understand how we could engage in the most exaggerated debate involving recriminations, picturesque and fantastic charges, appeals to prejudice, incitements to hatred, and insinuations of treason without tearing ourselves asunder. That we could determine to act, and to act in union, by such a process was beyond the comprehension of those unschooled in democratic practices and was, perhaps, the most significant factor in our mobilization for the war.

CHAPTER

1

Facing the Failure of Neutrality

IF HISTORY has any lessons, the lesson of the period from 1931 to 1939—from the Japanese movement into Manchuria to the German invasion of Poland—is not to be found in what we did but in what we did not do. Throughout this period opposing factions contended over what the foreign policy of the United States should be. The limited commitments which the Nation was disposed to undertake in foreign affairs created no need for important steps in the mobilization of Government for the contingency of war. The important question we had to decide was whether wars elsewhere in the world were of any concern to us and if so, what we proposed to do about it. The decisions taken on these issues demanded no substantial alteration of the governmental system. Only a few actions were taken of subsequent significance for governmental organization.

The Incubation of World Conflict

In the years preceding September 1939, when Germany invaded Poland, we were more inclined to feel annoyance with the march of events in Europe than to consider seriously their implications to us. Our own domestic problems were difficult and persistent and we did not welcome distractions from our efforts to solve them. As far as most of us were concerned, both Europe and Asia should be left to solve their own problems in their own ways. We found refuge in the hope that minor changes would soon produce new political equilibria. There were few who would have given credence to the suggestion that what appeared to be irresponsible minorities in Germany and Japan could eventually drive us into the malestrom of world conflict.

5

Before the Neutrality Act of 1935 there were a few forecasts—
penetrating but largely unheeded—of things to come. The Japanese
movement into Manchuria in 1931 began a chain of events which was
to bring us into war. While in sentiment the people of the United
States condemned Japanese aggression, the strongest feasible governmental policy was the doctrine of nonrecognition pronounced by
Henry L. Stimson, then Secretary of State, who correctly gauged the
ultimate significance of the new Japanese imperialism. Similarly,
most of us were slow to recognize the potentialities of the New Germany. Soon after the accession of the Nazis to power, some of our
diplomatic observers saw in the new government a serious threat to
the peace of the world. A prescient dispatch from Berlin in April
1934 informed the Secretary of State that the fundamental purpose
of the Nazis was "to secure a greater share of the world's future for
the Germans, the expansion of German territory, and growth of the
German race until it constitutes the largest and most powerful nation
in the world, and ultimately, according to some Nazi leaders, until it
dominates the entire globe."[1] The Nazis, the same observer reported,
"are determined to secure more power and territory in Europe."

In September 1934 the Ambassador in Italy reported that preparations for war were in motion. He predicted a defensive war "provoked" perhaps by "unruly" tribes.[2] In December 1934 the Ambassador in Japan reported that the aim of certain elements in the
Army and Navy, the patriotic societies, and the nationalistic groups
was "to obtain trade control and eventually predominant political
influence in China, the Philippines, the Straits Settlements, Siam,
and the Dutch East Indies, the Maritime Provinces and Vladivostok,
one step at a time, as in Korea and Manchuria, pausing intermittently
to consolidate and then continuing as soon as the intervening obstacles
can be overcome by diplomacy or force."[3] The best possible way to
reduce the risk of an eventual war, he thought, was to "be adequately
prepared."[4]

Generally we did not take much stock in such forecasts. Nor were
we inclined to arm ourselves sufficiently to translate our urging that
peace be maintained into language comprehensible to aggressors and
potential aggressors. In 1933, by Presidential allocations of public
works funds, and by regular appropriations, a naval construction program was undertaken of a size greater than the country had seen
since 1916. Yet a subsequent public works appropriation act prevented further use of such funds for naval or military purposes. The
Act of April 1935, contained a proviso that "no part of the appropri-

---

[1] U. S. Department of State, *Peace and War*, Washington, D. C.: Government Printing Office, 1942, pp. 211-212.
[2] *Ibid.*, p. 236.   [3] *Ibid.*, p. 239.   [4] *Ibid.*, p. 244.

ation made by this joint resolution shall be expended for munitions, warships, or military or naval matériel".[5]

Our deep aversion to war, joined with the notion that wars are fought to protect profits, led to the Neutrality Act of 1935 and its successor acts. The theory was that if we did no business in munitions with nations at war, our commercial interests would not become involved and we would not be brought to fight to protect them. If American vessels stayed out of danger zones and were not sunk, we would not become angry because they had been attacked. The Act, approved August 31, 1935,[6] made it "unlawful to export arms, ammunition, or implements of war" from the United States for the use of the countries at war when the existence of war had been proclaimed by the President. The law also made it illegal for munitions to be transported to any country at war on American vessels, empowered the President to regulate access of submarines of foreign nations to American waters and ports, and forbade United States citizens to travel on the vessels of belligerent nations when the President proclaimed that such abstention would promote the maintenance of peace.

In signing the act, the President commented in particular on the prohibition of exports of munitions to nations at war. The objective of avoiding being drawn into wars between other nations was, he said, wholly good, "but it is a fact that no Congress and no executive can foresee all possible future situations. History is filled with unforeseeable situations that call for some flexibility of action. It is conceivable that situations may arise in which the wholly inflexible provisions . . . of this act might have exactly the opposite effect from that which was intended." In other words, the inflexible provisions might drag us into war instead of keeping us out.[7]

The act prevented our munitions interests becoming allied with the cause of a belligerent, but it also gave notice to the world that aggressors need have no fear that our munitions industry would be drawn upon by nations with no arsenals of their own. The legislation thus did nothing to discourage the Italians who were manufacturing a crisis with Ethiopia at the time the bill was under consideration. In October 1935, Italy moved into Ethiopia, and, in keeping with the Neutrality Act, the President on October 5, proclaimed the existence of war between Italy and Ethiopia and prohibited the shipment of munitions to either belligerent. Another proclamation prohibited travel by United States citizens on vessels of either belligerent nation. Italy, well-equipped with munitions, was scarcely handi-

[5] 49 *Stat.* 115.
[6] 49 *Stat.* 1081.
[7] Roosevelt, Franklin D. *The Public Papers and Addresses of* . . . New York: Random House, 1938. Vol. 4, 1935, pp. 345–346.

capped by our action while we bowed out as a potential source of supplies to Ethiopia. The Government used its influence, short of becoming involved in war, in an attempt to restrain the aggressor. In this it was probably hewing to the line of public opinion in the United States for less than one-tenth of us, according to the opinion polls, favored military action against aggressor nations.[8]

Negotiation, warning, suasion were not enough to restrain the forces of aggression. Emboldened perhaps by the failure of efforts to develop collective measures to restrain Italian aggression, Hitler in violation of the Locarno Pact, in March 1936, occupied and fortified the demilitarized Rhineland. This threat found the democracies paralyzed and gave further encouragement to the forces of reaction. In July 1936 civil war broke out in Spain and soon almost all European countries were heavily involved emotionally. Many of them became directly involved by furnishing arms and ammunition and even troops to one side or another. Although the Neutrality Act did not apply to civil conflicts, the Administration adopted a policy of noninterference and discouraged the export of arms to Spain. This executive policy was ratified by Congress on January 8, 1937, when it adopted a joint resolution embargoing the export of arms to Spain during the civil war. In November 1936, Japan and Germany signed the Anti-Comintern Pact and it soon became the opinion of our diplomatic observers that Japan and Germany had engaged themselves to take parallel action in military matters. Even if all these things should lead to war, and very few people thought they would, a majority of us were, apparently, persuaded that we could stay out.[9]

Even after these events had made the nature of the emerging world situation much more apparent, we clung to the belief that perhaps we could avoid entanglement by minimizing our commercial dealings with belligerents. In May 1937 the Neutrality Act was broadened to authorize the President to prohibit the export to belligerents in American vessels of materials and articles other than direct war munitions. During the Italo-Ethiopian war, our exports of copper, trucks, and other items had increased. Such items were as essential as munitions for the conduct of war, but the law had not prevented their export. In addition, the Act of 1937 required that, if shipped in other vessels, such goods had to be paid for in advance. Another

---

[8] In October 1935, the American Institute of Public Opinion asked: "If one foreign nation insists upon attacking another, should the United States join with other nations to compel it to stop?" The replies were: Yes, 28 percent; no, 67 percent; no opinion, 5 percent. Of the 28 percent who favored our joining with others to check an aggressor, 65 percent favored economic and nonmilitary measures only, 31 percent were for military measures, if necessary, and 4 percent had no opinion on the issue.

[9] In December 1936, the American Institute of Public Opinion asked: "If there is another general European war, do you believe the United States can stay out?" The replies were: Yes, 60 percent; no, 36 percent; don't know, 4 percent.

major amendment prohibited the arming of American merchant vessels.[10]

The revised Neutrality Act doubtless reflected the desire of the overwhelming majority of the American people not to become involved in any foreign war. In May, when the act was adopted, the Spanish civil war still raged and it was becoming plain that in it were projected forces which almost inevitably would be arrayed at some time against each other in a struggle on a much grander scale. Yet according to a poll of American opinion, 8 out of 10 Americans were indifferent about the outcome of the Spanish conflict.[11]

The Neutrality Act of 1937 did not restrain Japanese aggression in China. In July 1937 the Marco Polo Bridge incident occurred and a large-scale Japanese movement into China was soon under way. To apply the terms of the Neutrality Act to the Sino-Japanese conflict would deprive the Chinese as well as the Japanese of munitions and materials of war. Shipments to one could not be embargoed without stopping the movement of goods to the other. The act did not become operative until the President should, in the words of the statute, "find that there exists a state of war between, or among, two or more foreign states . . . ." No such finding was made and goods continued to flow to both China and Japan.

While undeclared war went on in China and the Spanish civil war continued, the President made his notable "quarantine" address in Chicago on October 5, 1937. He remarked that the world political situation was "growing progressively worse." It was such as to "cause grave concern and anxiety." He cited interference by nations in the affairs of others, the ruthless murder of civilians by bombing, the sinking of ships without cause. He thought the "very foundations of civilization" were "seriously threatened." He warned that we should not "imagine that America will escape" if the rest of the world became embroiled. The peace-loving nations, he declared, "must make a concerted effort to uphold laws and principles on which alone peace can rest secure." He saw a spreading "epidemic of world lawlessness." He observed that when epidemics of disease spread, "the community approves and joins in a quarantine of the patients in order to protect the health of the community against the spread of the disease." He thought that the will of peace-loving nations had to be expressed "to the end that nations that may be tempted to violate their agreements and the rights of others will desist from such a cause."

[10] 50 *Stat*. 121.

[11] In May 1937, the AIPO conducted a poll on the following question: "Are your sympathies with either side in the present Spanish Civil War?" Twenty-one percent replied "Yes," while 79 percent were recorded as saying "No" or "Don't know enough about it."

The speech brought charges of "war mongering" from many sources, charges that were made at the time when the League of Nations was attempting futilely to end the undeclared war in the Far East. Nor was our complacency much disturbed by outright attack on American vessels, the Japanese bombing in December of the United States gunboat *Panay* and three United States merchant vessels on the Yangtze. The United States Government immediately initiated the appropriate diplomatic demand for apology and for indemnification, a demand which was promptly met. Yet the larger significance of the affair in the general sequence of events seemed to escape us.

All these developments in foreign relations did not occupy the center of the stage in American politics. Public interest and the major part of the efforts of the Government had since 1933 been concentrated on problems of domestic recovery and reform. The measures taken at the time of the inauguration of the new Administration in 1933 demanded almost the complete attention of the public and required a greater part of the effort of the Government. These emergency programs, and discussions over fundamental measures of domestic reform overshadowed the threats to peace. Our traditional spirit of non-participation in the affairs of other parts of the world was thus fortuitously reenforced by the course of domestic politics. Only as the world crisis approached its climax were we able to begin to mobilize our national opinion on foreign matters and to begin to realize that we had a vital stake in the events outside our boundaries.

Limited Preparedness

As the threats to world peace became more apparent, it became feasible to initiate a few measures of rearmament. Yet even limited measures of preparedness aroused no little opposition. In only one phase of defense preparation was it possible to proceed without having to overcome the charge of war mongering. The Merchant Marine Act of 1936 had laid the basis for a long-range program for the rebuilding and enlargement of the Merchant Marine. The Maritime Commission, in consultation with the Navy Department, developed a program for the construction of merchant vessels designed incidentally to meet defense requirements. In 1938, 37 ships were under construction for the Maritime Commission in addition to ships being built for private operators who were taking advantage of the subsidy plan provided by the Act of 1936. In the following year, 1939, the program was accelerated to compress into 2 years the previous 3-year program.

Proposals for increases in direct armaments, however, met a more determined opposition. In his annual message to Congress on January 3, 1938, the President said that it had become clear "that acts and policies of nations in other parts of the world have far-reaching effects not only upon their immediate neighbors but also on us." He observed that in "a world where stable civilization is actually threatened" a nation striving for peace had "to be strong enough to assure the observance of those fundamentals of peaceful solution of conflicts which are the only ultimate basis for orderly existence." A few weeks later he recommended some increase in both naval and land arms. "In the light of the increasing armaments of other nations," he found it his constitutional duty to report that our national defense was "inadequate for purposes of national security" and required "increase for that reason."

The modest recommendations by the President were adopted in substance by the Congress only after long discussion. The congressional hearings on the bill to authorize an increase of approximately 20 percent in the combat strength of the Navy indicated the beliefs of those who opposed greater preparedness. One type of belief was that "a wholly abnormal naval building program" would "intensify international tensions and distrust." Others opposed increasing the Navy "until the American people know what lies behind the increase and what is our present foreign policy." Another view was that the American people ought to know what "our Government would do if an undeclared war broke out in Europe." Others believed that the President had "set out on the road to collective action or quarantine that leads to war." The parade of witnesses before the congressional committees reflected the views, fears, and questions of many citizens.

While discussion on the naval expansion bill proceeded, the Nazis annexed Austria, and thus destroyed the strategic foundation for the existence of Czechoslovakia. The naval expansion provisions were finally adopted by the House of Representatives on March 21, 1938, by a vote of 294 to 100. The Senate acted on May 3 by a vote of 56 to 28.[12] The recommendations for increases in Army strength were carried out in the military appropriation bills.

During the summer of 1938, a war fever spread over Europe; it arose from fears about the intentions of a rearmed Germany. In all the countries bordering Germany, preparations for defense were accelerated and a general belief existed that war was imminent.

During the Munich crisis in the summer and fall of 1938, the President urged the governments concerned to seek a peaceful solution. He predicted that hostilities would cause the loss of millions of lives. At Munich, Britain and France agreed to the Nazi demand for the Sudetenland. Statesmen, realizing the gravity of their surrender, were amazed to find themselves hailed by their peoples as saviors.

---

[12] *Congressional Record*, vol. 83, pt. 4, p. 3767; pt. 6, p. 6135.

Hitler's antidemocratic strategy was working. Britain and France decided not to fight. Nor had Hitler any reason to suppose that the United States could or would oppose him in the near future.

Meanwhile, the Japanese conquest of China continued; our policy of nonrecognition of forced territorial charges and our efforts at persuasion appeared to restrain the Nipponese but little. In the summer of 1938 the Secretary of State requested a moral embargo by airplane manufacturers on the shipment of planes to countries which engaged in the bombing of civilian populations. Japan met these specifications and most shipments of planes soon stopped. In December the Export-Import Bank granted a loan of $25,000,000 to China to be used for the purchase of nonmunitions such as trucks, tires, gasoline, and machinery. At about the same time, Great Britain and the Soviet Union entered into agreements to furnish credit and supplies to the Chinese.

It was not easy to believe that the Munich agreement held promise for the maintenance of peace. In his annual message to the Congress on January 4, 1939, the President reported that it was "increasingly clear that world peace is not assured." "All about us," he said, "are threats of new aggression—military and economic." He declared that religion, democracy, and good faith were challenged by "storms from abroad. . . . There comes a time in the affairs of men when they must prepare to defend, not their homes alone, but the tenets of faith and humanity on which their churches, their governments, and their very civilization are founded." He said that we had learned that "the probability of attack is mightily decreased by the assurance of an ever ready defense."

On January 12, 1939, the President urged additional appropriations for national defense. He emphasized the "great change" which had come over conflicts between nations since the World War. He asked Congress to recall that even after our entry into the World War we "had more than a year of absolute peace at home without any threat of attack on this continent, to train men, to produce raw materials, to process them into munitions and supplies, and to forge the whole into fighting forces." It was necessary, he said, "for every American to restudy present defense against the possibilities of present offense against us." He asked for appropriations of about $525,000,000 as a "minimum program for the necessities of defense."[13]

Hitler had declared that Germany did not intend to annex Austria; in 1938, Austria was annexed. At the time of the Munich pact, he indicated that he had no further territorial ambitions and was prepared to guarantee the frontiers of Czechoslovakia. In March 1939, German troops occupied Czechoslovakia. In the next month,

[13] Roosevelt, Franklin D., *op. cit.*, 1939 vol., pp. 70–74.

Mussolini invaded Albania. The crisis atmosphere of the preceding summer again prevailed. The Government of the United States again appealed to Hitler and Mussolini for the maintenance of peace.

Recurrence of tension brought again a reconsideration of American neutrality policy. In his annual message in January 1939 the President had called attention to the actual effects of the neutrality policy. On May 27, 1939, the Secretary of State suggested to the Congress that a modification of the Neutrality Act was desirable and advocated the elimination of the arms embargo. The House Committee on

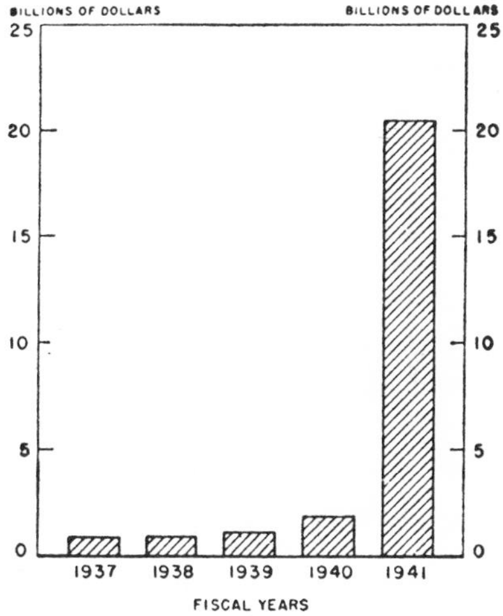

CHART 1. *Federal Appropriations for Defense Prior to Pearl Harbor.*
Source: Treasury Department.

Foreign Affairs reported a bill in agreement with the Secretary's recommendations, which precipitated a long and bitter debate. Failure to repeal the embargo, one Representative asserted, "will cause rejoicing in the capitals of the dictator nations, and will encourage the dictators to commit further acts of aggression upon the democratic nations, and may mean the outbreak of another world war."[14] The opposition adhered to the belief that the trade in arms would inevitably drag us into whatever war might come. The munitions makers, it was declared, would "look forward to again reaping unrestricted profits" and the mothers of America might "well shudder at the likely prospect of again sending their sons across the sea to die in the attempt to collect the debts owed these warlords. . . ."[15]

By a vote of 214 to 173, the House voted to retain the arms embargo.[16] The Secretary of State then issued another statement urging his original recommendations, stressing their importance in "the dis-

---

[14] *Congressional Record*, vol. 84, pt. 8, p. 8508.
[15] *Congressional Record*, vol. 84, pt. 8, p. 8498.
[16] *Congressional Record*, vol. 84, pt. 8, p. 8511.

couragement of the outbreak of war."[17] The Senate Committee on
Foreign Relations on July 11 decided by a narrow margin to take no
action on neutrality legislation until the following January. On
July 14, the President again urged Congress to act. He transmitted
with his request a statement by the Secretary of State, who asserted
that the arms embargo "plays into the hands of those nations which
have taken the lead in building up their fighting power." An aggressor nation well prepared for war would be encouraged in its depre-
dations because it would know that "its less well-prepared opponents
would be shut off from" supplies from neutrals.

After a White House conference on July 18, at which it was determined that Senate action on neutrality was impossible, a release announcing the results of the conference stated, "The President and the
Secretary of State maintained the definite position that failure by the
Senate to take action now would weaken the leadership of the United
States in exercising its potent influence in the cause of preserving peace
among other nations in the event of a new crisis in Europe between
now and next January."[18]

On August 21 it became known that Russia and Germany had
agreed to sign a nonaggression treaty. Believing herself free from
danger in the east, Germany was able to move. Appeals by the
United States to Germany, to Italy, and Poland to seek a peaceful
settlement were futile.

On September 1, German forces moved into Poland. On September
3, 1939, France and Britain, in fulfillment of their guarantees to
Poland, declared war on the Reich.

Strengthening Administrative Foundations

The role which the Government played in attempting to stave off
war in itself placed no unusual requirements on the machinery of administration. Diplomatic maneuvers and limited preparedness could
be carried on by the existing departments and agencies. Important
steps in administrative reorganization were taken, however, and considerable progress was made in the practice of Federal administration.
These changes were not made in preparation for war, but they stood
us in good stead when war came. Like improvements in public
health, in public education, in public highways, and in other services,
improvements in public administration to meet the needs of peace
strengthened us for defense and war.

In January 1937, the President transmitted to Congress a message
on the reorganization of the executive branch of the Government.

---

[17] U. S. Department of State, *op. cit.*, p. 465.
[18] Roosevelt, Franklin D., *op. cit.*, 1939 vol., p. 388.

He urged the adoption of a reorganization program in a message pointedly relating the matter of effective administration to national defense. "In these troubled years of world history," he said, "a self-government cannot long survive unless that government is an effective and efficient agency to serve mankind and carry out the will of the Nation. A government without good management is a house builded on sand." While democracy was being challenged by the temporarily triumphant doctrines of dictatorship, he asked, "Will it be said 'Democracy was a great dream, but it could not do the job?' Or shall we here and now, without further delay, make it our business to see that our American democracy is made efficient so that it will do the job that is required of it by the events of our time?"

After a delay of 2 years, the Reorganization Act of 1939 was adopted. It embodied only a part of the President's program of 1937. Under its procedures, the President with the approval of Congress, reassigned certain Government functions among the departments and agencies so that the number of agencies would be reduced and more efficient operation of the departments would result. The reduction in the number of agencies brought the governmental machine more nearly within the limits of control and direction by the President, even though certain important activities of the Government could not be touched under the authorizing statute.

Other actions in the reorganization program contributed even more to strengthening the President as manager of Federal Administration. The reorganization plan brought into being the Executive Office of the President in recognition of the growing burdens upon the President and of the increasing necessity that he be adequately equipped to exercise leadership and direction of the work of the Government as a whole. In this office were grouped the Bureau of the Budget, the National Resources Planning Board, the Office of Government Reports, the Liaison Office for Personnel Management, and the immediate White House Office. At the same time, the activities of the Bureau of the Budget were substantially enlarged to include the conduct of research "in the development of improved plans of administrative management" and advice to the President with regard to such matters. As the activities of the Executive Office were built up, the President came to be more nearly equipped with the machinery by which he could give the Federal Government the administrative flexibility essential in time of crisis.

The Executive order, signed September 8, 1939, which established the internal divisions of the Executive Office, provided that there should be in that Office, "in the event of a national emergency or threat of a national emergency, such office for emergency management as the President shall determine." The Presidential statement accompanying the Executive order noted that in periods of emergency it had "always been found necessary to establish administrative machinery in addition to that required for the normal work of the Government. Set up in a time of stress, these special facilities sometimes have worked at cross-purposes both within themselves and with the regular departments and agencies. In order that the Nation may not again be caught unaware, adequate resources for management should be provided in advance of such periods of emergency." The proviso of the Executive order was eventually to serve as one of the legal bases for the erection of the major part of the governmental machinery essential for defense and war. It was a valuable feature in that it permitted the Government to act promptly in time of emergency.

In other ways the foundations of administration were being strengthened. In the thirties, thousands of highly trained persons streamed into the civil service to perform the duties required by legislation enacted to meet the emergency requirements of peace. A major element in the program of administrative management of the President was the strengthening and extension of the merit system of employment in the public service. The result was that when the need came, the most competent corps of civil employees in the recent history of the Federal Government was available for utilization on emergency tasks. These civil servants were, of course, inadequate in number for the work which was to come, but the rapid infiltration of persons of talent into the civil service strengthened it for the test of war.

On the military side, during the thirties, the Army and Navy Munitions Board, proceeding independently, prepared successive revisions of its Industrial Mobilization Plan. Revisions were issued in 1931, 1933, 1936, and 1939. In August 1939, the Assistant Secretary of War appointed a War Resources Board to advise on further revision of the Industrial Mobilization Plan. This board consisted of Edward R. Stettinius, Jr., Karl T. Compton, Walter S. Gifford, Harold G. Moulton, John Lee Pratt, Robert E. Wood, and John Hancock. The Board reviewed the plan and submitted recommendations and suggestions. Shortly after the completion of its assignment, the Board was disbanded.

CHAPTER

2

Preparing for Defense

IN THE months that intervened between the invasion of Poland in September 1939, and the national election in November 1940, legislative foundations were laid for a more adequate system of national defense, but only after thorough debate which spread from the Senate and House chambers to every crossroads. Though creation of administrative machinery for mobilization was necessarily subordinated to the task of obtaining legislation and of promoting public discussion of the issues underlying legislative proposals, by November 1940, the first steps had been taken in the erection of a governmental machine for defense and for war.

The outbreak of war between the great powers found us still torn by conflicting emotions. If the opinion polls are to be believed, we thought Germany had caused the war. We thought Hitler's claim to the Polish corridor unjustified. We did not want to see England, France, and Poland agree to Germany's claims regarding Danzig. Less than a tenth of us believed that we should declare war on Germany at once.[1] A month after war broke out more than half the people believed we would not become involved. Our sympathies were overwhelmingly with the democracies, but our sympathies were not belligerent. Nor did we believe the chances of our becoming involved great enough to warrant strenuous efforts in preparation for our own defense.

---

[1] In September 1939, 81 percent of the respondents in a poll by the American Institute of Public Opinion placed responsibility for causing the war on Germany. In the preceding month the Institute had asked: "Do you think Hitler's claims to the Polish Corridor are justified?" The replies were: Yes, 10 percent; no, 61 percent; no opinion, 29 percent. In the same month, the Institute asked whether Germany's claims to Danzig should be accepted and the replies were: Yes, 9 percent; no, 68 percent; no opinion, 23 percent. In September, the Institute asked whether we should declare war on Germany at once and the replies were: Yes, 9 percent; no, 88 percent; no opinion, 3 percent.

On September 5, 1939, the President, in obedience to the Neutrality Act, prohibited the export of arms and munitions to France, Germany, Poland, the United Kingdom, India, Australia, and New Zealand.[2] In his address to Congress, summoned to an extra session on September 21, the President recounted the rise of aggression and reported: "The Executive Branch of the Government did its utmost, within our traditional policy of noninvolvement, to aid in averting the present appalling war. Having thus striven and failed, this Government must lose no time or effort to keep our Nation from being drawn into the war." He called for a repeal of the arms embargo provision of the Neutrality Act and a return to our traditional neutrality policy under the usages of international law. He advocated that certain other provisions of the Neutrality Act be retained such as the restriction on the movement of American vessels in war zones and of travel by American citizens on belligerent vessels.

On November 4, the President signed a revised Neutrality Act. The new Act repealed the embargo on the shipment of arms and munitions to belligerents and introduced the rule that no exports to belligerents could be made until all right, title, and interest was transferred to the consignee. This provision, popularly known as "cash-and-carry," had applied to articles other than arms and ammunition from the passage of the 1937 Neutrality Act until May 1, 1939. Prohibition of the arming of American merchant ships, limitation of travel by American citizens on vessels of nations at war, and restriction of the movement of American vessels into combat areas were continued in effect.[3]

With the adoption of the "cash-and-carry" principle, the British and French took steps to enlarge and to coordinate their purchasing operations in this country, and on December 6, the President established an Interdepartmental Committee for Coordination of Foreign and Domestic Military Purchases—generally known as the President's Liaison Committee—which consisted of representatives of the War Department, Navy Department, and Treasury Department. It operated under the direction of the Secretary of the Treasury and located sources of supply and ironed out competition between foreign purchasing and our own procurement programs. British and French contracts resulted in the construction of facilities for the production of armament and thus strengthened our own defense. To the maximum practicable degree the Committee took measures to assure that new factories erected with foreign funds would be equipped to produce goods to meet American military specifications.

---

[2] *4 Federal Register* 3809–12.
[3] *54 Stat.* 4.

On January 3, 1940, the President, in his annual message, said: "I am asking the Congress for Army and Navy increases which are based not on panic but on common sense. They are not as great as enthusiastic alarmists seek. They are not as small as unrealistic persons claiming superior private information would demand." In reporting the appropriation bill, the House Appropriations Committee recommended 57 new airplanes instead of 496. It eliminated an

CHART 2. *Foreign Government Contracts for Armaments Placed in the United States.*[1]

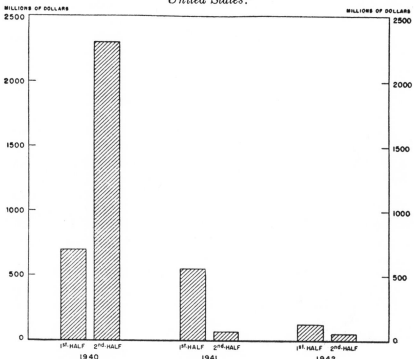

[1] Prior to 1940, foreign government contracts amounted to $118.1 million.
Source: Foreign Purchasing Missions and War Production Board.

item of some $12 million for the development of an air base in Alaska. In all, cuts totaling about 10 percent of the requests were made.[4] The Committee's recommendations were accepted by the House without serious protest. By the time the appropriations measures were considered by the Senate, the Nazis had begun moving westward and then all could see that the level of military expenditures proposed in January was far too low.

[4] House Report No. 1912, 76th Cong., 3d sess., Apr. 3, 1940.

The "phony" war came to an abrupt end in April and May 1940. Mechanized forces, employed on an unparalleled scale and with unprecedented skill, destroyed what had been thought to be the world's best armies, but the Maginot mentality in America, remote from the field of actual battle, was not crushed by falling bombs. It had to be worn down by the attrition of debate and by the realization that warfare had entered a new era. We had to revise our thinking about a great many things: about the security which the Atlantic assured us under these new conditions, about our position in world affairs, and about methods to finance and organize military production. We had to learn, in effect, to believe what we could see with our own eyes. That was not easy. For months following the opening of war in the west, we debated and disputed, making up our minds about what we should do at this juncture in world events.

The Nazis Move Westward

The German invasion of Denmark and Norway on April 9 appeared to us disturbing but not fatal, but the assault on the Low Countries on May 10 revealed unforeseen methods of making war. Within a week the Army of the Netherlands capitulated. The Belgians surrendered in less than 3 weeks. In little more than 30 days, France, considered to be one of the great land powers of the world, sued for an armistice. The British were driven from the continent. Italy entered the war. Disruption of the pattern of power in Europe had repercussions in the Far East. With the Netherlands and France conquered and with Britain occupied in her defense at home, their Far Eastern possessions became tempting objects of conquest. Even before the French-German armistice was signed in June 1940, the Japanese militarists began to exert pressure on French Indochina. In July, the British were brought to close the Burma Road. A Germany dominant on the continent and free to develop and utilize its resources could threaten the United States through the economic ties that bound the Latin-American countries to Europe.

The United States was probably in the most precarious position in its history. Yet to many of us the peril seemed remote. Voices proclaimed loudly that all this could never touch us; we had the Atlantic and Pacific for moats. We continued with unabated zest our political feuds even though these internal cleavages affected our ability to react quickly to changes in the international environment. The coincidence of the crisis with a presidential election further complicated matters. Everything that was done or left undone was open to charges of partisanship. On the other hand, the fact that the crisis occurred during the year of a presidential election insured the most alert and demanding public scrutiny and criticism of governmental policy.

The fall of the Netherlands, Belgium, and France did, however, demolish most of the powerful centers of opposition to the development of industrial facilities for production of defense equipment. By and large, the problem of rearmament, narrowly defined to exclude such questions as the draft, ceased to be one of mobilizing national consensus and became one of governmental and industrial organization for production. In this, some progress had been made already. Navy expenditures for the year ending June 30, 1940, were 46 percent greater than those for the fiscal year 1937–38. Over the same period, expenditures for the military functions of the War Department increased 54 percent. But this expansion, achieved against fairly strong opposition, was trifling in comparison with what had to be done.

The sweep of German armies over Western Europe also cleared the way for obtaining additional appropriations for national defense. When the President addressed Congress on May 16 to review military developments in Europe, he requested an immediate appropriation of $896,000,000 and additional authority to make contract obligations totaling $286,000,000. In response to this request, funds were made available by acts approved on June 11 and 13.[5] Shortly after the British forces were driven from the continent of Europe, the President made an "urgent and new recommendation" for the appropriation of still more money both for the further expansion of production facilities and for the purchase of additional weapons. Again Congress acted quickly. Including contract authorizations, about 1¾ billion dollars were made available by legislation approved on June 26.[6] On July 10, the President went to Congress again for additional appropriations and authorizations of almost 5 billion dollars. Two months later Congress made the necessary authorizations in an act approved September 9, 1940.[7] The delay between the request and the appropriation handicapped the defense program, particularly the construction of training facilities.

Advisory Commission to the Council of National Defense

As early as the fall of 1939, the President began to think about the administrative arrangements which might be necessary if we were forced to go to war. It was deemed inadvisable to seek from Congress positive legislation for industrial mobilization since, in a campaign year, such a request might set off a partisan debate and if anything resulted it might be restrictive legislation. Plans, therefore, had to be made within the existing statutory framework. The President

---

[5] 54 *Stat.* 265, 350.   [6] 54 *Stat.* 599.   [7] 54 *Stat.* 872.

decided to revive the Advisory Commission to the Council of National Defense. From the first World War, statutory authority remained for a Council of National Defense consisting of the Secretaries of War, Navy, Interior, Agriculture, Commerce and Labor. The statute authorized the President to appoint, upon nomination by the Council, an advisory commission "of not more than seven persons, each of whom shall have some special knowledge of some industry, public utility, or the development of some natural resource, or be otherwise specially qualified."[8]

As a first step, on May 25, 1940, he issued an administrative order formally establishing an Office for Emergency Management in the Executive Office of the President. The basis for this action had been laid by the Executive order defining the divisions of the Executive Office in connection with the general program of governmental reorganization in 1939. That order had provided, "in the event of a national emergency, or threat of national emergency," for "such office for emergency management as the President shall determine." The activation of the office served two important purposes. It provided the President with assistance in the coordination and direction of emergency agencies and provided authority for the establishment of such new agencies as had to be created. Most of the new administrative organizations necessary for defense and war originated as units of the Office for Emergency Management. At the time of the establishment of the OEM, the President designated William H. McReynolds, one of his administrative assistants, as Liaison Officer for Emergency Management with the function of directing the OEM the duties of which were to—

Assist the President in the clearance of information with respect to measures necessitated by the threatened emergency;

Maintain liaison between the President and the Council of National Defense and its Advisory Commission, and with such other agencies, public or private, as the President may direct, for the purpose of securing maximum utilization and coordination of agencies and facilities in meeting the threatened emergency:

Perform such additional duties as the President may direct.

On May 28, the President announced the reestablishment of the Advisory Commission to the Council of National Defense. It was to consist of the following "advisors": Industrial materials, Edward R. Stettinius, Jr.; industrial production, William S. Knudsen; employment, Sidney Hillman; farm products, Chester C. Davis; transportation, Ralph Budd; Price stabilization, Leon Henderson; and consumer protection, Harriett Elliott. The Liaison Officer for Emergency Management was designated as Commission secretary. Although the Commission in form was advisory to the Council of National

---

[8] *39 Stat.* 872.

Defense, in fact it was advisory to the President, for the Council remained dormant.

In creating the Commission, the President made an administrative determination which drew no little criticism from both his friends and enemies. Fundamentally, his decision was dictated by judgments of what was feasible in the general political circumstances—and in political matters the opinion of the President had always been accorded respect. Reliance on existing legislation made it possible to avoid seeking action from Congress, action which might, and probably would, have resulted in administrative inflexibility at a time when the utmost flexibility was required. Moreover, other and more important issues, such as selective service, needed to be given priority by Congress without the distraction of additional urgent Presidential requests.

At the time of the creation of the Commission, the domestic political situation was delicate. The national conventions were in the offing. Even preparation for defense was a matter of questionable popularity with a people that hated war. The Administration was being accused of leading the Nation to war in an underhand manner without disclosing its intentions. In describing his action, the President said:

This is not complete, immediate national mobilization. We are not talking at the present time about a draft system, either to draft money or men or women or all three. We are trying to expend about a billion and a quarter dollars more than the normal process. And in order to do that, it has seemed wise to put into effect what has been ready and planned for a long, long time, under an existing statute, without having to go and propose something entirely new in the way of legislation that would take weeks and months and a great deal of pro and con discussion, partisan and otherwise, and would probably end up in practically the same thing that we have on the statute books now.

Decision to revive the Advisory Commission meant a rejection of the Army-Navy Industrial Mobilization Plan. The plan, however, scarcely merited the build-up it had been given; it was a document dealing only in generalities with the problem of governmental organization for war and it was formulated for conditions unlike those which actually arose. It presumed the existence of a state of war under which almost any power could be had from Congress for the asking and under which a full-fledged war organization would have to be created. Neither of these conditions prevailed, and until war came, progress could be made only as public opinion crystallized into decision. Another crucial factor in the rejection of the "M-day" plan was its provision for a single administrator with vast powers over governmental organization and policy, far greater powers than those exercised by the Chairman of the War Industries Board in World War I. Delegation of such enormous powers would have made it difficult for the President to control the broad strategy of defense preparation and foreign economic policy during a most critical period. Such action would have constituted virtual abdication by the President and would have made him less able to meet his constitutional responsibilities. Moreover, the plan carried with it potentialities of far greater military influence in the management of governmental affairs than appeared either desirable or politic at the time. For these reasons, the plan seemed unattractive to the President. For the same reasons, his political opponents held the plan in high esteem.

The individual advisors set to work in their respective fields. In most instances, each advisor's job was twofold. He had to aid in getting a current job done. Perhaps more important, he had to make detailed studies and plans about what would have to be done if the country got into war. Only the advisors on industrial materials and industrial production faced questions demanding immediate answers. Labor supply was adequate. Price inflation was not an immediate danger. Farm products were not scarce. The transportation system was not under a strain. In these fields, the problem was one of preparation of plans for whatever might come. Each of the advisors built up small staffs which later became the foundation on which more elaborate war organizations were built.

In addition to the small organizations which grew up around each advisor, the Commission provided for the establishment of other organization units which were destined to become important parts of the administrative machinery for defense and war. The Council of National Defense had statutory authority to "organize subordinate bodies for its assistance in special investigations" and this power served as a legal basis for the creation of some emergency administrative agencies. The Council of National Defense on June 27, 1940, designated Donald M. Nelson as Coordinator of National Defense Purchases. He functioned in fact as a member of the Advisory Commission. Later he also became Director of the Small Business Activities Office, authorized by the Commission on October 23, 1940. At the outset, the Commission authorized the establishment of the Bureau of Research and Statistics, under the direction of Stacy May, to serve all the advisors. At the same time, Robert Horton became Director of Information for the NDAC. Late in July, Frank Bane, Executive Director of the Council of State Governments, became Director of the Division of State and Local Cooperation in the Office of the NDAC Secretary. The functions of this division included the maintenance of liaison with State and local defense councils and the absorption of some of the pressure from State and local groups for defense contracts. Other "subordinate bodies," to be mentioned subsequently in this chapter, were also established to aid the Advisory Commission or to carry on functions quite independently of the Commission.

Although the "advisors" were collectively called the Advisory Commission to the Council on National Defense, they were not intended to constitute a collegial body or to function as a group. In practice, the theory was not maintained that each advisor was to function independently within his own sphere. All the advisors were interested in all phases of defense policy and the Commission soon assumed collegial characteristics and functions. The advisors considered themselves to be a Commission, not just Presidential assistants created under a convenient statute, and so did Congress and the country. In the personnel of the Commission, and in its deliberations were reflected most of the significant political viewpoints of the time. And the deliberations of the Commission were certainly not without value in the process of developing reconciliations of some sharp differences in order that the defense effort might move along. Yet the efforts of the advisors to function as a Commission, a type of operation to which their mandate did not extend, contributed to their administrative difficulties.

Any judgment about the work of the Commission must necessarily be tentative. Administratively, it was by no means a perfect machine for the conduct of mobilization, but it was not designed to be. On the positive side, the advisors expedited the execution of the production and procurement program authorized at the time, brought new and needed personnel into the Government, initiated studies and surveys, defined the kinds of problems which might arise, and served as a practical administrative stop-gap. The Commission must be evaluated in the light of what was politically practicable at a time when the Nation, beset by considerable internal political turmoil, was making up its mind about what it would do in international affairs. During the summer of 1940 and even after Pearl Harbor, endless fears and ideological blinders restrained action. It required both debate and the further development of events to dissipate these restraints. Business was fearful; labor was anxious.

Issues in Getting Production Under Way

It was necessary to induce manufacturers to accept defense contracts. Only recently, businessmen who had manufactured munitions in the first World War had been subjected to investigations, and they were not anxious again to go through that kind of agony. Mr. Knudsen, the advisor on industrial production, Mr. Nelson, Coordinator of Purchases for the Commission, and other businessmen drawn into the Commission's work were able by pressure and persuasion to induce reluctant businessmen to take contracts for the construction of new defense plants and the production of military goods.

The War and Navy Departments, accustomed to small-scale, meticulous, and slow purchasing procedures, had to be shocked into altering their practices to meet the necessities of larger-scale operation. The advice, assistance, and urging of business experts, while not always welcomed by the service departments, brought modifications in their practices. Legislation was required to remove legal limitations on contracting officers and to permit the negotiation of contracts. Congress granted the necessary authority in several acts, but it was not easy for contracting officers, mindful of a reckoning to come for inevitable errors of judgment, to shake off their habitual methods of slow and careful action. The passage in June 1940 of a statute authorizing the President to order priority for deliveries under Army and Navy contracts gave them further support and strengthened our legislation for defense.[9]

One of the most important blocks to rapid action was the fear that productive facilities, especially for raw materials, would be expanded so much that the Nation would be left with excess capacity. This anxiety colored action within both industry and the Defense Commission. We were not, and we hoped not to be, in the war, but war or no war, the estimates of materials and facilities the crisis would demand to support military production and to maintain the essential civilian economy, were subjects of dispute. Quite apart from the technical problem of estimating quantities of materials and products required to maintain a given military effort over a given period of time, the determination of the new productive facilities we needed had to rest on a correct forecast of the trend of international events. What the trend was became the subject of heated controversy until Pearl Harbor. All sides accepted the proposition that some expansion in capacity was essential to produce commodities which had both civilian and military uses, but they differed about the particular industries to be expanded and about the degree of expansion. Emerging from a period in which our thinking was dominated by the problem of what to do about surpluses, we were cautious in our estimates of the future demands on our industries.

Private enterprise naturally was reluctant to invest its money in plants to produce weapons for a war that might not come, but we were not a nation traditionally disposed to invest public funds in manufacturing establishments. Government ownership of plants and machinery was anathema to many business and financial men, although some plane manufacturers were indifferent about how new factories were financed. After considerable discussion, Congress passed, and on June 25, the President approved, legislation which empowered the Reconstruction Finance Corporation—

---
[9] 54 *Stat.* 676.

(1) To make loans to, or, when requested by the Federal Loan Administrator with the approval of the President, purchase the capital stock of, any corporation (*a*) for the purpose of producing, acquiring, and carrying strategic and critical materials as defined by the President, and (*b*) for plant construction, expansion and equipment, and, working capital, to be used by the corporation in the manufacture of equipment and supplies necessary to the national defense, on such terms and conditions and with such maturities as the Corporation may determine; and

(2) When requested by the Federal Loan Administrator, with the approval of the President, to create or to organize a corporation or corporations, with power (*a*) to produce, acquire, and carry strategic and critical materials as defined by the President, (*b*) to purchase and lease land, to purchase, lease, build, and expand plants, and to purchase and produce equipment, supplies, and machinery, for the manufacture of arms, ammunition, and implements of war, (*c*) to lease such plants to private corporations to engage in such manufacture, and (*d*) if the President finds that it is necessary for a Government agency to engage in such manufacture, to engage in such manufacture itself. . . . [10]

Under this legislation, the Rubber Reserve Company and the Metals Reserve Company were established on June 28, 1940, as subsidiaries of the Reconstruction Finance Corporation. Creating of the Defense Plant Corporation and the Defense Supplies Corporation followed on August 22 and 29, respectively. By now the Reconstruction Finance Corporation had become, as large organizations tend to do, fixed in its ways, and it was proud of its record of making "sound" loans. With the encouragement of persons in the Defense Commission who disliked the idea of Government ownership of plants, the RFC wavered for some time before it decided that the Government might own outright a plant essential for national defense but not likely to be built by private investors.

At the same time that steps were being taken to get production of defense articles under way, measures were initiated quietly to mobilize the scientific brains of the country to develop new implements of war. On June 27, through an order of the Council of National Defense, the President established the National Defense Research Committee. The Committee was instructed to "correlate and support scientific research on the mechanisms and devices of warfare, except those relating to problems of flight included in the field of activities of the National Advisory Committee for Aeronautics".[11] The Committee rapidly entered into contracts with universities, industrial laboratories, and other scientific institutions to focus the scientific resources of the Nation on problems relating to the mechanisms and devices of warfare.

The process of getting the country squared away for rearmament was accompanied by prolonged and vitriolic debate over the terms on which various interests would participate in the defense program.

---

[10] 54 *Stat.* 573. [11] 5 *Federal Register* 2446.

Labor leaders thought that industry considered the emergency as a golden opportunity to liquidate labor unions and labor rights; and some industrialists undoubtedly were judged correctly. Industrialists (or some of them) thought that labor leaders saw in the emergency a golden opportunity to enlarge their domains and to hold up the Government until it met their terms; and some labor leaders undoubtedly were correctly gaged. Business was accused by labor, by politicians, and by others of conducting a "strike of capital" until they were able to get contracts on their terms. Everybody was clamoring for the Government to knock heads together; i. e., other people's heads.

The controversy crystallized around such specific issues as profit limitation, excess profits taxation, accelerated amortization for tax purposes of private investment in defense production facilities, and labor conditions to be attached to Government contracts. In the summer of 1940, these subjects were being discussed in the press, in Congress, and within the Administration. Their solution did not seem to be expedited materially by reflections on the Battle of Britain. Industrial groups were anxious to modify limitations on profits and to be assured that their investments would be amortized rapidly under the tax laws; they were somewhat less enthusiastic about settling the question of excess profits taxation. At the insistence of the President, consideration of excess profits taxation was coupled with legislation for accelerated tax amortization. Business might be permitted to write off costs of expansions necessary for defense purposes more rapidly than usual but the Government would have some protection through excess-profits taxes.

Final action on tax amortization did not come until the approval of legislation on October 8. The dispute over this subject turned out to be less important than it seemed for it developed that most war plant expansion was financed from public funds rather than by private investment. The administration of tax amortization legislation became a question largely of determining whether proposed expansions would be useful only for defense. Relatively liberal administration by the War and Navy Departments, anxious to get along with production, resulted in permission to some concerns to write off rapidly against high war profits the cost of facilities which would be usable in time of peace.

On Government policy toward labor, long and heated discussions occurred within the Advisory Commission, in the press, and on the hustings, for, it is to be remembered, this was a Presidential campaign year. Labor desired that hours of work should not be lengthened in order that idle workers might be absorbed in defense plants. It was more convenient for contractors to increase the hours of work than to put on double shifts; the War and Navy Departments sympathized with this point of view and also were impatient with the labor conditions attached to Government contracts under the Walsh-Healy Act. The National Labor Relations Act still was unpopular among employers many of whom would have welcomed an opportunity to use the defense program as a way around the legislation.

On August 31, the Advisory Commission to the Council on National Defense adopted a statement of principles on labor questions which was later transmitted to Congress by the President.[12] The Commission urged that the defense program be used to "reduce unemployment and otherwise strengthen the human fiber of our nation". It suggested that hours of work should be generally limited to 40 per week in order that the unemployed might be put to work. When more than 40 hours was necessary, overtime should be paid "in accordance with the local recognized practices." The Commission also concluded that defense work should comply with applicable Federal statutes such as the Walsh-Healy Act, the Fair Labor Standards Act, and the National Labor Relations Act as well as with State and local laws governing hours of work, wages, and related matters. The Commission declared against discrimination among workers because of age, sex, race, or color and suggested that adequate housing facilities be made available for employees. It reaffirmed a statement issued by the Chief of Ordnance of the United States Army on November 15, 1917, in which it was asserted that safeguards designed to protect labor should be retained in an emergency because they contributed to efficiency.

Progress in defense production from the fall of France to the end of 1940 was not impressive in terms of defense articles actually manufactured. Instead the period was one in which money was appropriated, contracts were awarded, war plant construction was put in motion, and other preliminaries to actual production were carried out. From June 1 to the end of December, almost $10.5 billion in contracts were awarded. Deliveries under these contracts were very small, of course, and the Government was ridiculed because, for example, it cited the number of planes "on order" as an indication of progress. An impression of the magnitude of total contract awards in the latter half of 1940 may be gained from the fact that these awards were over nine times the total amount spent for military purposes by the War and Navy Departments in the fiscal year ending June 30, 1938. Cash expenditures for all defense purposes in the month of December 1940 slightly exceeded the amount spent for naval purposes during the entire fiscal year ending June 30, 1938. Expansion was under way.

While the issues connected with getting production under way were being settled, other questions concerning the maintenance of

---

[12] *Congressional Record*, vol. 86, pt. 11, p. 12114.

the health and welfare of the civilian population were arising. Modern war had made obscure the line between the home front and the battle front and to mobilize the civilian population for defense necessitated special governmental actions in a variety of fields.

Housing was one of the first problems to emerge. The construction of new industrial plants, the erection of shipyards, and the expansion of employment in established industrial centers, stimulated movements of population which created heavy demands for shelter in centers of defense activity. In June 1940 the Central Housing Committee reported to the President that the provision of housing for workers should be undertaken "in order to avoid the enormous labor turnover and the hampering of production which was experienced in the last war".

At the time, a number of Government agencies were concerned with housing in one way or another. The Public Buildings Administration had a large construction organization which designed Government buildings and contracted for their construction. The United States Housing Authority had responsibility for low-cost family housing and the Farm Security Administration specialized in rural housing. The financing of housing was handled by the Federal Housing Administration, the Federal Home Loan Bank Board, and certain subsidiaries of the Reconstruction Finance Corporation.

The administrative problem was to focus the work and influence of all these housing agencies in the areas where developing defense activities were creating requirements for housing. The Central Housing Committee recommended that a Defense Housing Coordinator be named for the duration of the emergency. He would be connected with the Defense Advisory Commission and would be responsible for the planning and prosecution of a housing program through the existing governmental agencies. On July 21, the Defense Advisory Commission announced the appointment of Charles F. Palmer as housing coordinator to expedite housing construction and to coordinate the work of governmental housing agencies in defense centers. The coordinator within a few weeks had determined which local areas had the most urgent need for housing and should receive priority of attention by housing agencies. Steps were also soon taken to obtain appropriations for housing to be constructed directly by public agencies.

It was clear that intensification of defense activity would strain governmental health, welfare, recreational and related services and that they would have to be adapted to meet new kinds of problems. On November 28, 1940, the Federal Security Administrator was designated by order of the Council of National Defense as Coordinator of Health, Welfare, and Related Defense Activities. He was directed to "formulate and execute plans, policies, and programs designed to assure the provision of adequate services of this character to the Nation during the national-defense emergency; and to that end he shall coordinate the facilities of existing Federal agencies with respect to these several fields of action, and shall establish and maintain liaison with such other agencies, public or private, as he may deem necessary or desirable".[13]

Emergency Organization for External Affairs

Following the fall of France, and during the siege of Britain, two broad objectives animated our actions in external matters. The first was to keep Britain and her fleet in being as fighting entities. The second was to protect our Latin-American flank by economic and political action. After Dunkirk, "the British Isles were in effect defenseless so far as organized and equipped ground forces were concerned," the Chief of Staff later reported. "Practically all their field army equipment had been lost and an immediate invasion was threatened . . . For the United States the militaiy issue immediately at stake was the security of the British Fleet to dominate the Atlantic." The only sources from which immediate British needs for military equipment could be met even partially were the stocks of our Army and Navy. Steps were taken hastily to move rifles, field guns, machine guns, ammunition and other munitions to ports of embarkation, leaving the United States with enough World War stocks to equip 1,800,000 men.

The transfer of munitions enabled the British to meet their immediate crisis better equipped, but for the long pull greatly increased production in the United States was necessary to furnish a steady flow of war goods. Throughout the summer of 1940, British supply officers negotiated with the President's Liaison Committee and with officials of the Defense Commission to arrange for new facilities to produce tanks, planes, and other munitions. So far as practicable, the Government insisted that British orders should be in accord with specifications acceptable to both governments. Thus, as factories and machines came into production, we had the assurance that they would be capable of turning out war material which would be usable by American forces as well as by the British. Apart from this contribution to our national defense, the policy in the long run increased the efficiency of our productive capacity, for it reduced the variety of models of defense articles and equipment to be manufactured.

Even before Dunkirk, the British and French explored with the United States Government the possibility of acquiring a number of

---

[13] 5 *Federal Register* 4848.

the 200-odd destroyers which we had constructed for convoy duty in the First World War. The suggested transfer raised an issue painful to decide. The benefit to us of strengthening the British Navy had to be weighed against the probability that we might need the destroyers in the Pacific. Also, the proposal quickly became a subject of public discussion and strong blocs of opinion arrayed themselves on both sides.

The transfer proposal was coupled with the acquisition of naval and air bases on British possessions in the western hemisphere. Thus was suggested a way to handle the issue in a manner consonant with the domestic division of opinion. Isolationist leaders long had advocated acquisition of naval bases on nearby British possessions; interventionists were equally anxious that the pressing necessities of the British be met. The deal was made on September 2 by an exchange of notes between the British Ambassador and the Secretary of State. The right to bases in Newfoundland and Bermuda was granted freely to the United States. The right to bases in the Bahamas, Jamaica, St. Lucia, Trinidad, Antigua, and British Guiana was granted in exchange for 50 of our over-age destroyers.

Our program for external economic affairs had a negative aspect as well as the positive one of promoting production for export to friendly countries. The Government possessed a limited power to control exports, but it was necessary to broaden this authority to limit the exportation of materials which were required for our own production and to prevent the shipment of critical materials to aggressor countries. On July 2, the President approved an act which permitted him to prohibit or curtail the export of "any military equipment or munitions, or component parts thereof, or machinery, tools, or material, or supplies necessary for the manufacture, servicing, or operation thereof.. . . ." [14] On the day the act became effective, the President issued a military order designating Lt. Col. Russell L. Maxwell, United States Army, as Administrator of Export Control. The President also issued a proclamation listing materials, chemicals, products, and machine tools which were to be exported only under license. Subsequent proclamations enlarged this list. Licenses were issued by the Department of State in accordance with directives from the Administrator of Export Control.

The organization of the defense of the American republics was a matter of prime importance in the summer of 1940 because the Latin-American route offered the Germans their easiest approach to this hemisphere. It was necessary to combat Nazi economic and idealogical infiltration into the American republics as well as to take preventive military measures. In both objectives, the Good Neighbor Policy, which the Government had pursued consistently, stood us in good stead.

The Nazi advance in Western Europe brought final action on a bill to authorize the War and Navy Departments to manufacture and sell certain types of arms and munitions to the government of any American republic.[15] The legislation had been under consideration for a long time. It had been passed by the House on July 24, 1939, but did not become law until June 16, 1940. Its purpose was to make available to the American republics products manufactured in the United States by Government arsenals and factories, and thus to make the American republics less dependent on European sources of supply. This legislation was important chiefly as a gesture, since the course of events led to assistance to the Latin-American republics under the Lend-Lease Act, rather than under this act.

French, Dutch, and British possessions in Latin-America were potential bases for Axis operations. Two days after France requested an armistice, the Secretary of State transmitted to the German and Italian foreign offices a note indicating that the United States "would not recognize any transfer, and would not acquiesce in any attempt to transfer, any geographic region of the Western Hemisphere from one non-American power to another non-American power." On July 21, foreign ministers of the 21 American republics convened at Havana to consult about the difficulties and problems confronting them. The Declaration of Reciprocal Assistance and Cooperation for the Defense of the Nations of the Americas, as it emerged from the deliberations of the meeting, averred that any attempt by a non-American state against the territory or political independence of any American state would be "considered as an act of aggression against the States" signing the declaration. The signatory powers agreed to confer among themselves to agree upon measures in case such acts of aggression were committed.

While the Havana conference was in session, the President requested Congress to increase the lending power of the Export-Import Bank. He pointed out that blockades and counterblockades with the consequent disorganization of trade were causing distress in the countries of the Western Hemisphere which were unable to dispose of their commodities through their normal channels of trade. Legislation approved on September 26 increased the lending authority of the Bank from $200,000,000 to $700,000,000 and authorized it to lend up to $500,000,000 "to assist in the development of the resources, the stabilization of the economies, and orderly marketing of the products of the countries of the Western Hemisphere. . . ."[16]

---

[15] 54 *Stat.* 365.   [16] 54 *Stat.* 961.

Promotion of hemisphere solidarity demanded more effective coordination of governmental agencies concerned with various aspects of
our relations with the American republics. Although the State Department had great accomplishments to its credit in the promotion
of the Good Neighbor Policy, the traditional methods and limitations
of diplomacy made it necessary to supplement the Department's work.
The customs of diplomacy as well as its lack of legal authority restrained the State Department from participation in commercial,
cultural, and educational activities which might embarrass it in the
conduct of its normal business. Mr. Nelson Rockefeller and certain
associates proposed that there should be created an organization
which would not be hampered by the limitations of traditional diplomacy in the promotion of good will among the Latin American
republics. Their arguments were persuasive and the Office for Coordination of Commercial and Cultural Relations between the American Republics was established by order of the Council of National
Defense on August 16, 1940, with Mr. Rockefeller as Coordinator.
The Office was directed to serve as a central point for coordination of
the activities of Government departments and agencies which affected inter-American relations. It was also made responsible for
carrying on directly programs in "such fields as the arts and sciences,
education and travel, the radio, the press, and the cinema" which
would "further national defense and strengthen the bonds between
the nations of the Western Hemisphere".

By the order establishing his Office, the Coordinator was instructed
to—

(1) establish and maintain liaison between the Advisory Commission, the
several departments and establishments of the Government and with such other
agencies, public or private, as the Coordinator may deem necessary or desirable
to insure proper coordination of, and economy and efficiency in, the activities of
the Government with respect to Hemisphere defense, with particular reference to
the commercial and cultural aspects of the problem, and also shall be available
to assist in the coordination and carrying out of the purposes of Public Resolution
No. 83, Seventy-sixth Congress (H. J. Res. 367);

(2) be a member and chairman of the Interdepartmental Committee on Inter-
American Affairs, which shall include the president of the Export-Import Bank,
one designated from each of the following departments: State, Agriculture, Treasury, and Commerce, and such representatives from other agencies and departments
as may be needed from time to time, the Committee to consider and correlate proposals of the Government with respect to Hemisphere defense, commercial and
cultural relations and to make recommendations to the appropriate Government
departments and agencies;

(3) be responsible directly to the President, to whom he shall submit reports
and recommendations with respect to the activities of his office;

(4) review existing laws, coordinate research by the several Federal agencies,
and recommend to the Interdepartmental Committee such new legislation as

may be deemed essential to the effective realization of the basic objectives of the Government's program;

(5) be charged with the formulation and the execution of a program in cooperation with the State Department which, by effective use of governmental and private facilities in such fields as the arts and sciences, education and travel, radio, the press, and cinema, will further national defense and strengthen the bonds between the nations of the Western Hemisphere.[17]

Peacetime Selective Service

In an age of mechanized warfare a nation cannot "spring to arms." Men must be instructed thoroughly in the care and use of weapons and equipment often requiring great skill. But knowledge of the use of weapons and the operation of complex equipment is not enough; to become an effective team, officers and men must train together in large units under field conditions approximating those of actual military operations. In the spring of 1940, our land forces consisted of a small professional army, the National Guard, and some Reserves. Training of the regular army had been limited severely by the maintenance of the regular army in small groups at scattered posts which made it imposible to conduct field exercises with large bodies of troops. In fact, the first genuine corps and army maneuvers in the history of the Nation became possible in the late spring of 1940. The National Guard required intensive training to be brought to the proper condition, but it represented the most readily available source of additional military personnel.

In his message of May 31, asking for additional armament appropriations, the President recommended that Congress give him authority to call into active service such portions of the National Guard and Reserve as might be necessary. The request was made so that, if Congress adjourned, the President would have authority to meet contingencies which might arise during its absence from Washington. No action was taken immediately to meet the recommendation. Shortly after it was made, Italy entered the war and France surrendered. On July 29, the President reported to Congress that the "increasing seriousness of the international situation" demanded that the national defense structure should be "brought as rapidly as possible to the highest state of efficiency, in training as well as in equipment and materials." He requested Congress to authorize him to order Reserve officers to active duty and to call the National Guard to "active service for such period of intensive training as may be necessary to raise its efficiency to a point comparable with that of our small regular establishment." By legislation approved on August 27, 1940,[18] the President was granted power to call up the National

---

[17] 5 *Federal Register* 2938–39.   [18] 54 *Stat.* 858.

Guard and Reserve officers for 12 months of duty. By order of August 31, effective September 16, the President called into active military service certain elements of the National Guard, and subsequent orders brought other units into service.

Congress did not appropriate until September funds requested by the President early in July for construction of training facilities. The existing shortage of military camps made doubtful the wisdom of calling the National Guard into Federal service in September. Selective Service was, however, under consideration by Congress at the time and it was feared that to delay active duty for the Guard might result in further postponement or defeat of draft legislation.

Induction of the National Guard furnished a large block of personnel which could be trained, conditioned, and disciplined into an important addition to the defensive system. But even with this addition we had insufficient troops for defense. In the summer of 1940, the Administration felt that large numbers of men should be trained for military service. The issue was whether to rely on recruitment of volunteers or to adopt conscription. The introduction of compulsory military training in time of peace presented a grave issue which aroused prolonged debate in Congress and the country at large. The wisdom and necessity of the action were doubted by men of unquestioned sincerity. Thus a distinguished Senator declared—

. . . Mr. President, were I to be a party to riveting shackles of militarism upon the American people, and superimposing upon the American people in time of peace, the damnable system of conscription which has devastated and ruined Europe, I could not hope for any peace with myself hereafter.
. . .

Mr. President, this bill is supported by some of the ablest men in the Senate and in the country. When they come to reflect within a few months after their fever has abated and realize that they were hurried beyond necessity and hurried beyond the requirements of the hour, I venture the assertion that many if not most of those who vote for this bill will regret it, because they are men of conscience; and when the last hour comes and the last scene comes for them and they review their careers, they will say, "That is one vote I cast that I would recall if I could." [19]

Our traditional fear of militarism was a major basis of opposition to the proposal. Another objection, which applied also to other issues then under consideration, was the belief that military training was a step toward war:

More than a year ago—I think it was a year and a half or 2 years ago—I said that I would stand at this desk until the end against war; and I repeat that statement, Mr. President . . . I do not know whether the President wants all the power we are giving him here or not, but I know that we cannot give it to him and convince the American people that we are not ready and resigned and reconciled to the final, inevitable, short step of actually entering the war.[20]

---

[19] Senator Ashurst, *Congressional Record*, Vol. 86, pt. 10, pp. 11110–11.
[20] Senator George, *Congressional Record*, Vol. 86, pt. 10, pp. 11097–98.

The proposal to draft manpower inevitably suggested the conscription of property. Delays in the execution of defense contracts because of uncertainty about profits added fuel to the flames and brought demands by some members of Congress for the conscription of industry as well as men. With equal vigor others opposed the conscription of factories. For example:

> This is a most extraordinary provision for the confiscation, or at least the appropriation, of property. It modifies every concept of American law we have ever had, as does the draft law. If it were absolutely necessary in time of war, I should be in favor of it; but I do not believe the emergency is one which justifies the drafting of men. I shall refuse to vote for any measure to draft men, and I do not propose to vote for any measure to draft property.[11]

Debate on the issue was by no means restricted to the halls of Congress. Discussion flared throughout the country, but public opinion gradually crystallized in favor of the draft. The trend in

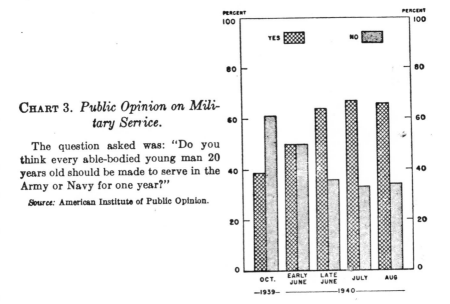

CHART 3. *Public Opinion on Military Service.*

The question asked was: "Do you think every able-bodied young man 20 years old should be made to serve in the Army or Navy for one year?"

Source: American Institute of Public Opinion.

opinion, as measured by the opinion polls, is shown by the chart on this page. Opinion became much more favorable after the fall of France, and the upward trend continued during the summer months of 1940. After thorough consideration of every phase of the problem Congress enacted selective service legislation which was approved on September 16; it included provisions permitting obligatory orders upon industry and empowering the Government, if necessary, to seize plants and operate them.

---

[11] Senator Taft, *Congressional Record*, Vol. 86, pt. 10, p. 11101.

Passage of the Selective Service Act made a huge administrative mechanism necessary for the selection and induction of personnel for military training. Preparatory work by the General Staff of the War Department under way since 1926 included the preliminary training of Reserve officeis and National Guard officers for the administration of selective service. As the passage of the bill approached, the President appointed a civilian committee to cooperate with the Joint Aimy and Navy Selective Service Committee with the consequence that plans which had been developed by the Joint Committee were further revised in the light of the viewpoint of the President's Committee. Once the plans were completed, the rapid creation of machinery for the administration of the legislation was made possible by the collaboration of State and local governments. On October 16, 30 days after the law became effective, more than 16 million men were registered at more than 125,000 registration points in the United States. In the creation of local boards to function in the administration of selective service after the initial listing of registrants, State Governors prepared lists of persons for nomination to the President in whom the power of appointment was vested. In each State a headquarters was established to supervise the work of local boards. Federal-State cooperation and the willingness of thousands of citizens to volunteer their services enabled the rapid erection of a far-flung administrative apparatus which was to function remarkably well in view of the magnitude of its job.

The Cumulation of Events

In the months following the President's message of May 16, 1940, the Nation slowly moved toward great decisions. This process of making up our national mind about what to do in the world crisis was reflected in a series of basic laws. Before the end of 1940 legislation had been enacted to alter the peacetime rules for letting production contracts, to fix new rules to prevent excessive profits on contracts, to permit the Government to undertake the procurement of raw materials and the construction of facilities, to appropriate huge sums of money for defense, to establish the selective service principle, and to deal with a variety of related subjects. When war came in December 1941 further legislative action was necessary, but the legislation essential to authorize preparation for defense had already been enacted. The situation which confronted the Nation had not been foreseen by those responsible for planning for mobilization. They had thought that industrial mobilization would not really get under way until after a declaration of war, a condition under which expression of the national will through legislation would present a different problem.

CHART 4. *Development of the War Organization.*

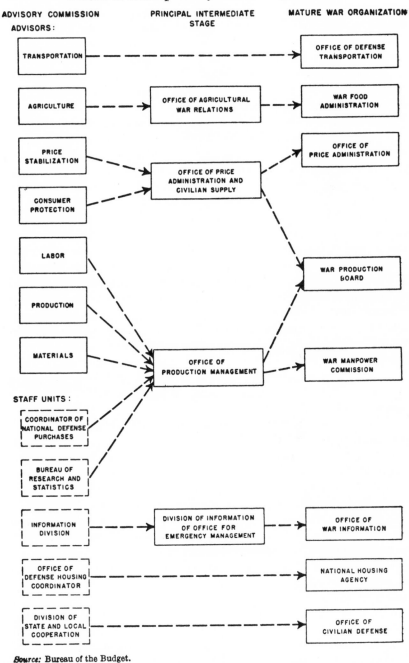

Source: Bureau of the Budget.

On the administrative side, the Government's defense actions in 1940 were limited to the establishment of partial administrative machinery for partial industrial mobilization. The general political divisions were reflected in the form and rate of development of the administrative machinery and in the designations of the principal personnel. Moreover, the inchoate nature of the administrative machinery was not unaffected by the uncertainty which remained in national purpose. Had there been more general expectation that we would be attacked and that a more rapid industrial mobilization should be undertaken, the governmental mechanisms would have been different. Nevertheless, the Defense Advisory Commission and its subsidiary organizations contained in embryonic form many of the agencies which were developed more fully later. In the small and fairly simple administrative mechanisms created in the summer of 1940 were to be found the seeds of the Office of Production Management, the Office of Price Administration and Civilian Supply, and the Office of Defense Transportation. Some of the functions later to be performed by the War Manpower Commission, particularly in the field of labor training, were got under way on a small scale. The Administrator of Export Control eventually furnished part of the Economic Defense Board organization. The Defense Housing Coordinator, established as an agency of the Defense Commission, later served as the core of the National Housing Agency. The Coordinator of Commercial and Cultural Relations between the American Republics, also created as a subsidiary of the Council of National Defense, was to have a continuous existence throughout the war. The Division of State and Local Cooperation later became the basis for the Office of Civilian Defense. The Reconstruction Finance Corporation set up various subsidiaries for defense purposes and began to work out policies and procedures. Building up the Selective Service System, in collaboration with the State governments, was a remarkable administrative performance involving the participation of more than 100,000 volunteer and unpaid workers throughout the Nation.

In the steps taken and not taken in 1940, there were many grievous miscalculations as well as actions which subsequent events proved to be wise. In the accumulation of stock piles and in the development of additional facilities for the production of raw materials, the goals were fixed far too low. Notable cases were rubber, aluminum, and steel. In general, miscalculations of this sort were premised on erroneous estimates of the probable course of international events and on unimaginative forecasts of the magnitude of the effort we would have to make. The trend of action was not uncolored by fears of surpluses and overcapacity. On the other hand, a vast program for the construction of plants to manufacture weapons of war was got under way, although by the end of 1940 only a trickle of arms was coming off the production line. The explanation and the lesson is that it takes time to build factories and to get them into operation. These variations in the rate of progress in the defense program pointed to the lack of sufficient coordination within the administration to assure common action on all fronts.

After the election of 1940 and the conclusion of Congressional debates on major issues of the mobilization policy, the time was ripe for further steps in development of the Government's machinery for industrial mobilization. The campaign, although conducted with great fervor and not a little asperity on both sides, strengthened the position of the Government. The campaign was remarkable, not for the divisions it revealed but for the range of agreement among both major parties which it demonstrated. On the general direction which the country should follow, there was substantial agreement, but there was warm dispute about which party could take us in that direction most effectively. Criticisms made in the campaign, experiences in operation, and the growth in the defense program itself all made it clear that further developments in the machinery of Government were in order.

CHAPTER

3

Laying Administrative Foundations

IN THE presidential campaign of 1940 there was no issue between the nominees of the two major parties on the question of material aid to nations resisting aggression. Within both parties, however, there remained opposition from people who insisted that events abroad need have no consequences for the United States. Against this belief leaders of the Administration directed a vigorous attack. The Secretary of State, in a radio address on October 26, insisted that we were "in the presence not of local or regional wars, but of an organized and determined movement for steadily expanding conquest." No nation, he asserted, could secure itself against the threat of attack except through formidable defense. Any contention that the United States should not furnish supplies to those defending themselves against barbaric attack constituted, he averred, a denial "of the inalienable right of self-defense." By aiding such nations we reduced the danger to ourselves.

The Secretary's diagnosis of the nature of the world conflict was quickly confirmed. In the last months of 1940 the contagion of aggression continued to spread. Late in October, Italy invaded Greece. In November, Romania joined the Axis powers. Bulgaria was threatened. The Axis drive into the Balkans menaced Britain's Mediterranean life line. On the Eastern front Germany had strong forces drawn up to reenforce her hope that the U. S. S. R. would accept the primacy of the Nazis in Europe.

The British were holding out alone. The diagnosis of Axis strategy was that Britain might be conquered; and, after that, Germany and Japan would be free to attack us from the East and the West. The situation in the Far East gave basis for the fear that Japan might take advantage of such an opportunity. If this estimate of Axis intentions

43

was correct, it was crucial that Britain should be kept in being. Our policy of aid to those resisting aggression, however, was limited by the "cash-and-carry" principle which had been adopted as part of a program to keep us out of war. We would aid Britain to the extent that she was able to pay for our help. As the end of 1940 approached, the uncommitted dollar balances of the British had almost disappeared. If the defense of Britain was vital to the defense of the United States, some way had to be found to aid her without requiring that she should pay spot cash for our assistance. The answer was found in the lend-lease idea.

Debate over lend-lease in the early months of 1941 overshadowed the administrative evolution occurring in the Government. Yet during 1941 almost the entire administrative structure essential for war, should it come, emerged. The Advisory Commission to the Council on National Defense gave way to agencies more suited to the changing tasks of administration. Men had been tested. Some had been found wanting and others proved themselves and could be advanced to positions of greater responsibility as the administrative machine was altered. The wisdom of maintaining a fluid administrative structure demonstrated itself as changes became necessary to meet new conditions. The first 7 months of 1941 saw the birth of the Office of Production Management, the Office of Price Administration and Civilian Suppply, the Coordinator of Information, the National Defense Mediation Board, the Petroleum Coordinator, the Office of Scientific Research and Development, the Office of Civilian Defense, and the Economic Defense Board. Most of these agencies came into existence as units of the Office for Emergency Management. New conditions required that new administrative arrangements be made quickly and thus showed the soundness of the broad administrative strategy of maintaining presidential initiative in matters of emergency governmental organization. The legal basis for this initiative had been provided with considerable prevision in 1939 in actions laying the basis for an office for emergency management should necessity arise. Thus, in addition to serving as a means for assisting the President in general management, the Office for Emergency Management became something of a holding company for emergency agencies and a legal device for permitting flexibility in emergency organization.

Lend-Lease Enacted

In his press conference of December 17, 1940, the President stated that methods were being devised to continue aid to Britain in spite of her disappearing dollar balances. He noted that British war orders resulted in the construction of new manufacturing facilities which increased our capacity to produce munitions and improved our defensive position. From a purely selfish point of view, British orders thus were a tremendous asset to the United States. The traditional ways of continuing these orders included private or public loans and gifts. But these were not the only ways. The President discussed with the representatives of the press types of arrangements which might be made that fitted neither of these categories and foreshadowed proposals which he was to make to Congress later.

In a radio broadcast on December 29, the President reviewed the position of the United States in the current crisis. He asserted that it was the purpose of the Axis powers "to dominate the rest of the world." He pointed to Great Britain's role in keeping the Axis powers out of the Western Hemisphere. He pointed to the fact that in Asia, the Japanese were being "engaged by the Chinese nation in another great defense." If Britain should fall, he said, the Axis would "be in a position to bring enormous military and naval resources against this hemisphere." He denied that the Nazis could be appeased. "The American appeasers," he said, "ignore the warning to be found in the fate of Austria, Czechoslovakia, Poland, Norway, Belgium, the Netherlands, Denmark, and France." He urged the utmost effort to meet the needs of the people of Europe who were defending themselves against the Axis. "Emphatically we must get these weapons to them in sufficient volume and quickly enough, so that we and our children will be saved the agony and suffering of war which others had had to endure. . . . We must be the great arsenal of democracy," the President said. "For us this is an emergency as serious as war itself." In his annual message on the State of the Union, delivered January 6, 1941, the President requested Congress to enact the lend-lease principle. ℓHe found it, "unhappily, necessary to report that the future and safety of our country and of our democracy" were "overwhelmingly involved in events far beyond our borders."

A bill to carry out the presidential recommendation was introduced on January 10, 1941, in the Senate by Senator Alben W. Barkley and in the House by Representative John W. McCormack. Consideration of the bill precipitated a debate which centered first in hearings before the House Committee on Foreign Affairs. The Secretary of State, the Secretary of War, the Secretary of the Navy, the Secretary of the Treasury, and the Director-General of the Office of Production Management testified in favor of the bill. The proposal was opposed, as it was supported, by all kinds of people. William R. Castle, former Under Secretary of State, thought the "real purpose" of the bill was "to create a dictatorship." [1] Gerald L. K. Smith, National

---

[1] U. S. Congress. House. Committee on Foreign Affairs. Hearings on H. R. 1776, 77th Congress, 1st Session, p. 483.

Chairman of the Committee of One Million, asserted that the bill would give the President powers which had "been granted only to the dictators of the world," and that it would be "the first step in sending from 1 to 5 million American boys across oceans to die on the battlefields of five continents." [2] William J. Grace, Chairman of The Citizens Keep America Out of War Committee, demanded that we use our resources to build an impregnable defense and that we "keep free from taking sides and inviting war through encouraging the continuance of fighting or through inflammatory denunciations of belligerents." [3] The two organizations with most influence in the controversy—The Committee to Defend America by Aiding the Allies and the America First Committee—expressed their views before the committees and in public debate. Wendell Willkie, the 1940 Republican presidential candidate, urged adoption of the principles of the bill.

Discussion of the bill revealed again not only the deep national hatred of war but also the deep sympathy of this country with the people of Britain and other nations resisting aggression. Unity prevailed on the necessity for promoting our own national defense. That aid to the victims of aggression would promote our defense, however, was a proposition challenged by at least a considerable minority. A demand for immediate intervention came from significant sectors of the people, but, on the whole, the Nation was united in aversion to war. Choice of a course of action was complicated further by memories of war debts and by a widespread belief that munitions makers were "merchants of death." Cross currents in the hopes and aspirations of the American people made the task of political leadership one of unprecedented difficulty. To a majority of the people and to a majority in Congress the bill offered a way by which we could aid the decent people of the world and have at least a chance of keeping out of war ourselves. On February 8, the House passed the bill by a vote of 260 to 165. On March 8, the Senate passed an amended version of the measure by a vote of 60 to 31. On March 11, the House concurred in the Senate amendments by a vote of 317 to 71. On the same day, the President approved the legislation.

Action on the lend-lease question, like action on other major issues, followed changes in public opinion. The public probably kept ahead of its government. The data recorded in chart 5 indicate the growth in 1940 of opinion favorable to aiding Britain even at the risk of war and the rise in the degree of expectation that we might become involved in war.

The Lend-Lease Law, an "Act further to promote the defense of the United States, and for other purposes" [4] placed heavy responsibilities

---

[1] *Ibid.*, pp. 538–539.   [3] *Ibid.*, p. 558.   [4] 55 *Stat.* 31.

upon the President. When he deemed it "in the interest of national defense," he was empowered to authorize the Secretary of War, the Secretary of the Navy, or the head of any other agency to manufacture or procure any "defense article" for "any country whose defense" the President deemed "vital to the defense of the United States." Likewise, he might authorize the transfer by Government departments of defense articles already on hand up to a value of $1,300,000,000. "Defense article" was defined broadly to include weapons, munitions, aircraft, vessels, machinery, tools, materials, supplies, or any agricultural, industrial or other commodity or article for defense. In addition, the President was empowered to direct Government departments to repair or recondition defense articles for governments whose defense he considered vital to our defense and to communicate "defense information," i. e., plans, specifications, designs, and other data, to any such government.

The terms and conditions under which any foreign government might receive aid were to be those which the President deemed "satisfactory." Reciprocal advantages to the United States might be "payment or repayment in kind or property, or any other direct

CHART 5. *Public Opinion on U. S. entry into the War.*

The questions asked were: "Do you think the U. S. will go into the war in Europe sometime before it is over, or do you think we will stay out of the war?"

"Which of these two things is more important for the U. S. to try to do— to keep out of the war ourselves or to help England even at the risk of getting into the war?"

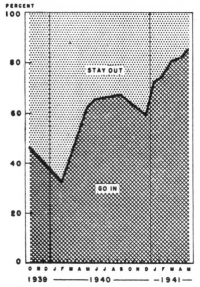
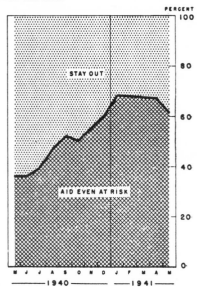

Source: American Institute of Public Opinion.

or indirect benefit which the President deemed "satisfactory." The President was required to report to Congress at 90-day intervals on operations under the act but he was not bound to include information which he deemed "incompatible with the public interest to disclose."

Additional responsibility was placed on the President by an act of March 27, which appropriated $7 billion for lend-lease purposes. This act recognized that procurement of articles for direct use by the United States would have to be merged with purchases for lend-lease purposes and that allocations to the United States and to other countries would have to be made when the goods were completed and ready for delivery. The appropriation act specified that defense articles purchased with lend-lease funds might be retained "in lieu of being disposed of to a foreign government, whenever in the judgment of the President the defense of the United States" would "be best served thereby." [5] The President thus had to divide our production between ourselves and countries whose defense was vital to our defense.

The gravity of the responsibilities placed upon the President by the Lend-Lease Act made the provision of machinery for its administration of special importance. Matters of national policy of first rate magnitude had to be decided and in the execution of the program through production, procurement and delivery of goods the collaboration of several major departments of Government had to be assured. Even before adoption of the act, in contemplation of its passage several plans of administration were developed within the Government. One proposal was to establish a Foreign Supply Policy Committee consisting of the Secretary of War, the Secretary of the Navy, the Secretary of the Treasury, and the Director-General of the Office of Production Management. This Committee would have advised the President on policies and would have supervised an Office of Foreign Supply which would have been responsible for handling the details. Another suggestion was to create an all-inclusive Defense Policy Board with a similar composition and mission. A third idea was to establish a Cabinet Committee on Defense Aid to the Democracies, which would have consisted of the Secretaries of State, Treasury, War, and the Navy, and would have advised and assisted the President in formulating policies and plans. This scheme would have established an Office of Defense Aid to serve as the agent of the President in seeing that the policies were executed by the various agencies of the Government.

All these plans apparently drew their inspiration in part from the liaison committee established by the President in December 1939, to coordinate foreign military purchases with the United States program.

[5] *55 Stat.* 53.

That committee had consisted of the Secretaries of the Treasury, War, and the Navy. The outcome of the discussions of these plans was the rejection of proposals for cabinet committees and other like bodies and the centering of responsibility squarely upon the President. By this means the President averted the almost inevitable embarrassment of being confronted with the recommendations of a cabinet committee influenced by the desires of Government departments for an immediate strengthening of our own defenses at the expense of a longer-term global strategy of keeping other nations in being as fighting entities. On March 27, 1941, the President designated Harry Hopkins "to advise and assist" him in carrying out the lend-lease program and on May 2 established by Executive order in the Office of Emergency Management a Division of Defense Aid Reports headed by an executive officer appointed by the President. The President retained the authority to make policy decisions, but he directed the Division of Defense Aid Reports to—

(a) Provide a central channel for the clearance of transactions and reports, and coordinate the processing of requests for aid under the act.

(b) Maintain such system of records and summary accounts to be approved by the Bureau of the Budget, as may be necessary for adequate administrative and financial control over operations under the act and as will currently reflect the status of all such operations.

(c) Prepare such reports as may be necessary to keep the President informed of progress under the act; assist in the preparation of reports pursuant to section 5B of the act; and serve generally as a clearinghouse of information for agencies participating in the program.

(d) Perform such other duties relating to defense aid activities as the President may from time to time prescribe.[6]

On May 6 the President signed a military order designating Maj. Gen. James H. Burns as Executive Officer of the Division of Defense Aid Reports.

The general system for administration of the Lend-Lease Act thus provided for retention by the President of control over lend-lease policy. Although the President was roundly criticized for keeping control in his hands, this arrangement was demanded by the kinds of policy decisions which had to be made. What countries should receive lend-lease aid? On what terms should they receive it? In what quantities should goods be transferred to particular countries? What weight should be given to the immediate necessities of our own military services in comparison with the advantages to be gained by aiding other countries? Only the President could decide these kinds of questions; they were not delegable. Operating authority, however, was freely delegated. Procurement was conducted by the depart-

---

[6] Executive Order No. 8751, May 2, 1941, 6 *Federal Register* 2301.

ments and agencies best fitted to buy particular articles or to arrange for their production. The Division of Defense Aid Reports coordinated requests for aid, kept records and accounts, and maintained liaison among the departments concerned with the execution of the program. Gradually as policies and lines of action were established, it became possible to identify and delegate subordinate issues of policy which could be decided within limits already fixed by the President. By regulation of June 20, 1941, the President authorized the executive officer of the Division of Defense Aid Reports to determine the value of defense articles, services, and information transferred or received by the United States.[7] By letter of July 26, the Executive Officer was empowered by the President to transfer defense articles in value of not over $15 million to any country whose defense the President previously had determined to be vital to the defense of the United States.

On August 29, the President issued a much broader authorization to the executive officer of the Division of Defense Aid Reports. Within the over-all allocation of funds made by the President, the executive officer was authorized to transfer, or to revoke transfers of, "defense articles and defense information other than aircraft, aircraft engines, antiaircraft guns, tanks, and vessels and defense information pertaining to such articles." The letter also authorized the executive officer to make adjustments within the aggregate amounts allocated by the President to the several procurement agencies by increasing or decreasing the quantities of articles to be purchased by such. agencies or by substituting other articles.

Agencies Evolving from the Advisory Commission

Concurrently with germination of the lend-lease idea, the adequacy of governmental machinery for direction of the defense program was under review. The National Defense Advisory Commission, established in May 1940 had been only a first step; the individual advisors were instructed to develop plans for action which might be required in their respective spheres. In the areas of interest of the individual advisors—industrial materials, industrial production, employment, farm products, transportation, price stabilization, and consumer protection—small staffs had been built up and extensive studies made of what might be required. In some fields, especially purchasing, production, and materials, considerable progress has been made—the critics were later proved right in claiming that it had not been enough. As work got under way the initial theories on which the Commission had been founded ceased to fit the facts. The Commission had been

---

[7] 6 *Federal Register* 3266.

designed to be advisory; it soon acquired operating functions in such areas as the approval of military contracts and the review of applications for accelerated tax amortization on defense production facilities. It had not been created as a Commission; a convenient statute had been used as the basis for the appointment of a series of individual advisors. Yet the Commission acquired a corporate personality and attempted to work as a group.

The enlargement of the national effort implicit in the lend-lease program made it advisable to provide more elaborate governmental machinery to handle the defense effort. Some of the questions regarded as only in the planning phase at the time of the creation of the Commission, such as price stabilization, were beginning to move into the action stage. Also on purely political grounds change seemed expedient. The Advisory Commission had been subjected to steady criticism on the ground that authority was divided and that the defense effort should be headed by a single individual other than the President. The factors which made inadvisable the designation of a single individual in May 1940 still existed at the end of the year. In American public life, even in time of national emergency, the supply of recognized leaders of national stature who are regarded as persons with views transcending their class or group interests seems to be extremely limited. Appointed officials new to politics are frequently regarded as representatives of particular social groups or classes. Persons known to be attached to the national interest and regarded by all groups as earnest defenders of the general interest are few. The make-up of the Advisory Commission was adapted to coping with these general considerations. Individually its members might be spokesmen for class, group or interest, but the impression collectively was that no single group enjoyed special advantages.

The reorganization of machinery for defense, plainly necessary by the end of 1940, presented problems of statesmanship far more complex than those concerning the administrative structure of the Government. The issue in large measure was who was going to run the defense program. Given the strength of special interests in American society and the shortage of leaders generally regarded as attached to the national interest, the issue of who was to control was posed sharply by the demand for the appointment of a single defense czar. This suggestion clothed a variety of motives. Some people believed that such an arrangement was absolutely essential but others advocated it in the hope that the President would abdicate a large part of his responsibility to some person more to their liking. As it became clear that there would be a reorganization—and that there was at least a chance for a defense "czar"—a desperate struggle for position got under way. Industrial and financial groups sought to gain control of the defense program. The War and Navy Departments in the main were allied with them. Other groups, with equal zeal, fought to retain their gains of the preceding years and to prevent domination of the Government by industrial and financial interests. Mr. Knudsen, Defense Commission advisor on industrial production, and Mr. Hillman, Defense Commission advisor on employment, came to be regarded as spearheads of the industrial and labor groups respectively. Personally they were quite willing to accept whatever role the President assigned to them, but others energetically promoted their candidacy for a dominant role.

The broad issues were pointed up in a plan which Mr. Knudsen proposed to the President at his request late in November 1940. Under this proposal a Director of Industrial Mobilization would have been placed in charge of administrative units dealing with planning, procurement, export and import control, raw materials, production, transportation, labor, price control, domestic requirements, and statistics. The plan was built on the idea that the Advisor on Industrial Production should become a Director of Industrial Mobilization, vested with power to supervise and direct almost the entire home front effort. In its essentials it restated the Army-Navy Industrial Mobilization Plan, a scheme already rejected by the President. It would have placed in the hands of the proposed Director of Industrial Mobilization the functions which eventually came to be performed by the War Production Board, the Office of Price Administration, the War Manpower Commission, the Foreign Economic Administration, and other agencies as well.

Apart from the administrative difficulties inherent in the management of an agency with such broad responsibilities, the designation of its chief would have presented a problem of acute difficulty in view of the belief prevailing generally that whoever managed the defense program would represent some class, group or interest. It is not astonishing that the controversy over administrative structure became surcharged with overtones of social conflict. A bitter political campaign had just been fought, and tempers and feelings were still high. A domestic political equilibrium had to be maintained to deal with lend-lease and other divisive issues which would arise in the months ahead. In Congress and out, there were disputes and fears about profits on defense contracts, and charges of a "strike of capital" against participation in the defense program except on its own terms had been made not without some color of truth. Under these circumstances, a decision on administrative organization tended to become a decision on which group should control the production program. In the calculus of the politics of democracy, a move too far in the direction of the interests of any one group might seriously weaken support of the Government in its efforts to deal with current and forthcoming crises.

The outcome was a decision which appeared to be a clear-cut victory for no single group. The President decided that the new agency—the Office of Production Management, a unit of the Office for Emergency Management—should concern itself only with production. It would assume the work of the Advisory Commission on industrial production, raw materials, and priorities and the activities of the Commission's Coordinator of National Defense Purchases. To it were shortly transferred the work of the Advisor on Employment and the Commission's Bureau of Research and Statistics, although these shifts were not included in the plan as first announced. Exports and imports, price control, consumer protection, agriculture, transportation, and other subjects would continue to be dealt with by existing agencies and officials. Again the concept of the Army-Navy Industrial Mobilization Plan of a home-front "czar" with extremely broad powers was rejected. At a press conference on December 20, 1940, the President outlined in general terms the structure of the new Office of Production Management, details of which were to be spelled out in an Executive order. In his discussion with the press, the President ridiculed the notion that there could be found one "Czar," "Poobah" or "Akhoond of Swat" who would embody all the characteristics necessary for handling defense mobilization. In the President's analysis the problem had three elements, that of the buyer and user combined and those of management and labor. The Office of Production Management was to consist of these "three elements, divided among four people—the Director, Mr. Knudsen, and the Associate Director, Mr. Hillman" and the Secretary of War and the Secretary of the Navy. Production, purchasing and priorities were to be under the policy supervision of these four persons.[8]

It was unusually difficult to phrase the presidential solution of the problem in an Executive order. The Bureau of the Budget, which was responsible for drafting the order, prepared at least a dozen drafts for discussion and clearance with the interested persons. In the process of negotiation it became plain that not all of these persons had understood the President's determinations in exactly the same way. Some person, whose identity not even the Secret Service could determine with certainty, gave the content of one confidential draft to a newspaper reporter in an apparent attempt to gain publicity that would force the hand of the President in the negotiations. The crux of the problem was the definition of the relationship between the Director-General and the Associate Director-General. It was clear that the

[8] Roosevelt, Franklin D. *The Public Papers and Addresses of* . . . New York: Macmillan Company, 1941. 1940 Vol., pp. 622–631.

Secretary of War, the Secretary of the Navy and Messrs. Knudsen and Hillman were equal in their capacity as members of the policy council of the OPM. The relative status of Messrs. Knudsen and Hillman in managing the OPM organization was a different matter. Formulation of this relation defied the skills of the drafting experts, and the President pencilled into their version the following language:

> The Director-General, in association with the Associate Director-General, and serving under the direction and supervision of the President, shall discharge and perform the administrative responsibilities and duties . . . vested in the Office of Production Management.

The President's exposition of the positions of the Director-General and the Associate Director-General at his press conference of January 7, 1941, gave no satisfaction to those who demanded a single-headed administration of the defense effort.

> I suppose the easiest way to put it is that these four people—the Office of Production Management, Knudsen, Hillman, and the two Secretaries—fix the policy and then Knudsen and Hillman carry it out, just like a law firm that has a case; say there are two partners, and they carry it out as a law firm. Anybody that knows anything about management will realize that that is the practical way to handle that kind of a matter, just like a law firm with two main partners.
>
> Q. Are they equals?
> The PRESIDENT. That's not the point; they're a firm. Is a firm equals? I don't know. See what I mean? Roosevelt and O'Connor was a law firm in New York; there were just two partners. I don't know whether we were equal or not. Probably we might have disagreed in regard to a catch question of that kind; but we never had a dispute or an argument.
>
>   *   *   *   *   *   *   *
>
> Q. Why is it you don't want a single, responsible head?
> The PRESIDENT. I have a single, responsible head; his name is Knudsen and Hillman.
> Q. Two heads.
> The PRESIDENT. No, that's one head. In other words, aren't you looking for trouble? Would you rather come to one law firm, or two?
> Q. I don't think that's comparable.
> The PRESIDENT. Just the same thing, exactly. Wait until you run into trouble.
> Q. I would rather avoid trouble.
> The PRESIDENT. I think they will. They think they will—that's an interesting thing.

Oddly enough they did avoid trouble. The partnership of a Danish immigrant turned assembly-line genius and a Lithuanian immigrant who had achieved eminence in the labor movement worked much better than the critics foresaw. It worked well enough so that each could contribute his special talents at a time when they were most needed, that is, when mass production techniques had to be planned into an expanding munitions industry accustomed to small-scale operation and when government policy had to take special account of the problems incident to the fitting of masses of people into new jobs. At the same time the partnership symbolized a domestic political coalition in the national interest.

The major functions placed in the Office of Production Management by the Executive order were to—

(a) Formulate and execute in the public interest all measures needful and appropriate in order (1) to increase, accelerate, and regulate the production and supply of materials, articles, and equipment and the provision of emergency plant facilities and services required for the national defense, and (2) to insure effective coordination of those activities of the several departments, corporations, and other agencies of the Government which are directly concerned therewith.

(b) Survey, analyze, and summarize for purposes of coordination the stated requirements of the War and Navy and other departments and agencies of the Government, and of foreign governments for materials, articles, and equipment needed for defense.

(c) Advise with respect to the plans and schedules of the various departments and agencies for the purchase of materials, articles, and equipment required for defense, to coordinate the placement of major defense orders and contracts and to keep informed of the progress of the various programs of production and supply.

(d) Plan and take all lawful steps necessary to assure the provision of an adequate supply of raw materials essential to the production of finished products needed for defense.

(e) Formulate plans for the mobilization for defense of the production facilities of the Nation, and to take all lawful action necessary to carry out such plans.

(f) Determine the adequacy of existing production facilities and to assure their maximum use; and, when necessary, to stimulate and plan the creation of such additional facilities and sources of production and supply as may be essential to increase and expedite defense production.

(g) Determine when, to what extent, and in what manner priorities shall be accorded to deliveries of material as provided in Section 2 (a) of the act entitled "An Act to Expedite National Defense and for other Purposes," approved June 28, 1940. Deliveries of material shall take priority, as provided in said act, in accordance with such determinations and the orders issued in pursuance thereof by the Office of Production Management.[9]

The functions of the Office of Production Management, as contemplated by the Executive order, were limited in various respects. The Office was concerned primarily with direct defense requirements; responsibility for civilian production was a gap in the administrative machinery to be filled later. The chief operating authority of the Office was the priorities power, a power which did not have to be used extensively until late in 1941. On other matters the Office stimulated, advised, planned, coordinated. With respect to the level of military production, the Office could only "survey, analyze, and summarize" the "stated" requirements of the War and Navy Departments. It could not raise the number of tanks or guns stated as required by the War Department, but it could criticize and it did. The Office could "coordinate" the work of Government agencies which had to carry on their operations in the light of total military needs. It

---

[9] Executive Order No. 8629, January 7, 1941, 6 *Federal Register* 191.

could, for example, stimulate and plan the construction of additional factories, smelters, and other productive facilities. It could advise on purchasing methods and policies. Legal power to place contracts for defense facilities and articles remained in the War and Navy Departments, the Maritime Commission, and the defense subsidiaries of the Reconstruction Finance Corporation. The OPM could view the program as a whole, attempt to anticipate future needs especially in raw materials, and try to see that the work of all government agencies contributed to meet these future needs. Its creation constituted a step in the necessarily slow development of a huge and complex governmental organization. This administrative machine was constituted necessarily of many parts but ways had to be found to tie them together into a working whole.

In some respects, the internal organization of the Office of Production Management presented more significant issues of an administrative character than did the much discussed dual leadership. The Office began with three operating divisions—Production; Purchases; and Priorities—which were inherited, more or less intact, from the Advisory Commission. For convenience in dealing with industry, it was recognized immediately that it would be better to organize along commodity lines, i. e., concentrate at one administrative point production, purchase, and priority functions relating to a particular commodity. It required, however, several months to reorganize a going administrative structure made immalleable both by normal rigidity of organizations and the attachment of the interests of strong personalities of the Office to the initial divisional system. The three operating divisions soon were supplemented by a Labor Division and a Bureau of Research and Statistics, both of which were created out of services transferred from the Advisory Commission.

Another element was added to the machinery for economic control by the creation of the Office of Price Administration and Civilian Supply by Executive order on April 11, 1941. This Office, which inherited the functions and staff of the advisor on price stabilization of the National Defense Advisory Commission, filled one of the gaps left by the establishment of the Office of Production Management which was to be concerned chiefly with military production. The following paragraph of the Executive order sets forth the main functions of OPACS, which was to—

Take all lawful steps necessary or appropriate in order (1) to prevent price spiraling, rising costs of living, profiteering, and inflation resulting from market conditions caused by the diversion of large segments of the Nation's resources to the defense program, by interruptions to normal sources of supply, or by other influences growing out of the emergency; (2) to prevent speculative accumulation, withholding, and hoarding of materials and commodities; (3) to stimulate provision of the necessary supply of materials and commodities required for civilian use, in such manner as not to conflict with the requirements of the War, Navy and other departments and agencies of the Government, and of foreign governments, for materials, articles and equipment needed for defense (such requirements are hereinafter referred to as "military defense needs"); and (4) after the satisfaction of military defense needs to provide, through the determination of policies and the formulation of plans, and programs, for the equitable distribution of the residual supply of such materials and commodities among competing civilian demands.[10]

The linking of price control and civilian supply in the Office arose from the fact that scarcities brought pressure on prices; control of the distribution of scarce supplies of OPACS would enable it to sterilize nonessential demand as well as to guide the flow of scarce supplies to the most essential civilian uses. The Office, however, depended upon OPM which possessed the priority power, for the execution of its programs for the "equitable distribution of the residual supply" of scarce materials and commodities among "competing civilian demands". The price stabilization functions of OPACS had to be improvised in contrast with the state of affairs contemplated by the Industrial Mobilization Plan. That plan had envisaged a state of war in which legislation could readily be obtained for any purpose. OPACS had no power to control prices. It had to do what it could in a period of defense preparation during a state of peace. On the whole, it was limited to persuasion in the control of prices and to administrative preparation and policy planning for the future. Its price edicts were, as the quip went, perfectly constitutional being solidly grounded on the right of freedom of speech. "Jaw-bone" price control, as it came to be known, excelled inaction, but the effects were not all that might be desired.

The Office of Production Management and the Office of Price Administration and Civilian Supply were the two largest agencies to grow out of the Advisory Commission to the Council on National Defense. During the first half of 1941, however, other administrative entities which had originated under the sponsorship of the Commission also gained a new status as the evolution of the administrative structure for defense proceeded. On January 11, the NDAC Defense Housing Coordinator was converted into the Division of Defense Housing Coordination in the Executive Office of the President. In the absence of authority to regroup the Government's housing agencies into a single department, a temporary administrative solution was found in the establishment of this Division to exercise supervision over them on behalf of the President. It was the duty of the Division to anticipate the need for housing in areas congested because of defense activities and to develop programs to meet these needs for execution by the appropriate housing agency.[11]

---

[10] Executive Order No. 8734, April 11, 1941, 6 *Federal Register* 1917.

[11] Executive Order No. 8632, Jan. 11, 1941, 6 *Federal Register* 295.

The Advisor on Agriculture of the Defense Commission felt, as the different parts of the Commission were sloughed off and transmuted into more elaborate organizations, that an office of food supply should be established as a division of the Department of Agriculture or as a part of the Office for Emergency Management. The President felt it "unadvisable . . . to risk creating the alarm that might arise from a broad survey of agricultural supplies." For the same reason he did not think we needed "to establish an office of food supply or a food administration" at the time. Instead the President abolished the Agricultural Division of NDAC in May 1941 and transferred its functions to an Office of Agricultural Defense Relations which was created in the Department of Agriculture at his request. This Office was to aid the Secretary in directing the work of the Department in accordance with defense needs.

In June the Office of Scientific Research and Development (another OEM agency) was established to carry on the work initiated by the National Defense Research Committee created earlier by order of the Council of National Defense. A National Defense Research Committee was continued in an advisory capacity. The Office was given a broader charter to mobilize the scientific personnel and resources of the nation in the conduct of scientific and medical research relating to national defense. Among the responsibilities assigned to the Office was the duty to—

Coordinate, aid, and, where desirable, supplement the experimental and other scientific and medical research activities relating to national defense carried on by the Departments of War and Navy and other departments and agencies of the Federal Government.

Develop broad and coordinated plans for the conduct of scientific research in the defense program, in collaboration with representatives of the War and Navy Departments; review existing scientific research programs formulated by the Departments of War and Navy and other agencies of the Government, and advise them with respect to the relationship of their proposed activities to the total research program.

Initiate and support scientific research on the mechanisms and devices of warfare with the objective of creating, developing, and improving instrumentalities, methods, and materials required for national defense.

Initiate and support scientific research on medical problems affecting the national defense.

The Director of the Office was aided by several advisory committees whose personnel was designed to bring into the closest collaboration governmental and private scientists. He was authorized to enter into contracts with commercial and university laboratories for investigations in order that the energies of the scientists of the Nation might be concentrated on questions whose solution would promote the national defense.[12]

---

[12] Executive Order No. 8807, June 28, 1941, 6 *Federal Register* 3207.

At the time that consideration was being given to the disposition of the Division of State and Local Cooperation of the Defense Commission, several other questions requiring cooperation with State and local governments were coming to a head. Some consideration was given to the transfer of the Division to OPM on the assumption that the Division and the State and local defense councils which it had fostered had a close connection with production problems. The problem of organizing civilian protection also was receiving a great deal of attention as the consequences of the bombing of English cities became apparent. In local areas in which defense production was bringing population congestion, the problem of developing adequate community facilities was becoming acute. A variety of objectives finally found expression in an Executive order of May 20 which replaced the Division of State and Local Cooperation by the Office of Civilian Defense. The Office was to—

Serve as the center for the coordination of Federal civilian defense activities which involve relationships between the Federal Government and State and local governments. . . .

Keep informed of problems which arise from the impact of the industrial and military defense effort upon local communities, and take necessary steps to secure the cooperation of appropriate Federal departments and agencies in dealing with such problems and in meeting the emergency needs of such communities.

Assist State and local governments in the establishment of State and local defense councils or other agencies designed to coordinate civilian defense activities.

With the assistance of the Board for Civilian Protection (which was established within the OCD by the Executive order), study and plan measures designed to afford adequate protection of life and property in the event of emergency. . . .

With the assistance of the Volunteer Participation Committee (also established by the Executive order) consider proposals, suggest plans, and promote activities designed to sustain the national morale and to provide opportunities for constructive civilian participation in the defense program. . . .[13]

On May 28, the day after he declared the existence of an unlimited national emergency, the President moved to round out another element of the organization for defense by designating the Secretary of the Interior as Petroleum Coordinator for National Defense. In his letter of designation the President noted that Government functions relating to petroleum were "divided among numerous officers and agencies of the Federal Government and the principal oil-producing States." To provide the necessary coordination among these officers, the Secretary was designated as Coordinator and instructed as a representative of the President, to obtain information about military and civilian needs for petroleum and its products and to make recommendations to the appropriate government agencies and to the industry to assure the maintenance of an adequate supply.[14]

---

[13] Executive Order No. 8757, May 20, 1941, 6 *Federal Register* 2517.
[14] 6 *Federal Register* 2760.

Growing Pains of the Production Program

Reorganization of administrative machinery for the guidance of production cleared the way for more vigorous efforts to increase the output of munitions and to speed the construction of factories and shipyards to increase our capacity to produce. On January 3, 1941, the President submitted to Congress the Annual Budget for the fiscal year 1942. Sixty-two percent of the estimated expenditures were to be for defense purposes. Supplemental authorizations and appropriations, however, increased these estimates rapidly. On January 16, the President called to the attention of Congress the necessity for an emergency ship construction program. He requested $350 million for shipbuilding facilities and cargo vessels. A series of additional authorizations and appropriations followed, including the $7 billion fund made available in March for lend-lease purposes. Events abroad made speed more and more urgent. In January the German air force ended British control of the Mediterranean. Early in February the Japanese obtained military concessions in Indo-China. In March Bulgaria joined the Axis. In April Germany invaded Yugoslavia and overwhelmed an heroic but weak resistance.

Although a larger and larger proportion of American resources was diverted to defense production, the acceleration of defense output seemed discouragingly slow. In the press and within the Administration a warm debate was waged over the rate of progress. Industrialists of the Office of Production Management were accused of being insufficiently bold in converting industry to military production and of fearing to enlarge facilities for the production of materials and other components of munitions lest industry be handicapped subsequently by overcapacity. Other groups within the Administration persistently demanded greater speed in the increase of munitions output. Industry was beginning to feel the prosperity flowing from defense spending and was somewhat reluctant to turn to production of war goods. The Administrator of the Office of Price Administration and Civilian Supply demanded heavy cuts in the production of automobiles and other consumer durable goods, and added fuel to the flames of intraadministration debate. The Director-General of the Office of Production Management prodded the War and Navy Departments to raise their sights and to request larger appropriations in order that more adequate production might be initiated. As early as May he also obtained agreement of the automobile industry that a cut of 20 percent would be made in automobile production for the year beginning in August. The Office of Production Management urged the Reconstruction Finance Corporation to expand its program for the construction of synthetic rubber plants and to expedite and enlarge its program for the stockpiling of strategic and critical materials. The President, from time to time, urged greater speed and indicated the direction which the defense production program should take. In May he asked an expansion in the output of critical tools. In July, soon after the German invasion of the U. S. S. R. he sought a prompt and substantial increase in tank output. At the same time, he requested diversion to munitions production of a "substantial part of large durable goods factories in America that are now manufacturing items to meet consumer needs".

In the midst of this discussion, munitions production steadily increased, and the dislocations attendant on diversion of resources to defense purposes began to be felt. Defense production was superimposed upon civilian production, which itself was stimulated by defense expenditures. The slack in the economy was taken up as idle men and industrial capacity were put to work on the defense program. Shortages began to occur as demands for materials increased, and during the first half of 1941 the Office of Production Management put into effect a comparatively mild priorities system. The OPM orders in the first two-thirds of 1941 were designed chiefly to assure that producers of materials gave preference to defense orders.

OPM Order M–1 which became effective March 22, 1941, required that producers of aluminum should give preference to defense orders and specified the sequence in which nondefense orders should be filled. In the following months copper, iron, steel, cork, certain chemicals, nickel, rayon, rubber, silk and other materials were brought under similar control. Exercise of the priority power had the incidental effect of enabling producers of the materials affected to give preference to defense orders without incurring liability for failures to fulfill pre-existing civilian contracts. In addition to requiring that preference be given to defense orders, the OPM in some instances prohibited use of the affected materials for less essential purposes.

Through various orders, the Office of Production Management also developed a ranking of products according to their essentiality. The Army-Navy Munitions Board was empowered by directive to assign specified ratings to military products, while the OPM itself assigned ratings to indirect defense and essential civilian products. Thus, producers of metal-working equipment were entitled to a higher rating than were manufacturers of farm machinery. The priority system developed by the autumn of 1941 was comparatively simple. It did not cover the entire industrial system and its chief effect was to control the sequence in which orders were filled.

Although by the end of the summer no general program for the conversion of entire industries to military production had been effectuated, the diversion of materials to military production through the priorities system made it increasingly difficult for many producers of nonmilitary goods to obtain materials. Small business concerns were affected most seriously. In May the Office of Production Management agreed that the contracting agencies should compel contractors to subcontract parts of their orders so as to utilize existing facilities of industry and to avert "priorities unemployment." In July, following criticism by the Senate Committee Investigating the National Defense Program, the OPM elevated its Defense Contract Service to the status of a Bureau and increased its efforts to bring about the participation of small business in defense production.

Expansion of defense production was accompanied by complex problems in industrial relations. The movement of workers to new industries which were clamoring for additional employees increased the bargaining power of labor and stimulated strikes. Competition of employers for workers placed pressures on wage scales. Long-term measures had to be devised to increase the labor force by training and by bringing additional people into the labor market.

In March the President established the National Defense Mediation Board to settle controversies between employers and employees. The Board consisted of three public members, four representatives of employees, and four representatives of employers. It was instructed to act when the Secretary of Labor certified that a dispute threatening the production or transportation of equipment or materials essential to national defense could not be adjusted by conciliation commissioners of the Department of Labor.[15] In June, the President for the first time used his power to assume control of a plant to prevent disruption of defense production by authorizing the Army to take over the North American aviation plant.

In the summer of 1941, the Office of Production Management inaugurated a program to coordinate and direct the work of Government agencies engaged in training workers for defense employment. New industrial techniques, particularly in the aircraft and shipbuilding industries, required that literally hundreds of thousands of workers should be trained in new skills. Both to make additional workers available and to quell unrest, efforts were inaugurated to prevent discrimination against minority groups by employers in defense industries. "No nation combating the increasing threat of totalitarianism," the President said, "can afford arbitrarily to exclude large segments of its population from its defense industries." This admonition was reenforced in June by creation of the Committee on Fair

---

[15] Executive Order No. 8716, Mar. 19, 1941, 6 *Federal Register* 1532.

Employment Practice which was to investigate and redress grievances growing out of departures from the policy against discrimination in employment on grounds of race, creed, color, or national origin.[16] To increase the working force further the Office of Production Management in August urged the employment of more women in industry.

Increasing demands for defense goods created greater demand for raw materials. The prospect of further increases in requirements encouraged speculative operations. The defense boom stimulated increases in wages which, in turn, tended to raise prices. The Office of Price Administration and Civilian Supply cajoled, persuaded and threatened in an effort to maintain a stable price level, but it was fighting a losing battle and, indeed was not equipped to do much more. In the months since its establishment, however, it had been preparing for more effective price control measures and conducting negotiations within the government to achieve consensus on the general outlines of an economic stabilization policy. On July 30 the President requested Congress to act. He recalled the consequences of failure to control prices in the first World War, traced the alarming increases in prices during 1941, and suggested lines of action. Legislation was needed to control prices, rents, and installment credit. For the maintenance of over-all economic stability, he declared that relatively stable wages also would be necessary and indicated the need for an adequate tax program as part of a general attack on inflation.[17]

Broadening of Economic Defense

Late in 1940 and early in 1941 Administration officials had under consideration the problem of better organization, and the adoption of sterner policies, for economic defense. At the beginning of 1941 the principal existing agency was the Office of Export Control. It could prevent shipments to unfriendly countries and a steadily increasing number of commodities had been embargoed. The embargo against shipment of iron and steel scrap, put into effect on October 16, 1940, had been preceded by a Japanese warning that it would be regarded as an "unfriendly act." [18] As supplies gradually were pinched off from Japan—the rate of curtailment being weighed against the state of our preparedness and judgments of Nipponese bellicosity—Japanese imports from South America rose sharply. In the last 6 months of 1940, the Japanese purchased almost a normal year's consumption of copper from South America. Heavy purchases of mercury were being

---

[16] Executive Order No. 8802, June 25, 1941, 6 *Federal Register* 3109.

[17] *Congressional Record*, vol. 87, pt. 6, p. 6427.

[18] U. S. Department of State, *Peace and War*, Washington, D. C.: Government Printing Office, 1942, p. 97.

CHART 6. *United States Exports by Country.*

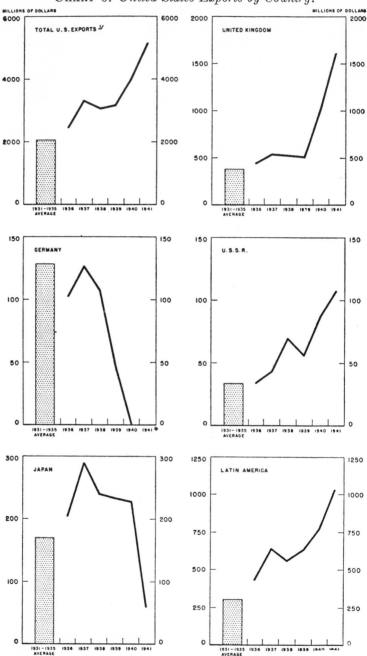

[1] Data include reexports.   Total U. S. exports include exports not shown separately.
 * Less than $100,000.

Source: Department of Commerce.

made in Mexico, apparently on German account for shipment through the U. S. S. R. As the British restricted the export of shellac from India, Japanese purchases in the United States increased. Something more than export control was required for our economic defense.

The economic defense of the United States required measures more positive than the negative device of export control. However, the formulation of lines of action and the timing of that action were conditioned by diplomatic and military factors as well as by the problem of making suitable administrative arrangements. Moreover, action was delayed by the necessity of giving priority to other matters, such as the settlement of the lend-lease question. From the administrative standpoint the problem of equipping the Government for economic defense involved issues of determining what agencies of the Government should participate in the program and how and by whom their endeavors should be coordinated into a consistent program. Early in January 1941 the Treasury Department prepared a proposal which would have made that Department the economic defense agency of the Government although it would have been advised by an "Economic Defense Board" consisting of the Secretaries of State, Treasury, War, Navy, and Commerce, and the Director-General of the Office of Production Management. Under this plan, the Secretary of the Treasury would have directed the administration of financial controls for freezing foreign funds, the coordination of foreign buying and shipping, and the licensing of exports. The proposal grew out of the Department's work in coordinating foreign purchases for the President's Liaison Committee, whose staff was alert to the possibilities of broadening the Committee's usefulness.

As was customary in such matters, the draft order submitted by the Treasury was discussed by the Director of the Budget on behalf of the President with other agencies of the Government concerned. In these negotiations various objections were made to the proposal. In some quarters the Treasury approach was viewed as too narrow because it did not encompass such matters as preclusive buying. In others, its reliance on financial techniques—as in the licensing of financial transactions—was regarded as too indirect an approach to economic defense. It was asserted that, since the task, in considerable measure, was one of coordinating the work of Government agencies concerned with economic defense, it was doubtful that one of these agencies could bring the others into agreement on any comprehensive plan of action. That the cabinet committee proposed to guide the policies of the Treasury could be effective was doubted. It was felt also that the matter could not be dealt with very well before arrangements were made to carry out the lend-lease program. In military circles a sentiment existed that the entire economic defense program should be developed by the Office of Export Control, a view to which the chief officials of this agency were not averse, since they were military men themselves. Some officials thought that something like the War Trade Board of World War I should be created. In short, while it stimulated consideration of the problem, the Treasury proposal was not acceptable to other officials who would have to collaborate in any program of economic defense.

The Administrator of Export Control proposed that a program of economic defense should be organized around his office. He gained some support within the Government but the general reaction of civilian officials was negative. In April the Administrator presented a budget which contemplated the development of a broad program of economic defense including import control, shipping control, preclusive purchasing and related international trade programs. In passing on the financial request, the President limited the Office to its existing functions.

The proposal of the Administrator of Export Control was countered on May 5 by a plan submitted by the Secretary of State, the Secretary of the Treasury and the Attorney General to create an Economic Defense Committee consisting of these three officials. The Committee would have supervised the control of foreign funds by the Treasury, the approval of exports by the State Department, and the work of the Administrator of Export Control. The plan clearly was not broad enough to cover the entire economic defense front. However, on the basis of this and other proposals the Director of the Bureau of the Budget developed another plan, and by the end of the month he had received from the President instructions to consult with interested officials in the development of an arrangement for economic defense.

As study of the problem of economic defense organization proceeded, the tempo of events in foreign affairs accelerated. On May 27, the President declared a state of unlimited emergency. On the same day, in an address to the governing board of the Pan American Union, he asserted that the war was "approaching the brink of the Western Hemisphere . . ." In June, Axis funds were frozen and this Government requested the closing of German and Italian consulates. The freezing of funds was an action of prime importance in economic defense for it aided greatly to prevent the financing of propaganda and the operations of secret agents of unfriendly powers. On June 22, 1941, Germany invaded the U. S. S. R.

During June several schemes were prepared. The dispute between military and civilians for control of economic defense continued. The Administrator of Export Control proposed an Executive order toward the end of June to establish an Office of Foreign Trade Control with the Vice President as Director and himself as executive officer. Early in July the President decided that the Vice President was to be in charge of a new economic defense agency. After this decision the final terms of the order to establish the Economic Defense Board were quickly agreed upon, and the order was issued on July 30. The debate about what an economic defense agency should do and who should control it resulted in an interagency board with authority to establish policies to guide agencies with economic defense functions. This was to become a familiar pattern of operation. In the complex situation many departments of government were inevitably concerned with almost every significant problem of defense. Yet their work had to be directed toward common objectives and a board consisting of the chiefs of the interested departments furnished a convenient means for consultation about proposed lines of action. The Economic Defense Board, built on these principles, consisted of the Vice President as Chairman, the Secretary of State, the Secretary of the Treasury, the Secretary of War, the Attorney General, the Secretary of the Navy, the Secretary of Agriculture, and the Secretary of Commerce. The order defined "economic defense" as—

the conduct, in the interest of national defense, of international economic activities including those relating to exports, imports, the acquisition and disposition of materials and commodities from foreign countries including preclusive buying, transactions in foreign exchange and foreign-owned or foreign-controlled property, international investments and extensions of credit, shipping and transportation of goods among countries, the international aspects of patents, international communications pertaining to commerce, and other foreign economic matters.

The chief responsibilities of the Board were to:

(*a*) Advise the President as to economic defense measures to be taken or functions to be performed which are essential to the effective defense of the nation.

(*b*) Coordinate the policies and actions of the several departments and agencies carrying on activities relating to economic defense in order to assure unity and balance in the application of such measures.

(*c*) Develop integrated economic defense plans and programs for coordinated action by the departments and agencies concerned and use all appropriate means to assure that such plans and programs are carried into effect by such departments and agencies.

(*d*) Make investigations and advise the President on the relationship of economic defense . . . measures to post-war economic reconstruction and on the steps to be taken to protect the trade position of the United States and to expedite the establishment of sound, peacetime international economic relationships.

(*e*) Review proposed or existing legislation relating to or affecting economic defense and, with the approval of the President, recommend such additional legislation as may be necessary or desirable.[19]

---

[19] Executive Order No. 8839, July 30, 1941, *Federal Register* 3823.

As arrangements were being completed for better organization for economic defense, another aspect of governmental machinery relating to foreign affairs—our intelligence system—was receiving attention. The Government had no real intelligence system, although several agencies of Government had been long concerned with the collection of information affecting the national security. Yet no agency had responsibility for collecting and analyzing all such information and putting it into meaningful form for the President and other high officials of the government. The existing arrangements left the information that was collected scattered among secretive governmental units and provided no means for piecing the puzzle together to assure the most complete data on which to base governmental decision. On July 11, by military order, the President established a Coordinator of Information "with authority to collect and analyze all information and data, which may bear upon national security; to correlate such information and data, and to make such information and data available to the President and to such departments and officials of the Government as the President may determine . . ." Old-line Government agencies did not especially relish the rise of a rival to coordinate intelligence operations; the creation of the Coordinator, however, was illustrative of the problem faced by a Chief Executive in managing the huge Federal administrative machine to serve the ends of national policy. The organization erected by the Coordinator later grew into the Office of Strategic Services while the functions developed by the Coordinator in short-wave broadcasting to foreign countries eventually became a part of the Office of War Information.

During the first 7 months of 1941 there was a diminution of dissension and a corresponding sharpening of national purpose. The Lend-Lease Act embodied the most important new national policy adopted during this period; to make it effective some reorganization of the governmental structure was necessary. As the international situation deteriorated through the summer it became possible to take more vigorous steps in our defense through foreign trade measures. In the pulling and hauling within the Administration that accompanied these organizational adjustments, problems unforeseen by industrial mobilization planners were encountered. These were fundamentally the political problems of maintaining a working balance among the many groups represented in any national administration. Industrial and labor groups competed for dominance and the services attempted to gain control of important nonmilitary activities. The administrative arrangements which were developed reflected attempts to strike a balance among these groups and interests. The necessity of organizing for defense during a period of peace made it inevitable that disputes and controversies over the correctness of national policy would color and delay administrative action. When the year was half over there was much unfinished business. A rudimentary system for production control had been established; machinery for price control had been erected but it had no powers; the mechanisms for the coordination of economic defense activities existed on paper but they required development and elaboration. As these steps were being taken the international situation grew in tenseness while in domestic politics a crisis approached as the year's service of men in military training neared completion. Further important administrative adjustments were indicated but they had to await determination of whether the military force already built up would be dissipated.

4

Rounding Out Defense Organization

I N THE summer of 1941, it became fairly clear that Japan was not disposed to work out a peaceful settlement in the Far East. The German attack on Russia which began in June, if successful, would remove the threat from the East and give the Nazis freedom of action in the West. In the Pacific, we had no friend of sufficient strength to hold off the Japanese until we could raise and deploy military forces. It was imperative that, while giving all aid possible to the British, Russians, and Chinese, we retain and enlarge the armed forces that had been built up. Our vital interests in the Pacific were threatened by impending Japanese moves. The capacity of the Russians to resist was a factor yet unknown. The freedom of our ships to sail the seas had been challenged. In this perilous situation, we were threatened with the dissipation of our military forces. The expiration of the year of training provided by the Selective Service and Training Act of 1940 was approaching. It was of paramount importance that the existing forces be maintained; their continuance in service required action by Congress. Although many other issues were urgent, these questions had to be subordinated for a time to the primary problem of obtaining decision on the basic matter of keeping under arms such forces as we had.

On July 21, the President asked for legislation to authorize continuance in service of selectees, National Guard and Reserve components of the Army and the retired personnel of the Regular Army. He also asked for the removal of restrictions on the number of selectees that might be inducted each year for training and service.

Today [the President said] it is imperative that I should officially report to the Congress what the Congress undoubtedly knows: That the international situation is not less grave but is far more grave than it was a year ago.   It is so grave, in my opinion, and in the opinion of all who are conversant with the facts, that the Army should be maintained in effective strength and without diminution of its effective numbers in a complete state of readiness. . .[1]

This proposal was the occasion for widespread propaganda questioning the President's good faith in making this request.   It was charged that he was seeking to build up a dictatorship and to lead the Nation into war without its consent.   It was denied that the interests of the United States were threatened by the military developments daily taking place in Europe and Asia.

In the great congressional debate on the question, the opposition asserted that the Nation was not imperiled and that there was a moral obligation to release men who had been inducted for training with the expectation that their period of service would be completed in 12 months.   The following comment of undoubted sincerity by a respected and able Senator was typical:

I cannot, for the life of me, see in what respect the United States is in greater danger of invasion, greater danger of attack, or more pressed for time in training men for military service than it was a year ago, when we were assured that training for a year was the answer to our problem of preparing the land forces.   I am strongly for national defense, but I cannot and will not vote to keep these boys in service, for possible expeditionary forces to Europe, Asia, and Africa, unless and until Congress authorizes such a program.   When Congress declares war as the Constitution provides I shall do everything possible to win the war.   Until that time comes, I shall do everything possible to keep America out of the present war, and I intend to vote against draft-time extension.[2]

The Senate took favorable action by the ample margin of 45 to 30,[3] but in the House the outcome appeared to be uncertain.   A minority of members of the House Committee on Military Affairs doubted that the Nation was in danger: ". . . it is our opinion that the crisis today is not as grave as it was one year ago or when the selectees were first inducted into the military service." [4]   Similar comments recurred in the House debate.   One member spoke for many when he asserted: "I am convinced that unless we go out looking for trouble with a chip on our shoulder we need have no immediate fear of being attacked or involved in war." [5]

By a vote of 203 to 202, the House on August 12 acted favorably on a bill to authorize the continuance in service of inductees and other personnel which had been called to the colors.   After this crucial decision by the narrowest possible margin, the Government was free to

[1] *Congressional Record*, vol. 87, pt. 6, p. 6149.
[2] Senator Capper, *Congressional Record*, vol. 87, pt. 6, p. 6816.
[3] *Congressional Record*, vol. 87, pt. 6, p. 6881.
[4] *Congressional Record*, vol. 87, pt. 6, p. 7001.
[5] *Congressional Record*, vol. 87, pt. 6, p. 6908.

make dispositions of troops as the circumstances warranted and to move on various domestic questions which had been crying for attention but which had been postponed until settlement of the paramount question of the maintenance of the forces in being. During the following weeks further steps were taken quickly in the improvement of defense organization; several major agencies acquired, in the essentials, the form and functions which they were to exercise, under other names, during the entire war. This stage had been reached by a zigzag route and had necessitated involved judgments concerning the state of public opinion, the desires and strength of different elements within the Administration and the public generally, and the changing needs of governmental management as the defense program grew. The complex process by which the administrative mechanisms for defense were built suggests that under circumstances of uncertainty of national purpose a full-blown organization for defense or for war cannot be erected in time of peace without placing severe strains on the coalition of interests supporting the Government. However that may be, as these administrative steps were taken, further attacks on American vessels occurred. The international situation became worse rather than better. The stimulus of heightening danger and the shifts of personnel and organization made it possible to accelerate all phases of preparation for defense in the months before Pearl Harbor.

Centering Responsibility for Priorities

In rounding out the defense organization, refinement of organization for the guidance of production received first attention in the establishment of the Supply Priorities and Allocations Board by Executive order of August 28, 1941.[6] This action was the culmination of several streams of development. The Office of Production Management, created early in 1941, had been under pointed public attack, partly because it was headed by a "partnership" consisting of a Director General and an Associate Director General. In fact, the "partnership" was not at the root of the troubles of OPM. Action on this point, however, would relieve tension induced by criticism. In reality, a more significant problem was that of working out a proper division of functions between the Office of Production Management and the Office of Price Administration and Civilian Supply.

The Office of Production Management had received by delegation at the time of its creation the priority power vested in the President by an act of 1940, i. e., the power to compel priority in delivery for Army and Navy orders over orders for private account or export. It soon became apparent that this authority was inadequate and on May 31,

---

[6] Executive Order No. 8875, Aug. 28, 1941, 6 *Federal Register* 4484.

1941, the President's priority power was broadened. The new statute gave power to require that priority be granted to certain orders not placed directly by the Army and Navy. Thus, orders for the "Government of any country whose defense the President" deemed vital "to the defense of the United States" might be granted priority. Orders "necessary or appropriate to promote the defense of the United States," such as those for housing in defense production areas, might receive priority. The new statute also enabled the assignment of priority ratings to subcontracts or suborders necessary to fulfill a rated prime contract. Finally, the statute granted power to allocate scarce materials in such manner as might "be necessary or appropriate in the public interest and to promote the national defense." Thus, specific authority to determine the relative essentiality of different civilian uses of materials and commodities was granted. Whatever doubt existed about the legal power to determine whether scarce aluminum should be used in juke boxes or cooking utensils was resolved.

The statutory authorization to the President to exercise a broader range of priority power made it necessary that he delegate that power for detailed administration. The necessity for delegation in turn precipitated the issue of redefinition of relations between the Office of Production Management and the Office of Price Administration and Civilian Supply. The decision of this question raised again the problem of Presidential mediation between two powerful groups within the Administration. When the Office of Production Management was created the President delegated to it the narrow priority power which he then possessed. The OPM had been charged only with concern for military production and presently, in April 1941 the Office of Price Administration and Civilian Supply was given cognizance of production to meet essential civilian needs. OPACS was directed to stimulate provision of required civilian goods in a manner not to conflict with military defense needs. After these defense needs had been met, OPACS was empowered to plan for the equitable distribution of the residual supply of materials among competing civilian demands, OPACS had no powers, however, to direct industry to effectuate these distributions. OPM had the power to direct the steel industry, for example, to give priority to particular orders; OPACS had the power to tell the OPM how it should direct industry to dispose of materials and supplies remaining after defense needs had been met. The practical solution of the problems inherent in such a relationship between two new and growing governmental organizations naturally was accompanied by friction, but under these provisions during the summer OPACS issued numerous programs for the guidance of OPM. For example, it ordered that, after defense needs had been met, "deliveries of material and equipment necessary for the construction of locomotives" should "be given preference over all material and equipment going into any other civilian use." Under the existing administrative arrangements, it then became the responsibility of OPM to apply this policy in reviewing applications for priority in the acquisition of materials for different civilian uses. OPM officials disliked to have to execute programs formulated by OPACS and the administrative arrangement did contain inherent difficulties. More significant in the friction between the two agencies, however, was the fact that the jurisdiction of OPACS over civilian needs gave it license to be critical of the rate of progress by OPM in converting civilian industry to defense purposes.

Rivalries between OPM and OPACS as well as the suitability of the division of authority between them under an expanding production program became involved in the consideration of how the President should delegate the broadened priority authority. To whom was the power to be delegated and how would the delegation affect relations of the Office of Production Management and the Office of Price Administration and Civilian Supply? The solution of these questions gave rise to a bitter controversy between two factions within the Administration. The Office of Price Administration and Civilian Supply, headed by Leon Henderson, and manned chiefly by career civil servants and personnel from universities and research institutions, was widely regarded as a New Deal agency. The Office of Production Management, on the other hand, had filled most of its key positions with persons from business and industry. Although they were charged with protection of the civilian economy, the OPACS personnel fought a continuing battle to reduce civilian production in order that defense output might be increased. The Office of Production Management was accused of delaying the defense effort, of underestimating requirements for materials and facilities, and of hesitating to take bold measures for expansion lest industry find itself with overcapacity after the war. Undoubtedly, there was some truth in these charges. The top personnel of OPM was considerably ahead of the Army and Navy in their estimates of defense needs. Among subordinate officials in the organization, however, there were those who, like people generally, were dubious about the necessity for preparedness. Because of the different composition of the two agencies their conflict came to be pictured as a debate over the level of effort that should be devoted to defense preparation.

Another basic element in the complex administrative and political situation was the growing scarcity of resources. Although small by later standards, military production was beginning to interfere with production for other purposes. We did not have enough to meet all needs. It was becoming necessary to formulate a broad economic strategy. How could what we had be used to the greatest national advantage? To what extent, for example, should we devote our materials and manufacturing capacity to meet the needs of railroads; and how should their needs be weighed against that for automobiles? How should domestic civilian and military requirements be treated in relation to those of friendly nations in this hemisphere and elsewhere? All these needs had to be weighed against other export requirements mixed with diplomatic considerations. How much tin could we spare to persuade Portugal not to help the Axis? Was it more important that we devote materials to the manufacture of short-wave transmitters for propaganda broadcasts or that we use them for Signal Corps equipment? Questions of priority in the broadest sense were becoming urgent.

The composition of the Council of the Office of Production Management—the Secretary of War, the Secretary of the Navy, and the Director General and Associate Director General of the Office of Production Management—was not one to assure due consideration of all factors involved in the allocation of resources. The Council was weighted in favor of the Army and the Navy, while the defense of the United States required that careful attention also be given to export and lend-lease needs. With the increase of pressure on our resources, it was becoming necessary to provide a more appropriate mechanism to settle issues of allocation, a consideration which was urged by the Director of the Bureau of the Budget. Mr. Bernard Baruch also urged the centralization of priority authority and the control over production—both civilian and military—in a single agency.

The complex situation was not made simpler by the inevitable struggle among individuals for position, or, perhaps more accurately, the struggle of their friends in their behalf. If responsibility for production management and for determination of broad policy for allocation of resources were to be more highly centralized, some individuals would gain in power; others would lose. Moreover, individuals were still on trial. Sooner or later, enormous authority had to be vested in a single individual, but who should that individual be? The leading figures in defense organization had demonstrated qualities both of strength and weakness. For the heavy responsibilities which were ahead, no person stood head and shoulders above his associates. Considerations looking toward a further trial of individuals, therefore, worked their way into the solution of administrative issues presented by the dispute between the Office of Production Management and the Office of Price Administration and Civilian Supply.

After Congress had extended the service of the armed forces and after the conference with Mr. Churchill that resulted in the Atlantic

Charter had been concluded, the President was free to devote attention to problems of production organization. The Director of the Bureau of the Budget had been conducting studies and negotiations for some time and on August 18 he presented to the President several alternative plans together with a statement of the issues and considerations involved. The formulation of a solution required several transfers of high-ranking personnel to positions to which their talents were more suited and the modification of proposals based purely on administrative considerations by factors of political feasibility. In the negotiation of the final details and the necessary personnel adjustments, the President relied upon Judge Samuel I. Rosenman, his special counsel.

The diverse ingredients of the situation produced the Supply Priorities and Allocations Board, a policy group superimposed over the Office of Production Management. It consisted of the Chairman of the Economic Defense Board, as chairman, the Director General and Associate Director General of the Office of Production Management, the Price Administrator, the Secretary of War, the Secretary of the Navy, and the Special Assistant to the President supervising the Lend-Lease Program. The general administrative theory of SPAB was that the chief officials of the principal agencies with stakes in the allocation of our resources would be brought together for consultation, in order, as the Executive order read, "to assure unity of policy and coordinated consideration of all relevant factors involved in the supply and allocation of materials and commodities among the various phases of the defense program and competing civilian demands." The Secretaries of War and Navy could speak for direct military needs. The chairman of the Economic Defense Board and the Special Assistant to the President supervising the lend-lease program could participate with knowledge of the urgency of export needs. The Price Administrator (who also headed the OPM Division of Civilian Supply) could contribute information on essential civilian needs as well as indirect defense needs and could bring to bear in the deliberations of the Board considerations of economic stabilization. The participation of the Director General and Associate Director General of OPM was calculated to assure a coordination with the general program of requirements of the work of OPM in stimulating the construction of new facilities, in programming the import of strategic and critical materials, and in allocating the available supplies of goods and materials among competing uses. Later the Secretary of Commerce, under whose direction RFC subsidiaries constructed plants, imported materials, and conducted other operations to increase supplies, was designated as a member of the Board in an effort to assure better coordination of his actions with the general program of industrial requirements.

The Board, acting in accordance with the basic defense policies of the President, was directed to:

(a) Determine the total requirements of materials and commodities needed respectively for defense, civilian and all other purposes; establish policies for the fulfillment of such requirements, and, where necessary, make recommendations to the President relative thereto.

(b) Determine policies and make regulations governing allocations and priorities with respect to the procurement, production, transmission, or transportation of materials, articles, power, fuel, and other commodities among military, economic defense, defense aid, civilian, and other major demands of the total defense program.

Mr. Donald M. Nelson, who had been Coordinator of National Defense Purchases for the Advisory Commission and Director of the OPM Division of Purchases, was made Executive Director of the Board. In all these positions his stature had grown and he showed promise of bridging the gap between conflicting groups within the Administration. He was designated as Executive Director of the Board with the hope that he would later be able to assume heavier responsibilities, should the necessity arise.

The functions of the Office of Price Administration and Civilian Supply in the allocation of the residual supplies of materials among competing civilian uses were transferred to the Office of Production Management in which a Division of Civilian Supply was established. This Division was headed by Mr. Leon Henderson, who also became in his capacity of Price Administrator a member of the Supply Priorities and Allocations Board where he could participate in policy deliberations. The Office of Price Administration and Civilian Supply became simply the Office of Price Administration. The Chairman of the Economic Defense Board, the Vice President, was made Chairman of SPAB partly to avoid a clear victory for either of the contending factions and partly because of his zeal for preparedness. The Executive order also centered the administration of all types of priority policy in the Office of Production Management and made this office, acting under general policies fixed by SPAB, superior to other governmental agencies whose collaboration was required to effectuate priorities actions.

From a purely administrative point of view, the organization erected by the order of August 28 left much to be desired. Critics pointed out that Mr. Nelson, as Executive Director of SPAB, was a subordinate of Mr. Knudsen when Mr. Knudsen was acting as a member of the Board and perhaps was an administrative superior of Mr. Knudsen when Mr. Knudsen was acting as Director General of the Office of Production Management. As Director of the Division of Civilian Supply of OPM, Mr. Henderson was a subordinate of Mr. Knudsen, but when he attended sessions of SPAB, he met Mr. Knudsen as an equal. However involved the administrative structure was, the maneuvers eventuating in the establishment of SPAB were steps which gradually were bringing together into a working whole elements of the Administration which had diverse notions about how the defense program should be managed. No one of these groups had either the right view or all the skills required, but step by step they were brought to work together as the administrative structure evolved. Moreover, admirers of the niceties of logical administrative charts are sometimes confounded. Defense production was 15 percent more in September than in August when SPAB was created; it was 26 percent greater in October than in August. No causal relation can be inferred between the order of August 28 and the upward production trend. On the other hand, in evaluating production organization at the time such figures are not to be ignored.

The composition of SPAB created a situation more favorable to the Administration's policy of aid to Russia. The Council of the Office of Production Management was weighted against aiding Russia. Inclusion of Messrs. Wallace, Henderson, and Hopkins in the membership of SPAB strengthened the hand of the President in checking the disinclination of the armed forces to allocate industrial materials to Russia.

Transfer of the civilian supply function from the Office of Price Administration and Civilian Supply, made virtually irrevocable the administrative separation of price control from production control. This basic decision was made without a great deal of consideration of its future consequences although there was an awareness that the way was being prepared for some administrative difficulty. It was contended in some quarters that control over price and production should be in the same hands. Practically, there were drawbacks. Organizations such as the Office of Production Management, were by their nature colored strongly by producer interests which ordinarily are not enthusiastic about price control. An agency such as the Office of Price Administration could develop a vital interest in price control, and its staff, by design, consisted chiefly of persons divorced from producer interests. It cannot be said, however, that such calculations were dominant in the separation of price and production control. That action was the culmination of a sequence of administrative actions which began with the assignment of functions in the National Defense Advisory Commission. The adviser on price stabilization of the Advisory Commission established himself as the chief exponent of price control and as a man who understood some of the complexities of the problem and who was courageous enough to undertake an unpopular but essential task.

Speeding the Production Tempo

With the organization for determination of production policy refurbished and improved by reassignment of personnel, the way was clear to proceed more vigorously and more rapidly with the production program.   There was no sharp break with the general direction of movement during the first two-thirds of the year, but the tempo was accelerated during the few months before Pearl Harbor.   A strenuous effort was made to reconsider the Nation's needs for raw materials and to meet these needs by increasing imports and domestic capacity. The problem of allocating resources among civilian, military, and foreign uses became increasingly difficult with the competition most keen between military and Russian requirements.   Measures were adopted to divert larger quantities of materials from domestic civilian production to military uses.

SPAB inaugurated a systematic review of requirements for raw materials particularly and began to initiate measures to augment supplies.   The problem of measuring requirements had two basic aspects: What did we need in the way of military items—guns, tanks, planes, ships, and so forth?   What raw materials did we require to meet these needs and other needs which might be placed upon the economy by war?

The question of requirements for military equipment and supplies was one for the military authorities, but the production agency continued to urge the services to raise their sights.   In the middle of September Mr. Knudsen reminded the War Department that he had remarked repeatedly on the inadequacy of the program for antitank guns and other ordnance items and declared it was imperative that the production objectives should be adjusted upwards.

What materials and facilities would be needed to produce war goods and to maintain the civilian economy if war should come?   SPAB addressed itself to this matter with the assistance of the staff of the Bureau of Research and Statistics of the Office of Production Management.   The accuracy of estimates of requirements rested fundamentally on the assumption about the size of the defense effort we might have to make, about the volume of equipment and supplies we might have to furnish to others, and about what would be needed to keep the civilian economy functioning.   Once these assumptions were made, an enormously difficult statistical problem had to be solved in translating guns into tons of steel, ammunition into pounds of copper, planes into quantities of different types of aluminum.   It was not enough to say that we needed tremendous amounts of everything.   It would be senseless to devote effort to producing steel for plane motors without attempting to produce enough aluminum to make airframes in the appropriate numbers. For the importation of materials, there was so much shipping space and no more. All the space could not be used for bauxite; cryolite also had to be on hand for use in processing the bauxite. The materials program had to be balanced with proper emphasis on all its phases.

At the insistence of the services, the Army-Navy Munitions Board, was made responsible for estimating the quantities and delivery dates of raw materials required for military items. Figures presented initially by the services were practically worthless. An OPM staff report prepared in August noted—

The unreasonable character of the Industrial Mobilization Plan estimates may be evidenced by the fact that total military needs of aluminum for 2 years of maximum effort for the 4-million-man Army was less than 500 million pounds; for copper the total was 25,000 tons; for silk 13 million pounds. At the present time it appears that the requirements for aluminum for military purposes will be considerably more than 1 billion pounds; for copper nearly 1 million tons; for nickel 180 million pounds (total supply); and silk 3 million pounds. Obviously the Industrial Mobilization Plan estimates for the 4-million-man effort bear no relationship to the realistic demands under the present program.

Insofar as the Navy is concerned, most of the estimates we have received represent guess work. There is neither the basic material for doing the job satisfactorily nor the inclination to develop the staff needed for estimating raw materials needed in the Navy Department. Time after time a check of the estimates has indicated the need for almost unbelievable revision upward or downward in the originally submitted figures. As long ago as last fall we discussed these problems with the Navy and time after time they were shown that the estimates were completely out of line with any realistic approximations. Practically no progress in this direction has been made in the Navy Department.

One of the first undertakings of the Supply Priorities and Allocations Board was a frontal assault on the question of requirements. No immediate progress was made in improving the estimates from the military but civilian judgment could be substituted. At the end of September 1941, for example, the Board considered a staff report on steel requirements and supply which stated—

Existing estimates of military and civilian requirements are extremely diverse because of the many different assumptions, many of them necessarily combining the unsociable qualities of being both imaginary and arbitrary, on which they are based . . .

Estimates of Army requirements in 1942 are based on the report of the Army-Navy Munitions Board. These data were adjusted upward for some supply arms . . .

Navy estimates are based on reports from the Navy Department, again with upward adjustments . . . For example, a higher steel requirement for Navy building is estimated than that shown by the Bureau of Ships which showed decreasing quarterly requirements throughout 1942. Furthermore, Navy estimates for ammunition provided for reserves (on ship and shore) to match the expansion of the fleet without any allowance for expenditure other than target practice.

Because of the current situation in the Atlantic area, these figures were doubled for large projectiles and trebled for antiaircraft projectiles.

The Board instituted a systematic review of the supply-requirements position of all materials likely to be critical and adopted policies which seemed to be appropriate. Indicative of the shift in attitude was the order of October 2 to increase steel capacity by 10 million tons a year. In this and many other questions the linkage between order and action was not always effective; the threat of overcapacity aroused resistance, both administrative and industrial. After all, perhaps there might not be a war. Action was under way, however, and in some instances considerable progress was made in stockpiling and in the development of new capacity.

SPAB had the job of determining requirements and of initiating measures to increase supply. It also had the job of dividing what we had among competing uses. Frictions over division increased as the pressure on supply became greater. The issue was most acute in allocations between Russian requirements and those of the United States military forces. On October 7, 1941, the President approved the Moscow Protocol under which it was agreed to furnish certain materials to Russia. On October 23, SPAB issued orders for allocation of materials and equipment to meet the protocol undertakings. But the Board had to reaffirm its decision at almost every meeting over opposition from the Navy Department. In November, the Secretary of the Navy opposed transfer of aluminum to Russia with the argument that its industrial areas were in danger of conquest; but the Board ordered aluminum sent to Russia and suggested that perhaps the Navy could use something other than aluminum for furniture on its warships. Machine tools also were allocated to Russia over strong Navy protest. In carrying out the Moscow Protocol commitments, the Board was acting under specific Presidential instructions. During November, the President also rejected a proposal by the Secretaries of War and Navy to establish a super-priorities committee on which the armed services would have been dominant and from which the members of SPAB who supported the President's Russian policy would have been missing.

The movement of events was giving more and more strength to those who sought more adequate defense production, and in the latter part of 1941 the Office of Production Management and the procurement branches of the services were occupied with scheduling an enlarged munitions program. On August 25 the First Supplemental National Defense Appropriation Act, 1942, was approved and over $6 billion additional were made available for War, Navy, and maritime production and procurement.[7] In October, the Second Supplemental

---

[7] *55 Stat.* 669.

National Defense Appropriation Act, 1942, became effective and made available almost $6 billion more for military and other defense-aid items.[8] Meantime, the Reconstruction Finance Corporation had been authorized to issue an additional $1.5 billion in notes to finance activities of its subsidiaries in the construction of war plants and in the purchase of strategic and critical materials.[9] All these appropriations reflected a sharp upward revision of needs and the realization that enormous productive power remained untapped. Intense criticisms that production was "too little and too late" in Congress and in the country stimulated official action.

SPAB was responsible for making broad allocations of resources among military, civilian, and foreign requirements. As defense production increased SPAB had to reduce the quantities of materials going into certain types of civilian production. At first, military production had been superimposed upon civilian production which, in turn, was stimulated by defense expenditures. Gradually the point was reached at which further increases of defense production required positive limitations on, or prohibitions of, civilian production. Early in 1941 preference had been given to military uses of metals and other commodities and certain uses of materials had been prohibited. In the last months of the year more direct measures had to be taken to limit civilian production. A warm controversy had existed between OPM and OPACS particularly over the conversion of the automobile industry and in August curtailments to go into effect by November 30 had been announced. In September, October, and November, limitation orders affecting other industries were issued. On October 9, restrictions on nonessential building and construction were announced. On October 21, the use of copper in most civilian products was prohibited. The consumer-durable goods industries began to be subjected to limitations on production in order that they might be converted to military production and that consumption of metals in their products might be stopped or reduced. Refrigerators, vacuum cleaners, metal office furniture and equipment were among the products whose manufacture was placed under limitation orders.[10]

As more and more materials were drawn into high priority armament production, dislocations began to be felt in the industrial system. Small business concerns and their spokesmen became more vocal as time went on and protests were heard that procurement officers discriminated in favor of large enterprise in the award of contracts. Large concerns did receive the lion's share of war business, but whether they received a share disproportionate to their share in peacetime production is difficult to calculate. Moreover, it is probable that the

---

[8] 55 *Stat.* 745.
[9] 55 *Stat.* 744.

immediate impact of the change-over from normal production to defense production struck little business harder than it did big business. A considerable time lag was inevitable before subcontracts filtered down to small concerns. Whatever one concludes from the tangled mass of fact, the failure to plan and to organize adequately for utilizing the facilities of small concerns illustrates a type of difficulty often overlooked by mobilization planners. The deprivations and connected reactions consequent upon the operations of mobilization may endanger the entire process. Dramatic action was needed and, in September, the President established within the Office of Production Management, a Contract Distribution Division.[11] This Division which succeeded the OPM's Defense Contract Service and was a precursor of the Smaller War Plants Corporation, conducted a spectacular campaign of publicity to bring to the attention of small manufacturers the opportunities to use their plants in the production of "bits and pieces." Its work allayed the anxieties of small businessmen to some extent but it was merely another in a series of agencies that did not succeed completely in coping with the problem of utilizing the facilities of the thousands of small business enterprises, a problem of extreme administrative complexity.

Further Steps in Economic Defense Organization

Reorganization of the machinery for the general oversight of production and distribution made necessary some changes in the Administration of our foreign economic affairs. Under the general scheme of the Supply Priorities and Allocations Board foreign requirements were to be weighed against other needs in determining general economic strategy. No agency existed with responsibility or staff to assemble export requirements in a systematic way. Moreover, as the demands on our resources increased, positive measures became necessary to insure that friendly nations received goods essential for the stability of their economies. Friendly nations had been able to purchase to meet their needs in the open market; now it became necessary that they have a priority status in order to obtain goods. We had to develop a policy in accordance with which priority would be granted. The Office of Export Control had been operating primarily with the negative policy of preventing the shipment of goods to unfriendly nations and persons. This Office and the Division of Controls of the Department of State administered export control in confused collaboration which required clarification. The Economic Defense Board, which had been established at the end of July, was a policy

---

10 Senate Document No. 161, 77th Cong., 2d sess., p. 23.

11 Executive Order No. 8891, Sept. 4, 1941, 6 *Federal Register* 4623.

coordinating body. Its creation had been a stop-gap in maneuvers among agencies and factions within the Administration for primacy in economic foreign policy, and its establishment check-mated those who wished military control of that policy.

In its early consideration of ways to meet some of these problems, the Supply Priorities and Allocations Board agreed on September 3 in a preliminary fashion that the Office of Export Control should become a part of the Office of Production Management. Export requirements could thus be brought into the general supply-requirements calculations and the OPM could grant priority ratings which would assure the delivery of sufficient goods to meet the essential needs of friendly nations. This move was checked after the Bureau of the Budget pointed out the importance of export control in the larger context of economic foreign policy and defense and the general relation of SPAB to exports contemplated by the plan underlying the creation of SPAB. On September 16 SPAB agreed to request the President to designate an agency to provide it with total requirements for exports other than defense aid.

On September 15 an Executive order was issued which enlarged the role of the Economic Defense Board by transferring to it the functions and staffs of the Office of Export Control and the Division of Controls of the Department of State.[12] By this action the Economic Defense Board became an operating agency as well as a general planning and coordinating body. It could execute its export policies through the licensing of shipments. It could prevent goods reaching our enemies and it could give preference to our friends. The way was paved for removing some of the confusion created by the division of functions between the Office of Export Control and the Division of Controls of the Department of State. The order left unsolved the vexing problem of assuring reflection of the interests of the Department of State in the policies of the Economic Defense Board. It also left import policy, determined by the Board, to be executed by the defense subsidiaries of the RFC, a relationship subsequently to cause trouble.

The order of September 15 directed the Economic Defense Board to "obtain, develop, and determine over-all estimates of materials and commodities required for export purposes in the interest of the economic defense of the Nation," with the exception of exports under lend-lease, and to advise the Supply Priorities and Allocations Board of such estimated requirements. This action laid the basis for over-all estimates of export needs and their presentation to SPAB which could weigh them against military, civilian, and other requirements. The order also directed the Economic Defense Board to "provide a central clearing service" to which export requests could be made and to "ob-

---

[12] Executive Order No. 8900, Sept. 15, 1941, 6 *Federal Register* 4795.

tain clearance for such proposals from the several Federal agencies concerned with the control of exports and financial transactions incidental thereto."

The Vice President announced on September 17 that the new arrangement assured that the Office of Export Control would "be more closely integrated into the broader work of the Economic Defense Board. . ." He stated: "The international crisis requires a determined intensification of our policy of preventing shipments to Axis-dominated countries. At the same time, we must help see to it that other nations in that part of the world which is still free get enough goods to maintain the stability of their own economies insofar as that is possible. This is particularly important in the western hemisphere."

Since the Economic Defense Board had only limited responsibilities in lend-lease transactions, Latin American requirements loomed large in its export work. In this area, the Board was a potential competitor of the Coordinator of Inter-American Affairs whose office had been concerned with our economic policy in this part of the world. By agreement between the Coordinator and the Vice President, the Coordinator was made a member of the Economic Defense Board and the staff of the Coordinator's Commercial and Financial Division was merged with the executive personnel of the Board engaged in western hemisphere matters. The combined unit was to report to the Executive Director of the Board in some matters, to the Coordinator in others.

Export policy toward the American Republics was one of the first matters to receive the attention of the Supplies Priorities and Allocations Board. These countries were cut off from their normal European sources of supply and maintenance of their friendship was a fundamental element in American policy. The Economic Defense Board recommended to SPAB that the American Republics be treated equally with civilians in the United States and this became the general policy. Presidential instructions in April had directed the Office of Production Management to "make appropriate provision for the satisfaction of essential Latin American requirements for industrial and consumer nonmilitary goods and materials." As supplies became more scarce, the policy required refinement in detail but the general standard of parity furnished a basis for judgment. Thus, if steel were not available for the construction of amusement parks in the United States, it would not be exported to another American Republic for that purpose. In turn, Latin American countries adopted export control systems of their own to prevent the flow of defense materials and articles outside the hemisphere.

Simultaneously with reorganization of the machinery for production control, a change in the method of handling lend-lease affairs was announced.   Mr. Edward R. Stettinius, Jr., was transferred from the Division of Priorities of the Office of Production Management to head the administration of lend-lease.   As an interim arrangement, to serve until the general administrative problems would be reexamined, Mr. Stettinius was designated on September 16 as Special Assistant to the President in connection with the lend-lease program, thus formalizing an arrangement previously announced.   Lend-lease continued to be a matter of high policy and White House oversight was maintained.   In a letter to Mr. Stettinius, signed concurrently with the letter of designation, the President wrote: "Harry Hopkins is, of course, familiar with the administration of lend-lease, and I hope you will consult with him and with me where matters of major policy arise."

The Office of Lend-Lease Administration was formally established by Executive order of October 28, 1941.   OLLA absorbed the Division of Defense Aid Reports.   Power delegated to the Office enabled it to handle many matters which until then had required the signature of the President.   The order read: "Subject to such policies as the President may from time to time prescribe, the Administrator is hereby authorized and directed . . . to exercise any power or authority conferred upon the President by the [Lend-Lease] act and by the Defense Aid Supplemental Appropriation Act 1941, and any acts amendatory or supplemental thereto, with respect to any nation whose defense the President shall have found to be vital to the defense of the United States."

In the preparation of the Executive order defining the powers of the OLLA, modifications of the initial draft reflected efforts to cope with the administrative problems created by the existence of three major agencies concerned with foreign affairs.   The interest of the State Department found expression in the provision of the final order that "the master agreement with each nation receiving lend-lease aid, setting forth the general terms and conditions under which such nation is to receive such aid, shall be negotiated by the State Department, with the advice of the Economic Defense Board and the Office of Lend-Lease Administration."   Similarly, a measure of coordination between the Office and the Economic Defense Board was envisaged by the provision that the Lend-Lease Administrator should "make appropriate arrangements with the Economic Defense Board for the review and clearance of lend-lease transactions which affect the economic defense of the United States as defined in Executive Order No. 8839 of July 30, 1941."

With these organizational changes, the Government was better equipped administratively to handle economic foreign policy, in the fields of both defense aid and general exports.   Provisions of the

Neutrality Act of 1939, however, hampered the movement of goods to nations fighting the Axis. That act prohibited carriage by American vessels of passengers, articles, or materials to any nation at war. It provided for the establishment by the President of combat areas into which American vessels and citizens were forbidden to travel. It also prohibited the arming of American merchant vessels.[13] These and other restrictions had been enacted on the theory that the United States could keep out of war by such self-restraint. On October 9 the President requested Congress to modify the act of 1939. He asserted that the policy of aiding enemies of the Axis was obstructed by limitations on the operation of the American merchant marine. Defense articles were becoming available in greater and greater quantities but their delivery was becoming more and more difficult. Removal of the restriction on arming merchant vessels, the President said, was "a matter of immediate necessity and extreme urgency".[14]

The President's message precipitated a bitter debate within and outside Congress. The chief contention of opponents of revision was that the Nation was being led into war step by step. A leader of the opposition stated the position in this way:

. . . I consider the pending Senate decision as substantially settling the question whether America deliberately and consciously shall go all the way into a shooting war, probably upon two oceans. The ultimate acknowledgment by Congress of a state of war, I fear, will be a mere formality, ratifying a precipitated fact if we approve the needless provocation and trend inherent in this proposed action.[15]

This theme recurred in the House and the Senate debates with such subsidiary contentions as that there was no need to arm merchant vessels since the defensive capacity of armed vessels was slight. Favorable action was taken by the House on October 17, by a vote of 259 to 138,[16] and by the Senate on November 7, 1941, by a vote of 50 to 37.[17] House concurrence with Senate amendments was won by a small margin, 212 to 194, on November 13.[18] The action of Congress was approved by the President on November 17. Sections 2, 3, and 6 of the Neutrality Act of 1939 were repealed and the President was authorized to arm American merchant vessels for the duration of the emergency he had proclaimed on May 27.[19]

The action by Congress followed a change in public opinion on the advisability of using American ships to transport goods to the victims of aggression. At an earlier time the majority sentiment, as measured

[13] 54 *Stat.* 4.
[14] *Congressional Record*, vol. 87, pt. 7, p. 7769.
[15] Senator Vandenberg. *Congressional Record* vol. 87, pt. 8. p. 8251.
[16] *Congressional Record*, vol. 87, pt. 7, p. 8041.
[17] *Congressional Record*, vol. 87, pt. 8, p. 8680.
[18] *Congressional Record*, vol. 87, pt. 8, p. 8891.
[19] 55 *Stat.* 764.

by the polls, was to keep American ships out of danger areas, but this
view was modified with the trend of events and the closer and closer
identification of our interests with those of Britain.   The trend of
opinion appears in chart 7.

The tempo of events speeded up during consideration of revision of
the Neutrality Act.   Between the time the question was raised by the
President and the approval of the act, the U. S. S. *Kearney* was at-

CHART 7. *Public Opinion on Aid to Great Britain.*

The question asked was: "Should the Neutrality Act be changed to permit
American Merchant ships with American crews to carry war materials to Britain?"

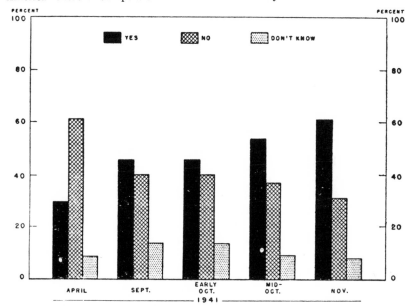

Source: American Institute of Public Opinion.

tacked, a more hostile cabinet assumed office in Japan, the *Reuben
James* was torpedoed, Ambassador Grew warned that Japan might
"resort with dangerous and dramatic suddenness to measures which
might make inevitable war with the United States," and Secretary
Hull informed the Cabinet that relations between the United States and
Japan were extremely critical.

Beginnings of Information Coordination

The debate over revision of the Neutrality Act again brought
sharply to attention the problem of maintaining an adequate flow of
straightforward information to the public about the policies and intentions of the Government.   This problem always exists, but it is

accentuated in time of crisis when tempers run high and the public mind is divided. The structure of the American Government provides in Congress a forum in which it is possible to attack Administration leaders, to question their motives, and to doubt their integrity without providing an opportunity for face-to-face debate between critics and those responsible for the conduct of administration. On the other hand, leaders of the Administration can continue desultory ways without having to meet face-to-face the criticism of men in Congress who are equally devoted to the general welfare. Yet dissemination of information to the public by the Administration is apt to be regarded as propaganda and to be viewed with suspicion by the people, the Congress, and the press. Ministries of propaganda and enlightenment have no place in the American tradition. Nevertheless, a government has a responsibility to tell the people what it is doing and why. Moving into the area of legitimate government information work presented delicate problems and, as in other situations, the Government policy was to tread lightly lest other, more important, objectives be jeopardized.

In July the Office of Civilian Defense proposed to the President that it establish a Bureau of Facts and Figures to be charged with morale activities. The Bureau would analyze the types of information being disseminated and would conduct an aggressive campaign of information to correct errors, to answer charges, and to inform the people. The proposal contemplated that the Bureau of Facts and Figures would handle broadcasts to other nations, but this function was given to the Coordinator of Information. The OCD proposal also encroached somewhat on the jurisdiction of the Division of Information in the Office for Emergency Management which did information work for the principal emergency war agencies.

Preliminary steps were taken to establish the proposed activities within the Office of Civilian Defense, but by September those engaged in the operation were persuaded that a different approach was necessary. The President drafted Mr. Archibald MacLeish to undertake the work as head of the Office of Facts and Figures which was established by Executive order of October 24, 1941.[20] The Office was directed to "formulate programs designed to facilitate a widespread and accurate understanding of the status and progress of the national-defense effort and of the defense policies and activities of the Government." The problem of coordinating information programs of different departments of the Government was touched on in an instruction to "advise with the several departments and agencies of the Government concerning the dissemination of such defense information." The departments and agencies were also ordered to make

---

[20] Executive Order No. 8922, Oct. 24, 1941, 6 *Federal Register* 5477.

available to the Office information and data "to facilitate the most coherent and comprehensive presentation to the Nation of the facts and figures of national defense."

The powers and responsibilities of the Office were inadequate to coordinate the information activities of Government agencies, as later events demonstrated. Its functions were limited to suit the circumstances of the time, but creation of the OFF constituted a step toward coordination. The nature of the job was described by the Director of the Office a few days after his appointment:

> I think that it is easier to talk about the job in terms of its distinctions from certain other jobs of a like kind that have been done or are being done. The first distinction, perhaps, and the easiest, is to distinguish it from the Creel operation. In the First World War all the departments of Government spoke through one mouthpiece, and, therefore, the question of a common Government policy on information didn't come up.
>
> In this war the Administration is very strongly determined to have the departments speak through their own mouthpieces, their own information services, maintaining their autonomy; and hence, the problem of a common information policy does very decidedly come up. The job of the Office of Facts and Figures is to try to develop and work out that policy.
>
> I'd like to make one other distinction, which I don't think is necessary but which I'd like to make for my own satisfaction, the distinction between this kind of operation and the propaganda office of a totalitarian state. I think the difference is the difference between the strategy of terror and the strategy of truth.
>
> . . . The Office of Facts and Figures is established, as I understand, upon the assumption that the people of a self-governing country are entitled to the fullest possible statement of facts and figures bearing upon conditions with which their Government is faced.

The State of Affairs on December 7, 1941

The attack on Pearl Harbor both vindicated and condemned the policy of the United States. The predictions that the United States was in danger of attack were fulfilled, but neither foresight nor intelligence had been adequate to foresee with certainty the exact time and place of attack. The voices which had demanded preparation were justified by the turn of events, but we had not been able to mobilize industrial or military strength sufficient to permit quick assumption of the offensive.

The entire policy of the Government had been conditioned by the necessity of maintaining the delicate domestic balance between those who unalterably opposed preparatory measures and those who enthusiastically advocated virtual declaration of war. No substantial body of opinion had been entirely satisfied with the policy of the Government. Those who condemned measures to appease Japan were countered by those in and out of the Government who wanted to play for time. Those who demanded more assistance to Britain were opposed by those who still twisted the lion's tail. Those who urged more rapid mobilization were met with the argument that mobilization inevitably meant war rather than defense. All these shades of opinion were reflected in the Congress and they could not be ignored. Yet the singleness of purpose of the Administration and of like-minded members of both parties in Congress provided sufficient political consensus to permit substantial preparation for what did happen.

Defense measures prosecuted from the middle of 1940 to Pearl Harbor produced a degree of preparedness which was high in comparison with the country's condition upon its entry into World War I. All types of armament actually were coming from the factories in

CHART 8. *Expenditures of the Federal Government.*

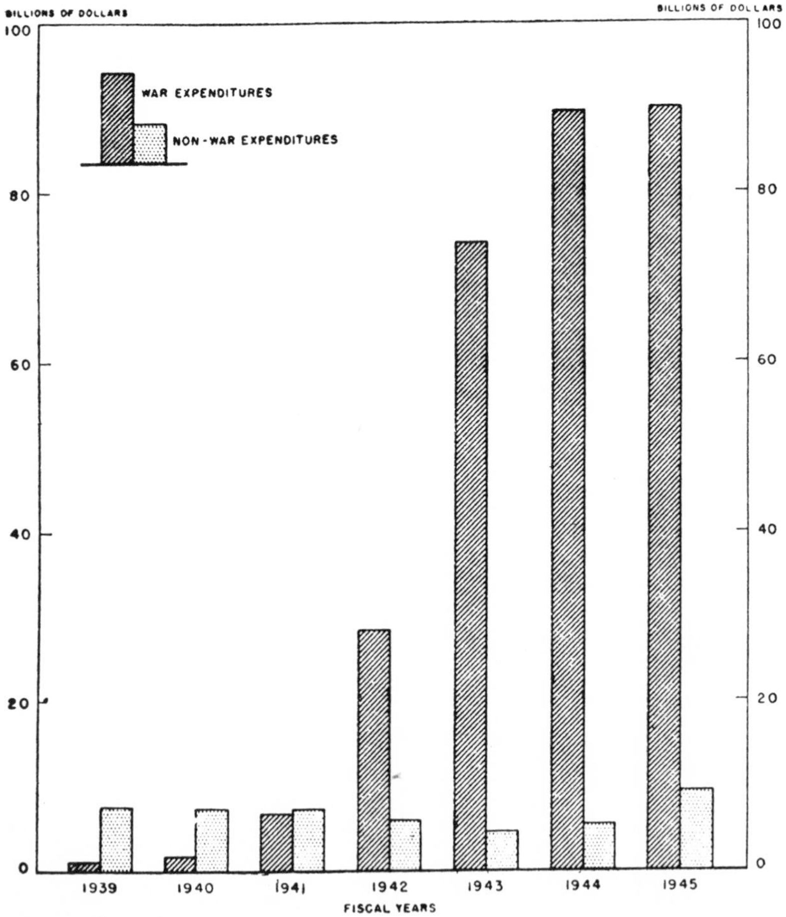

Source: Bureau of the Budget.

December 1941; in World War I, we depended on our Allies for many types of finished munitions even to the end of hostilities. Expenditures for war in 1941 totaled $6.7 billions (chart 8). In December 1941 such expenditures had reached a monthly rate of almost $2 billions, reflecting the rapid acceleration of the defense program. Munitions production in that month had reached a rate of a billion dollars a year (chart 9). From January 1941 to December 1941 munitions production increased by approximately 225 percent. In November 1941 2,200 planes and 5,500 plane engines were delivered. Thus plane production was at an annual rate of almost 25,000. Current produc-

CHART 9. *Munitions Production Prior to Pearl Harbor.*

[1945 Standard Dollar Weights]

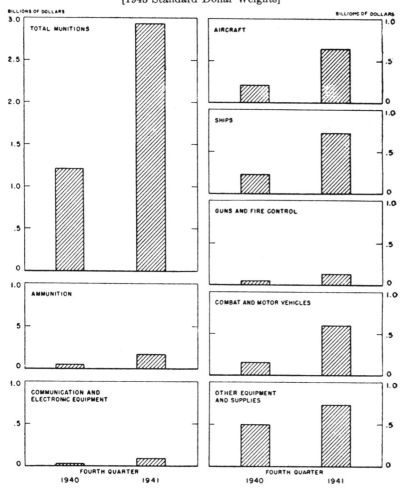

Source: Civilian Production Administration (formerly War Production Board).

tion, however, was an incomplete measure of accomplishment, for construction was under way on plants and facilities which soon would be ready to add to the flow of war goods.   The groundwork had been laid for the rapid rate of increase of output which was to occur in the following year.

We had also, a substantial military force inducted and in training. At the end of 1941, the total strength of the Army and Navy exceeded 2 million (chart 10).   An immense program to construct camps and other training facilities was under way.   Facilities for training of additional forces were either ready or under construction.

In the matter of the conversion of the Government to the necessities of war, great progress had been made.   Although the Government

CHART 10. *Growth of the Armed Forces.*

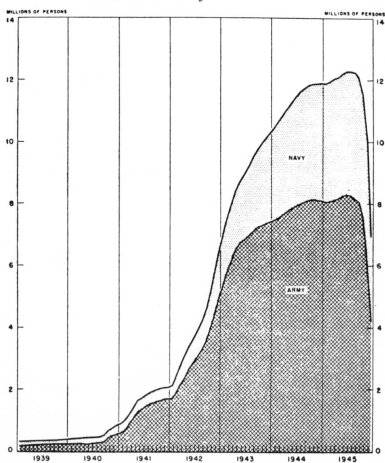

Source: Department of Labor.

had been criticized consistently for the nature and slowness of its administrative actions, the fact remained that the agencies destined to become the major war agencies had been built up. These organizations could not spring up overnight. Men had to be persuaded to come to Washington and working organizations had to be developed. These men had to acquire or develop a perspective bigger than their company or industry before they could be fully effective. The steps by which we reached the administrative status existing at the time of Pearl Harbor coincided roughly with expansions in the defense program which, in turn, placed different kinds of demands on the Government's administrative system. Further, the evolution of administrative structure had been tangled with the problem of political leadership and with the Presidential problem of maintaining a balance among different elements and different departments within the Administration. The broad issue of public versus military control of the Government repeatedly arose. Although many administrative changes were to be made subsequently, by December 7 a working organization had been established which was staffed by persons who had learned a great deal about how to operate and what needed to be done. This organization could be modified readily as emerging conditions required.

The Nation had the benefit of a year or 18 months of preparatory measures. The advantages of this readiness, imperfect though it was, can perhaps be measured if one speculates on the consequences that might have followed had we been unable to land in Guadalcanal and in North Africa until late in 1943 instead of in 1942 or had we been unable to mount a force adequate to invade Western Europe until the summer of 1945 instead of 1944.

PART

Two

DEFENSIVE WAR

Defensive War

ON DECEMBER 8, 1941, in an address delivered to a joint session of the two houses of Congress, the President said: "Yesterday, December 7, 1941—a date which will live in infamy—the United States of America was suddenly and deliberately attacked by naval and air forces of the Empire of Japan." He related that even while the àttack was in preparation and naval vessels in movement toward Hawaii, "the Japanese Government . . . deliberately sought to deceive the United States by false statements and expressions of hope for continued peace." He reported that Japanese forces had also launched attacks against Malaya, Hongkong, Guam, the Philippine Islands, Wake Island, and Midway Island. "Japan has, therefore, undertaken a surprise offensive extending throughout the Pacific area." He asked that "Congress declare that, since the unprovoked and dastardly attack by Japan on Sunday, December 7, a state of war has existed between the United States and the Japanese Empire."

The Senate, without dissent, and the House, with one member voting nay, resolved that

. . . the state of war between the United States and the Imperial Government of Japan which has thus been thrust upon the United States is hereby formally declared; and the President is hereby authorized and directed to employ the entire naval and military forces of the United States and the resources of the Government to carry on war against the Imperial Government of Japan; and, to bring the conflict to a successful termination, all of the resources of the country are hereby pledged by the Congress of the United States.

On the morning of December 11, Germany declared war against the United States. "The long known and the long expected," the President said in his message to Congress on the same day, "has thus taken place. The forces endeavoring to enslave the entire world now are moving toward this hemisphere." He mentioned, in passing, that Italy had also declared war against the United States. The President requested "Congress to recognize a state of war between the United States and Germany and between the United States and Italy." The House and the Senate acted on the same day.

Aggression against us in the Pacific and declarations of war from Berlin and Rome gave an entirely different tone to domestic political debate as was evidenced by the Congressional discussion of our declarations of war. Those who had consistently predicted that we might

99

become victims of aggression and had advocated that we should prepare for the worst did not gloat. Those who had denied the likelihood of attack were the first to admit the error of their views. "The time for debate and controversy within America has passed," one member of Congress declared, and many others spoke in the same tone. "The time for action has come. Interventionists and noninterventionists must cease criminations and recriminations, charges and countercharges against each other, and present a united front behind the President and the Government in the conduct of the war." [1] The Nation closed ranks. Unity of objective replaced division. To this outcome the prewar policy of the Administration doubtless contributed. That policy had followed great shifts in public opinion as influenced by the course of events and had not been pushed so rapidly as to antagonize irrevocably opposition elements.

Although the Nation was prepared more adequately than it would have been had the Government accepted the counsel of those who contended that the war could become no affair of ours, we were compelled to fight a defensive war for many months following the disaster at Pearl Harbor. The Japanese successes left our western approaches vulnerable and preference was given to the movement of forces to strengthen our defenses along the West Coast, Panama, Hawaii, and in Alaska. Our untenable position in the Philippines made it necessary to fight a delaying action there—Bataan fell April 9, Corregidor on May 6—and to concentrate our efforts in deploying forces to defend the route to Australia and in building up a force on that continent. Early in May in the Battle of the Coral Sea, Japanese movement toward Australia was checked, and in the next month in the battle near Midway heavy naval losses were inflicted on the Japanese.

Meanwhile, forces were being sent to the British Isles to aid in warding off a possible cross-channel attack and American aerial attacks against the continent were inaugurated on July 4, 1942. In Europe the war was not going well for the United Nations. The Russian winter offensive in the north pushed the Nazis back from Moscow. In the south, however, the Germans pushed the entire southern end of the Russian line eastward during the summer. They captured Sevastopol in July and advanced into the Caucasus. In September the siege of Stalingrad began. In North Africa Rommel launched his offensive in May and drove the British into Egypt where they made a stand at El Alamein in July.

While the forces at our command were being deployed to check our enemies until we could attack, on every phase of the home front the tempo of activity was speeded up and measures were undertaken better to adapt the Government to the requirements of war. In the

---

[1] Hamilton Fish, *Congressional Record*, vol. 87, pt. 9, p. 9520.

declaration of war, Congress had pledged "all of the resources of the country" to "bring the conflict to a successful termination." The days of guns and butter were over. To fulfill the pledge of all of our resources, it was necessary to do much more than we had in the period of defense preparation. Our resources had to be devoted in large measure to munitions of war. They had to be diverted from all civilian uses save those essential to the maintenance of the civilian economy as a production organization to support the fighting front. New factories had to be built; new sources of materials had to be developed. To do all these things and others, new governmental organizations had to be developed; existing ones had to be reorganized and tightened up. More effective economic controls had to be exerted to make sure that things essential to war were produced. Means had to be devised to keep within limits the dangers of inflation ever present in war. Systems had to be set up to assure—by rationing or otherwise—the fair distribution of scarce commodities among the civilian population. Arrangements for recruiting workers for factories producing needed items had to be improved. Ways and means had to be devised to keep the people informed of what the Government was doing and to prevent the dissemination of information which would give aid and comfort to the enemy.

These and other like issues had to be dealt with during the first 9 months of 1942. Fortunately, we did not begin the war without considerable administrative, as well as military, preparation. In large measure, it was only necessary to expand and refine the governmental machinery which had evolved since May 1940. The strain of total mobilization, however, required the development of some new governmental machinery, the establishment of new legal and administrative techniques, and the settlement of a series of domestic political issues arising chiefly from the problem of assuring an equality of sacrifice in meeting the pledge of our total resources.

The chapters of Part II that follow outline broadly the major administrative developments of the first 10 months of 1942. In this period the principal adjustments required to fit the emergency governmental machinery built up before Pearl Harbor for the needs of war were made. The chief new agencies demanded by the conditions of war were established. The mobilization of national resources was rapidly extended toward more complete exertion of national effort.

CHAPTER

5

Accelerating Production

THE ATTACK at Pearl Harbor and the war declarations which
followed put an end to the inhibiting doubts which beset our
national policy and action during the preceding year. Though
few grasped the meaning of "total war" even after war was declared,
all were ready to exert every effort and to make sacrifices for eventual
victory. There was a single national purpose as clear and dominant
as can be found in the history of any people.

On all sides it was recognized that war production was an extremely
important factor in building the military power both of ourselves and
of our allies. Even so, the President's clarion call for 60,000 planes,
45,000 tanks, 20,000 antiaircraft guns and 8,000,000 tons of shipping
in the single year 1942 almost took the breath away from many war
chieftains, industrial leaders, and production economists. "He set
the sights so high indeed," said Hanson Baldwin, the military expert
of the New York *Times*, "that it will be an industrial miracle if we
achieve these goals." Baldwin thought that we might double, but
would hardly treble, our plane production in a single year.

In spite of the doubts and timorous counsels of practical and expert
men, the President set our goals high, and the Nation drove forward
as a unit for "all-out" war production.

In this the Nation already had a running start in the production,
contracts, controls, administrative machinery, and experience of the
defense days. At the time war was declared we were already de-
voting about 15 percent of our industrial production to war, (chart
11), a start of the greatest significance both in speeding the production
build-up and in determining the administrative machinery and the
personnel of our war administration. The gradual development of
administrative organization and processes in the defense period per-

103

mitted a smooth change-over to war conditions. Sharper definitions of responsibility, broadening of authority, and renaming of existing agencies and officials could be accomplished without interrupting the acceleration of their activities.

Immediate Administrative Adjustments

The new drive for production under war conditions called for the immediate abandonment of the slow processes of debate, consultation, board action, and the inconclusive influence of advisory interdepartmental agencies, and for the substitution of administrators with authority to act with dispatch, and power to command both public agencies and private enterprises to do their parts in the national effort.

Within a few months after the outbreak of war, a series of changes in the war-production machinery of the Government of the United States was made. In some instances these changes were made by the President under the power he possessed to organize and reorganize the agencies within the Office for Emergency Management. In other

CHART 11. *Industrial Production.*

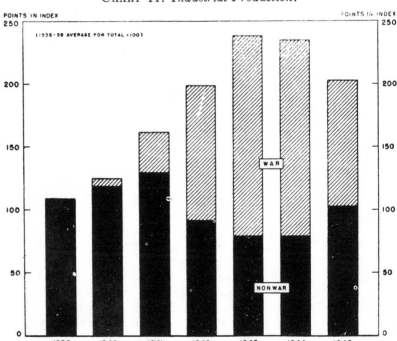

Source: Board of Governors of the Federal Reserve System.

instances, he acted under authority granted by the First War Powers Act [1] which enabled him to reassign the functions of departments and agencies established by statute. The extension of this power by Congress permitted the accomplishment of some administrative changes which were overdue but had not been feasible earlier because of lack of power in the Executive to act.

The War Production Board was created with all the President's powers over industry, production, raw materials, factories, machine tools, priorities, allocations, and rationing. The Office of Production Management and the Supply Priorities and Allocations Board were abolished, and their duties and personnel were transferred to WPB. The Army-Navy Munitions Board was ordered to report to the President "through the Chairman of the WPB." [2]

All the powers of WPB were placed in the hands of one man, Donald M. Nelson. The "Board" itself was purely advisory, and served to bring around the council table for weekly meetings the top production representatives of the War, Navy, and Commerce Departments, the Board of Economic Warfare, and the Price Administrator as well as a representative of the White House.

The Office of Price Administration was placed on a statutory basis with power to stabilize prices, eliminate hoarding, and prevent speculation.[3] All the powers of the OPA were assigned to the Administrator, Leon Henderson. OPA was also given the administration of rationing by Donald Nelson, through WPB Directive No. 1 of January 24, 1942.

The War Manpower Commission came into being on April 18, 1942, with broad coordinating and "directive" powers over manpower, labor assignment to industry, employment and training, and all agencies of the Government dealing with the use of manpower in the war effort were placed under the Commission.[4] Such powers as the Commission had—and these did not include the right to draft, assign, or punish civilian workers—were entrusted to the Chairman of the WMC, Paul V. McNutt, "after consultation with" an interdepartmental commission representing War, Navy, Agriculture, Labor, War Production Board, National Housing Agency, Office of Defense Transportation, War Shipping Administration, the Civil Service Commission, and the Federal Security Agency. Other advisory committees were set up including a Management-Labor Policy Committee, a Women's Advisory Committee. The Committee on Fair Employment Practice, which had been established in June 1941 to eliminate racial discrimina-

---

[1] Adopted by Congress, Dec. 18, 1941.
[2] Executive Order No. 9024, Jan. 16, 1942, 7 *Federal Register* 329; Executive Order No. 9040, Jan. 24, 1942, 7 *Federal Register* 527; Executive Order No. 9125, Apr. 7, 1942, 7 *Federal Register* 2719.
[3] 56 *Stat.* 29.
[4] Executive Order No. 9139, Apr. 18, 1942, 7 *Federal Register* 2919.

tion in employment, was a part of the WPB until July 30, 1942, when it was brought into WMC.[5]

The National War Labor Board was established on the foundations of the National Defense Mediation Board, on January 12, 1942.[6] The Board was made up of 12 members, 4 representing the public, 4 the employee, and 4 the employer and was given final jurisdiction over all labor disputes and over wage and salary rates except as to the railroads.

The Office of Defense Transportation, the creation of which had been under consideration prior to Pearl Harbor, was set up under Joseph B. Eastman as Director to exercise the President's powers over the coordination and direction of all "domestic transportation systems."[7] These powers were subsequently extended to cover "all rubber-borne" civilian transportation, including the use of private cars.[8]

The War Shipping Administration was created on February 7, 1942, to operate and maintain shipping owned by the United States and to allocate all vessels under the United States flag or subject to United States control, to provide insurance, and to administer priorities in shipping in accordance with such schedules as might be transmitted by the WPB.[9] The Administrator was Admiral Emory S. Land. Lewis W. Douglas, as his deputy, handled ship utilization and priorities.

The National Housing Agency was created to bring under one Administrator, John B. Blandford, Jr., all the housing planning, construction, management, and financing agencies of the Government and to supersede the Division of Defense Housing Coordination which had been established within the OEM.[10]

The Civil Service Commission on March 15, 1942, issued regulations to facilitate the recruitment of additional personnel needed to man the war agencies. All new appointments became "war service" appointments and could be made under rules and administrative arrangements permitting expeditious action. The action by the Commission was the culmination of a series of measures beginning in mid 1940 and was taken under broad authority delegated by the President.[11]

---

[5] Presidential Letter of July 30, 1942. (FEPC established by Executive Order No. 8802, June 25, 1942, 6 *Federal Register* 125.)

[6] Executive Order No. 9017, Jan. 12, 1942, 7 *Federal Register* 237.

[7] Executive Order No. 8989, Dec. 18, 1941, 6 *Federal Register* 6725.

[8] Executive Order No. 9156, May 2, 1942, 7 *Federal Register* 3349.

[9] Executive Order No. 9054, Feb. 7, 1942, 7 *Federal Register* 837.

[10] Executive Order No. 9070, Feb. 24, 1942, 7 *Federal Register* 1529; Executive Order No. 8632, Jan. 11, 1941, 6 *Federal Register* 295.

[11] Executive Order No. 9063, Feb. 16, 1942, 7 *Federal Register* 1075.

Reorganization of the Procurement Services

The creation of the WPB did not, as a matter of fact, shift the procurement activities from Army Ordnance, the Bureau of Ships, the Quartermaster, Treasury Department, the Bureau of Supplies and Accounts, the Navy Bureau of Ordnance, the Army Air Corps, the Maritime Commission, or the other independent procurement authorities which were concerned with placing contracts for war materials, construction, and supplies. The power to take over all these activities was assigned to the WPB by its Executive order, but Mr. Nelson had no intention of assuming the procurement and contracting functions. As he said to the Truman Committee:

I have gone even to the point of being overzealous in seeing that the contracting power is kept within the Army and Navy.

We had one of two courses to take when we took this job. Many urged that we set up a buying organization independent of the Army and Navy. I knew, sir, that that would be just dead wrong and didn't even consider it for 5 minutes, because it would have been impossible to have gotten the type of men that we wanted to come here and do that job with the contracting power without having subjected themselves to great criticism. So, in setting it up, we were very careful not to take a bit of authority away from the Army or the Navy. As a matter of fact, we enhanced that authority.[12]

It was also Mr. Nelson's view that the effort to take over procurement in 1942 would only have slowed up production which had already reached a monthly total of $2.2 billion by January.[13]

To handle the procurement functions thus left with the Services, the Maritime Commission, the Department of Agriculture, and the Treasury, there was need for immediate reorganization within each of these agencies.

The major reorganization was in the War Department. As part of the realignment of the Department in February 1942, General Brehon Somervell was placed in charge of the newly created Services of Supply, which was the title given to the basket in which were placed the Engineers, the Medical Corps, the Signal Corps, the Quartermaster, the Ordnance Department, and a number of other offices which were not part of the Ground Forces or the Air Forces. The SOS, which was later entitled the Army Service Forces, thus included all the procurement functions of the Army with the exception of specialized aircraft procurement, which remained with the Army Air Forces, and the coordination and control functions of the Joint Army and Navy Munitions Board which, under the chairmanship of Ferdinand Eberstadt, represented the Under Secretary of War and

[12] U. S. Congress. Senate. Special Committee Investigating the National Defense Program. 77th Cong., 1st sess., Hearings on S. Res. 71, pt. 12, p. 5089. Statement of Donald M. Nelson.
[13] Ibid., p. 5228.

the Under Secretary of the Navy. Due to the partial abstinence of the Navy, the ANMB never moved out of the War Department, and was in reality an agency of General Somervell's office.

The reorganization of the Navy Department came on January 30, 1942. As part of this shift, Vice Admiral S. M. Robinson was placed in charge of the Office of Procurement and Material and thus handled liaison with WPB on most procurement matters. While the Bureau of Ships, Bureau of Ordnance, and other major functional divisions of the Navy Department continued to exercise their autonomy in procurement matters, in contrast to the degree of central control imposed on procurement units in the War Department, Admiral Robinson did supply a center of leadership on Navy procurement at least in relationships with the WPB.

Treasury Procurement, which, in addition to the supplies needed by the Government of the United States for its regular services, bought nonagricultural and nonmunitions items for lend-lease, had been newly staffed and newly organized in 1940. This structure went into the war period with few changes except for the addition of personnel.

The Maritime Commission was divided into two separate organizations to handle its work.[14] This division was accomplished by setting up the War Shipping Administration to allocate tonnage, enforce priorities, administer marine insurance, and procure and manage the American-controlled merchant marine, public and private. All construction of ships, and this included some naval craft along with the stupendous program of merchant shipping, remained a function of the Maritime Commission, and was placed under the immediate supervision of Rear Admiral Vickery. Rear Admiral Land remained as Chairman of the Commission and also served as Administrator of the War Shipping Administration, although construction, involving as it did both contract work and the management of the Government shipyards, absorbed the bulk of his time.

The reorganization of the food-procurement program came through the establishment in the Department of Agriculture of the Agricultural Marketing Administration which was designed to handle all lend-lease agricultural procurement, and to supervise the market expansion program, the market stabilization program, and market services and regulation.[15] The actual procurement of lend-lease foods was through the Federal Surplus Commodity Corporation.

With these changes in the procurement agencies, all of which came before the end of February, the Government was organized for its war procurement tasks. The system comprehended two elements:

---

[14] Executive Order No. 9054, Feb. 7, 1942, 7 *Federal Register* 837.
[15] Executive Order No. 9069, Feb. 23, 1942, 7 *Federal Register* 1409.

a half dozen independent procurement units which were, with the important exception of the Army Service Forces, also users of the commodities procured and a coordinating unit, the WPB, with authority to take over the procurement functions, and to issue overriding directives.

Transition to War Production Board

In taking over SPAB, OPM, and the new powers which went to make up the WPB, it was Mr. Nelson's policy to rule gently and use as much of the prior personnel and machinery as possible. He feared the loss of momentum, and the delays incident to new organization and new men.

In place of the Director General and Associate Director General of OPM, there was now a single head with all power. In place of the debating and resolving SPAB, all of the authority and responsibility went to Nelson, though most of the same people still sat as his advisors in the WPB.

Personnel changes in WPB were minor except at the top. Mr. William S. Knudsen, though greatly handicapped by the mounting problems of his weak and bifurcated organization, had made a great contribution especially toward the expansion of facilities. He went to the War Department with the rank of Lieutenant General to be the top advisor on production.

All of the OPM and SPAB activities were continued in WPB though the effort to tie labor into the operation was curtailed with the disappearance of Mr. Hillman as a codirector. He continued nominally to head the Labor Division, but actually dropped out of the picture. Mr. Hillman's health was bad, and he soon indicated his desire to resign. He remained, however, until further functions were transferred out of WPB in the creation of the WMC. At that time the President recognized that the assignment was no longer in keeping with his stature and in a telegram to Hillman at a hospital in Washington asked him to become instead a "Special Assistant" to the President "in labor matters."

Another shift was the abandonment of Floyd Odlum's vigorous campaign for "contract distribution." Odlum disappeared, his elaborate organization was absorbed, for the time being, in other divisions of WPB and the papers and radio were no longer filled with his exhortations for the enlistment of the small manufacturer in munitions production.

In the shift from OPM to WPB the most important developments were, however, not the activities which were deemphasized or dropped, but the new activities which were given an organizational basis. These were the Requirements Committee, the Planning Committee, and the pulling together in a single organization of Industry Operations and of Priorities. The Field Service was established, as was a Bureau of Government Requirements. Otherwise, the organization units devoted to production, purchases, civilian supply, materials, and statistics went on much as before.

Under these new arrangements, the Planning Committee, under Robert Nathan, freed from all administrative responsibility, was designed to analyze what was happening, study the impact of the production program on the American economy, and make suggestions to the chairman on major policy matters. The Requirements Committee, on the other hand, was given a more restricted and immediately practical role. It was given the task of adding up the raw material requirements of all the claimants, getting the requests cut back so that they would not exceed the supplies, and then dividing up the supplies, commodity by commodity, among the claimants so as to produce the most satisfactory total result. Each 3-month period was treated as a separate unit, and the effort made to allocate to each claimant agency enough steel to go with its copper, enough nickel to go with its rubber. The Requirements Committee reflected another step in the institutionalization of arrangements for the allocation of our total resources among competing uses. This general objective had been one of the dominant purposes in the creation of the Supply Priorities and Allocations Board. With the rapid growth of munitions production and the increasing pressure upon our resources, it was imperative that better means be found to make allocations of resources. The Requirements Committee, like SPAB, was plagued by the inadequacy of data on which to base decisions and by the inadequacy of arrangements to assure that its broad decisions were executed in detail.

While the Planning Committee was a small cohesive group of men of broad comprehension of policy problems, the Requirements Committee was made up of representatives of the leading claimants, each fighting to keep the other fellow's piece of the material pie small and his own big. Though the decision always rested with Mr. Nelson's representative in this struggle, the lion's share went to meet immediate military demands, to the undue sacrifice at times of equally good claims of the railroads, of housing for workers, mining machinery and agricultural tools, or of aid to the Allies.

In the new WPB set-up, the materials branches, like those concerned with steel, copper, and aluminum, were part of the same broad organization as the Requirements Committee. They were thus responsible for passing out the critical raw materials to the users in general accordance with the determinations of the Chairman of the Requirements Committee as certified to them.

The materials branches were primarily responsible also for inducing or forcing conservation in the use of their particular material, although there were also especial sections of WPB concerned with conservation and revision of specifications. While the WPB thus had some influence on the simplification of specifications to make production easier, the most effective work of this sort was done by civilian manufacturing experts who were made a part of the military procurement offices under the "infiltration" policy mentioned below.

The demands for steel, copper, aluminum, and other materials came to the producers and raw material handlers through an entirely different channel. This demand started with the placing of contracts by the extremely active and independent procurement agencies—the Army Services Forces, the various Navy bureaus, the Maritime Commission, and Treasury Procurement. These contracts carried with them priorities; that is, rights to have components and materials ahead of anyone else who did not have an equal or higher priority rating. The final authority to control the issuance of priorities was in WPB. In order not to disturb a going system and cause delay, Mr. Nelson continued the priority system which had been built up under the Office of Production Management, and immediately authorized the Army-Navy Munitions Board to assign priorities to all Army, Navy, Maritime, and Coast Guard procurement. These priorities were "extensible"; that is, any contractor who had an "A" priority order could place that priority on any material which he in his own judgment decided that he needed to do the work. All other priorities, including a great many secondary priorities for military end products, were assigned through the Priorities Division and the industry divisions of WPB, all of which were now placed under the supervision of Mr. J. S. Knowlson. The priority power was thus officially delegated to him.

In the early days of WPB, manufacturers who needed priority assistance to get hold of steel, aluminum, valves, motors, wire, lumber, cement, wheelbarrows, refrigerators, paint brushes, or other items required for production would fill out an application explaining for what they needed the material or article, and on the basis of the rating on an approved list of the thing they were making, they would receive a high priority, a low priority, or no priority. Originally these applications, except for those handled by ANMB, all came in to Washington, as many as 130,000 a week during June 1942, and they were "processed" through the industry branches and the priority division, rated, and sent back to the plants and factories of America. Later on, a considerable part of this work was decentralized to the field.

The Impact of Unlimited Procurement

Under the traditional American system, industry does not produce war munitions until there are Government orders; Government orders are not placed until there are appropriations; and appropriations are not made until requests based on estimates and supporting information are submitted to Congress for action. In fact, in peacetime, the control over the whole process centers in the appropriation by Congress. It was natural, therefore, for procurement officers not to take vigorous action to raise war production before appropriations were

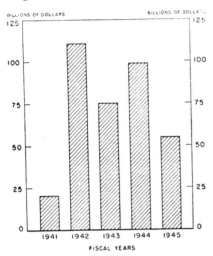

CHART 12. *Federal Appropriations for War.*

Source: Treasury Department.

available. Not only was this against the whole tradition of the past, but it would, if carried far enough, have been a criminal offense. But any restriction, real or imagined, imposed by appropriations, disappeared after the declaration of war. Appropriations were made in lump sums, so that appropriation language no longer limited the military agencies in their war activities.

While Congress had slowed up the building of training camps only a few months earlier, it now acted with great dispatch. Within 6 months, almost $100,000,000,000 was appropriated, and in the next 4 months another $60,000,000,000 was added (chart 12). Of these stupendous authorizations, the Army received $95 billion, the Navy $50 billion, lend-lease $5 billion, and the Maritime Commission $3.5 billion. Never before or since, have such immense financial authorizations been given in so short a period.

By spring the floodgates were open. Equipped with virtually unlimited financial authorizations, the procurement agencies went to work to place their contracts with the industries of America. This was not too difficult. Industry was now eager to get into war work, especially as the WPB materials orders and limitation orders began to interfere with normal production of civilian items. The services were equipped with high priorities, which gave the contractors confidence that they would be able to get the materials and components they required, price arrangements were generous and elastic, and the manufacturers were not unwilling, under pressure, to sign additional contracts even when their plants were already full, hoping to expand, or find some other method of discharging their inflated obligations. With this combination of circumstances, over $100 billion of contracts were placed in the first 6 months of 1942.[16] In other words, industry signed up to deliver for war more than the total production of the American economy in the Nation's most prosperous and productive prior year. At the time there were also some $20 billion of orders outstanding, mostly for munitions. The new orders included $68 billion for munitions, $12.6 billions for industrial expansion, and $6.9 billions for military construction.[17]

Under this flood of war orders, a number of things were bound to happen, and did happen.

First, it became utterly impossible to produce everything ordered at any time in any near future. It was an industrial impossibility. The total called for was in excess of our industrial capacity.

Second, there was a resulting collision between the various production programs and between the men who were responsible for them. Merchant ships took steel from the Navy, and the landing craft cut into both. The Navy took aluminum from aircraft. Rubber took valves from escort vessels, from petroleum, and from the Navy. The pipe lines took steel from ships, new tools, and the railroads. And at every turn there were foreign demands to be met as well as requirements for new plants.

Third, all semblance of balance in the production program disappeared because of the different rates of contracting and of production that resulted from the scramble to place orders. If there ever had been a planned balance between men, ships, tanks, planes, supplies, weapons, ammunition, and new facilities, and there is no evidence that there was, that balance disappeared in the differential time required to develop the orders, the differential energies of the various procurement officers, and the differential difficulties of getting production out.

Fourth, there was terrific waste in conversion. After a tragically slow start, many a plant was changed over to war production when its normal product was more needed than its new product. Locomotive plants went into tank production, when locomotives were more neces-

16 WPB, *Report on Production*, 1942, p. 27.   17 *Ibid.*, p. 27.

sary—but the Tank Division did not know this.   Truck plants began to produce airplanes, a change that caused shortages of trucks later on. In some cases, plants were converted at great cost of steel and copper, when a fraction of the precious metals involved would have brought a greater return at some other place in the economy.   The scramble for a production we could not attain, brought us waste instead.

Fifth, we built many new factories, and expanded many others, which we could not use and did not need.   Many of these factories we could not supply with labor or with raw materials, or if we had, we would not have been able to fly the planes or shoot the ammunition that would have come out of them.   But in the process we used up critical materials and manpower which might better have gone into something else.   In the light of the tremendous contracts outstanding especially in the early part of 1942, however, these plants seemed necessary to some people, and under the system they were given high priorities.   In most cases they were also financed by the Government. The result was, however, an overconcentration of contracts in the larger corporations and a failure to fully utilize the facilities of many small manufacturers whose plants could have produced "bits and pieces." [18]   It did not escape the attention of Congress that better utilization of small plants could have reduced the necessary expansion of facilities.

Finally, the priority system broke down because of "priority inflation."   People with military contracts had the right to take more scarce materials and components than there were, so that a priority or an allocation became nothing more than a "hunting license." In other words, those who were issuing priorities did not limit their high-ranking authorizations within the allocations given them by the Requirements Committee.   In fact, there was very little connection between the two, partly because the allocations were based on a quarterly time schedule, while the priorities carried no terminal date and were good at any time.

Whether it would have been possible, within the time available, by better planning of procurement to prevent the consequence of indiscriminate placement of contracts without delaying the advance of production is a complex question.   The determination of the construction program for ordnance plants, for example, required not only that we know in what quantities and at what times a particular ordnance item would be needed, but also that the output rate of plants

---

[18] Up to December 1942, 71 percent of all war contracts had been awarded to the 100 largest contractors. See in this connection U. S. Congress, Senate. *Economic Concentration and World War II.* Report of the Smaller War Plants Corporation to the Special Committee to Study Problems of American Small Business. 79th Cong., 2d sess., No. 6.

A Department of Commerce survey in the spring of 1943 indicated substantial unused capacity in the hands of small business firms. *Survey of Current Business,* July 1943, pp. 19–24; Sept. 1943, pp. 19–24.

producing by new methods and on unprecedented scales be predicted. Control over other types of procurement would have required types of data, such as the usage of materials in the manufacture of particular items, and administrative techniques not yet developed. Whatever the hypothetical possibilities might have been, the general policy in the first few months of the war was to permit the placement of contracts until difficulties developed. Then the War Production Board proceeded to deal with the problems born of experience.

CHART 13. *Productive Facility Expansion by Source of Funds.*

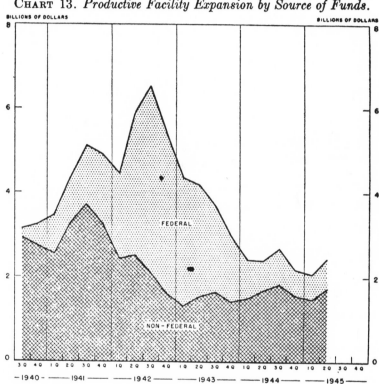

BILLIONS OF DOLLARS

FEDERAL

NON-FEDERAL

3Q 4Q 1Q 2Q 3Q 4Q 1Q 2Q 3Q 4Q 1Q 2Q 3Q 4Q 1Q 2Q 3Q 4Q 1Q 2Q 3Q 4Q

—1940— —1941— —1942— —1943— —1944— —1945—

Source: Civilian Production Administration (formerly War Production Board).

Facilities

The problem of factory construction and expansion received early attention. In the middle of March 1942 the Planning Committee reported that facilities expansion was out of balance and would run ahead of all possible use. In spite of control measures initiated by WPB, the same warning had to be repeated on May 6 and again on June 12. In April Order L–41 prohibited all further facilities expansion without prior WPB approval. Under this order, projects initiated on request of the services received automatic approval. A number of expansions were stopped, however, like the Higgins Shipyards project, and a rather ineffective committee was set up to cut back all facilities which could not come into production by the middle of 1943.[19]　The problem was discussed in the War Production Board itself, and it was generally agreed that further expansion of facilities was undesirable with certain exceptions designed to meet specific critical shortages.　The chief expansions of this sort were for aviation gasoline and synthetic rubber.

As a result of these efforts, there was a sharp reduction after the

CHART 14. *Manufacturing Facility Expansion by Industry*
[Third Quarter 1940 through Second Quarter 1945.]

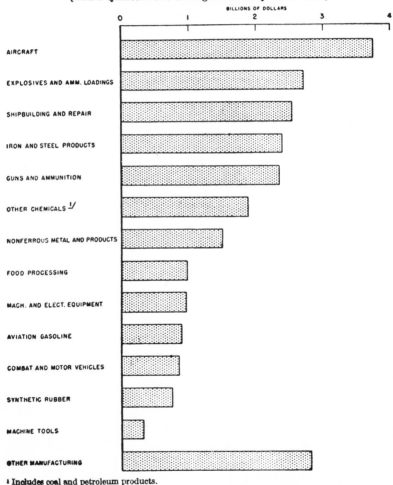

¹ Includes coal and petroleum products.

Source: Civilian Production Administration (formerly War Production Board).

¹⁹ WPB, *Minutes*, June 16, 1942.

middle of 1942 in facilities expansions initiated. Six months later actual construction and then tooling up began to drop off as well. By this time we had finished building the bulk of our aircraft, ammunition, steel, aluminum, magnesium, petroleum, shipbuilding, and other plants, as well as our military camps and establishments and wartime housing, street, water and sewer works.

Eventually the facilities program was brought into reasonable balance more by material shortages, suasion, and debate than by the exercise of controls.

Feasibility

The effort to bring the total of all war production programs somewhere within the realm of possibility was also initiated by a report of March 17, 1942, from the Planning Committee and the Bureau of Research and Statistics. After extensive discussion of the question, Mr. Nelson took the whole problem to the President and insisted that the services must review and revise their programs themselves to bring them into "do-able" limits.

The major difficulty at the time was steel plate. To meet this difficulty, the President on July 4 authorized Mr. Nelson to cut back the ship program in accordance with his judgment and to work out the details.

Production bottlenecks became even more serious during the summer of 1942 when many programs were in difficulty and scores of production lines were closed down because of competition for components. The solution of the problem of keeping the production program within the limits of feasibility did not come until later in 1942.

Materials Control

The excessive demands placed on the production system in the early months of 1942 brought out latent weaknesses in priorities procedures which had been adequate for a less ambitious program. These procedures, in a variety of forms, had the common objective of channeling the available supply of materials into the types of production considered most essential. The system of controls went through a series of trial-and-error evolutionary changes. Soon after the establishment of WPB, its staff began a thorough investigation to devise more suitable methods of control to meet the requirements of large-scale production for war. At the outset, it inherited from the Office of Production Management a system of controls which, after additional growth, included the following major elements:

I. PROHIBITIONS

(a) *Materials orders* prohibiting the use of scarce materials in the manufacture of given articles, such as chrome in auto trim or baby carriages. About 400 of these were issued during the war, the bulk of them in 1942.

(*b*) *Limitation orders* which limited or prohibited the manufacture or use of specified articles except on military contracts. About 350 limitation orders were issued during the war, most of them in 1942.

(*c*) *Inventory limitation orders.*

II. Priorities

Priorities were general instructions to producers and dealers requiring them to fill orders bearing a higher rating before they fill orders of a lower rating. In any industrial queue, those with priorities went directly to the head of the line, no matter how many others were there ahead of them.

The system started in the summer of 1940, when special military orders were given priorities, and the Army-Navy Munitions Board issued a "critical list." This was extended in March 1941 by Priority Administrative Order No. 1 issued by OPM. The first priorities were simply A, B, and C, each letter with 10 subdivisions, which took precedence in that order. As soon as the A's began to crowd each other in some factories, new systems of lettering came in with A–1–a, etc., and finally AA's and AAA's.

III. Allocations

Allocations were used as the basis of control where the entire supply of a commodity like copper or wood pulp was brought under accounting control by the War Production Board and was completely budgeted on a time and quantity basis, and withdrawals for any purpose were prohibited except in accordance with a WPB authorization.

IV. Apportionment

Apportionment was used as the basis of control where the WPB in effect took direct ownership of a specified commodity, like crude rubber, and issued the material to specific manufacturers as required.

V. Order Board (Delivery) Control

In some individual factories, WPB reviewed orders on hand, canceled or rearranged deliveries; determined in what order things would be manufactured or delivered.

VI. Scheduling

In "scheduling," WPB worked directly with the management to get out required production on a timetable, arranging to have required material and components on hand to meet the timetable.

VII. OVERRIDING DIRECTIVES

Specific orders to deliver a specific article or quantity of commodities at or during a given time in spite of all other orders or controls were known as "overriding directives". (Used for components for escort vessels, landing craft, to deal with unforeseen emergencies.)

VIII. INTEGRATED CONTROL

Finally, the effort was made to limit procurements by manufacturers of a selected list of critical materials to a quantity in balance to complete articles required on a balanced program basis. (Production requirements plan and later controlled materials plan.)

These eight types of production controls were developed step by step starting with I and II and ending up with VI, VII, and VIII. In the end, all eight were being used side by side, or layer on layer, though the major emphasis shifted from priorities (II) to integrated control, scheduling, and, in emergencies, to overriding directives (VI, VII and VIII).

Production Requirements Plan

Under PRP, mentioned above as the first example of integrated control, the effort was made to introduce a horizontal control of materials for each plant directly by the War Production Board. Under PRP, each manufacturer filed a schedule of his products, showing the items and their priority rating, a list of critical materials used by him for these items and of the quantities on hand, a statement of his orders ahead and their priority rating, and finally, a statement of his material, and other requirements on a monthly basis for the immediate future. These PRP schedules, or "books," were filed in Washington, where the totals required of each critical material were added up to see whether and how much they overran the total national available supply for the months ahead. This total picture was then reviewed by the Requirements Committee and its staff. Broad allocations of critical items were made by programs. On this basis, the individual schedules were then cut down, and the individual manufacturer given authority to procure so much steel, and so much aluminum, copper, or other materials, or so many components containing such materials, during the ensuing 3-month period. Under this plan, it was possible to relate the amounts of different commodities given each plant so that if copper had to be cut, a particular plant would not be given steel which it could not use in view of its copper cut. Also, inventories were taken into account on a plant basis in relation to the work of that plant. This Production Requirements Plan system was first developed and used voluntarily by a few manufacturers as early as December 3, 1941, under the Office of Production Management. When the priority system broke down in the spring of 1942, PRP was, on June 2 by order of the War Production Board, made mandatory for all metals industries (some 30,000 plants) beginning with the third quarter of 1942.

There were, however, grave doubts as to the workability of the system both within WPB and in the services. Inasmuch as the system, if it succeeded, would completely supersede the vertical system of special military priorities elaborately built up by the Army-Navy Munitions Board, the opposition of the Army and the ANMB to the plan may have arisen from mixed motives.

The opponents of PRP thought the system would be too complicated to administer, especially from a central point; that the general run of manufacturers could not fill out the blanks as they did not know what part of what metals went into which priority articles; that the manufacturers of components seldom knew where their products would ultimately go; and that the system would get in the way of future changes in the war production program, or of new contracts, as the cutting up of the steel pie, for example, would rest on the individual orders already on the books of the producers when the apportionment was made. It was pointed out that a producer who failed to file, or whose "book" was lost, would be closed down even if he was making a critically needed part for a Norden bombsight.

The proponents of PRP admitted that the first few quarters would be far from satisfactory, but maintained that industry would soon learn, and would be greatly relieved to escape from the old welter of priority paper. As to future changes and new contracts, these would carry with them their own new allotments. The Production Requirements Plan planned to hold back a considerable "kitty" to meet emergencies and to deal with errors, and was confident that complete accounting, a full use of excess inventories, and the development of balanced apportionments would gain so much material for the programs that needed help that priority inflation would be cured, and a great increase in production would result.

In any case, with the situation getting rapidly worse, and with no alternative in sight, Mr. Nelson decided to go ahead with PRP, and issued his order accordingly.

Reorganization of War Production Board

After the usual "honeymoon period" of public and official approbation, criticisms of WPB began to be heard. These arose chiefly from within WPB, from the Army, and from Congress and the Truman Committee.

Within WPB there was a considerable feeling of frustration. Businessmen within WPB "could not get decisions," were harried by "impractical planners," and by "other divisions," and by "politicians" who "knew nothing about the business." Moreover, they were "investigated to death" and "suspected." The economists and career public servants were dissatisfied with the "resistance to conversion," the lack of "comprehensive production plans based on strategy," and the freedom of the WPB industry branches which enabled each one "to have its own policies and its own strategy for winning the war."

From the services, chiefly the Army, came the criticism of "bad" and "weak" management, blame for every procurement muddle or production delay, and the continual insistence that the real needs of the war were being sacrificed to "soft civilian desires."

Congressional criticism centered on slowness in conversion, production delays, injury to small business, kow-towing to the Army, and the inefficiencies and special interests of dollar-a-year men. The most celebrated "case" of the Congressional investigations was Mr. Guthrie, a businessman who resigned from WPB on March 14 because of disagreements arising over "the conservation of wool, the rate of conversion to war work of the refrigerator, radio, carpet, upholstery, automobile fabric, tire cord, and nylon industries, and the delays in the allocation of cotton textile manufacturing capacity to war and essential civilian production." [20] While Mr. Nelson permitted Mr. Guthrie to resign to maintain peace in the family, the public excitement created was electric. The Planning Committee report on conversion, which in effect agreed with Mr. Guthrie on important matters of policy, was released to all WPB branches, almost as a directive; limitation orders began to pour out; and many of the "business as usual" executives disappeared from the scene. Things moved so fast from this point on, that Mr. Nelson was able to say on April 21 that the conversion program would be completed by the end of May.

In this connection, Mr. Nelson stated to the Truman Committee:

I purposely set up the WPB so that there are all shades of opinion in it . . . I think we must have all shades of opinion from businessmen who are conservative, businessmen who are liberal, professors, economists, public servants, people of all kinds, because this job of conversion, this job of shutting off civilian production is not an easy thing, sir, nor is it to be toyed with lightly * * * Only time will tell, and only history can record, whether we have been too slow or too rapid. In my opinion, it is about right.[21]

---

[20] U. S. Congress. Senate. Special Committee Investigating the National Defense Program. 77th Cong., 1st sess., Hearings on S. Res. 71, pt. 12, p. 4959.

[21] *Ibid.*, p. 5083.

On the whole, these criticisms helped rather than hindered the WPB, and the resulting "exposures" seemed to enhance rather than lessen the stature of the Chairman.

On July 4, 1942, Mr. Nelson showed to the President and secured his approval of the first systematic and comprehensive reorganization of WPB, developed in part to meet the criticism of his organization and in part to fit its developing work load. The organization inherited from the OPM had been continued, with the modifications already noted. With the major push of contracting well under way and with measures in motion to deal with other immediate problems, attention could be given to the further adaptation of the organization.

The new organization differed from the old in the following important particulars:

The number of executives reporting to the Chairman of WPB was reduced from eight to three, not counting the eight staff agencies.

New emphasis was given to connections with the military and with the international agencies in the materials and production fields.

Far greater emphasis was placed upon the industry and materials branches, with the expectation that each would be the primary center of control within WPB for programming, and priority administration, for the industry it represented, subject, of course, to the broad policy controls of the Requirements Committee and the Program Bureau.

All the industry branches and the materials branches were brought into a single family under the Director General for Operations, to whom the Priorities Bureau as well as the priorities power was assigned. This put an end to the independent materials division, tied the materials branches in with the industry branches, and with the administration of priorities.

All requirements and program functions, except those of the Planning Committee and of the Office of Civilian Supply, were brought together under the new post of Vice Chairman for Program Determination. This officer, working closely with the Chairman, was to review all production programs, bring them within feasible limits, cut the critical materials pie up among the claimants in accordance with approved programs, and give such determinations, allocations, and policy instructions to the Director General for Operations as he might need in managing the priorities and supervising the activities of the industry branches.

The Office of Deputy Chairman on Program Progress was provided for, designed to make a continuous critical and constructive study for the Chairman of all major production schedules in relation to programs, and of all activities of the War Production Board in relation to the policies of the Chairman. This part of the plan, however, was never put into effect, although certain of the functions were carried on in the Office of the Chairman and in the planning and statistics divisions.

At one time it had been planned to place the Planning Committee and the Office of Civilian Supply in the program set-up, and the Statistics Bureau in the program progress office. Mr. Nelson decided, however, after discussion with the heads of the three agencies that they should continue to report directly to him.

The position of labor in the WPB was considerably strengthened by the creation of a Labor Advisory Committee attached to the Labor Production Division, and the establishment of labor advisors from the Labor Production Division to serve in and work with each of the more important industry divisions.

The reorganization plan as thus prepared was based on the Chairman's own experience in the Office of Production Management and the War Production Board. The technical work was entrusted to the WPB Office of Organizational Planning. An advisory committee of business executives reviewed and approved the outlines of the plan. The Bureau of the Budget, though approving the plan, saw three weaknesses:

(1) the failure to combine both programming and operations under a single deputy to the Chairman, (2) the too great adjustment of the plan to fit individuals, and (3) the failure to make a larger place for labor.

The plan as a whole was, however, well received by the staff of WPB, and the country, and went into operation gradually.

Field Organization

A field organization with about 100 district offices grouped under 14 regional headquarters had been set up under OPM, and was continued and expanded under WPB. This field organization had 4,000 employees in August 1942 when its structure was redefined under the new organization of WPB. These employees were primarily engaged in explaining WPB regulations and forms to the businessmen of America, "processing" their papers, helping them to make out applications for materials, establish contacts with procurement representatives, break production bottlenecks, solve technical problems, and to secure contracts or subcontracts, or machinery or money and thus to get into war production. The field offices made surveys of open capacity in factories, took part in the conservation programs, looked for unused inventories, aided the scrap iron and aluminum drives,[22] set up the local Labor-Management Committees, aided in the prepara-

---

[22] The scrap rubber drive was initiated by the Petroleum Coordinator, working through the gasoline distributors.

tion of appeals, and issued local publicity to speed up production. They were also one of the channels between the producers and Washington, performing services for the manufacturers, and gathering information for Washington. Many contacts were direct, however, especially in the case of the big corporations who had their representatives in Washington. Until early in 1943, when field offices were authorized to make priority decision up to specified limits, virtually all decisions were made in Washington, and the field was, in fact, an advisory and service agency without power.

Within WPB in Washington, the field organization did have a single point of contact through an Office of Field Operations under the Vice Chairman for Operations. The field operation was a waif through 1942, however, having little or no part in top management counsels, and finding itself continually confronted with new decisions, programs, and regulations which were often first heard of in the field through the newspapers. Certain of the divisions of WPB in Washington, moreover, were inclined to send out their own experts into the field to handle their own contacts direct. This was perhaps natural under the circumstances, because the organization was new, the men did not know each other, and the central divisions wanted technical work done precisely as they directed without interference or "coordination" with overlapping programs. This frustration was greatly increased by the striking difference in organizational structure in Washington as compared with the field. Operations in Washington were set up largely on an industry and commodity basis, with some functional staff services or program units; the field was set up with operations on a functional basis of its own geared somewhat to the programs. As a result, in the early days, a Washington operations branch chief had no opposite number to look to in the field, and an engineer in the field had a dozen conflicting demands on his time from as many administrative units at Washington.

The fine accomplishment of the field organization in these days is more a tribute to the quality and spirit of the men engaged in the work than in the soundness of its structure or supervision.

Appeals and Enforcement

An important feature of the War Production Board as it developed was the establishment of the Appeals Division, under Arthur N. Holcombe, which reported to the program Vice Chairman, and had jurisdiction over all individual appeals from manifest hardship cases arising under the application of WPB orders by field representatives or branch chiefs in Washington. The Appeals Board took testimony, heard the arguments of aggrieved businessmen, labor leaders, their attorneys and Congressmen and local political officers, as well as the technicians of WPB, and rendered decisions which were, as a matter of policy, never overruled by Chairman Nelson, though they frequently amounted to individual amendments of administrative determinations or of general rules.

No doubt in part because of the existence of this impartial safety valve, and in part because of the eagerness of most industrialists to do what they were told was for the best interests of the country, the general problem of enforcement of WPB regulations was not too serious. A few test cases were successfully carried through the courts by the General Counsel, John Lord O'Brian, who was completely responsible for all legal work both in Washington and in the field, having stipulated from the first that no lawyers could be appointed in WPB except by him and in his department.

Under this system, enforcement was largely administrative and persuasive and appeals were handled by an impartial tribunal within WPB rather than through the courts.

Operating Policies of WPB

The War Production Board took over from the Office of Production Management or developed a number of operating policies of considerable importance. These related especially to the priority power, the limitation of its own scope, the use of other agencies, dollar-a-year men, industry committees, labor, and the civilian economy.

Though it is difficult to do justice to these policies in limited space, a brief comment on each is required.

From the very first, Mr. Nelson maintained that "the priority power is indivisible." He repeatedly fought to prevent any other agency of the Government from being given the right to determine who should have, and when they should have, any materials, machines, factories, or components. In this fight, he was in the main victorious though several agencies ultimately acquired the power of allotment within totals set by the WPB and thus subject to its control on major and over-all allocations.

Another important policy of the WPB was the limitation of its own scope. The orders defining the powers of WPB were extremely broad. They covered the entire economy. Nonetheless, it was the Chairman's policy not to exercise or develop those powers unless they controlled production to the needs of war. Illustrations of such self-limitation are found in WPB cooperation in developing both the War Food Administration and the War Manpower Commission despite the fact that these agencies cut directly into WPB operations. Similarly in the international field, WPB made no effort to occupy the primary position, though the power was there.

The War Production Board was also eager to make use of other agencies as far as possible. The Chairman left procurement to the former procurement agencies as has been explained above; and as part of this policy encouraged the transfer of WPB's ablest procurement men to the procurement offices where they were generally absorbed.

This WPB policy, of relinquishing control of its staff members to the procurement agencies, came under the scrutiny of the Truman Committee, which leaned strongly toward the view that all procurement was a business function and must be under the control of businessmen, not career military men. Mr. Nelson insisted that this had been achieved under his policy, and that the civilians whom he had sent from WPB and the business world to the Army and the Navy had done and were doing for the services exactly what the Congress was after. While the Truman Committee was never satisfied, Mr. Nelson stuck to his guns, and continued to leave the procurement function, the making of specifications and the contracts, entirely in the hands of the services, strengthened as they were by the addition of many men of outstanding experience from the business world and from WPB.

The War Production Board delegated the review of defense contracts to the Joint Army and Navy Munitions Board. On March 10, 1942, WPB delegated the whole system of military priorities to the ANMB, though this soon brought on an inflation and collapse of the system. WPB delegated the enforcement of consumer rationing to the Office of Price Administration, and assisted the War Manpower Commission to develop its controls over manpower, although manpower factors eventually became a major element in the strategy of industrial production.

The greatest resignation of power by WPB, however, was its readiness to let the grand outlines of the production program be determined by the services without their development of firm, comprehensive, or balanced programs related to military strategy or industrial feasibility. Mr. Nelson found that neither the Army nor the Navy had comprehensive plans, and he decided that to demand them would only slow up the war effort. The War Production Board knew little about the strategy considerations. Apparently this was also true of the procurement officers, who let landing craft fall disastrously behind at a crucial period, while they were pushing for other things which used up the steel. When Mr. Nelson found that the failure of the military to plan or to keep reasonably within the productive capacity of American industry was leading to a dangerous situation, he called for a show-down, for the limitation of facilities construction, for the cut-back of contract authorizations, and established in the Controlled Materials Plan a substitute for the priorities system, which tied together the allocation for critical materials and the "tickets" issued against the allocation. This is described in a later chapter. He also set up definite scheduling in the factories under WPB control for many of the critical items like airplanes, motors, valves, and even certain types of ships. But in working all this out, WPB left it entirely up to the services to make their own cut-backs and their own distribution of priorities within those reduced programs.

The problem of dollar-a-year men came up early in Mr. Nelson's administration. On January 28, 1942, 2 weeks after taking over the WPB, he told the Truman Committee, whose January 15 report demanding a single head for war production and criticizing dollar-a-year men was just out, that he could not possibly organize war production without the dollar-a-year men furnished to the Government by industry. He also stated that no man from an industry would be permitted to make a decision involving his own company, and that the head of no industry division or branch would come directly from that industry. While this policy did serve to protect the WPB from letting each industry run its own affairs to suit itself, and flout the public interest, it meant that many an industry branch was under the direction or nominal direction of a man who knew little or nothing about the industry or its important elements and personalities.

A somewhat similar problem arose in setting up industry advisory committees. These were established for every major industry, with over 750 before the end. In order to guard against antitrust suits and to protect the integrity of WPB, the OPM policy of regarding these committees as purely advisory was reaffirmed and strengthened. In addition, the members paid their own expenses, were given no confidential information or decisions, and were carefully selected to represent all sections, sizes, and levels of the business.[23] Paid employees of trade associations were excluded. Under these policies, private industrial and business associations were not used by WPB to assist in mobilizing war production. This same policy was followed throughout the Government with two exceptions: the Office of Defense Transportation which relied on the organized railroad industry to run the railroads; and the Petroleum Administration for War which relied on the organized petroleum industry to run the oil industry.

The labor policy of WPB was a mixture from the first. The Chairman clearly wanted to bring labor into the operation although he had difficulty in discovering a satisfactory method. Particularly difficult was the question of the responsibilities of these men. Should they serve as "representatives" of Labor, or should they perform functions for the Government in the manner in which business men were sup-

---

[23] The representatives of distant small businesses, however, generally were absent.

posed to operate? He set up a Labor Division, followed this by attaching labor advisors to the industry branches, and trying to put men suggested by organized labor in certain administrative posts. Working with labor, he set up the Labor-Management Committee program to increase labor-management cooperation throughout the country. Finally, under pressure from CIO, he set up two labor vice chairmen, one to deal with manpower (Clinton Golden), and one to deal with labor and production (Joseph Keenan). In spite of these moves by the Chairman, the rank and file of WPB manifested no desire to work with labor, and the labor representatives felt that they were "on the outside looking in." The Chairman's efforts were greatly impeded because labor leaders, like corporate general managers and presidents, wanted high posts and titles, and, unlike men from industry, were not able to free themselves full time and work continuously until they became part of a working team, although there were a few exceptions.

War Production Board policies on the civilian economy were consistent from first to last. The Chairman was convinced that the highest levels of industrial production come only from an economy that is well supplied with machinery, repair parts, power, and transport facilities, homes for workers, water, sewers, and utilities, and a generous standard of necessities. And within limits, he was determined to let each man determine those necessities for himself. Mr. Nelson was always far ahead of the industry branches of his organization in pushing for conversion of the metals industries to war production, although he never went as far as some of his economists. He was always in opposition to the Army on short-sighted restrictions of steel for the railroads, for agricultural machinery, and for industrial spare parts. To help him watch the course of events and to protect these and other aspects of the civilian economy, the Chairman maintained and listened to a separate organization, the Office of Civilian Supply, which operated under Leon Henderson and Joseph Wiener during the period under review. This organization was maintained intact in spite of its paltry direct accomplishments, its continual friction with the Requirements Committee, with the industry divisions, and with the Army—this being its chief accomplishment—and the questions of the Bureau of the Budget as to whether the agency was still necessary.

It was recognized, however, that the Office of Civilian Supply, although it had no program of civilian requirements in those days, was the foremost proponent of speedy conversion and all-out war production and the most effective critic within the WPB of special interests and special industries.

The end result of Mr. Nelson's program for civilian consumption may be summarized as follows: We stopped making most kinds of durable goods, like autos and washing machines and ordinary housing and made our old equipment do; we maintained or slightly increased the production of food, clothing, repair and maintenance items, although far less than the consumers would have gladly bought with their greatly increased earnings. As a result, those who wanted to buy new cars and houses could not get them, and those who formerly had plenty of choice foods, shoes, clothing, and service, found they had to share them with others who under full employment had the money to buy.

The Army and the Economy

As shown by the Industrial Mobilization Plan, it was the doctrine of the Army that the military should take direct control of all elements of the economy needed for war, once war was declared. Under "total" war, this would include total control of the Nation, its manpower, its facilities, its economy. Starting with this simple and "logical" concept, and being absolutely certain from 1939 on that war was coming, it was natural that the generals and colonels and majors, even those drawn from civilian life, were dissatisfied with the President's slow approach to war mobilization and with his reliance upon civilian personnel in all of the posts which were concerned with labor, industry, public opinion, and the economy. In spite of these decisions by the President, the Army never gave up the effort to increase its control in these areas.

In December 1941, when OPM and SPAB were approaching their end, the Secretary of War, the Secretary of the Navy, and the two military chiefs of staff sent the President a strong proposal calling for the creation of a new top priorities committee which would eliminate most of the civilians, especially those who were sending materials to our allies abroad and to neutral nations, and would substitute complete control by the military. When this suggestion fell by the wayside with the creation of WPB after the declaration of war, General Somervell found time to prepare an elaborate plan for the organization of WPB which would have placed complete control of WPB and of the economy under the Joint Chiefs of Staff. This was sent to Mr. Nelson on May 15, 1942. In rejecting the central idea, Mr. Nelson wrote a long and closely reasoned letter which said "The battle for production is the primary responsibility of the Chairman of the War Production Board in much the same sense that the military battles are the primary responsibility of the military chiefs."

When the effort to take over the WPB failed, the Army decided not to disband the Joint Army and Navy Munitions Board, which had always been considered as an interim organization, slated for absorption by an over-all agency like WPB, but to keep the agency to champion the requirements of the services against the civilians. The Army also suggested that Mr. Nelson take over aggressive and efficient Mr. Ferdinand Eberstadt who was the chairman of the ANMB as his deputy in charge of WPB operations. When Mr. Nelson did not take General Somervell's advice on the July 4 reorganization of WPB, however, Mr. Eberstadt declined the appointment because the Requirements Committee and the program functions were not designed to be under him, but were independent of and above the post of Director General of Operations which was offered him.

The inability of the Army and the Navy to make any comprehensive, consistent, balanced, or reasonably stable plans, coupled with the tremendous advance contracting in the spring and summer of 1942, and the unrestrained use of the priority powers delegated by WPB to the ANMB, intensified the Army's and Navy's difficulties with civilian control, and civilian difficulties with the Army and the Navy. The Army seems to have made many complaints on production delays to the President, a few of which were relayed to WPB in one form or another. On several occasions, the Army secured letters from the President so directing WPB as to limit its controls and to expand the powers of the ANMB. An illustration is a letter of May 1, 1942, under which the Army sought not only to assume control over a new system of high military priorities through the ANMB but also the right to review and reject any granting of similar top priorities to other than military items.

Though this right of review was rejected by WPB, the matter was in dispute for many months, and the ANMB so handled its new high-ranking priority system, established in June in accordance with the President's letter, that the production of many essential but non-military items, like locomotives and freight cars, and even some maritime items was seriously upset for a time.

The relation of military operations to war production was not understood in 1942. Memoranda were written severally by advisors of the Secretary of War, of the Director of the Bureau of the Budget, and of the Chairman of the War Production Board all insisting that production schedules must rest on military strategy, and that any other method of approach was indefensible and wasteful. The military concluded from this approach that the economy must be controlled by the military, because strategy could not be confided to civilians, and many a priority argument was closed by junior officers with hints of strategy considerations which could not be disclosed. The civilian advisors, however, argued that the civilian tops of the WPB must not only be informed on strategy, but that they must participate in its final formulation, because strategy must rest in part on production possibilities. The futility of the argument at the time was not disclosed until General Marshall, in his epochal report of June 30, 1945, indicated that the major strategy of the war was still under discussion until the middle of August 1942, when the invasion of Africa was determined upon. In fact, it was not until May 1943 that the plan of invading Northern Europe "was translated into firm commitments".[24] In other words, the whole production build-up of 1941 and 1942 was not, and could not be, based on strategy, because strategy was inevitably being constrained by our enemies and by the plight of our Allies. We were manufacturing munitions "for the shelf," for equipping armies and squadrons, and not for specific operations the strength and date of which could be forecast even by the chiefs of staff.

Allied Cooperation

An important war production development of 1942 was the establishment of a series of cooperative international agencies designed to bring about a quicker and more economical use of the combined resources of the major Allies. These agencies were:

The *Munitions Assignments Board*, which had the power to determine to what nations munitions should be dispatched as they came from the factory.

The *Combined Shipping Adjustment Board* with units in Washington and London, which served as bases for the exchange of information on shipping allocations within the United States and United Kingdom shipping pools.

The *Combined Raw Materials Board*, which conferred on the raw material resources and needs of the world under the control of the Allies, and developed a working arrangement for their international apportionment.

The *Combined Food Board*, which conferred on the food resources and needs of the world and developed a working arrangement for their international apportionment.

The *Combined Production and Resources Board*, which conferred on the war production needs, resources, and problems of the Allies and developed working arrangements for the better use of certain resources and facilities.

These five boards working in the field of munitions, shipping, resources, and war production were balanced in the military field by the combined Chiefs of Staff, the creation of which was announced by Mr. Churchill on January 27, 1942. The first three boards above

---

[24] U. S. General Staff. *General Marshall's Report: The Winning of the War in Europe and the Pacific.* Washington, D. C., G. P. O., 1945, p. 10.

were announced the previous day in Washington, while the two latter boards were established on June 9, when Mr. Lyttleton, the British Minister of Production, was in Washington.

The structure of these boards is of interest in international affairs. Except for the Munitions Assignments Board, the board members in each case were made up of the responsible United States and United Kingdom administrators in a given field and there was a single staff for each board made up of alternate United States and United Kingdom experts. In theory at any rate, when a combined board sat, deliberated, and reached a decision, which by nature had to be unanimous, each member of the board could move back to his own office and carry out his end of the agreement reached.

Soon after the creation of the boards, Canada was brought into the Food and Raw Materials Boards. The U. S. S. R. never joined, but secured its goods under "protocols," which were signed from time to time.

The experience with these boards frequently demonstrated to the American members the admirable nature of the staff work and the excellent coordination of the policy lines available to the British members. The British members and staffs were seldom, if ever, uninformed on recent top-side decisions, and never in pursuit of contradictory major policies. The British, moreover, appeared to be acquainted with major military strategy and programs of which our members, including the military, were often innocent.

*   *   *   *   *

The United States production build-up which commenced with the attack on Pearl Harbor and extended through the summer of 1942 was one of the great accomplishments of the war, and one of the major elements in making possible the offensives which brought the final victory.

Up until Pearl Harbor, the monthly rate of increase in war production and construction had been not over $100 million a month. For December this was raised to $440 million, and from that point on each month showed a gain over the prior month of something like $400 million for a period of 9 months, when the rate was markedly reduced for a time. For the period under review, war production per month arose from less than $1.5 billion to almost $5 billion, and the percentage of the economy engaged in war production rose from 15 percent to about 33 percent, a stupendous shift-over of the American economy within a period of less than a year.

This result was accomplished by national unity and determination, high production goals, unlimited authorizations by Congress, and the gradual evolution of the War Production Board, with its controls of materials, components, and other aspects of industry.

During this period, the new facilities for production and military purposes were in the main completed, although the control of facilities was inadequate, and considerable waste was incurred.

The major part of war production came, however, from the conversion of nonwar industries to war production. Although the changeover was delayed by "business as usual" pressures, conversion was completed about as fast as the procurement officers could get orders in shape.

When war production began to absorb some 20 percent of the total economy, simple priorities proved no longer adequate as a protection of military requirements. From this point on, the various war programs came into sharper competition with each other, and controls had to be devised over facilities, machine tools, steel, aluminum, copper, other materials, and components. Even with these controls bottlenecks could not be avoided, and efforts were initiated to estab lish integrated production control.

In the creation of the War Production Board, all power over procurement, except for food, and over production and industry were placed in the hands of a single administrator responsible to the President alone. Procurement—the making of the contracts for production—was delegated to the armed services, the Maritime Commission, and other procuring agencies, however; and the WPB endeavored to control the size of the procurement program and through a series of controls over the use of materials to manage the economy. During this period, no controls over manpower were used.

The structure of WPB followed this philosophy, and placed its emphasis on planning, the balancing of requirements for materials, and upon the operations of its industry and materials branches.

While certain policies were under continual fire by the Army, and various sins of omission were brought to light, especially by the Truman Committee, on the whole the War Production Board held the respect of industry and the confidence of the American people, as the nation pushed forward successfully to meet the ambitious production goals set by the President.

CHAPTER

6

Transporting the Goods

REGARDING the transportation problems of a many-front war, President Roosevelt said in his radio address of February 23, 1942:

The broad oceans which have been heralded in the past as our protection from attack have become endless battlefields on which we are constantly being challenged by our enemies.

We must all understand and face the hard fact that our job now is to fight at distances which extend all the way around the globe.

We fight at these vast distances because that is where our enemies are. Until our flow of supplies gives us clear superiority we must keep on striking our enemies wherever and whenever we can meet them, even if, for a while, we have to yield ground . . .

We must fight at these vast distances to protect our supply lines and our lines of communication with our Allies—protect these lines from the enemies who are bending every ounce of their strength, striving against time, to cut them.

Our entrance into the war intensified the race between the United Nations' merchant shipbuilding program and the Axis submarines, surface raiders, and long-range bombers; it magnified the problems involved in allocating shipping space; and it brought many new domestic transportation problems. Our transportation resources had to be mobilized for all-out war. Close coordination had to be established between shipping needs, ship construction, ship utilization, and movement of men and materials to war factories, training camps, and ports. The defense period had failed to produce these coordinating mechanisms.

Shipbuilding

Allied sinkings were particularly heavy in Atlantic waters. Because of a deficiency of escort vessels, the United States Navy was not

135

prepared to perform an adequte job of convoying. For some months
the fate of the war hung in the balance. The total Allied ship tonnage
sunk was larger than that built. At the time of Pearl Harbor, the
United Nations had 45,000,000 deadweight tons of shipping of which
12,000,000 tons were under United States control. During 1941 the
Axis powers sank 3,100,000 tons of United Nations' shipping and in
1942 three times as much. Further losses would imperil Allied life
lines. The American Navy had to increase the number of antisubmarine vessels and put into operation new techniques for reducing
sinkings, and the Maritime Commission had to stimulate the shipbuilding industry to perform miracles of ship construction.

The war needs of the United Nations for merchant shipping were
beyond anything the world had previously known. Military supply
to combat theaters around the world required water transportation
over vast distances for men and material. In addition, there were
the needs of our Allies for food, materials, and munitions. As Admiral
Land, Chairman of the United States Maritime Commission, put it:
"There is no limit to the need for ships in a total, global war." [1]

Under arrangements made by President Roosevelt with Prime
Minister Churchill shortly after Pearl Harbor, the task of building
merchant vessels fell largely to the United States, while the British
yards constructed British naval vessels.[2]

Since mass construction of oceangoing ships requires many months
of careful preparation, the United States benefited from the foresight
in having started before Pearl Harbor both long-range and emergency
ship-construction programs. No other type of defense construction
takes so long to get under way. The year following the passage of
the Merchant Marine Act of 1936, the United States Maritime Commission inaugurated a long-range shipbuilding program calling for
construction of 50 high-speed standard merchant ships a year for
10 years. These ships were to have up-to-date turbines and gears
and to be equipped with the most modern loading devices. Their
construction was subsidized and fixed-sum contracts were used in
letting the bids. Following the fall of France in July 1940, this
program was stepped up to 200 ships a year. Events moved swiftly
and these plans soon proved inadequate for the assumed needs of
national defense. Great Britain was in danger of falling if aid were
not forthcoming. The standard ships took too long to construct
and their main propulsive engines were of the type needed also by
the Navy.

The National Defense Advisory Commission recognized the need
for an emergency shipbuilding program and on July 2, 1940, persuaded

[1] U. S. Congress, House. Committee on Appropriations. *Independent Offices Appropriation Bill for 1944.* Hearings, . . . 78th Cong., 1st sess., p. 681.
[2] Ibid., p. 699.

Rear Admiral Land, Chairman of the Maritime Commission, to assume, in addition to his regular duties, the directorship of a newly created Shipbuilding Section of its Production Division. Admiral Land and William S. Knudsen of the Advisory Commission recommended to the President the mass production of a simple-design emergency steel cargo vessel called the Liberty ship and unofficially named the "Ugly Duckling." The plans for this ship were adapted from a British tramp-steamer type and called for the older triple-expansion reciprocating engine, steam-driven winches, and other auxiliary equipment no longer used on standard ships or naval vessels. Its speed was slow, 11 knots, and its cargo capacity about 10,000 dead-weight tons. Elimination of refinements found on standard vessels made it possible to use prefabrication and subassembly methods. After some experimentation, full use was also made of welding instead of riveting. To build a welded ship would require less steel, fewer trained shipyard workers, and less time.

On December 28, 1940, the President allocated $500,000 in cash and $36,000,000 in contract authorization from his emergency fund to

CHART 15. *U. S. Merchant Ship Construction and Sinkings.*

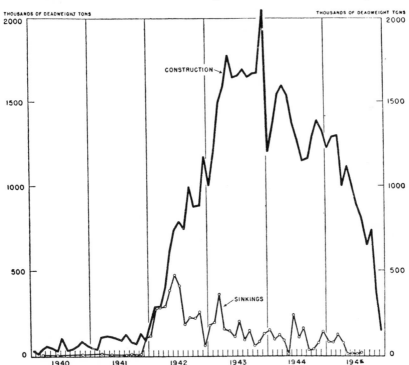

Source: United States Maritime Commission.

enable the Maritime Commission to start work on the new program. Congressional approval for construction of 200 Liberty ships followed in an act passed on February 6, 1941, which included authority to negotiate construction contracts without competitive bidding and to adjust outstanding construction contracts.[3] The authority to negotiate contracts meant that the Commission could use a cost-plus-a-fee contract in place of a fixed-sum contract. At the hearing on this legislation, several Congressmen raised objections to the cost-plus system which had led to abuses in World War I. Admiral Land explained that in view of rising and uncertain costs for labor and materials, it was not possible to get shipbuilding companies to make fixed-sum bids for emergency ship construction. He contended that the negotiated contract was the only type of procedure that could be utilized to procure emergency ships quickly under existing conditions of pressing need and congestion of facilities.

In order to transport the increasing volume of strategic materials and lend-lease aid, later appropriation acts passed in March, August, October, and December increased the program to 1,200 vessels of approximately 13,000,000 dead-weight tons.

To carry out its emergency ship construction program, the Maritime Commission had to create almost a complete new shipbuilding industry because existing yards had prior commitments either to the Commission itself or to the Navy. Admiral Land recommended that the number of new shipyards be kept to a minimum so as to reduce the requirements for overhead management. In line with this recommendation, the Advisory Commission proposed to the President on December 27, 1940, the expansion of shipbuilding facilities in four localities. Within four months, the number of new shipyards proposed for the emergency program was increased from four to nine. They were financed by the Maritime Commission. By October 15, contracts had been let in 19 different yards for 131 new shipways, of which 107 were for the emergency program and 24 for the long-range program.

While at first the Maritime Commission left procurement of materials for constructing shipyards and ships to a single private company, it found itself drawn into procurement through the need to furnish expediting assistance. Enlarged shipbuilding programs of both the Navy and the Maritime Commission encountered shortages of machine tools, steel, propulsion machinery, and valves. The reluctance of the steel industry to expand, the slowness of the Office of Production Management in pushing this expansion, failure of the armed services and the Maritime Commission to anticipate clearly

---

[3] *55 Stat.* 5–6.

their needs for steel and components, and the rivalry between programs contributed to these shortages.

The Maritime Commission had to face keen competition from the armed services in procuring materials for shipbuilding. It was not until the spring of 1941 that the Commission was given representation on the Priorities Committee of the Army and Navy Munitions Board. Shortly after this, the Director of Priorities of the Office of Production Management gave merchant shipbuilding priority parity with the Army and Navy. In spite of this parity, the Commission was at a disadvantage as compared with the Navy which had started its program earlier and which enjoyed greater prestige among manufacturers. The Commission did not obtain mandatory priorities until August 1941.

From July 1, 1940, to December 31, 1941, some 136 merchant ships aggregating 1,551,000 deadweight tons were delivered. While this was an impressive achievement, it was less than had been scheduled and was far short of war needs. The War Production Board Planning Committee reported in June 1942 that failure of ship completions to meet schedules was due to inadequate steel deliveries, slow development of production in new yards, failure of older yards to accept new standards of speed, inadequate production of propulsion machinery, and conversion of merchant ships to naval categories. It recommended coordination of production planning, procurement, and allocations of all agencies securing ships materials; placing of Government representatives in plants of major suppliers to deal with distribution of steel plates, and a larger staff for the Maritime Commission.[4]

Of the ambitious Liberty ship program, only seven ships were completed during 1941 and five of these were for the British. But the necessary groundwork had been laid for vast increases in shipbuilding which was to reach its peak in a year and a half.

After Pearl Harbor, the shipbuilding program was progressively advanced to meet growing needs arising out of greater demands for aid and increasing sinkings by German submarines. In his address to Congress of January 6, 1942, the President said that he had ordered immediate steps to be taken "to increase our production rate of merchant ships so rapidly that in this year, 1942, we shall build 8,000,000 deadweight tons as compared with a 1941 production of 1,100,000. We shall continue that increase so that next year, 1943, we shall build 10,000,000 tons." A month later, another 6,000,000 deadweight tons were added to the program and by June 30, 1942, a further directive had been given the Maritime Commission to add

---

[4] WPB, *Digest of Minutes*, June 30, 1942, p. 42. In January Admiral Land reported to Mr. Knudsen that delays were caused by (1) lack of steel, (2) strikes, (3) late delivery of cranes in new shipyards, (4) failure of valve manufacturers to produce valves and fittings, (5) late delivery of turbines and gears for stan d ard ships, and (6) failures in main ship machinery delivery.

another 3,000,000 deadweight tons. These additions brought the total program for the calendar year 1943 to 19,000,000 deadweight tons.

The achievement of this unprecedented merchant shipbuilding program was to involve the solution of difficult management, manpower, and materials problems.

The appropriations acts granting contract authority to the Maritime Commission were only the first step. It was up to the Commission to work out the terms of the shipbuilding contracts and find reliable companies to accept them. The contracts for the Liberty ships were of the cost-plus-base-fee type under which the contractor received a base fee subject, within maximum and minimum limits, to a bonus or penalty for delivery ahead of or behind contract delivery date, and with bonus or penalty for man-hour record below or above an agreed standard. Such contracts were made possible by emergency legislation which gave the Commission authority to negotiate construction contracts without competitive bidding. The Commission insisted that the cost-plus-base-fee contract which placed a high premium on speed and volume of construction was necessary to fulfill its obligations.

Analyses of comparative performance by individual yards awarded contracts showed marked variations in efficiency. The best yards building Liberty vessels showed a production record for all deliveries during their operating history, of from two to three times that of the poorest yards.[5] Further detailed analysis of yard showings on Liberty ships in production time, man-hours, and cost per ship, for equivalent construction experience, indicated similar wide variations. In general, good management meant good performance records. Low performance records and management shortcomings were in part the result of cost-plus-base-fee contract terms which permitted the yard operator an assured net return regardless of total production cost, which was borne by the Federal Government. Profits were earned almost entirely for management, with relatively small contractor investment, and, in addition, allowed costs included very high executive salaries in many yards. In a few cases the Truman Committee discovered what it thought was "rapacity, greed, fraud, and negligence" and it referred these findings to the Department of Justice for appropriate action.[6] In addition, the Truman Committee recommended renegotiation of fee contracts with several companies which had poor production records.

In shipbuilding such manpower problems as recruitment, training,

[5] As measured by average lightweight tons per way-month, that is, the actual weight of the ship without cargo, fuel, or stores.
[6] Senate Report No. 10, pt. 16, 78th Cong., 2d sess., p. 271.

CHART 16. *Ship Deliveries under U. S. Maritime Commission Program.*

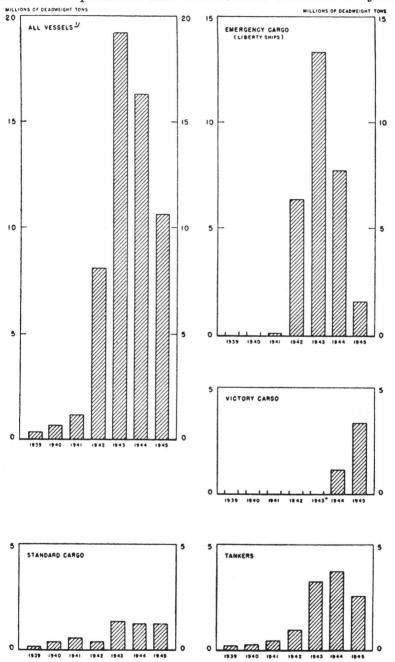

¹ Includes also combination (cargo and passenger), military type, and minor vessels not shown separately.
Includes vessels for private and foreign accounts.
Source: U. S. Maritime Commission.

wage stabilization, and turn-over were similar to those in other fields of war production which are discussed elsewhere.

Of peculiar importance in shipbuilding was the training function. Before the defense period more than one-half of the shipyard workers were skilled and the length of apprenticeship was from 3 to 4 years. More than 90 percent of the workers recruited in 1942 had to be trained for the jobs they were to perform.

During 1942 the merchant shipbuilding program was delayed at times by shortages of steel and of such components as gears, turbines, engines, and valves. After December 17, 1941, the Army and Navy Munitions Board no longer granted merchant vessels an equal priority with naval construction. Since the total supply of steel at the time was below the total requirements, the Maritime Commission as a claimant for the shipyards was in an unfavorable position. Appeals were made by the Commission to the Army and Navy Munitions Board for equal status, but no change was made despite the judgment of Admiral King that there was little use in producing all the materials of war unless we could transport them abroad. The launching and completion of merchant ships were repeatedly delayed by inadequate and tardy deliveries of steel plates and propulsion machinery.[7] The contract with the Higgins Company for the construction of Liberty ships was canceled because of a lack of steel.

The weak priority position of the Maritime Commission was partly the result of inadequate representation on the Army and Navy Munitions Board. Representatives of the Commission were outvoted by representatives of the Army and Navy. Within the War Production Board, the Planning Committee protested against the inferior priorities of the Maritime Commission and urged the Shipbuilding Division to adopt more energetic measures in aiding the Commission. The unequal priority treatment meant that aircraft escort carriers being constructed by the Maritime Commission carried a lower priority than similar Navy construction and that the Navy could set back the delivery of needed components for merchant ships by placing orders in plants booked solidly with Maritime orders. So serious did the situation become in the summer of 1942 when Congress authorized naval construction in excess of the President's program, that the President looked into the matter personally and directed Donald Nelson, Secretary Knox, and Admiral Land to confer and "settle the matter." At the conference, it was decided to prosecute both the Maritime Commission and Navy programs as scheduled. The deficit in steel plate would be borne by other programs which would be reviewed by the Joint Chiefs of Staff.

During the first 9 months after Pearl Harbor, the deliveries of new

[7] WPB, *Minutes*, Feb. 17, 1942, and Feb. 23, 1942.

ships were behind schedule and they failed to offset Allied losses. The United Nations Merchant fleet fell to a low point of 43,000,000 tons in August. Lack of shipping was a major limiting factor in the prosecution of the war.

Shipbuilding problems, however, were being solved. The curve of ship deliveries was rising rapidly. In September a turning point was reached. During the calendar year 1942 the President's goal of 8,000,000 tons, set in January, was met (chart 16). American shipyards shattered all established shipbuilding records. Whereas in 1941, the average time taken to deliver a Liberty ship had been 355 days, by the end of 1942 the average was reduced to 56 days and the Oregon Shipbuilding Corporation, one of the Henry J. Kaiser companies, had completed a ship in the record time of 14 days.

Allocating Shipping Space

As the United Nations' supply of vessel tonnage diminished and the demand for cargo space rose, efficient use of available shipping facilities became a matter of major importance. Within a month after Pearl Harbor, shipping demands outweighed the available supply by better than 2 to 1. The issues involved in the use of ships were of a top policy character; i. e., the fulfillment of the Russian protocol, the support of the British campaign, the reinforcement of the Philippine area and Australia, and the movement of troops to various bases, as well as to England. Normal commercial practices were entirely inadequate to meet these demands. It would have been the height of folly for Government agencies to bid against each other for shipping space and thus skyrocket shipping costs. Furthermore, the shipping companies could not afford to take war risks and they might refuse to handle the most urgent cargoes. Proper allocation of shipping tonnage required Government coordination by a system of priority ratings for cargoes. The Government had to determine the cargoes to be moved both in the import and export trades, to coordinate the two, to determine the ports to be used, and to route the traffic.

Import and export control, shipping control, cargo control, and port control were the chief tools available to insure the best use of shipping to bring strategic materials to this country and to carry munitions and supplies to our Allies where they were needed most. Cargo control meant determining the type of commodity which would move in the available shipping space and the order of priority in which such commodities would move. Shipping control or operations control called for the scheduling, routing, and loading of merchant vessels so as to guarantee their maximum utilization. Port control called for the close coordination between shipping, storage, and domestic transportation facilities. The right cargoes had to be available for outgoing vessels, and proper arrangements had to be made to handle incoming cargoes. Steps had to be taken to avoid port congestion. At the same time, there had to be enough surplus goods in storage at the ports so that the ships could be promptly and correctly loaded.

Cargo, operations, and port control had to be closely related, but at the time of Pearl Harbor these controls were scattered among a number of old-line and emergency agencies. Definite answers had not been given to a number of administrative questions. Should transportation and war production be controlled by the same agency? What should be the relationship between shipping priorities and materials priorities administration? Should the armed forces have their own ships? Should the armed forces have the final word as to the use of shipping? Should ocean shipping and domestic transportation be controlled by the same agency? What should be the relationship between the American shipping pool and the Allied shipping pool? Within 3 months answers were given to most of these questions. The answers had their roots in events which preceded the actual outbreak of war.

When the emergency shipbuilding program was started, a number of leading Government officials discussed ship-operation problems with the President. On January 15, 1941, Secretary Hull urged the President to make some provision for establishing priorities on shipping in order to expedite acquisition of critical materials. Shortly after this, Admiral Land, supported by Secretary Jones and others, recommended to the President that the Chairman of the Maritime Commission be named by Executive order as Director of Ocean Shipping with instructions to utilize the Maritime Commission and its staff in dealing with all problems of ocean transportation. At the same time, Admiral Land pointed out that there were "no existing statutory provisions adequate to devise and implement control of shipping facilities in foreign commerce; i. e., priorities of space and shipments, routes, discharging facilities, and storage tonnage," and he indicated a willingness to submit a draft of such legislation.

The Attorney General and the Bureau of the Budget investigated the proposal to establish a Division of Ocean Shipping Management in the Office of Production Management and reported to the President that it was not "legally or administratively feasible." It was pointed out that under existing laws the powers vested in the Maritime Commission could not be transferred by Executive order, that there was no statutory authority in existence for directing the movement of ships, except as the Commission operated its own ships or exercised certain indirect controls, that control over ship movements should not be vested in OPM while that office was concerned with the import of defense materials, that there were other important elements in shipping policy, that the proposed Executive order illustrated the immediate need for a Division of Defense Economics which would consider shipping policy as one device for controlling trade, and that an administrative order might designate the Chairman of the Maritime Commission as an aide of the President on shipping matters.

Instead of an Executive order, the President, on February 10, 1941, requested Admiral Land, with the assistance of other Government departments involved, to take proper steps to secure the maximum utilization of our merchant tonnage. He said: "I particularly request you to give all assistance and cooperation to the Office of Production Management in expediting the shipping of materials which are essential to our production program."[8] The President thus specifically mentioned that the Maritime Commission should cooperate with OPM in working out shipping priorities.

To carry out the President's directive, the Maritime Commission established a Division of Emergency Shipping on February 28, 1941. This Division was charged with supervising all emergency shipping problems and maintaining liaison with the War, Navy, and State Departments, the Office of Production Management, the Rubber and Metals Reserve Corporations of the Reconstruction Finance Corporation, and other governmental departments and agencies with respect to emergency activities of ship transportation. It also supervised negotiation of sales, charters, transfers, reallocations, reassignment, and acquisition of vessel tonnage. A small staff was recruited from the shipping industry. In the beginning the Division had no field staff and conducted business on an informal basis with no systematic record keeping and no analysis of performance. It asked the various shipping companies to cooperate in the defense effort on a voluntary basis. Some companies refused to substitute defense cargoes for more profitable nondefense cargoes.

In handling export cargoes, the Maritime Commission was guided by demands of the Army, Navy, lend-lease authorities, Coordinator of Inter-American Affairs, British Purchasing Commission, and private shippers. Especially important were the lend-lease requests following the President's directive in April that at least 2 million tons of shipping be obtained to aid the British. Much of this shipping was secured on the basis of informal negotiations with interested shipping companies and was put into service on the Red Sea route to aid the British in their Mediterranean campaign. The British signed the contracts but payments came out of lend-lease funds. Subsequent

---

[8] National Defense Advisory Commission, *Defense*, Feb. 18, 1941, vol. 2, p. 9.

investigations showed that the companies found the contracts highly profitable. One operator, for instance, obtained a net return for a voyage which was nearly six times the return for operation of the same vessel in the intercoastal trade in 1940 for a similar period of time.[9]

On the import side, the President directed the Maritime Commission to cooperate with the Office of Production Management on cargo priorities. OPM was concerned with shipping, since it allocated critical materials upon their delivery into this country. Beginning in April, it sent to the Commission brief lists of priorities for materials which it was trying to stock pile. In June it established a Shipping Liaison Section to present systematic priorities to the Commission for essential imports. At the request of the Commission, the priority lists were cleared with other agencies by the Shipping Priorities Advisory Committee, which included representatives of the Commission, the State Department, the Federal Loan Agency, the Office of Price Administration and Civilian Supply, the Department of Agriculture, the Office of the Coordinator of Inter-American Affairs, and OPM. W. Y. Elliott, the Chief of the Shipping Liaison Section and the Secretary of the Committee, became the driving force behind the import priorities work.

As the Shipping Priorities Advisory Committee broadened its experience, it saw the need for coordinating its activities with the stockpiling work of the Reconstruction Finance Corporation. A second informal committee, called the Cargo Clearance Committee, was created to deal with stock-piling problems. This committee, also known as the Clayton Committee, from its chairman, William Clayton, included representatives of the Maritime Commission, the Reconstruction Finance Corporation, the Department of State, and from time to time other agencies.

The relative responsibilities of the Office of Production Management and the Maritime Commission for import priorities were the subject of prolonged negotiations. OPM contended that priority powers were indivisible, but Congress in the Ship Warrants Act, approved July 14, 1941, gave the Commission authority to provide for priorities in transportation by merchant vessels in the interests of national defense. The law was similar to a British law which had been found effective in controlling neutral shipping. Warrants issued

---

[9] The Red Sea charters were made between the shipping companies and the British Ministry of War Transport in April 1941, on the basis of rates approved by the Maritime Commission. As later events showed, the risks were not as great as anticipated. The Commission requested the companies to agree to a voluntary do nward revision of rates. U. S. Congress. House. Committee on Merchant Marine and Fisheries. *Red Sea Space Charter Rates*. Hearings . . . 78th Cong., 1st sess., on H. Res. 52, p. 243. The Commission was criticized for not requisitioning the ships in 1941 after it was given the powers of requisition. U. S. Congress. House. Committee on Appropriations. *Independent Offices Appropriation Bill for 1944*. Hearings . . . 78th Cong., 2d sess., pp. 754-757.

by the Commission entitled ships to priorities in the use of facilities of loading, discharging or storage of cargoes, fueling, drydocking, and repairing in American ports. To secure a warrant, the ship company had to agree to the Commission's conditions regarding voyages, cargoes and rates.[10] OPM was not mentioned in the law but the President in a letter of August 26 asked Admiral Land to use OPM as a channel for schedules of shipping priorities. The Executive order establishing the Supply Priorities and Allocations Board, issued 2 days later, further strengthened the position of OPM in dealing with the Commission regarding shipping priorities.[11]

Differences arose between the Maritime Commission and the Office of Production Management regarding the administration of the legislation and Presidential directives on shipping priorities. Mr. Elliott and his group in OPM kept pressing the Commission for greater performance in picking up foreign cargoes on the import priorities list. The Commission took the position that the Priorities Advisory Committee could advise but not direct the Commission regarding what should be imported. The Committee, which was guided by Mr. Elliott, found it difficult to obtain the information it needed to operate. It found unsatisfactory the figures collected by the Commission and other agencies regarding goods available abroad and actual imports. It also took exception to the Commission's reluctance to interfere with the shipment of profitable nonessential cargoes. It urged the Commission to use its powers to increase the importation of low-rate high-priority cargoes.

The declaration of war found the United States unprepared to meet the greatly increased demands placed upon its ocean shipping. The War and Navy Departments began to press their claims for shipping as against those of the Lend-Lease Administration. With plans being discussed for expeditionary forces to Africa, Britain, and Australia, it was evident that military developments would put a tremendous strain on shipping facilities which were already inadequate for our rearmament needs and for delivery of lend-lease aid.

The situation was rendered more difficult by uncertainties about who was to be responsible for shipping and how such responsibilities were to be administered. In addition to the questions regarding the role of the Office of Production Management, the Maritime Commission, and the Economic Defense Board in cargo control, there was the question regarding the divided direction of shipping. Both the Army and the Navy had expanded their own merchant fleet operations by purchase and by charter.

The bulk of the American foreign fleet still operated under private

---

[10] 55 *Stat.* 591.
[11] **Executive** Order No. 8875, Aug. 28, 1941, 6 *Federal Register* 4181.

control, subject only to mild restraints exercised by the Division of Emergency Shipping of the Maritime Commission. Scarcely any use had been made as yet of the powers under the Ship Warrants Act and the requisitioning sections of the Merchant Marine Act. During the defense period many American vessels had been sold or transferred to foreign registry in order to get around provisions of the Neutrality Act. Repeal of the restrictive provisions on shipping in this act in November, and the declaration of war in December brought the entire American Merchant Marine into United Nations war service without the necessity of change of registry.

At the outbreak of war, imperfect coordination existed between the American and British shipping authorities. Informal working relationships had been established between the two countries but there was no machinery for settlement of disagreements. While there was a mutual exchange of information as to records and cargoes, each country maintained responsibility for the operation of its own facilities.

Proposals to establish an agency to handle both import and export problems were rejected because of interagency disagreements. On December 17, 1941, the President asked William L. Batt, Director of the Materials Division of OPM, to organize an interdepartmental conference on raw materials. Mr. Batt assumed that his control of raw materials necessarily involved responsibility for control of shipping. Henry Wallace and Milo Perkins of the Board of Economic Warfare were not willing to accept this assumption. On the other hand, the agencies dealing with stockpiling and shipping problems were opposed to granting the Board of Economic Warfare exclusive control over cargo. Another important development was the foreseeable demand by the Army and Navy for increased diversion of shipping. The execution of the plans for sending and convoying expeditionary forces to Africa, Great Britain, and Australia would place a tremendous strain on shipping facilities.

Recognizing the need for action, President Roosevelt established on December 8, 1941, the Strategic Shipping Board by the following letter:

This Board will be composed of the Chairman of the Maritime Commission, the Chief of Staff, the Chief of Naval Operations, and Mr. Harry Hopkins. It should establish policies for and plan the allocation of merchant shipping to meet military and civilian requirements, and coordinate these activities of the War and Navy Departments and the Maritime Commission. Operations should remain in the hands of existing organizations.

The Board should consult with representatives of the OLLA and other agencies of the Government responsible for processing or planning the procurement, production, import and export of defense articles and materials. Representatives of the governments receiving assistance under the Lend-Lease Act should likewise be consulted.

The Strategic Shipping Board soon encountered difficulties which made it clear that a more systematic organization was necessary. Secretaries Stimson and Knox in a joint letter to the President on January 13, 1942, pointed out some limitations of the Board. In the first place, the power of decision lay with the Board rather than a single person. Since no Executive organization could be established under the directive of the Board, the members of the Board delegated action to subordinates who were members of existing organizations having conflicting interests. Actual control of private shipping was not vested in the Board and control of shipping in the hands of the armed services remained in those organizations. Control in the field was divided and existing private shipping agencies were uncoordinated. For these reasons, Secretaries Stimson and Knox urged the President to establish a Central Shipping Administration with Admiral Land as Administrator.

With their letter, the Secretaries submitted a draft of an Executive order which provided for control by a new agency of all oceangoing vessels of the United States with certain exceptions, for the transfer of functions concerned with maritime affairs from other Government departments to the new agency under the provisions of the War Powers Act, and for allocation of vessels in compliance with the joint decisions of the Secretary of War and the Secretary of the Navy. Admiral Land objected to the provision in the proposed order placing him under the control of the military authorities, since it allowed him no discretion in carrying out Presidential and other high nonmilitary directives for allocating ships. Harry Hopkins opposed the same clause since he thought it would not result in sufficient consideration to lend-lease. The Maritime Commission prepared a draft of an order to meet this and other objections.

President Roosevelt submitted both drafts of the proposed order to the Director of the Bureau of the Budget for further consideration. After long and difficult negotiations, the Bureau of the Budget worked out a new draft which embodied the essential features of the Maritime Commission proposal. This draft failed to receive the approval of the War Department. In a memorandum of February 5, 1942, to the President the Director of the Bureau of the Budget said:

The attached Executive order establishes a War Shipping Administration in the Office for Emergency Management. This order has been prepared in the Bureau of the Budget and represents a reworking of drafts which were submitted: (*a*) Jointly by the Army and Navy and (*b*) by the Chairman of the Maritime Commission.

The functions, duties, and powers now vested in the Maritime Commission, with respect to ship allocation and operation are transferred to the War Shipping Administration under authority of the First War Powers Act. The Administrator is authorized to allocate and control the operation and use of all ocean vessels under the flag or control of the United States, *except* combatant vessels of the Army and Navy, fleet auxiliaries of the Navy and transports owned by the Army and Navy.

The order has been cleared with and approved by Secretary Knox and Admiral Land. I also understand that Harry Hopkins is strongly in favor of this draft as now presented. However, Secretary Stimson has requested that the Army and Navy be given greater control over the decisions of the Administrator in allocating vessels by inserting language which would require that the allocations of the Administrator comply with "strategic military requirements as determined by the joint decision of the War and Navy Departments." Both Admiral Land and Harry Hopkins feel that this sentence so weakens the position of the Administrator that an order including such a provision would be ineffective. We concur in the view of Land and Hopkins and thus recommend that you sign the order as submitted.

The President took the view that the war being waged was global in character and that the closest cooperation with our Allies was needed. This he thought could be better achieved by establishing a civilian agency in charge of all shipping which would give proper weight to lend-lease. American military control of shipping would tend to slight the imperative demands of Russia, Great Britain, and China. The President signed the proposed order creating the War Shipping Administration on February 7, 1942.[12] Two days later Admiral Land, still retaining his chairmanship of the Maritime Commission, was appointed Administrator of the new agency.

The responsibility of the War Shipping Administration under the Executive order extended to all phases of shipping including purchase or requisition of vessels for its own use or use of the Army, Navy, or other Government agencies; the repairing, arming, and degaussing of vessels controlled by War Shipping Administration and Allied vessels under Lend-Lease provision; conversion of vessels to troop transports, hospital ships, and to other special purposes; providing ship personnel; operating, loading, discharging and general control of the movement of these ships; administering of marine and war risk insurance laws and funds; and control of terminal and port facilities, forwarding and related matters.

Creation of a new war agency to exercise these functions had a number of advantages. Emergency shipping powers which had been vested in the Maritime Commission were now concentrated in a single individual. The new agency would be free from the restraints in the Merchant Marine Act regarding the recruitment of personnel from the shipping industry. This act prohibited the hiring of people from the shipping industry on a dollar-a-year basis. WSA was not bound by these provisions and made a general practice of hiring men from the industry.

---

[12] Executive Order No. 9054, Feb. 7, 1942, 7 *Federal Register* 837.

The executive order authorized the Administrator to allocate shipping within the limits of "strategic military requirements," as he interpreted them. In arranging for imports, he was to be guided by schedules transmitted from the War Production Board. The exact relations between ocean and coastwise shipping were left to negotiations between the Administrator and the Director of the Office of Defense Transportation.

The order designated the Administrator to represent the United States Government in dealing with the British Ministry of War Transport in matters relating to the use of shipping. On January 26, 1942, while negotiations regarding the Executive order were still in process, the President announced prospective formation of the Combined Shipping Adjustment Board. Actually, two boards were established, one in Washington and the other in London. While in principle the shipping resources of the two countries were pooled, in practice each country directed its own shipping. The British representative in Washington did not have power to commit the British shipping pool. Such decisions could only be made by the British Ministry of War Transport in London. Similarly, the American member on the London Board could not commit the United States pool. The allocation of American shipping was in the hands of the War Shipping Administration in Washington. In 1942 the British pool was two and a half times larger than the American pool, but as the American shipbuilding program got under way this ratio changed in favor of the American pool.

The elaborate plans made by the British representative in Washington, Sir Arthur Salter, for the staffing of the Combined Shipping Adjustment Board did not materialize. In practice, the Board made a general review of the utilization of vessels in an effort to discover ways of saving tonnage through the elimination of duplication and the prevention of cross-hauling. Its findings were purely advisory. In addition to holding formal meetings, British and American representatives carried on many confidential and informal negotiations. To the American representatives, the Board was a disappointment because it did not provide a joint shipping pool. Efforts within the War Department to enlarge and strengthen the Board came to naught.

One of the main problems facing the War Shipping Administration was the lack of an accurate record of where United Nations ships were, what they were doing, and to what extent they could be assigned to other purposes. To remedy inadequacies of shipping data, Admiral Land appointed as his adviser Lewis W. Douglas, insurance executive and former Director of the Bureau of the Budget, who had been brought to Washington by Harry Hopkins to assist in lend-lease activities. Mr. Douglas found lend-lease and shipping problems inseparable. His job with the War Shipping Administration was to prepare a picture of the American shipping situation and to establish the basic statistical and reporting procedures which would make possible current appraisals of the shipping operations. This work was slow in getting under way because Mr. Douglas at first had no control over the operating divisions of War Shipping Administration. In a report of April 25, 1942, to the President on wartime transportation, the Liaison Officer for Emergency Management said:

> The general administration of WSA is thus marked by an almost complete lack of planning and effective management. Problems directly affecting the Nation's survival are being met on a day-to-day basis without adequate information for proper decisions. This has resulted in needless waste in the past and the waste will continue until effective management methods are instituted. * * * At the moment, some of the information essential to proper allocation and efficient management of our shipping is beginning to be assembled. This has come about since the appointment of Mr. Lewis Douglas as Chief Adviser of WSA.

In May Mr. Douglas was appointed Deputy Administrator for vessel utilization and planning and this gave him the needed control over operations. By fall marked improvement had been made in the statistical picture and advance planning was under way. Lack of cooperation on the part of the Navy, however, was still a handicap in compiling information about ships.

In allocating shipping tonnage, Mr. Douglas stated that Presidential directives were given first priority. For instance, the President made shipping to meet the Russian protocol a first priority and this was carried out at the expense of the Red Sea operations. After the President's instructions, requests from the military authorities came next, then lend-lease orders, and finally civilian requirements. In practice, Mr. Douglas, after consultation with the agencies concerned, made the day-to-day decisions on allocations. In performing this function WSA was subjected to continual pressure from agencies interested in securing greater allocations. Dissatisfaction with Mr. Douglas' decisions led in some cases to attempts to have them set aside by higher authority. In an effort to alleviate this pressure, he sought directives from top military and civilian officials in making the most vital decisions.

In early 1942 the Army attempted to gain control of all inland and off-shore transportation. After a series of conferences, a compromise was reached under which representatives of the War Department, War Shipping Administration, Office of Defense Transportation, and the British Ministry of War Transport were to sit as a Daily Operations Committee controlling the movement of both inland and off-shore transportation. On June 13, 1942, an agreement was signed by the Army Transport Service and War Shipping Administration covering the interdepartmental relationship between the Army and WSA so as to form a basis for full and complete cooperation in connection with the purchase, charter, use, and operation of vessels and terminal facilities. On imports the War Production Board continued to furnish priority lists and the Board of Economic Warfare was the key agency on exports not under the control of military authorities or lend-lease.

Active participation by the United States in the war necessitated total Government control of all oceangoing tonnage. On April 18, 1942, the WSA issued an order making all American owned or controlled ships subject to requisition. It proceeded at once to take over either actual title or the unlimited right of use of all privately owned oceangoing vessels within our jurisdiction. Private ship companies became operating agents for the Government. Elaborate legal and accounting arrangements were necessary to take care of acquisition costs, charter rates, operating costs, stevedoring contracts, repairs contracts, and insurance rates. Regarding problems encountered by the Administration in getting under way, the Truman Committee reported:

> The War Shipping Administration candidly admits that many difficulties have been encountered in the loading and handling of ships and that many blunders were made, especially in the earlier months. This was to be expected because of the transition that had to be made from peacetime cargoes handled by private merchants to war cargoes of different types handled by Government agencies. The frankness of the War Shipping Administration in admitting and hastening to correct its mistakes presents a refreshing contrast to the attitude of some war agencies.[13]

One of the most serious problems in connection with effective operation of American ocean ships was that of providing the necessary seamen and officers. During the early months of our war effort, sailings of many ships were delayed because of inadequate crews. An interdepartmental committee composed of representatives of the State and Justice Departments and the War Shipping Administration analyzed these problems. Recruiting and training of merchant seamen had been a function of the Maritime Commission, which had delegated the actual operation of schools to the Coast Guard. On the recommendation of the Bureau of the Budget, which had made a study of maritime training and related problems, the President issued on February 22, 1942, an Executive order transferring training to the United States Coast Guard.[14] Recruitment functions left with the Commission were transferred to the War Shipping Administration, which established a Recruitment and Manning Organization to

[13] Senate Report No. 10, pt. 16, 78th Cong., 2d sess., p. 281.
[14] Executive Order No. 9083, Feb. 28, 1942, 7 *Federal Register* 1609.

create and operate pools of American seamen in a few principal ports. There was no question about the responsibility of the War Shipping Administration for manning vessels in the sense of hiring a specific man for a specific voyage.

Admiral Land and his associates were never reconciled to the transfer of the training function to the Coast Guard. They continued to agitate for the return of this program to their jurisdiction. Maritime unions, fearing militarization of the merchant fleet, supported the position of the War Shipping Administration. As a result, the President signed on July 11, 1942, an Executive order transferring the training functions from the Coast Guard to War Shipping Administration.[15] Cooperative arrangements were developed between the United States Employment Service and the Recruitment and Manning Organization for the registration of seamen. In the actual hiring of seamen, union hiring halls were used in accordance with collective bargaining agreements. Individual discipline cases continued to be handled by the Coast Guard.

During the first 9 months of the war, many improvements were made in the ocean shipping situation. Establishment of the War Shipping Administration hastened the leasing and acquisition of ships by the Government so that they could be employed more effectively for war transport. The Maritime Commission was left free to concentrate on shipbuilding. Shipping was converted from a "business as usual" to an all-out war basis. American shipping was not monopolized by the Armed Services but was devoted to the needs of all the Allies. Close relations were established with the British shipping pool. Vast improvements were made in the procedures for maintaining current information on the location of ships and cargoes. Sailing delays due to manpower shortages were practically eliminated.

Maximum utilization of shipping in the American pool, however, was not achieved during this period. This was especially true of the ships under the control of the Army and the Navy. The War Shipping Administration order did not unify control over all American-controlled ships and it contained no ready-made formula for solving shipping space allocation problems. Friction still existed between War Shipping Administration, War Production Board, Lend-Lease Administration, Foreign Economic Administration, and the armed services over requirements, exchanges of information, loading methods and the general problems of shipping and cargo control. As the War Shipping Administration gained experience and the size of the American shipping pool increased, these frictions interfered less and less with the job of delivering the greatest quantity of war goods ever moved in history.

---

[15] Executive Order No. 9198, July 11, 1942, 7 *Federal Register* 5383.

Domestic Transportation

Ocean transportation shortages were felt by our Allies first. Domestic transportation shortages soon affected the lives of every man, woman and child in the United States. The swift advance of the Japanese on the rubber-producing areas, sinking of coastal vessels-- especially tankers, growing shortage of gasoline on the eastern seaboard, orders stopping the manufacture of motor vehicles for civilian use, manpower shortages in the transportation field, curtailment of civilian air traffic, growing obsolescence of railway equipment, and rationing of tires, automobiles, and gasoline brought home to all the transport dislocations of a many-front war.

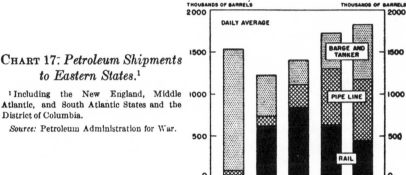

CHART 17: *Petroleum Shipments to Eastern States.*[1]

[1] Including the New England, Middle Atlantic, and South Atlantic States and the District of Columbia.

Source: Petroleum Administration for War.

Domestic transportation requirements at the time of Pearl Harbor were much heavier than at the time of the declaration of war in 1917. The armed forces were larger, ports on all our seacoasts were used for the shipping of men and materials, war industries involved more displacement of population and greater freight tonnages, coastal shipping was more successfully attacked by the enemy, and the railroads had less equipment with which to meet the emergency. Since coastwise and intercoastal shipping was subject to attack by the enemy and to requisition by the Armed Forces and War Shipping Administration, it practically disappeared during 1942. This meant a greatly increased burden upon the railroads.

Particularly threatening to inland transportation was the enemy action against petroleum tankers. Normally the eastern States consumed approximately 1,500,000 barrels of petroleum or petroleum products daily and of this supply about 95 percent moved by tankers from the southwestern oil fields and refineries (chart 17). By May this supply had been more than cut in half. The long tanker haul from the Gulf of Mexico had to be given up because escort vessels could not be spared from convoy duty in the Atlantic and Pacific. Steel, manufacturing facilities, and labor could not be immediately diverted to the manufacture of railroad tank cars, barges, and pipe lines without disrupting the flow of supplies to the Pacific and to our Allies fighting the Nazis. If we were to prosecute the war successfully and conserve our limited supply of rubber, it was not possible to consume oil and gasoline at home in the quantities to which we had become accustomed.

Another major question which faced the country in these fateful days was whether our transportation resources were adequate for total warfare. There were differences of opinion among the experts regarding the capacity of our transport. Some contended that we had a surplus of transportation capacity, while others held that there were serious shortages and a danger of a general break-down of the war machinery on that account.

Prior to the war there existed no machinery capable of dealing with the domestic transportation system as a whole. The Association of American Railroads had certain voluntary controls over car supply and movements. The Interstate Commerce Commission had broad emergency powers which might have been used to promote a more economical flow of railway traffic and a more efficient distribution of cars. But the Commission was not in a position to require advance preparation to meet defense needs. Besides, as an 11-member quasi-judicial regulatory body, the Commission was not fitted for fast action; neither was its staff geared to a defense program. It did not have full regulatory powers over intrastate and local carriers. This was especially important in the local transportation field. While these powers could have been given to the Commission, it was thought better to give them to a temporary war agency which would be abolished after the emergency and raise no questions about the Federal Government continuing in this field. The motor carrier groups were not so well organized as the railroads and limited themselves to voluntary organization to meet emergencies.

The Division of Transportation of the Advisory Commission to the Council of National Defense, established on May 29, 1940, was the last of the staff units of the Advisory Commission to be absorbed into other administrative agencies. Ralph Budd, railroad executive, served as Commissioner until after Pearl Harbor when the Office of Defense Transportation was established. The Division never had a large staff and it relied heavily upon consultants, advisory committees, and the cooperation of other agencies and the transportation industry.

Mr. Budd and his associates believed that the Division of Transportation could be most useful by acting in an advisory and coordinating capacity. They assumed that existing transportation facilities were adequate for national defense since there was a surplus of transportation capacity and that a large staff would duplicate the work of the Interstate Commerce Commission and other agencies and get in the way of private management. The Division relied upon the Association of American Railroads for advice, information, and active support of its policies. Much of its comparatively conservative advice on car supply was based on statistical data furnished by the AAR Car Service Division. The Division established a Central Motor Transportation Committee which headed up a Nation-wide organization composed of 16 district committees. Within the Central Committee and also in each district committee were included representatives of the public, of for-hire trucking, private trucking, and bus operations. The Division also set up a Tank Car Service Committee in anticipation of the diversion of tankers from the Gulf East Coast oil service. Activities of the Division included making of recommendations regarding needed railroad equipment, assisting transportation companies to secure priorities for equipment, and furnishing advice on such matters as port congestion, grain shipments, increasing the movement of ore, stock piling of coal, collection of iron and steel scrap, and prevention of sabotage.[16]

As the defense program got under way, the Division of Transportation became a less suitable instrument for coordinating domestic transportation. Provision of information and advice was not sufficient to meet the growing needs. The staff of the Division thought largely in terms of railroad problems and looked upon other forms of transportation as secondary—as in normal times they perhaps are. Other agencies began to move into the transportation field on a piece-meal basis.

In the spring of 1941 the staffs of the Bureau of the Budget and the National Resources Planning Board made a study of transportation and concluded that certain critical problems were developing. They contended that allowance should be made for diversion of coastwise and intercoastal ship tonnage, for possible shortages of tonnage on the Great Lakes, for increasing demands on port facilities, and for other contingencies of an emergency period. They foresaw the need for insuring an adequate supply of petroleum and its products to Atlantic coast points following withdrawal of tankers. Among possible programs and actions, they mentioned the short-routing of traffic, placing restrictions on the use of equipment for storage, pooling and reallocating car supplies, shifting locomotives to hard-pressed roads, diverting tonnage around congested terminals, and coordinating all inland transport with movements at the ports.

Plans for the reorganization of the defense transportation field were pushed by the National Resources Planning Board, the Bureau

[16] **Activities** of the NDAC Transportation Division, Sept. 11, 1941 (mimeo.).

of the Budget, and other agencies in the spring of 1941. The staff of the Planning Board recommended the establishment of a new agency within the Office for Emergency Management to carry on both emergency planning and action functions under the direction of a man with broad experience who was not a top executive in a transportation industry. When officials of the Office of Production Management sought to absorb the Transportation Division of the Advisory Commission, the staff of the Bureau opposed this move on the ground that the transportation function was of broad importance to the entire defense program and they proposed an Executive order establishing a separate transportation agency whose functions would extend to ocean shipping as well as land transport facilities and would include the exercise of certain authorities of the President over transportation priorities.

The question was threshed out by the President's advisers during the summer and fall and the plan subsequently proposed was modified in the light of their discussions. It was decided that the powers of the new office be confined to domestic transportation because of the difficulty of getting someone who could supervise both inland and ocean transportation, that priorities in movements would be directed by the Office of Production Management and the Supply Priorities and Allocations Board and carried out by the new office, and that the new office would be responsible for negotiating rate adjustments.

The Bureau of the Budget draft of an order incorporating these changes was ready on December 5, 1941, and was signed by the President the 18th of the month.

Executive Order No. 8989 established the Office of Defense Transportation and authorized it to coordinate the transportation policies and activities of the railroad, motor, inland waterway, pipe line, air transport, and coastwise and intercoastal shipping industries; to keep close watch on domestic transportation in connection with the war effort; to protect the interests of such transportation before other agencies of the Government, particularly the Office of Production Management; to do everything possible to promote the maximum utilization of transportation facilities; and to this end to require action by orders, where necessary.

From the beginning of the negotiations concerning the Executive order, Mr. Joseph Eastman, Chairman of the Interstate Commerce Commission, was regarded by the President's advisers as the logical man to head the new agency. He was not connected with any transportation group but he was thoroughly familiar with the problems in the field and had the confidence of the industry. Mr. Budd was among those who urged Mr. Eastman's appointment. The President announced Mr. Eastman's acceptance of the responsibility on January 2, 1942.

As Director of the Office of Defense Transportation, Mr. Eastman exercised his wide powers with marked caution. He and his associates, many of whom came with him from ICC, believed that actual management should remain in private hands and that existing operating practices should be left undisturbed wherever possible. He also held that transportation priorities were administratively impractical and should be avoided.

After Pearl Harbor, freight traffic reached new highs but there was comparatively little congestion and no general system of priority orders was invoked by the Office of Defense Transportation. As in World War I, it was essential that congestion at the ports be prevented. The Association of American Railroads worked out elaborate procedures for keeping in touch with possible danger points and cooperated closely with ODT, ICC, WSA, the Armed Forces, and shippers to prevent serious accumulations of cars under load. ODT organized on March 18, 1942, a Transportation Control Committee, representing interested Government agencies, to control the movement of freight to the ports in such a manner as to meet the established shipping schedules. The Committee met daily and issued permits to the various procurement agencies and shippers in accordance with the shipping space which had been allocated to them. ODT sent members of its own staff to keep a constant watch over traffic in all major ports and by General Order No. 16A established a unit permit system on export cargo and named as its agents for the issuance of such unit permits Transportation Division, Bureau of Supplies and Accounts, Navy Department; Division of Cargo Clearance, War Shipping Administration; Transport Controller, Canada; and Traffic Control Division, Transportation Corps, War Department. The Army Transport Chief stated that the Army was in actual control of its traffic and that the Committee was relatively powerless to interfere. While the War Department domination of this rail traffic was criticized in some quarters, the results in preventing congestion at and near the ports were of the greatest importance.

In contrast to the situation in 1917, no great demand developed for large and rapid increases in railroad rates. Although railroad rates were increased only moderately in 1942, railroad earnings were high. Mr. Eastman ascribed this to the greater success the Government had in 1942 in resisting inflation and to the fact that dense traffic combined with close approach to maximum utilization of facilities was productive of highly economical operation.[17] In ac-

---
[17] Eastman, Joseph B., "Public Administration of Transportation under War Conditions," *American Economic Review*, March 1944, pt. 2, vol. 34, p. 91.

cordance with the provisions of Executive Order No. 8989, ODT represented the Government interest in negotiating rates with domestic transportation carriers. In the performance of this function it established a joint force of rate clerks with OPA and sponsored the creation of the Traffic Executive Chairmen's Committee by the traffic associations.

Because of the enormous amount of freight that had to be transported during the war, coupled with the limited amount of equipment to handle this extraordinary load, ODT had to issue regulations that would result in fuller use of railroad equipment than was common in peacetime. Among the orders issued was one requiring heavier loading of less-than-carload of freight.[18] This order, which restricted the forwarding of such cars unless loaded with minimum weights was instrumental in preventing a shortage of box cars.[19] A similar shortage in refrigerator cars was avoided by an arrangement set up by ODT in cooperation with the car owners, ICC, and the Association of American Railroads, which provided practical pooling of all refrigerator cars, regardless of ownership. ICC issued a service order to carry out this plan.[20]

Another responsibility imposed on ODT was to survey and ascertain present and anticipated storage and warehousing requirements and encourage the provision of increased storage facilities where necessary. After Pearl Harbor, the capacity to produce was greater than the capacity to transport and well-ordered storage arrangements had to be provided. ODT had no authority to compel the storage industry to provide for ample storage space, nor could it legally build and operate this space itself, but it persuaded the industry to create Federal warehouse associations which pooled existing resources of warehouses, it induced such procurement agencies as the Army, Navy, and Lend-Lease Administration to construct new warehouses, and it cooperated with ICC and the Department of Agriculture in solving grain storage shortages.

The war disrupted the normal pattern of railway movement. New industries and military establishments were created on sites which had not been railroad centers and there were increasing movements of freight to ports for shipment abroad. These conditions modified and sometimes reversed the direction of loaded and empty car movement. Obstructions could be averted most effectively by a centralized supervisory authority continuously informed of conditions likely to affect the free flow of traffic, and using such information to remove them.

---

[18] ODT General Order No. 1, Mar. 23, 1942.

[19] ODT estimated that for periods May–December 1942, and for the calendar years 1943, 1944, and 1945, the average loading (tons) was over 9, whereas in 1941 it was 5.5.

[20] ICC Service Order No 95, Nov. 9, 1942, 7 *Federal Register* 9257.

To provide this supervision, ODT established the Traffic Channels Plan which was essentially a daily reporting system based on a purely voluntary arrangement between the carriers and ODT. No order was promulgated by ODT to enforce it. In the western territory, however, war activities were unusually disruptive of normal railroad traffic and it was felt that to improve utilization of equipment and to prevent congestion and delay, traffic had to be diverted or rerouted over rail lines with excess capacity. The Association of American Railroads proposed the extension of the functions of its Car Service Division to include rerouting and diversion. It was decided, however, that such an activity would violate the antitrust laws. While both

CHART 18. *Passenger Traffic on Railroads.*

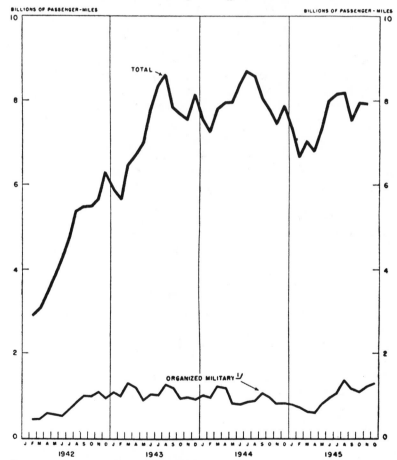

1 Includes organized military groups of 40 or more only.

Source: Interstate Commerce Commission and Association of American Railroads.

ODT and ICC had some jurisdiction in the field, they decided to act jointly through a common agent.[21]

One of the most difficult problems faced by ODT shortly after Pearl Harbor was the transportation of petroleum products from the southwestern oil-producing districts to the eastern seaboard territory following the withdrawal of intercoastal tankers from this trade. The Liquid Transport Department of ODT, originally called the Division of Petroleum and Other Liquids, was the only Division organized along commodity lines. Early in the war, it concentrated on the substitution of railroad tank cars for oceangoing tankers. The amazing increase in the shipment of oil by tank car was facilitated by close supervision of the car supply by ODT; by substitution of tank trucks for tank cars on short hauls; and by scheduling of trainload movements, all with the cooperation of the railroads, the shippers, and the Office of Petroleum Coordinator. The tank car rail movement increased from 70,000 barrels a day before Pearl Harbor to more than 850,000 barrels per day 8 months later. But the railroad equipment was old and the use of tank cars costly. In 1941 the Supply Priorities and Allocations Board twice refused to approve the construction of pipe lines from the Texas oil fields to the East Coast. Differences of opinion were expressed regarding location and use of such lines. On June 10, 1942, however, WPB, on the recommendation of the Petroleum Administrator for War and ODT, authorized the allocation of materials for pipe-line construction. A little more than a year later the 24-inch line was in operation and the pressure on the railroads was lightened.

While railway passenger-miles were 83 percent higher in 1942 than in 1941 the railroads had to operate with virtually the same passenger-carrying equipment. ODT had to see that essential military and civilian passengers were accommodated and that a disproportionate share of railway facilities was not diverted to pleasure travel. It sought to achieve these objectives without resort to a compulsory priority system or any scheme requiring the rationing of passenger travel. It rejected such rigid controls on the ground that they would create serious administrative problems, particularly with the increasing shortage of manpower, and would involve many hardships. ODT issued one order prohibiting replacing of train service by bus service without its approval and another freezing all railway passenger schedules and prohibiting railroads, with certain exceptions, from running any special passenger trains or giving other special services. In addition, ODT urged the railroads to adopt voluntary measures of

---

[21] ICC Service Order No. 99, Feb. 3, 1943, 8 *Federal Register* 1652. The Army requested exemption from some of the provisions of this act for its freight. This was granted by ODT Certificate of Preference and Priority in Transportation No 2, dated Jan. 19, 1944. It marked a departure from ODT's policy of not using priorities.

their own to conserve passenger equipment.[22]   Through the cooperation of business and professional organizations, about two-thirds of
the normal conventions and group meetings were eliminated or
greatly reduced.   ODT prohibited use of special passenger facilities
for athletic and other recreational events.   It also conducted educational campaigns to induce the general public to refrain from unnecessary travel and it urged the Government and industries to spread
vacations throughout the year.

Local Transport

Within a few months after his appointment, Mr. Eastman recognized the responsibility of his office for regularly established local
transportation even though this subject was not expressly mentioned
in Executive Order No. 8989.   He saw that something had to be done
to improve the local transit facilities in areas where new war plants
or training centers were established.   As prospects for securing additional equipment were poor, ODT had to secure the maximum utilization of existing rapid transit systems, street railways, interurban railways, trolley buses, local, suburban and school buses, taxicabs, for-
hire cars, ferries and local water carriers, and other local passenger
services.

In order to conserve local transport equipment and to direct it into
channels of essential use, ODT issued a series of orders regulating
the substitution of buses for streetcars and the chartering of buses by
groups for their exclusive use, banning sightseeing buses, eliminating
duplications of service, curtailing schedules and service for elimination
of wasteful operation, requiring proper maintenance of equipment and
maximum loading, and requiring carriers in competitive service over
parallel, or closely parallel routes, to formulate joint action plans for
the maximum utilization of equipment.   The joint action plans were
submitted to the Department of Justice for clearance as to the enforcement of the antitrust law.[23]   Other orders banned automobile racing,
restricting the number of taxicabs and the number of taxicab services,
and regulated the use of rental cars.   In addition, public and operator
cooperation was sought for securing the adoption of staggered hours,
restoration of abandoned streetcar services, diversion of rubber-
borne traffic to street railway routes, turn-back service, fewer stops on
bus and streetcar routes, street traffic control, and other conservation
measures.

While the increased burdens placed upon local mass transit systems
in many places were staggering, ODT took the position that it would

---

[22] In 1945, ODT felt obliged to issue a number of orders clamping down on facilities for unnecessary travel
and uneconomic operation of railroad passenger equipment.

[23] After July 20, 1943, joint action plans were put into effect under WPB Blanket Certificate No. 99.

not attempt to obtain priorities for the construction of new street-cars, trolley coaches, and motor buses until all possible means of making fuller use of existing equipment had been exhausted. WPB authorized the completion in 1942 of only 350 streetcars, 400 trolley coaches, and 9,000 buses, in each case consideiably less than the number recommended by ODT.

Private Passenger Cars

The attack at Pearl Harbor called for immediate action to conserve existing rubber stockpiles since it cut off substantially all of the Nation's sources of crude rubber. Some 27 million passenger automobiles, comprising an essential part of our transportation system, had to be kept on the road. Failure to provide tires for these vehicles would keep war workers from their factories and ultimately would mean a break-down in the whole transport system.

At first Mr. Eastman was unable to take comprehensive action on rubber-borne traffic problems. Subsequently and in cooperation with the Chairman of the Highway Traffic Advisory Committee of the War Department, he sponsored conservation of rubber-borne car equipment by promoting group riding, slower speeds, changes in traffic signals, and staggered hours for industry.

On December 11, 1941, the Office of Production Management stopped the sale, transfer, and delivery of new tires, and, on December 27, authorized the Office of Price Administation to ration automobile tires.

The rationing of tires involved administrative problems of vast proportions, chief among which was the creation of an organization capable of rationing commodities in communities throughout the country. The first step was taken on December 16 when State Governors were notified that it would be necessary to begin rationing on January 2 and that the rationing organization would be built around State defense councils. By December 19 outlines of the plan had been drawn: the Office of Price Administration would develop "policies, regulations, and necessary informational data" and distribute this information among the defense councils; the job of setting up community organizations would be handled by State defense councils; and local boards established by local defense councils would be responsible for seeing that tires were made available to persons entitled to them urder regulations issued by the national office of OPA. By January 5, 1942, less than a month after the declaration of war, the organization had been developed sufficiently to permit sale of automobile tires under the rationing system. Monthly quotas were established for each State and county and eligibility lists issued to guide the tire rationing boards in distributing tires and

CHART 19. *Transportation Activity.*[1]

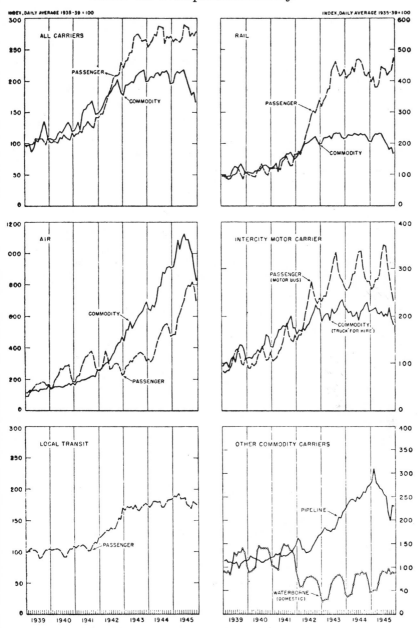

[1] Indexes for commodity and passenger traffic (except local transit) are based upon ton-miles and passenger miles respectively; index for local transit is based upon number of passengers.

Source: Department of Commerce.

tubes to the most essential users.   Similar mechanisms were worked out for rationing of automobiles.

Before the tire and automobile rationing program had become well established, a second threat to inland transportation developed; enemy action against petroleum tankers created a gasoline shortage on the eastern seaboard.   On May 15, 1942, an emergency gasoline rationing plan was put into effect on the eastern seaboard.   Applications were filed and ration cards distributed through public schools. The system was admittedly crude and was designed as a stop-gap measure to reduce gasoline consumption pending the development of a coupon rationing system.   It was not sufficiently flexible to permit "tailoring" of rations to individual needs.   Educational campaigns did not completely eliminate evasion of the rationing regulations by the public and they were less successful in curtailing pleasure driving.

The relation between ODT and OPA became an important issue after the signing of an Executive order giving ODT authority over "all rubber-borne transportation facilities, including passenger cars, buses, taxicabs, and trucks".[24]   As OPA began to ration cars, tires, and gasoline, it was apparent that it was making decisions which affected "rubber-borne transportation facilities" but which also came within the jurisdiction of the ODT.   The amount of gasoline allowed an owner of a truck fleet by OPA might not be sufficient to transport essential war freight.   Similarly, there was no mechanism in the rationing system "to bring about rationalization of rubber-borne traffic."   At the outset, therefore, gasoline, tires, and automobiles were rationed as commodities rather than as factors of transportation.

By action of WPB, May 2, 1942, OPA was directed to implement insofar as administratively practicable any policies or programs formulated by ODT.   OPA, however, continued to develop its rationing plans; ODT moved slowly in formulating any transportation policy for passenger cars; and, as a result, transportation policy for which ODT was legally responsible was being fixed by OPA.

A survey made in the summer of 1942 of the Federal agencies concerned with the supply of local transportation facilities revealed the general impression that the Office of Defense Transportation had shown a lack of understanding of the full implications of the rubber shortage, had an inadequate staff to cope with its responsibilities, and had demonstrated a lack of imagination and energy in attacking the local transportation problem.

By June, however, mandatory gasoline rationing extending throughout the Nation was demanded by many in order to reduce consumption of rubber tires and maintain essential transportation facilities. A report of the Petroleum Industry War Council, made on May 27,

---

[24] Executive Order No. 9156, May 2, 1942, 7 *Federal Register* 3349.

estimated that without additional rubber for automobile tires and without reduction of speed and mileage, the number of cars in use would decline to 9 million by the end of 1943 and to slightly over 1 million by the end of 1944. After thorough discussion of this situation, and of ways in which it might be solved, members of the War Production Board were of the opinion that Nation-wide compulsory rationing was the only solution. Pending further discussion of this measure, the Office of Price Administration was directed to move ahead as rapidly as possible with a more fully developed rationing system for the Eastern area.[25]

At meetings held in June and July, the President would not approve Nation-wide rationing of gasoline but suggested instead that a major conservation program covering tires and gasoline be instituted by means of an intensive public information campaign.

This campaign did not have the desired results, however, and by August the rubber supply situation had become so crucial that the President appointed a special committee to study the supply problem and to recommend action. On September 10, 1942, the Baruch Committee reported that the situation was so grave that "unless corrective measures are taken immediately this country will face both a military and civilian collapse". The Committee concluded that "gas rationing is the only way to save rubber." It recommended that a new Nation-wide rationing system of gasoline be devised so that the average annual mileage could be held to a maximum of 5,000 miles.

The importance of immediate action, stressed by the Baruch Committee, tended to resolve the question of OPA–ODT responsibility in favor of OPA. OPA local boards, established at first to ration automobile tires, comprised a field organization which could undertake the administration of a rationing system designed to limit individual car owners to essential mileage. OPA had acquired considerable experience in rationing and the "permanent" eastern area plan could be extended without difficulty. ODT, on the other hand, had no rationing experience and was just beginning to build up its field organization. Under these circumstances the job of administering the Nation-wide rationing plan was delegated to OPA. The problem of the relation between the ODT's rationalization policies and the OPA rationing program had yet to be solved.

Motor Transport

In the field of motor transport, the Office of Defense Transportation was given additional responsibilities by an Executive order of May 2, 1942, which directed it to "formulate measures to conserve

───────

[25] WPB, *Minutes*, June 2, 1942.

and assure maximum utilization of the existing supply of civilian transportation services dependent upon rubber, including the limitation of the use of rubber-borne transportation facilities in non-essential civilian activities, and regulation of the use or distribution of such transportation facilities among essential activities."[26] This order, supplementing but not supplanting the rationing authority delegated to the Office of Price Administration by the War Production Board, was aimed to help a sick industry. Trucks were wearing out rapidly and new equipment was not being made. The operation of trucks under war rules was not always profitable.

The dispersed organization of the motor transport industry made unworkable the administration of a general and simplified policy of control uniformly applicable to all carriers. Many thousands of private and contract carriers were involved and they were comparatively unfamiliar with the operation of controls. At first it was hoped that limited supplies of vehicles, parts, tires, and gasoline could be conserved by issuance of general orders regulating mileage operated and loads carried. Reliance was placed upon voluntary cooperation of the industry and only a relatively small field staff was contemplated. It soon became evident, however, that an industry with over 4,000,000 private owners and 600,000 public carriers engaged in such varied activities could not be controlled successfully by any such blanket system of regulation.

The Office of Defense Transportation decided that necessary savings in tire mileage and in equipment use could be achieved only by a more flexible technique administered on a decentralized basis. It developed a plan for issuing to all commercial truck operators a Certificate of War Necessity which would be required in order to obtain gasoline, tires, parts, and other essential materials. The basic principle of the program was the elimination of waste through full loading of equipment and curtailment of unessential mileage. In reviewing the operations of these vehicles, ODT sought to eliminate such wasteful practices as daily delivery and "call-backs". Observance of the 35-mile-an-hour speed limit was also made a condition for receiving a Certificate of Necessity. This ODT order was difficult to enforce since the local authorities failed to report violations except in rare cases. A survey of highway speeds showed widespread nonobservance of the order. Local war price and rationing boards were directed to issue gasoline coupons in accordance with mileage granted by ODT. The plan was applied first to the eastern gas rationing area, but later it was extended to the entire country. ODT had to increase greatly its field force to administer the certificates. In spite of this, the plan was inconvenient to small operators, and in 1944

[26] Executive Order No. 9156, May 2, 1942, 7 *Federal Register* 3349.

ODT turned the work over to the OPA local boards. In applying the plan to farm vehicle operators, ODT relied upon the county war boards of the Department of Agriculture.

Water Transportation

The use of water transportation to supplement overloaded rail and highway facilities was an obvious way in which the transportation crisis could be alleviated. Iron ore traffic on the Great Lakes was given priority over grain and coal shipments with the result that during the 1942 season a record-breaking total of 92,000,000 tons of iron ore was moved from the Minnesota iron ranges to the steel mills on the southern shores of the lakes. While many barges on the country's rivers and canals were idle at the time of Pearl Harbor, they were being used close to capacity 6 months later. The greatest exception was south-bound movement down the Ohio and Mississippi Rivers. Attempts to induce the Maritime Commission to use barges to transport steel southward were unsuccessful. The Commission refused to cooperate on the grounds that the barges were slow and their use would hold up the shipbuilding program.

ODT issued orders designed to increase shipment of ore at the expense of grain and steel shipments but WPB pressed for a general priority system. As in other fields, ODT shied away from using general priority powers for water transportation.

Our waterways carried only a small fraction of the freight that was moved during the first 9 months of the war. In addition to iron ore, oil, coal, sulphur, scrap iron, and heavy general merchandise were carried by water. At certain crucial centers, however, water transport constituted an important part of our surplus carrying capacity which enabled the Government to meet war requirements.

Transportation Manpower

As far as manpower problems were concerned, the Office of Defense Transportation acted as a coordinating agency, bringing to bear whatever technical knowledge and economic data it possessed and enlisting the aid and cooperation of those Federal agencies responsible for the operating phases of the Government's manpower program. The Office with certain exceptions,[27] did not operate transportation systems, nor did it regard itself as a labor recruiting agency, a training agency, or a mediator of labor disputes. It worked with the Federal agencies concerned with such matters, aiming not to duplicate the work of any of them. Thus, it kept the War Manpower Commission

---

[27] Certain transportation properties were taken over and managed because of strike situations. They were: Toledo, Peoria & Western R. R.; American Railroad of Puerto Rico; Illinois Central R. R.

informed regarding current over-all manpower requirements of transportation industries, it cooperated with Selective Service System to determine occupational deferment policies for essential occupations in the transportation industries, it tried to induce the transportation companies to take full advantage of the United States Employment Service and the Railroad Employment Service, and it facilitated the settlement of labor disputes by urging use of the Conciliation Service and by furnishing information and technical advice to the War Labor Board.

ODT encouraged transportation industries to adopt on a voluntary basis such personnel policies as would insure the maintenance of an adequate staff of employees. At the end of 1942 there were 2,700,000 Americans working in for-hire transportation jobs within the country —an increase of 200,000 over December 31, 1941—and turn-over was considerable, particularly among the poorly paid maintenance-of-way laborers. Both the railroad and the trucking industries formed joint labor management committees to consider, with representatives of the Office of Defense Transportation, not only manpower problems, but also problems of maximum utilization of materials and equipment. ODT helped influence the transportation industries and unions to open up jobs for women and Negroes. Women "motorettes" and "conductorettes" invaded the local transportation field. It encouraged the establishment of adequate training and upgrading programs. The lack of any direct labor representation in the Office was criticized in labor quarters while the lack of vigorous action against labor rules and practices which were wasteful of manpower was criticized in management circles. In this as in other fields, the Office of Defense Transportation did not disturb existing practices.

General Considerations

Any final estimate of the Office of Defense Transportation must take into account the limited nature of its jurisdiction of which Mr. Eastman was fully aware. He indicated that his No. 1 problem was to assure the carriers supplies for repairs and maintenance and "whatever new equipment and facilities may be necessary to meet the demands of an increasing traffic." He had to appear before the Requirements Committee of the War Production Board to plead for the critical materials needed by the transportation industries and later in 1942 his office became the claimant agency of domestic transportation for such materials. He made it clear that WPB would be responsible for a transportation break-down in case that the needs of the transportation industry for equipment and repairs were not met. In the spring of 1942 the War Production Board turned down the request for additional railway passenger cars and greatly curtailed the request for freight cars and locomotives on the assumption that there would be a surplus of transportation capacity.

Other important transportation questions were outside the jurisdiction of the Office of Defense Transportation. Authority over rates and charges rested with either the Interstate Commerce Commission, the Civil Aeronautics Board, State, or municipal regulatory authorities, or the Office of Price Administration. The Interstate Commerce Commission also had broad emergency powers over both railroad-car service and motor-transport service. Mention has already been made of ·the responsibilities in the domestic transportation field of the armed services, the labor agencies, the Maritime Commission, the War Shipping Administration, the Petroleum Administrator for War, the Defense Housing Coordinator, the Department of Agriculture, and the Rubber Director. In describing the position of his agency, Mr. Eastman said:

> It is, for example, the claimant agency of domestic transportation for critical materials before the War Production Board, for rubber before the Rubber Director, for gasoline before the Petroleum Administrator for War, and for coal before the Solid Fuels Administrator. It has representatives on both the War Production Board and the War Manpower Commission. It can negotiate voluntary rate adjustments with the carriers and make representations as to rates before the regulatory authorities. On wages alone it has no chips in the game whatsoever. The whole set-up is, of course, far from perfect, but I do not criticise it on the ground that authority over transportation is somewhat divided. Matters such as critical materials, wages, prices, and manpower are of such general importance over the whole range of the war effort that they cannot wisely be left to individual treatment by commodities or services.[28]

The Government agencies charged with primary responsibility for transporting goods during the war were set up before or within 2 months after Pearl Harbor. This prompt action would not have been possible without the careful planning and consideration of the issues during the defense period. In fact, the shipbuilding program might have been delayed a whole year if it had started from scratch after December 7, 1941. Before Pearl Harbor, the President had decided not to establish an office of transport after the British model that combined control over domestic transportation and ocean shipping. He had about decided upon an emergency domestic transportation agency apart from the emergency production agency and apart from the established transportation regulatory agency. While considerable thought had been given to shipping priorities and shipping control, prewar plans were less definite in this field than in the domestic transportation field.

The War Powers Act enabled the President to transfer the necessary powers to establish the Office of Defense Transportation and the

---

■ Eastman, Joseph B., *op. cit.*, p. 89.

War Shipping Administration. Both of these emergency agencies placed great emphasis upon cooperation with other Government agencies and with the transportation industries. Apparently, the theory was held that American private enterprise under suitable contract terms and with the necessary Government aid in securing critical materials could build all the ships needed to win the war, that private shipping companies under suitable charters and naval protection could operate these ships on any routes required by the grand war strategy, and that the private domestic carriers were fully capable of so pooling and utilizing their existing facilities with certain needed replacements that they would be able to handle the movement of men and goods needed to win the war. While these theories were challenged and more drastic measures were demanded, serious transportation break-downs were averted, even though narrowly. With certain curtailments of nonessential travel, the existing transportation equipment plus the newly built emergency ships met the requirements of a global war.

CHAPTER

7

Mobilizing Labor

THE PROBLEMS of raw material supply, transportation, and production planning, discussed in previous chapters, had become urgent before Pearl Harbor. Our labor reserves, however, were so ample that no acute problems of labor supply appeared until later. Shortages of unskilled and industrial workers did not become acute until 1943, and then only in a few production areas. At no time were labor shortages so critical as the shortages of raw materials, machine tools, components, ships, freight cars, and other items which necessitated tight control programs in those fields.

These facts account in part for the relative slowness in the development of a national manpower agency, the limited authority granted to this agency, and its relatively slight influence on the labor market. The year 1942 was a period of discussion and tentative experiment. Officials concerned with manpower were shadowboxing with a problem which had not yet developed. There was a great output of plans and much controversy over what should be done and who should do it, but few actions of any importance were taken. Yet this lack of action did not appreciably retard war production. Workers continued to show up at the factories, employers continued to hire and train them, and Government for the most part observed the process from the sidelines.

The period from June 1940 to December 1941 was marked primarily by a reduction in unemployment from some 9 million to about 4 million. The absorption of the unemployed plus the normal growth of the labor force made possible an expansion of some 5 million in employment and the addition of a million and a half to the armed forces. When war began, unemployment was still about 3 million higher than the unavoidable minimum. There had yet been no drain on the large reserve of women not in the labor force; indeed, the number of women in the labor force in December 1941 was substantially less than it had been a year before. Nor had there been any net transference of labor out of agriculture, trade, service, and other industries which were relatively overmanned at this time. Hours had not been lengthened beyond 40 except in shipbuilding, machine-tool production, and a few other key industries. In short, there were still in December 1941 extensive labor reserves which could be drawn on to meet increasing labor requirements.

It should not be inferred that no labor-supply problems were encountered during the defense period. As early as the fall of 1940 shortages of skilled workers, particularly in the metal trades, developed in many parts of the country. But employers gradually adjusted to this situation by breaking down and simplifying skilled jobs, installing training programs, and accelerating the promotion of partly trained workers. Their efforts were furthered by training programs sponsored by several Federal agencies, of which the most important were the Office of Education in the Federal Security Agency and the Training-Within-Industry organization which operated successively under

CHART 20. *The Labor Force.*

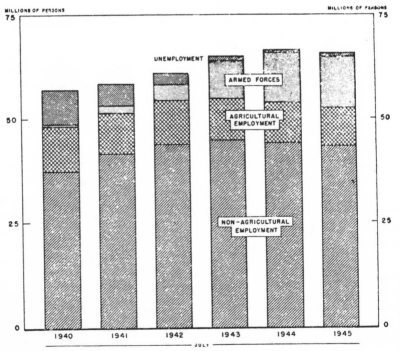

Source: Department of Commerce and Department of Labor.

the NDAC, OPM, WPB, and finally under the War Manpower Commission.

The outbreak of war caused a sharp increase in the prospective manpower requirements of war industry and the armed services. Estimates prepared in the spring of 1942 [1] indicated that the number employed and in the services would have to be increased from the 51.6 million of December 1941 to 60.3 million in December 1943.[2] To meet these requirements there were available the various types of labor reserve noted above, and it did not appear that there would be a deficiency in aggregate labor supply. The problem was rather that, because of the concentration of production facilities in certain areas, the geographical distribution of labor requirements differed considerably from the distribution of the labor force. Labor supplies could be matched with demand only through large-scale migration of labor which had been under way since 1940 and was still continuing. The influx of workers into centers of war industry resulted in serious congestion of housing, transportation, and other community services. By early 1942 some areas had already reached the point at which it was not physically possible to absorb more workers in spite of mounting labor demands. In these areas there was a problem of recruiting as many people as possible for war work, directing them to the most essential jobs, and preventing unnecessary shifts of workers from one plant to another.

The problem was not sufficiently acute, however, to arouse serious concern among production and procurement officials. Facilities and materials were the important production bottlenecks. While it was conceded that labor might become a problem at some point, the time seemed remote and meanwhile there were other things to do. Nor was industry seriously concerned about its ability to hire enough workers. While employers in many cities formed agreements not to pirate labor from each other and welcomed Government approval of such agreements, they did not favor any governmental restrictions on management's traditional right to hire and fire. Planning for a national manpower agency went forward in an atmosphere charged with the feeling that there probably was no problem of labor supply, and that even if such a problem existed, employers could handle it by their own efforts with perhaps some assistance from organized labor.

---

[1] Social Security Board. Bureau of Employment Security. *Estimates of Manpower Requirements to December 1943*, June 12, 1942. Chart.

[2] This estimate proved to be reasonably accurate as regards the total; the number actually employed and in the services in December 1943, was 61:3 million. As would be expected, there were errors in the components of the total; employment in manufacturing, for example, was overestimated by about 2 million, while the number who would be in the services was underestimated by 1.3 million. These errors, however, came close to canceling out.

A more immediate problem during 1942 was the prevention of strikes in war industries. Action to this end was taken immediately on the outbreak of war. A conference of representative leaders of labor and management prepared the way for the creation, early in January 1942, of a National War Labor Board with authority to arbitrate unsettled disputes in industries affecting war production. By the end of 1942 the administrative organization and main policies of the Board had settled into a pattern which was to remain substantially unchanged throughout the war. This development will be traced after a discussion of the steps taken to deal with the problems of labor supply.

Early Labor Supply Organization

The creation of the War Manpower Commission in April 1942 must be viewed against the background of previous organization in this field. A dozen major federal agencies and many others of lesser importance had been concerned with labor supply problems since the beginning of the defense program. The Selective Service System, created by act of Congress on September 16, 1940,[3] was responsible for inducting men of the number and types required by the armed services.[4] Through its network of some 6,500 local boards, it had by December 7, 1941, registered 17 million men aged 21 to 35 and inducted more than a million of these (chart 21). During the next year the number of registrants was to increase to almost 30 million men aged 18 to 45, and the number inducted to more than 5 million. By December 1941 the selection system and administrative procedures of Selective Service had become well established. The early creation of a military manpower organization which had 2 years to develop its procedures and policies before an agency for mobilizing industrial manpower was created, resulted in a bifurcation of manpower administration which was to continue throughout the war.

The War and Navy Departments also had a direct influence on the recruitment and use of labor. They were enlisting large numbers of men for military service at their own recruitment stations. They were engaged in recruiting a civilian labor force which at the peak was to number more than two million persons employed in arsenals, navy yards, and in other types of industrial and clerical work. Finally, they had a direct interest in the labor supply problems of their contractors. Contracting officers representing the procurement

---

[3] 54 *Stat.* 885.

[4] From October 1940, through January 1943, the Selective Service System furnished men only to the Army, while the Navy secured all of its personnel through voluntary enlistment. After the termination of voluntary enlistment pursuant to Executive Order No. 9279, Dec. 5, 1942 (7 *Federal Register* 10177) the System furnished men to the Navy as well.

CHART 21. *Military Inductions through Selective Service.*

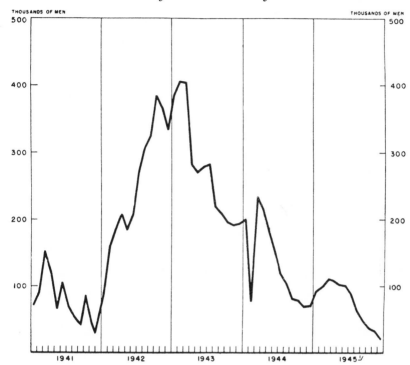

THOUSANDS OF MEN

THOUSANDS OF MEN

[1] Only 22,195 registrants were inducted during December 1945, because there were no inductions from December 21, 1945, to January 1, 1946.

Source: Selective Service System.

agencies in the plants, as well as staff specialists in labor supply,[5] provided advice and persuasion on manpower matters, particularly where labor shortages threatened to prevent the plant from meeting delivery schedules.

Primary responsibility for recruitment, selection, and training of industrial labor rested with the thousands of employers in war industry. Their steadily intensified competition for labor was indicated by a sharp increase in turn-over rates and especially in the number of voluntary quits.[6] Hiring away of other firm's workers was widely stigmatized as "labor piracy" and voluntary "antipirating agreements" were made by employers in many areas during 1940 and 1941,

---

[5] In the Army, these were field representatives of the Labor Branch of the Industrial Personnel Division of the Army Service Forces; in the Navy this work was centered in the Shore Establishments Civilian Personnel Division (transferred in February 1944 to the Office of Procurement and Material).

[6] The quit rate per hundred employees in manufacturing was 0.66 in January 1940; 1.31 in January 1941; 2.36 in January 1942; and 4.45 in January 1943—approximately a geometric rate of increase. Separations for other reasons remained substantially stable at about 2.7 throughout this period.

but these agreements tended to give way under the intense pressure of demand for labor.

As the pool of unemployed and readily available workers shrank, employers turned increasingly to the United States Employment Service for assistance. This Service, a Nation-wide system of public employment offices operated by the States under Federal grants-in-aid, had in June 1940, some 1,500 full-time and 3,100 part-time offices with more than 18,000 employees. Neither the number of offices nor the number of employees increased appreciably during the defense and war years. The placement work performed by the Service, however, increased greatly. Placements rose from about 4½ million in the fiscal year 1940 to more than 8 million in the fiscal year 1942. The Service also gave increased attention to developing advance estimates of labor demand and supplies in important industrial areas, and to improving its established procedures for meeting labor shortages in one area by recruiting workers from other areas.

The Employment Service remained throughout the war the most important civilian agency concerned with labor supply. The War Manpower Commission in its final form was basically a reconstituted employment service under new top management and with the addition of certain training functions transferred from other agencies. It is therefore important to point out certain disabilities with which the Employment Service entered the war period, and which were never entirely overcome.

First, the 48 State employment services which composed the system varied greatly in quality of personnel and facilities, repute in the community, and volume of placement activity. After the State services were brought under direct Federal control in December 1941 [7] efforts were made to strengthen some of the weaker ones by bringing in experienced personnel from other States. It was not feasible to go far in this direction, however, and the quality of the Service continued uneven. Moreover, since the loan of the State services to the Federal Government was expected to end with the war, many employment service officials continued to look for guidance to the State capitol rather than to Washington. This divided allegiance frequently interfered with national policies on such matters as free movement of labor across State lines, relations with organized labor,

---

[7] Before this time the Social Security Board, through its control of grants-in-aid, was able to prescribe minimum standards of fiscal and personnel administration for the State services. It also provided technical advice and assistance on operating problems, but had no direct control over operations. On Dec. 19, 1941, the President requested each of the Governors to lend the facilities of the State employment service to the Federal Government for the duration of the war. The Governors consented, though in a few cases somewhat reluctantly. The Director of the United States Employment Service in the Social Security Board thus acquired direct authority over the State employment service directors, which was exercised through representatives in the regional offices of the Board.

prevention of hiring discrimination against Negroes and aliens, and provision of uniform safeguards for workers under controlled hiring plans.

Second, the Employment Service had developed during a depression period in which its main activity was to register the unemployed and refer them to public works projects. Private employers made little use of the Service during the thirties and tended to regard it as a part of the relief system, and many workers had the same attitude. These community attitudes caused the Service to be held in rather low esteem by many Army, Navy, and Selective Service officials. Efforts by the Employment Service to make itself the focus of labor-supply activities were met by skepticism or even opposition from other Government agencies as well as from industry and labor. The operations of the Service provided considerable ground for such skepticism. Procedures developed to ration scarce jobs among a large number of unemployed registrants were not well adapted to a situation in which jobs exceeded workers. The process of desk interviewing, completing a detailed application, filing the application, then combing the file to fill each employer order was very time-consuming. As the pressure of placement work mounted, the Service did simplify its procedures and eliminate many unnecessary operations. The slowness with which this was done, however, provided some basis for criticism of the Service by other Government agencies.

Third, the Employment Service had a serious manpower problem of its own. From 1940 on there was a vast demand for persons skilled in interviewing, testing, hiring, occupational analysis, and other techniques of personnel management. Jobs could be had in private industry, the armed services, and other Federal agencies at salaries much above those paid by most of the States. Many of the most capable and energetic people in the Service left it during 1941 and 1942. While from a broad viewpoint some of this movement may have been in the national interest, it meant that the Service had a very large recruitment and training problem and was constantly being thrown off balance by the loss of key personnel.

Several other Federal agencies were engaged on a smaller scale in recruiting and placing workers. The Civil Service Commission recruited people for Government service and was responsible also for reviewing the appointment of persons recruited directly by Federal agencies. The Department of Agriculture, operating through county agents, county war boards, and the Farm Security Administration, played a large part in the recruitment of agricultural labor and after January 1943 had exclusive operating responsibility in this field. The Railroad Retirement Board maintained a system of employment offices for railroad workers, while responsibility for manning the merchant fleet rested first with the Maritime Commission and, after February 1942, with the War Shipping Administration.

Several agencies assisted employers in training workers and supervisors for new wartime tasks.   In June 1940 the United States Office of Education initiated a program of vocational education in occupations related to the defense program.[8]   Local vocational schools, using funds administered by the Office of Education, provided pre-employment courses for unemployed workers and young people, and supplementary training for workers already employed who wished to increase their skill.   In August 1940 the Training-Within-Industry Service was established under the NDAC.   Its objective was to provide a consulting service to disseminate the best industrial training experience throughout the country.   It would not do training itself, but would advise industry on training methods.   It early decided to restrict itself to advising on the training of supervisors, who would then be able to train production workers.   The Apprentice Training Service of the Department of Labor intensified its efforts to establish apprenticeship programs for the training of skilled workers.   The National Youth Administration, the Civilian Conservation Corps, and the Works Progress Administration endeavored to relate their training programs more closely to the needs of defense production.

During the life of the NDAC responsibility for maintaining general supervision over these labor supply activities rested with Mr. Sidney Hillman.   A few months after the Office of Production Management was created, the NDAC staff became the Labor Division of OPM and continued to function under Mr. Hillman's direction.   The Labor Division's charter of authority was a letter from the President to Mr. Hillman [9] instructing him "to undertake the full responsibility of getting the necessary workers into the industries claiming manpower shortages."   The main device used for this purpose was a National Labor Supply Committee on which all of the interested agencies except Selective Service were represented.   This was paralleled by 12 regional labor supply committees under the chairmanship of the regional representative of the Bureau of Employment Security of the Social Security Board.   The purpose of the national and regional committees was to pool information on labor supply problems, analyze the problems and decide on methods of meeting them, issue instructions to the various agencies, and check on the performance of the assigned tasks.[10]   Concretely this meant getting agreement be-

---

[8] This was financed by an initial appropriation of 15 million dollars in the Second Deficiency Appropriation Act 1940.   (54 *Stat.* 628).

[9] May 28, 1941.

[10] OPM Labor Division, Labor Supply Branch: *Circulars* No. 1, July 1, 1941; No. 2, July 9, 1941; and No. 3, July 9, 1941.

tween vocational schools and local Employment Service offices on selection of people for job training and their eventual placement in employment; getting agreement between the Civil Service Commission and the Employment Service on recruitment of workers for arsenals and Navy Yards; and securing interagency cooperation on dozens of other specific problems.

The actual influence of these committees fell below their objectives. Some increase in interagency cooperation on particular local problems was achieved, and a good deal of useful information was exchanged. But for the most part, each operating agency continued to work along lines which it had already charted. Meetings of the National Committee, which had been fairly frequent at first, had fallen to one per month by September 1941.

The lack of concrete accomplishment by the OPM Labor Division was due partly to administrative weaknesses. The Labor Supply Committee was too large and diversified in membership to be more than a debating society, and its members had vested interests in maintaining their respective agencies' control over their present labor supply functions. The Labor Division itself did not have a clear-cut administrative organization, labor supply activities being scattered among at least six separate branches of the Division. The principal operating agency, the United States Employment Service, was blanketed under the top-heavy administrative structure of the Federal Security Agency The complicated administrative relationships within FSA and between it and the Labor Division involved great delay and endless argument over proper channels of communication and lines of responsibility. Three of the most important agencies concerned with manpower problems—Selective Service, the War Department, and the Navy Department—were entirely beyond the Labor Division's sphere of influence. Within the civilian sphere, its authority over the all-important Federal Security Agency was very nominal. Federal Security, fortified by its technical knowledge and administrative control of employment service operations, was able to resist the intrusion into this field of people whom it regarded as amateurs.

Perhaps more important than organizational difficulties, however, was the fact that the problem which the Labor Division was supposed to deal with was still a year or more in the future. Labor was still in plentiful supply. The Division predicted that serious shortages might develop and urged that precautionary actions be taken. But with millions still unemployed and war not yet certain, these pleas made little impression on production and procurement officials preoccupied with shortages which were already visible.

During the fall of 1941 the Bureau of the Budget studied the problem of improving administrative organization in this field and presented several proposals to the OPM Labor Division and the Social Security Board. None of these proposals was acceptable to both agencies, however, and the only concrete development was the appointment on November 29, 1941, of a new full-time director of the E ployment Service, John Corson.

Creation of the War Manpower Commission

The outbreak of war had two immediate effects on labor-supply organization: first, steps already noted were taken to bring the state employment services under direct Federal operation; second, several groups proposed the creation of a new manpower agency by Executive order. Federal Security Administrator Paul V. McNutt raised the problem of manpower organization at a cabinet meeting early in December and the President appointed a cabinet committee of three to investigate manpower mobilization in its entirety. The cabinet committee report, largely prepared by the staff of the Social Security Board, was submitted by Mr. McNutt on December 31, 1941. This report proposed the creation of a Manpower Mobilization Board with policy-determining functions, but was rather vague concerning the extent to which this Board would have authority over existing agencies. On the same day the Director of the Budget informed the President that the Bureau of the Budget was interested in manpower administration, and was instructed to proceed with development of the Bureau's proposals.

There was a clear need to insure that the various labor-supply agencies were not duplicating the work of each other or operating at cross purposes, that, for example, the Civil Service Commission was not trying to place certain men in navy yards while the Employment Service was trying to place the same men in private shipyards or that men were not drafted by Selective Service who were performing key jobs in a war industry. But this objective did not provide any clear guidance in determining the necessary administrative organization. The main question which had to be decided was whether the new manpower agency should have direct responsibility for recruiting and placing workers or whether it should simply issue instructions to other agencies as the Labor Division of the Office of Production Management had attempted to do. Some persons believed that it would be necessary in the reasonably near future to impose compulsory labor-market controls on the British pattern and advocated a strong operating organization to which the Employment Service, the Selective Service System, and other labor-supply agencies would be transferred outright. Those who did not believe in the necessity or wisdom of compulsory controls proposed a manpower board with purely policy-forming functions, with operating responsibility continuing to rest chiefly in the Federal Security Agency.

After a month of discussion, a compromise plan was prepared by the Bureau of the Budget for submission to the President. Consolidation of existing agencies within the manpower agency was limited to the Selective Service System, the labor-supply functions of the Labor Division of WPB, and certain statistical functions of the Bureau of Labor Statistics. Other agencies were "to conform to such policies, directives, regulations, and standards as the Administrator may prescribe in the execution of the powers vested in him."

The plan was discussed with the President by Mr. McNutt and the Director of the Bureau of the Budget on February 7 and was approved in principle. It was not signed, however, possibly because the President wished to expose it to the criticism of the agencies and private groups on whom its successful operation would depend. In any event, the unsigned order speedily became a center of contention. The heads of agencies which were to lose functions opposed the transfer of any of their operations to the manpower agency. Mr. Hillman and Secretary Perkins, indeed, contended that there was no need for establishment of a new agency. The President's "labor cabinet" [11] which was consulted on the matter, drafted a proposal suggesting that manpower organization be placed within the Department of Labor subject to the direction of a policy board consisting of four representatives of labor, four of industry, and one each from the War Department, Navy Department and Selective Service. They also wished a number of labor standards and policies written into the Executive order.

The pull and tug of the twenty-some government agencies in the labor supply field, as well as the pressure from labor and management groups, grew with delay in signing the order. By the end of March the situation had grown so confused that the President appointed a group of four—Judge Samuel Rosenman, Justice William Douglas, Anna Rosenberg, and Harold Smith—to recommend a plan of manpower organization and nominate a candidate for manpower administrator. The Bureau of the Budget's original proposal of February 7 emerged from the deliberations of this group relatively intact. The authority of the proposed War Manpower Commission was strengthened by giving its chairman power to "issue such policy and operating directives as may be necessary." The chairman was empowered to act without the consent of the Commission, though he was required to consult it. On the other hand, the new agency was weakened by

---

[11] Composed of three AFL and three CIO representatives.

allowing Selective Service to retain its independent status. The United States Employment Service also remained in the Federal Security Agency. The labor supply functions of the Labor Division of the War Production Board were transferred to the Manpower Commission, while the training functions of the Division were transferred to the Federal Security Agency.

The order creating the War Manpower Commission under the chairmanship of Federal Security Administrator McNutt was signed by the President on April 18.[12] This order did not create an operating manpower organization. Such an organization was not wanted by the heads of existing agencies dealing with labor supply, nor did strong support for the idea appear from any other quarter. The President therefore proceeded to place a loose policy canopy over the operating agencies as a possible prelude to outright amalgamation at some later date.

The idea of a unified manpower administration, however, was by no means dead. It was revived within 2 or 3 months and made rapid headway during the fall of 1942. A series of Executive orders, culminating in Executive Order No. 9279, December 5, 1942, transformed the War Manpower Commission from a policy forum into an operating agency. For all practical purposes the history of the Commission dates from December 5 rather than from April 18.

Evolution of the War Manpower Commission, May–November, 1942

The new Commission inherited not only most of the WPB Labor Division's personnel and functions but also most of its basic difficulties. Shortages of labor were not yet serious in most parts of the country. While turn-over was rising, most employers continued to feel that they could meet their own labor-recruitment problems and to oppose any suggestion of Government control over hiring. This attitude was shared for the most part by labor leaders, procurement officials, and members of the Congress. While a somewhat vague demand for a manpower program was voiced occasionally in Congress and in the press, specific controls by which such a program might have been effectuated were opposed as an undemocratic interference with the right to work and to hire.

There remained also the difficulty of coordinating the activities of powerful operating agencies which had been busy for almost 2 years in building independent organizations and programs. WMC had virtually no voice in procurement policies which determined the size and location of the industrial labor demand or in decisions concerning the number and kinds of men to be withdrawn for military service.

---

[12] Executive Order No. 9139, Apr. 18, 1942, 7 *Federal Register* 2919.

The Selective Service System and the labor supply organizations of the War and Navy Departments remained largely autonomous. The inclusion in the WMC staff of many Federal Security officials by no means solved the problem of relationships with that agency. Instead, it precipitated a continuing controversy over whether the WMC should develop a large staff of its own or whether it should remain an appendage of the Federal Security Agency. It seemed self-evident to the FSA group that the Employment Service must become the central operating stem of any manpower agency, but this position was challenged by the newcomers from WPB and elsewhere. This controversy was partly responsible for the failure of WMC to develop a strong field organization during 1942; and without this the essentially local problem of labor supply could not be tackled effectively.

The situation was not helped by a complex organization structure which permitted the coexistence of three top officials—a deputy chairman, an executive director, and a director of operations—each of whom had his own sources of strength and each of whom had independent access to the chairman. This arrangement naturally produced frequent controversy over policy and organization, serious diffusion of authority and responsibility, much duplication of effort, and even issuance of conflicting statements and instructions.

These circumstances largely explain the ineffectiveness of the Commission during its first 7 months of existence. The various operating agencies continued to function along established lines; but their accomplishments were in no sense accomplishments of the WMC. The United States Employment Service, for example, took additional steps during this period to streamline its operations and give priority in service to war industries, steadily increased its volume of placements, further developed its techniques for expediting interstate movement of labor, attempted to stimulate the transference of draft registrants to war industries, and expanded its lists of essential activities and occupations. These developments, however, were a continuation of trends which had been under way since 1940.

Barred from effective action, the Commission turned to introspective discussion of its own organization and functions. Should it continue to function as a policy forum or should it endeavor to absorb the operating agencies and move into the field of action? If the latter course were chosen, should the Commission operate by persuasion and voluntary agreement or should Congress be asked to provide it with compulsory authority through a "national service act"? Much of the time of top WMC officials during the latter part of 1942 was spent in discussing these matters. Until they had been resolved both organizational and program development were bound to mark time.

The question of an operating versus a coordinating agency had been thoroughly discussed before the creation of WMC and had been resolved in favor of a coördinating body. This policy was approved at the time by both the Chairman of the Federal Security Agency and the Chairman of the Social Security Board, who were to become Chairman and Executive Director respectively of WMC. By August, however, these officials were of the opinion that the employment service and war training functions of the Federal Security Agency should be transferred outright to the Manpower Commission. This change of opinion was probably due in part to the difficulty which the Federal Security Agency had experienced in getting appropriations for the United States Employment Service.[13] Considerations of administrative convenience were also involved. It became increasingly clear that the Employment Service would necessarily be the main operating arm of WMC; possession of mere coordinating authority over the Service made it difficult to secure adjustments in methods and to introduce new personnel into the Service as rapidly as circumstances required.

On August 19, the Chairman of WMC transmitted to the President a proposed Executive order transferring to the War Manpower Commission all employment office and defense training functions vested in the Federal Security Agency. The President signed this order on September 17, after some alterations had been made. Agencies transferred outright to the WMC included the Employment Service, the National Youth Administration, the Apprenticeship Training Service, and the Training-Within-Industry Service.[14] The order also transferred supervisory authority over the Office from the Federal Security Administrator to the Chairman of the WMC; i. e., from Mr. McNutt in one capacity to Mr. McNutt in another capacity.

This order did not repair the most obvious deficiency in national manpower organization: the separation between the task of recruitment for the armed services and the task of meeting the manpower needs of industry and agriculture. Provision was indeed made at about this time for discussion of the planned over-all size of the

---

[13] The State unemployment compensation directors had long suspected the Social Security Board of intent to federalize both employment service and unemployment compensation operations, and were determined to prevent it from retaining control of the State employment services after the war. When the Board came to Congress for an appropriation for employment service operations during the fiscal year 1943, the State directors succeeded in writing into the bill a specific statement that the State Services must be returned after the war, and a further provision that the salaries of employment service workers could not be raised above the level prevailing for State employees in the respective States. Employment Service workers were thus materially worse off as a result of federalization. They were now subject to the 48-hour Federal workweek and a 5 percent retirement deduction, while their basic salaries remained unchanged. The Service continued to be an easy recruiting ground for more highly paid jobs in industry and in other Federal agencies. Between January and June 1942 some States lost more than a third of their personnel, including many key officials.

[14] Executive Order No. 9247, Sept. 17, 1942, 7 *Federal Register* 7379.

armed forces among the Chairman of the War Production Board, the Chairman of the War Manpower Commission, and the Joint Chiefs of Staff, with differences of opinion to be resolved by decision of the President. The War and Navy Departments were planning at this time to attain a peak strength of 10.8 million men. After WMC and WPB officials had expressed doubt that the civilian labor force remaining would be adequate to equip and supply armed forces of this size, the President issued his instructions for consultation on the matter. The Chiefs of Staff did not recede from their objective of 10.8 million and their plans were approved by the President. There remained, however, the problem of selecting the number of men allotted to the Services in such a way as to cause minimum disruption of essential production. Over this vital matter, WMC had no control and little influence. The most essential civilian worker could volunteer for military service at his own discretion. The service departments, and particularly the Navy, opposed any restrictions on voluntary enlistment. Selective Service deferment policy was not subject to WMC control—indeed the actions of local Selective Service boards were not effectively controlled even from the national headquarters of the system. Moreover, the Selective Service System was in competition with WMC for the position of over-all manpower agency. There was considerable sentiment in Congress and in the press for vesting manpower controls in Selective Service rather than WMC if and when compulsory controls were adopted.[15]

During August and early September these problems were discussed intensively by the Management-Labor Policy Committee of WMC,[16] which had by this time supplanted the Commission itself as the main forum for policy discussions. At the same time, the Committee was clarifying its position on the explosive issue of national service legislation. Since its actions on these two matters were closely linked, it is necessary to review briefly the background of the national service controversy before carrying forward the story of topside manpower policy.

Discussion of the possible need for a national service act had been under way within WMC since June. The idea had strong support

---

[15] For example, S.2805, introduced by Senator Austin on Sept. 25, 1942. This bill would have empowered local Selective Service boards to assign to production work any man between the ages of 18 and 65, subject, to the established appeals machinery of the Selective Service System. Several other bills to the same general effect were introduced in the House and Senate during 1942 and 1943.

[16] This Committee, appointed by the Chairman in June 1942, consisted of four management and four labor members presided over by the Deputy Chairman of WMC. The Committee contained several very able individuals, and its members were both closer to and more directly concerned with matters of labor supply than the Commission members. Thus while it had been originally conceived as a purely consultative body, it soon proceeded on its own motion to discuss in detail all important actions proposed by the WMC staff and also to propound manpower programs of its own.

both within WMC and in the War and Navy Departments, though there were wide differences of opinion on the details of the legislation. War and Navy officials tended to favor an act similar to the Selective Service Act, which would require registration of all persons within certain age-groups and their assignment to essential work through the local Selective Service boards. The bulk of opinion within WMC favored an act similar to the British national service act, which would impose obligations on employers as well as workers and would use the Employment Service as the central administrative agency.

In August the Chairman of WMC transmitted recommendations on this subject to the President and was instructed to develop the proposals further in consultation with the Management-Labor Committee. Mr. McNutt then convened the Committee and requested its advice. Discussion soon revealed that both the labor and management members of the Committee were strongly opposed to national service legislation, and this opposition remained unshaken through weeks of subsequent discussion. As an alternative to legislation, the Committee recommended a program which included termination of voluntary enlistments, centralization of military and civilian labor supply functions in a single agency, and formulation of a program for allocating scarce labor supplies on a voluntary basis.

The President had taken no public position on national service legislation and as late as October 30 told his press conference that no decision had been reached and that studies of the whole situation were continuing. It had become clear, however, that Congress was disinclined to vest compulsory powers in the War Manpower Commission. The opposition of management and labor groups to such proposals had also become increasingly clear. Reports of the WMC Management-Labor Committee's attitude had appeared in the press. On October 30, President Green, of the AFL; President Murray, of the CIO; and Julius Luhrsen, of the Railway Labor Executives Association, took a strong position in opposition to national service. This view was expressed to the President at about the same time in meetings of his "labor cabinet" and discussions with individual labor leaders. Early in November the President informed Chairman McNutt that he had decided not to push for national service legislation.

Mr. McNutt had been the chief public proponent of such legislation. In August, without waiting for the Management-Labor Committee's report on the subject, he had stated publicly his belief that some type of national service system was inevitable. He repeated this view in numerous speeches and public statements during September and October, though he expressed opposition to a bill introduced by Senator Austin which would have entrusted administration of national service to the Selective Service System (testimony before the Senate Military Affairs Committee on S. 2805, Oct. 21, 1942). Mr. McNutt appears to have been influenced in this direction by members of his staff who favored national service legislation, and the President seems also to have encouraged him to test public opinion on the subject.

With the national service issue out of the way, the President turned to consideration of proposed executive orders on manpower. The order finally issued on December 5 [17] was based on a draft prepared by WMC officials. Among other things it (*a*) provided for transfer of the Selective Service System to WMC; (*b*) required the appointment of a Management-Labor Policy Committee of 16 representatives of industrial management, labor, and agriculture, and directed the Chairman to consult with this Committee before taking any action; [18] (*c*) provided for termination of voluntary enlistment; (*d*) gave WMC control over policies for military training programs carried on in nonmilitary educational institutions; (*e*) gave WMC authority to regulate all hiring and recruitment of workers in any area designated as critical by the Chairman; (*f*) required all departments and agencies of the Government to take such action as the Chairman, after consultation with the agency in question, might determine to be necessary to promote compliance with WMC regulations. This last provision was weakened, however, by a qualifying clause—"subject to appeal to the President or to such agent or agency as the President may designate."

This order established the War Manpower Commission as an operating agency with a clear mandate to regulate the hiring of labor for civilian work through the Employment Service and to control the recruitment of military manpower through the Selective Service System. It set the stage for more rapid development of field organization and for a complete reorganization of WMC headquarters during December 1942. The order also committed the Administration definitely to a program of mobilizing civilian manpower by voluntary methods rather than through the applications of punitive sanctions authorized by national service legislation. The issue was not, however, finally resolved at this time. It was to recur several times during the next 3 years, and proposals for national service were not finally abandoned until April 1945.

---

[17] Executive Order No. 9279, Dec. 5, 1942, 7 *Federal Register* 10177.

[18] The first Executive order made no mention of such a committee. The existing committee was appointed by the chairman on his own motion in June 1942. As a matter of practice, the committee had been consulted on all important actions since that date; and had itself taken the initiative on more than one occasion. During the controversy over national service legislation, however, the committee was told at one point that it had no legal standing and that consultation with it was merely a matter of courtesy on the part of the chairman. The labor members were particularly piqued by this and demanded that the chairman write the committee into the new Executive order, which he agreed to do.

Adjustment of Industrial Disputes

More insistent than the problem of labor supply was the problem of preventing strikes and lockouts which would interfere with defense production. Industrial disputes, which usually increase during periods of rising industrial activity, grew in number during the first winter of the defense program (chart 22). To reinforce the work of existing Federal agencies in this field, the President on March 19, 1941, appointed a National Defense Mediation Board [19] consisting of

CHART 22. *Worker Idleness Due to Strikes.*

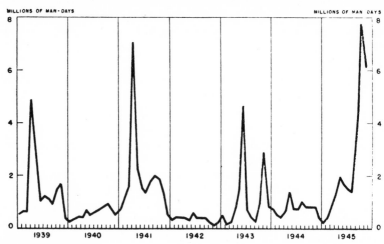

MILLIONS OF MAN-DAYS   MILLIONS OF MAN DAYS

Source: Department of Labor.

four management, four labor, and three public members. The Board was authorized to further the settlement of disputes by collective bargaining between the parties; if this failed, it might suggest voluntary arbitration; if both methods failed, it was to prepare findings of fact and recommendations, which could be made public. Disputes were to reach the Board only through certification by the Secretary of Labor after the United States Conciliation Service had been unable to settle them.

During its 10 months of life the Board received 118 cases, of which 96 had been adjusted when it ceased operation. The remainder were transferred to its successor, the National War Labor Board. Under the guidance of Chairman W. H. Davis, a vigorous advocate of mediation and voluntary collective bargaining, the Board attempted to work out in each case a solution agreeable to the parties. A substantial majority of the cases was disposed of by agreement of the parties

[19] Executive Order No. 8716, Mar. 19, 1941, 6 *Federal Register* 1532–33.

either before or during Board hearings, and formal recommendations were made in only 30 cases. A formal recommendation by the Board was usually complied with forthwith, though in a few cases a special appeal by the Chairman or a prominent labor member of the Board was necessary to secure labor's acceptance of Board decisions. In only three cases was intervention by the President necessary to secure compliance.[20]

The Mediation Board became inoperative early in November 1941 after the resignation of its two CIO members following a Board decision in the "captive" coal mine cases, involving the United Mine Workers of America and several leading steel companies operating coal mines in the Southern Appalachian area.[21] The Mine Workers had demanded that the steel companies sign the standard "Appalachian Agreement" already concluded with other employers in the area and which contained a union shop clause. The companies had refused to agree to the union shop. Although more than 95 percent of the workers in the "captive" mines were already union members, both parties persisted in their position and the case was certified to the Board. After hearings before a Board panel and later before the full Board, punctuated by two strikes in the mines, the Board finally decided not to recommend the union shop on the ground that it was not essential to protect the security of the union.[22] The Board's decision was supported by the President in a conference with union and steel industry officials on November 14, in which he said among other things: "I tell you frankly that the Government of the United States will not order, nor will Congress pass legislation ordering, a so-called closed shop."[23] The CIO, with which the United Mine Workers was affiliated at that time, denounced the decision in strong terms. The two CIO members of the Board, who had dissented from the November 10 decision, submitted their resignations and thereby made effective functioning of the Board impossible. While cases

---

[20] In the *North American Aviation* case, the union called a strike during mediation in violation of an agreement with the Board. In the *Federal Shipbuilding* case, the employer refused to accept a recommendation for inclusion of a maintenance of membership clause in the contract. In the *Air Associates* case, the employer refused to accept a recommendation that striking employees be returned to work without discrimination. The President by Executive order directed the Navy to take possession of the Federal Shipbuilding yards, while the other two plants were placed under Army control.

[21] Case No. 20 B. Hearings, Sept. 17-19, 24-25, Oct. 7-9, Oct. 31-Nov. 10. Final recommendations of the Board issued Nov. 10. Strikes Sept. 15-22, Oct. 27-Nov. 3, Nov. 17-24, 1941.

[22] Department of Labor. Bureau of Labor Statistics. Bulletin No. 714, *Report on the Work of the National Defense Mediation Board, Mar. 19, 1941–Jan. 12, 1942*. Opinion of Chairman W. H. Davis, in National Defense Mediation Board Case No. 20 B, Nov. 10, 1941, pp. 122-126.

[23] The text of the President's statement appears in Bureau of Labor Statistics Bulletin No. 714, *Report on the Work of the National Defense Mediation Board, Mar. 19, 1941–Jan. 12, 1942*. This report also contains the other documents pertinent to this case. After another strike in protest against the Board's deicision, the union on Nov. 22, accepted the President's proposal that a three-man arbitration board be appointed to adjudicate the dispute. This board, consisting of John Steelman, John L. Lewis, and Benjamin Fairless, on Dec. 7 issued a 2 to 1 decision in favor of a union-shop clause.

continued to be certified and the Board continued to exist, it remained inactive pending clarification of its status.

The outbreak of war made it imperative to revive the Board or to find some alternative method of preventing strikes. Congressional interest in strike prevention, which had been aroused by the coal mine dispute, grew still stronger after Pearl Harbor, and it appeared likely that drastic antistrike legislation would be passed unless immediate action was taken by the Executive Branch.[24] On December 14, the President invited 12 employers and 12 union officials to attend a conference on wartime labor relations, which was to convene in Washington on December 17.[25] Chairman Davis of the National Defense Mediation Board was named moderator of the conference and Senator Elbert Thomas, chairman of the Senate Committee on Education and Labor, was made associate moderator.

The object of the conference was to secure from the labor and management representatives an agreement that they would not resort to strikes or lock-outs during the war and that they would submit unsettled disputes to a Government agency. It quickly developed that there was general agreement on these objectives. The conference bogged down, however, on the union-shop issue which had wrecked the NDMB. Labor representatives insisted that extension of the union shop be recognized as a legitimate union objective in wartime, and that the proposed war labor board have authority to adjudicate union-shop demands; their hope was that the Board would grant such demands or at least go some distance in this direction. The employers insisted just as strongly that the union shop should not be made a subject of Government arbitration. They also proposed at first that open- and closed-shop arrangements be frozen for the duration of the war, which was the policy followed in World War I. They later modified their proposal, however, to provide that existing union-shop contracts were not to be disturbed and that new union-shop contracts might be arrived at by voluntary negotiations between unions and employers.

This deadlock presented the President with a difficult problem. A new Board could not be created without deciding, at least by implication, whether its jurisdiction was to include disputes over the union shop. Yet to decide either way on this issue might alienate one of the

---

[24] On Dec. 3, the House by a vote of 252 to 136 passed H. R. 6066, introduced by Representative Smith of Virginia. This bill provided for a 60-day notice for the calling of a strike, a secret strike ballot under Government supervision and calling of a strike only after a majority vote, freezing of open and closed-shop arrangements for the duration, severe restrictions on picketing, prohibition of jurisdictional and sympathy strikes and of all boycotts, registration and filing of financial reports by all unions, and numerous other controls over union activities. The bill went to the Senate Committee on Education and Labor, which had this and several similar measures under consideration at the time of Pearl Harbor.

[25] Six of the labor officials were nominated by the AFL and six by the CIO. The employers were chosen in consultation with the chairman of the Advisory Council of the Department of Commerce.

groups on whom successful operation of tripartite Board would depend. Moreover, if the new Board was to arbitrate union-shop disputes, it might speedily founder on this issue as its predecessor had done.

When Mr. Davis advised the President on December 22 that an impassé had been reached, the President instructed him to reconvene the conference at 2 p. m. the following day. During the morning of December 23 the President met with Mr. Davis and Senator Thomas. When the conference met at 2 o'clock, Mr. Davis read to it a letter from the President accepting their "general points of agreement" that there should be no strikes or lock-outs and that a War Labor Board should be created to handle industrial disputes. While there was no direct mention of the union-shop issue, the letter clearly implied that no subject of dispute should be excluded from consideration by the Board. It was thus in effect a decision for the labor position. The employer members of the conference issued a public statement in which, while accepting the decision to create a War Labor Board, they reiterated their view that it should not accept union-shop disputes and reserved the right to argue this point before the Board.

The Executive order creating the National War Labor Board was drafted in the Bureau of the Budget in consultation with Mr. Davis, Mr. Hillman, Secretary Perkins, and others. The chief question which arose was whether any general principles should be laid down to guide the Board in deciding disputed issues—for example, wage demands—or whether the Board should be left entirely free to develop its own criteria. Mr. Davis, a firm believer in the common-law approach, argued for the latter course and in the end this view prevailed. As finally issued on January 12, the order provided merely that "the Board shall finally determine the dispute, and for this purpose may use mediation, voluntary arbitration, or arbitration under rules established by the Board." [26]

In imposing what amounted to compulsory arbitration the order went beyond anything contemplated by the members of the December conference. Both the industry and labor proposals at that conference envisaged a body similar to the National Defense Mediation Board which, in the event of continued disagreement between labor and management, would have authority merely to make public its findings and recommendations. Under the Executive order, however, the War Labor Board was made final arbitrator of all disputes and the

---

[26] Executive Order No. 9017, Jan. 12, 1942, 7 *Federal Register* 237. The Board was to consist of four industry, four labor, and four public members. The Board was authorized to take jurisdiction of a dispute after a certification by the Secretary of Labor that the Conciliation Service had been unable to settle it or, after consultation with the Secretary, the Board might take jurisdiction on its own motion. All employees, records, and funds of the National Defense Mediation Board were transferred to the NWLB, and W. H. Davis, who was chairman of the NDMB for the last 6 months of its life, became chairman of the NWLB.

full force of the President's war powers was placed behind its decisions.
Decisions of the Board could be enforced, and were subsequently enforced in several important cases, through seizure of plants and their
operation by the War Department, the Navy Department, or some
other Government agency. The Board thus became a regulatory
rather than a mediatory body, with authority over wages, hours,
conditions, and all the other terms of union agreements. Suspension
of strikes meant virtual suspension of collective bargaining for the
duration of the war and the substitution of Government decisions
for the results of union-employer negotiation. The public members
of the Board were faced inescapably with the problem of how far they
should compel employers to grant demands which the unions would
normally at a time of high employment have been able to win by
striking, but which they could not longer win in this way because of
the no-strike pledge.

The most insistent union demands confronting the Board were for
wage increases and the union shop. The reiteration of the same demands and arguments gradually convinced the public members that
strictly case-by-case approach was impossible and that guiding principles must be developed on these issues. The basic policies of the
Board with respect to wages and union status were hammered out
during the first 8 or 9 months of its operation and were not greatly
changed in later years. Feeling ran high on both issues, and either
could have wrecked the Board by bringing about the resignation of
the industry or labor members. Only the insight and skill of the
public members, and particularly of Chairman Davis, made possible
the development of compromises which won acquiescence if not full
agreement.

The issue of union status was not new to the public members,
several of whom had been members of the National Defense Mediation
Board. Even had the public members wished to grant labor's
demands for a union shop, they were precluded from doing so by the
intense opposition of industry to this provision and by the President's
statement of November 14 that the Government would not compel
workers to join a union. On the other hand, they felt that at a time
when Government was preventing the unions from winning their
demands by direct action, the unions deserved some protection against
possible employer attacks and membership dissatisfaction.

After a few months of experimentation, the Board hit on a compromise which gave some measure of union security without going as far
as a union shop. This was the "maintenance of membership clause,"
which had appeared in a few union agreements before 1940 and had
been recommended by the National Defense Mediation Board in a
number of cases. It did not require nonmembers of the union to join,

but did require people already in the union to remain in it for the duration of the union contract as a condition of employment. As a result of criticism by industry members of the Board, the clause was shortly amended to include an "escape period." This permitted any union member to resign from the union within a stated period— usually 15 days—after a Board decision ordering maintenance of membership. The industry members regularly dissented from all Board orders on this subject, but their dissent was considerably less vehement after the escape provision was added.

With a few outstanding exceptions, the employers appearing before the Board accepted and complied with Board policy on this matter, though the great majority were in hearty disagreement with it. On several occasions leading industrialists endeavored to persuade the President to bring about a change in the Board's policy. The President declined, however, to override the judgment of the public members. By the fall of 1942 the crisis had been passed and Board policy on this issue had settled into a form which remained virtually unaltered for the remainder of the war.[27]

In the field of union security the Board was free to work out its own compromises. Regarding wages, however, it was obliged to work within the confines of the national price stabilization policy. Moreover, because of continued increases in the cost of living, the Board remained throughout the war under almost continuous labor pressure to permit increases in wage rates. In spite of recurring wage crises, however, and in spite of numerous concessions to the labor viewpoint, the basic principles of wage adjustment worked out during the summer and fall of 1942 remained as the general framework of Board policy until the end.

The National Defense Mediation Board had no wage policy. Committed to settling disputes through voluntary agreement of the parties wherever possible, it looked with favor on any wage schedule which the parties could be brought to accept. Indeed, throughout 1941 the Office of Price Administration was much more interested in stabilization of wages than NDMB. Mr. Henderson, however, opposed suggestions advanced by Mr. Baruch and others during the summer of 1941 that OPA be given wage-control functions and urged the President to handle this problem through existing labor agencies or a special Board. The President's message to Congress on price control delivered July 30, 1941, implied that this approach would be followed

---

[27] It should be understood that maintenance of membership was ordered only where an open shop had previously prevailed and the union was demanding a union shop. Where a union shop had previously been in effect, the Board would not order any weakening of the union shop in a new contract. So numerous were Board orders on maintenance of membership, however, that a survey of union agreements in the summer of 1945 indicated that maintenance of membership clauses, almost unknown before the war, were actually more frequent than union-shop clauses.

and did not recommend that wage control be included in the proposed legislation. An amendment to the price control bill introduced by Representative Gore which would have frozen wages along with prices and rents was defeated in the House. As finally enacted on January 30, 1942, the bill contained only one vague reference, inserted in the Senate, to the subject of wages:

> It shall be the policy of those departments and agencies of the Government dealing with wages . . . within the limits of their authority and jurisdiction, to work toward a stabilization of prices, fair and equitable wages, and cost of production.

The War Labor Board thus entered on its work without any clear instructions on wage policy from Congress or the President. Frequent discussions of this subject by the Board during February and March revealed much disagreement and uncertainty. The industry members favored immediate establishment of a general wage policy directed toward stabilizing wage rates at the level of January 1, 1942, with exceptions only to correct substantial wage disparities in an industry or to relieve actual hardship. The labor members, sensing that any general wage policy would tend in the direction of a wage "freeze," opposed establishment of a general policy and argued for continuation of the case-by-case approach used by the NDMB. Mr. Henderson on several occasions urged the Board to adopt a firm wage control policy in order to make price control effective. Since OPA had not yet established any direct control over the cost of living, and since the Board had no instructions on wages from the President, the public members did not feel able to override labor's objections to wage control. The Board therefore continued for several months longer to operate on a case-by-case basis, and the general level of wages continued to rise at an accelerating rate.

The strategic position of the public members was improved by the President's seven point anti-inflation program submitted to Congress on April 27, 1942, and by the almost simultaneous announcement by OPA of a general maximum price regulation designed to freeze retail prices at March 1942 levels. The public members were now able to argue convincingly that, if retail prices were effectively stabilized, wage increases would no longer be necessary to protect the workers' standard of living, and also that unless wage increases were controlled the price stabilization program could not succeed. They had also the support of a statement by the President in the anti-inflation message that "we must stabilize the remuneration received by individuals for their work. . . . I believe that stabilizing the cost of living will mean that wages in general can and should be kept at existing scales."

During May and June there was intensive discussion of how to apply the intent of the President's program to specific wage disputes before the Board. In these discussions were developed the criteria which the Board was later to use in passing on wage increases and which were eventually formalized in Executive orders.

There emerged, first, the notion of a "standard wage", i. e., a wage which was fair and equitable as of some base date. The base date eventually chosen was January 1, 1941, which marked the end of a period of relative stability in wage rates and living costs. But between January 1, 1941, and May 1, 1942, the cost of living index had risen by almost 15 percent. Were workers receiving a "standard wage" on January 1, 1941, thereby entitled to a wage increase of 15

CHART 23. *Straight-time Wage Rates Paid in Manufacturing Industries*

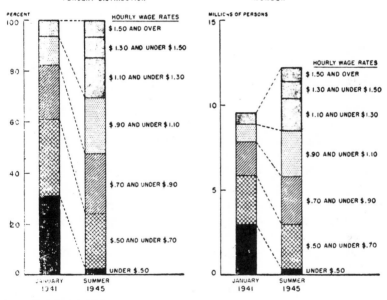

Source: Department of Labor.

percent in order to keep pace with the cost of living? The Office of Price Administration argued strongly in the negative, on the ground that the real living standards of all economic groups—including workers—were bound to fall during wartime and that any effort to prevent such a fall would be inflationary. In early discussions of the matter in the Board, Chairman Davis seemed also to be of the opinion that cost of living increases should not be fully offset. But in the precedent-making Little Steel cases decided July 16, 1942, the Board used the full 15 percent in computing the wage increase which should be allowed the steelworkers. The explanation offered in the Board's opinion was that most workers had already received increases of 15 percent or more and that it would be inequitable not to allow as much to the steelworkers.

This decision was rapidly generalized into the so-called Little Steel formula, under which any group of workers whose straight-time hourly earnings had increased by less than 15 percent since January 1, 1941, was entitled to increases sufficient to bring them up to this level. Nothing was said at this time as to whether the wage formula would be adjusted upward if the cost of living continued to rise. The opinion in the Little Steel case, however, and other statements of the public members implied that it would not be altered. In spite of intense labor pressure on several occasions, the Little Steel formula did remain unchanged and constituted the cardinal point of WLB wage policy until the end of the war.

The story of wage stabilization from early 1943 until the end of the war is essentially the story of how the public members of the Board, the directors of OES and OWMR, and the President himself, conducted an elastic defense of the Little Steel formula. Onslaughts on the formula were countered by (1) intensified efforts to stabilize or reduce the cost of living. The extension of dollar-and-cents price ceilings and the attempted roll-back of food prices in April-May 1943 were directly related to AFL and CIO demands for abandonment of the Little Steel formula. After the National War Labor Board had formally voted down such a demand on March 22, the President's "labor cabinet" met with him on April 1 and told him they were not renewing their request for wage increases but were asking instead for reductions in food prices to the level of September 15, 1942. Immediately following this conference, the OPA programs just mentioned were inaugurated. (2) Increasing workers' take-home pay without increasing basic wage rates through fairly generous grants of incentive wage systems, night-shift differentials, paid holidays, vacations with pay, and other "fringe" wage demands. Members of the Administration whose primary concern was with price stabilization tended to feel that the Board went too far in this direction and attempted to limit its discretion. The public members of the Board felt that they had to go some distance to maintain labor support of the Board, and insisted that they be given considerable latitude. On the whole, the public members were fairly successful in walking a tightrope between OPA and OES on one side and the labor organizations on the other; and labor discontent was held within limits without disrupting price ceilings. (3) Liberalizing other parts of the Board's wage policy such as the policy toward substandard wage rates. Such changes permitted large groups of workers to obtain general wage increases without any alteration of the Little Steel formula.

Two other grounds on which wage increases might be justified were worked out during this formative period. Even though a group of workers had received a 15 percent increase since January 1941, they might receive a further increase if their wage rates were "substandard," i. e., inadequate to support a minimum level of decent living. This was accepted by the public members from the beginning as a valid basis for wage increases. The first major application of the principle was in the granting of a general increase of 7½ cents per hour to the

CHART 24. *Earnings in Manufacturing Industries.*

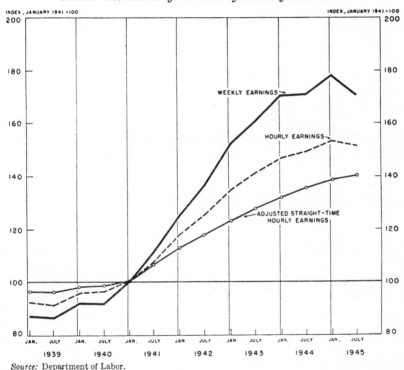

Source: Department of Labor.

cotton textile workers. It was also laid down at an early point that wage increases might be necessary to correct "inequalities" or "inequities", i. e., wage rates seriously out of line with rates paid by other plants for similar work, or rates for one job in a plant which were out of line with other rates in the same plant. This principle, however, remained rather unclear for some time. It was not at all certain in the summer of 1942, for example, whether it was inequities within an industry or an area which were to be eliminated, nor was it clear how much levelling-up of rates was required to eliminate an inequity.

A fourth basis for wage increases—to induce workers to move to or remain on critical war jobs—was early urged on the Board by WMC,

WPB, and the procurement agencies. The Board adopted an increasingly cautious attitude toward such proposals as their potentialities became apparent. Policy on this subject was clarified relatively late—October and November 1942—and included two points: first, as a general rule the Board would not adjust wage rates to influence the flow of labor; second, it would consider action in critical situations provided the War Manpower Commission had taken all actions within its power and provided it could be shown that wage adjustments would actually increase labor supplies in the plant in question. These limitations were imposed to prevent WMC from relying on manipulation of wage rates to solve labor shortages instead of undertaking direct regulation of the movement of labor.[28] The Board was able to maintain this position in part because wage rates in munitions industries had risen considerably more than wages in other industries before wage stabilization was undertaken, and wage differentials were favorable to a flow of labor into war industries.

The President's message of April 27 had called for stabilization of all wage rates. The War Labor Board had jurisdiction, however, only over wage rates coming before it in dispute cases. Neither it nor any other agency had authority to control wage increases made voluntarily by employers. This problem was discussed repeatedly at interagency meetings during the summer of 1942, but no action was taken until the President on September 7 asked Congress to amend the Price Control Act so as to permit tighter control of farm prices and of wage regulation. The history of this message, of the amended act passed by Congress on October 2, and of the stabilization order issued by the President on October 3 is outlined in Chapter 9. In order to round out the story of wage control, it is necessary merely to recall that the Executive order gave the War Labor Board jurisdiction over all wage rates and not merely those involved in labor disputes, and that it forbade wage increases above the level of September 15, 1942, without the approval of the Board. The Board was directed to approve increases only when "necessary to correct maladjustments or inequalities," i. e., maladjustments relative to the cost of living, covered by the Little Steel formula; "to eliminate substandards of living"; "to correct gross inequities," i. e., unreasonable inequalities of wage rates between plants or within plants; or "to aid in the effective prosecution of the war" by facilitating the flow of manpower in desired directions. The exceptions written into the order thus corresponded with the four grounds for wage increases which the Board had de-

---

[28] The first important action taken on this ground was the granting on Oct. 16 of a $1-a-day increase to nonferrous metal miners in the mountain States, where critical shortages of miners existed. This action was taken, however, only after the War Manpower Commission had issued an order "freezing" nonferrous metal workers in their jobs. It was in connection with this case that the Board enunciated its policy of acting on manpower problems only in support of action taken by the agencies directly concerned.

veloped in previous months. On November 6, the Board, in outlining its detailed procedures for wage regulation, took occasion to restate and elaborate these four principles.[29] They were to remain central to Board policy for the next 3 years, and argument was to center mainly about detailed modification and reinterpretation of them.

The order of October 3, which greatly increased the Board's workload, forced it to lighten its burden by a sweeping program of decentralization. During the next few months 10 regional Boards were established and given initial jurisdiction over voluntary applications for wage increases and also over dispute cases except those of national importance which the national Board might take on its own motion. Authority over particular industries was delegated to panels or commissions in the building construction, shipbuilding, trucking, and west-coast lumber industries. Industries placed under a commission were thereby removed from the jurisdiction of the regional boards, which operated on a territorial basis; discussion of the relative emphasis which should be placed on industrial and territorial units continued throughout the life of the Board, with the tendency being to create more and more industry units. Finally, the Board delegated to the War Department, the Navy Department, and a long list of other Government agencies authority over the wage rates of their own employees.[30]

In general, it can be said that the Board moved faster and farther in the direction of decentralization than most of the other war agencies. Decision on the less important disputes and wage applications was brought closer to the parties, and the time of the national Board was freed for consideration of major issues. This was true not only as regards delegation of authority to the field, but also as regards the Washington organization itself. Over the course of time appeals from regional board and industry commission decisions came to be heard by a tripartite appeals committee, whose recommendations were almost invariably accepted by the Board; authority for many wage decisions was delegated to the Chief of the Wage Stabilization Division and finally a group of alternate Board members was created to handle most of the routine work-flow. The time of the "Big Board" was thus freed to an unusual extent for extended discussion of major policy issues. The price of these gains was considerable variation in the application of Board policy—particularly wage policy—from one

---

[29] NWLB Press Release B-284, Nov. 6, 1942.

[30] The main steps by which this decentralization program was accomplished are described in the following NWLB orders and releases: General Orders 14 (7 *Federal Register* 9860), 17 (7 *Federal Register* 10204), 18 (7 *Federal Register* 10204), 19 (7 *Federal Register* 10518), 20 (7 *Federal Register* 10519), 21 (7 *Federal Register* 10519) 24 (7 *Federal Register* 11109), 25 (7 *Federal Register* 11109), and 13-A (7 *Federal Register* 10770); also Press Releases B-273, B-309, B-312, B-350, B-357, B-360, B-380, B-394, B-396, and B-423.

industry or region to the next, and a rather lengthy appeal procedure from local panel to regional board to national appeals committee to national Board, with occasional ricochetting of cases back and forth between these levels.

By the end of 1942, then, the Board had surmounted the initial crises over union security and wage policy, won substantial acceptance from labor and management, worked out a modus vivendi with other Government agencies in bordering fields, received an extension of its jurisdiction to cover all wage rates, developed the broad outlines of its wage strategy, and shaken down its administrative organization into semifinal form. The only subsequent events requiring consideration in this history were the occasional crises in wage policy alluded to above.

CHAPTER

8

Informing the Public

TWO DAYS after Pearl Harbor, President Roosevelt in a press conference outlined the policy of the Government in issuing war news. News to be released must be true, but also it must not give aid and comfort to the enemy. He added that the decision to release or not to release war news was up to the heads of the War and Navy Departments. On the same day in a radio address to the American people, he said in part:

We are now in this war. We are all in it all the way. Every single man, woman, and child is a partner in the most tremendous undertaking of our American history. We must share together the bad news and the good news, the defeats and the victories—the changing fortunes of war.

. . . This Government will put its trust in the stamina of the American people, and will give the facts to the public as soon as two conditions have been fulfilled: First, that the information has been definitely and officially confirmed; and, second, that the release of the information at the time it is received will not prove valuable to the enemy directly or indirectly.

To carry out these policies the Government had to set up machinery for safeguarding information and to expand greatly the facilities available for the dissemination of information both at home and abroad. On the domestic front it was the job of the information agencies to help keep 130 million Americans working full speed to get the war work done, whether this involved carrying a rifle, piloting a plane, producing food, working in a factory, or sitting at a desk. Abroad, it was the job of these agencies to help keep the United Nations working together with maximum effort toward common goals, and to convince the world that in the long run the United Nations could not be beaten, and that a fair peace could be realized only with a United Nations' victory.

On all of these topics the Government had to provide as much information as possible, consistent with military safety, to maintain
the highest degree of truth and at the same time to be persuasive, to
provide information at the right time, to distribute this information
on the broadest possible scale, and through as many communication
channels as possible, and to counteract enemy propaganda at home and
abroad.

The German, Italian, and Japanese Governments attempted to sow
seeds of disunion among the Allies.   Axis short-wave radios sought to
create distrust between England and the United States, to portray
the Nazi attack upon Russia as a crusade against communism and to
spread the view in this country, as well as in Asia, that both Britain
and America were engaged in a racial war against the colored peoples
of the earth.   Soon after Pearl Harbor, a Nazi broadcaster to America
shouted: "British naval circles are finding encouragement in the defeat
suffered by the United States."[1]   German broadcasts charged that
landing of American troops in North Ireland in January 1942 was
timed "to coincide with Roosevelt's gradual absorption of Australia
and Canada," that "American foreign policy is dictated from Down-
ing Street rather than from Washington, and will leave America holding the bag," and that "the British Empire is dissolving like a lump
of sugar into Roosevelt's teacup".   Special efforts were also made to
disrupt Western Hemisphere amity by accusing the United States of
imperialist aims in Latin America.

The Axis propagandists found fertile soil for some of their disruptive activities in the pessimism, intolerance, and apathy of certain
elements of the American people.   Surveys of the press and samples
of current public opinion show that signs of frustration and dissension became apparent in certain sections all too soon after Pearl
Harbor.   While the majority recognized the seriousness of the war,
were determined to win it, and approached post-war problems with
a high measure of idealism, certain elements sought to limit American
participation in the war to the protection of American territory,
portrayed the British as craven, incompetent, and responsible for
American involvement in the conflict, pictured Russia as a menace
to Western civilization, and sought to undermine public confidence
in the good faith of the United States Government.

Confidential Government surveys showed that the United States
faced such information problems as the following: an insufficient
recognition in some quarters of the need for waging offensive rather
than defensive warfare; a tendency to underestimate the enemy and
the magnitude of the war job; considerable distrust of the British
and Russians and some lack of faith in their future cooperation;

---

[1] Federal Communications Commission Monitoring Digest, Dec. 15, 1941 (mimeo).

ignorance of the nature and interrelationships of the economic controls necessary to regulate the cost of living; failure to comprehend the need to curb excess buying power as a means of preventing inflation; a widespread lack of mutual confidence between groups, particularly between labor and other groups; and a feeling on the part of a substantial minority that the Government was giving the people inadequate information about military and naval events.

The handling of the news regarding the attack on Pearl Harbor presented in acute form most of the information problems facing our Government at war. It was imperative to keep the Japanese from finding out anything about damage done that would be of use to them. The public relations offices of the Army and Navy imposed a strict silence at first and referred the newsmen to the White House, which furnished a statement giving few details. American newspapers and broadcasters employed accounts of the disaster obtained from Japanese sources. Although these sources were identified, the use of them conveyed to the public an enemy version of the events which raised doubts about the adequacy and accuracy of American official information. While Secretary Knox issued a report a week later which was based on first-hand observations, and while a special Board of Inquiry headed by Supreme Court Justice Roberts made a report in January, rumors exaggerating the damage persisted and the President had to deny these rumors in his radio talk of February 23, 1942.

Under a regime of freedom of the press, success in the dissemination of war information depends in last analysis upon securing the cooperation of the press and radio. If Government releases are to be run as news items, if Government messages are to be broadcast to radio listeners, or if Government themes are to be shown in the newsreels or in motion picture shorts, the industries concerned must volunteer their services. Negatively, the Government had to rely upon the voluntary cooperation of the press and radio to refrain from publishing materials which would serve the purposes of the enemy.

In time of war, the person in the United States who can command the fullest cooperation of the press and radio is the President. Franklin D. Roosevelt's audiences now became world-wide. To unequalled American radio audiences were added the listeners to American and British short-wave broadcasts.

On the psychological front as well as the military front President Roosevelt carried the battle to the enemy. In his radio address of December 9, 1941, he defined the role of the United States as reaching far beyond mere defense against unwarranted attack:

The true goal we seek is far above and beyond the ugly field of battle. When we resort to force, as now we must, we are determined that this force shall be directed toward ultimate good as well as against immediate evil. We Americans are not destroyers—we are builders. We are now in the midst of a war, not for conquest, not for vengeance, but for a world in which this nation, and all that this nation represents, will be safe for our children. We are going to win the war, and we are going to win the peace that follows.

Most of the press and radio commentators followed the President's lead in picturing the war in planetary terms, accepting the kinship of all peoples fighting fascism, and defining our goal as nothing less than total victory. In his address of January 6, 1942, the President amplified his position and listed the following war themes: All-out production, civilian sacrifices, offensive warfare, protection of the four freedoms, the nature of the conspiracy against us and against our way of life, the counter-strategy of the United Nations, and the necessity for guarding against complacency on the one hand and defeatism on the other. In his radio address on Washington's Birthday, the President took up the cause of the United Nations and made an eloquent plea for cooperation and comradeship with our Allies. Among other important addresses that the President made during the first 9 months of the war should be mentioned his radio address of April 28, 1942, outlining a seven-point program for control of the cost of living.

It was the task of the information agencies to follow the President's lead and carry the war of words to the enemy. Among the organization questions to be decided were whether censorship and information activities should be combined, whether domestic and foreign information should be disseminated by the same agency, and whether there should be a centralized war information office which would serve all of the war agencies.

Censorship

The attack on Pearl Harbor found the United States with no organization to prevent valuable information from reaching the enemy since censorship was not regarded as a proper function for our Government in time of peace. The First War Powers Act conferred on the President the powers of censorship. He had to decide how and by whom these powers would be exercised. He was faced with the question whether to follow in the footsteps of President Wilson, who, in World War I, delegated to George Creel, Chairman of the Committee on Public Information, responsibility for both war information and voluntary censorship. Mr. Creel's office laid down the rules for the voluntary censorship of the press and was also a central source for war information. The British experience with its Ministry of Information which combined censorship and propaganda functions had not been particularly happy.

While no censorship organization existed, plans had been worked on for more than 20 years by representatives of the Army, Navy, Post Office, and Justice Departments. Early in 1941 the Joint Army and Navy Board presented to President Roosevelt a plan for censorship in case of war which provided that the President appoint a Director of Censorship who would have no responsibility for issuing information. The plan did not stipulate that the Director should be a civilian, although such a provision had been in the plan of the old Censorship Board of World War I. Under the 1941 plan, the President was to designate an Army officer as chief postal and wire censor and a Navy officer as chief radio and cable censor. The President approved this plan on June 4, 1941, and appointed a committee the following November under the chairmanship of the Postmaster General to work out the details. The Committee asked the Director of the Federal Bureau of Investigation to make a comprehensive study of the subject. This study, completed on December 7, recommended that there should be no restrictions on the President in the selection of a Director who would be given absolute authority over censorship.

President Roosevelt established the Office of Censorship on December 19, 1941, by Executive order under the authority of the First War Powers Act.[2] In announcing the establishment of the Office of Censorship and the appointment of Byron Price, Associated Press executive, as Director of Censorship, he said:

All Americans abhor censorship, just as they abhor war. But the experience of this and of all other nations has demonstrated that some degree of censorship is essential in wartime, and we are at war.

The important thing now is that such forms of censorship as are necessary shall be administered effectively and in harmony with the best interests of our free institutions.

The order read in part as follows:

The Director of Censorship shall cause to be censored, in his absolute discretion, communications by mail, cable, radio, or other means of transmission passing between the United States and any foreign country or which may be carried by any vessel or other means of transportation touching at any port, place, or territory of the United States and bound to or from any foreign country, in accordance with such rules and regulations as the President shall from time to time prescribe.

The Office of Censorship had two main objectives. One was to prevent the transmission in or out of the country of information which might be useful to the enemy. This function included the interception of information regarding sabotage, espionage, and subversive activities, and the prevention of the entrance of harmful propaganda. The other objective was to obtain information from the communications examined which might be of value to the prose-

---

[2] Executive Order No. 8985, Dec. 19, 1941, 6 *Federal Register* 6625, and 55 *Stat.* 838.

cution of the war; i. e., intercepts on conditions in enemy countries, on attempted evasion of export and import regulations, on enemy shipping, on available sources of war materials, on new industrial developments of military importance, and on financial transactions that were related to the war. The agency was entirely divorced from the job of giving out information.

Censorship operations actually began on December 7, 1941, when the President directed the Navy Department to censor cable and radio communications and the War Department to censor postal communications going in and out of the country. When the Office of Censorship was established, a Cable Division under the leadership of naval officers and a Postal Division under the leadership of Army officers became the two principal operating divisions.

Voluntary censorship of the domestic press and radio was authorized, not by the Executive order, but by a Presidential letter to the Director of Censorship on January 27, 1942. The letter stated:

As President of the United States and Commander in Chief of the Army and Navy, I hereby authorize and direct you in your capacity as Director of Censorship to coordinate the efforts of the domestic press and radio in voluntarily withholding from publication military and other information which should not be released in the interest of the effective prosecution of the war.

Press and radio censorship was accomplished by the issuance of codes stating what might and might not be published and requesting voluntary compliance of press and radio. To a great extent, the War and Navy Departments and the Maritime Commission determined the kind of restrictions which went into these codes. While most of the military information was censored at source by the Army and the Navy, it was possible for the private news agencies to get information from nonofficial sources about troops, ships, fortifications, and war production which would be of value to the enemy. The Office of Censorship established a small Press Division and a small Radio Division to formulate the codes and guide their interpretation.

The Press Division developed the following principles to govern its administration of voluntary censorship:

1. Voluntary censorship must deal only with questions involving war security.

2. It must never base a request on any security consideration which may be questionable. The danger to security must be real, and must be backed by a solid and reasonable explanation.

3. It must avoid any interference whatever with editorial opinion. Such opinion could not possibly be controlled on a voluntary basis, even if it were desirable.

4. It must never be influenced by nonsecurity considerations of policy or public needs. Any involvement in these fields would destroy effectiveness elsewhere.

5. It must make no request which would put the press in the position of policing or withholding from publication the utterances of responsible public officials.

6. It must make every effort to avoid multiple censorship and on no account must withhold from the American public any information which has been generally disseminated abroad.

7. It must never undertake to vouch for the truth or accuracy of any news story. The embarrassments would be too great for a voluntary system, based on security, to survive.

8. It must never undertake to regulate release dates or other matters of newspaper ethics. To do so would encourage Government interference of a considerable and possibly uncontrollable character.

9. It must be absolutely impartial and consistent. If any censor is to maintain a position of influence, his blue pencil must know no brother among competitors.

10. It must operate openly, advising the public of every request made of the press. To do otherwise would undermine public confidence and foster unwarranted suspicion both against the Government and the press.[3]

During the first 8 months of 1942 the Press and Radio Divisions of the Office of Censorship were busy keeping the news services informed about how the codes applied to particular events. The sinkings of ships off the Atlantic Coast by German submarines, the shelling of the southern California coast by a Japanese submarine, the burning of the *Normandie* in New York Harbor, the visits of Churchill and Molotov to the United States, and the constant danger of the inadvertent publication of military addresses presented censorship problems that had to be solved promptly by these Divisions. The Office of Censorship answered questions and called attention to violations. It had no powers of compulsion over domestic press and radio.

A central question facing the Office of Censorship was whether it would censor other Government agencies. Stephen B. Early, Secretary to the President, thought it would, but the Censorship Policy Board, and interdepartmental committee established by the Office of Censorship Executive order, decided at a meeting, January 7, 1942, that the Office of Censorship should not censor, either by review or the enunciation of general principles, information released by Government agencies. It furthermore determined that the principles concerning the release of information by the Government should be developed by the Office of Facts and Figures.[4]

The Office of Facts and Figures issued a number of statements on what information might be released by Government agencies without endangering security but never satisfactorily solved the problem. The first statement on January 17, 1942, endeavored to insure that the policy controlling Government publication of procurement information would be consistent with the policy established by the Director of Censorship for the voluntary cooperation of press and radio. Active

[3] Office of Censorship. *A Report on the Office of Censorship.* Washington, D. C.: Government Printing Office, 1945. (Historical Reports on War Administration, Series 1) pp. 42–43.
[4] Office of Censorship. *Censorship Policy Board Minutes,* Jan. 7, 1942.

in formulating the policy were the Army, the Navy, the War Production Board, and the Division of Statistical Standards of the Bureau of the Budget. In March OFF issued a still more comprehensive statement of policy on war information covering news of military action as well as news of war production.

So skillfully did the Office of Censorship work out the administration of voluntary censorship of press and radio that there were few complaints from the public. Surprisingly, the Director of Censorship was frequently found on the side of news agencies urging the War and Navy Departments to be more liberal in their releases of war news. There were violations of the codes, particularly by small newspapers which inadvertently published news about native sons in the armed services, but these violations were minor, and it was not necessary to resort to compulsory censorship of press and radio in order to safeguard national security.

Although the creation of the Office of Censorship theoretically separated the powers of censorship and the duty of issuing information, and appeared to set up one supreme authority for censorship, these powers were already widely disseminated. Though the Office of Censorship could issue codes of security regulations, and intercept communications to citizens or communications abroad, it could not deal with Government censorship at source; that is, the refusal of a Government agency or official to issue information. Every information agency was in one sense a censor since it had the power of deliberate choice of what it would issue and how it would issue it. Actually, too, there was delegation of the power of censorship. The Office of Facts and Figures outlined the principles to govern the issuance of Government releases, and the public relations departments of the Navy and the Army both had the power of censorship over military releases and all communications that dealt with military personnel.

Domestic Information Agencies and the War

The Office of Censorship was a new and independent war agency which had no peacetime counterpart. The dissemination of war information, on the other hand, was carried on by agencies and offices which had been established on a piece-meal basis before Pearl Harbor. These agencies lacked adequate powers to do a war information job and they got in each other's way. The advent of the war made necessary a realignment of both responsibility and organization in order that consistent and accurate war information could be carried to the people of the United States and of the world.

In World War I President Wilson delegated to George Creel, Chairman of the Committee on Public Information, the responsibility for keeping the public informed regarding the war effort. Mr. Creel's office was the central source for all war information, including the releases put out by the State, War, and Navy Departments.[5] President Roosevelt did not set up any central organization at first. He followed the familiar pattern of establishing a series of parallel agencies whose powers or fields of authority were not sharply limited, both because of the urgency of the need, which allowed little time for organization, and because the functions of public information in a global war were not yet clarified. The handling of military information was left in the War and Navy Departments and the handling of diplomatic information in the State Department. The War Department Bureau of Public Relations was established by a memorandum from the Secretary of War, dated February 11, 1941, which placed all agencies of the War Department dealing in public relations or related matters under the supervision of the Bureau. Public relations offices were established in the headquarters of each theatre of operations to provide continuous access to important announcements by commanding generals overseas. The Office of Public Relations of the Navy Department was established in the Office of the Secretary on May 1, 1941, and was expanded after Pearl Harbor to meet wartime needs. The War and Navy Departments together devised a system of accrediting war correspondents which facilitated the sending of reporters to all the fighting fronts.

In addition to the information offices of the State, War, and Navy Departments, five other agencies were working on defense information. The Division of Information· of the Office for Emergency Management provided central information facilities for the OEM agencies; the Office of Facts and Figures formulated war information programs and acted as a clearing house for certain types of domestic information; the Office of Government Reports handled inquiries coming from State and local governments, citizens' organizations and the public; the Foreign Information Service of the Coordinator of Information disseminated information to all foreign countries other than the Latin American; and the Coordinator of Inter-American Affairs sent information to the American republics.

The Division of Information of the Office for Emergency Management which was in operation from March 5, 1941, until June 13, 1942, was organized on the theory that there should be a centralized information service rather than information offices in each emergency agency. Robert W. Horton, a journalist with Government experience, served as Director of the OEM Division of Information from its inception. He and his staff held that a central information service would minimize agency and agency-head glorification, afford an opportunity to check possible conflicts in advance of their occurrence, and would permit the most economical use of information manpower. In Washington centralization meant a central press room reserved for reporters, a central distribution system for releases, pictures, posters, and other information materials, and centralized facilities for producing information with information men assigned to individual emergency agencies but responsible to Mr. Horton in the central office. It was the function of the men assigned to different agencies to prepare releases and answer questions regarding developments for their agencies.

The staff of the OEM Division of Information assigned to the War Production Board, for example, was charged with reporting, interpreting and explaining the manifold activities of WPB. Among the subjects covered were the conversion of peacetime industries to war production; the curtailment of normal production; the conservation of raw materials and expansion programs; the rubber, metal, paper, and other salvage campaigns; the preparation of military production schedules; subcontracting; programs to benefit small businesses and industries; requisitioning of inventories and idle stocks; clearing of major war contracts; and the preparation of programs drafted to preserve the minimum civilian economy in time of war.

One of the accomplishments of the Division of Information was the initiation of the War Production Drive. Shortly after his appointment as Chairman of WPB, Mr. Nelson requested the Division of Information to plan a national campaign to spur production. On February 2, 1942, he took this matter up with the Committee on War Information of the Office of Facts and Figures, which agreed that the program should have goals and incentives for individual companies and for individual workers. The Division of Information worked out a plan for a War Production Headquarters to administer the drive. General policies were determined by a joint policy committee composed of representatives of the Army, the Navy, the Maritime Commission, and the War Production Board. By June 1942 nearly 100 labor-management committees had been established, a number of important labor unions had participated in the drive, slogan contests had been held all over the country, and an individual awards program was started in order to encourage the submission of suggestions by workers. Manufacturers testified that the drive was having favorable results.

The OEM Division of Information paved the way for the first general production report, which was issued in July 1942, after many delays and numerous clearances with the armed forces. For more than 6 months, representatives of the Division of Information, the Office of Facts and Figures, and the Division of Statistics of WPB discussed what kind of production information could be made public. The Committee on War Information of the Office of Facts and Figures had the question on its agenda during the same period.

The staff of the OEM Division of Information assigned to the Office of Price Administration found its work vastly increased by the declaration of war. With the coming of rationing and price actions on consumer goods, this staff had to carry on the educational campaigns to inform the public why such actions were necessary, how they would be carried out, and what the ordinary citizen would do to adjust himself to the new situation.

Long before the general maximum price regulation was announced, the information staff indicated that the implementation of the program would require, in order to secure general public and businessman acceptance, a very comprehensive publicity and promotion campaign. When the regulation was ready, materials were distributed in advance for simultaneous release in Washington and the field. As far as newspaper coverage was concerned, the informatio1 campaign was highly successful. Some papers carried the full text of the regulation and hundreds of others carried the text of the release. This type of coverage more effectively reached the large urban retail stores than the small retail stores in the rural areas. It was also more effective in securing general compliance with the principle of a ceiling than it was in securing compliance with the details of administration, such as price posting and record keeping. The staff of the Division felt that in order to secure compliance with technical instructions, it was necessary to supplement a general information campaign with a direct check-up by Government officials at each retail establishment.

Very early, the various agencies began to demand the right to have their own information offices on the plea that to comprehend adequately what they were doing, the information officers had to belong to the staff of the agency. The break-down of the central information service began with the Office of Civilian Defense. One of the reasons for this was that OCD was in part an information agency utilizing the techniques of group discussion, face-to-face contacts, and local distribution. Dean James M. Landis, who replaced Mayor LaGuardia as Director of OCD in February 1942, early expressed the desire to run his own information office since he felt that information was the heart of the OCD program and to be effective in promoting OCD projects and programs, such an office would have to be part of the organization. The Office of Civilian Defense had a difficult Federal-State-local relations problem which required persuasion and interpretative information. While OCD was responsible for civilian defense policies and programs at the national level, it had to work through State, county, and city governments in order to reach the great mass

of the people and to make use of the protective facilities organized
by these governments. OCD had no direct authority over such
governmental units but could only suggest what they should do in
the way of cooperation.

OCD was allowed to set up its own information office, called the
Public Advice and Counsel Division, after some negotiations with the
Bureau of the Budget. The staff of the OEM Division of Information
assigned to OCD was reassigned to other duties on February 7, 1942.

While the OEM Division of Information concentrated its resources
most heavily upon the information needs of the Office of Price Administration and the War Production Board, it also provided central information services for many other emergency agencies. It assumed
responsiblity for the information work of the Office of Lend-Lease
Administration, the Combined Raw Materials Board, the Office of
Defense Transportation, the Alien Property Custodian, and the War
Relocation Authority, and it established liaison service with the
Coordinator of Inter-American Affairs, the Coordinator of Information, the Economic Defense Board, the Office of Agricultural War
Relations, the Office of Scientific Research and Development, and the
Office of Defense Health and Welfare Services. The liaison services
involved the furnishing of basic source materials and the coordination
of information programs.

In the spring of 1942 information campaigns were organized on
conversion, rationing, salvage, and "hush hush" by the Division
of Information. The last-mentioned campaign aimed to impress upon
both military and civilian personnel the importance of refraining from
loose talk which might aid the enemy. In these campaigns, the
widest possible coverage and effect were sought by the coordinated
use and timing of releases, radio programs, pamphlets, posters,
speeches, motion pictures, and other media. Such campaigns depended upon the cooperation of the press, the national advertisers,
the broadcasting companies, and the motion-picture companies, since
it was not in the American tradition for the Government to buy
newspaper space, radio time, or news-reel footage to put over a war
program. The fullest use of the information campaign technique was
not achieved during this period because the Division of Information
did not have an adequate staff to do the job and it had no control
over the Office of Facts and Figures and the old-line departments.

During the earliest days of the war, the central information services
rendered by the OEM Division of Information were regarded as
generally satisfactory by the Office of Price Administration, the War
Production Board, and a number of other emergency agencies. As the
information tasks grew, the pressure for agency information offices
increased. It was again argued that if information was to aid adminis-

tration, it had to be in the hands of persons who understood all the ramifications of the specific program, who possessed zeal for the special prosecution of that program, and who were just as subject to the control of the agency head as any other employee of the agency. Not only the Office of Civilian Defense, but the Office of Defense Health and Welfare Services and the Division of Defense Housing Coordination sought their own information units.

The Office of Facts and Figures, established under Archibald Mac-Leish, Librarian of Congress, shortly before the attack on Pearl Harbor, was designed to coordinate defense information functions on the home front. Its authority was not fully recognized, however, by the Division of Information within the Office for Emergency Management which handled publicity and releases for the war agencies. At first it concerned itself with information policies.

The organization of OFF consisted of the (interdepartmental) Committee on War Information, a board, and four operating bureaus. Represented on the Committee were the State, War, Navy, Treasury, and Justice Departments, the Coordinator of Information, the Coordinator of Inter-American Affairs, the Office of Government Reports, the Office of Lend-Lease Administration, the Office of Civilian Defense, and the Office for Emergency Management. The Board of Facts and Figures included the eight OFF deputy directors, the heads of the operating bureaus, the Director of the Office of Government Reports, the Director of the Foreign Information Service of the Coordinator of Information, and a market research consultant.

The Committee on War Information tried to act as the war information planning agency on the domestic front. It advised war agencies on information matters, formulated general principles regarding the security of war information, outlined general propaganda objectives in the domestic field, including counter-propaganda themes, reviewed the findings of the OFF Bureau of Intelligence regarding the status of domestic public opinion and the nature of the enemy propaganda, suggested subjects for the Bureau of Intelligence to investigate, suggested topics for publications and radio programs, defined the functions of OFF in the fields of speech clearance, in the coordination of radio programs, and in the coordination of the production and distribution of posters, endeavored to get more war information from the Army, the Navy, and the civilian war agencies, drew up principles to guide the use of advertising by war agencies, and considered the handling of minority groups in the United States.

The Board of Facts and Figures, as contrasted with the Committee on War Information, was more concerned with the details of information campaigns, methods of meeting criticisms of OFF, procedures for carrying out different assignments, the relationship of OFF to other agencies concerned with domestic information and morale problems, the utilization of OFF reports, relationships between Government information officers, and the determination of the use to be made of different media.   The President's message on the State of the Union was taken as the basis of an over-all information program and in connection with the President's anti-inflation speech, meetings were arranged with the representatives of the departments concerned.

OFF served as a clearing house for the press, radio, and motion picture industries endeavoring to aid the war effort.   Since there was nothing in its Executive order on this function, it had to work out ways of securing the maximum cooperation with the industries with a minimum of friction with other governmental agencies.

By a letter from Stephen B. Early, Secretary to the President, dated January 16, 1942, OFF acquired certain coordinating functions over Government requests for radio time.   To prevent duplication of effort within the radio field, OFF prepared an over-all schedule of the radio plans of each Federal agency.   In cooperation with the radio industry an allocation plan was prepared which provided for an orderly distribution of, and proper emphasis on war themes in radio programs.

The powers of OFF were extended to the clearance of speeches by high-ranking officials by a letter from Mr. Early.   At its meeting of January 19, 1942, the Committee on War Information authorized Mr. MacLeish to send a letter to the President calling attention to such statements as those made recently by Secretary of Commerce Jones on rubber, by Secretary of Agriculture Wickard on sugar, and by Secretary of the Navy Knox on the Pacific front, and recommending that the President establish a method of clearing such statements so as to avoid intragovernmental conflicts.   On January 29, 1942, Mr. Early authorized OFF to undertake this function.

In the poster field OFF acquired clearance powers by negotiating voluntary agreements with the war agencies which, in planning their poster programs, discovered that they needed some system for allocating the available space among the various Government agencies.

Mr. MacLeish urged his staff to promote in their contacts with Government information officers an understanding of the importance of clearing with each other proposed press releases when they involved interests or activities of agencies other than their own.[2]   In practice, OFF failed to secure the full cooperation of the OEM Division of Information and of other important war information offices.   Its powers to coordinate the relations of the war agencies with the press on over-all matters were strictly limited.   It did not issue many

---

[2] Office of Facts and Figures.   Board of Facts and Figures, *Minutes*, Mar. 31, 1942.

press releases itself and those which it did were largely concerned with counterpropaganda. Since it did not have a clear directive to do a war news clearance job, it relied chiefly upon persuasion.

The shortcomings of the OFF Executive order were abundantly clear to Mr. MacLeish. In a letter to the Director of the Bureau of the Budget, dated February 20, 1942, he urged the liquidation of OFF and the establishment of a stronger agency which would combine the functions of other agencies in the field of war information.

A third domestic information agency was the Office of Government Reports, established in the Executive Office of the President in 1939, some of whose activities originated in the National Emergency Council established in 1933. The Director of OGR was Lowell Mellett, former editor of the Washington Daily News. While the OGR central press-clipping services, public, inquiry offices, and field services which included public-opinion reporting, the handling of Federal-State relationships, and the reporting on Washington-field administrative problems, were established as peacetime activities, they were greatly expanded after the attack of Pearl Harbor. The public-opinion reporting facilities of the field offices were used to analyze war production, price control, and rationing problems, thus duplicating some of the assignments of the OFF Bureau of Intelligence.

Before war was declared, OGR had established contacts with the motion-picture industry through a National Defense Committee representing motion-picture producers, distributors, and exhibitors. After Pearl Harbor this committee changed its name to the War Activities Committee and suggested to the President that someone be appointed coordinator of motion pictures for the United States Government. By a letter, dated December 18, 1941, the President appointed Mr. Mellett as Coordinator of Government Films and directed him to act as the liaison officer of the Federal Government with the motion-picture industry, to clear the Government's civilian films, to plan Government motion-picture production and distribution, and to consult with all Government departments in connection with film production and distribution programs and consult with and advise motion-picture producers of ways and means in which they could most usefully serve in the national effort. In carrying out these functions, OGR maintained close liaison with OFF.

Foreign Information

To the confusion on the domestic war information front was added confusion in handling overseas information. There was no agreement on what the relationship should be between foreign and domestic information activities, on how foreign information policies should be determined, or on how these policies should be carried out.

Whereas the domestic information agencies relied heavily upon the voluntary cooperation of the press, radio, and motion-picture industries, it was soon clear that the disruption of international communications by the war would make it necessary for our Government to distribute information abroad in order to reach the peoples of enemy, occupied, neutral, and Allied countries.' While some of the commercial news services were continued on a reduced basis in neutral and Allied countries, the Government had to supplement these services in order to combat the insidious influences of Axis propaganda.

When the Japanese struck at Pearl Harbor, the dissemination of information abroad was in the hands of two emergency agencies, the Office of the Coordinator⁄of Inter-American Affairs, which confined such activities to Latin America, and the Office of the Coordinator of Information, which operated in the rest of the world. Since it was imperative that Government information sent outside of the country conform with our foreign policy and military strategy, the State, War, and Navy Departments helped coordinate the activities of these two agencies.

The information programs directed toward Latin America were within the jurisdiction of the Coordinator of Inter-American Affairs, Nelson Rockefeller, who, since August 16, 1940, had operated a well-rounded program for the development of good inter-American relations. The press, radio, and motion-picture activities of the CIAA were regarded as an integral part of its general cultural and commercial relations program which was worked out in close cooperation with the State Department. The separate treatment of the Western Hemisphere was reaffirmed in the Executive order of July 30, 1941, which established CIAA in OEM. When war was declared, Mr. Rockefeller's agency helped convince the Latin Americans that hemisphere solidarity was necessary for hemisphere defense. CIAA was particularly effective in supplementing the commercial news services with special features, local information activities, film distribution, and advertising.

The Office of the Coordinator of Information, established by military order of the President on July 11, 1941, had been assigned two main functions. One was the coordination of intelligence materials from all sources, including the armed forces, and the other was the transmission of information abroad except to Latin America. The military order automatically placed the Office under the Joint Chiefs of Staff, and thus provided for a greater degree of security. The overseas information function was not specifically granted by the order but was based on an understanding between the Coordinator, Col. (later Gen.)

William J. Donovan, and the President. The agency was directed by the President not to engage in domestic information activities.

To carry out the overseas information program, Colonel Donovan established a Foreign Information Service and appointed Robert Sherwood to direct it. In accordance with policies which were cleared with the State, War, and Navy Departments, and in close cooperation with the British Government, this Service undertook to spread the gospel of democracy and the cause of the United Nations throughout the world except in Latin America. The Service contended that a democratic country cannot successfully undertake a Goebbels-deception type of foreign propaganda and that truth was the only effective basis for American foreign information, although the facts thus disseminated had to be carefully interpreted and timed on basis of a strategy entirely different from that involved in domestic information work. It concentrated on giving volume, tone, and meaning to an American approach. Radio programs were presented as "The Voice of America," not as the voice of this or that refugee or immigrant group. Use was made of President Roosevelt as a symbol of American idealism. While emphasis was placed upon American power, equal attention was given to the American aim to end the war under circumstances which would make a real peace possible.

Mr. Sherwood was keenly aware of the need for coordinating our overseas efforts. He felt that the news-gathering functions of his Service were duplicated by the OEM Division of Information and by CIAA. This duplication, he said, would be unnecessary if some system could be worked out whereby his organization could get the news it needed to operate. He was also aware that his unit, OFF, CIAA, and the OEM Division of Information duplicated each other in their contacts with other governmental agencies.

At the outbreak of war, both the Rockefeller and the Donovan agencies were developing the use of short-wave broadcast facilities in their foreign information programs. Since the short-wave radio, no matter how carefully it may be beamed toward a given country, can be picked up by neighboring countries, the general and detailed operational policies of the two agencies had to be harmonized. Any discrepancy between the broadcasts to South America and the rest of the world would be quickly picked up by the enemy and used to discredit American information in general. For instance, there were differences between the two agencies as to the emphasis to be placed on news regarding our aid to Russia. The Latin American countries were jealous of Russian aid because of their own shipping shortages. Close coordination between the two agencies was also necessary because of the shortage of radio equipment and technical personnel.

Establishment of OWI

The confusion in handling war information, both domestic and foreign, was such that demands for a reorganization came from all quarters. A number of Presidential advisers recognized that the situation was unsatisfactory and took steps to see that the lines of responsibility were more specifically fixed and that a coordinating mechanism was established.

The staff of the Bureau of the Budget proposed a draft of an Executive order providing that the following agencies or functions should be consolidated into a proposed Office of War Information: the Office of Facts and Figures, the Foreign Information Service of the Coordinator of Information, the functions of the Coordinator of Inter-American Affairs relating to the dissemination of information, the functions of the Director of the Office of Government Reports in his capacity as Coordinator of Government Films, and the general functions of the Division of Information of the Office for Emergency Management. War agencies of the Office for Emergency Management received their own press and publications services and set up their own information offices. This assignment of local offices meant the abandonment of the centralized information services which the OEM Division of Information had been performing for WPB, OPA, and other war agencies. The main features of this draft were eventually adopted but the process of negotiating acceptance took time.

A memorandum on the reorganization of the war-information services was sent to the President on March 7, 1942, by the Director of the Bureau of the Budget. The memorandum said in part:

This multiplicity of general war information agencies has resulted in conflict and duplications in the flow of war information to the American public and to other nations. An example of present duplication is the dual coverage of the official news each day, once for domestic (by OEM) and once for foreign use (by COI). Furthermore, there is uncertainty with respect to areas of responsibility and authorized points of clearance.

Much information released daily is still of the "agency glorification" type and is not designed to implement an over-all war information policy. There is competition in obtaining funds, building staffs, and preempting special fields of information. Conflicts in press releases have been numerous, as for example, the contradictory statements recently issued on the rubber situation. Coordination between domestic and foreign information programs has been weak. Finally, there has been too much reliance placed on "making the press" as opposed to the development of information programs designed to stimulate citizen understanding of the war effort. Thus, there has been overemphasis on reporting, and underemphasis on long-range planning, interpretation, and program effectuation.

While it is neither desirable nor necessary to concentrate all of the Government's information facilities in a single operating agency, it is nevertheless imperative that some single agency be responsible for policy coordination and for providing centralized control over Government use of such media as the radio, motion pictures, and posters.   The plan recommended in the attached Executive order, therefore, provides for decentralization to the individual war agencies of information work relating specifically to their own activities.   On the other hand, it provides for the centralization of general war information work and of Government sponsored radio, motion-picture, and poster programs.   .   .   .

The Office of War Information would be headed by a Director appointed by the President.   The Director would be assisted by a Committee on War Information Policy which would formulate basic war-information policies and plans to govern the various agencies in the development and dissemination of war information.

The most important policy issue involved in the proposed plan concerns the transfer of the information activities of Mr. Rockefeller's office.   I believe that the control of short-wave broadcasting facilities and the general control of foreign information policy should properly be located in the new office.   However, inasmuch as the information activities of the Coordinator of Inter-American Affairs are an integral part of the program of that Office, I think it may be advisable to arrange for the Coordinator of Inter-American Affairs to continue the operation of radio and other information programs for the American Republics, subject to policy and program control by the Office of War Information.   In effect, the Coordinator of Inter-American Affairs would, under this arrangement, serve as the agent or deputy of the Director of the Office of War Information in carrying out such programs.

It was hoped that after considering this memorandum the President would be prepared to act on the Executive order.   The Director of the Bureau of the Budget and Judge Samuel Rosenman, special adviser to the President, discussed the draft of the order with the President who, however, was reluctant to move on the matter and raised a number of questions concerning the transfer of the Foreign Information Service of the Coordinator of Information, and of the Coordinator of Inter-American Affairs.

The relation of the activities of the Coordinator of Inter-American Affairs to the proposed Office of War Information was discussed vigorously for over 2 months.   Mr. Rockefeller opposed the transfer of the information activities of his agency on the ground that they were an integral part of an over-all program being carried out in cooperation with the Department of State.   Since we had a distinctive foreign policy in the Western Hemisphere, something could be said for this point of view.   Under Secretary of State Sumner Welles, in a letter to the President dated March 17, 1942, supported this position, indicating that these activities were being handled in a successful and satisfactory manner and that any transfer would result in a protracted period of confusion at the very moment when it was all-important that our relation with the other American Republics should be unimpaired by lack of efficiency or lack of knowledge on the part of the appropriate officials of this Government.   At a White House conference on May 15, the President agreed to leave the CIAA out of the proposed order.

Another problem presented by the original plan of the Bureau of the Budget for an Office of War Information concerned the place of the Foreign Information Service of the Coordinator of Information. The plan finally adopted, however, called for the transfer of the Foreign Information Service to the Office of War Information and the creation of an Office of Strategic Services under the joint Chiefs of Staff out of the other functions of the Coordinator of Information.

Those opposed to an over-all information agency argued that domestic and foreign information should be separate because the differences in aims, purpose, and methods in each field called for a difference in administration, that foreign information should be employed as a weapon of war and should be effectively allied with the military services, and that a tie-up between domestic and foreign information agencies would endanger security, impair the effectiveness of psychological warfare, and risk the exposure of our plans and methods to the enemy. Those in favor of the proposed information agency took the position that the United States should send abroad the same type of information that it released at home since it was impossible under conditions of democratic freedom of speech to divorce the two operations, that both programs should be based on the strategy of truth, and that the control of information policy should be with the civilian rather than the military authorities. The latter arguments prevailed.

The transfer of the Office of Government Reports to the Office of War Information grew out of attacks made on OGR in the spring of 1942. On February 2, 1942, President Roosevelt suggested to Lowell Mellett, Director of OGR, that a central information center be established in Washington. This proposal became a target for the critics of the Administration. Since he wanted to avoid bringing any disfavor upon the Executive Office of the President, Mr. Mellett went to the President about the matter and they agreed that OGR should be merged with the new information agency.

Sometime in May the President indicated that he wanted the whole of OGR transferred in the new order. All the subsequent drafts of the order so provided. The staff of the Bureau of the Budget observed that the press-clipping service was related to the media analysis work being done by OFF and the public inquiry service was related to a similar function performed by the OEM Division of Information. As for field services, the public opinion reporting functions were paralleled by some of the OFF functions and the local public inquiry work was similar to work done by the OEM field services. In addition the transfer would eliminate duplications in services to weekly newspapers and in liaison with Government information agencies.

The negotiations conducted in May regarding the proposed order left the question of its issuance in doubt. At the same time that these discussions were being carried on, the Bureau of the Budget was considering the 1943 budget estimates for all the emergency agencies concerned. In a memorandum sent to the President, on June 1, 1942, the Director of the Bureau of the Budget linked the need for the proposed Office of War Information with the budget problems involved.

This memorandum made a distinct impression upon the President. He asked for additional data about the budgetary situation of the information agencies. In the meantime, negotiations were going forward with reference to the choice of the Director of the proposed Office of War Information. Before signing an order, the President liked to associate the terms of the order with the person who was to carry them out. When Elmer Davis, radio news commentator, agreed to direct the new agency, the President signed the Executive order, effective June 13, 1942.[7] The establishment of a centralizing authority at this time—just before our first offensive in the Pacific—channelized the flow of public information at a critical period, yet it did not entail recruitment of an entirely new staff since full use was made of preexisting agencies and trained personnel.

OWI as a Coordinating Agency

According to the order, the Director of the new Office of War Information was given the authority, subject to policies laid down by the President and to the provision excluding the CIAA, to issue directives to all departments and agencies of the Government on all matters pertaining to their informational services, and to formulate and carry out, through the use of press, radio, motion pictures, and other facilities, information programs designed to facilitate the development of an informed and intelligent understanding, at home and abroad, of the status and progress of the war effort and of the war policies, activities, and aims of the Government.

The new Office of War Information, during the first few months of its existence, had to plan for expansion in certain vital operations, satisfy the information needs of the war agencies by keeping production going, and physically and administratively consolidate the constituent parts of the organization. These were not easy tasks and it took 2 years to bring some of them under control.

The decision not to concentrate full responsibility for war information activities in a single agency as was done in World War I meant that OWI had to solve many problems of coordination. The new

---

[7] Executive Order No. 9182, June 13, 1942, 7 *Federal Register* 4468.

agency had to establish satisfactory working relationships with the Office of Censorship, the Department of State, CIAA, the armed services, the civilian war agencies, and other agencies having war information programs.

When OWI was set up, incomplete coordination existed between the Office of Censorship and the information agencies on the types of information to be withheld from publication. It had not been decided whether the same rules that applied to private sources would apply to information originating from Government sources. On November 15, 1942, the two agencies agreed that outgoing OWI short-wave broadcasts would be censored for security only, and not for policy, and that in the domestic field OWI would exercise an affirmative function only, and would, in no case, ask newspapers or broadcasters to withhold anything from distribution.

The exclusion of CIAA information activities from the jurisdiction of OWI did not remove the need for coordinating the information work of the two agencies, especially in the short-wave broadcasting field. When OWI took over the Foreign Information Service of the Coordinator of Information, it continued negotiations with the Rockefeller group for the leasing and construction of short-wave broadcasting facilities. The two agencies and the Federal Communications Commission agreed that OWI would assume all responsibility, budgetary included, for the facilities expansion program. On November 1, 1942, just before the Allied invasion of North Africa, contracts were signed by CIAA and OWI, leasing virtually all the short-wave broadcasting facilities in the United States. An agreement between the two agencies regarding the operation of these facilities was not reached until several months later.

As far as relations with Armed Services were concerned, Mr. Davis indicated that he had no intention of interfering with communiqués of the War and Navy Department. He did not regard it as his function to determine finally what type of information imperiled national security. Nevertheless, he met daily with appropriate Army and Navy officials to stimulate the fullest possible dissemination of information involving military and naval actions.

In the field of psychological warfare, negotiations were carried on between OWI, the Office of Strategic Services, and the Joint Chiefs of Staff to settle questions about the division of labor between them. A satisfactory solution of the problems involved was not reached until the theatre commanders established psychological warfare branches, embracing all activities concerned whether civilian or military, British or American. In the meantime, OWI rapidly expanded its information activities directed abroad. It increased its production of short-wave radio programs, press-wireless dispatches, publications,

CHART 25. *Consolidation of Information Agencies.*[1]

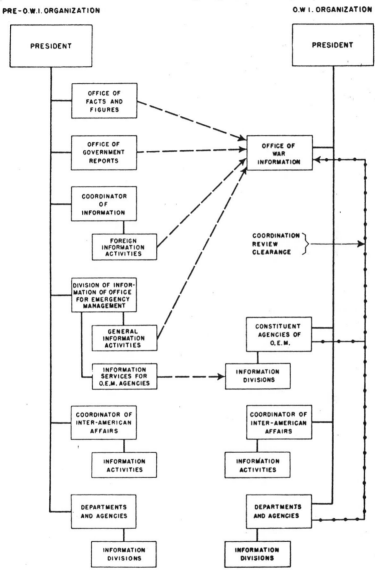

PRE-O.W.I. ORGANIZATION

O.W.I. ORGANIZATION

PRESIDENT

PRESIDENT

OFFICE OF
FACTS AND
FIGURES

OFFICE OF
GOVERNMENT
REPORTS

COORDINATOR
OF
INFORMATION

FOREIGN
INFORMATION
ACTIVITIES

OFFICE OF
WAR
INFORMATION

COORDINATION
REVIEW
CLEARANCE

DIVISION OF INFOR-
MATION OF OFFICE
FOR EMERGENCY
MANAGEMENT

GENERAL
INFORMATION
ACTIVITIES

CONSTITUENT
AGENCIES OF
O.E.M.

INFORMATION
SERVICES FOR
O.E.M. AGENCIES

INFORMATION
DIVISIONS

COORDINATOR OF
INTER-AMERICAN
AFFAIRS

COORDINATOR OF
INTER-AMERICAN
AFFAIRS

INFORMATION
ACTIVITIES

INFORMATION
ACTIVITIES

DEPARTMENTS
AND AGENCIES

DEPARTMENTS
AND AGENCIES

INFORMATION
DIVISIONS

INFORMATION
DIVISIONS

[1] Does not include the functions of voluntary censorship of mass media and of censorship of international communications between civilians which were performed by the Office of Censorship after December 1941.

Source: Bureau of the Budget.

leaflets, posters, motion pictures, exhibits, and other information materials. Machinery was established to clear overseas propaganda directives with the War, Navy and State Departments.

On the domestic front, the decision to have agency information offices meant that OWI had to perfect methods of coordinating the war informational activities of all Federal departments and agencies. On July 10, 1942, Mr. Davis issued a regulation which defined the clearance procedures to be used in connection with news releases, addresses, publications, radio, motion pictures, posters, and other graphics, advertising, foreign-language services, and comprehensive war information. The regulation provided that. "news releases relating significantly to the war effort or dealing with activities broader than the authorized work of the initiating agency shall, where possible, be prepared by the appropriate Federal department or agency for clearance and issuance by the News Bureau of the Office of War Information." It also directed the officers of the Federal departments and agencies "to maintain an open-door policy in their relations with representatives of the press, radio, and other media." [8] How well this was being done was indicated by the President in his letter to department and agency heads ordering them to cease public conflict. He said in part:

In dealing with the many complex war problems which we face today, it is unavoidable that there be wide differences of opinion between agencies of the Federal Government—opinions sincerely and honestly held. However, too often in recent months, responsible officials of the Government have made public criticism of other agencies of the Government; and have made public statements based either on inadequate information or on failure to appreciate all the aspects of a complex subject which is only partially within their jurisdiction.

One of the duties prescribed for the Office of War Information is the coordination of war informational activities of all Federal departments and agencies, for the purpose of assuring an accurate and consistent flow of war information to the public and the world at large and for the added purpose of eliminating conflict and confusion among the departments and agencies of the Government in the matter of their public relations. Elmer Davis, Director of this Office, tells me that so far as written statements from departments and agencies are concerned, very satisfactory progress toward this objective is being made. But, he points out that the attainment of the objective is being gravely hampered by verbal statements dealing with matters touching more than one department or agency made by high officials in press conferences and elsewhere—statements which do not contribute either to the accuracy or the consistency of public information.[9]

The Office of War Information also faced the problem of devising a formula for determining the place of the information staffs of the constituent agencies. In Washington the staffs of the Division of Information, Office of Emergency Management, who had been serving different war agencies, were transferred to the agencies they

---

[8] OWI Regulation No. 1, July 10, 1942.   [9] White House Press Release, Aug. 21, 1942.

served. The Office of Price Administration, the War Production Board, and the other emergency agencies expanded their information staffs and set up tight controls over the release of information. OPA especially found it necessary to guard against "leaks" of information regarding rationing because of the danger of "runs" and hoarding. In the field, OWI continued for a year to provide central services for the emergency agencies. Office of War Information field offices did not expand rapidly enough to perform all the information services which the constituent agencies regarded as necessary. Consequently, constant pressure was exerted by such agencies as OPA to establish agency field information services. Action by Congress in the spring of 1943 turned over the local information function to the constituent agencies.

Throughout its career OWI faced a constant series of problems; it necessarily wielded large powers both in this country and abroad that wakened misgivings in Congress and rivalries in the information services of the various war agencies; it found it difficult to satisfy the demands of the press, the radio, and the moving-picture industries; and, finally, even though its duties as an organization were those of coordination, it was itself an amalgamation of four preexisting agencies; i. e., the Office of Facts and Figures, the Office of Government Reports, the Division of Information of the Office for Emergency Management, and the Foreign Information Service Branch of the Office of the Coordinator of Information. Over 2,000 people were involved; OWI could not use the services of all of them, particularly in domestic information activities, nor could it preserve the organizations under which they had worked. One of the first tasks facing the newly appointed Director, Elmer Davis, was that of creating a working organization and the establishment of new lines of authority. To aid him he had Milton Eisenhower, brother of General Eisenhower, who was at that time Director of the War Relocation Authority and who had been Director of the Office of Information of the Department of Agriculture.

The first organization plan, the result of a series of conferences in the Bureau of the Budget, was set forth in an Office of War Information Staff Order No. 1, July 10, 1942. It established three branches with an Assistant Director for each branch: the Domestic Branch, a Policy and Development Branch, and the Overseas Branch.

The Domestic Branch, headed by Gardner Cowles, Jr., was built upon the central information services of the Division of Information of OEM, the operating bureaus of OFF, and the service functions and motion-picture activities of OGR. Robert Horton, former Director of the Division of Information of OEM, and Lowell Mellett, former Director of OGR, accepted subordinate posts in the new Domestic

Branch, the former as head of the News Bureau and the latter as head of the Motion Picture Bureau.

The Overseas Branch was placed in charge of Robert Sherwood, who had been the head of the Foreign Information Service of the Office of the Coordinator of Information. It included those parts of the COI which had been concerned with open overseas information activities as contrasted with secret activities. Excepted was the news-gathering staff in Washington, which was transferred to the News Bureau of the Domestic Branch. Operating activities in New York and San Francisco were continued under Mr. Sherwood.

The third branch, the Policy Development Branch, was headed by Archibald MacLeish, former Director of OFF. He had under him the former OFF deputies for departmental liaison and the OFF Bureau of Intelligence. This branch had two primary functions; one was to conduct public-opinion research and the other to develop major information policies for the other two branches. In practice, the Bureau of Intelligence was limited almost entirely to work for the Domestic Branch. Staff Order No. 2, September 11, 1942, transferred practically the entire operating staff of the Policy Development Branch to the Domestic Branch and abolished the Policy Development Branch by implication. Mr. MacLeish continued to serve as Assistant Director on Developing Policies until his resignation on January 30, 1943. With his resignation, the function of coordinating policies of the remaining two branches was absorbed in the Director's Office.

Meanwhile, the Domestic Branch was riven from within and assailed from outside. The branch suffered first from a succession of directors. While Mr. Davis gave to the director of the branch a free hand, the kind of men that he selected for the post accepted the responsibility only under the condition that they serve for a year or less. They worked in highly competitive fields in private life and were unable to stay away from them too long. The first director, for instance, was a newspaper executive who had experience running a daily, a magazine, and a radio station. He accepted the appointment only after a direct appeal from the President and on the condition that he return to his private affairs within a year. The high turn-over in directors meant that there was a lack of continuity in the leadership of the Branch.[10] By the time that one man learned the ropes, it was necessary to break in a new director.

The internal problems of the branch had repercussions upon its relations with Congress. Under various reorganizations some of the

---

[10] The directors and their terms were as follows: Gardner Cowles, July 1942 to May 15, 1943; Palmer Hoyt, May 16 to Dec. 31, 1943; George W. Healy, Jr., Jan. 4 to Sept. 8, 1944; Neil Dalton, Sept. 8, 1944, to abolition of OWI on Aug. 31, 1945.

professional staff grew restive. A number of writers who had formerly been directly under Mr. MacLeish in the OFF felt that they were too far removed from Mr. Davis himself. The writers resigned in a body and issued a blast against the Director of the Domestic Branch. In his final report to the President on the war, Mr. Davis wrote grimly but illuminatingly of the incident:

> It might be pertinent here to note one personnel problem which came up again and again, in both our domestic and our overseas branches, for which we never found a solution. It is not a problem peculiar to OWI; it has afflicted in greater or less degree every ministry of information in a free country. It is the problem of the brilliant and zealous individual who cannot work as part of a team.
> OWI was not only a team itself but part of a larger team, the Government of the United States at war. We were directed to perform our duties "consistently with the war information policies of the President and with the foreign policies of the United States"; and within the framework of those policies, certain principles of execution and lines of action had to be laid down by the head of OWI. Now an information agency, in a war which was in some of its aspects ideological, naturally attracted many free-lance writers and others who had been used to working by themselves and had always jealously cherished their personal integrity and freedom of expression. Such a man is very apt to insist that he must proclaim the truth as he sees it; if you tell him that so long as he works for the Government he must proclaim the truth as the President and the Secretary of State see it, he may feel that this is an intolerable limitation on his freedom of thought and speech. In that case, he must go.

In the spring of 1943 the Domestic Branch faced serious opposition in Congress. The branch was attacked because its internal bickering leading to the resignation of the pamphlet writers, information production activities including pamphlet writing and documentary motion-picture production, and its potentialities as an administration defender made it a target for those opposing the President. The four pamphlets arousing Congressional ire were an anti-inflation tract, a tax primer, a discussion of Negroes and the war, and a cartoon history of President Roosevelt. The latter was not a product of the Domestic Branch and was only distributed abroad. Only with reference to the anti-inflation booklet did the OWI officials admit that they were in error. They defended the other two pamphlets as within the province of their general mandate. As a warning gesture, the House of Representatives abolished the Domestic Branch but it concurred in the restoration of the branch by the Senate. The appropriation finally passed forbade the production of pamphlets, abolished the OWI field offices, and by reason of the drastic cut in funds limited the branch to coordinating activities.

After it had been cut back so severely, the Domestic Branch dropped the production of motion-picture documentaries, posters, and pamphlets, and discontinued its news services in field offices. Other agencies, particularly the Office of Price Administration, greatly expanded their information services in the field. The Domestic Branch became essentially a coordinating agency which plannned Government information campaigns on war needs in cooperation with other Government agencies and the communication industries.

The Overseas Branch was destined to be the largest and the most lasting part of OWI. Its personnel accompanied our victorious armies all over the world as members of combat propaganda teams and moved into liberated areas in order to furnish a true picture of America's role in the victory and the new world organization to come. Just prior to V–E Day it had more than 8,400 employees of whom about one-half were citizens of foreign countries employed locally abroad in minor capacities.

The fundamental problems facing the branch concerned the integration of our foreign propaganda with our foreign policy and military strategy; the bridging of the spacial distance between Washington and New York, San Francisco, London, Algiers, Cairo, Brisbane, Chungking, New Delhi, Teheran, and other outposts; and the selection of the propaganda appeals and media best adapted to save lives and shorten the war.

Since the OWI officials thought that they had a clear mandate to control all information activities aimed at the enemy, they were greatly upset by the issuance of a directive by the Joint Chiefs of Staff on December 22, 1942, setting up a Board of Strategy on Military Psychological Warfare on which the Office of Strategic Services was the key agency. Mr. Davis protested this order on the ground that it conflicted with the Executive order under which he was operating. The matter was referred to the President, who clarified the situation by issuing on March 9, 1943, an Executive order placing full responsibility in OWI for foreign propaganda activities involving dissemination of information. Under this order, OWI contended that it had power to direct secret as well as open propaganda, utilizing the undercover (cloak and dagger) personnel of OSS. The Joint Chiefs of Staff notified OWI that they would coordinate military activity with propaganda by direct liaison. Programs in a theatre of military operations were under the control of the theatre commander. Later it became necessary to point out to a theatre commander from time to time that he had no authority to reverse the general propaganda objectives of the United States as laid down by the Washington Planning Board on which the Joint Chiefs of Staff and the Department of State were represented. On the combat propaganda teams, representatives of OWI, the Army, the British Political Warfare Executive, and the British Army worked well together. Whatever differences there were between OWI and OSS regarding black propaganda did not interfere with operations and were formally composed by an agreement between the agencies reached in the spring of 1944 under which OWI recognized OSS's jurisdiction over secret propaganda.

The liaison between OWI and the Department of State presented many problems throughout the war. While the OWI Executive order directed Mr. Davis to perform his functions in a manner consistent with the foreign policy of the United States, it did not specify how OWI could find out what our foreign policy was. OWI officials contended that our foreign policy was determined by the President's speeches and other pronouncements which they could interpret as well as the State Department. In other words, they were reluctant to concede the Department's role in enunciating our foreign policy. Friction developed on both sides. OWI officials felt that the Department of State did not keep them fully informed as to developments abroad and the Department of State officials felt that OWI disregarded their directives and used confidential information for propaganda purposes for which it was not intended. In addition, OWI chafed under the passport regulations and the censorship of materials going by diplomatic pouch. The Department of State could prevent OWI personnel or OWI leaflets from going abroad.

The disagreements between OWI and the Department of State also extended to policies. Top officials of the Overseas Branch were outspokenly critical of the friendly policy toward Vichy France, Franco, and the King of Italy. These differences came out into the open in connection with the famous "moronic little King" broadcast sent out by OWI on July 25, 1943, the day on which the fall of Mussolini was announced. The phrase was taken from the broadcast of a commentator, George Grafton, and was broadcast to London to show a trend in American public opinion. It was picked up by the New York Times where it was read by President Roosevelt who made it one of the subjects at his next press conference. OWI was rebuked for not following our foreign policy, but it developed that the Overseas Branch officials had not been informed regarding the negotiations between our Government and the King of Italy. There was no consensus of opinion as to whether the propaganda directives on that day had been properly cleared with the Department of State. The Director of the Overseas Branch, who knew nothing of the broadcast at the time, admitted that it had been in bad taste.

Disharmony between the Overseas Branch and the Department of State was in part the result of the independence of the branch from the office of the director. This independence was inherited from the Foreign Information Service of the Coordinator of Information. In the summer of 1943, the branch proposed a staff order which would have formalized current tendencies by practically removing the entire authority over foreign operations to the New York Office. The

Director of OWI pointed out that any reorganization must proceed from the major premise that the seat of the Government was in Washington and so were the headquarters of OWI.

Following the appointment of Edward Klauber as Associate Director of OWI on December 1, 1943, steps were taken to strengthen the leadership of the Director's office over the Overseas Branch. As Mr. Davis put it before the House Committee:

> After some discussion the situation was solved by a reorganization which established a clear line of authority and responsibility from the Director of OWI through the Director of the Overseas Branch and straight on down through the organization. Mr. Sherwood's authority as Director of the Branch, subject to the over-all responsibility of the head of the agency, is as complete as ever; but he is now assisted in his supervision of its operations by an Executive Director and an Assistant Executive Director—respectively Mr. Barrett and Mr. Barnard, who had proved themselves two of our ablest bureau chiefs. They are responsible to Mr. Sherwood and relieve him of much detail, enabling him to concentrate on the planning and execution of propaganda and information policies—at which in my opinion he is outstandingly gifted. At the same time, I accepted the resignations of three executives of the Overseas Branch, who, though able men, and of unquestioned devotion to the national interest and to the general objectives of OWI, were in my opinion lacking in some of the qualities required for good teamwork. Our present organization shows every promise of functioning very effectively.[11]

During the month of February, 1944, the Overseas Branch was reorganized in connection with the preparation of its 1945 budget estimates. The Editorial Board in New York was abolished and steps were taken to bring about the centralization of intelligence and planning activities in Washington. The changes were made in order to strengthen the control of the Director's office and to reduce the possibility of independent action in New York which was not in conformance with OWI policies as determined in Washington. On March 27, Staff Order No. 29 was issued to carry out these objectives: The Washington office of the Director of the branch was strengthened by the addition of an Executive Director and an Assistant Executive Director who were responsible for the supervision of production activities in New York and San Francisco, three deputy directors in a staff relationship who were responsible for the formulation of propaganda and information policy for specified areas, and a chief of liaison who was responsible for coordinating policy and intelligence liaison with agencies of the United States and other governments. Instead of a deputy director for Atlantic operations in New York, there was a chief of the New York Office. A review board was set up in Washington to review all major proposals regarding policy. A New York Board of Review was also established, as an "extension" of the Wash-

[11] U. S. Congress. House Committee on Appropriations. *National War Agencies Appropriations Bill, 1945.* Hearings . . . 78th Cong., 1st sess., pt. 2, p. 11.

CHART 26. *Public Opinion on War Information.*

The question asked was: "Do you think the Government is giving the public as much information as it should about the fighting in this war?"

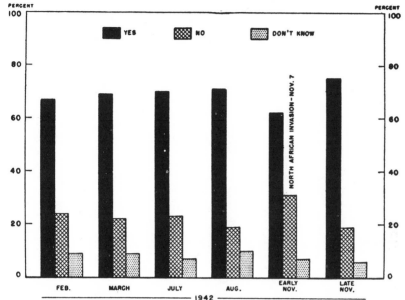

Source: Office of War Information.

ington board. While the machinery set up was cumbersome and failed to break sharply with the past, it represented an effort to centralize control over policy and operations.

The strengthening of topside management in OWI enabled the agency to improve greatly its relations with the Department of State. Representatives of the Department felt that they were really consulted regarding the OWI propaganda directives and they also had greater confidence in OWI's efforts to follow the directives laid down by the Planning Board in Washington.

Long before VE-day, OWI was ready with plans for the liquidation of European psychological warfare operations, for the control over information media in the conquered countries, the correction of distorted information in liberated countries and the continuation of psychological warfare in the Pacific. These plans were much more carefully worked out than those presented by some of the other agencies engaged in similar activities.

CHAPTER

9

Fighting Inflation

MONTHS before the declaration of war, leaders in business and Government were fully aware that stringent action would have to be taken to prevent a run-away inflation. There was, however, no general agreement about the kind of action which should be taken. The big farm organizations opposed control of farm prices; labor resisted wage controls in the face of rising profits and living costs; and manufacturers were alarmed by the prospect of heavier taxes. The public wanted the Government to hold down the cost of living, but there was little realization that inflation controls would require the sacrifice of immediate financial gains for the more lasting benefits of a stable economy. These attitudes were prevalent in the period January-October 1942, when the Government was trying to work out its inflation-control program.

When war came on December 7, 1941, the Administration lacked adequate authority to control prices. During the defense period OPA attempted to hold down prices by getting the cooperation of businessmen. But the lack of real sanctions which could be used against companies refusing to cooperate penalized businessmen who foresaw the dangers of inflation and were anxious to prevent it. Furthermore, these voluntary measures at best exerted a restraining influence on only a few commodity prices. The general economic situation, however, required action covering a wide range of commodities. From September 1939 to December 1941 the price of 28 basic commodities affecting manufacturing and living costs increased by almost one-fourth. During 1941, increases in the cost of living averaged a little less than 1 percent each month, and wholesale price increases somewhat more than 1 percent (charts 27 and 28). Also, in 1941, farm prices rose by at least one-fourth, and wages,

235

salaries, and income payments by about one-fifth. These increases
were stimulated in large part by the European war and by our own
war expenditures which, in December 1941, amounted to $2 billion.
After the declaration of war, the dangers of inflation seemed more
real. The President's goals announced on January 6—50,000 planes,
45,000 tanks, 20,000 antiaircraft guns and 8 million tons of shipping—
would triple our monthly rate of war expenditures by the end of 1942
and would build up inflationary pressures in two ways. First, these
goals could be met only by a diversion of material, labor, and manufacturing facilities from the production of consumer goods and services,
which would reduce consumer supplies drastically. Second, dollars
spent for tanks, ships, and other implements of war would flow back
to the public in the form of wages, salaries, profits, and dividends

CHART 27. *Consumer's Price Index.*

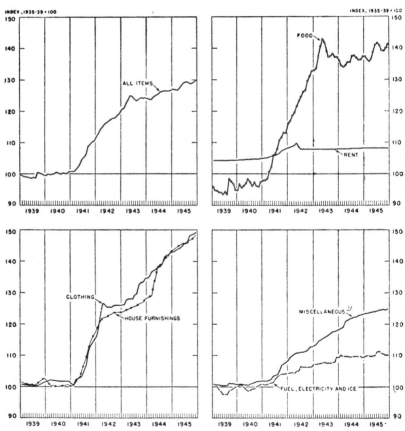

[1] Includes transportation, medical care, recreation, personal and household care.

Source: Department of Labor.

and would increase consumer demand for scarce goods and services. Expressed in terms of dollars, consumer demand in 1942 would exceed available supply by about $17 billion. The resulting pressure on price levels would be tremendous and would have to be controlled in some fashion if we were to maintain a stable economy.

There were two general approaches to the problem of economic stabilization. The first, proposed and strongly advocated by Bernard Baruch, required imposition of a general ceiling on "prices, rents, wages, commission fees, interest rates"—in short, on the "price of every item of commerce or service." The chief advantage of this method was the comprehensive nature of the control. Each citizen would be "treated alike as part of one nation joined in a great emergency and every segment of our economy, agriculture, labor, business" would be treated "as parts of a single, living sensitive organism." The quality of sacrifice implicit in this plan might be expected to gain acceptance, if not active support, from powerful farm, labor and industrial organizations which normally were suspicious of each other and of Government regulation.

An essential condition of the Baruch plan was that the general ceiling be established on "some date on which the normal operations of the law of supply and demand can be said to have controlled prices," before factors such as material and labor shortages had distorted "normal" price relationships. If this were done, it would be necessary only to adjust prices which, for one reason or another, were not at satisfactory levels on the base date. Ideally, a general ceiling should have been issued early in 1941, coincident with the development of priorities machinery for dividing up supplies of scarce raw materials. It is doubtful whether such action would have been supported by a nation generally unaware of the impact which the European war would have on our own economy. If a general ceiling were established in 1942, it would have been necessary to freeze prices at levels prevailing in 1941. The facilities required to administer the "price roll-back" implied in such action had not been established when war was declared and later experience showed that it is practically impossible to effect a roll-back.

The alternative to a general ceiling was, to use Baruch's phrase, "piecemeal price fixing." Under this plan ceilings would be placed on the prices of commodities as and when they exhibited inflationary behavior. It was thought that this selective approach would permit the prices of individual commodities to rise when increased supplies were needed for defense production. Moreover, the Government would be able to deal with dangerous price rises as they occurred without regulating the entire economy. For this reason it was particularly suited to the needs of the "limited national emergency, all-measures-short-of-war" period, when stable prices depended on cooperation between Government and business.

Commodity price controls, in practice, could not prevent increases in the cost of living as long as consumer purchasing power exceeded the available supply of goods. It was necessary, therefore, to supplement price control with other anti-inflation devices—wage stabilization, "a considerable increase in taxation, a decided stepping up of the savings program, and a reduction in installment credit."[1] Failure to

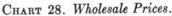

CHART 28. *Wholesale Prices.*

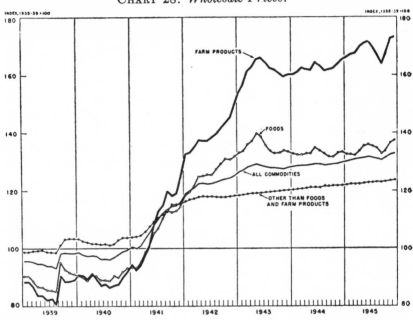

Source: Department of Labor.

deal vigorously and effectively with any one of these related problems would handicap effective action on the others. Failure to tax excess profits or stabilize living costs or control wages would be the signal for powerful pressure groups to seek special benefits which were incompatible with national objectives and probably injurious to their own ultimate welfare. The influence of these groups in Congress would make legislative approval of rigorous antiinflation measures more difficult to obtain. Finally, the operations of various Government agencies entrusted with separate phases of economic stabilization would have to be related to a coherent stabilization policy and perhaps tied together through common administrative direction.

---

[1] United States Congress. House. Committee on Banking and Currency. Hearings (revised)on H. R. 5479, 77th Cong., 1st sess., p. 186. Leon Henderson.

Whichever method of stabilization was chosen, the technical problems were formidable. In July 1941, however when there was still doubt about the public's willingness to accept stringent economic regulation, the selective method of control seemed especially attractive. Price-control officials frequently stated that selective controls would not do the whole job and that supplementary actions would have to follow, such as wage and credit controls and heavier taxes. But OPA's limited experience seemed to indicate that price ceilings extended to a wide range of commodities would go a long way toward holding down the cost of living. Probably with this limited objective in mind, a bill embodying the principles of selective price control was submitted to Congress on July 30, 1941, and, after 3 months of investigation and discussion, was passed by the House of Representatives shortly before the Japanese attack.

At this point, the bill, which, after all, had been shaped months before the declaration of war, might have been reexamined to see whether it would meet the requirements of a war economy. Events pressed in another direction. With the President fully occupied by military matters and OPA officials thrown into a series of actions directed against a wave of speculative price increases, it is not surprising that the situation was not reappraised and that a drive for immediate enactment of the pending bill began in the Senate. By the end of January the Emergency Price Control Act of 1942 had been passed by Congress and signed by the President.

After passage of the Price Control Act the character of economic stabilization problems shifted somewhat. During the period January-October 1942, with which this chapter is concerned, the chief problems were (1) to obtain legislative authorization for more effective control over the prices of agricultural commodities (2) to formulate a stabilization policy which would encompass prices, wages, rents, and war finance; and (3) to establish the administrative facilities required to put the coordinated stabilization program into effect.

Emergency Price Control Act of 1942

On December 9, 1941, Mr. Henderson presented to the Senate Committee on Banking and Currency the case for a strong price-control law. Legislation authorizing an expanded price-control program was deemed necessary as a step toward more general antiinflation measures. The experience of "every nation at war," whether a "democracy or a totalitarian government," was adduced to show that economic stabilization was as essential to effective prosecution of the war as staffing the armed forces or providing material for war production.

High-level industrial production could not be maintained in face of uncontrolled inflation. Rapid and continued rises in the cost of living would create unrest among workers and would have a disruptive effect on civilian morale generally. Uncontrolled price rises also would increase substantially the cost of the war. According to an estimate of Bernard Baruch, inflation increased by about 40 percent the cost to the American taxpayers of World War I. Mr. Henderson estimated that approximately $13 billion of the $67 billion authorized for munitions and armaments as of December 1941 would be absorbed by price increases. Price control thus was necessary "from the standpoint of cost." Finally Mr. Henderson pointed out that "all wars in this country have produced an inflationary period followed by a deflation which paralyzed recovery." An effort should be made to prevent a repetition of the depression which followed the World War I, with widespread business failures, farm foreclosures, and untold human suffering.[2]

Principal issues developed by Congressional consideration of the price-control bill were whether wage stabilization would be included in the bill and be administered by the price-control agency, and whether agricultural products would be subject to the same controls and agricultural prices stabilized at the same levels as other commodities.

The failure of the President in July 1941 to request control over wages as well as over commodity prices stirred up opposition to price-control legislation. In his July message recommending passage of price-control legislation, the President had said, "we may expect the wholehearted and voluntary cooperation of labor only when it has been assured a reasonable and stable income in terms of the things money will buy and equal restraint on the part of all others who participate in the defense program."[3] Labor would forego wage increases if the cost of living and the profits of industry were held in bounds. A somewhat different view of the wage-control problem was given by the spokesman of the Congress of Industrial Organizations:

> An attempt to institute wage control would bring in its wake the break-down of voluntary collective bargaining, the establishment of dictatorial controls over labor and industry, and the destruction of a free democratic labor movement.[4]

The strength of organized labor's opposition to wage control was openly recognized by Leon Henderson who said, "I must confess that personally I have particularly tried to avoid having it in a price bill, lest it complicate an already difficult job."[5]

---

[2] U. S. Congress. Senate. Committee on Banking and Currency. Hearings on H. R. 5990, 77th Cong., 1st sess., p. 16.
[3] House Document No. 332, 77th Cong., 1st sess.
[4] U. S. Congress. House. Committee on Banking and Currency. Hearings (revised) on H. R. 5479, 77th Cong., 1st sess., p. 1553.
[5] U. S. Congress. Senate. Committee on Banking and Currency. Hearings on H. R. 5990, 77th Cong., 1st sess., p. 165.

The strategy of the farm organizations was to point out these defects in the legislation and to urge Congressmen to vote against the bill.[6] No attempt was made to get the bill amended so as to provide for control of wages as well as farm prices. Although the Senate Committee on Banking and Currency had in its membership Senators who were customarily apprehensive on behalf of farm interests, a key member pointed out that none of his colleagues had proposed that the bill be amended to include wage controls, and that such an amendment was not offered on the floor of the Senate.[7]

Instead of using their influence to get before Congress an amendment broadening the scope of the price control bill, the farm organizations concentrated their attention on the bill's provisions authorizing control of agricultural prices. Early drafts of the bill did not contain special limitations on the authority of the price administrator to set ceilings on farm prices. Later there was written in a limitation which would have allowed the administrator to fix the price of any farm commodity which had reached parity levels. Preliminary discussions between OPACS staff and farm groups were on the basis of a 100 percent of parity standard.[8] Prior to introduction of the bill and after conference with Congressional leaders, Leon Henderson accepted a revision which authorized price ceilings only on agricultural commodities which had reached 110 percent of parity. The bill, as introduced, contained this limitation.[9] Later the board of directors of the American Farm Bureau Federation adopted a resolution which stated that, in order to maintain the average price of farm produce at parity levels, "no price ceiling should be established on any agricultural commodity or the products thereof at a price less than 110 percent of parity." [10]

To a considerable extent the agricultural price issue was a direct offspring of the agricultural policies which the Government had followed since 1933. Parity of farm income with that of industry and labor became the goal of the Government as well as of the big farm pressure groups. Various forms of subsidies—soil conservation and incentive payments, crop loans—were utilized to give the farmer a larger share of the national income than he could get by selling his crops in the normal market. These measures were devised to cope with an agricultural problem of which huge surpluses were symptomatic. The tendency to think of the farm problem as primarily one

[6] *Congressional Record*, vol. 87, pt. 9, p. 9207.
[7] *New York Times*, Feb. 5, 1942, p. 20, cols. 2 and 6. Senator Prentiss M. Brown in a letter to the editor.
[8] U. S. Congress. Senate. Committee on Banking and Currency. Hearings on H. R. 5990, 775th Cong., 1st sess., p. 140.
[9] U. S. Congress. House. Committee on Banking and Currency. Hearings (revised) on H. R. 5479, 77th Cong., 1st sess., p. 1112.
[10] *Ibid.*, p. 1389. The date of the resolution was Sept. 10, 1941.

of surpluses made it difficult to see clearly what policies should be pursued in dealing with short supplies.

For this reason Mr. Henderson, while not enthusiastic about the 110 percent of parity provision, thought it a "workable standard." Before the attack on Pearl Harbor he testified:

> . . . in a number of agricultural commodities what you are going to have, rather than the difficulty of their being too high, is that they are still going to think they are too low. . . . We have fairly ample stocks of most agricultural commodities.[11]

Although the outbreak of war was in itself a warning that planning for food as well as for industrial production should be reexamined, expert opinion continued in the belief that supplies of most agricultural commodities were more than ample for war needs. Former President Herbert Hoover, the Food Administrator of World War I, on December 16 said "the question of putting a ceiling higher than parity is more or less academic, because the Department with all its pushing up of the floor has not been able to get up to parity yet." [12] This view was shared by the Secretary of Agriculture.

After the attack on Pearl Harbor, Leon Henderson urged Congress to restore the original provision of the price-control bill authorizing the price administrator to fix agricultural prices at parity levels. The bill passed by the House of Representatives provided that prices for agricultural commodities could not be set below: (1) 110 percent of parity; (2) the market price on July 29, 1941; or (3) the average price during the period July 1, 1919, to June 30, 1929. The first of these limitations, Mr. Henderson said, had been inserted in recognition of the Government's policy of guaranteeing parity prices to farmers, and the second, to prevent a reduction of farm prices below levels existing when the bill was introduced. The third limitation, however, had been added in final passage of the bill, with very little discussion of its effect. He pointed out that these limitations, taken together, would allow the average farm price level of 27 major farm products to rise to 116.6 percent of parity, a rise above prevailing levels of about 12 percent of parity, before controls could be established. Mr. Henderson requested the Senate Committee on Banking and Currency to eliminate the "110 percent of parity" and the "average price during July 1, 1919, to June 30, 1929" provisions of the House version of the Price Control bill.[13]

The majority of farmers would have accepted parity as the standard, according to public-opinion polls. In a survey made in November 1941, 52 percent of the farmers indicated their satisfaction with the

[11] Ibid., pp. 650–51.
[12] U. S. Congress. Senate. Committee on Banking and Currency. Hearings on H. R. 5990, 77th Cong., 1st sess., p. 421.
[13] Ibid., p. 126.

prevailing price levels.[14] The American Farm Bureau Federation, however, was adamant on the 110-percent-of-parity limitation. It claimed that this restriction was necessary in order to prevent the average price of farm commodities from falling below parity and in support of its position it cited the Secretary of Agriculture, who had said, "The real purpose of restricting ceilings to a point somewhat above parity is to make it reasonably sure that all farmers will have an opportunity to get parity," and "It happens to be the expressed policy of Congress and the Administration to achieve and maintain farm prices at parity."[15] The fact that Mr. Henderson had given the 110-percent provision his approval was also noted. This difference of opinion between representatives of the Executive Branch on the question of agricultural prices undoubtedly weakened the Administration's effort to provide effective control of agricultural prices.

On December 10, the day after Mr. Henderson urged the adoption of a strong price-control bill, the Office of Price Administration placed price ceilings on approximately all types of fats and oils. Many of these fats and oils were normally imported from the Pacific area. With the threat of Japanese blockade of these sources, a wave of speculative buying swept the market. The resultant sharp price increases called for immediate action. Since fats and oils are highly interchangeable, the Office of Price Administration had to put ceilings on both domestically produced and imported commodities. Under the theory of control incorporated in the pending price bill, it was necessary to fix prices as of a base date when a normal price relation between the various types of fats and oils existed.[16] The prices set for cottonseed oil and lard were the closing exchange prices as of November 26, 1941.

Issuance of this price schedule, while it was an essential step, stirred up opposition to price stabilization. Four days after the regulation was announced the President of the American Farm Bureau Federation indicated his displeasure:

> Mr. Henderson not only has failed to keep his agreement with regard to the 110 percent provision, but during the last few days he fixed prices on fats and oils without consulting the proper officials of the Department of Agriculture. If he is going to administer this program in this manner, I am not in favor of giving him this wide discretionary authority. I am not. Positively am not.

Certainty that the demands of war would wipe out agricultural surpluses and that special measures would have to be taken to obtain

---

[14] *Public Opinion Quarterly*, vol. 5, No. 4, p. 667.

[15] For the Farm Bureau's position following the declaration of war, see testimony of O'Neal in Senate Committee on Banking and Currency Hearings, p. 429. Secretary Wickard's statement before the House Committee (see House Committee on Banking and Currency Hearings, pp. 20, 71, et seq.) was made a part of the Senate Committee record by O'Neal.

[16] Price Schedule No. 53, 6 *Federal Register* 6409.

maximum production of foodstuffs gave Mr. O'Neal a new argument:

> . . . Price ceilings placed on agriculture should be fixed in such a way as to be consistent with the need of the Nation for additional food production. It is well known that the Secretary of Agriculture is asking for increased production of fats and oils. Arbitrary action by Mr. Henderson in fixing prices on fats and oils without consulting the proper officials of the Department of Agriculture is a positive indication that he is not properly coordinating his efforts . . . with those of the Secretary . . . [17]

On December 17, a resolution was introduced in the Senate requesting the Office of Price Administration to rescind its fats and oils order pending final action on the price-control bill. In spite of the fact that between August 1939 and December 1941 cottonseed oil prices had risen 137 percent and lard prices 76 percent, the Cotton Belt and Corn Belt Congressmen were bombarded by protests from their constituents.[18] The President of the National Cotton Council was quoted on the floor of the Senate as stating that the action of OPA "constitutes a serious breach of good faith on the part of a Governmental agency."[19] Economic pressures and special interests did not become less active as the Japanese military machine moved into new areas of conquest.

The possibility of delegating to the Secretary of Agriculture responsibility over agricultural prices was given serious consideration. Beginning with the National Defense Advisory Commission, authority over prices had been withheld from agencies responsible for production. This policy was based on the tendency of production agencies to become identified with the interests of producers. There were particularly strong reasons for placing price-control functions outside the Department of Agriculture. Over a long period of years the Department has sought to improve the economic position of farmers and to make rural life more attractive and satisfying. Its efforts to increase farm prices did not always accord with the desires of consumers and the food distribution trade, in whom it had only a secondary interest. These efforts, moreover, were supported in Congress by the "farm bloc" and by effectively organized farm pressure groups as well as by the Executive branch. Against this background, it seemed that a new price-control agency would be in a better position than the Department of Agriculture to hold down agricultural prices. This decision was acceptable to the Department until it appeared that demands would wipe out food surpluses and push prices above prevailing levels.

---

[17] U. S. Congress. Senate. Committee on Banking and Currency. Hearings on H. R. 5990, 77th Cong., 1st sess., p. 443.

[18] *Congressional Record*, Vol. 87, pt. 9, p. 9900. For price data, see U. S. Department of Labor, *Wartime Prices*, part I, p. 57.

[19] *Congressional Record*, vol. 87, pt. 9, p. 9901.

After the declaration of war, the Secretary of Agriculture changed his position on the question of agricultural price controls. In an off-the-record appearance before the Senate Committee on Banking and Currency, Secretary Wickard reaffirmed his approval of the price-control bill's objectives. He went on to say that since his earlier testimony the United States had become involved in the war; the bill, therefore, should be examined in light of the need for abundant production. His statement continued:

. . . If it is rightly used, the control of prices can help to get farm production. It can help prevent inflation . . . On the other hand, price management in wartime must be skillfully used and synchronized with the production effort. Otherwise it may interfere with the production effort and therefore do more harm than good.

The Secretary described some of the steps taken by the Department of Agriculture to obtain greater production and urged that the Government grant price inducements to agriculture as well as industry. He then indicated his doubt as to the ability of the Department of Agriculture and the Office of Price Administration to join in a program which called for increased farm production and a stabilization of food prices and the cost of living:

To take care of changing conditions, we have had to adjust prices of many products almost daily. It is a delicate and difficult job at best. What would it be like if another set of price controllers were to move into the field? The Department's operations in this intricate and important field should be complicated no more than they are at present.

I must say that the Office of Price Administration has informed the Department that it will, if necessary, change price ceilings. But this raises a question. If the Department of Agriculture must revise the price ceilings on farm products set by the Office of Price Administration, why not let the Department fix the ceilings in the first place? [20]

A few days after the Secretary of Agriculture's appearance, an amendment was submitted in the Senate which would give the Secretary of Agriculture and the Price Administrator coordinate responsibility for the stabilization of farm prices.[21] In commenting on this proposal Senator Prentiss M. Brown, who presided over most of the hearings before the Committee on Banking and Currency, said:

. . . We thought we were doing what Mr. O'Neal wanted, within reason, we thought we were doing what the Senator from Alabama wanted, and we thought this controversy was pretty largely out of the window. Not only that, but we were also doing all the Secretary of Agriculture asked.[22]

---

[20] Department of Agriculture. Press Release. Statement of Claude R. Wickard, Secretary of Agriculture, before the Senate Banking Committee and Currency Subcommittee on H. R. 5990, Jan 2, 1942.
[21] *Congressional Record*, vol. 88, pt. 1, p. 7. One of several amendments introduced by Senator Bankhead on Jan. 5, 1942.
[22] Senator Prentiss M. Brown, *Congressional Record*, vol. 88, pt. 1, p. 175.

The position of Mr. O'Neal and the American Farm Bureau Federation was not long in doubt. Telegrams went to all Members of the Senate stating:

This amendment imperatively necessary to keep faith with pledges of Congress and Administration to millions of farmers who are mobilizing in an all-out effort to produce adequate food and fiber to win the war. Without this amendment entire agricultural production for defense program stands in jeopardy. This amendment also necessary in order to prevent dual authority in the administration of agricultural programs.[23]

The President was unable to stem the drive to divide control over the stabilization of farm prices. A provision requiring the Price Administrator to obtain prior approval of the Secretary of Agriculture of action affecting agricultural commodities was passed by a 48 to 37 vote of the Senate.[24] It was also accepted by the House.

Because of fundamentally different attitudes, OPA and Agriculture frequently disagreed about control of food prices, with the result that stabilization and food-production policies required continuous adjustment throughout the war.

One section of the bill which attracted relatively little attention at the time of the debates later assumed major significance. The bill submitted to the Congress contained a provision authorizing the use of subsidies for the purpose of obtaining maximum production or preventing price increases. It was contemplated that the Government would purchase commodities where necessary and resell at a lower price; a revolving fund was proposed in order to facilitate such buying and selling operations. The Price Control Act authorized subsidies for the purpose of bringing out marginal production but prohibited their use for preventing price increases.[25] Under this authority supplies of copper, lead, zinc, and other strategic materials were expanded by payment of Government premiums on all production above quotas which generally were based on 1941 output. High-cost mines were brought into production without granting the price increases which they would have required to operate under OPA ceilings. This device, known as the premium price plan, stimulated increased production, helped to stabilize prices of metal products, and saved the Government millions of dollars on purchases of metal war matériel and in general proved to be one of the most successful of the wartime programs.

The act as finally passed was characterized by the President as "all in all a workable one." The Office of Price Administration was established under the direction of a single head, the Price Administrator. It was given the responsibility for the prevention of excessive

[23] *Congressional Record*, vol. 88, pt. 1, p. 179.
[24] Ibid., p. 189.
[25] 56 *Stat.* 26–27.

and speculative price increases, price dislocations, and inflationary tendencies. In effecting these purposes the Price Administrator was authorized to establish maximum prices which would be generally fair and equitable and in doing so to give consideration to the prices prevailing between October 1 and October 15, 1941.

Special limitations were imposed on the Administrator's powers over agricultural commodities. Maximum prices could not be established for an agricultural commodity until the price of the commodity had reached the highest of the following prices: (1) 110 percent of parity or a comparable price; (2) the market price as of October 1, 1941; (3) the market price as of December 15, 1941; and (4) the average price for such commodity during the period July 1, 1919, to June 30, 1929.[26] As mentioned previously, approval of the Secretary of Agriculture was a prerequisite to the fixing of any price for an agricultural commodity.

The Price Control Act also authorized the Price Administrator to establish maximum rents for housing accommodations in areas where defense activities had affected rent levels. Under this provision the following procedure was established by OPA: (1) the agency designated war-boom communities as defense rental areas and specified the levels at which rents should be stabilized; (2) a 60-day waiting period followed this designation, during which the recommended stabilization might be achieved by voluntary action of landlords or by State or local regulation; (3) if rents were not stabilized within 60 days, Federal regulation was extended to the area and OPA designated a maximum rent date which was "generally fair and equitable" and which gave due consideration to rents prevailing on April 1, 1941, or April 1, 1940, if defense activities had inflated rents prior to April 1941; (4) within approximately 60 days after designation of the maximum rent date all rental units in a defense rental area were registered with OPA; and (5) the registered rent became the legal maximum rent for the duration of the war unless an increase was approved by OPA.

The Price Control Act gave OPA several alternative methods of enforcing its regulations: (1) Any person convicted of violating a price or rent order was subject to a maximum penalty of 1 year imprisonment and $5,000 fine. (2) Federal district, State, and territorial courts were authorized to issue writs enjoining violation or ordering compliance with regulations. (3) A person subject to a price and rent regulation could be licensed by OPA; by violating the regulation and upon suspension of the license by an authorized court, the person

---

[26] The explanation of why these alternative ceilings were written into the law is in the following: (1) 110 percent of parity gave the most favorable price for wheat, corn, oats, barley, sweetpotatoes, soybeans, peanuts, flaxseed; (2) October 1, 1941, was most favorable for cottonseed and certain types of tobacco; (3) December 15, prices were highest for rice, eggs, beef cattle, veal-calves, and wool; and (4) the 1919-1920 average gave the highest prices for potatoes, edible dry beans, cotton, live chickens, and lambs.

would forfeit for as long as 1 year his right to deal in the regulated commodity. (4) Finally, any consumer who had been charged more than the amount allowed by a price or rent regulation might sue the seller for treble damages—three times the amount of the overcharge or $50, whichever was higher.

These provisions of the Price Control Act gave OPA an unusual assortment of enforcement tools. But as its area of control widened, the effectiveness of control depended upon the willingness of retailers, landlords, consumers, and tenants to comply voluntarily with price and regulations rather than upon formal enforcement action.

Special provisions were included for the protection of private rights of individuals. Any person subject to a price or rent regulation could file with the Price Administrator a protest, accompanied by evidence supporting his contention that the regulation was unfair as applied to him. Within a reasonable period of time (generally 30 days) the Price Administrator was required to act on the protest and if the protest was denied, the individual had the right of appeal to an Emergency Court of Appeals which was created by the act. This court consisted of three judges appointed by the Chief Justice of the Supreme Court from Federal district and circuit courts and thus was certain to be highly competent. The Emergency Court of Appeals had exclusive jurisdiction, subject to final review by the Supreme Court, to determine the validity of OPA price and rent regulations. This provision expedited judicial review of OPA administrative acts, permitted continuous operation of regulations pending review by the Emergency Court, and safeguarded individual rights as fully as was consistent with wartime conditions. Subsequent dissatisfaction with this procedure was caused by OPA's inability to review quickly the protests which poured in regularly. The procedure itself was fundamentally sound.

Formulation of Stabilization Policy

Although the Price Control Act on the whole was satisfactory, the Government still lacked authority and a program to hold down the cost of living. The chief weakness in the price-control area was the limitation which had been imposed on the pricing of agricultural commodities. But there were as yet no supplementary controls over wages and little had been done to relate war finance to the requirements of the economic stabilization program. A series of crises showed that action on these matters could not long be delayed.

The first crisis was caused by the Government's attempt to hold farm prices at current levels. Upon signing the Price Control Act, the President said, "I feel that most farmers realize that when **farm** prices go much above parity, danger is ahead." He stated that he was giving the legislation his approval with the understanding, "confirmed by Congressional leaders," that the bill contained nothing which could be construed "as a limitation on the existing powers of governmental agencies . . . to make sales of agricultural commodities in the normal conduct of their operations." The Government owned large stocks of grain and cotton which had been acquired in its attempts to maintain farm prices during periods of surpluses. By timely disposition of these supplies it would be possible both to relieve shortages and to restrain shortage-induced price increases. Soon after the President signed the Price Control Act, Secretary of Agriculture Wickard announced that the Government would undertake such a program. Under the plan, the Department would attempt to stabilize farm-produce prices which had not yet reached 110 percent of parity or the other levels stipulated in the Price Control Act and which, therefore, could not be controlled by OPA price ceilings.

Immediately after this announcement cotton prices on the exchanges dropped substantially. The Senate Committee on Agriculture called the Secretary of Agriculture before it in an attempt to ascertain what modifications in the program might be possible. After a meeting of several farm organization representatives, the Senate Committee reported favorably a bill prohibiting the disposition of Government-owned stocks of cotton and grain below parity prices.[27]

The policy on the disposition of surpluses was calculated to prevent increases in the price of food. Corn and wheat producers were receiving parity income as the result of Government benefit payments. If feed prices were allowed to rise, milk prices also would have to be increased. Higher feed costs would mean either price increases for poultry and hog producers or the abandonment of increased production programs for these basic foodstuffs. By careful disposition of surplus stocks, a $1 billion rise in the annual cost of living could be prevented, the Secretary of Agriculture believed.

Meanwhile, labor's drive for wage increases commanded attention. While the price-control legislation was before Congress, a conference of industry and labor representatives was called by the President. Out of this conference came the "no-strike, no-lock-out pledge"—the promise of organized labor and management that for the duration of the war, labor disputes would be settled without work interruption. It was also agreed that the National Mediation Board should be superseded by a new agency responsible for the adjustments of disputes. By Executive order, issued on January 12, 1942, the President established the National War Labor Board, composed of four repre-

---

[27] *Congressional Record*, vol. 88, pt. 1, p. 1188. The bill was S. 2255 and the report was Senate Report No. 1054; See *New York Times*, Feb. 1, 1942, p. 1, col. 1.

sentatives each from labor, management, and the public, with the function of deciding labor disputes which could not be settled by other methods.

The WLB order did not contain any statement of national wage policy to guide settlement of wage disagreements. The Board, like other departments of the Federal Government dealing with wage matters, was directed by the Price Control Act "to work toward a stabilization of prices, fair and equitable wages, and cost of production." In the absence of policy standards such as those set forth in the Price Control Act with respect to price levels, the threat of further increase in the cost of living accentuated the administrative difficulties of the War Labor Board. Cases began to pile up before the Board had established an organization to handle them. Workers became impatient at the delays which seemed more exasperating as the cost of living surged upward. Wildcat strikes broke out, contrary to the no-strike pledge and beyond the control of the leaders who had given the pledge.

Further action on the stabilization front was imperative. A program for such action had been given in the President's budget message for 1943. The Chief Executive set a $56 billion goal for war expenditures, proposed a $7 billion tax program, and requested a $2 billion increase in the Social Security program. On the subject of inflation controls, he said:

An integrated program, including direct price controls, a flexible tax policy, allocation, rationing, and credit controls, together with producers' and consumers' cooperation will enable us to finance the war effort without danger of inflation. This is a difficult task. But it must be done and it can be done.[28]

The President instructed the Director of the Bureau of the Budget on March 16, 1942, to take the lead in developing an integrated anti-inflation program. The Treasury, Office of Price Administration, Federal Reserve Board, Department of Agriculture, and the Bureau of the Budget were to cooperate in formulating the program. The President appointed a committee, with the Vice President as chairman, which, in accordance with the President's instruction, began to "work fast."

Ten days later, March 26, 1942, a preliminary memorandum prepared by staff of the Bureau of the Budget was sent to the President. In urging the adoption of a "war program to prevent inflation" the document stated:

Bold and concerted action is required. Inflation cannot be stopped as long as wage increases, as well as rising Government expenditures, create additional purchasing power. Wage increases cannot be stopped as long as prices rise. The price rise cannot be stopped unless part of the rapidly increasing purchasing power is absorbed by fiscal measures. Fiscal measures cannot be effective as long as

---

[28] *Congressional Record*, vol. 88, pt. 1, p. 40.

businessmen, wage earners, and farmers can make up for taxes by increasing their incomes. Only simultaneous action on all fronts can stop the inflationary spiral.

The essential steps proposed were to freeze prices as of April 1; to freeze all basic wage and salary rates, except those below 40 cents an hour; to request Congress to levy heavier taxes, including, in addition to the $7 billion program of the budget message, $2 billion of personal income taxes to be withheld by employers, and a retail sales tax to raise $2.5 billion; to seek early congressional consideration of the proposed $2 billion expansion of the Social Security programs; to request immediate repeal of the 110 percent of parity provision of the Price Control Act, and subsequently to freeze all farm prices; and to adopt other inflation controls, such as extension of rationing, control of inventory accumulations, and limitation of installment buying of non-rationed goods.

Officials working on the anti-inflation program disagreed about what policies to recommend to the President. The Secretary of Treasury objected especially to a retail sales tax, lowered income-tax exemptions, compulsory savings, and a wage freeze. He was particularly concerned about the effect on pending tax legislation of a request for additional taxes. In a letter to the President he stated:

> Any substantial changes in this [tax] program proposed by the Administration, would greatly confuse the situation, delay enactment, and on these accounts, materially increase during the interval inflationary tendencies. There is little or no prospect of increasing the tax yield beyond the amount asked for in the Treasury program.

A compulsory savings policy would, the Treasury believed, destroy its voluntary savings program. Arrangements had been made with labor and management for pay-roll deduction purchases of bonds and there was a large investment of personnel, planning, and advertising materials in the voluntary program.

Opposition of Secretary Morgenthau weakened the effort to formulate an effective program of action. He disagreed with and did not sign a memorandum submitted to the President on April 18 by the other members of the committee, who said "We have come to the conclusion that partial programs will not work and that only a simultaneous attack on prices, rents, wages, profits, and mass purchasing power will suffice". The committee's program included (1) an immediate ceiling on all prices; (2) proclamation of a policy of stabilization of all wage rates above 40 cents an hour; (3) prevention of unreasonable wartime corporate profits by the tightening of excess-profits-tax provisions, strict application of the internal revenue laws which prohibit deductions of "unreasonable" salaries, and a ceiling of $50,000 after taxes on individual income; and (4) absorption of $10 billion

CHART 29. *Sources of Federal Funds: Tax Receipts and Borrowings.*

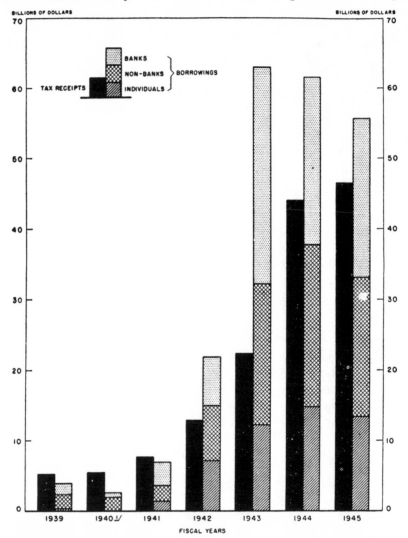

¹ Total held by non-banks includes .1 billion dollars which represents the net change in individual holdings.

Source: Bureau of the Budget.

excess purchasing power by a compulsory "universal savings plan," lowering of personal income-tax exemptions, and the expansion of the Social Security program. In conclusion, the memorandum stated, "Only a program as drastic and broad as that here outlined can stop inflation. Any lesser program must fail. Such failure will be a major defeat."

The pessimistic tone of the memorandum was justified by economic developments since the declaration of war. From December 1941 to March 1942 food costs rose 4.9 percent and clothing prices 7.7 percent. By March the prices of these commodities were approximately 20 percent higher than 1 year earlier. These increases had taken place in spite of the extension of formal price controls by the Office of Price Administration, and they were greater than during any similar period of the previous year. The rapid movement of workers to war production jobs during February and March contributed to the rising level of income payments. While the production of consumer goods declined sharply, retail sales continued at high levels (chart 30). Most of the ingredients for a run-away inflation were present.

Seven Point Anti-Inflation Program

On April 27 the President sent to the Congress his seven-point program to stabilize the cost of living. The message was not specific in all of its proposals, presumably because of the inability of the Wallace committee to agree on a detailed program and because of Secretary Morgenthau's opposition to compulsory savings, a heavier tax program, and a wage freeze. "To keep the cost of living from spiraling upward," the President said, "we must:

1. . . . tax heavily, and in that process keep personal and corporate profits at a reasonable rate, the word "reasonable" being defined at a low level.
2. . . . fix ceilings on the prices which consumers, retailers, wholesalers, and manufacturers pay for the things they buy; and ceilings on rents for dwellings in all areas affected by war industries.
3. . . . stabilize the remuneration received by individuals for their work.
4. . . . stabilize the prices received by growers for the products of their lands.
5. . . . we must encourage all citizens to contribute to the cost of winning this war by purchasing war bonds with their earnings instead of using those earnings to buy articles which are not essential.
6. . . . we must ration all essential commodities of which there is a scarcity, so that they may be distributed fairly among consumers and not merely in accordance with financial ability to pay high prices for them.
7. . . . we must discourage credit and installment buying, and encourage the paying off of debts, mortgages, and other obligations . . .[29]

The authority and administrative facilities of the Office of Price Administration were available to carry out points 2 and 6—to estab-

---

[29] House Document No. 716, 77th Cong., 2d sess., p. 3.

lish general price ceilings, control rents, and ration scarce commodities. The tax program and revision of farm price controls depended
upon Congressional action which the President requested. Either
Congress or the Executive might stabilize wages, the other crucial
part of the anti-inflation program.

OPA Action Under the Seven-Point Program

The first and major action under the seven-point program was taken
by OPA. On April 28, it issued the General Maximum Price Regulation which set the highest price charged in March 1942 as a ceiling
over virtually every commodity purchased by the ordinary consumer.
The GMPR was supplemented by 18 price regulations issued the
same day and covering specific commodities such as solid fuels, nonferrous castings, paper and paper products, farm equipment, and
construction and road maintenance equipment. An order designating
302 defense rental areas also was issued, bringing to 323 the areas
designated since passage of the Price Control Act.

CHART 30. *Retail Sales.*

Source: Department of Commerce.

Largely because of the newness of the OPA organization, these regulations were more sweeping than the agency could administer effectively. Although staffing of the national office was reasonably adequate by the summer of 1942, weaknesses of internal organization and of administrative personnel seriously impaired the agency's operations. First, separate organizational status had been given to specialized technical personnel, such as lawyers, accountants, and information staff, and to price, rent, and rationing activities. This form of organization produced an excess layering of clearance and gave to daily operations some of the less attractive aspects of international negotiation. Simple differences of opinion among staff working on common problems were the subject of prolonged discussion or were referred for decision to the Price Administrator or his senior deputy. The coordinate organization and responsibility of the legal staff with the price, rent, and rationing departments was particularly unfortunate. Getting agreement between the lawyers and program personnel on policy questions frequently occupied the staff for months and the lawyers' concern over possible litigation resulted in regulations which were unduly technical in form and difficult for the public to

CHART 31. *Retail Inventories.*

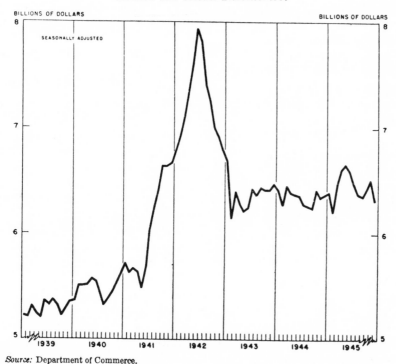

Source: Department of Commerce.

understand.   Second, the agency lacked experienced administrative
talent at the center.   Price Administrator Henderson necessarily was
preoccupied with high policy questions and with relations with
Congress, other agencies, and the public.   Thus the job of pulling
together the price, rent, rationing, legal, and information departments
and of providing administrative leadership for the whole organization
fell to the senior deputy.   The internal organization of OPA thus
accentuated difficulties which the top personnel were not equipped
to handle.   Third, OPA programs called for the printing and distribution of vast quantities of regulations, registration forms, coupon books,
and information bulletins.   The agency was handicapped in this
vital area by the weaknesses of the Government's facilities for handling
printing and distribution jobs of such vast proportions.

Administration of the General Maximum Price Regulation and other
price regulations required processing of hundreds of price adjustment
petitions alleging hardship.   The national office lacked facilities to
assemble and analyze data relevant to these cases and no general
policies had been laid down to guide the personnel in granting adjustments.   As a result, the national office during the summer of 1942
found itself swamped with work which it was not equipped to handle,
which delayed solution of pressing administrative problems, and which
interrupted essential development of new price-control techniques.
One result was to delay for months the anticipated replacement of
the "general freeze" with new tailor-made price regulations; e. g.,
dollars-and-cents regulations, which finally replaced GMPR for many
commodities.

The OPA field organization was even less ready to absorb the administrative load incident to the seven-point program.   When it became
necessary to ration tires after Pearl Harbor, OPA, with the assistance
of rationing administrators appointed by State governors, established
a Nation-wide network of 8,000 local rationing boards.   As additional
programs were undertaken—automobiles, sugar, typewriters—the
rationing organization expanded to include 48 State offices.   Later
district offices were also organized, conforming more or less to industrial
and commercial areas.   The district offices, of which there were 25
by the summer of 1942, were expected ultimately to administer price
controls in the field.   Rent control was administered through area
offices which were independent of both State and district offices.
All of the subordinate field offices—State, district, rent area—fell
within the immediate supervisory jurisdiction of regional offices, of
which there were eight by the end of July.   Many of the district
offices had been "opened" but in no sense were ready for business.
Although the General Maximum Price Regulation had been in preparation for months, there was little opportunity to discuss its initial

provisions with field staff (indeed, there were few with whom it might have been discussed) or to provide field offices with information useful in answering public inquiries.

Provision for supervision of the field organization added to the confusion engendered by the loosely constructed organization. Until March 1942 responsibility for field operations was lodged in a Division of Field Operations through which all instructions, regulations, procedures, and the like were channeled to field offices. After the Division was abolished in March, the major program divisions communicated directly with price, rent, and rationing personnel in the field offices, frequently without informing regional administrators and state and district directors of their actions. Responsibility for supervision of the field organization was undertaken by the Senior Deputy Administrator who also was responsible for general management of the Washington office. These combined responsibilities were so burdensome that inadequate attention was given to administrative problems at both the Washington and field office levels.

Although OPA's administrative inadequacies were to be expected in a new and rapidly expanding organization and were also present in other war agencies, they were especially significant in OPA because that agency had to carry the major responsibility for economic stabilization. As long as OPA's administrative deficiencies remained, price control rested on the ability of the Price Administrator to achieve compliance by securing the cooperation of business and the general public.

The President's indication in his April 27 message that rationing would be resorted to only when there was an inadequate supply of an essential commodity represented an important policy decision. The Secretary of Treasury, in his argument against a stiff, integrated anti-inflation program, had urged the use of rationing on a wide scale in order to reduce competition between consumers for scarce goods. Limited experience with rationing had shown that, in view of administrative complexities and public resistance to any rationing not clearly justified by shortages, rationing should be used only in limited and urgent cases.

Taxation

In his seven-point anti-inflation message the President had said "we must tax heavily." There were two reasons for heavier taxes. First, a very large part of war costs should be met out of current incomes of the American people which, because of vast Government expenditures, would reach record levels. In the spring of 1942, it appeared that war expenditures in the fiscal year 1943 would be about

$70 billion and the revenues from existing taxes about $18.3 billion. These estimates had led the Wallace anti-inflation committee, appointed by the President in March, to recommend new taxes totaling $11.6 billion and a $2 billion increase in social security taxes. Under this program we would have paid about 42 percent of war costs out of current revenues and about 58 percent by borrowing.

The second reason for taxing heavily was that OPA price, rent, and rationing controls needed to be reinforced by a tax program which would reduce substantially excess consumer purchasing power. If a large share of the war were financed out of current income, there would be less competition between consumers for scarce goods such as food and clothing.

The Treasury in March 1942 submitted to Congress a new tax program calling for $7.6 billion in new taxes, about two-thirds of the amount recommended by the Wallace committee. Secretary Morgenthau was unwilling to support a more substantial increase in taxes, presumably on the assumption that Congress would be unfriendly to a larger increase. In his testimony he said, "The new revenue act must help to check inflation, for nothing in the economic field can interfere with the war effort as much as an uncontrolled rise in prices". He went on, however, to say that "taxes alone" cannot prevent inflation and "the sooner we come to complete rationing the better, as far as inflation goes".[30]

The Wallace committee had suggested a retail sales tax to raise $2.5 billion. This proposal was not acceptable to the Treasury and was also opposed by labor and consumer organizations. It was supported before the Ways and Means Committee by the witness for the National Association of Manufacturers, who also commented adversely on taxation as an anti-inflation measure:

Of course, we recognize that a tax on consumption would add to the cost of goods. But this in itself cannot bring about inflation. If you will pardon the language, we need only some plain old-fashioned American guts to stop inflation before it really gets under way. We can do this by putting a ceiling—at whatever point this ceiling may be—on the prices of agricultural products, manufactured goods, labor, commodities, and rents . . .

We cannot believe that the millions of patriotic American farmers and working men object to these proper means of controlling inflation, and it is our sincere belief that they are ready to join manufacturers in the acceptance of any rigorous controls which threats of inflation may require.

We have little sympathy for suggestions to take from people in this country a sizable portion of their savings and earnings just because of the theoretical effect on inflation; especially since the direct means of controlling inflation have yet to be taken and given thorough trial.[31]

────────────
[30] U. S. Congress. House. Committee on Ways and Means. Hearings on Revenue Revision of 1942 (revised), pp. 2 et seq.

[31] Ibid., p. 274. Statement of J. Cheever Cowdin, Chairman of the Committee on Government Finance of the National Association of Manufacturers.

The Treasury proposed to finance about 63 percent of the war by expanding its voluntary bond purchase program. At the request of Secretary Morgenthau, officials of the General Motors Corporation, and union representatives of General Motors' employees appeared before the committee and described the elaborate campaign which had been developed for the sale of war bonds. Union officials testified to their belief in the advantages of the voluntary system and the relation between voluntary methods, morale, and production. At the conclusion of the presentation the chairmen of the House and Senate committees gave their support to the voluntary savings program, about which the President had said: "I prefer . . . to keep the voluntary plan in effect as long as possible." During the first 3 months of 1942 bond sales to individuals totaled only $2.3 billion, and for the quarter ending September 30 only $2.47 billion. Savings bonds sales accounted for less than one-fifth of the amount borrowed during July–September. During the summer, while Congress deliberated on the tax bill, bond purchases did not relieve notably the pressure on price ceilings.

The Revenue Act of 1942 became law in October and would provide, according to estimates, approximately $3.6 billion additional revenue in the fiscal year 1943.[32] This increase was about half of the amount which the President had requested. The United States would pay about 26 percent of war expenditures by taxation, as compared with 53 percent in Great Britain and 55 percent in Canada. To absorb some of the excess purchasing power, the new act levied a "victory tax" of 5 percent on income in excess of $12 per week, to be withheld from the individual's pay check.

Food Price Control

The Office of Price Administration faced two difficulties in controlling food prices: First, commodities such as poultry, eggs, sheep and lambs, milk and milk products and wheat products, including flour, could not be brought under General Maximum Price Regulations because of the Price Control Act's restriction on pricing agricultural commodities. The cost of living could not be stabilized until the prices of these basic foods were brought under control and with this objective the President's seven-point message requested Congress to restore the "original and excellent" goal of parity for American farmers.

Second, there was the problem of the "squeeze" under the General Maximum Price Regulations. GMPR was intended to hold prices generally at March 1942 levels. As retailers began to replenish

[32] 56 *Stat.* 798.

stocks of canned fruits and vegetables, they found that ceiling prices of their supplies were higher than the retail price ceilings. For one retailer, for example, the retail sales price of asparagus was $1.75 per case, the wholesale price $2 per case. Farm prices and labor costs were up about 10 percent each and transportation costs were 5 percent higher than in the previous year. Such substantial increases could not be absorbed by canners, but if they were passed on to retailers, retail price ceilings would have to be raised. The problem of the "squeeze" reached the crisis stage in May and June when, with record crops in the fields, packers and distributors threatened to strike until their prices were raised.

There were three possible solutions for this problem. The first possibility was one frequently urged by retailers caught in the "squeeze": March ceilings might be raised to allow retailers to pass on to consumers the higher prices which had been granted to processors. If applied generally, this policy would have made it impossible to hold the price line. A second alternative was to remove canned fruits and vegetables from price controls. The chief argument advanced for this action was that consumers would be brought to a realization that OPA could not control the cost of living under the farm price provisions of the Price Control Act. Removal of controls,

CHART 32. *Disposition of Total Income Payments of Individuals:*

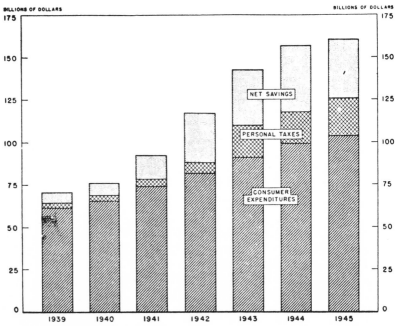

BILLIONS OF DOLLARS   BILLIONS OF DOLLARS

NET SAVINGS

PERSONAL TAXES

CONSUMER EXPENDITURES

1939 1940 1941 1942 1943 1944 1945

Source: Department of Commerce.

however, would have made more difficult the eventual stabilization of food costs. A third alternative was to hold the line at March price levels and to absorb increased costs through Government subsidies.

Although OPA favored Government subsidies to relieve the "squeeze," this alternative also was questionable In view of the legislative history of section 3 of the Price Control Act, which indicated a clear congressional intent to provide flexible prices for agricultural commodities, it was difficult to see how the Executive Branch could maintain fixed prices for agricultural commodities by subsidy payments. The authority of the Department of Agriculture in the maintenance of maximum prices was also a complicating factor. Through the Commodity Credit Corporation, the Department had about $450 million and unquestioned authority to subsidize for the purpose of increasing production or guaranteeing minimum prices to farmers. But use of these funds to maintain fixed food prices contrary to congressional policy might jeopardize the program for subsidizing food production.

A clear-cut solution was not possible. On June 19, 1942, the President advised the Secretary of Agriculture of his anxiety that "every possible administrative step be taken to maintain price ceilings established under the General Maximum Price Regulation, and, at the same time, secure the necessary volume of agricultural production." His letter continued:

> Pending clarification of the policy of Congress on this question, I am asking you to use Commodity Credit Corporation funds, or funds available to the Department . . . for the purpose of making purchases for resale at a possible loss in those instances in which the situation is so critical that some sort of action needs to be taken in the very near future.
>
> You should also promptly advise congressional leaders of your plans in order to be assured that they have full understanding of the program and will facilitate legislation necessary for its success.

The President also sent a letter to Price Administrator Henderson, saying:

> I would like to have you work very closely with the Department of Agriculture on this program and render every possible assistance to the end that we maintain the highest possible production of food commodities while holding the cost of living at present levels.

It was hoped that the immediate emergency (the 1942 pack of fruits and vegetables) might be handled in the manner suggested by the President. This solution, however, depended on the willingness of Congress to maintain food price ceilings and to authorize subsidies for that purpose. Since passage of the Price Control Act in January, Congress on a number of occasions had asserted its opposition to more rigorous control of farm prices. This position was especially clear in an amendment to the appropriation bill for the Office of Price Administration which restated and strengthened the 110 percent of parity and other restrictive provisions of section 3 of the Price Control Act.[33] After conferences between congressional leaders, the Secretary of Agriculture and the Price Administrator, it was concluded that the available funds of the Department of Agriculture should not be used to maintain price ceilings until the specific question had been fully discussed by Congress.

Accordingly, the Office of Price Administration made such adjustments in the price ceilings as were necessary to move 1942 crops of fruits and vegetables. A Gallup survey made in June showed that 58 percent of the farmers were satisfied with the prices which their crops were bringing. But Executive agencies were obliged to conform to legislative policy of flexible prices for agricultural commodities.

Wage Stabilization

Upward adjustments of food prices did not, however, contribute to stabilization of the cost of living, or to the stabilization of wages. The April 27 message of the President dealt with wage matters in these terms:

> . . . all stabilization or adjustment of wages will be settled by the War Labor Board machinery which has been generally accepted by the industry and labor for the settlement of all disputes . . . the existing machinery . . . will, of course, continue to give due consideration to inequalities and the elimination of substandards of living.[34]

This statement did not provide a national wage policy. When were there inequalities? Does an inequality exist when there are differences between one wage group and another? If so, it would be impossible to prevent an inflationary spiral.

Allocation of authority among the agencies interested in wage stabilization was not clear-cut. The War Labor Board necessarily would have to develop wage standards in the process of settling disputes. The Board, however, seemed overwhelmed by the number and complexity of the cases referred to it in the first half of 1942. While it was attempting to settle some of these disputes, other agencies moved on the wage stabilization problem. On May 22 the Department of Labor announced an agreement for the building trades which stabilized wages on Government war construction at rates paid under collective bargaining agreements on July 1. The Labor Production Division of the War Production Board sponsored a wage stabilization agreement in the shipbuilding industry and planned to extend these arrangements to other areas. The primary objective of WPB's wage

[33] 56 *Stat.* 704.
[34] House Document No. 716, 77th Cong., 2d sess.

activities was to increase production by developing a stable labor force, reducing turnover and migration, and facilitating the training of new employees for industrial work. A secondary objective was to stabilize wages at levels which would help check inflationary pressures.

These objectives were to some degree incompatible and it was not clear just how all of them could be achieved. In a tight labor market it would be difficult, if not impossible, to increase some wages and reduce others. Adjustment by collective bargaining between unions and employers normally resulted in higher wage levels.

A conference of the airframe industry held on the West coast in July illustrated the conflicting objectives among the several Government agencies interested in wage stabilization. The War Manpower Commission was primarily interested in questions of labor supply, the War Production Board in the expansion of production. "Price as usual" during a production crisis was as reprehensible as "business as usual." This attitude was repugnant to OPA's position and could not be fitted into the general economic stabilization program. Divergent views of Government officials confused labor and employer representatives, who requested a statement clarifying the Government's standards of wage stabilization as set forth in the April 27 anti-inflation message.

A definition consonant with the requirements of price stabilization was supplied by the OPA representative:

Wage stabilization means no wage increases except to eliminate inequalities and substandards of living . . . The Government will require that compelling evidence be produced before assenting to any increase.[35]

Since the union officials had presented requests for substantial wage increases, the effect of this statement was such that the conference adjourned and the Government representatives returned to Washington to work out a method of relating high-level production, price ceilings, and wage stabilization.

On July 16 the turbulent labor situation was eased temporarily by the War Labor Board's decision in the Little Steel wage dispute. While this case was pending, the Board was almost destroyed by a labor threat to withdraw its representatives from the Board—a crisis which was prevented by Presidential intervention. Public opinion had been outraged by a series of strikes in February and March which endangered the program for conversion to military production. To deal with this situation WLB proposed to raise hourly wage rates only where wage increases had not kept pace with the 15 percent rise in the cost of living between January 1941, and May 1942. Exceptions to this rule would be granted only to remove inequalities or substandard conditions. According to a Government public-opinion

[35] OPA Press Release 273, July 13, 1942. Statement of Richard V. Gilbert.

survey, this formula was acceptable to a majority of workers: 60 percent of the workers were in favor of stabilizing wages at current levels. Of these, 37 percent insisted that the cost of living be kept in line with wages.

The Office of Price Administration was less enthusiastic about the War Labor Board's formula for tying wages to the cost of living. Such a scheme would tend to maintain prewar standards of living—an expectation which was perhaps not justifiable in a war for survival. Under the formula, large blocks of workers would be entitled to wage adjustments. Such adjustments would complicate the task of the price-control agency in two ways: (1) unit labor costs, which had risen by an average of 1.3 percent per month from January to May, might force revisions of price ceilings which the agency was not equipped to handle; and (2) without compulsory savings or a stiff tax law, the gap between consumer income and the supply of consumer goods would steadily widen.

Credit Controls

On May 6, 1942, the Board of Governors of the Federal Reserve System revised and strengthened its Regulation W which restricted purchases of consumers' durable goods through installment payments, charge accounts, and other forms of credit. The regulation had been issued in August 1941 under authority of an Executive order, and was intended to slow down the record buying which threatened to deplete inventories of consumers' goods.[36] Although credit controls were reasonably effective, they did not reach the people who could afford to pay cash for the goods they wanted. For this reason credit controls were of minor importance in the fight against inflation.

To summarize, the seven-point program was an attempt to deal simultaneously with all major aspects of the inflation problem—price and rent levels, wages, finance. The principal achievement was the issuance by the Office of Price Administration of the General Maximum Price Regulation and accompanying price and rent regulations. By July, however, it was apparent that the plan would fail because follow-up action on several points had not been taken. OPA's difficulty in administering the General Maximum Price Regulation was aggravated by the lack of supporting action specified in the President's message. Excess purchasing power created pressure under price ceilings as Congress debated a new tax bill and postponed action on revision of the 110 percent of parity limitation of the Price Control Act. Bond sales to individuals, chosen as an alternative to compulsory

---

[36] Executive Order No. 8843, Aug. 9, 1941, 6 *Federal Register* 4035-37; Regulation W, August 21, 1941, 6 *Federal Register* 4443, revised May 6, 1942, 7 *Federal Register* 3351-57.

savings, accounted for a small part of total Government borrowing. As long as the 110 percent restriction remained, OPA could not place ceilings on basic foodstuffs and the cost of living would continue to rise. Meanwhile, labor would drive for wage increases at least equal to those allowable under the Little Steel formula.

Stabilization Act of 1942

With the break-down of the seven-point program, another drive for coordination of anti-inflation activities was begun. By the end of July it was apparent that the Little Steel formula for granting wage increases was an invitation to some of the farm organization leaders to get still higher prices for farm produce. Labor leaders considered any substantial rise in the cost of living an invitation to seek further wage increases. Congress was anxious to get out of Washington. The normal midsummer recess seemed even more appealing in view of the November Congressional elections. By the end of July, many Congressmen had gone home during an unofficial recess to which the President had agreed.

OPA began to push for action by the Executive branch to ease the stabilization crisis and presented to Judge Rosenman a proposal at the White House for tightening up farm price and wage controls. The memorandum stated that the cost of living could not be stablized "unless all major elements . . . including wages and agricultural commodities, are subject to common stabilization." It recommended establishment of an administrative board to formulate wage stabilization policies and to issue directives to Federal agencies responsible for wage regulation, and the use of subsidies to maintain OPA price ceilings. The proposal was rejected because, without legislation authorizing such use of subsidies, the rise in the cost of living could not be halted. Also, creation of another labor agency was administratively unjustifiable and would probably contribute to rather than minimize labor unrest.

The desirability of creating an agency to coordinate actions of various agencies responsible for parts of the stabilization program was explored. Such an agency would be useful only if authority could be found to stop the rise in the cost of living. After discussions among White House and Bureau of the Budget staff, a draft order was prepared in August, creating an Office of Economic Stabilization; prohibiting wage increases except where necessary to eliminate substandards of living or inequalities or to restore real wage rates as they existed on January 1, 1944; and authorizing the Administrator of OES to fix agricultural prices at the higher of two levels—market price or parity price as computed by the Secretary of Agriculture.

The proposed authority over farm prices in effect would amend by Executive order the 110 percent of parity and other limitations of the price-control act. The legal grounds for such action were explained to the Senate in the following terms:

> Remember that the Second War Powers Act was passed in March 1942, a little over a month after the price-control bill was passed, and, therefore, it supersedes the Price Control Act as to any matters with respect to which the two may conflict.
>
> I have composed in sentence form a paraphrase of the provisions of the act which apply to the present situation:
>
> > That whenever the President is satisfied that the fulfillments of requirements for the defense of the United States will result in a shortage in the supply of any material . . . he may allot such material in such manner . . . upon such conditions . . .
>
> What can that mean other than the conditions of the price, terms, and so forth, by which the materials and supplies will reach the public for private account, will reach the Army, and will reach the lend-lease operations?
>
> I can conceive of no language which could be written in general terms which would give the President of the United States greater power over the economic life, the service of supply, and the prices of things we have to buy and sell, than would the language contained in the Second War Powers Act.[37]

There was little doubt of public willingness to accept responsibilities incident to the stabilization program. In August 70 percent of the people interviewed in a Gallup survey thought that every family not on relief should pay substantially heavier taxes. The efforts of the OPA to control the cost of living were commended by 54 percent. And 71 percent approved the freezing of wages, salaries, and food costs, with no appreciable difference between the attitude of farm and urban dwellers.[38]

Voices were raised in opposition to the type of Executive action that had been proposed. The executive board of the Congress of Industrial Organizations sent to the White House a resolution opposing the "naming of any czar or supreme dictator to regulate the economic affairs of the Nation," criticizing the tax proposals of the Senate Finance Committee, and stating that "failure to adopt a sound tax program will defeat the entire national economic program".[39] A Republican Senator was quoted as saying that the President should seek laws to bring farm-price-ceiling restrictions down to 100 percent of parity and that the War Labor Board should be given authority to pass on voluntary wage increases; he condemned those who argued that the President could "take any action he wanted to under his war powers".[40] There were indications that amendment of the Price Control Act by Executive order would be made a campaign issue in

---

[37] Senator Prentiss M. Brown, *Congressional Record*, vol. 88, pt. 6, pp. 7407-09.

[38] *Public Opinion Quarterly*, vol. 6, no. 4, p. 452.

[39] *New York Times*, Sept. 2, 1942, p. 16, col. 3.

[40] *New York Times*, Aug. 28, 1942, p. 1, col. 1, Senator Taft.

the November congressional elections. Presidential advisers, confident of the willingness of the public to accept more drastic economic sacrifice and perturbed by the seriousness of the stabilization crisis, urged the President to issue the proposed order.

Their recommendation was rejected by the President and on September 7, he asked Congress for an immediate revision of the Price Control Act. On the question of the use of Executive authority to obtain control of farm prices, he said "the course which I am following in this case is consistent with my sense of responsibility as President in time of war, and with my deep and unalterable devotion to the processes of democracy." Again he pointed out that real stabilization could be achieved only by concerted action on all seven of the anti-inflation fronts. As in April, such action depended upon enactment of an adequate tax program, and a law permitting the fixing of price ceilings on farm products at parity prices. The President called attention to the fact that Congress had not acted on this essential legislation and that further delay would endanger the economy. He said that the Price Control Act restrictions on the pricing of farm commodities meant that "the lowest average level for all farm commodities at which ceilings may be imposed is not 110 percent, but 116 percent of parity." Since price ceilings wer established in May 1942, food costs—controlled and uncontrolled—had risen 1¼ percent per month; exempt commodities had risen an average of 3½ percent per month since May. The rise in uncontrolled food prices, he said, "has been so drastic as to constitute an immediate threat to the whole price structure, to the entire cost of living, and to any attempt to stabilize wages." Wages could not be stabilized unless the cost of food and clothing and shelter was also stabilized.

The President requested Congress to pass legislation authorizing him to stabilize the cost of living, including the price of all farm commodities.

I ask the Congress to take this action by the first of October. Inaction on your part by that date will leave me with an inescapable responsibility to the people of this country to see to it that the war effort is no longer imperiled by threat of economic chaos.

In the event that the Congress should fail to act, and act adequately, I shall accept the responsibility, and I will act.

At the same time that farm prices are stabilized, wages can and will be stabilized also. This I will do.[41]

Congressional comment on the President's message was unfavorable. It was said that the President's challenge was "an even worse method of approaching the problem than to issue an Executive order directly"; the assertion that the President possessed authority to set aside the parity limitation and to fix wages and salaries was described as

---

[41] *Congressional Record*, vol. 88. pt. 5, p. 7042.

revolutionary, as leading to dictatorship, and as foreign to American constitutional principles. Failure to control wages was said to be the fault of the Executive and not of the Congress. The request for legislative control of farm prices but not for wages was noted: "There is much about agriculture, little about labor." A threat to national unity was seen: "It is unfortunate that when we are straining every nerve to win the war on every continent on earth, the people should be divided by an attempt to override the Constitution." The "you do it or I will" tone of the message provoked the comment that "the responsibility cannot be adroitly transferred exclusively to these halls." The charge that the Congress had failed to act on the two phases of the stabilization program which required legislation was said to invite "highly unfair implications which are unwarranted in fact." [42]

Within a short time, Congressmen were on their way back to Washington and by September 21 bills had been introduced, hearings had been held, and measures had been reported to the House and Senate. Debate began immediately. Minor issues were administration of the Price Control Act by the Office of Price Administration, failure of the Executive Branch to stabilize wages following the passage of the Price Control Act, the extent to which discretionary authority would be granted to "correct gross inequities," and the possibility of preventing inflation without establishing controls over all segments of the economy.

The paramount issue was whether the law fixing the method of computing parity should be changed to include farm labor costs. The parity formula, originally provided in the Agricultural Adjustment Act of 1933, had been changed from time to time, depending upon general economic conditions and the kind of Government program needed to give farmers a larger share of the national income. Inclusion of farm labor costs in the formula would have required further rises in agricultural commodity prices before controls could be imposed. This method of obtaining higher prices for farm produce was suggested in November 1941 by the chairman of the House Committee on Agriculture. He expressed his satisfaction with the 110 percent of parity saying: "I cannot understand how those of us who represent the farmers of the country could ask more." He expressed dissatisfaction, however, with the method used by the Department of Agriculture in computing parity stating:

As far as I am concerned the Department [of Agriculture] is using the wrong formulas in fixing parity prices on farm products. The Department does not add anything for farm labor nor does the Department take into consideration in seeing to it that the parity prices will give the farmers a just proportion of the national

[42] Ibid., pp. 7046–49.

income. The job of working out a fair and proper formula is going to be up to my committee.[43]

The possibility of a drive to get higher prices also had been foreseen in the President's Labor Day message, in which he said, "In computing parity, we should continue to use the computations of the Bureau of Agricultural Economics made under the law as it stands today."

Congress was deluged with telegrams and letters urging that the parity formula law be changed to include farm labor costs. The American Farm Bureau Federation, National Grange, National Council of Farmer Cooperatives, and the National Cooperative Milk Producers Federation all supported revision.[44] These pressures were so intense that the chairman of the Senate Banking and Currency Committee felt that it was necessary to remind his colleagues that "we do not hear from the vast majority of the American people." [45] Protests of Senators against pressure tactics provoked the response that leaders of farm organizations "are elected by farmer members of their organizations" and express the convictions and recommendations of millions of farmers.[46] Farm labor shortages, rising labor costs incident thereto, and the Government's program for increased food production were cited in support of the proposed revision.

The farm organizations were willing to reduce the 110-percent-of-parity restriction as recommended by the President, provided the cost of farm labor was included in the parity price. Agreement to accept a "reduction" of this price was no real concession. Rises in industrial wages themselves did not mean that agriculture was in a relatively less favorable position since "automatically parity goes up as industrial wages increase, because it is not a question so much of prices, as of relative parity of purchasing power as between the present time and the base period of 1909 to 1914." [47] Estimates by the Department of Agriculture indicated that inclusion of farm labor in in the parity formula in fact would raise the 110-percent limitation to 112 percent. "If we are going to do that," said Senator Taft, "why do we not abandon the entire joint resolution? . . . [It] is an act which on its face would make the Senate look ridiculous." Nevertheless, Congress accepted the amendment to change the parity law by votes of 284 to 96 in the House and 48 to 43 in the Senate.[48]

As the October 1 deadline approached, the White House considered the action that should be taken if Congress should order the inclusion of farm labor costs in the parity formula and thereby give another

[43] *Congressional Record,* vol. 87, pt. 9, pp. 9228–29.

[44] *Congressional Record,* vol. 88, pt. 6, p. 7244.

[45] Ibid., p. 7408.

[46] *New York Times,* Sept. 26, 1942, p. 1, col. 4. Messrs. Goss, Teague, Babcock, O'Neal, and Holman to Senators Thomas (Oklahoma) and Hatch.

[47] Senator Barkley, *Congressional Record,* vol. 88, pt. 6, p. 7246.

[48] *Congressional Record,* vol. 88, pt. 6, p. 7251. This was not a vote on final passage of the bill.

boost to the inflationary spiral. A Presidential veto and issuance of the September draft Executive order seemed probable. In the Senate supporters of the anti-inflation program noted the possibility of a veto and devised a compromise which would permit the revision of price ceilings by the President to cover the increased production costs. Farm-organization leaders opposed the compromise, arguing that there was nothing in the record of price control to indicate that the Presidential authority would be used to make such revisions. The compromise was accepted, however, and the Stabilization Act was sent to the White House on October 2.

This act, an amendment to the Price Control Act of 1942, directed the President to issue before November 1 a "general order stabilizing prices, wages, and salaries affecting the cost of living;" as far as practicable such stabilization was to be on the basis of the levels of September 15, 1942. Adjustments were authorized to the extent found necessary by the President to "aid in the effective prosecution of the war or to correct gross inequities." [49]

The act provided that price ceilings for agricultural commodities could not be set below the higher of two prices: (1) parity or comparable prices as determined and adjusted by the Secretary of Agriculture; and (2) the highest price received by producers between January 1, 1942, and September 15, 1942. The act required that prices fixed for processed commodities should reflect to the grower the higher of these two prices and allow a generally fair and equitable margin for the processor. The compromise on the addition of farm labor costs to parity required that they should be given "adequate weighting" in fixing maximum prices for agricultural commodities and that these prices be adjusted where "it appears that such modification is necessary to increase the production of such commodity for war purposes, or where by reason of increased labor or other costs to the producers . . . incurred since January 1, 1941, the maximum prices . . . will not reflect such increased costs." Other sections dealt with the prevention of a postwar collapse of agricultural prices and increased the crop-loan rate from 85 to 90 percent of parity.

The act fixed the highest wage levels existing between January 1, 1942, and September 15, 1942 (the same base period as that required for farm prices) as a floor below which wage and salary ceilings could not be set except where adjustments in wages and salaries were necessary to correct gross inequities and to aid in the prosecution of the war. Also, a basis for control of common-carrier and utility rates was established in the act.

In signing the bill on October 2, the President stated:

The Congress has done its part in helping substantially to stabilize the cost of

---

[49] *56 Stat.* 765.

living. The new legislation removes the exemption of certain foods, agricultural commodities, and related products from the price control of the Emergency Price Control Act. . . . It leaves the parity principle unimpaired. It reaffirms the powers of the executive over wages and salaries. It establishes a floor for wages and for farm prices.

I am certain that from now on this substantial stabilization of the cost of living will assist greatly in bringing the war to a successful conclusion, will make the transition to peace conditions easier after the war, and will receive the whole-hearted approval of farmers, workers, and housewives in every part of the country.[50]

Office of Economic Stabilization

Following through on the directive of Congress to issue a general stabilization order before November 1, the President on October 3 signed an Executive order establishing the Office of Economic Stabilization, headed by the Economic Stabilization Director.[51] An Economic Stabilization Board was set up to advise and consult with the Director. It comprised the Secretaries of Treasury, Agriculture, Commerce, and Labor, the Chairman of the Board of Governors of the Federal Reserve System, the Director of the Budget, the Price Administrator, the Chairman of the War Labor Board, and two representatives each of labor, management, and agriculture, appointed by the President.

The October Executive order established the following administrative pattern for management of the stabilization program: The Director of OES, on behalf and with the support of the President, would formulate general programs and reconcile conflicting policies and disagreements among agencies whose actions affected economic stabilization. These agencies, such as WLB, OPA, and Agriculture, would retain primary responsibility within their jurisdictions, but would be subject to policy directives of OES. Under this pattern OES would not need a large staff, but as stated by the order, would "so far as possible, utilize the information, data, and staff services of other Federal Departments and agencies which have activities or functions related to national economic policy." Justice Byrnes resigned from the Supreme Court in order to take the post of Economic Stabilization Director. In announcing his appointment on October 3, the President characterized the job of the Director as "one of the most important in the country," and as calling "primarily for judicial consideration." The organization of the Office "will therefore be small because the administrative action will be carried out by the existing agencies."

With the objective of stabilizing "the cost of living in accordance with the act of October 2, 1942," the Director of the Office of Economic

---

[50] White House Press Release, Oct. 3, 1942.

[51] Executive Order No. 9250, Oct. 3, 1942, 7 *Federal Register* 7871.

Stabilization was instructed to develop "a comprehensive national economic policy relating to control of civilian purchasing power, prices, rents, wages, profits, rationing, subsidies, and all related matters."

The National War Labor Board was designated as the agency to carry out the wage policy of the order, which was to prevent "any increase in the wage rate prevailing on September 15, 1942, unless such increase is necessary to correct maladjustments or inequalities, to eliminate substandards of living, to correct gross inequities, or to aid in the effective prosecution of the war " Any wage increase which might require a change in an OPA price ceiling would have to be approved by the Director of OES as well as by the War Labor Board.   Notice of all proposed increases in wage rates were to be filed with WLB.

The Secretary of Agriculture and the Price Administrator were made jointly responsible for control of agricultural commodity prices and were directed to stabilize them "so far as practicable, on the basis of levels which existed on September 15, 1942, and in compliance with the act of October 2, 1942."   Disagreements between the Secretary and the Price Administrator were to be resolved by the Director of OES.

The Director was authorized "to take necessary action, and to issue the appropriate regulations, so that, insofar as practicable, no salary shall be authorized to the extent that it exceeds $25,000 after the payment of taxes."   The purpose of limiting salaries was "to correct gross inequities and to provide for greater equality in contributing to the war effort."   Action taken by OES under this provision subsequently was reversed by Congress.

The order also instructed the Price Administrator to "determine price ceilings in such a manner that profits are prevented which in his judgment are unreasonable or exorbitant."   This provision likewise was criticized by Congress and industry which from time to time questioned whether OPA was using its powers to reform business and eliminate free enterprise under the guise of necessary wartime regulations.

Also, on October 3, the President sent two letters to the Office of Price Administration.   The first instructed the Price Administrator to "establish ceiling prices for eggs, chickens, butter, cheese, potatoes, flour, and such foods as can be controlled under existing laws."   The Price Administrator was directed to consult with the Secretary of Agriculture in formulating agricultural price regulations.   The President also instructed the Office of Price Administration to take steps necessary to establish rent control throughout the Nation, in rural as well as urban areas.   "In such areas as you deem appropriate to reduce current rents, I am sure you will proceed to take such action as may be necessary. . . . This Government is determined," the Chief Executive said, "to use all of its power to prevent any avoidable rise in the cost of living."

In this manner the Government developed its stabilization program and established the administrative arrangements required to carry it into effect. We were to rely on price, rent, and wage controls as principal stabilization tools and on borrowing rather than taxation to finance the war. Failure to tax heavily would handicap operation of price and wage controls and, in months to come, produce other inflation crises. Failure to establish effective controls over wages would endanger the entire stabilization effort.

In tackling these problems the Government was anxious that the social and economic gains of the preceding decade be retained as. nearly intact as possible and in this design it was supported by determined and vigorous leaders of labor and farm organizations. These reforms were not established so firmly that there were not some who hoped to eliminate them. As large incomes enabled many families for the first time to obtain an adequate diet, and as we undertook to supply large quantities of food and clothing to our Allies, agriculture found the prosperity which it had sought during the years following the Great Depression. Leaders of labor and farm groups attempted, during 1942, to advance and consolidate the immediate economic interests of their constituents. Throughout this period farmers and laborers appeared to see more clearly and more quickly than their leaders the social and economic adjustments required by total war. The ordinary consumer—the white-collar worker, the Government clerk, the pensioner—who would suffer most by an uncontrolled rise in the cost of living, was so ineffectively represented in Congress that his interests actually were neglected. The byplay of these pressures before and after the enactment of the Price Control Act demonstrated clearly the necessity for skilled political management in achieving economic stabilization.

PART

THREE

Full Tide of War

Full Tide of War

THE AUTUMN of 1942 marked the peak of Axis expansion. In the South Pacific the Japanese had occupied much of New Guinea and were threatening Australia. In the North they had taken several islands in the Aleutians in a thrust toward the North American continent. In Africa the Germans had slashed into Egypt and were stalled at El Alamein. In Russia the success of the great eastward drive of the Nazis hinged on the outcome of the siege of Stalingrad to which the Germans committed 22 divisions in September. In Europe Allied air warfare had not yet seriously inconvenienced the Axis in its exploitation of the resources of the continent. Yet the nadir of Allied fortunes had been reached. On all fronts the United Nations were able in the latter half of 1942 to check the Axis spread and to make a start on the long road to victory. In August the Marines landed in Guadalcanal in a desperate gamble and successfully resisted Japanese efforts to drive them from the island. In October, after reenforcing and reequipping their forces, the British at El Alamein initiated an offensive that was to drive the Germans from Egypt and westward to Tunisia. Early in November American forces landed in Northwest Africa in an action coordinated with the British offensive from the east, the two moves being designed to pinch the Nazis between the British and American armies. In November the Russians put in motion a vast encircling movement to relieve Stalingrad and to crush the Nazis in the East. It was not until May 1943 that attacks could be mounted to drive the Japanese from American islands in the North Pacific and by that time island-hopping tactics were under way in the South Pacific.

By the time these military operations were in motion the wartime structure of the American Government had taken form. The problems of administration that were to arise after the fall of 1942 were of a different order than those which had been involved in establishing and staffing the wartime agencies. New problems arose in the coordination of the going mechanisms of government and a few major rearrangements of organization had to be made to deal with new issues. But in the main after the fall of 1942 the problem of administration became one of management of the machinery which had been established. Most of the critical problems that emerged flowed from

277

the economic and political effects of the burdens placed on the American economy by the preparations for the military campaigns under way and for those scheduled for the future. During 1942 our production of military and war-related goods for ourselves and our allies rose sharply toward the peak which was reached in 1943. As military operations got under way and as the initiation of other actions approached the demands for war matériel became more imperious. The demand for goods for war use, the needs of a prosperous civilian population, and the reduction in the production of many types of articles for civilian use brought greater and greater pressure upon price levels. The expansion of production was taking up the slack in the economy and scarcities of materials became serious while a prospective shortage of manpower loomed. The civilian population began to feel the pinch of war and the problem of supplying the home front became more difficult.

All of these things had their repercussions in the organization and administration of the Government on the home front. The pressure on prices and wages required the establishment of mechanisms to gear together the agencies of Government with powers useful in stabilizing the economy. Early in October 1942, the Office of Economic Stabilization was established with authority to take the leadership in directing the activities of Government agencies with powers to affect stabilization. The intensification of the competition for the output of the American productive system required improved mechanisms and procedures to allocate the supply of goods to different uses. New and better procedures were developed by the War Production Board for these purposes. A crisis in petroleum brought a reorganization of the governmental agencies concerned with petroleum and its products. Toward the end of 1942 the increasing demands on American agriculture brought a reorganization of the agencies of Government concerned with food production and distribution. The declining quantities of goods available for civilian use required the institution of broader rationing programs. In September 1942, it was decided to ration gasoline on a Nation-wide basis. In the spring of 1943, shoes, meats, and processed foods were rationed.

10

Regulating the Flow of Materials

AN IMPORTANT change took place in the American economy between the spring of 1942 and the fall of that year. This change was gradual, but nonetheless dramatic. It consisted of the disappearance of slackness in most elements of our productive system and the development of a tight economy in which war production demands apparently exceeded the Nation's capacity. The most urgent production programs of the military, naval, and air forces, and those of the shipping and lend-lease agencies were in violent collision. The required increases in total production, or in individual types of production, could not be achieved through the comparatively simple solutions used in the prior winter and spring.

In the fall of 1942 and winter of 1942–43, four solutions were advocated for dealing with this new and extremely difficult problem of expanding war production in a tight economy.

The first proposal, put forward even before the summer, and readvanced from time to time later, whenever difficulties developed, was the elimination of civilian responsibility for managing the economy and the transfer of that power to the military.

The second type of reaction was the desperate effort to get quick action in solving any immediate problem by giving the responsibility in a limited field to one man along with a broad grant of powers so that he might act with vigor and dispatch. The best illustration of this answer to the problem of war production in a tight economy was the creation of the Office of Rubber Director, although other "czars" were set up, and still others suggested from time to time.

The third method was the development under WPB of comprehensive integrated controls requiring also the reduction of programs to feasible limits, their timing on the basis of needs, and the elimination or postponement of unbalanced programs.

The fourth method was the development under the War Production Board of the direct and indirect management of production, especially through the control of scheduling.

It is the purpose of this chapter to review these four methods of approach and to show how each one of these solutions played its part in the development of the final pattern of American war production, a system of controls which on the total record achieved extraordinary success.

Proposals for Military Control

As chapter 5 explains, the idea of military control of the economy in time of war was firmly held and vigorously advocated by officials of the War and Nàvy Departments and the military chiefs at various times from 1939 on. During the summer and fall of 1942 scores, if not hundreds, of production lines were closed down for brief periods when the flow of materials ceasèd, and the conflict of high military priorities threatened to strangle the entire war production program, military and civilian. These temporary crises called forth strenuous new demands from some quarters for military control of the economy. Proposed plans brought WPB under the Joint Chiefs of Staff, or replaced Mr. Nelson by a military officer or at least by a man with less susceptibility to foreign demands and civilian requirements whose primary concern would be for the military program.

Through all this discussion the issues were perfectly plain, though they were frequently overlooked even by those who were most deeply involved. The choice was between flexible civilian supervision over military production and procurement or military domination over the supply of materials, materiél, essential civilian goods, and manpower. Though there were times when it looked as if the only way out of the controversy lay in giving the military final control over the total economy, the President and the Congress, supported by the Truman Committee, were never persuaded to make the change.

While the military forces were not accorded final control over the economy, extensive war production powers were given to the military establishments from time to time. While these are described elsewhere in this study, it is appropriate to note certain of these powers here.

It was noted in chapter 5 that the War Production Board delegated the entire procurement function to the military services, the Maritime Commission, and other purchasing agencies. Extensive delegation of the right to issue priorities was a necessary consequence. Military and naval personnel reporting to high Army and Navy officers or to the Army-Navy Munitions Board were brought directly into the WPB offices all through the organization where they might not only observe but also influence, if not control, WPB activities and decisions. And finally, military personnel were given central advisory posts on the War Production Board itself, on the extremely important Production Executive Committee which became the major power in WPB after February 1943, and on the Requirements Committee, as well as on the Divisional Requirements committees. Military personnel served also on the Area Production Urgency committees and in other field office posts. In this way the military agencies were not only represented at every point within the civilian agency designed to control the economy, but were in a position to delay or recommend action, both on top policy decisions and in the smallest details, if the action proposed did not suit their views or desires.

Whenever a particular drive for military demands of the economy failed as the result of Presidential decision, or because of specific action by the Chairman of the War Production Board in asserting his powers, the military leaders took another approach to secure the same result; they never abandoned the sincere conviction that they could run things better and more expeditiously than could the civilians. This approach was involved, for example, in the transition from the Production Requirements Plan to the Controlled Materials Plan, as is explained below. Similarly, when the WPB, after a bitter struggle in which the President made the decision, reestablished its right to control production schedules, the military promptly reestablished, if it did not actually extend, its influence through the Production Executive Committee and the staff which surrounded the Executive Vice Chairman.

War Production Czars

The second answer, in a tight economy, to confusion and delay in war production was the setting up of men with conspicuous authority and specific limited duties. These men came to be known as the "czars." The best illustrations are the Rubber Director, the Petroleum Administrator, the Solid Fuels Administrator, and the War Food Administrator. At various times czars were suggested also for lumber, steel, aluminum, civilian supplies, and electric power.

In every case the history was the same: A serious shortage with its attendant confusion would develop; the columnists and the public generally became alarmed; officials with conflicting authorities or ideas each proposed his own solution, or failed to present immediately a clear simple plan of action; Congress often commenced to investigate; and sooner or later someone would come forward with a dramatic plan for solving the particular issue by giving one man all the power necessary to do the job. The author of this plan ignored the existing organization of production and the chaos that dictatorial powers in one field could cause in the whole war economy. Corrective reasoning was generally supplied by the Director of the Bureau of the Budget, by the Chairman of the War Production Board, or by the Price Administrator, who represented the agencies most concerned by these moves.

This development of czars is well illustrated in the following accounts of the origin and experience of the Rubber and Petroleum Administrations. The somewhat similar story of the development of the War Food Administration is presented in the next chapter.

Oil

Of the three commodities, rubber, food, and oil, oil was the most critical. We had lost our supplies in the Far East; the Germans had the rich Russian fields; and submarines were sinking our tankers in sight of the Atlantic shores. Our own and Allied demands for oil had domestic repercussions which led to mobilization of government and industry to grapple with petroleum problems, first of transportation, and then of production and distribution.

The pressure for a wartime "oil czar" stems from developments of the spring of 1941. At that time, the most pressing domestic petroleum problem was to bring adequate amounts of oil to the Atlantic coast area. Nearly all such supplies had been brought in by tankers

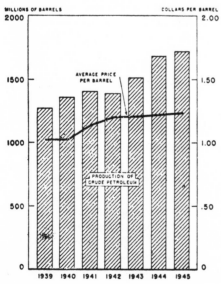

CHART 33. *Price and Production of Crude Petroleum.*

1945 data preliminary.
Source: Department of the Interior.

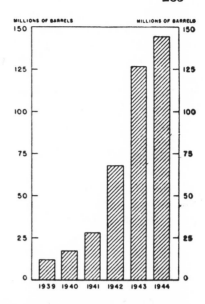

CHART 34. *Sales of Fuel Oil to the Military Services.*[1]

[1] 1945 data not available.

Source: Department of the Interior.

operating, principally, from Gulf coast ports. A supply crisis was created by allocation early in May of 50 of these vessels to carry oil from Gulf and Caribbean ports to northern ports where the cargo was transferred to ships under a foreign flag for trans-Atlantic shipment, chiefly to Great Britain. The deficit in transportation facilities could be met by expansion of rail movements, by construction of additional tankers, and by extension of pipe lines, but all these solutions required time and there was immediate need to make more efficient use of existing facilities both to meet current requirements and to build up reserves for the winter ahead. Other problems which demanded attention included efficient development of petroleum reserves, optimum balance in refinery operations, and elimination of cross hauling of petroleum and its products.

Something obviously had to be done. The chief difficulty was that a good many Federal agencies had coordinate interests in oil and its distribution. Furthermore, coordination could not offer a decisive solution. The Department of the Interior had jurisdiction over production of oil on public lands and Indian Reservations, forecast consumer demand for oil, and engaged in research. The Navy Department administered naval petroleum reserves and was one of the principal consumers of petroleum. The Maritime Commission had charge of tanker transportation and the ICC had jurisdiction over rail and inland barge-line oil movements. In addition, the War Department, OPM (which had set up an industry committee for oil), the Office of Price Administration and Civilian Supply, Lend-Lease, and other defense organizations had an interest in petroleum.

On May 28, 1941, a day after he had declared the existence of an unlimited national emergency, the President sent a letter to the Secretary of the Interior naming him Petroleum Coordinator for National Defense,[1] with wide advisory powers but with little operational control. It was obvious that the President recognized both the need for coordination and the threat to the established forms of organization.

This choice was influenced by the Department's long standing interest in oil, its available staff, its contacts with the industry, and the President's confidence in Mr. Ickes. The Coordinator was charged with two types of functions: He was to assemble data about needs for petroleum and about factors and actions affecting its supply. He was also to consult with, and recommend to Federal agencies, State governments, and the industry, action needed to maintain adequate supplies. The President requested some 20 Federal agencies concerned with petroleum to give the Coordinator antecedent advice of proposed actions which might affect oil supplies and to notify him of meetings dealing with its problems so that he might make recommendations. The letter did not transfer powers to the Coordinator from other agencies already dealing with phases of the petroleum problem. It simply set up an organization in which available information about petroleum could be brought together and through which proposed actions for dealing with oil problems would be cleared. Thus, assignment of authority over the defense production program continued to be distributed on functional lines, but an advisory organization with an interest in the total petroleum problem was set up to make recommendations to operating agencies which were dealing only with parts of that problem. If, for example, the Coordinator thought that unnecessary drilling of wells was consuming steel that could be used better for pipe lines, he could recommend that OPM issue orders to prohibit such drilling, but he could not command.

In organizing his office, the Petroleum Coordinator drew on staff of the Interior Department, and also on the oil industry, from which he selected his Deputy Coordinator and other officers, and constituted a national Petroleum Industry Council and District Advisory Committees. Under terms of an agreement with the Department of Justice, which was responsible for enforcement of the antitrust laws, he made extensive use of these groups in planning and executing programs. In the months before our declarations of war, OPC made Nation-wide surveys of capacities for production, transportation, refining, distribution, and equipment and supply requirements of the oil industry. It prepared and executed plans for expansion of high-octane gasoline production facilities and for supplying petroleum to Great Britain and

---

[1] 6 *Federal Register* 2760. On Apr. 18, 1942, the President changed Mr. Ickes' oil title to Petroleum Coordinator for War.

the Soviet Union. For OPM, OPC acted as an industry branch, advising, recommending, and passing on priority applications, preference ratings, and limitation and curtailment orders. American entrance into the war aggravated these and other problems with which OPC was grappling and made their solution more difficult.

Public annoyance with inconveniences and conflicting statements about supplies of gasoline and fuel oil, the petroleum industry's dissatisfaction with actions of Government agencies—particularly with OPA's price policies, and the Petroleum Coordinator's desire for greater authority for discharging his responsibilities led to attempts to strengthen the powers of the Office of Petroleum Coordinator. In Congress, an unenacted bill would have vested in a National Petroleum Administrator "all functions of the War Production Board and its Chairman, of the Price Administrator, and of the Office of Defense Transportation, relating to the production, transportation, distribution, sale, or price of petroleum." In the Executive Branch, the Petroleum Coordinator spearheaded the drive for greater OPC authority. As early as September 1941 the President had rejected his request to delegate to the Coordinator power to determine priorities and allocation of supplies for crude petroleum and natural gas. In 1942, however, the Petroleum Coordinator succeeded partially in his renewed efforts to increase his authority.

As an organization to collect information and to make recommendations, OPC experienced difficulties in its relations with a number of other agencies. OPC, which had tackled oil transport problems several months before the creation of ODT, was inclined to feel

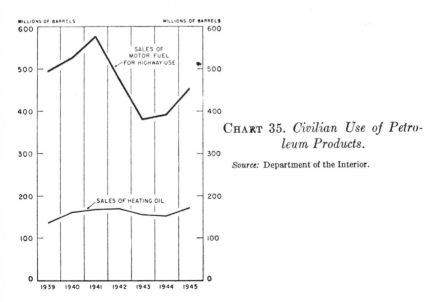

CHART 35. *Civilian Use of Petroleum Products.*

Source: Department of the Interior.

that tank cars could be treated largely apart from other transportation facilities, a view with which ODT, which had over-all jurisdiction was not inclined to agree. There was friction between OPC and the Board of Economic Warfare over matters such as supplies for oil producers in foreign countries. In WPB, which continued the OPM practice of using OPC for processing priority applications and recommending limitation and conservation orders, there was general agreement on high priorities for materials needed for high-octane gasoline plants to supply the needs of our huge plane-production program; but there were differences over other issues, particularly the construction of pipe lines, steel for which competed with material for bombs, tanks, ships, and other military requirements. OPC relations with OPA were strained by continuing differences over the urgency, extent,

CHART 36. *Production of Motor Fuel.*

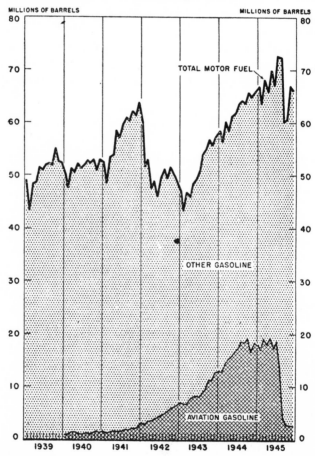

Source: Department of the Interior.

and methods of oil rationing about which the agencies issued conflicting press releases. OPC also felt that OPA was too slow in approving price increases to offset higher costs of transportation (resulting from shifts in movement of petroleum from water to land) and less profitable refinery yields. These interagency frictions, especially those over prices, came to the attention of the President who asked the Petroleum Coordinator if there were any way all the handling of oil could be put in one place. In reply, the Coordinator wrote, on August 19, 1942, that, although a great deal had been accomplished under his existing powers, it was necessary to centralize authority over oil more clearly and positively. To accomplish this purpose he submitted a draft of an Executive order to create a Petroleum Administration for War.

The President referred this draft to the Bureau of the Budget which undertook to reconcile the views of the agencies affected, a process that required the 4 months between August and December 1942, when an Executive order, considerably less sweeping than the orignial proposal, was issued. Since these negotiations involved one of the major threats to the established pattern for war production, it will be useful to use them as an example and to review them in some detail to bring out the character of the controversy over functional and commodity organization. Two related issues may be distinguished: location of the petroleum agency, and the scope of its authority.

The Coordinator had proposed to place the new Petroleum Administration in the Executive Office of the President rather than in the Department of the Interior, though, like OPC, it could have been given independent status with direct access to the Secretary and freedom from internal departmental routines. The Bureau of the Budget thought it would be a fiction to locate the new Petroleum Administrator in the Executive Office and preferred an autonomous agency within the Department of the Interior. A third solution, advocated by the War and Navy Departments, OPA, and WPB (whose chairman's earlier attempts to get it adopted had failed) was to put the oil agency in WPB, on terms similar to those applying to the recently established Office of Rubber Director, so that its activities might be related better to actions affecting the rest of American industry. The Petroleum Coordinator, who had turned down an invitation to become a member of the War Production Board, was reported to have conceded the logic of such an argument but to have objected to incorporation of his agency into WPB as long as its then chairman, with whom he did not get along well, remained in office. Another obstacle to the transfer of the oil organization to WPB was confusion in the Board resulting from an internal reorganization in the fall of

1942.   In the end, the Petroleum Administration was set up technically outside the Executive Office, the Interior Department, and WPB;
and its head was authorized to report directly to the President.

More significant than location, however, were the powers of the
Petroleum Administration.   The Coordinator had written to the
President that his draft order did not expand existing OPC authority
substantially except over prices other than those to consumers, and
in the exercise of priority powers within the oil industry.   Possibly
because language in the proposed order was not sufficiently clear,
possibly because they were excessively suspicious of potential en-
croachments on their own jurisdictions, other agencies affected pro-
fessed to read much greater power into the draft order than did the
Petroleum Coordinator.   The latter expressed willingness to modify
the document, which underwent extensive revision before it was
issued.   The basic issue, as noted already, was the principle to be
followed in organization for war production.   The Coordinator advocated that authority to take action, as distinguished from making
recommendations, to a substantial extent should be vested in the
petroleum agency.   Other agencies, with economy-wide responsibilities, objected strongly to diffusion of authority over production,
transportation, price stabilization, foreign trade, and other functions
which cut across all industries and commodities.   The Bureau of the
Budget sided with these agencies on the grounds, summarized in a
memorandum to the President, that the functional principle had been
followed in organization since the start of mobilization; that it would
be utterly confusing to try to employ simultaneously both functional
and commodity or industry organizations; and that drastic change
of the basic pattern in the midst of war would create confusion and
result in stoppages that the country could ill afford.   The difficulties
inherent in the organization suggested by the Petroleum Coordinator
can be brought out best by a review of his original far-reaching proposals, the reactions of other agencies that were affected, and the much
more moderate provisions of the Executive order finally issued on
December 2, 1942.[2]   More than a dozen agencies had a substantial
interest in the powers of the proposed petroleum agency, but the
broad issues of "commodity" versus "functional" organization will be
posed clearly enough by consideration of provisions applicable to only
five of them.

Transportation.—The order submitted by the Coordinator would
have authorized the Petroleum Administrator to issue and enforce
specific directives to the oil industry on the transportation of petroleum.   The War Shipping Administration and the Office of Defense

---

[2] Executive Order No. 9276, Dec. 2, 1942, 7 *Federal Register* 10091.

Transportation would have determined the number of tankers, barges, tank cars, and tank trucks available to transport petroleum, but the Petroleum Administrator, in collaboration with these agencies and the War and Navy Departments, would have allocated these facilities among the various services and among units of the petroleum industry. He would have been empowered to direct the construction and operation of petroleum pipelines. Also, he would have advised the War Production Board Chairman what materials were needed for transportation of petroleum.

Detailed control of specific operations such as that proposed by the Coordinator ran counter to the prevailing conception of war production organization, under which supply agencies merely set goals for total movements, and very likely would have interfered with attempts to achieve a balanced and over-all plan for the flow of traffic.

The War Shipping Administration, which had been dealing directly with the Army, Navy, and lend-lease in allocating tankers, objected to establishment of a second agency to allocate shipping, and declared its intention to continue to be guided by OPC recommendations in making allocations to units of the oil industry. Under the order issued by the President, the Petroleum Administrator was merely to consult WSA about tanker assignments and to recommend allocations of available vessels.

The Director of the Office of Defense Transportation found it "difficult . . . to see how an important part of transportation can be wisely separated from the total transportation without adding to duplication and conflict and without impairing the effectiveness of public control." His objections were met substantially in the order finally issued. Transportation was excluded specifically from definition of the oil industry over which the Petroleum Administrator was given certain powers. ODT was to continue to make recommendations to WPB for materials needed for transportation not only of oil but also of other products. Instead of allocating barges, tank cars, and tank trucks among units of the oil industry, the Administrator was simply to designate the quantity and kinds of petroleum to be shipped and received by those in the industry and to certify these designations to the Office of Defense Transportation for provision of necessary transportation. The Petroleum Administrator's authority over pipe lines, also, was limited: he was to review plans for their construction, approve those he thought necessary, and recommend material requirements to the War Production Board; and he was to direct their physical operation to the extent of prescribing the petroleum to be transported, and the direction of flow, through such pipe lines. These powers were subject to ODT's existing authority to provide additional transportation facilities and equipment to coordinate and direct domestic traffic movements.

Economic Warfare.—The Coordinator proposed to give the Petroleum Administrator authority to determine, in collaboration with the State Department, Lend-Lease Administration, and the Board of Economic Warfare, the amounts of oil required by foreign nations. The Executive Director of BEW criticized this provision, among others, on the ground that "any economic warfare program depends largely for its success upon the authority to coordinate and direct the movement of all goods in international commerce." Control of the flow of oil was a vital weapon whose use had to be coordinated with that of others in the economic arsenal. Collaboration between BEW and OPC already was provided to some extent through OPC's membership in BEW's Foreign Petroleum Policy Committee.

In the end, the Petroleum Administrator was empowered merely to collaborate with agencies authorized to determine plans and policies for foreign petroleum activities; and his orders to the domestic industry with respect to their foreign activities were to conform to such plans and policies. The Administrator, however, was to be the channel of communication on foreign petroleum between Federal agencies and the oil industry.

Price Control.—The oil industry's dissatisfaction with prices allowed by the Office of Price Administration for petroleum products was one of the principal motives behind the proposal to set up an "oil czar," from whom the industry expected more sympathetic treatment. To this end, the Coordinator's draft order would have transferred from the Price Administrator to the Petroleum Administrator the former's powers over petroleum prices under the Emergency Price Control Act of 1942. The sole qualification was the Price Administrator's approval of prices to ultimate consumers, in reviewing which he was to consider only their effect on general price levels. If the Petroleum Administrator, whose principal responsibility was to provide adequate supplies of oil, had been given this power, it was not unlikely that he would have given more consideration than had OPA to use of prices to facilitate operations of the oil industry and less attention to the general problem of stabilization and prevention of inflation. The Price Administrator pointed out that the power of approval left to him would be "wholly ineffectual" because prices to ultimate consumers are determined largely by prices at earlier levels, over which he would have no control, and because it would be difficult or impossible to demonstrate concretely a threat to the general price level.

In the final order, the Price Administrator's authority was preserved and the Petroleum Administrator was limited largely to advisory functions. The latter was to compile data about petroleum prices, to consult with the former, and to recommend revisions of petroleum prices to him. The Price Administrator, in turn was to advise with the Petroleum Administrator before establishing or changing oil price schedules.

Rationing.—The Coordinator's draft order would have required the Petroleum Administrator's approval of oil rationing orders before they were issued. Thus, one agency would have been authorized to approve the methods of another agency with general responsibility for administering the rationing program. The Price Administrator pointed out that "detailed policy formulation cannot be successfully separated from the actual administration and operation of programs . . . Apart from the evil of divided responsibility, the additional time consumed in clearance is not unimportant." As the Executive order was issued by the President, it provided simply that the Petroleum Administrator should be advised of all proposals for civilian rationing and that he should consult with rationing authorities in their development.

Priorities and allocations.—The proposed Executive order would have vested in the Petroleum Administrator substantial powers which were being exercised by the War Production Board Chairman. The Petroleum Administrator would have obtained determinations of military oil requirements from the War and Navy Departments, and, in collaboration with others, would have determined the amounts needed by foreign countries and for essential industrial and civilian uses. He would have advised the WPB Chairman about material necessary to meet these requirements; and he would have issued directives to distribute materials allotted to the industry by the WPB Chairman. He would have had general authority to issue and enforce specific directives to the oil industry on practically all phases of its operations.

The WPB Chairman opposed the draft order strongly on the ground that it would interfere with his exercise of priority and allocation powers. He suggested that, instead of strengthening OPC as a separate agency, it would be "more efficient and rational" to transfer it to WPB. This shift was not made, but the President decided that WPB should retain full control over materials and priorities.

Under terms of the Executive order finally issued and agreed to by the WPB Chairman,[3] the Petroleum Administrator had the following authority and functions: (1) He was to obtain estimates of oil requirements, compile and analyze them, and submit them to WPB with recommendations for allocations. After the WPB Requirements

---

[3] WPB Directive No. 30, Aug. 18, 1943.

Committee determined oil allocations to the several claimant agencies, the Petroleum Administration for War was to act as a War Production Board operating division in implementing them. When rationing was adopted to maintain adequate supplies of petroleum the Petroleum Administrator was to determine, after advising with WPB, the areas and times of rationing and the amounts of oil to be available for it. (2) The Petroleum Administrator was to prepare and recommend estimates of material needed by the industry to make available petroleum to meet the oil allocations he recommended; and he was to control distribution within the industry of the material made available to it. (3) Finally, the Administrator was given authority generally to issue to the industry, and to enforce, directives and orders dealing with production, refining, treating, storage, shipment, receipt, and distribution of petroleum and its products.

The effects of this grant of authority which was to be exercised subject to policies and directives of the WPB Chairman, were less far-reaching than they appeared. To a very substantial extent, WPB had recognized OPC as an industry division and had followed its recommendations with respect to the oil industry's material needs and the allocation of petroleum. Formal recognition of PAW as an operating division of WPB, by giving the Petroleum Administrator authority to issue directives to the industry, however, did relieve the Board of certain time-consuming functions.

The Executive order on petroleum issued in December 1942 watered down the draft submitted by the Petroleum Coordinator in August by limiting the PAW's functions largely to advice and recommendations. It safeguarded the powers of other agencies further by reciting their authorities, which the order was not to be interpreted as limiting. The attempt to create an oil "czar," then, had only a very moderate success. Those, like the oil industry, who favored the Petroleum Coordinator's original draft failed in the attempt to exempt petroleum from the authority exercised over all commodities by agencies set up to deal with production, prices, and other "functions" that cut across all industries and commodities. Thus, the basic functional pattern of organization for war production was retained despite the position of PAW outside of WPB [4]—though the issue was soon to be fought again in connection with coal. Ickes became, in fact, a liaison agent between the oil industry and the WPB.

---

[4] The Rubber Director reported directly to the WPB Chairman even after the latter appointed an Executive Vice Chairman. WPB General Administrative Order No. 2-80, Feb. 26, 1943. The Senate Special Committee Investigating the National Defense Program declared that, as a result of the Petroleum Administrator's direct responsibility to the President and of his complicated relations with the WPB Chairman, "The lines of authority are confusing even on paper. As a practical matter they breed disputes . . ." Senate Report No. 10, 78th Cong., 1st sess., pt. 9, pp. 4–5.

Rubber

Like oil, rubber was a commodity for which there were universal demands many of which could not be filled; but while in petroleum and solid fuels the principal bottlenecks were transportation and labor, in rubber the most critical factor was the raw material. Over ninety percent of our crude rubber imports were cut off when the Japanese attacked Pearl Harbor, and prospects of substitute supplies from South America were uncertain. Facilities to process scrap rubber were limited and reclaimed rubber could not be used in all cases as a substitute for crude rubber. The country was "basically dependent upon synthetic rubber," as the following data make amply clear: [5] On July 1, 1942, there were on hand 578,000 long tons of crude rubber, with imports of 53,000 tons more expected by January 1, 1944, making a total supply of 631,000 tons. Without allowance for passenger automobile tires, military and other essential demands between July 1942 and January 1944, amounted to 842,000 tons. Thus, the deficit to be met by synthetic rubber was 211,000 tons. Little of this could be produced during 1942. Under programs already scheduled, however, it was estimated that during 1943 manufacture would amount to about 400,000 tons of buna-S, 30,000 tons of neoprene, 62,000 tons of butyl, and 24,000 tons of thiokol—enough synthetic rubber to offset likely deficits in crude rubber during the critical year 1943. Only neoprene and buna-S were suitable for combat and heavy-duty tires. The schedules for these synthetics would provide a safety margin of 100,000 tons; but, if they lagged as much as 4 months, there would not be enough to meet all military needs. These were narrow limits, indeed, to meet the requirements of mechanized warfare and the need to keep civilian America on wheels. Concern with the problem found expression both in Congressional and in Executive action.

Late in July 1942 Congress passed S. 2600, a bill to create a new, independent rubber supply agency headed by a director appointed by the President with Senatorial approval. The agency was to provide a supply of rubber, which, added to other sources, would be adequate to meet military and (apparently, all) civilian needs. It was also to provide an adequate supply of alcohol produced from agricultural products. The agency would have been empowered to provide the plants and materials needed for making synthetic rubber; and materials which its director certified he needed would have had priority over all other deliveries. In vetoing this measure on August 6, 1942, the President set out forcefully the case against diffusion of the priorities and allocations powers which, by delegation, he had

<hr>

[5] House Document No. 836, 77th Cong., 2d sess., Sept. 10, 1942, *The Rubber Situation*, containing the Report of the Rubber Survey Committee.

concentrated in the War Production Board "in order to carry on
a unified, integrated, and efficient program of war production." He
pointed out that plants already were being constructed by the RFC's
Rubber Reserve Company and the Defense Plant Corporation under
a WPB program to establish capacity to manufacture 800,000 tons
of synthetic rubber annually. The President took note of charges
that "the manufacture of synthetic rubber from grain has been
hamstrung by selfish business interests" and of "many conflicting
statements of fact concerning all the elements of the rubber situation."
He informed Congress that he had appointed a committee, consisting
of Bernard M. Baruch, James B. Conant, and Karl T. Compton, to
investigate the whole problem and to make recommendations to him.

In its report to the President on September 10, 1942,[6] the Rubber

CHART 37. *New Supplies of Rubber.*

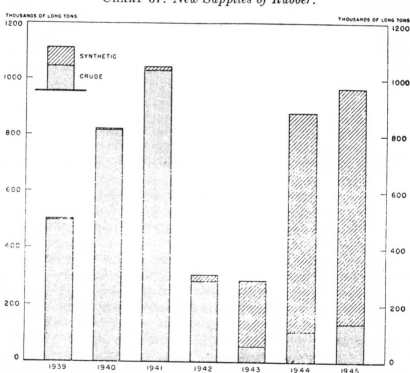

Source: Office of Rubber Reserve and Civilian Production Administration.

Survey Committee reviewed estimates of requirements and supplies,
recommended measures for conservation and production of rubber, and
proposed administrative reorganization. To conserve the available

---

[6] Ibid.

supply of rubber, the Committee outlined a rationing program that included gasoline rationing as "the only way of saving rubber." To increase supplies, the Committee recommended that the existing synthetic program should be "bulled through" and that an additional margin of safety should be provided by increasing the program from 800,000 to 1,100,000 tons annual capacity. To insure that the program would be carried through effectively, the Committee advocated an immediate administrative reorganization.

The Committee cited the following examples of poor administration under the existing set-up: Conflict between the Rubber Reserve Company and the Office of Petroleum Coordinator had delayed the bringing in of new facilities for production of butadiene, a component of buna-S. Under an agreement with four large rubber companies, only Rubber Reserve could give out information about synthetic rubber processes to others; but the WPB Rubber Branch had to work 6 weeks to get such data released. In spite of Soviet offers to make it available, information about long-used Russian methods for making synthetic rubber had not been obtained. None of the agencies carrying out the $600,000,000 rubber program had set up a clearly recognized group of experts to make technical decisions in the highly complicated program.

To overcome difficulties such as these, the Committee recommended "complete reorganization and consolidation of the governmental agencies concerned with the rubber program." It was critical of WPB's handling of the rubber problem and, at first, was inclined to propose an independent Rubber Administrator who would report to the President through the Chairman of WPB. After discussion with members of the Bureau of the Budget, however, who pointed out the objections to transferring priority and other powers from the central production agency to one concerned with only a single commodity, the Committee decided to recommend that the Rubber Director should be located within the general framework of WPB and that the Board's Chairman should delegate to him complete authority over manufacture of rubber. These and related recommendations were incorporated in orders issued subsequently by the President and the WPB Chairman.

Executive Order No. 9246, drafted in the Bureau of the Budget and signed by the President on September 17, 1942,[7] contained the following provisions: The Chairman of WPB was directed to assume full responsibility for, and control over, all phases of the Nation's rubber program. Within WPB and under its Chairman, there was to be a Rubber Director to administer the program. The Director was authorized to direct other Government agencies, including RFC, OPC, BEW, ODT, OPA, and Agriculture, to execute aspects of the

[7] *7 Federal Register* 7379.

rubber program and these agencies were instructed to give full compliance to his directives. Plant construction was to be supervised by the Rubber Reserve Company. OPC was to do developmental research on butadiene from oil and to supervise operation of butadiene plants. The Price Administrator's powers under the Emergency Price Control Act of 1942, however, were not limited by the Executive order.

On September 15, WPB Chairman Nelson appointed William M. Jeffers, President of the Union Pacific Railroad, to be Rubber Administrator in complete charge of the entire program. Five days later, he delegated to the Rubber Director all the powers conferred on him by Executive Order No. 9246. He abolished the Office of Coordinator for Rubber and the Rubber and Rubber Products Branch in WPB, whose functions, personnel, and records were inherited by the Rubber Director. Later, the rubber functions of the Division of Civilian Supply were transferred to the Office of Rubber Director, which continued to operate until September 1944, when it was replaced by a Rubber Bureau under the WPB Operations Vice Chairman.[8]

The Rubber Office had been created within WPB, so the functional pattern of the war production organization had been preserved. Structural symmetry, however, did not insure harmony among various parts of the Government's machinery for industrial mobilization. On the contrary, the Director's aggressiveness in "bulling through" the Baruch Committee program brought him into collision with administrators who had responsibility for other phases of the war program and also with members of Congress. Two general problems were involved. First, it was necessary to relate the Office of Rubber Director to the rest of the WPB organization. Second, the program for construction of rubber plants had to be integrated with other programs, such as those for aircraft and escort vessels, which competed for materials and components required for such plants.

Since the Rubber Director was part of the WPB organization, it is not surprising that, in some ways, fuller authority was delegated to him than was vested in the oil and coal "czars" who were outside the Board. In effect, the definition of the Director's authority amounted to slicing rubber out of the general structure of the WPB.[9] Though the surgery was less extreme than the Rubber Director sought, from time to time, the position of the Rubber Director's office (ORD) was more favorable than that of WPB industry branches for other commod-

---

[8] The production of synthetic rubber amounted to 8,383 long tons in 1941, 22,434 in 1942, 231,722 tons in 1943, and 753,111 in 1944. *War Production in 1944*, Report of the Chairman of the WPB, June, 1945, p. 138.
[9] General Administrative Orders Nos. 2–62, Oct. 20, 1942, and 2–70, Dec. 8, 1942.

ities.[10] (1) Requirements: ORD was designated as the claimant agency before the WPB Requirements Committee for critical materials and facilities needed for construction and alteration of rubber plants and for raw materials needed in rubber manufacture. Construction requirements were to be presented' through the Facilities Bureau, while those for maintenance and operation were to go through regular channels, though the Rubber Director had wanted to bypass them. (2) Allotments and allocations: (a) The Rubber Director was authorized to allot rubber among claimant agencies and for civilian requirements, with the advice of a Rubber Requirements Committee consisting of the principal using agencies and ORD's Domestic Requirements Section. Allotments were to be submitted to the WPB Requirements Committee for determination of their consistency with over-all production programs approved by the Board. After determining allotments, the Rubber Director was authorized to make specific allocations of rubber to manufacturers and for civilian requirements. For this purpose, for issuance of limitation orders, and for control of rubber stock piles, the WPB Chairman delegated priorities powers to him. (b) The Rubber Director's request for authority to allot critical materials for construction, maintenance, and operation of specific rubber plants was not approved by the WPB Chairman, who later specified that the Rubber Director's authority did not extend to distribution of materials other than rubber or its products even when they were for use in rubber production. This reservation meant that the power to allocate the critical component parts required by competing war production programs would remain concentrated within WPB.

Final Status of Czars

The rise of commodity czars resulted from a very real need of industry for liaison agents with production agencies. At first the czars threatened the existence of a functional stabilization, but in the end they strengthened it. Jeffers' insistence on securing components for his rubber factories emphasized the need for a unified control over all processes of production, rather than control through allocation of materials. Similarly, Secretary Ickes' demands for complete control over petroleum and its pricing and allocation ended by giving him extensive control over petroleum and its production

---

[10] The Senate Special Committee Investigating the National Defense Program remarked that "a rubber czar was set up, within the War Production Board, to be sure, but still more or less autonomous" since, in spite of his responsibility to the WPB Chairman, he "was given power himself to issue directives to the various agencies. The Chairman of the War Production Board was requested by the Commander in Chief to divest himself of concern with the rubber program. Therefore, practically speaking, the Chairman of the War Production Board has had only tenuous authority over the Rubber Director although technically he is the boss." Senate Report No. 10, 78th Cong., 1st sess., pt. 9, pp. 2–4.

and distribution, but within the existing framework of production. The WPB controlled materials, and the OPA, prices.

The adjudication of these attempts to establish one-man controls over commodities also illustrates the difficulty in trying to find a definite pattern in the flexible system of our wartime administration. Both Ickes and Jeffers became liaison agents between an industry and the Government, but one reported directly to the President; the other remained subordinate to WPB—the decision reached showed the care with which the President tried to fit the case to the man, to the industry, and the real need.

Thus, in the long run, in spite of the publicity given to the czars, very few were set up, and these few were extensively tied into the general structure of the over-all war production controls. In World War II, there were in the United States no such centers of single commodity authority as were represented by the independent food and fuel administrations of the prior war.

Comprehensive and Integrated Controls

The third answer to the difficulties of production in a tight economy was the effort to develop new integrated controls for the whole war production program. This effort involved new methods of comprehensive programming, cutting programs back to feasible totals, balancing production within these totals, allocating materials on a time schedule, month by month, and quarter by quarter, and clearing production bottlenecks with new scheduling and directive powers.

The steps by which this third method of approach was finally carried through, and the organizational changes which it required in the structure of the WPB, are described in the following pages of this chapter.

The Time Element

When the stringency of the economy compelled a decrease in production plans, program planners had to introduce the element of time into their calculations. A stated production requirement might stand still. If the total requirement had to be reduced, however, closer attention had to be given to maintaining a balance within each program and between the various programs. While this was highly desirable from the first, it was imperative as soon as the time element was introduced, so that at given target dates for major military actions there might be available a balanced complement of troops, transports, escorts, landing ships, mechanized equipment, air protection, guns, ammunition, gasoline, quartermaster and medical supplies, and a certain flow of services, munitions, and supplies for the operation from that point on. All of this called for "synchronizing the flow of material with the time element of the program"—to take a phrase from Donald Nelson. It was the time element which thus made it necessary to interrelate the programs.

Though this synchronization was generally recorded in terms of materials, the top decisions were actually made in airplanes, tanks, ships, high-octane gas, pipe lines, and other end products which were to be finished by a given date.

Program Cut-Backs

A major first step in getting war production on a maximum basis, strangely enough, was the reduction of the grand totals sought in a given period. These reductions in major production programs carried the expressive title of "cut-backs."

Our economy is apparently much like the camel and ceases to keep going when the load is increased by "the last straw." The problems arise with the high-pressure demands by individual procurement officers, each of whom "must" get his tanks, or rifles, or shoes, or landing barges, or packing boxes, or beef, by a given date in the near future, and who is convinced that no other demand is half so pressing as his. This is followed by the placing of contracts wherever a producer can be found. The producer then starts to hire workmen, get more machinery to increase his output, and to place orders for steel, wool, lumber, ball bearings, leather, oil, valves, and everything else. As these orders accumulate, they exceed the possible capacity of the suppliers of raw materials, and these start to expand, hiring more men and ordering more machinery. The machine-tool manufacturers and the mines in turn are in the same fix; they cannot fill their orders without expanding. And so it goes, everybody getting in the way of everybody else, until, instead of increased production, there is the threat of industrial self-strangulation in the effort to do more than is possible. In the end nobody can operate efficiently because everybody is out of something—coal, or steel, or manpower, or machinery, or cotton, or paint, or soda, or any one of the other thousand things which must be available at the right time, the right place, and in the right quantity to keep the wheels turning and the goods flowing.

Some statistics will show that we were heading into just such a situation during the early years of the war. When WPB added up the production programs of the various services in January 1942, incomplete as were these programs, it found they came to about $60 billion for the year 1942, over against a theoretical feasibility estimate of about $40 billion. While American labor and industry fooled the experts and actually produced 10 percent more than the theoretical maximum, that was still far short of the $60 billion sought by the

CHART 38. *Production of Selected Basic Commodities.*[1]

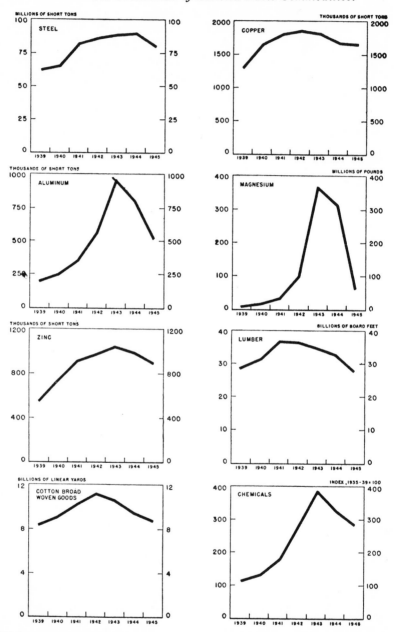

[1] Data for copper, aluminum, magnesium, and zinc include primary production and secondary production from old scrap only.

Source: American Iron and Steel Institute; Department of the Interior; Department of Commerce; Board of Governors of the Federal Reserve System; Civilian Production Administration (formerly War Production Board).

services in their scramble for equipment. Similarly, the figure for 1943 was even worse, being some $45 billion out of estimated balance. Such discrepancies were not mere "straws"; they were sure to break the camel's back.[11]

No amount of juggling things around or establishing controls could meet this situation. There is no way of adjusting a load which is simply too heavy to carry. So the answer was cut-backs, without which all the rest of the program of control and Government guidance was futile. The story of the Army supply program which covers well over half of the total war production for 1942 is revealing. On February 1, 1942, it was set at $62 billion for the year 1942. This was cut on April 6 to $45 billion, and on May 29 to $38 billion. On September 1, however, the program was pushed up to $40 billion, only to be cut back to $31 billion on November 12, approximately the actual production achieved for the year.[12]

Similarly the aircraft program went through many permutations, measured both in numbers and in weight, as the new models became heavier and faster. On numbers alone, from January 31, 1942, to July 12, 1945, there were 16 "schedules," numbered from 8–I to W–15, four of which had both "initial" and "ultimate" objectives. Production for 1942 was scheduled all the way from 68 thousand planes to 47 thousand planes in four programs; 1943 saw 10 different schedules running from 88 thousand planes up to 109 thousand, and then back again to 86 thousand. The merchant marine program, however, went through the year 1942 at about 8 million tons, substantially as originally planned, though at one stage it was temporarily lifted to 9 million tons.

These and other program reductions, though made by the services under WPB pressure, were not accepted without a most vigorous struggle, a struggle fought in terms of steel, copper, aluminum, tin, and other strategic materials.

Review of Programs

Next in importance to "cut-backs" was the systematic review of programs by the impartial staffs of the WPB to see if the claimants really needed as much as they asked, and as fast as they asked it. This critical review of material demands, not only brought about important reductions in inflated demands, but also revealed the all too-human propensity of energetic supply officers, determined not to fail in their assignments, to overlook completely the needs of other services and other needs of the total economy. At the very beginning there were failures to plan for enough, but from February

---

[11] War Production Board. *Wartime Production Achievements, and the Reconversion Outlook.* Report of the Chairman of WPB, Oct. 9, 1945, p. 11.

[12] War Production Board, *Minutes,* Dec. 1, 1942.

1942 on, the errors were all the other way, the tendency to overorder, to overcompute in translating from tanks to tons of steel, for example, to overestimate the needs for spares and the use of ammunition, except for the foreign orders, and above all, to set completion dates ahead of real needs based on other complementary parts of the total program was almost universal.   Many supply officers were caught trying to complete in 1942 end products which would have been stored for 2 years before they were scheduled for shipment, while the steel, textiles, and valves going into them were holding up articles which turned out to be critically needed in 1943 for the African landings. In certain shipyards, steel was found which could not be put in place for 18 months, at the very time that escort vessels for combating the submarines were in immediate demand.   Many contracts for components also were permitted to run after the major end product had been superseded.

It was not unexpected to find that few, if any, supply officers knew about, thought about, or cared about any other part of the program than their own.   But it was surprising to discover how passionate, tricky, and ill-balanced men can become because of short-sighted overloyalty to their own programs.   Most of the anguish of war-torn Washington arose not from the inherent difficulties of organizing for war, but from the frictions engendered by energetic men who sought the success of their own programs, had no time or inclination to think about the total effort or its many interrelated parts, and had no ability to discriminate between the exasperating obstacles of inertia and the essential barriers of coordination.   In such situations, the impartial review of programs and schedules by men concerned only with the total success of the whole war production program proved not only essential, but actually more often than not, helpful for the individual programs thus brought into better balance within themselves.

Program Balance

The effort to introduce balance into the conflicting production programs thus became a major necessity in the fall of 1942.   While various glaring inconsistencies had been pointed out before by the WPB Planning Committee and others, the first full-scale attack on the problem came through the reports of the Bureau of Statistics at the meetings of the War Production Board on August 18, September 22, and November 24, 1942.   At the last meeting, Stacy May, Chief of the Statistics Bureau, not only exposed the wide gap between first-of-month schedules and actual deliveries under the unbalanced and unrealistic programming, but demonstrated that the situation was getting steadily worse, and pinned the blame directly on the procurement officers of the Army, Navy, and Air Forces. In the meantime, at the Board meeting of October 6, Robert Nathan presented the feasibility report of the Planning Committee, showing that the sum total of unbalanced programs, which stood at $115 billion for 1943, was beyond the realm of possibility.

The following further conclusions from this report of the Planning Committee deserve repetition:

> The analysis reveals imbalance in the sense that production is well above schedules for some easy items; and significantly below for the harder items with which the easy items are to be combined to yield a usable end-product. This is an inevitable consequence of a huge program flooding the channels of production without a careful, unified control . . .
>
> While the pressing problem for the immediate future is to correct this imbalance by curbing the items that are ahead of schedules and concentrating effort on the items that are behind, we must not overlook the fundamental basic source of the trouble. There can be no efficient production control without production schedules; there can be no meaningful production schedule without a set of well-formulated and properly screened and tested objectives, spelled out over time and in respect of the relative importance of the various categories and end products; and there can be no such set of objectives unless there is a competent body, taking responsibility for formulating them in broad terms, and seeing to it that the spelling out in detail does not contravene the fundamental considerations that determined the program in its broad outlines . . .
>
> What we urgently need is an authoritative body that would represent fully and competently the strategic, economic, and political (in the sense of broadly social) factors that must jointly determine a well-formulated production program . . .

While high goals were recognized as an incentive for all-out production, WPB took the position that impossible goals had become dangerous because they (1) throw production out of balance, (2) justify excess production capacity, (3) result in failure to meet targets for other and often more important parts of the program, (4) produce inflexibility, (5) increase difficulty of effectively controlling flow and distribution, and (6) prevent coordination of production program with those of other nations.[13]

While various generals, admirals, and under secretaries rose at subsequent meetings of the Board to defend their own programs and to demand the elimination of various civilian products, they did go back to their offices and begin to introduce some balance and some recognition of feasible time limits into their own production programs, and the Chairman of WPB, with the backing of the President, asked the joint Chiefs of Staff to revise their total program. Mr. Nelson also concluded that WPB would have to take over and exercise a greater degree of control over the balancing and timing of programs one against the other.

---

[13] War Production Board, *Minutes*, Oct. 6, 1942.

This balancing, and the elimination of production bottlenecks arising from lack of balance and timing were sought through two important innovations, the introduction of the Controlled Materials Plan under Mr. Ferdinand Eberstadt, and the introduction of controlled scheduling under Mr. Charles Wilson, both of whom were appointed Vice Chairmen of WPB during the third week in September, 1942.

Reorganization of WPB

The appointment of Mr. Eberstadt and Mr. Wilson, with the duties assigned them, constituted a major reorganization of WPB, a reorganization which called forth from Mr. Bernard Baruch in a telegram of October 1 to the President these glowing words:

> I feel that the WPB is now at last reorganized on the proper lines and headed in the right direction, and that in the next 60 days we will see the commencement of a large increase in production in every line that we wanted. I feel much encouraged on the production outlook.

The new organization was, however, not put into administrative orders immediately because of the difficulty of drawing a sharp dividing line between the functions assigned to the vice chairman in charge of program and the flow of materials, Mr. Eberstadt; and the vice chairman in charge of production and scheduling, Mr. Wilson.

November 11 Reorganization Order

Mr. Eberstadt proceeded immediately to standardize, clarify, and integrate the industry and material divisions and the programming activities put under his direction. This was accomplished in part through the issuance on November 11, 1942, of a WPB administrative order drawn by Mr. Eberstadt with the staff aid of Maj. Gen. C. F. Robinson from the Army Service Forces Control Division, the WPB Office of Organization Planning and representatives of the Bureau of the Budget.[14]

There were several important elements in this new organizational set-up. First of all programming and operations, which had existed independently and on the same plane of authority under the prior organization, were now brought together under a single authority, that of the program vice chairman. This meant that Mr. Eberstadt would sit as the presiding officer of the Requirements Committee, listen to the claims advanced by the Army, the Navy, the Air Forces, the Maritime Commission, the Land-Lease Administration, and the Office of Civilian Supply, consult with his own program experts, make a tentative decision, clear it with Mr. Nelson if sufficiently important,

---

14 General Administrative Order 2–65.

and then issue orders to the materials divisions and to the industry divisions, all of which were under his immediate direction, to operate the industrial economy accordingly. Making the decision and carrying it out were tied up in the same bundle, under one man.

The second important step in the new organization was the establishment of the sovereignty of the materials and industrial divisions. This was done through five administrative devices. First, the titles were changed from "branch" to "division," an important step upward in the semantics of Washington bureaucracy; second, each division was given primary responsibility for maximizing the production in its area, and for handling virtually all relations of the industry as such with WPB; third, the division directed the flow of allocated materials in its area, making specific allotments under the broad determinations of the Requirements Committee and the program chairman, except as these were covered by the claimant agencies; fourth, if the WPB maintained order-board or scheduling control over the products of any industry, the management of these were assigned to the appropriate producing division; and finally, the division was made the point of focus for reconciling competing demands, and for this purpose had its own subrequirements committee, patterned after the parent committee of claimants and was responsible for working out the total program of requirements, production, allocation, and distribution. The major divisions were also equipped with their own lawyers, labor advisors, civilian requirements experts, and statisticians, all of whom were assigned by the staff bureaus and offices under which they served.

The third important step in strengthening the operating divisions was the curtailment of the defined responsibilities of the special program units, such as those dealing with scrap and salvage, simplification and substitution, redistribution and inventories, stockpiling and shipping, resources protection, facilities and construction, concentration of industry and civilian supply. These units were bluntly told that they were from that time on "staff divisions," and that it was their function to:

(a) Advise the vice chairman, the director general for operations, and their immediate subordinates.

(b) Formulate policies, programs, plans, and procedures.

(c) Advise and service the industry divisions and the regional offices.

(d) Follow up the execution of functions in the industry divisions and the regional offices.

(e) Perform those phases of the functions where centralization of performance is unavoidable.

Furthermore, it was specifically stated that "all performance phases of the functions assigned to the vice chairman are carried out by the industry divisions and the regional offices, with minor unavoidable exceptions."

The fourth important step in building up the status of the operating divisions, and perhaps the most important, was, however, Mr. Eberstadt's methods of management. He meant what he said in the new organizational order, and in his daily operations leaned heavily on the materials and industrial divisional chiefs and their divisional requirements committees to carry on the major operating functions of WPB in Washington. Thus, under the November 11 plan, each industry division became a small WPB in its own area, with its own small requirements committee representing the chief claimants and endeavoring to work out a balanced program within the overriding decisions of the top requirements committee.

The Controlled Materials Plan

When Mr. Eberstadt originally took hold, the WPB system of control over the flow of materials was undergoing transition from the priorities system to the production requirements plan, described in chapter 5. The essential element of PRP, as is shown below, was the monthly allotment to each plant by WPB of the amounts of materials required to meet its approved production schedules in view of its past experience and its inventories. Beautiful as was this plan on paper, it was under vigorous attack as administratively unworkable by some large industrialists and by the chief claimants, particularly the Army Service Forces. The PRP reports did disclose, however, large excess inventories and had a beneficial effect on production in many quarters.

Nonetheless, the new vice chairman went immediately to work to develop and enforce a new system of material control. In this he had aid from several sources. The WPB Steel Committee returned from England and reported on September 22, urging, among other things, the adoption of the British system of steel allocations. At the same time, a group of automotive engineers worked out and presented a "warrant plan" under which each prime contractor would be given warrants for the critical materials and components called for under his war contracts. The services, in contrast, thought that the only solution was to be found in giving each major claimant a fixed percentage allocation of each critical material, and then leaving it to that claimant to flow "his" material to the contractors working for him.

Mr. Eberstadt brought these various groups together behind locked doors, including some British advisors who were flown over for the purpose, and came out with a compromise and composite system which was approved by Mr. Nelson and presented as the Controlled Materials Plan on November 2, 1942, to become partially effective

April 1, 1943, and fully effective July 1, 1943. Extensive CMP schools were immediately organized both in Washington and in the field to train WPB, Army and Navy representatives, and businessmen in their new duties and the procedures under the Controlled Materials Plan.

Fundamental Principles of Production Control

In order to appreciate fully the significance of Mr. Eberstadt's epochal reforms, it is necessary to view this last change against the prior history of war-production controls, even at the risk of repeating what has been chronicled earlier. Two elements are involved: first, the strategy of control; i. e., where do you take hold of the economy? And, second, the tactics of operation; i. e., how shall you manage your controls?

The Strategy of Control.—The WPB program of November 1942, like its predecessors, was based almost exclusively upon materials. The new plan for managing the industrial economy, designed to get out the maximum war production, was entitled the "Controlled Materials Plan," the clearest possible recognition of its central purpose.[15]

There are many other possible points of control in an economy, such as contracts, appropriations, financing, production schedules and utilization of power, transportation, plant and manpower. Of all these, Mr. Eberstadt seized but one: materials and components, and these he dominated by completely controlling steel, aluminum, and copper, with other commodities added later. Under the CMP, the whole industrial economy of America was steered by taking control of these few key materials as a rudder. Virtually everything else was expected to fall in place naturally and inevitably.

The tactics of operation.—There was an equally clear philosophy back of the new technique of production control. This can best be seen by examining the changing principles underlying American production controls from 1940 to the Controlled Materials Plan of November 1942.

In spite of the tremendous complexity of the American economy and the involved nature of the war production controls which gradually

---

[15] The concentration of WPB controls in one area, namely materials, was accentuated by two other decisions of Mr. Nelson during the latter part of 1942. These were the decisions: (a) to transfer out of WPB such power as it might theoretically have exercised over the allocation of manpower, and (b) to relinquish as far as possible power over food and agriculture. Closely as these problems were related to war production, it was apparently Mr. Nelson's feeling that WPB should be kept as simple as possible, that it was already "too big," and that his interests could be adequately protected by continuing to control materials and by being represented on the advisory boards which dealt with manpower and with food and agriculture. The transfer of these functions was effectuated in the fall and winter of 1942-43; Manpower by Executive Order No. 9247, Sept. 17, 1942, 7 *Federal Register* 7379, and Executive Order No. 9279, Dec. 5, 1942, 7 *Federal Register* 10177; Food and Agriculture by Executive Order No. 9280, Dec. 5, 1942, 7 *Federal Register* 10179.

came into being, the essentials of the four kinds of control which were established through the OPM and WPB are not difficult to understand when stated in their simplest terms.

These four systems were:

1. Control by *Priorities*.
2. Control by *Unrelated Allocation* of short items by independent materials and commodity divisions of WPB.
3. Control by *Integrated Allocation under PRP* by the Requirements Committee and the WPB materials and commodity divisions.
4. Control by *Integrated Allocation under CMP* by the Requirements Committee, working primarily through the Procurement Agencies, namely, the Army, Navy, Air Forces, Maritime Commission, etc.

The accompanying diagrams (charts 39 and 40) bring out the points of contrast between the two latter systems. In both diagrams the WPB organization is shown in skeletal form on the left. The key function of the Requirements Committee is illustrated with the responsibility for "cutting the material pie" among the various claimants, and as the advisor of the program vice chairman and the Chairman of WPB who had the final say.

The twelve "claimants," each with their own war or essential civilian production programs, are represented by the four boxes to the right.

The circles which fill the bottom of the diagram represent in very simplified form the tens of thousands of independent contractors, large and small, who go to make up the American economy, most of whom in one way or another did some direct or indirect war work.

The dotted black lines from the claimants to the circles, and between the circles represent the prime contracts and their subcontracts for war production.

Chart 39 shows the skeleton of the first effort that was made to eliminate the confusion and inefficiency of unrelated priorities and allocations by substituting a comprehensive and integrated system of allocation. The system was known as the Production Requirements Plan, because under it each producer was required to make a single comprehensive statement to WPB of all his requirements on a monthly and quarterly basis, as is explained in chapter 5. This flow of incoming information on requirements is shown by the alternate dash lines. After the total requirements as shown by these PRP statements had been added up, the material pie was cut, and apportioned, plant by plant, in the light of the total war production program, by the Requirements Committee and the program vice chairman. Authorizations to

CHART 39. *General Scheme of Production Control Under Production Priorities Plan.*

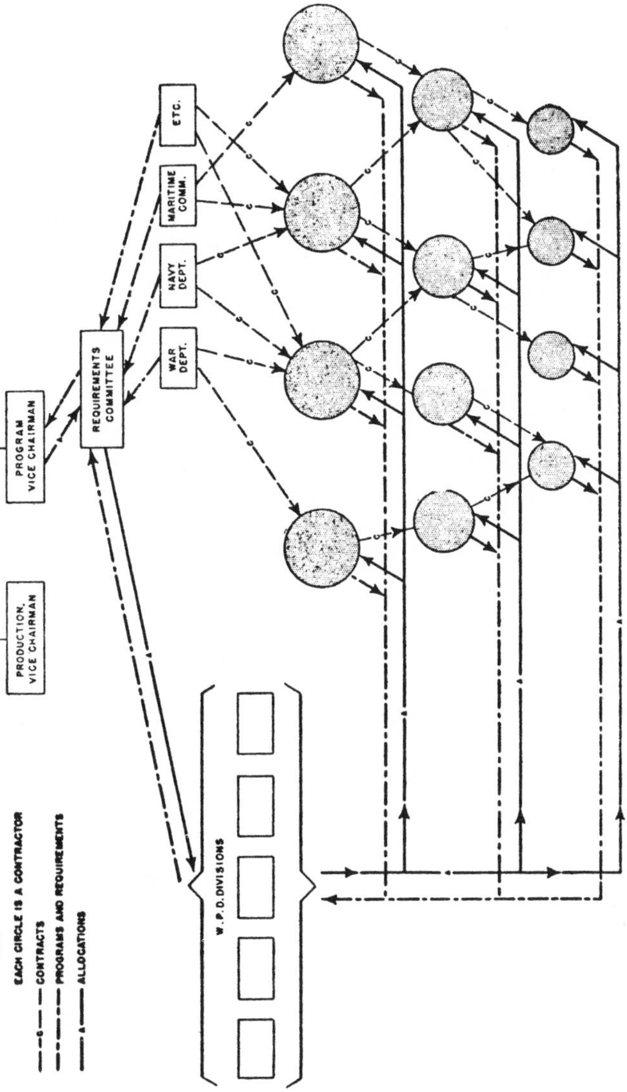

KEY

EACH CIRCLE IS A CONTRACTOR

—o—— CONTRACTS

—·—·— PROGRAMS AND REQUIREMENTS

————— ALLOCATIONS

W.P.B. CHAIRMAN

PROGRAM VICE CHAIRMAN

PRODUCTION, VICE CHAIRMAN

REQUIREMENTS COMMITTEE

WAR DEPT.

NAVY DEPT.

MARITIME COMM.

ETC.

W.P.D. DIVISIONS

Source: Bureau of the Budget.

buy and use critical materials were thus granted to every producer direct from WPB.

These allocations, which went out chiefly through the WPB industry divisions, were designed to take the place ultimately of both the specific allocations and the flood of priorities.

This system was tried experimentally beginning in December 1941 and was made mandatory for some 10,000 larger war contractors beginning with October 1942.

Chart 40 presents graphically the CMP system which Mr. Eberstadt installed, and which became effective in place of the PRP with the first quarter of 1943, and was continued for 10 quarter years to the end of the war.

Under this last development, requirements were gathered and stated by the "claimants," the material pie was cut by the Requirements Committee and the program vice chairman, and the stream of allocations flowed down to the 12 major claimants as lump-sum allotments under each of the controlled materials. Each claimant then made a suballocation to his prime contractor; each prime contractor made a further allocation to his subcontractors; and each subcontractor allotted to his sub-subcontractor, to the final link of the chain. Thus, the allocations followed the same lines as the contracts, and were managed, within the broad totals set by the WPB, by each of the major procurement agencies, the Army, the Navy, the Air Resources Control Office, the Maritime Commission, and the Foreign Economic Administration, etc.

There were, however, certain types of production which could not well be handled through this distribution of allocations—the chain was too long. Therefore, requirements for maintenance, repairs, and operations of industries, including the mines and mills, and for the civilian economy generally, were computed chiefly by the operations vice chairman, and the allocations were enforced through this office and through other divisions of WPB.

In chart 40, the flow of incoming information on requirements is shown in alternate dash lines, reaching the Requirements Committee chiefly from the claimants; i. e., the procurement services. The allocations are shown in lines marked "A," though only one set has been filled in to avoid pictorial confusion.

Perhaps these diagrams will aid in making clearer the underlying significance of the final evolution of the WPB material control techniques.

In passing from priorities to allocation, we passed from a queue system, with the military program entitled to go to the head of the line, to a rationing system, under which selected commodities were separately rationed. In passing from these multiple allocations to

CHART 40. *General Scheme of Production Control Under Controlled Materials Plan.*

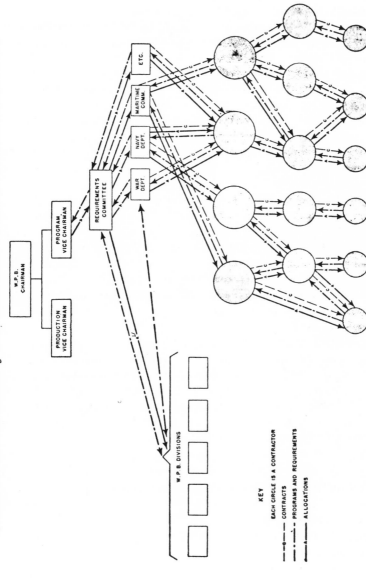

KEY

EACH CIRCLE IS A CONTRACTOR
——c—— CONTRACTS
—··—··— PROGRAMS AND REQUIREMENTS
———— ALLOCATIONS

[1] To simplify the chart, allocation of B products by Industry Divisions to Contractors is not shown.

Source: Bureau of the Budget.

PRP, we passed from the unrelated rationing systems to a comprehensive and integrated rationing system, under which allocations of one commodity were related to allocations of another commodity, plant by plant and program by program, under the complete administration of the WPB itself. The final change was to shift the detailed administration of allocations from the WPB to the claimant agencies, chiefly the Army, Navy, Air Forces, and Maritime Commission, and to delegate the secondary power of allocation to the prime contractors, who passed the allocations on down through the industrial system.

The power which this transferred to the military services and to the prime contractors was, however, not quite as sweeping as these diagrams indicate, because two other types of control not shown on these charts were developing just as the final shift was being made in the controlled-materials system. These two new areas of control were scheduling and manpower allocation. The nature of these controls is described below and in chapter 14.

Under the Controlled Materials Plan as thus worked out, the WPB announced that it would "bring about the adjustment of production programs to conform to materials supply" and that "each manufacturer receiving an authorized order or authorized delivery schedule for his product will receive an allotment of the materials which he and his subcontractors must buy in order to fill the order."

Scheduling production.—The fourth answer for the problem of maximum war production in a tight economy was the direct control by WPB of the main military production programs. Direct control involved three important activities: (1) sitting down with the military chiefs, reviewing their programs, contracts, and production schedules, and requiring them to make adjustments designed to get a better over-all result; (2) sitting down with the managers of plants which were producing the important military products, and authorizing or directing them to take the necessary action in their own plants to get out maximum production regardless of contracts, or the demands of individual procurement officers and their expediters; and (3) taking more or less complete control of the production schedules and deliveries of the manufacturers of intermediate products like valves, ball bearings, motors, crankshafts, and steel and aluminum alloys and shapes; i. e., components.

The man selected by the President and Mr. Nelson to develop and manage these production controls was Charles W. Wilson, president of the General Electric Co.

Jurisdictional controversy.—When Mr. Wilson went to work toward the end of September 1942 on this important and difficult assignment, he found it extremely difficult to get under way. The whole Washington situation and the complicated division of work between the

WPB and the services, and within WPB, were not only baffling, but exasperating to a man fresh from the outside. The basic reason for delay was, however, the loss by WPB of its powers over production both through inaction and by the delegation of the contracting power to the procurement services early in 1942. Thus, Mr. Wilson as production vice chairman had to reassert and recapture the primary authority of WPB over all production, a move the military authorities resisted openly as well as covertly. Thus, while Mr. Eberstadt was moving ahead rapidly with the backing of the Army, Mr. Wilson was fighting a jurisdictional conflict over the basic powers of the WPB. The ensuing interagency struggle between "coordinators" and "operators" was labeled widely as another show-down fight between the civilians and the military. The controversy ended in a compromise under terms of which the WPB production vice chairman, Mr. Wilson, was to be—

responsible for and . . . direct the scheduling of the various production programs of the Army, Navy, Maritime Commission, and other agencies participating in the national war production program, in order to ensure that program schedules do not conflict, are in balance, are consistent with the maximum productive possibilities of the national economy, and are in accord with the strategic requirements of the Chiefs of Staff.

In discharging these functions with respect to end products and their components, he was to have the advice and assistance of a Production Executive Committee consisting of himself, as chairman, the WPB program vice chairman (in charge of materials), the vice chairman of the Maritime Commission, and two representatives each of the War and Navy Departments. His directives were to be issued through the military supply services. In addition to these duties of general supervision, the production vice chairman was charged with central supervision and direction of the production programs for aircraft, escort vessels, and radio and detection equipment. In dealing with aircraft, he was to be advised and assisted by a board comprising himself, as chairman, two representatives of the War Department, and one of the Navy Department. Again, he was to issue directives through the supply branches of the Armed Forces.[16]

With the Production Executive Committee, Mr. Wilson had an organization through which he could coordinate all production. But the most immediate problem facing him involved only one small but extremely important part of production, that of component parts, such as valves or motors. For many vital programs, components were relatively more scarce than materials. Thus, for example, there might be ample supplies of steel for all the ships to be built for a particular quarter, but insufficient valves or motors. Forgings, boilers,

---

[16] OWI-WD-ND-WPB Press Release WPB-2207, Dec. 4, 1942; WPB General Administrative Orders Nos. 2-71, 2-72, 2-73, Dec. 9, 1942.

gages, heat exchangers, turbines, blowers, pumps, and bearings were equally necessary for ships and the manufacture of airplanes, for rubber factories, and the production of farm machinery. Unless the production of components was carefully scheduled, and unless the components themselves were distributed against immediate need, proper allocation of raw materials did not prevent bottlenecks in production.

How difficult it was to schedule the production and delivery of critical common components will be suggested by recalling the range of these "middlemen of manufacture."

The components going into the finished products necessary for modern war range all the way from minute jewel bearings for delicate instruments to huge steel castings and forgings, from tiny fractional horsepower electric motors to mammoth marine turbines, and many of these components, such as engines and pumps, winches, motor controls, and axles, have subcomponents of their own, each of which must be produced and delivered in proper quantity and on schedule or some vital end product will be delayed.[17]

For this purpose, neither the Production Requirements Plan nor the Controlled Materials Plan was adequate. These systems had been installed to distribute materials among competing end-product programs. They were not designed to assure the best detailed use of components which continued to flow under the priority contracts. Thus the new systems could not insure that orders for parts would be filled in accordance with the relative urgency of various end-product programs. A manufacturer with AA–1 ratings for more components than he could supply at once was compelled to fill orders according to the date he received them. As a result, the Navy, for example, might get electrical equipment for ships which would not be launched for another year while the Army waited its turn to have an order for an urgent program filled. These problems were aggravated by the armed services' underestimation of their requirements for components, so that production was not increased soon enough to meet needs. In addition, there was a tendency among claimant agencies to inflate the amounts, and to advance the dates for delivery, of their end-product and component needs, partly as a means to stimulate production. In other cases, claimants and contractors failed to place orders early enough to permit their production to be increased sufficiently and their distribution to be scheduled properly.

To meet these difficulties, the War Production Board undertook to obtain more timely determination of requirements and to scale them down to actual needs to secure prompter placement of orders, to increase capacity to produce components, and to effect better distribution of available components. Even before the winter of 1942–43,

---

17 War Production Board. *War Production in 1944*, June 1945, p. 53.

the Board had been obliged to schedule production and distribution of certain components in short supply, such as machine tools, compressors, turbo-blowers, and jewel bearings. Now it proceeded to "codify" the process and to extend its coverage. This was done under WPB General Scheduling Order M–293 of February 26, 1943,[18] and the Component Scheduling Plan of June 1, 1943, both of which latèr underwent considerable revision, though their basic features remained. Under these arrangements, WPB sought to detei mine more precisely the actual requirements of claimants for components and to establish and freeze firmly schedules for their production and delivery.

General Scheduling Order M–293 listed the critical components to which delays in fulfilling end-product programs approved by WPB had been attributed. On the basis of scarcity and need, these components were grouped into three categories: undesignated, "X" and "Y." Manufacturers of the first, and least critical, group were to make regular opei ation reports to WPB, showing productive capacity, and orders filled, received, shipped, canceled, and scheduled for the specific period designated. Manufacturers of "X" items were required to submit not only these operational reports but also delivery schedules, and they were allowed to deliver components only under schedules approved by WPB. Most items in the "Y" group, which was the most critical, already were under WPB scheduling orders. Anyone who wanted to place an order for one of these components first had to obtain approval of WPB, which might specify the plant in which it was to be placed. Orders so authorized had to be accepted by the manufacturer if regular price and terms were met. Schedules approved by the Board under Ordei M–293 could be "frozen"—i. e., protected from interference by rerating and expediting—though they were subject to change by further WPB directives.

On the basis of information submitted on forms required for operation of its Order M–293, WPB, through its industry divisions and Production Scheduling Division, was able to determine expected production and requested deliveries over a future period for a group of manufacturers. It could transfer orders among plants making a component if some were overloaded and others were operating below full capacity. When total supply was not enough to meet total demand, the Board tried to increase manufacture by eliminating labor and material bottlenecks; and it undertook to correlate pioduction and distribution of components more closely with actual relative urgencies of need.

To effect such correlation, it was necessary to determine the particular end products into which the components were going and the "lead time" required for each component of the products. For this

---

[18] OWI–WPB Press Release WPB–2690, Feb. 27, 1943.

purpose, the WPB industry divisions brought in representatives of claimant agencies to go over the orders of component manufacturers and to justfy their orders on the basis of concrete end-product programs and realistic time schedules. Results of this procedure, however, were not enough to meet the problem. The information needed for adjusting schedules was not always available; and there was no formal procedure to facilitate interchange of vital data about components among contractors, claimant agencies, and WPB. To deal with some of these deficiencies, the Board, on June 1, 1943, put into effect its Component Scheduling Plan.

The Component Scheduling Plan (CSP) was a voluntary cooperative scheme focused on critical components and subcomponents for a limited number of military programs including ships, tanks, and rubber plants. It introduced "vertical," as distinguished from the prevailing "horizontal" or interplant, scheduling, a shift in some ways analagous to that from PRP to CMP for control of materials. The purposes of CSP were to develop realistic unit requirements for each product and to identify the programmed items or projects for which components on order were intended. Information on requirements, contract numbers, and end products was transmitted by the prime contractor to his subcontractors, by them to their subcontractors, and so on.[19] Each manufacturer in the contracting chain thus was given the relation in time and quantity between the components he was to supply and the end products into which they would go. These arrangements facilitated verification of requirements and adjustment of delivery schedules by WPB. Orders approved by the Board under the CSP procedure could be frozen into schedules established under WPB Order M–293.

General Scheduling Order M–293 was revised on September 17, 1943. To the three categories of components mentioned already, there was added a "Z" classification consisting of items which had been handled under the Component Scheduling Plan. The CSP procedure was made mandatory by requiring contractors and subcontractors to fill out CSP forms on instructions from claimant agencies. In addition, certain "X" and "Y" components were moved into the undesignated category in order to simplify reporting by manufacturers. Detailed data were required only from producers in greatest difficulty and on types and sizes of components which were most critical. In February 1944, the "Z" classification was dropped and the vertical scheduling procedure for special programs was simplified because the paper burden and time involved were found to make this system unworkable. At the same time, procedures for reporting requirements for "X" components were simplified further. Those for "Y" items continued as they were, but the number of components affected declined.[20]

Collision Between Production and Materials Controls

These developments in the scheduling of production and delivery of components required adjustments in organization of the War production Board. The basic problem was to relate effectively the controls exercised over manufacture of end products through distribution of component parts with controls employed to allocate materials for these products since, in many cases, both these elements of production were critically short. It was desirable, for example, that production schedules obtained by WPB should be in a form that would serve both systems of control. It was important, also, that critical materials and components both should be directed to the specific manufacturing plants which would use them most promptly and effectively. Within WPB, however, the two types of control were in separate hands. The program vice chairman, Mr. Eberstadt, exercised authority over allocation of materials, while the production vice chairman, Mr. Wilson, had responsibility for production of end products and components.[21] The WPB Chairman recognized that these responsibilities were "closely interwoven" and that "each official must consult the other in many cases."[22] He sought, therefore, to define relations between them so that allotment of materials and scheduling of production would be integrated properly; but circumstances were such that this effort was not successful. WPB Chairman Nelson had declared that the relation between the program and production vice chairmen "has not and does not promote conflict."[23] Neither such reassuring statements nor his instructions for consultation and cooperation between the two officials, however, were enough to insure the coordination that was needed in the war production program. Apart from difficulties inherent in division of authority and provisions for its coordination,[24] there were other factors which interfered with

---

[20] W PB Press Release WPB–4952, Feb. 10, 1944 (OWI).

[21] Duties of the program vice chairman are stated in WPB General Administrative Order No. 265, Nov. 11, 1942. Those of the production vice chairman are included in WPB General Administrative Orders Nos. 2-71, 2-72, 2-73 and 2-74, Dec. 9, 1942.

[22] OWI-WPB Press Release WPB–2065, Oct. 26, 1942.

[23] Ibid.

[24] The production vice chairman was to obtain the advice of the program vice chairman with respect to (1) points at which proposed war production plans, programs, and schedules seemed likely to exceed production possibilities because of material shortages, and (2) readjustments that might meet material limitations effectively. He was to arrange with Army, Navy, and Maritime Commission that their schedules and claims for materials should be in harmony with production plans, programs, and schedules he had approved or released. Allotment requests submitted by these claimant agencies were to be reviewed by the WPB Requirements Committee, Program Bureau, and Controlled Materials Divisions to determine their consistency with production schedules approved by the production vice chairman and their relation to total supplies of materials. When the program vice chairman made determinations for distribution of materials that required reduction in approved production schedules, the production vice chairman was to ensure that such schedules were adjusted appropriately. (WPB General Administrative Order No. 2-73, Dec. 9, 1942.)

integration of the two systems required for control of production of end products. Among them were the presence in WPB of two "strong men" in coordinate positions with closely related functions, the playing of "palace politics" in the organization, and repercussions of controversies between WPB and the military procurement agencies.

The potential frictions inherent in this situation came to a head in a struggle for jurisdiction over WPB industry divisions. These units were used for scheduling production as well as for allocating materials (especially for CMP "B" products, which were common to many end products). Difficulties were almost inevitable in attempts by the divisions to serve satisfactorily two masters who did not see eye to eye: The program vice chairman, Mr. Eberstadt, had jurisdiction over most of the divisions and was responsible for allocating resources to end product programs. The production vice chairman, Mr. Wilson, had responsibilities for production of these end products and their components. The WPB Aircraft and Radio Industry Divisions and the Office of Progress Reports had been placed under his direction when WPB extended its control over production of these military products early in December 1942.[25] Not long after, Mr. Wilson sought to have other WPB divisions put under his jurisdiction in order to assist him more effectively in meeting his general responsibilities for the war production program. He was reported to have complained, for example, that the sizes and shapes of the raw aluminum supplied under Mr. Eberstadt's direction were such that they could not be turned into the extrusions needed for production of airplanes under his supervision.[26] On February 4, 1943, WPB Chairman Nelson transferred to the production vice chairman the Shipbuilding, General Industrial Equipment, Tools, Automotive, Safety, and Technical Supplies, Aluminum and Magnesium, and Facilities Divisions and the Facilities Bureau, all of which previously had been under the program vice chairman.[27] These shifts were a result of Mr. Wilson's insistence and a recognition of the increasing importance of production scheduling and the declining relative urgency of materials control in the war supply program. The process was completed less than 2 weeks later when the WPB Chairman asked the program vice chairman for his resignation and designated Mr. Wilson Executive Vice Chairman in charge of functions formerly performed by himself over production and by Mr. Eberstadt over materials.[28] Chairman Nelson justified the reorganization with the argument that—

[25] WPB General Administrative Orders Nos. 2–71, 2–72, 2–73, 2–74, Dec. 9, 1942.
[26] *New York Times*, Feburary 17, 1943, p. 11, column 4.
[27] WPB General Administrative Orders Nos. 2–76, 2–77.
[28] WPB General Administrative Orders Nos. 2–71, 2–72, 2–73, and OPVC Administrative Order No. 2. But see also Nelson, Donald M., *Arsenal of Democracy*, N. Y. 1946, p. 388 ff.

CHART 41. *United States Munitions Production*

[Average Monthly Rate, by Quarters, in 1945 Standard Dollar Weights]

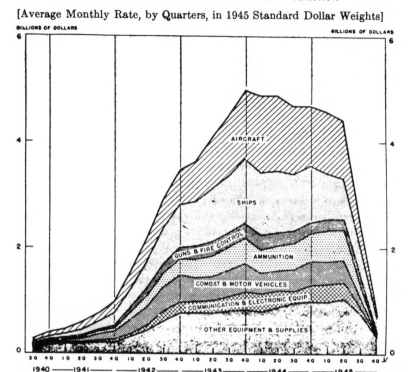

BILLIONS OF DOLLARS   BILLIONS OF DOLLARS

AIRCRAFT

SHIPS

GUNS & FIRE CONTROL

AMMUNITION

COMBAT & MOTOR VEHICLES

COMMUNICATION & ELECTRONIC EQUIP.

OTHER EQUIPMENT & SUPPLIES

1940 ——1941—— ——1942—— ——1943—— ——1944—— ——1945——

¹ 1945 data preliminary.

Source: Civilian Production Administration (formerly War Production Board).

Because our entire effort must now center about the production lines, and because this involves the closest control over scheduling, it is essential that two things be true—first, that a production man be in full charge; second, that all related problems be within the jurisdiction of that production man.

. . . The man in charge of production cannot discharge his duties adequately unless he also controls the flow of materials into production channels.

In other words, materials control and production control today are all one integrated job. They cannot be considered separately. They must be directed as one job, not two.[29]

Another element in the reorganization, however, was the relationship between the WPB and the military. The latter were reported to be seeking Mr. Nelson's ouster from the WPB chairmanship, and Mr. Eberstadt, a former official of the Army and Navy Munitions Board, was believed to be in sympathy with them.

With this final evolution, the WPB reached its ultimate wartime

---

[29] OWI-WPB Press Release WPB-2558, Feb. 16, 1943.

development and proceeded with new vigor and unity of direction to drive production upward from month to month, until direct military production reached toward the close of the year an annual rate of over $62 billion, a figure previously considered impossible by many experts and higher than the combined efforts of the other Allies.

11

Food for War

P RIOR to midsummer 1942 few people realized that global warfare would tax to the limit our agricultural resources. In 1939 an immediate result of the European war had been to reduce foreign demand for American agricultural produce. Our normally large surplus of commodities such as wheat, corn, and cotton, of which we had approximately a 2-years' supply, increased with each harvest. We also began to pile up stocks of other commodities for which there previously had been substantial export markets. After the declaration of war, however, Pacific sources of sugar, oil, fruit, and other foodstuffs were cut off and soon it became apparent that American agriculture, as well as American industry, would have to be mobilized in a great productive effort.

By the fall of 1942 existing arrangements for handling food problems had become inadequate. Shortages of meat, fats, and oils, dairy products, and canned foods were bringing home to consumers the effect of war on food supply. These shortages were simply another indication of the growing intensity of the war on all fronts. Military operations then under way in North Africa, Guadalcanal, and El Alamein, and planned for Italy, Western Europe and the Japanese Islands, could be supported only by the most efficient use of all our resources, including food. This pressure brought a reorganization of the War Production Board and a refinement of production scheduling techniques. It likewise required fuller utilization of manpower and better control over the production and distribution of agricultural commodities.

The principal problems in mobilizing food were similar to those which had to be solved in mobilizing steel, copper, manpower, manufacturing facilities, and other strategic resources. Since there was not enough food to satisfy all needs, available supplies had to be divided among competing uses according to essentiality. Farmers had to be persuaded to use their land and equipment for the production of war-essential crops. Farm produce had to be channeled to processors in proper amounts and to wholesalers and retailers for equitable distribution to consumers. The agencies responsible for performing these jobs had to be tied in with the general civilian war organization and coordinated with the activities of other agencies dealing with related problems. The story of how these problems were handled should be placed against a background of the food situation as it appeared in the fall of 1942.

The Department of Agriculture estimated in September 1942 that total food production in the coming year would be substantially above the average for the prewar period 1935–39. Increased production of meat, for example, was estimated at 49 percent above the prewar average, or 24 billion pounds. Production estimates showed substantial increases for other foods.

Food shortages were certain in spite of this favorable production picture. In Europe, Russia, and China there would be malnutrition and actual starvation. In the United States, the people would eat more than they had ever eaten before, but would not be able to get as much as they would wish to buy. The Department of Agriculture estimated that spendable income in 1943 would be about 65 percent above 1935–39 levels, much of it in the hands of lower income groups who never had been able to afford an adequate diet. Moreover, because of the disappearance from the market of new cars, washing machines, radios, and other durable goods, spendable income available for the purchase of food would be about 97 percent higher than the 1935–39 level. Again in terms of meat, this meant that the estimated supply of 140 pounds per person would be 14 pounds more than the prewar average but 24 pounds less than the potential 1943 civilian demand of 164 pounds per capita (charts 42 and 43).

Expanding military requirements also contributed to developing food shortages. By the end of 1942 it had been determined that military plans for 1943 would require an Army of 8.2 million and a Navy of approximately 1.8 million men. A military force of this size would consume enormous quantities of food. Navy menus, for example, provided each 1,000 sailors with monthly allotments of 32,000 pounds of meat, 2,400 pounds of butter, 4,500 pounds of eggs, and 800 pounds of cheese, in addition to large quantities of dry groceries and fresh fruits and vegetables.[1] These menus gave each sailor more

---

[1] U. S. Navy. Supplies and Accounts Memorandum No. 416, May 1937, "Items and Quantities to be Carried by Ships," reprinted and in use, 1942.

CHART 42. *Per Capita Consumption of Selected Foods.*[1]

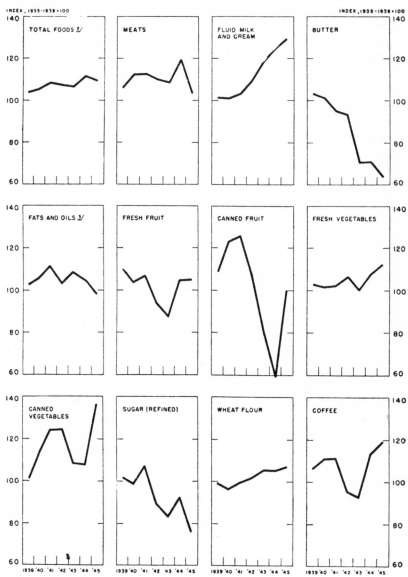

[1] Data for 1945 are preliminary. On calendar year basis except for canned fruits and vegetables which are on a pack year basis beginning in the year designated, and fresh citrus fruits which are for the crop year beginning in October of the previous year.

[2] Includes foods not shown separately on the chart.

[3] Excludes butter.

Source: Department of Agriculture.

than twice as much meat, three-fourths again as much butter, one-third again as many eggs, and two-thirds again as much cheese as the average citizen ate in 1942.

Another heavy drain on our food supplies came from the necessity of keeping our allies, chiefly Great Britain and Russia, in the war. Shortly after the fall of France the President had declared, "We will extend to the opponents of force the material resources of this nation" and, through lend-lease arrangements, we began to ship foodstuffs to Great Britain. Russia had lost the Ukrainain sugar and grain-producing areas a few weeks after the Nazi invasion and, in the 1942 summer offensive, the Germans captured the great North Caucasian agricultural area. Large quantities of fats and oils and grain were needed to keep the Red Army in the field and by December 1942 these requirements were so urgent that at times food was given precedence over steel in the assignment of shipping space. To keep British and Russian diets at the subsistence level in 1943 would take about 10 percent of our total food supply.

Finally, the invasion of North Africa on November 8, 1942, posed for the first time the problem of food for liberated peoples. In contrast to the Germans and Japanese, who were busily engaged in stripping resources of conquered territories, the President stated: "Every aid possible will be given to restore each of the liberated countries to soundness and strength, so that each may make its full contribution to United Nations' victory." [2]

Aid to our allies, maintenance of the health and efficiency of the civilian population, and full utilization of food as an instrument of warfare required changes in the Government's peacetime food organization. Prior to the declaration of war, when there was little awareness that food would become scarce, administrative problems involving agricultural commodities were handled within the rudimentary defense organization of the Department of Agriculture. As the tempo of the war increased in the months following Pearl Harbor, it became necessary to coordinate the various agencies whose actions affected in one way or another the production and distribution of farm produce. At first, this coordination was provided by WPB but by the fall of 1942, it was apparent that a more effective food organization was needed. On December 5, 1942, the President by Executive order directed the Secretary of Agriculture to "assume full responsibility for and control over the Nation's food program."[3] This order set the pattern of the War Food Administration for the crucial war years. The pages which follow relate the administrative developments preceding the

[2] Office of Lend-Lease Administration. *Seventh Report to Congress on Lend-Lease Operations*, for the period ended Dec. 11, 1942, p. 6.
[3] Executive Order No. 9280, Dec. 5, 1942, 7 *Federal Register* 10179.

CHART 43. *Production of Selected Foods.*[1]

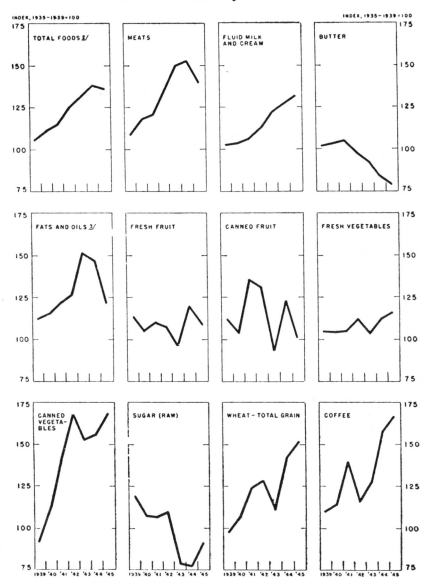

[1] Data for 1945 are preliminary. On calendar year basis except for canned fruits and vegetables which are on a pack year basis beginning in the year designated, and fresh citrus fruits which are for the crop year beginning in October of the previous year.
[2] Includes foods not shown separately on the chart.
[3] Excludes butter.
Source: Department of Agriculture.

issuance of the Food order and discuss some major problems confronting the Secretary of Agriculture in the first 3 months of 1943.

Administrative Developments Prior to December 1942

Immediately after the Nazi attack on Poland and the declaration of war by France and Great Britain, Secretary of Agriculture Wallace set up an advisory council (comprising representatives of farm organizations, the food industry, and consumer representatives) to advise the Government on the wartime problems of American agriculture. The advisory council's approach was that such adjustment in agricultural practices as might be required should come through voluntary cooperation between Government and the food industry rather than by the imposition of regulations and orders. The possibility of using the council as an instrument of such cooperation was lost when a fatal disagreement developed between the representatives of the farm organizations and representatives of the food trade over a food supply organization plan prepared by members of the trade and over the Secretary's proposal to support hog prices at a level which farm organizations feared would become a ceiling.

The next development came as the Nazis swept through the low countries and France: Mr. Chester C. Davis was appointed Agricultural adviser of the National Defense Advisory Commission. Under the President's concept of the NDAC, the agricultural adviser's function was to advise the President on all aspects of agriculture in relation to the defense program. Mr. Davis advised on matters such as the disposition of surpluses, place of the farm populations in the defense program, and the development of new agricultural products for defense. All operating functions of the Department of Agriculture remained intact.

As the parts of the National Defense Advisory Commission began to be transmuted into more formal Government agencies, such as the Office of Production Management, the question of what to do with the NDAC Agricultural Division arose. Mr. Davis suggested to the President on March 6, 1941, that an office of food supply be established, either as a part of the Office for Emergency Management and coordinate with the Office of Production Management, or as a division of the Department of Agriculture. The statutory responsibilities of the Secretary of Agriculture with respect to production, storage, and distribution of food, and the availability of trained personnel in the Department were cited as reasons for setting up the office in the Department of Agriculture. Under the Davis plan, the food organization would have been headed by a strong administrator reporting to the Secretary of Agriculture but acting under a Presidential directive; it would gather and maintain current information in regard to food supplies and requirements; and formulate and execute the Government's food program.

The President did not set up the office of food which Davis recommended. He stated that "the work of taking coordinated action with regard to food should be done in the Department of Agriculture" because they "have the facilities for this work" and because there would be "danger of confusion and duplication" if this work were done outside. The President added that, since the British were interested in obtaining only a few commodities and information about them was quite complete, "it seems inadvisable just now to risk creating the alarm that might arise from a broad survey of agricultural supplies. . . . For the same reason, I do not think that we need to establish an office of food supply or a food administration at this time." This decision was contrary to the general pattern which the President followed in establishing international agencies outside the Department of State, and the War Labor Board outside the Labor Department.

Instead, the President abolished the Agricultural Division of the National Defense Advisory Commission in May, 1941, and transferred its function to an Office of Agricultural Defense Relations which was placed, at the President's request, in the immediate office of the Secretary of Agriculture. The President described the wartime job of the USDA as follows: "first, the guarantee of an adequate supply of food for the needs of this nation and supplemental needs of those nations whose defense is essential to this country, and, second, the provision of sufficient agricultural raw materials for expanded defense production". [4] The President's letter stated that OADR should be considered "an integral part of the emergency defense organization" and outlined broad functions which would have OADR an over-all defense organization for the Department of Agriculture. In practice however, OADR was confined to liaison with WPB and OPA on priority and price problems.

The food production function emphasized by the President fitted easily into the Department's peacetime activities. For more than 50 years, improvement of agricultural production had been a major objective of the Department and since 1933, the Department had engaged actively in planning and controlling the kinds and amounts of farm produce and in helping the farmer market his crops. On December 11, 1941, the Secretary announced a broad reorganization of the Department, under which the various agencies responsible for these activities were regrouped for the purpose of providing better coordination. He established the Agricultural Marketing Adminis-

---

[4] Office for Emergency Management. *Handbook*, 1942, pp. 66–67. Letter from President Roosevelt to Secretary Wickard, May 1941, establishing the Office for Agricultural War Relations.

tration and Agricultural Conservation and Adjustment Administration. He authorized county defense boards composed of representatives from all Federal agricultural agencies within a county. The county representative of the Agricultural Adjustment Administration served as chairman. The boards, which later became known as war boards, had as a principal objective the coordination of agricultural defense activities at the county level. They were not notably successful in achieving coordination, largely because the chairman of the boards had no authority over the representatives of the constituent agencies.

There was no serious disagreement between Agriculture and OPA until after the declarations of war. The Secretary of Agriculture's membership on the Price Administration Committee of the Office of Price Administration and Civilian Supply gave him an opportunity to consult with and advise the Price Administrator on agricultural price policy.[5] Meanwhile, the Price Administrator had adopted the policy of changing price schedules where such changes were necessary to expedite the flow of any material,[6] and had stated, on April 30, 1941, "I will recognize what the Congress and the present Administration have always recognized and written into law—namely, that the prices of many farm products in the past years have been too low to provide the farmer with a decent wage for his labor".[7] Within this policy framework the Department of Agriculture and the Office of Price Administration and Civilian Supply collaborated actively in curtailing speculative sales of sugar futures and in dealing with price rises and emerging shortages of cotton textiles.

After establishment of the War Production Board on January 16, 1942, responsibility for management of the food supply was distributed among several war agencies whose authority limited that of the Department of Agriculture. The Department was active in planning the general outlines of farm production and the use of agricultural resources. Facilities of the Commodity Credit Corporation and the Agricultural Marketing Administration, which had been developed for the procurement and distribution of surplus agricultural commodities, were used in purchasing for Lend-Lease. Under the Emergency Price Control Act of 1942, the Secretary of Agriculture shared with the Price Administrator responsibility for the issuance of maximum price regulations affecting agricultural commodities. Food functions of the War Production Board were exercised through several industry branches of the Materials and Industry Operation Division and through the Requirements Committee. The most important of these activities

---

[5] Executive Order No. 8734, Apr. 11, 1941, 6 *Federal Register* 1917.
[6] Office of Price Administration and Civilian Supply. Minutes of Price Administration Committee, June 11, 1941.
[7] Leon Henderson to Representative Cannon, Apr. 30, 1941. OEM Press Release PM345, May 1, 1941.

were formulation of estimates of food and fiber requirements for industrial purposes; control of the amount of industrial capacity, raw materials, and labor used in the manufacture of farm machinery and food-processing equipment; and assignment of shipping space for importation of agricultural products in critically short supply. The Office of Price Administration was responsible for preventing inflationary price rises in agricultural products and for rationing scarce food supplies when directed to do so by the Chairman of the War Production Board. Agencies concerned with foreign relations, such as the Department of State, the Board of Economic Warfare, and the Lend-Lease Administration, were interested in procuring foreign supplies and in shipping food to the Allies and friendly neutrals. Farm labor eligible for military service was controlled by the Selective Service System.

This distribution of authority did not give any single agency clear-cut authority to plan for future emergencies but it seemed to be reasonably adequate as long as there was an abundance of food. As supply diminished, however, officials began to think of a greater concentration of authority. Acting under instructions of Mr. Harry Hopkins, early in 1942, representatives of the Bureau of the Budget and the Departments of Agriculture and Justice drafted an Executive order centralizing food management powers in the Department of Agriculture. The impetus for this particular proposal had come largely from persons interested in more effective arrangements for handling lend-lease purchases. Documents accompanying the draft order stated that the Department had established "working relations with existing food procurement agencies of friendly nations" and that it was desirable for this Government to have a single agency with which foreign missions could work. Action on the proposal was delayed pending study of the general organization of our foreign economic activities.

A few weeks later this issue—the way in which management of domestic food supply should be related to foreign trade in food—came up in a proposal for alleviation of a critical shortage of fats and oils. The Chairman of the War Production Board recommended that the Department of Agriculture take over the job of ascertaining the available supplies of fats and oils; of determining minimum requirements for industrial and consumer uses; and of devising a program to reduce consumption and to distribute available supplies among the most essential users. The Secretary of Agriculture was unwilling to undertake this responsibility "unless there is control of foreign purchases in the same agency which has responsibility for domestic production." He pointed out that imports of fats and oils became a part of our total supply and that purchases abroad should be "synchronized with foreign purchases of the British." The issue, according to the Secretary, was not "one of being able to work satisfactorily with the Board of Economic Warfare or with any other agency. It is simply a matter of centralizing and consolidating responsibility in the interest of speedy and effective action."

Complete authority for food management could not be concentrated in a single agency because solutions devised for food problems would have a profound effect on matters equally vital to successful prosecution of the war which could not be handled effectively by a food agency. Thus, "speedy action" could not be taken on fats and oils without reference to industrial and military requirements for glycerin, a byproduct of soap. Some of the factors which had to be considered in estimating total food requirements were: (1) size of the Army and Navy and the disposition of military forces; (2) time schedules for the invasion and occupation of enemy-held territory; (3) migration of the civilian population and increased employment in physically exacting jobs in heavy industry; (4) production schedules for industrial alcohol, synthetic rubber, and explosives; and (5) allotments to be made to the civilian populace. Estimates of supply had to take into account availability of foreign products as well as various factors affecting domestic production. In carrying out a food-production program, it was necessary to determine which commodities were most essential to conduct of the war; to persuade millions of farmers to plant essential war crops and to take risks involved in shifting to new crops; to balance the need for imported foodstuffs against requirements for manganese and chrome and to assign shipping space accordingly; to divide the Nation's labor force among farms, factories, and the military services; to decide whether plants should continue to make farm machinery and food processing equipment or convert to production of tanks and guns; and to decide whether chemicals should be used to manufacture antityphus and antimalaria insecticides or refrigerants for food storage facilities. In controlling food distribution provision had to be made for equalizing supplies between the country's producing and consuming areas; procuring food for military services without disruption of local markets and in accordance with seasonal fluctuations of supply; and for moving raw foodstuffs to processors so that luxury commodities were not produced at the expense of necessities or supplies of processed foods were not taken out of the ordinary trade channels.

Detailed decisions on all such matters had a common objective: mobilization of the Nation's resources so that the greatest and swiftest possible destruction could be brought down upon our enemies. This objective required the daily adjustment and fitting together of essential interests and activities of the Joint Chiefs of Staff, the War, Navy,

State, and Agricultural Departments, the War Production Board, Office of Price Administration, and other war agencies. Consolidation of authority over food, transportation, or manpower could eliminate some problems but, at the *same time, it would create many others. There was no escape from the problem of adjustment among war agencies. If the Department of Agriculture were given responsibility over foreign trade in food, as suggested by the Secretary, its decisions and actions would have to be related to work of the military, diplomatic, and economic missions abroad—and to the work of agencies responsible for fuel, rubber, minerals, and so forth if the suggestion were extended to other commodities. At the time the Department sought control over foreign purchases of food, an effort was being made to "centralize and consolidate" authority over foreign economic affairs. The conflicting plans of organization were essentially irreconcilable. This did not mean, however, that administrative arrangements for food management could not be clarified and strengthened.

The next step in the development of the war food organization was the establishment on June 4, 1942, of the Food Requirements Committee reporting to the Chairman of the War Production Board.[8] The Committee was headed by the Secretary of Agriculture and comprised representatives of the War, State, and Navy Departments, the Office of Price Administration, the Board of Economic Warfare, the Office of Lend-Lease Administration, and three WPB representatives. Under the general direction of the Chairman of the War Production Board, the Chairman of the Food Requirements Committee was authorized to determine the total food needs and the amount required to balance supply and need, and to divide food supplies among the several users—Army, Navy, foreign nations, civilians, and Government agencies. The WPB Requirements Committee retained its authority over supplies and equipment needed in the production of food, with the Chairman of the Food Requirements Committee supplying information and advice on amounts required to carry out the food-production program. If the Chairman of the Food Requirements Committee disagreed with the Chairman of the WPB Requirements Committee over division of agricultural products between food and industrial uses, the Chairman of the War Production Board decided the issue.

Food-production plans were formulated by the Food Requirements Committee and were carried out by the Department of Agriculture and War Production Board. The Department was responsible generally for growing food, adjusting domestic agricultural production, importing foodstuffs, and formulating food-conservation programs.

---

[8] WPB Press Release 1295, June 5, 1942.

The War Production Board Food Division was responsible for directing the processing of raw foodstuffs—for example, the manufacture of candy, soft drinks, and bakery products. Processing of nonfoods derived from agricultural materials, such as soap and clothing, was under the direction of the WPB Materials Division. The Office of Civilian Requirements had a staff working on civilian requirements for various kinds of food. Each agency was responsible for controlling distribution of the commodities within its jurisdiction. The Office of Price Administration, however, was designated the agency which, subject to the directives of the War Production Board, would be in charge of consumer rationing.

The Food Requirements Committee, however, did not prove to be an effective administrative device. At the outset there was a problem of making the new committee a part of the WPB organization. The personnel of the WPB was drawn largely from industry, and its attention and major interest were industrial production rather than food supply and management. At times, internal conflicts and confusion incident to rapid expansion of the agency made it difficult to obtain decisions within the War Production Board. For example, action on the fats and oils problem (which in considerable measure had been the immediate impetus for the setting up of the Food Requirements Committee) was delayed for months while questions of jurisdiction, the necessity for action, and the kind of action to be taken were thrashed out within the Food Requirements Committee, the Requirements Committee, the food branches, and the Civilian Supply Division. The Requirements Committee tended to schedule in great detail the material and equipment needed for the food production program. Under this practice matters such as steel for milk cans and farm fencing were the subject of lengthy negotiations within the War Production Board. Although some of these delays were due to the primitive production scheduling techniques in use at the time, they imposed an additional burden on the Food Requirements Committee which probably would have failed under the most favorable circumstances.

These difficulties (which were less serious than might have been expected in a new agency with a job of such magnitude) were matched by weaknesses within the Food Requirements Committee structure. The Chairman of the Committee was responsible to the Chairman of the War Production Board but, as Secretary of Agriculture he directed a department which, by reason of its standing with farmers, was a strong candidate for the food administration job. The Chairman of the Committee designated the Office of Agricultural War Relations as staff to the Food Requirements Committee. This group consisted of top-policy assistants to the Secretary who, aside from their work with the Food Requirements Committee, were primarily concerned with the programs and operations of the Department of Agriculture. Partially as a result of this double demand on the time of the staff, the Food Requirements Committee was slow in estimating total food requirements and in laying out a 1943 production plan. Meanwhile, requirements for particular commodities were considered in the absence of any plan for total requirements; the Department of Agriculture continued its work in supply and requirements planning and there seemed to be no systematic effort to fit the two activities together.

Weaknesses in the Food Requirement's Committee were apparent in its method of handling emerging meat shortages. Although the Committee's responsibility was supply and distribution, the OPA representative was an employee of the price department and, because in part of the loose internal organization of the OPA, was not able to speak with authority about rationing matters. In July, the Chairman of the Food Requirements Committee stated that general supplies of meat were adequate but that the OPA should be in a position to begin rationing in approximately 1 year.[9] In September he recommended that OPA begin rationing as quickly as possible; late in October the Food Requirements Committee announced that meat would be rationed in December. Technical difficulties, such as the printing and distribution of approximately 130 million ration books, made it impossible to start rationing on the announced date and an interim "voluntary rationing" plan had to be devised. Part of the difficulty was undoubtedly due to faulty statistics on meat supply. But more effective cooperation between the Food Requirements Committee and OPA rationing officials would have simplified the problem of stretching limited supplies until rationing could be started on March 29, 1943.

Difficulties in pricing food commodities, which also involved the relations of the Department of Agriculture and the Office of Price Administration, became acute in the summer of 1942. Questions such as the levels at which maximum prices should be fixed, the coverage of the commodities to be controlled, farmer liability under penalty provisions of price regulations, and relations between OPA food price ceilings and Department of Agriculture crop loans and price support payments programs arose continuously between the two agencies. The Food Requirements Committee had no authority in food price matters and in the absence of some central point where decisions could be made, these interagency problems were the subject of lengthy negotiations between the agencies involved. The rather loose internal organization which characterized both the Department of Agriculture

---

[9] WPB. *Minutes of Food Requirements Committee*, July 31, 1942.

and the Office of Price Administration frequently prolonged these discussions by making it difficult to obtain clear-cut statements of agency points of view.

This particular deficiency—lack of a device for reconciling disagreements of food price policy—was dealt with in the Stabilization Order of October 3, 1942, by giving the Economic Stabilization Director authority to settle differences between the Department of Agriculture and the Office of Price Administration.[10] With the establishment of OES, important segments of the food management function were dispersed among the War Production Board, the Department of Agriculture, the Office of Economic Stabilization, and the Office of Price Administration. Under these arrangements differences between the Price Administrator and the Secretary of Agriculture were referred to the Chairman of the War Production Board if they involved supply or distribution policies, but to the Director of Economic Stabilization if they involved the pricing of agricultural commodities. The pull and tug which these arrangements permitted and the shortening of food supplies called for additional action.

The War Production Board, supported by representatives of the food distribution trade, sought to consolidate and strengthen its food functions. On October 24, the Chairman recommended the establishment within the WPB of a Food Director with powers comparable to those of the Rubber Director. The statutory powers of the Department of Agriculture and of the Office of Price Administration would not have been affected by Nelson's proposal but "central direction and coordination" would have been given to the food program "in all of its phases." "Without such central direction," Nelson wrote, "there is sure to be lost motion and disastrous delay in solving this vital problem."

The Secretary of Agriculture opposed establishment of a Food Administrator as suggested by Chairman Nelson of the War Production Board. A WPB Food Administrator "could not possibly coordinate the food programs of the United States and the United Nations." The Secretary noted that his positions as cochairman of the Combined Food Board and chairman of the WPB Food Requirements Committee provided "a focal point at which to deal with the problems of supply, production, exchange, and shipping of food" and that a Food Administrator had "already been set up through the establishment of the Food Requirements Committee." The food situation could be handled satisfactorily without formation of "another large administration which would duplicate and conflict with agencies

---

10 Executive Order No. 9250, Oct. 3, 1942, 7 *Federal Register* 7871. The relevant language follows: "Subject to the directives on policy of the Director, the price of agricultural commodities shall be established or maintained or adjusted jointly by the Secretary of Agriculture and the Price Administrator; and any disagreement between them shall be resolved by the Director."

already in existence." As an alternative, Mr. Wickard proposed to strengthen the Food Requirements Committee by giving it authority to see that its decisions were carried out; and to transfer from the War Production Board to the Department of Agriculture "power to issue orders for the allocation, reservation, and rationing of food" and power "to decide the agency that will administer an allocation or reservation order." Authority to "fix prices and do all consumer rationing" would be retained by the Office of Price Administration.

The proposals of Nelson and Wickard did not provide a clear-cut basis for action. Appointment of a Food Director within the War Production Board would have been consistent with WPB's role as mobilizer of the Nation's economic resources and made possible better

CHART 44. *Prices Received by Farmers.*

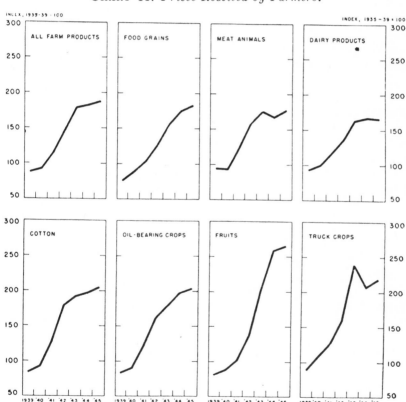

Source: Department of Agriculture.

cooperation among WPB units interested in various aspects of agricultural production. As long as the Department of Agriculture and the Office of Price Administration by statutory authorization controlled important segments of food programs, however, it was not likely that a WPB Food Director could give unified direction to the food program "in all of its phases." The Wickard proposal for "strengthening" the WPB Food Requirements Committee at first glance seemed to retain the concept of the War Production Board as *the* economic mobilization agency. But transfer of food allocation authority to the Department of Agriculture, as suggested by the Secretary, actually would have deprived the War Production Board of control over food. Authority to carry out WPB decisions, made by the Food Requirements Committee, would have been in the hands of another agency—the Department of Agriculture. Since Wickard served as Chairman of the Food Requirements Committee and as Secretary of Agriculture, decisions relating to farm production presumably could be executed without such a transfer. Decisions on processing and distribution matters probably could have been carried out satisfactorily by WPB. Although the Department of Agriculture unquestionably had the support of farmers and farm organizations, it had not established effective relations with food processors and distributors.

A variety of influential organizations and persons favored the transfer of food management responsibility to the Department of Agriculture. The President of the American Federation of Labor supported the Secretary of Agriculture for the post of Food Administrator in testimony before a Congressional committee and a similar recommendation was sent to the White House by the Congress of Industrial Organizations, and the Railway Brotherhoods. The National Farmers Union and former President Herbert Hoover were also on record in favor of centralizing wartime food responsibilities under the Secretary of Agriculture. Other organizations, such as the National Association of Manufacturers, the National Council of Farmer Cooperatives, the National Grange, and the American Farm Bureau Federation also urged the establishment of a strong food administration, located within either the Department of Agriculture or the Office of Economic Stabilization.[11] Of the three major alternatives—the Department of Agriculture, the War Production Board, and the Office of Economic Stabilization—the President selected the Department of Agriculture and issued the Food Order of December 5.

---

[11] Secretary Wickard also suggested the transfer of the Food Requirements Committee from the War Production Board and its reestablishment by Executive order in the Office of Economic Stabilization.

Operations Under the Food Order of December 5, 1942

The organization established under Executive Order No. 9280 was built around the four major jobs which the Secretary of Agriculture was directed to perform: (1) determination of the total national and foreign food requirements; (2) formulation and execution of a production program to supply food in quantities sufficient to meet total requirements; (3) establishment of allocation and priority controls to bring about proper distribution of available food supplies; and (4) procurement of food for the military services and other Government agencies.

Within the Department of Agriculture operating agencies concerned primarily with production, such as the Farm Security Administration and the Agricultural Conservation and Adjustment Administration, were transferred to a new Food Production Administration. The Agricultural Marketing Administration and other agencies concerned primarily with distribution were transferred to a new Food Distribution Administration. Each of these administrations was directed and supervised by an Administrator appointed by the Secretary of Agriculture. Organizational arrangements were completed by the abolition of the Food Requirements Committee of the War Production Board, the appointment of a Food Advisory Committee to the Secretary which included representatives of the military services, State Department, Lend-Lease Administration, and the Board of Economic Warfare, and by transfer to Agriculture of War Production Board activities and personnel concerned with food.

This food organization was essentially the Department of Agriculture, its components somewhat rearranged and its personnel augmented by specialists transferred from WPB. The Department of Agriculture provides the single example in World War II of an existing agency undertaking to plan and administer a major segment of the war economy. In other fields, new agencies were established to handle jobs which might have been given to such organizations as the Departments of State or Commerce, or the Interstate Commerce Commission. The experience of the food administrations thus is valuable in showing some of the uses and limitations of an "old line" department in war administration.

During the first quarter of 1943, the general outline of war food policies was shaped. Some of the policies dealt with fundamental questions of long-run significance, such as the extent to which existing production, social, and economic patterns of American agriculture should be adjusted to war conditions. Other policies were concerned with more immediate problems: the rising demand for agricultural commodities; the necessity for more equitable distribution of food; uncertainty that rich harvests made possible by unusually favorable weather in 1941 and 1942 would be repeated in 1943; and the availability of processing and-storage facilities. In dealing with these matters, the Department of Agriculture was called upon to develop new points of view and new conceptions of the "farm problem." The balance of the chapter describes the Department's response to this new situation.

Programming Agricultural Production

The Department was only partially successful in getting farmers to produce essential foods in adequate amounts. Total food production established new records and production of crops such as peanuts and soybeans, rich sources of essential oils, likewise increased substantially. But throughout the war many farmers used imported fertilizer, labor deferred from military service, and fertile land to grow short-staple cotton, of which there was a surplus, watermelons and other low-priority crops.

As we have seen, the War Production Board had to deal with one difficulty after another in bringing into balance its various production programs for raw materials, components, and end products. The scheduling of agricultural production was a much more complex job, because of a number of factors which the Department of Agriculture could not easily control. First, several million small producers, many of them operating family-type farms, comprised the "manufacturing plant." The "little fellows" of industry, it will be recalled, were not drawn into war production with notable success, even with special measures such as subcontracting drives and the Smaller War Plants Corporation, etc. Second, these millions of farmers were accustomed to certain crops and had learned the most satisfactory way of growing them and of minimizing dangers of loss. They were reluctant to plant new crops unless convinced that the Government really wanted them and was willing to help out by supplying necessary machinery and by underwriting a substantial part of the risk. In this attitude the farmers did not differ from the manufacturers who insisted on cost-plus contracts and priority assistance in obtaining machinery and raw materials. Third, traditional production patterns were reflected in "parity" legislation passed since 1933 and designed to bolster the prices of basic crops such as cotton, corn, wheat, rice, and tobacco. Fourth, officials of the Department of Agriculture who had helped formulate parity legislation and were responsible for its administration were accustomed to work within the parity framework. They were slow to see that 1933 techniques, developed to deal with surpluses and low prices, were not relevant in a war economy of scarcity and high prices. Finally, the parity structure was guarded jealously by potent farm-pressure groups and by a bloc of Congressmen whose Democratic leaders, by reason of seniority, were chairmen of powerful House and Senate Committees.

All of these factors conditioned the process of scheduling food production, the first step of which involved the determination of over-all requirements.

Requirements

Section 1–a of the December order directed the Secretary of Agriculture to ascertain "the military, other governmental, civilian, and foreign requirements for food, both for human and animal consumption and for industrial uses." The organization for, and procedure to be followed in, the determination of requirements were outlined by the Secretary on January 26, 1943. Requirements for all claimants were assembled and adjusted by the Director of Food Distribution and reviewed by the Secretary of Agriculture and the Food Advisory Committee. Foreign governments purchasing through lend-lease arrangements submitted their estimates directly to the Food Distribution Administration; the Department of State and the Board of Economic Warfare acted as claimants for foreign governments buying on their own account, and as a general practice other users submitted their estimates directly to FDA. The Combined Food Board, established in June 1942 and consisting of representatives of the United States and the United Kingdom, provided information on world supply and advised on allocations of particular commodities. Preliminary adjustments were worked out by the Requirements and Allocations Branch of the FDA in collaboration with the Production Programs Branch of the Food Production Administration, with final review by the Food Advisory Committee established by the Executive order.[12] In practice these arrangements did not produce realistic estimates of food requirements, especially of military requirements.

The determination of military food requirements involved new problems. There was little experience to point the way to realistic supply planning for a military force of more than 10 million men which was expected to fight all over the world. In practice, the first step toward estimates of total requirements was to plan basic menus in collaboration with the country's best food specialists. Menus had to be devised which would maintain the energy and stamina of men convoying in the North Atlantic, engaging the Japanese in the South Pacific, and fighting Nazis in the North African desert and on the continent of Europe. Factors such as seasonal fluctuations in supply,

---

[12] Department of Agriculture, Office of the Secretary, Memorandum No. 1068, Jan. 26, 1943.

availability of shipping, refrigeration and storage space, and the food preferences of soldiers and sailors also were important.

The second step in estimating military food requirements was to obtain reasonably accurate statements of total strength, and, especially for the Army, some indication of the distribution of personnel among the several theatres of operations. This information was vital to requirements planning but frequently was not available to the requirements staff. Decisions on the grand strategy of the war were made by the heads of State and the Joint Chiefs of Staff at levels far removed from the persons responsible for estimating food requirements. Accurate planned manpower figures for the Army were not regularly available for food requirements purposes, because of the partial failure of Services of Supply to distribute manpower figures to authorized persons. Variation in daily camp strength contributed to wastage of substantial quantities of food, particularly in the first years of the war.

Navy estimates of requirements were based primarily on past (largely peacetime) experience and on "planned average personnel." Wartime changes, such as food lost with ship sinkings, transfers of food in combat areas to ships of our Allies, and the feeding of Army personnel from Navy stocks and Navy personnel from Army stocks contributed to the inaccuracy of Navy food requirements figures.

In practice, the procurement device known as the "set-aside order" tended to exaggerate the size of military food requirements. Set-aside orders required the processor to set aside a stated percentage of his output for Government purchase, to insure that the military would be able to buy the food it needed. Such orders generally were prepared before total production figures were known, and it was thought necessary to add a generous "safety factor" to the estimate of requirements. As a result, the military requirements which the set-aside percentages represented tended to be liberal when, as in 1941 and 1942, crop yields met or exceeded production goals. War Production Board Order M-86 was an example of requirements estimates inflated through the set-aside order device: several million cases of the 1942 pack of vegetables, fruit, and milk later were turned back to civilian account.

In addition to these technical problems, the Department of Agriculture, a civilian agency, was not in a position to question military estimates of the food required by the broad strategy for the conduct of the war. Particularly with food relatively abundant, as it was in January 1943, it was difficult to reduce the requests of the Army and Navy. The Secretary of Agriculture spoke for the people in saying "our first obligation is to our own fighting forces." [13]

---

[13] Ibid.

Foreign requirements were determined in large measure by military and diplomatic considerations of the highest order. Conversations between President Roosevelt, Prime Minister Churchill, and Marshal Stalin resulted in long-run commitments which gave an air of inviolability to the requests of Russia and Great Britain but which were not useful in determining the accuracy of specific estimates. Instead, the quantities of food shipped to these countries were determined principally by the availability of merchant and escort vessels. Estimates of foreign food requirements were based only partially on nutritional needs. Major consideration was given to the availability of shipping which in turn varied with the rate at which Liberty ships left the ways, the length of convoy routes, and the effectiveness of antisubmarine measures. Early in 1943, the principal foreign-requirements problem was to obtain definite statements of Russian requirements, consolidate them with the requests of other Allies, and balance the total program against the available food supply and shipping space.

Formulation of relief requirements for liberated countries involved organizational and administrative considerations as well as the availability of shipping. The secret of the North African invasion was so well kept that responsible civilian agencies were unable to plan necessary relief operations. On December 4, 1942, the President established within the Department of State the Office of Foreign Relief and Rehabilitation Operations and appointed Governor Herbert Lehman as Director.[14] Following the establishment of OFRRO there were, in addition to the Army and the Red Cross, three agencies actively interested in the food program for North Africa—State, Lend-Lease, and the Board of Economic Warfare. None had been made responsible for planning the food requirements and appearing as claimant before the Department of Agriculture.

The North African Economic Board, established in a preliminary attempt to integrate the various foreign missions operating in Africa, was also outside the requirements-allocation process. Requirements submitted by the Board were treated as a matter for procurement rather than for review, possible reduction, and incorporation in the requirements estimates. The North African Economic Board requests, however, were not a part of the program of any recognized claimant agency, and, for a time, they were handled as "unallocated emergencies" and charged against contingency reserves. Similarly, requests from OFRRO for a monthly allocation of 10 billion pounds of cheese and for large quantities of fats and oils were accepted with the understanding that compensating adjustments would be made in the requirements of other foreign countries, principally Great Britain.

---

[14] State Department, Departmental Order No. 1114, Dec. 4, 1942.

Estimates of civilian food needs were prepared and justiefid by Civilian Food Requirements Branch of the Food Distribution Administration. Planning of civilian food needs had to take into account the fact that no single item of food is indispensable and no particular quantity is a minimum requirement, provided other foods are available. Sectional and cultural variations in eating habits and individual likes and dislikes were limiting factors altering patterns of civilian consumption. Had it been possible to develop a minimum diet for civilians, to prescribe standard menus, and to estimate civilian requirements on the basis of per capita allowances, the problem of arranging the distributive system so as to provide each individual with necessary food would have remained. Consumer rationing would reserve for each person his share of rationed foods, but devices such as community or plant feeding, school lunches, and a food-stamp plan would be needed if consumers in the lowest income groups were to get their allotted shares.

In the formative stages of the requirements process, there was a tendency to view civilian requirements as the residuum that remained after more pressing needs had been met. The difficulty of obtaining precise statements of minimum civilian requirements, high production levels, and the more easily perceptible relation between victory and military and foreign requirements contributed to this attitude. Pressure to control rigorously military or foreign requirements was at a minimum so long as the civilian residuum was sufficient to maintain consumption at or above prewar levels. In the absence of an articulate and effective consumer production organization the long-standing policy of the Department of Agriculture of increasing the amounts of farm products used by the ordinary consumer was perhaps the one factor which tended to give full expression to civilian requirements. Sharp rises in purchasing power had eliminated the necessity for special measures to increase civilian consumption; but it was important to postwar agricultural prosperity that high-level consumption habits be established.

Production Organization

The second major responsibility delegated to the Secretary of Agriculture by Executive Order No. 9280 was to "formulate and carry out a program designed to furnish a supply of food adequate to meet such requirements, including the allocation of the agricultural productive resources of the Nation for this purpose." Experience in production planning which the Department had acquired since 1933 would be useful in its new undertaking; but the existing organization would be severely strained by the magnitude of the war food job. Because of defects previously discussed, the requirements estimates were not very useful in building up production goals. The individual farmer had to be brought into the production program so that he would produce the crops which were most needed and which, with his resources of land, labor, and machinery, he could produce most efficiently. In mobilizing the farmers, the Department met resistance (in some areas organized) to changes in customary farming methods and crop patterns. And it had to work through a ·cumbersome administrative structure of four field organizations (Extension Service, Agricultural Adjustment Agency, Farm Security Administration, and Soil Conservation Service) which diffused and made less effective its contacts with farm groups.

The Executive order of December 5 attempted to deal in a broad way with the organizational problem by establishing a Food Production Administration, comprising the Agricultural Conservation and Adjustment Administration (except the Sugar Agency), the Farm Credit Administration, the Farm Security Administration, and parts of the Bureau of Agricultural Economics, the Office of Agricultural War Relations, and the food production activities of the War Production Board.[15] Mr. H. W. Parisius was appointed Director of Food Production with the job of devising an organization scheme which would "consolidate or integrate" and mobilize under single direction, the various departmental activities concerned primarily with production.[16]

The principal agencies involved were the Agricultural Adjustment Agency, the Farm Credit Administration, the Soil Conservation Service and the Farm Security Administration. The Agricultural Adjustment Agency had, under the Soil Conservation and Domstice Allotment Act, general responsibility for promoting soil conservation practices, adjusting crop acreages, and for improving the economic position of the farmer through commodity loans and various types of subsidy payments. It had an organization which extended from Washington to the individual farmer and employed on a part-time basis approximately 100,000 farmers in addition to a staff of full-time Federal employees. The Farm Credit Administration made loans to farmers, ranchers, and farmer cooperatives, and conducted its business on sound banking principles which required suitable security as a prerequisite for a loan. The Soil Conservation Service tried to get farmers to use methods which would reduce soil erosion. The Farm Security Administration had a field organization with some

---

[15] Executive Order No. 9280, Dec. 5, 1942, 7 *Federal Register* 10179. The WPB personnel concerned primarily with food production matters as determined by the Director of the Bureau of the Budget, Jan. 8, 1943, and by Memorandum No. 1054, Supplement No. 1, Jan. 16, 1943, were transferred to Food Production Administration and those concerned with distribution were transferred to Food Distribution Administration.

[16] Department of Agriculture, Office of the Secretary, Memorandum No. 1054, Dec. 10, 1942.

2,700 field offices, and a staff of 11,000. It was set up to assist low income rural families to become self-supporting, and to finance at nominal service charges the purchase of farms by farm tenants, share-croppers, and laborers. As successor to the Resettlement Administration, Farm Security was responsible for the management of Government-owned or sponsored resettlement projects, and it also provided transportation and shelter to migrant workers. In the main the supporters of'the Agricultural Adjustment Agency and the Farm Credit Administration were the larger, more successful farm operators; the Farm Security Administaration concentrated its efforts on small family-type farms which, with more efficient management, could contribute substantially to the food supply.

Mr. Parisius' effort to integrate the diverse interests and points of view of these agencies was abortive. First, he proposed to Secretary Wickard that the work of the Food Production Administration in Washington be grouped in two broad divisions concerned principally with production adjustment, credit, and farm labor. The field organizations of Farm Credit, Farm Security, Soil Conservation Service, and AAA also would be consolidated in a unified field organization serving the entire Food Production Administration. Nine regions, following closely the Farm Security regional pattern, would be established, with actual operations conducted through State and county offices. To supervise this consolidated field organization, Mr. Parisius proposed the name of C. B. Baldwin, Administrator of Farm Security Administration.

The Secretary apparently was not enthusiastic about this plan, especially the suggestion that Mr. Baldwin head the FPA field organization. He approved, however, the unification of the field organization. Secretary Wickard later decided that a sweeping reorganization should be postponed until June 1, presumably until after the planting season. Meanwhile, personnel of the Agricultural Adjustment Agency became suspicious of the Parisius proposal, because of the suggested consolidation of the field staffs of AAA and Farm Security.

After Secretary Wickard's decision not to push immediately a general reorganization of the food production agencies, Mr. Parisius recommended consolidation of the loan activities of Farm Security and Farm Credit. He hoped to facilitate this reorganization by appointing as chief of the Financing Branch a person from Farm Credit who would be acceptable to personnel of the Farm Security Administration.

This proposal, which fell far short of any real unification of the Department's food production activities, met institutional resistances which were fortified by strong external economic interests. Under normal conditions approximately 40 percent of the farmers produce

85 to 90 percent of the volume and value of crops for commercial distribution and about 60 percent of the farmers produce only 10 to 15 percent of the volume. The Farm Security Administration and its supporters urged that the main effort (supervision, manpower, credit, machinery, and fertilizer) be directed toward bringing these small farmers into production of food for market. Operators of large farms already were producing at near capacity and were facing a diminishing labor supply. Mr. Parisius had estimated that 1943 goals could be increased 20 percent by his program. The opponents of the plan argued that the maximum increase would be about 12 to 15 percent; that it would be limited to dairy products, meats, and vegetables; that feed shortages then appearing would make it impracticable to expand meat and dairy production. They concluded that the effort would not be worth while in view of the small amount of produce that would result. After rejection of his second proposal, Mr. Parisius resigned as Director of the Food Production Administration 5 weeks after his appointment. Subsequently the Secretary appointed M. Clifford Townsend, former Governor of Indiana, and, at the time of his appointment, Administrator of AAA, to the Food Production job. A. G. Black, Governor of the Farm Credit Administration, was designated to serve also as "Associate Director of Food Production in Charge of Production Loans," with the loan activities of the Farm Security Administration remaining under the control of the Administrator of FSA.

To help farmers for whom ordinary credit facilities were not available, the Farm Credit Administration later revived the Regional Agricultural Credit Corporation, established in 1933 but, in 1943, in the last stages of liquidation. Through this agency a farmer could obtain a loan or an advance on his crop with the approval of the chairman of his county war board and the county loan representative of the Farm Credit Administration. Such loans were available for the purchase of needed equipment or to finance the production of an essential war crop and did not have to be repaid in the event of a crop failure. This was undoubtedly a step in the direction of bringing the small farmer into production of crops for the market, as proposed by Parisius, but it was not part of a coordinated drive.

The controversy over the mobilization of small farmers behind war food programs had repercussions outside the Department of Agriculture. Parisius' plan of using the Farm Security Administration staff accustomed to working with small farmers as a nucleus for a unified field organization was contrary to the American Farm Bureau Federation's views about how the Department's field activities should be organized. Beginning in 1940, Farm Bureau leaders had urged Congress to coordinate field activities of the various Agriculture agencies through State and county Extension Service offices. Departmental officials were lukewarm toward this proposal, principally because it would have transferred administration of Federal programs to Extension personnel primarily responsible to State institutions.

The Farm Bureau did not like the idea of consolidating departmental field activities on a regional office pattern such as Farm Security's, since this would have eliminated the strongest argument (operation of several loosely coordinated agencies within the same area and in some cases on the same farm) for their State-county extension. There was also objection to FSA programs designed to help the small farmers and farm laborers improve their economic position. These attitudes provided an interesting contrast to those of pressure groups which pushed for subcontracting to small business.

A substantial group in Congress was in favor of curtailing rather than expanding Farm Security activities. Consideration of Agriculture's 1944 appropriation, pending in February 1943, was the occasion of an almost successful Congressional drive to abolish FSA and divide its functions between the Extension Service and the Farm Credit Administration.[17]

The Secretary's uncertainty about the merger of Farm Security, Soil Conservation, Farm Credit, and AAA field forces and pressures from Congress and the Farm Bureau help to explain why the Department in the spring of 1943 fumbled the opportunity to organize itself more effectively for work with farmers. Whatever the merits of the Parisius proposals, the objective was sound and with his resignation, the Department apparently decided to go through the war with a minimum of change in its field organizations. Food programs had to be carried to the farmer through several field organizations whose personnel were not accustomed to working closely together and who in some cases were not so disposed. This proved to be a major handicap to effective operation in the food field.

Production Management

The first step in production management was the conversion of requirements figures into production goals for each important farm product. If we could obtain, for example, reliable estimates of how much meat, dairy products, and vegetables would be required to meet domestic civilian, military, and lend-lease needs, we could determine how many head of cattle should be marketed, whether dairy herds should be increased or reduced, how much livestock would be needed,

---

[17] U. S. Congress. House. Committee on Appropriations. Agriculture Department Appropriation Bill for 1944. Hearings . . . 78th Cong., 1st sess.; and U. S. Congress. House. Select Committee to Investigate Activities of the Farm Security Administration . . . pursuant to H. Res. 119. Hearings . . . 78th Cong., 1st sess.

the acreage of vegetables to be planted, and so on. As pointed out elsewhere, estimates of requirements were not accurate enough to be of much assistance in managing food supplies. This deficiency, however, was only one of several factors which impaired production planning.

Production goals were an outgrowth of "outlook" statements which the Department had issued for many years, containing estimates of "expected" production and probable prices for each important agricultural commodity. In the fall of 1941 the Department established an Inter-Bureau Production Goals Committee with commodity subcommittees to prepare systematic estimates of probable production and to recommend production adjustments in light of future needs. In the summer of 1942 the function was transferred to the Office of Agricultural War Relations and, after the December food order, to the Production Programs Branch of the Food Production Administration.[18]

The close relationship between the production planning and requirements functions led, in March 1943, to the establishment of a joint requirements and production planning staff. Associated with this staff were a number of commodity committees, established to consider questions of supply and production feasibility and to prepare national "production goals." After the national goals were set, the Production Programs Branch fixed State goals, "based on historical sources of food and known acreage." State goals were broken into county goals by State AAA committees and the State war boards. Under these arrangements great weight was given to established patterns of production. Goals tended to be fixed at levels which fitted easily into farmers' attitudes, plans, and habits. Proposed goals were reviewed by representatives of the principal agencies of the Department, who were sensitive to changes in agency programs which the goals might require. Rather than risk increases which might glut the market and reduce farmers' income commodity specialists tended to take a conservative view of consumer demand and to favor stabilization of production at levels which would support favorable prices. As a consequence of such factors, announced goals did not always indicate that a maximum of vigor and imagination had guided their formation. Representatives of the Commodity Credit Corporation might reasonably be conservative in reviewing recommendations for greatly expanded production. If expected demand failed to materialize, the CCC would be called upon to buy up the surplus, and the huge prewar stocks, which it had been able to dispose of after the outbreak of war in Europe, was a sufficient reminder that the margin between a shortage and a surplus is sometimes narrow. Goals also

---

[18] Department of Agriculture. Food Production Memorandum No. 2, Jan. 22, 1943.

were affected by regional considerations. For example, representatives of the southern region of the Agricultural Adjustment Agency believed that southern farmers should be encouraged to increase milk production and that processing facilities should be expanded to handle the increase. Scarcity of labor and materials, and the fact that the program would have built up resources for postwar competition with the middle western dairy region were factors in the rejection of the program. Considerable weight was also given to competition between States and between crops.

The next step, after production goals had been fixed, was to get the desired acreage planted. When a county representative of AAA visited farmers to talk about plans for the coming year, he asked them to accept their proportionate share of the county goals. In this way national goals were translated into goals for the individual farm. Sometimes it was enough simply to tell the farmer how he could best help in the war. But if he was asked to shift to a new crop, he expected, and properly so, that the Government would assume some of the risk incurred by the shift. As an inducement the Department used commodity loans, price supports, direct Government purchases, and subsidies. This type of device was not developed especially for this purpose but was inherited from the depression years when the Government began to push farm prices up toward the parity level.

The purpose of parity price legislation, first enacted in 1933, was to improve the economic position of the American farmer. Following the collapse of farm values in the 1920's, the objective of the Government and of farm-pressure organizations was to establish and maintain a balance between the price of farm produce and the price of goods and services which the farmer bought. By law, this "parity price" relationship is defined in terms of agricultural prices during a base period, 1910–14, and is tied to five so-called basic crops—corn, wheat, cotton, rice, and tobacco. Two things should be noted: First, price relationships which existed in 1910–14 have no necessary relation to the price structure needed in 1943 to bring out production for war. Second, the basic crops have strong political implications. To large sections of the country, prosperity means high prices for wheat, cotton, or tobacco. During a Democratic Administration, important committee chairmanships are held, under the seniority rule, by Congressmen from the cotton belt, a one-party and a one-crop area. The "farm bloc," comprising Democrats as well as Republicans, is particularly anxious that no action be taken by the Government which will affect adversely the income of farmer constituents. For this reason, actions affecting basic crops are conditioned by political factors of a bipartisan character.

CHART 45. *Production Goals and Actual Production of Selected Agricultural Crops.*

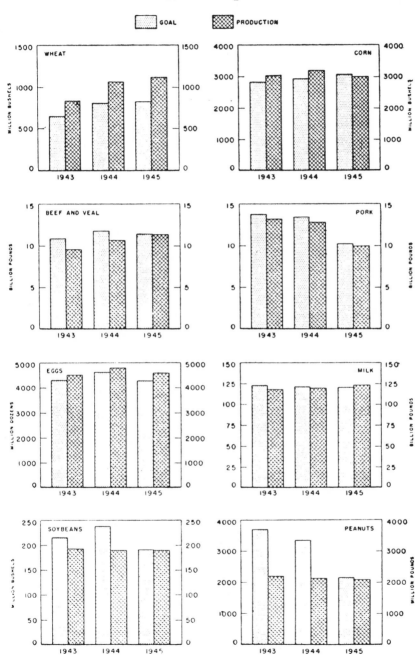

Source: Department of Agriculture.

Programs to maintain parity prices are operated through the Commodity Credit Corporation. During the depression, Congress authorized CCC to loan money on crops or buy them in the open market when the prices fell below designated levels. Although the objective of the original legislation, passed in 1933, was "parity," the Secretary of Agriculture was authorized to determine the rates at which loans would be made. In 1938, Congress stipulated a range of from 52 percent to 75 percent of parity for loan rates on corn, cotton, and wheat. Under the leadership of Senator Bankhead and other members of the farm bloc, acting with the full support of pressure organizations such as the American Farm Bureau Federation, Congress in May 1941 raised the minimum loan rates for basic commodities to 85 percent of parity. A year later, in the Stabilization Act, passed at the request of the President to provide for more effective control of farm prices by OPA, the loan rate was raised to 90 percent, with the proviso that 85 percent loans could be made if the higher figure would hamper livestock feeding. The effect of these congressional enactments was to guarantee successively higher prices for the so-called basic crops.

The same development took place with respect to "nonbasic" crops, the price of which the Department of Agriculture was also authorized to support. In July 1941, by a provision known as the Stegall amendment, Congress directed the Secretary of Agriculture, for the period of the emergency and when he found it necessary to encourage expansion of production of any nonbasic commodity, to support its price "through commodity loan, purchase, or other operation" at not less than 85 percent of parity or comparable price. This provision was amended by the Stabilization Act of 1942, which reiterated the limitation that price supports could be used only when necessary to encourage expanded production and raised the rate from 85 percent to 90 percent of parity.

At first glance it might appear that this legislation gave the Department all necessary authority to induce farmers to grow the things needed in a war economy. Actually, parity legislation was an obstacle to effective food management which was not overcome during the war. It meant that prices of basic crops were maintained regardless of demand and that the relation between the prices of basic and nonbasic commodities was not governed by relative need for the commodities. For example, high loan rates on wheat in areas in which a substitute crop could be grown had the effect of keeping land in wheat when other crops were needed more than wheat. To get around this difficulty, the Department had to establish unnecessarily high loan rates on the commodity for which increased production was desired. Similarly, price supports had to be set far above the 90 percent of parity minimum stipulated in the Stabilization Act simply because the 90 percent price was not high enough to get farmers to shift from cotton and other crops, the price of which was also being maintained at 90 percent of parity by Government guarantee.

The Department was reluctant to use fully its authority under the Stegall amendment, except where greatly expanded production was urgently needed. It felt that short of a clear and urgent need, demand was so uncertain that it could not afford to commit the limited resources of the Commodity Credit Corporation to a price support program.

These limitations led the Department to propose an "incentive payment" plan to supplement the commodity loan and price support programs. The fate of the proposal can best be told in terms of cotton.

Opposition to incentive payments, arising in part from cotton ginners, seed crushers, and others interested in continued high levels of cotton production, was uncompromising. Congressmen pointed to the large surplus of corn and wheat, to the recent removal of production and marketing restrictions by the Department of Agriculture, and claimed that there was no reasonable basis for distinguishing between corn, wheat, and cotton. Cotton was said to be an essential war crop in view of the shortage of oil and protein food which cottonseed oil and meal would alleviate.[19]

Answers to these objections were reasonably clear cut. If the controls were removed, increased production of cotton would be confined to the Southwest and to the short fiber variety for which there was limited demand. Cotton is a relatively costly source of oil and meal. Average Georgia yields during 1937–41 showed that one acre each of cotton, soybeans, and peanuts would produce, respectively, 72, 168, and 215 pounds of oil. From the standpoint of the manpower required, each man-hour used to produce 1 pound of cottonseed oil would produce 3.7 pounds of soybean oil and 5.7 pounds of peanut oil. Also, as compared with peanuts and soybeans, relatively large amounts of land and manpower were required to produce cottonseed meal for animal feed.

Even though it could be demonstrated that cotton was a relatively inefficient source of oil and protein, some way had to be found of getting cotton farmers to plant other crops. On January 26, 1943, Secretary Wickard announced "an extensive war-production program of incentive payments totaling approximately $100,000,000, designed to obtain greater production of food and fiber crops vital to the war

---

[19] U. S. Congress. House. Committee on Appropriations. **Agriculture Department Appropriation Bill for 1944.** Hearings . . . 78th Cong., 1st Sess., p. 784.

effort." To finance this program, the Department requested an additional $100,000,000 for expenditure under the Soil Conservation and Domestic Allotment Act. The necessity for the program was outlined by the Director of the Food Production Administration:

> One of the major problems today is getting farmers to grow new crops which are needed more urgently than increased production of their usual crops. Frankly it takes more than just a price incentive to get a farmer to shift from the production of a crop with which he is familiar to a new crop requiring different skills, and, from the point of view of the farmer, a risk which is not involved in the crops which he normally raises.[20]

Actually the program planned for 1943 represented a compromise between those who wanted to maintain existing production patterns and those who thought production should be shifted to meet the more pressing war needs. Subsidy payments to cotton and tobacco producers were planned in the amount of $84 million; only $78 million were projected for potatoes, fresh vegetables, soybeans, dried peas and beans, and sweetpotatoes.

The weight of the National Grange, American Farm Bureau Federation, and National Council of Farmer Cooperatives was thrown against the incentive-payment plan. The Master of the National Grange criticized the "subsidy" aspects of the plan and argued that prices should be permitted to rise to levels which would induce farmers to shift to war-essential crops. The president of the Farm Bureau presented resolutions of his organization urging the elimination of all "subsidies used to . . . achieve maximum production" and the "continuation of commodity loans and price supports at 90 percent of parity or at higher levels if necessary to get needed production." If adopted, these recommendations would continue the subsidies which had been built around prevailing production patterns and prevent the use of other subsidies as tools for altering such patterns.

Congress objected to the use of departmental funds for a program which it had not specifically approved, refused to appropriate funds for the incentive-payment plan and wrote into the 1944 Agriculture Department Appropriation Act a specific prohibition against incentive payments.[21]

Congressional inflexibility toward modification of the parity structure compelled the country to operate under a price system wherein the relations between the prices of various commodities were determined by patterns existing in 1910–14 rather than by current requirements. Upward adjustment of the loan rates from 75 percent to 90 percent of parity and rejection of incentive payments meant high

---

[20] Ibid., p. 688.

[21] 57 *Stat.* 392: "No part of said appropriation or any other appropriation in this Act shall be used for incentive or production adjustment payments" except for soil conservation and water conservation payments.

prices for produce for which there was little need and even higher prices for products of significant wartime value. Moreover, market prices seldom indicated the essentiality of crops because prices were controlled for the purpose of holding down the cost of living, a policy which Congress had likewise approved. As a result, commodities which provided the most nutrients for the manpower, fertilizer, and land expended, such as fresh vegetables and dairy products, were the commodities for which stable prices were sought. As increased purchasing power pushed up the prices of luxury foodstuffs, such as watermelons, farmers and processors were encouraged to allot acreage and facilities to products which probably should not be grown in wartime. Fruits needed for canning and freezing were taken out of the markets at high prices for immediate consumption or for use in making ice cream. Conflicting legislative policy made it virtually impossible to use price effectively as an instrument of production management.

Production Management and Price Stabilization

The dilemma of how to increase farmers' income and stabilize the cost of living at the same time was the source of administrative difficulty between the Department of Agriculture and the Office of Price Administration. After passage of the Emergency Price Control Act of 1942, which required the Secretary of Agriculture's prior approval to price controls over agricultural commodities, a price committee was set up within the Department of Agriculture to serve as liaison with the Office of Price Administration on agricultural pricing problems. As a matter of practice, however, disagreements on important policy questions were handled between the offices of the Secretary of Agriculture and the Price Administrator, and technical problems were discussed directly by the staffs of the agencies. Action was facilitated by appointment of Mr. Howard Tolley, Chief of the Bureau of Agricultural Economics, as Director of the OPA Food Price Division. He served in a dual capacity for several months before returning to the Department of Agriculture in 1942. By late 1942 the original Agriculture price committee had become inactive.

Since there was a fundamental difference in attitudes about prices, disagreements between the two agencies continued. As in peacetime, the Department of Agriculture tended to rely on price increases to adjust production, direct distribution, and facilitate procurement. But rising levels of agricultural prices and of living costs made the Office of Price Administration more and more reluctant to grant price increases.

After issuance of the December 1942 food order, another attempt was made to expedite the handling of disagreements between the two agencies. A "memorandum of understanding" was signed on December 11, 1942, under which the Office of Price Administration agreed to consult the Department on all pending price regulations affecting processed as well as agricultural conmodities; and the Department agreed to consult OPA on actions relating to marketing agreements, regulations, and support price programs. Deadlocked issues were to be referred to the Office of Economic Stabilization for decision.

Difficulties under this interagency agreement arose from the fact that the internal organization of the Department of Agriculture and the Office of Price Administration made it difficult to bring differences to the point of decision. Within the Department the individuals experienced on price problems were dispersed through several sets of commodity branches in the Food Production Administration, the Food Distribution Administration, the Commodity Credit Corporation, and the Bureau of Agricultural Economics. During the early part of 1943, no administrative device had been worked out for pulling the price specialists together and developing a departmental policy on commodity pricing. Within the Office of Price Administration, knowledge and points of view about food price problems were dispersed among business specialists, lawyers, and economists. As in the Department of Agriculture, it was difficult to obtain decisions on price questions.

The Office of Economic Stabilization was not equipped to take an active role in the formulation of food programs. The diffusion of responsibility within the Department of Agriculture and the Office of Price Administration generally meant that questions of price policy were the subject of prolonged negotiation between various levels of the two organizations. On occasion, differences were discussed with the Office of Economic Stabilization at some intermediate stage of negotiations, but OES preferred to take jurisdiction only after agency disagreements had become sharply defined and were susceptible of arbitration. This method of operation conformed to the President's characterization of the job of Director of Economic Stabilization as one calling "primarily for judicial consideration." It also fitted naturally into the training and attitudes of the judges and lawyers who comprised the staff of the office through 1944. Under this concept, OES did not take a notably active part in reconciling the fundamental conflict between the stabilization program and the pricing system administered by the Department of Agriculture. Generally it did not anticipate issues before they arose or attempted to obtain agreement before issues developed into actual controversies.

Material, Supplies, and Equipment

The Food Order of December 5 attempted to split between WPB and Agriculture control over material needed for food production. Section 8 authorized the Secretary of Agriculture to exercise with respect to food and "any other material or facility" the priority and allocation powers delegated to the President by the Second War Powers Act, when such exercise was determined by the Secretary to be necessary to carry out the provisions of the Executive order. If the WPB Chairman disagreed with a proposed priority action, the disagreement was to be referred to the President or his agent for resolution. A somewhat different relation was delineated by section 2, which authorized the Secretary of Agriculture to "recommend to the Chairman of the War Production Board the amounts and types of nonfood materials, supplies, and equipment necessary for carrying out the food program." The Chairman of WPB was directed to consider these recommendations in allocating specific amounts of nonfood materials, supplies, and equipment to food programs and to use WPB powers to bring about their use in accordance with the Secretary's determinations.

Exercise of these powers by the Secretary would have disrupted the organization which had been created to direct mobilization of the nation's industrial resources. Some of the implications were described by staff of WPB as follows: under section 8 the Secretary of Agriculture "might allocate any material or facility—whether steel, copper, aluminum, rubber, machine tools, or machinery—whenever he considers it necessary for the effectuation of the food program"; he might "undertake to allocate steel and rubber to the manufacture of an increased supply of agricultural machinery irrespective of the needs of the airplane, tank, and ship programs, the Russian protocol, the repair and maintenance of railways, etc."; he "might allocate to the manufacture of agricultural-equipment facilities which are now engaged or are scheduled to be used, in the manufacture of tanks or half-track vehicles"; and he might "allocate certain chemicals, or chemical manufacturing facilities, to the manufacture of certain types of fertilizer, irrespective of the competing needs of the ammunition and chemical-warfare-production programs."

The absurdity and danger of duplicate priority systems was recognized by the Secretary of Agriculture who agreed to accept WPB controls over supplies needed for food production. Under an agreement between Agriculture and the War Production Board, the Secretary submitted to WPB detailed quarterly estimates of nonfood materials, supplies, and equipment. These estimates, like those of the War and Navy Departments and other claimant agencies, were reviewed by the divisional requirements committees and the staff of the program vice chairman. Requirements of Agriculture were then considered by the Program Adjustment Committee and WPB Requirements Committee and allocations of materials were made by the WPB Program Vice Chairman for production of agricultural equipment and related products at the same time that allocations were made for other production programs. Proposals for new facilities—food processing plants, irrigation projects, and the like—were reviewed by the WPB Facilities Bureau and the Facilities Committee as were proposals for new steel mills, railway improvements, and other industrial plants. In general, therefore, industrial and construction requirements for the food program were reviewed and scheduled by the War Production Board in much the same manner as requirements for the other nonmilitary sectors of the economy. This arrangement, essential to effective central allocation of the Nation's industrial resources, was maintained in spite of the Executive order of December 5 granting allocation and priority powers to the Secretary of Agriculture.

The Department of Agriculture was restive under this control and the question of whether proper amounts of farm equipment were being produced often became a subject for public and congressional discussion.[22] On occasion, the arrangement seemed to delay unduly the execution of food programs. The process, however, was a necessary part of a central control over the allocation of industrial materials and facilities; and adjustment of competing requirements for these items became more essential and more time-consuming as supplies diminished. Meanwhile, operating relations between WPB and Agriculture were improved by establishment within Agriculture of an Office of Materials and Facilities which consolidated the food agency's requirements for materials, supplies, and equipment and presented to WPB unified estimates of material needed for food programs. Relations between the two agencies also improved as Agriculture personnel became more familiar with WPB policies and procedures.

Importation of Food

Control of food imports provided another example of the limited extent to which responsibility for food supply could be centered in a single agency. Beginning in the summer of 1941, the Office of Production Management (predecessor to the War-Production Board)

[22] U. S. Congress. Senate. Committee on Agriculture and Forestry. Hearings before a subcommittee on the Food Supply of the United States. 78th Cong., 1st sess.; also Senate Report No. 10, 78th Cong., 1st sess.

developed priority schedules which rated imported materials according to their importance in the war-production program. The lists were prepared in consultation with representatives of other agencies also interested in imports and were used by the Maritime Commission as a guide in loading vessels for trips to the United States. The order establishing the War Shipping Administration formalized WPB's function of transmitting import priority schedules to WSA. In October 1942 the Stockpile and Transportation Division was established within WPB to continue the preparation of import schedules, which guided the WSA in assigning vessels to bring such materials to this country.

The Food Order of December 5 authorized the Secretary of Agriculture to determine priorities relating to imports of food for "human and animal consumption." Directives for the "importation of food for industrial uses" were to be issued jointly by the Chairman of WPB and the Secretary of Agriculture. "Importation of materials, supplies, and equipment required for the war production program and the civilian economy" would remain under the authority of the War Production Board.[23]

The effect of these provisions was to make the Secretary of Agriculture more or less coordinate with the Chairman of WPB in determining what should be imported on available ships. As in the case of allocation of nonfood materials and facilities, the result would have been the establishment of duplicate priority controls; and two agencies would have had authority to control the same shipping space. Since only a few food commodities have no industrial use, the order would have required joint action by WPB and Agriculture for the bulk of food imports. Disagreement between the agencies on these import schedules would have been thrown to the War Shipping Administration for decision; and WSA had no responsibility for industrial production or food supply and could have had little information on which to base its decisions.

Again it was necessary to modify the Executive order by informal arrangement between the Department of Agriculture and the War Production Board. By May 1943 preliminary determinations of quotas and ratings for imported food commodities were being made by the food agency with WPB participation through representation on Agriculture's Committee on Foreign Purchase and Importation. Preliminary schedules for particular commodities were reviewed by the appropriate subcommittee of the Interdepartmental Shipping Priorities Advisory Committee. Recommendations of the subcommittees, headed by representatives of Agriculture, were reviewed by the full committee, the chairman of which was the Director of the

[23] Executive Order No. 9280, sec. 5, Dec. 5, 1942, 7 *Federal Register* 10179.

WPB Division of Stockpiling and Transportation. Determinations
of the interdepartmental committee which were unsatisfactory to
Agriculture were settled by negotiations between WPB and Agriculture or, if necessary, by appeal to the Office of Economic Stabilization. These arrangements left with WPB general responsibility for
issuing directives to the War Shipping Administration.

Farm Labor

Allocation of the Nation's manpower among competing uses such
as war plants, the armed services, food production, and other essential
civilian uses, is discussed in chapters 7 and 14. At this point it is
desirable simply to mention some of the more important developments
affecting farm labor. As early as 1940, while many experts were still
unconcerned about the necessity for increasing food production, farm
labor was being drawn off the farms by higher paying jobs in war
industries and by the military services. Later, chiefly as a result
of pressures generated by public concern over possible food shortages,
special measures were taken to maintain essential workers on the farm.
A provision of the Stabilization Act of 1942 was intended to help
the farmer compete for labor by requiring that OPA price ceilings be
adjusted to take into account production cost increases resulting from
higher wage rates.[24] Congress also required local draft boards to
defer "any worker necessary to and regularly engaged" in agricultural
occupation essential to the war effort and by September 1943 more
than 2 million had been deferred from military service.

By directive of the War Manpower Commission, the Secretary of
Agriculture acquired full operating responsibility for agricultural labor
programs. Under this authority the Department imported laborers
from Mexico, the Bahama Islands, Barbados, Newfoundland, and
Jamaica, brought about a fuller utilization of migrant farm workers,
directed the use of prisoners of war in food production, and in other
ways supplemented the pool of farm workers. In spite of all of these
actions, the labor supply continued to shrink. Nevertheless, farmers
achieved new records of food production, made possible by unusually
favorable weather conditions and by more skillful operation of farms.

Control of Distribution

The December Food Order directed the Secretary of Agriculture to
"take all appropriate steps to insure the efficient and proper distribution of the available supply of food." The priorities and allocation
powers of the Second War Powers Act were delegated to the Secretary
insofar as food for human or animal consumption was concerned.

---

[24] *56 Stat.* 765.

Under these powers the Secretary was responsible for determining "the need and the amount of food available for civilian rationing." The order provided, however, that rationing programs would be carried out through the Office of Price Administration with respect to "the sale, transfer, or other disposition of food by any person to an ultimate consumer" or by "any person who sells at retail." The Secretary was expected to consult with the Price Administrator "before determining the time, extent, and other conditions of civilian rationing."

Rationing

Distribution of the food rationing job between Agriculture and OPA involved, as did the problem of allocating nonfood materials and facilities, a fundamental question about the civilian organization for war. The Office of Price Administration in January 1942 had established local rationing boards throughout the country and had been designated by WPB as the consumer rationing organization of the Government.[25] Acting under directives from the War Production Board, OPA was rationing tires, automobiles, typewriters, and gasoline and was planning meat and processed foods rationing programs. Establishment of the Petroleum Administration for War and designation of the Department of Agriculture as the principal food agency required reexamination of the relation between these commodity "czars" and OPA, the rationing agency.

Staff of the Department of Agriculture interpreted the Executive order to mean that the Secretary had been given complete responsibility for food distribution as well as for food production. It was argued that in most instances the Department would need to retain control over distribution down to the retail level. "The Department must be assured that the allocation of foods for civilians' use at the processor and wholesale level will not interfere with the over-all allocation of foods for other purposes." Such assurance might be had if the Department issued orders dividing up the food supply at each level of the distribution system down to the wholesalers. If this were done, the shares assigned for military lend-lease and foreign governments would be protected from diversion into civilian markets. Accordingly, Agriculture took a narrow view of the consumer rationing functions of the Office of Price Administration: its job would be chiefly to develop and distribute ration books and forms; register consumers and retailers, and provide them with instructions and information; operate the ration coupon banking system; prevent used rationing coupons from getting back into circulation; handle indi-

---

[25] WPB Directive No. 1, Jan. 24, 1942, 7 *Federal Register* 562.

vidual adjustments within general policies laid down by Agriculture; and enforce rationing regulations.

The Office of Price Administration took the position that it would have to be given all the authority necessary to insure that meat supplies would be available to meet coupon demand. "The OPA is the only agency that actually deals with the public"; "it must bear the brunt of criticism." An allocation control system, administered by Agriculture, which would allow distributors a certain percentage of the supply which they handled in a designated base period might not move food into areas crowded with migrant war workers. The number of ration coupons cashed in a given area provided a more precise guide to food demand. The OPA argued, therefore, that meat should be distributed, from the primary distributor down to the retailer, only in exchange for ration coupons or certificates. Under such a system the OPA said it would have to have jurisdiction over all levels of distribution beginning with deliveries by primary distributors; handle all relations with industry groups subject to rationing regulations; make decisions on methods of rationing, procedures to be followed, adjustments of point values, and other administrative questions; and to release all public information about rationing actions and programs.

For several weeks following approval of the December order, representatives of the Department of Agriculture, the Office of Price Administration, and the Bureau of the Budget worked to establish a satisfactory agreement on the rationing function. Both Agriculture and OPA were adamant in their views. On January 10, 1943, the Secretary of Agriculture expressed to Director Byrnes of the Office of Economic Stabilization grave concern "over the almost certain development of food shortages in many areas of the country within the next few months." He stated that Agriculture "had urged the rationing of fats and oils as early as March 1942," and the rationing of meat in August 1942. The letter continued:

> General authority with respect to rationing was recently vested in me by the President's Food Order. However, the order directs me to exercise this authority with respect to rationing through the Office of Price Administration . . . In our efforts during the past few weeks to formulate a working relationship with the Office of Price Administration under the Food Order, representatives of the Office of Price Administration have taken the view that the office must have full control over domestic food distribution from processor to consumer . . . I feel that it is necessary that steps are taken to make it clear that I have complete authority to carry out the civilian food programs, including all phases of consumer rationing. Because of the precarious civilian food situation, I ask your assistance in seeing that this matter is clarified at the earliest possible moment.

Accompanying the letter to Justice Byrnes was a draft Executive order transferring to Agriculture the personnel, property, records, and funds of the Office of Price Administration primarily concerned with and available for civilian rationing of food. The Secretary proposed to utilize "local rationing boards and other facilities and personnel concerned with the actual carrying out of rationing programs" which would remain in the Office of Price Administration.

This proposal, under which Agriculture would develop rationing programs in detail and operate them through the field organization of OPA, was administratively impracticable. In the field, OPA would have had to make day-to-day adjustments required to fit policies to local needs: adaptation of rationing policy to operating experience would have become a matter for interagency negotiation. If adopted for food, pressures would have developed to extend the pattern to oil and gasoline and perhaps to rubber and other rationed commodities. Thus, the Office of Price Administration would have had to administer programs devised by several different agencies—the Department of Agriculture, Petroleum Administration for War, and the Office of Rubber Director. Adjustment of these agencies' requirements would have meant extended discussion and compromise over issues of administrative detail which, in many cases, the Office of Economic Stabilization would have had to settle. OES was not equipped to take over an operating job of such magnitude. For these reasons, efforts to devise a different solution continued.

Finally, on February 12, 1943, an agreement defining the functions of the two agencies was signed by Secretary Wickard and Price Administrator Brown. Under this agreement the Department of Agriculture was recognized as having exclusive "responsibility for determining supplies of foods available for civilian consumption and for allocating supplies accordingly," and for determining the need for and time and extent of civilian rationing. The Office of Price Administration was given primary responsibility for developing the rationing programs, and for determining rationing techniques and procedures. On the major point in dispute, the agreement provided that the "Department shall have complete responsibility for the determination of over-all allocations for civilian use and for determining individual processor quotas. The OPA shall have responsibility for directing the flow of rationed commodities within such quotas and allocations from the time the commodity is placed in a form ready for distribution by the processor."

The agreement also provided for the establishment of a "Food Rationing Policy Committee" consisting of representatives of the Food Distribution and Food Production Administrations of the Department and the Rationing Department of the Office of Price Administration. This Committee was set up to consider problems of concern to both agencies requiring joint consideration of policy; it was not given any authority to discuss matters which the agreement clearly delegated to either of the agencies. Specific matters mentioned for the Committee's attention were the handling of publicity, industry relations, and the desirability and feasibility of providing additional rations for workers in heavy industries such as coal mining and lumbering. In practice, the Committee did not become an active agent of interagency collaboration, partly because the interagency agreement provided a satisfactory basis for day-to-day operations.

These negotiations, which occupied top officials of the agencies for almost 3 months, did not delay work on pending rationing programs. While the relative responsibilities of Agriculture and OPA were being discussed, the agencies were attempting to devise some method of eliminating local meat shortages. The amount of livestock that large commercial slaughterers could process had been limited by a "restriction order," issued in October 1942 by OPA for the purpose of reinforcing price controls. The meat which passed through these plants was graded for quality by Department of Agriculture personnel and the plants were inspected for compliance with Federal sanitation regulations. Federally-inspected slaughterers processed most of the country's meat supply as well as all of the meat acceptable under Army and Navy procurement specifications and for shipment across State lines. Similar quota restrictions were not imposed on slaughtering by thousands of local and farm slaughterers who normally account for a very small percentage of the country's meat supply.

In April 1943 the food agency took over administration of the restriction order. Suits against nonquota slaughterers which OPA had begun were dropped. County war boards were authorized to issue permits to farm butchers and local slaughterers who had not been required to register under the original order. This system of permits, it was thought, would limit the business done by small slaughterers, increase the flow of meat to federally inspected plants, facilitate purchases of meat by the military, and relieve meat shortages in deficit areas. Agriculture personnel, however, tended to issue permits without suitable investigation, with the result that enforcement of price and rationing controls over numerous and widely dispersed small slaughterers was impossible.

The perfunctory nature of these controls had two consequences of significance to the Government's meat programs for the balance of the war. (1) Small slaughterers increased in numbers and expanded their businesses tremendously. They found it relatively easy to evade price and rationing regulations; and, by paying higher than ceiling prices, they were able to buy the better grades of livestock which formerly went to the large packers. Illegal prices paid for livestock and passed on to wholesalers and retailers, frequently without the use of ration currency, stimulated black-market operations. (2) An insufficient supply of meat passed through federally inspected plants. Since the Army and Navy bought only from such plants, they had difficulty in buying the meat which they needed. Also, severe shortages appeared in heavily populated cities that normally imported federally inspected meat from out-of-State producing areas. The institution of consumer rationing in March 1943 was expected to relieve some of the pressure on price and rationing regulations by making the availability of ration coupons a major factor in distribution. But absence of effective control over small slaughterers soon made it virtually impossible for available personnel to enforce OPA controls over the thousands of distributors whose meat supply came from local slaughterers. Thus, the problems of meat supply and distribution which aroused so much concern in 1944 and 1945 were due in large part to the failure to solve the slaughter control problem in 1943.

Procurement

Early in 1943 attention was also directed to the Government's food procurement activities which were being consolidated in the Army and the Department of Agriculture. The Army bought perishable foods through 34 local market centers and nonperishables through three large quartermaster depots. The Navy had begun to turn to Army market centers for perishable commodities but nonperishables were bought through its own organization. Army supply officers in small camps and stations were also authorized to buy locally without going through a market center. Food for merchant ships under the War Shipping Administration's jurisdiction was bought by the companies operating the ships.

Under the December food order, the Secretary of Agriculture was to correlate procurement by Federal agencies so that there would be a minimum of disturbance to local supplies. In January the Food Distribution Administration established an Inter-Agency Food Procurement Committee with representatives from the principal agencies interested in or affected by Federal procurement operations. The Committee operated through a series of subcommittees appointed to study particular commodity problems and to recommend action to be taken by the procurement agencies. It was the view of those responsible for procurement operations that establishment of the inter-agency committee would provide all necessary coordination. In the months which followed, the procurement problem became more and more one of locating supplies to meet the needs of the military services and foreign governments. The Committee was not in a position to deal with these general shortage problems which had their source in more fundamental aspects of food policy. Nevertheless, it was drawn into consideration of matters such as requirements and production, and tended to dissipate its energies and influence in areas in which it had no jurisdiction. The problem of coordinating Federal food procurement was not much further advanced toward solution.

Responsibility for purchases by the Department of Agriculture was given to the Food Distribution Administration and was carried out by the staff of the Agricultural Marketing Administration transferred to FDA by the December 5 food order. The Agricultural Marketing Administration and its predecessor agencies were originally set up to handle the various marketing and distribution activities of the Department. An objective of these activities was the improvement of the farmers' economic position by disposal of agricultural surpluses. Less than 6 months before the Germans attacked Poland, the Department launched an experimental food stamp plan for surplus farm produce disposal through the regular channels of trade. The immediate effect of the war was to cut off export markets and to add to existing surpluses which were further enlarged by the huge crops in 1940–42. Thus, the major problem confronting the Department and its marketing-distribution agencies during this period was the disposition of excess supplies. An organization which so recently had been preoccupied with surplus commodities would require careful direction if its operations were to be fitted into the management of tight supply.

The allocations of foodstuffs which came out of the Department's requirements-allocation procedure were not followed rigorously by either the Food Distribution Administration or the Army. On the foreign side the difficulty of obtaining definite statements or requirements made it virtually impossible to plan procurement. Foreign missions submitted their estimates to the Food Distribution Administration through the Program Liaison Branch which was itself in the stream of procurement operations. Under this arrangement the procurement staff was informed at all times of requests made by foreign governments and was in a position to place contracts in anticipation of final allocations. This practice of "forward buying" made it possible for the Food Distribution Administration to have foodstuffs on hand to meet the rapidly changing shipping situation. It could also divert to the Army and Navy supplies earmarked for foreign shipment. The obstacles which had arisen in the requirements-allocation function did not have serious consequences while total supplies were adequate and the procurement agencies engaged in forward buying. This manner of operation, however, required frequent changes in the amounts allocated to claimants and created additional problems in distributing scarce food supplies in accordance with an over-all allocation plan.

Although the structure of the food organization was determined by the actions taken from December 1942 to March 1943, one important change occurred. An Executive order of March 26, 1943, removed from the Secretary of Agriculture the direction of the war food program.[26] This order established within the Department of Agriculture an Administration of Food Production and Distribution (later renamed the War Food Administration),[27] under the direction of an administrator appointed by, and directly responsible to, the President. All of the powers delegated to the Secretary by the food order of December 5 were transferred to the Administrator. Although this arrangement violated organizational theory, the Food Administrator and the Secretary of Agriculture worked together without friction largely because of the personalities involved. WFA remained a nominal part of the Department until its abolition in June 1945.

The general pattern of administration already described persisted until near the end of the war when the specter of stock piles again rose. During the years 1944–45, actions of the War Food Administration alternately reflected fear of excessive food surpluses and concern over food shortages. Food production in 1944 established new records and generally was 38 percent above the average for 1935–39. In the spring of 1944, it was generally believed that the war in Europe would be over by the end of the year. On this assumption the military substantially curtailed food procurement. Reduction of military purchases accompanied record marketing of hogs, and created a glut in the stockyards and processing plants. To ease this situation, zero point values were set in May for all veal, lamb, and pork cuts, all beef cuts, except steaks and roasts, and all canned meats and fish.

With this relaxation of meat rationing, civilians in 1944 ate 2.5 billion pounds more than had been fixed in the original civilian requirements estimates. Per capita meat consumption in 1944 was approximately 150 pounds, as compared with the prewar average of 126 pounds. After removal of point values in May, consumption rose to an annual rate of 160 pounds, and it was estimated that there was purchasing power to support annual consumption of 170 pounds. The rise in consumption meant that meat which should have been canned or stored for a "lean" period was eaten during the spring and summer. During May, June, and July of 1944, for example, pork canning under Federal inspection fell to 56 percent of the amount canned in the same months of 1943. By August the surplus had

---

[26] Executive Order No. 9322, Mar. 26, 1943, 8 *Federal Register* 3807.
[27] Executive Order No. 9334, Apr. 19, 1943, 8 *Federal Register* 5423.

been reduced sufficiently to require restoration of point values on most cuts of meat.

In August, however, it appeared that victory in Europe was perhaps only a few weeks away. A sudden ending of the war would find the food "pipe lines" full and supported by embarrassingly large stock piles. The policy of "liquid inventories," also called the bare-shelf policy, was applied to eliminate surpluses which, if released by the Army, might flood the market and depress postwar prices. Almost all processed foods were removed from rationing in September 1944.

By eating too much in 1944, we created a "food crisis" in 1945. By the spring of 1945 a severe meat shortage had appeared and congressional committees were appointed to ascertain its cause and to devise corrective action. The findings and recommendations of the Anderson Committee pointed to administrative and policy failures as factors in the meat shortage.[28]

The Committee found substantial evidence of widespread violation of meat price and rationing regulations, or black-market operations. For example, nationally operating packers could not buy livestock at market prices and sell beef at OPA ceilings without taking a loss. These packers had been forced to reduce their volume of business. Meanwhile small, nonfederally inspected packers were able to increase their business for the period ending February 28, 1945, "in some cases six to eight, and in one case, to ten times" the amount done in the previous year. The expanded business of these small slaughterers was a prolific source of price and rationing violations.

This situation was brought about by WFA's failure to establish control over the entrance of new slaughterers into business and over the volume of business done by existing slaughterers. "From September 1, 1943, to January 24, 1945, an applicant for a license need only show that he had adequate facilities and met sanitary requirements." By May 1944 "all regulations had been removed from farmers, who could then slaughter anything without any permit. They were free from restrictions on slaughter for sale." By January 24, 1945, when the War Food Administration again made an effort to get some control over slaughtering by issuing licenses only when the applicant could show that the issuance would advance the war effort, so many slaughterers were already in business that existing conditions were not improved. OPA simply could not enforce price ceilings or rationing regulations in the absence of a control at the slaughterer level which would channel meat to legitimate distributors.[29]

[28] House Report No. 504, 79th Cong., 1st sess. Representative Clinton Anderson was named chairman of the Special Committee to Investigate Food Shortages for the House of Representatives, 1945. The report of this committee was favorably received, and when Secretary Wickard resigned, President Truman appointed Mr. Anderson to the post of Secretary of Agriculture.

[29] House Report No. 504, 79th Cong., 1st sess., pp. 13–14.

In February 1945 an effort was made to restrict the volume of business of nonfederally inspected slaughterers by withholding subsidies when the volume of business exceeded a specified maximum. The Anderson Committee pointed out that the subsidy which was lost for exceeding the maximum was only a small fraction of the profits that could be made in black-market operations. The black market was not notably reduced by this device.

The Committee recommended a review of all slaughtering permits, and War Food Administration at once transferred to OPA the job of administering slaughtering controls. We were then back to the situation which existed in April 1943, when Agriculture took over administration of OPA's Meat Restriction Order No. 1. In appraising this part of the food machinery, the Committee stated:

> Without doubt the permit system as it was operated was a prolific source of black-market meat and drained off good beef which would otherwise have found its way into legitimate trade channels and to the counters of those retail stores that have tried to observe legal price ceilings.[30]

On the subject of price ceilings, the Committee emphasized its belief that "the greatest mistake made in the control of meat prices was to begin by pricing at the retail level and then working backward."[31]

As early as August 1942 Price Administrator Henderson had requested Secretary Wickard's approval of livestock ceilings and subsequently the proposal was discussed periodically between OPA and the food agency. In these negotiations the food agency consistently opposed ceilings on live cattle and hogs. In part, this opposition grew out of a reluctance to have any maximum prices which would be enforceable against farmers. The Office of Price Administration wanted livestock ceilings because it believed that they would relieve pressure on processor and distributor ceilings and thereby simplify the OPA enforcement job. Agriculture took the position that livestock ceilings were impracticable and unenforceable and that by undermining the farmers' confidence in food-production programs, they would tend to reduce production. This view was also held by the American National Livestock Association, the National Grange, and other livestock producing and marketing groups. The lack of control at the producer level caused the Office of Price Administration to hold onto ceilings which undoubtedly did discourage production or processing. With so little control, it seemed necessary to retain the regulations which were in effect.

The Anderson Committee reported that "one of the fundamental mistakes made in the war-food program was in the failure to expand cold-storage space in keeping with the increases in production which

[30] Ibid., p. 14.
[31] Ibid., p. 15.

farmers were asked to make." Lack of storage space affected production as well as distribution. Having announced a support-price program to encourage increased production, the War Food Administration frequently found that facilities were not available to store the commodities it would have to buy in order to maintain market prices at the support level. Departmental officials then began to think in terms of curtailing production to proportions which could be handled in available storage space. When prices fell below support levels guaranteed by the Department, farmers also lost confidence in Departmental programs and tended to reduce production below levels set by the Department. For example, in 1944 the Department asked farmers to produce 20 percent fewer hogs than they had in 1943, but farmers actually reduced their pig crop by 30 percent.[32]

The agriculture subcommittee of the House Appropriations Committee, under the chairmanship of Congressman Tarver, made a special study of the warehousing and storage operations of the War Food Administration. The committee reported that "many errors of judgment and administration" necessarily occurred in carrying out a vast emergency program for which "administrative machinery had to be assembled hurriedly." Not all of these mistakes were unavoidable, however, and matters such as the failure to develop a properly managed inspection service to determine whether warehouses were suitable for food storage, unnecessary transfers of food between warehouses, inadequate inventory and financial records, and poor coordination and supervision of component parts of WFA were cited as examples of faulty administration which should have been corrected.[33]

During the 1945 "food crisis," pressure also developed to curtail food shipments to foreign countries. On March 12, 1945, Director of War Mobilization and Reconversion Byrnes appointed an Interagency Committee on Foreign Shipments to reexamine our foreign commitments in light of existing food supplies. The Committee, under Chairman Leo Crowley of FEA, consisted of representatives of Army, Navy, Foreign Economic Administration, War Food Administration, War Production Board, War Shipping Administration, and the Department of State. In its first report, the Committee stated that "stocks were not built up to the maximum possible extent last year (1944) to meet this emergency, in part due to insufficient storage facilities. Instead, we consumed our food at a record rate, 9 percent over prewar years." The report went on to say that military needs would be greater in 1945 than in 1944, and that millions of people in Europe, recently liberated by Allied armies, were living on starvation

[32] Ibid., p. 14.
[33] House Report No. 816, 79th Cong., 1st sess.

diets, in some areas on "no more than one-fourth the daily minimum requirements." Because of world food shortages, the "most that can be accomplished is to provide such foods as will tide the people of Europe over their immediate difficulties." [34]

On the subject of our own civilian requirements, the Committee stated that "the American people would, were it available, consume greater quantities of food in 1945 than were consumed in 1944." We could afford to reduce our consumption without risk of malnutrition. But because of the increased demand for food, "the maintenance of an effective rationing system is an essential condition for the distribution of adequate food supplies to all Americans in the period ahead." [35]

After the German surrender in May and the Japanese surrender in August 1945, the Government moved swiftly to relax rationing controls. Within a few months only sugar remained on the ration list. Thus, unexpected military developments and the speedy removal of wartime controls forestalled for the American people the consequences of inadequate food organization, policies, and operations. We emerged from the "war for survival" the best fed of all the major Allied nations.

Six months after VJ-day, however, there was another "food crisis," this time involving actual starvation of millions of people in Europe and Asia.

[34] U. S. Interagency Committee on Foreign Shipments. First Food Report to the Director of the Office of War Mobilization and Reconversion, Apr. 30, 1945.

[35] Ibid.

Coordinating the War Agencies

THE PROBLEM of top direction of the war agencies of the Government became acute in the early months of 1943. Issues which could not be handled by any single administrative agency multiplied. Their solution required purposeful and coordinated guidance of action by related agencies. The upward pressure on prices was bringing a continued increase in the cost of living which stimulated strikes and threats of strikes. The munitions production curve was climbing rapidly. Less and less was available for non-military uses and a much more careful allocation of resources among civilian uses was required. The experts began to speak of "bedrock" civilian requirements. The effects of conversion of industry to war were being keenly felt. Farmers, for example, were expressing deep dissatisfaction about the declining output of farm machinery.

Although problems at home were becoming more critical, urgent military and diplomatic matters made it difficult for the President to give uninterrupted attention to the management of home-front affairs. His participation in international negotiations such as the Casablanca Conference required time. Questions of broad military strategy were demanding his attention. The Axis forces in Northern Africa were being driven toward surrender. Preparations for the taking of Sicily and Italy were under way and plans for the eventual invasion of the continent from Britain were taking shape.

The combination of increasingly difficult problems in the top management of the war agencies on the home front and demands on the President's time by his strategic and diplomatic duties led to the establishment of the Office of War Mobilization in May 1943. The creation of this Office constituted a formal recognition of the gradual enlargement of the duties of James F. Byrnes who had been designated

Director of Economic Stabilization in October 1942. Though he was appointed to assist the President in the management of Government agencies concerned with economic stabilization, his duties grew to include a broader range of functions. In the early months of 1943, for example, he participated in the settlement of disputes among the commodity czars. With his elevation to the post of Director of War Mobilization, he came to be popularly known as the "Assistant President."

The question of machinery to aid the President in the direction of the Government had been under almost constant discussion since the establishment of the National Defense Advisory Commission in 1940. During the life of the Commission, a clamor was raised for "one-man" control. Eventually in the Office of War Mobilization a type of "one-man" control developed, but it was of a character not contemplated by either critics or responsible officials in 1940. It was the final product of successive stages of a tortuous evolution, an evolution feasible under a flexible administrative system which could sooner or later be adapted to emerging demands and which could be molded within the changing limits of practical feasibility. In 1941 the Office of Production Management began to take form as a central agency to coordinate the defense program. A step toward more comprehensive direction was taken in the creation of the Supply Priorities and Allocations Board late in August 1941. The War Production Board, established in January 1942, inherited the powers of SPAB and OPM and was granted additional authority.

None of these agencies gave general satisfaction or was entirely adequate. Discussion of the problem of central direction continued and was voluminous and heated but often neither perceptive nor helpful. It reached peaks of intensity at times when things did not seem to be going well. Congressional committees, newspaper editors, and critics of the administration came forward, from time to time, with plans to improve the administration of the war activities of the Government. Most of these reformers oversimplified the problem. The plan of action proposed was usually very simple: empower a single man to direct the war effort. Such a formula was a catharsis for frustration and persons hostile to the President took satisfaction from proposals which might deprive him of his powers as Chief Executive. Most of the advocates of this ready and simple remedy for the ills of the Government ignored or were quite unaware of the complexities of the problem for which they glibly proposed solutions. Some of them also would advocate with equal zeal the establishment of "czars" for particular segments of the economy apparently without realizing the inconsistency of advocating both a multiplicity of czardoms and a war effort tightly knit under central direction.

Amateur administrative reformers were not alone in their erroneous estimates of how to manage the Government as a whole. The problem, in fact, was without precedent in the United States and plans and systems were the product of groping by fallible men into unfolding events. A common error of judgment was in the timing of advocated changes. Thus, those who in 1940 urged a highly centralized direction were demanding something which did not become really essential or possible until Pearl Harbor. Those who sought in 1942 still greater centralization of power within the Government were attempting to cope with problems which did not become critical until late in 1943. Though the development of machinery for the general direction of the Government paralleled the rise of conditions which required new types of general coordination, there was a lag in organizational adjustment caused by slowness in comprehending emerging conditions and in contriving administrative machinery to deal with them.

In the early stages of the defense program one of the chief tasks of the President was to arrange the organization of Government to deal with forthcoming problems. By a fortunate coincidence of events the Executive Office of the President was established shortly before large-scale preparations for defense began. Its largest component, the Bureau of the Budget was charged, among other things, with assisting the President in dealing with problems of organization. Its work in this field was most significant in 1940 and 1941 and early 1942 when the basic administrative machinery for the war economy was being created. The Bureau of the Budget studied emerging problems that seemed to require additions to, or alterations in, the machinery of government. It reviewed proposals originating in the departments and formulated plans on its own initiative or at the specific request of the President. In other instances it attempted, on behalf of the President, to negotiate agreement among the principal officials of the administration about changes in governmental machinery which were of concern to him. The extensive work of the Bureau in the development of plans for administrative organization, the drafting of orders for the establishment of new agencies, and the establishment of new agencies as working entities demonstrated the soundness of the judgment of the President's Committee on Administrative Management when it foresaw a need for greatly enlarged staff assistance to the President.

The Bureau of the Budget was an extremely valuable instrument to aid the President in establishing new governmental machinery and in modifying it as occasion demanded. Yet once the administrative mechanisms were set up and became going enterprises, the problem of presidential direction of the administration took on a different color. The central problem became one of creating adequate means by which the operations of these agencies could be directed and coordinated to achieve the broad national objectives imposed by the changing pattern of events.

Policing the Battle for Resources

Organization for top direction of the Government was not an easy problem to solve at the times when it became critical. Nor is it one to be simply explained or described in retrospect. In seeking to understand the various measures taken to coordinate the work of Government in the war economy, two fundamental factors must be kept in mind. First, to assure the maximum war potential our resources had to be devoted to the purposes which would contribute most to our national strength. Second, a large number of agencies of Government had to make decisions about the uses to which we put our resources.

A few words of elaboration will perhaps make plain the significance of these propositions. Our resources; i. e., our manpower, our factories and machines, our ships and railroads, our minerals and materials, were scarce. With them we could not do everything that we wanted to do. We had to make choices. For example, would our military potential be strengthened more by using, say, 100,000 men to produce planes, to fight in the infantry, or to produce food for our allies?

Of necessity, many Government departments and officials were concerned in settling such questions. The huge job of managing our resources had to be divided among many agencies. If one man could have passed on every question and seen that his decisions were executed, we would have had no problem of top management of the Government war agencies. That was manifestly impossible. Yet, if all agencies of the Government were permitted to proceed independently, the situation would be something like the operation of a single bank account on which many people were authorized to draw checks. The account soon would be overdrawn and there would be no means of seeing that the money was spent most efficiently in promotion of joint enterprises. Hence, there was the difficult task of organizing at some central point ways and means for directing the work of all agencies of Government in such a manner that their individual actions would conform to a grand design for the best use of our strength to win the war.

Deciding how to use our resources most effectively is not simply a matter of determining that one objective is more important than another. An intricate balance must be maintained among many different objectives. The machinery of Government must synchronize its operations on several fronts. Within the strictly military sphere, we must have the right number of rifles and cannon, the right number of tanks and planes, and the right quantities of ammunition. Or, to put the matter in another way, ammunition without enough guns or too many guns for the available ammunition would be wasteful. We must also have the proper tonnage of merchant shipping to transport our armies to the fields of battle and the correct naval strength to enable the Navy to perform the tasks assigned to it in the prosecution of war.

The civilian population is as much a part of the fighting strength of the nation as the uniformed forces. Hence, we must have the proper quantities of food, clothing, shelter, and other essential goods to sustain the civilian population in order that the flow of weapons may be maintained. The mobilization of maximum strength requires also that our allies and friendly nations be furnished with military equipment and materials and supplies necessary to enable them to carry their part in the common effort. Our manpower has to be assigned appropriately to the military services, to industry and to agriculture. If proper decisions are not made on all these questions, we might have a larger Army than our munitions industry can supply, a larger or a smaller merchant marine than necessary to carry the armies and materials which we have, too much or too little to maintain the civilian population, or a surplus in some things and a deficit in others.

Decisions on all these matters must also be thought of in a perspective of time. Raw materials and human effort are not convertible into factories, guns, and ships overnight. We must plan ahead to make sure that we have arsenals to produce the right quantity of a given weapon at the right time. We must have housing completed for arsenal workers at the time they must be on hand to man the machines. All the equipment and supplies necessary for a particular campaign must be transported to the right place at the right time. Thus, an extraordinarily complex flow of actions, from the mine, through the industrial system, to the battle front, must be taken in orderly sequence to focus our strength at the chosen times and places.

To make the decisions affecting all these matters, there were many different agencies of Government. The War and Navy Departments had primary responsibility for obtaining the weapons and equipment necessary to perform the strategic tasks assigned to them. The Maritime Commission had responsibility for the development of the merchant marine. The Department of Agriculture had long been vested with responsibilities in planning the production of food and other agricultural products. With the threat of war, the permanent agencies of Government were supplemented by the creation of emergency organizations. The Department of State was paralleled by the Board of Economic Warfare and the Office of Lend-Lease Administration, both having heavy responsibilities in foreign economic affairs.

Alongside the Department of Labor there was established the War Manpower Commission with broad authority for the mobilization of manpower for war purposes and the National War Labor Board with authority over industrial disputes. The Reconstruction Finance Corporation was supplemented by the establishment of a group of subsidiaries to import strategic and critical materials and to finance construction of facilities to produce materials and other commodities.

The problem of general management of the Government was to direct the work of all these agencies so that the end results would constitute the most effective utilization of our resources for war. We could use steel for tanks or ships or locomotives. We could use shipping space to bring in manganese, industrial diamonds or bananas. We could use manpower on the farm, in the factory, or in the Army.

The most acute thinking on how to gear together the decisions of all the Government agencies on these many questions was stimulated by American experience in the First World War. In his report on the operation of the War Industries Board, and in other writings, Mr. Bernard Baruch expounded the doctrine of priority as a synchronizing force. Some of the inadequate understanding of the significance of Mr. Baruch's broad ideas came from the popular use of the word "priority" to denote a piece of paper which entitled a man to buy a ton of aluminum. In fact Mr. Baruch used the word in several senses.

From the standpoint of broad governmental policy, the determination of priority involved judgments about the proportion of our resources which should be devoted to aid our allies rather than for use by our own forces, judgments about the level of production which should be maintained for domestic civilian use at the expense of direct military production, judgments about the extent to which we should develop a merchant marine at the expense of the Navy or vice versa. The making of broad decisions on these matters of necessity controlled many subordinate issues. Thus, if there were to be so many destroyers, there had to be the appropriate number of guns to equip them. The determination of priority in this broad sense usually is accomplished by an analysis of requirements and supply. The process of analysis requires a tabulation of the needs of all the Government programs which draw upon the economy. Alongside these tabulations are then placed estimates of the total available supply of steel, aluminum, copper, or components. If the needs of all programs of the Government can be met within the available supply, no problem of priority arises. In fact, however, all the stated requirements can never be met and it is necessary to make a broad determination to have, say, a smaller military effort or a more straitened civilian economy than was initially proposed. The analysis of requirements and supply also permits informed decisions on expansions of supply.

Priority in the broad sense of the preceding paragraphs differs from the use of the priority power to control the flow of material and commodities through the production system. The flow of materials and commodities, of course, must be in accord with the general program of production but in this narrower sense, the exercise of the priority power means that the producer of copper, for example, is instructed by Government order, about the persons to whom he may deliver his product, and in what quantities. Or the producer of electric motors is instructed to deliver a certain portion of his output to a producer of Navy planes and another portion of his output to producers of refrigerators for use in housing in crowded war production areas. The priority power also is used to assign facilities to various types of production or to prohibit their use in the production of nonessential items. These devices contribute to the disciplining of the industrial system in line with requirements of the over-all economic program.

In still another sense the term "priority" is used to describe a directive from one Government agency to another to assure operation in accordance with the central economic plan. Thus, the public employment agencies may be guided by a system of priorities in referral of available manpower. The procurement agencies may be limited in the quantities which they may purchase in keeping with the conclusions arrived at through the analysis of requirements and supply. Other governmental agencies which affect the operation of the economic system likewise may be governed by a system of directives or priorities calculated to synchronize the effects of all their operations.

From the standpoint of the top management of the Government, only the determination of very broad priorities affecting the distribution of the resources of the country and the determination of related priorities governing the activities of other agencies of the Government are significant. By trial and error and through the force of events as the war program developed, these problems of priority were dealt with in administrative machinery and procedures. During the period of the National Defense Advisory Commission, the demands on our resources were so small that it was not necessary to calculate with extreme care how we should utilize what we had. The beginnings of systematic central coordination of the Government's procurement and production activities are to be found in the Office of Production Management. The order establishing this Office issued in January 1941, directed it to—

A. Formulate and execute in the public interest all measures needful and appropriate in order (1) to increase, accelerate, and regulate the production and supply of materials, articles, and equipment and the provision of emergency plant facilities and services required for the national defense, and (2) to insure effective coordination of those activities of the several departments, corporations, and other agencies of the Government which are directly concerned therewith.

B. Survey, analyze, and summarize for purposes of coordination the stated requirements of the War and Navy and other Departments and agencies of the Government, and of foreign governments for materials, articles, and equipment needed for defense.

When the Office of Price Administration and Civilian Supply was established in April 1941, an attempt was made to define its powers in such a manner that its allocation work would be coordinated with the work of the Office of Production Management. OPACS was to allocate among civilian uses the residual supply which remained after military and other defense requirements were met. Thus OPACS might determine whether the available supply of steel for civilian use should be used in the manufacture of locomotives or threshers.

A next step in the development of machinery for coordination of activities of the Government was taken in establishment of the Supply Priorities and Allocations Board late in August 1941. By this action, a policy board, representative of the major agencies concerned with the defense program, was superimposed over the Office of Production Management and the civilian allocation function of OPACS was transferred to the Office of Production Management. SPAB was directed to "determine the total requirements of materials and commodities needed respectively for defense, civilian, and all other purposes; establish policies for the fulfillment of such requirements, and, where necessary, make recommendations to the President relative thereto." The Board included the heads of the agencies primarily concerned with industrial production: the Secretary of War, the Secretary of the Navy, the Special Assistant to the President supervising the defense-aid program and the Chairman of the Economic Defense Board. In addition, the Director General and Associate Director General of the Office of Production Management and the Administrator of the Office of Price Administration were members. The Board thus was designed to bring together the responsible officials concerned with the military sphere, with civilian supply, and with export and economic warfare policy. The implicit theory was that a unified policy would emerge from this type of administrative machinery.

The order establishing the Board also attempted to define its relations with other agencies which exercised powers affecting the economy. It was empowered to make allocations of materials and other commodities among military, economic defense, defense aid, and civilian claimants of the defense program. Theoretically, it could by this means determine the emphasis to be given to these various aspects of the Government's program. The Office of Production Management, subject to the policies of the Board, was authorized "with reference to specific priority authorities vested by law in established departments and agencies of the Government" to "certify to such departments and agencies, when the Office of Production Management deemed such action necessary to national defense, that preferential treatment is essential for certain materials, commodities, facilities, or services." OPM also was authorized to determine priorities to be followed by the Maritime Commission in the allocation of import space on merchant vessels. Under administrative arrangements developed during the summer of 1941, the detailed findings of OPM, derived from analysis of requirements and supply, could be transmitted to the Maritime Commission for its guidance in lifting cargo for import. The Executive order was silent on the relationship of the Board to the Reconstruction Finance Corporation and its subsidiaries which financed the construction of plants and the acquisition of materials. It was essential that these activities be conducted in accordance with the findings of the analysis of supply and requirements; working arrangements were in existence, although they did not operate without friction. The correction of this kind of situation probably was contemplated by the clause of the Executive order which provided that the Board should establish policies for the fulfillment of requirements and "where necessary, make recommendations to the President relative thereto."

After Pearl Harbor it became possible to take further steps in organization for coordination and on January 16, 1942, the War Production Board was established. The Board inherited the powers of the Office of Production Management and of the Supply Priorities and Allocations Board. Its powers were vested in the Chairman of the Board, who was advised by the members of the Board, which consisted, among others, of the Secretary of War, the Secretary of the Navy, the Federal Loan Administrator, the Price Administrator, the Chairman of the Board of Economic Warfare, and the Special Assistant to the President supervising the defense aid program.[1] The Chairman of the Board was authorized to "exercise general direction over the war procurement and production program" and to "determine the policies, plans, procedures, and methods of the several Federal departments, establishments, and agencies in respect to war procurement and production." He also was authorized to exercise all the powers which had theretofore been vested in the predecessor agencies.

Almost from the outset the powers vested in the Chairman of the

---

[1] At the outset the Board also included the Director General and the Associate Director General of the Office of Production Management. With the abolition of these offices these officials ceased to be members of the Board but subsequently other officials were added to its membership.

War Production Board were challenged by other Government agencies. The opposition, led by the War Department, did not subscribe to the doctrine that war is too important a matter to be left to the military. Scarcely had the War Production Board begun operations when the War Department proposed a reorganization of WPB and hotly criticized the Chairman of the Board. In the summer of 1942, the Joint Army and Navy Munitions Board almost succeeded in a coup to require its concurrence in the principal actions by the War Production Board. Thus was inaugurated a running fight between the War Department and the War Production Board which was to continue for several years. It was fought through the press by spokesmen for the War Department, who consistently sought to create an attitude which belittled the principal officials of WPB and challenged its technical ability. Under cover, other efforts were made to bring about the removal of WPB officials and to undermine their status within the Government.

Apart from the more or less inevitable resistance of the military to civilian control from any source, the powers vested in the War Production Board and the general theory of one-man control of the allocation of our industrial resources were subject to limitations which had not been clearly foreseen. If the Chairman of the War Production Board could determine in his own right the resources which the military agencies received, he could determine what kind of war was to be fought. He could, for example, have determined the relative emphasis upon military effort in the air and on the ground. He would have become, in effect, Commander in Chief. The determination of questions of broad strategy had to be reconciled with the power of the Chairman of the War Production Board for the coordination of our industrial effort by agreement with the Joint Chiefs of Staff, a mechanism for the coordination of military operations. If it became impossible, by pinching other segments of the economy, to meet the needs of all aspects of proposed military programs, the Joint Chiefs of Staff would determine what adjustments should be made among the various elements of the military production program.

The War Production Board limited itself to certain types of questions. Its experts submitted the programs of the military agencies for the production of weapons and munitions to a most-searching review. Ordinarily, however, even the highest officials of the War Production Board had no knowledge of the strategic plans which were to be effectuated with the items to be produced; hence, their criticisms were limited to matters suggested by the internal evidence of the military production programs. If, for example, the quantity of spare parts scheduled to be produced for a known quantity of tanks appeared to be too large, they could raise questions and suggest that battle experience should be brought to bear on spare planning as soon as practicable. If a greater quantity of bombs was scheduled to be manufactured than possibly could be transported by the bomber force to be available, that discrepancy could be pointed out. Continuing searching criticism often brought appropriate alterations by the military agencies.

It was extremely difficult for a civilian agency to question projects justified on grounds of military necessity. Many such undertakings turned out to be a highly uneconomical application of resources even from the strictly military point of view, but the challenge of civilian coordinators to this sort of project tended to be criticism rather than authoritative disapproval. A good example is the *Canol* project which was initiated in 1942 at about the time of the high tide of Japanese expansion. The project involved construction of an oil products distribution system for the Alcan Highway, oil-well development in Canada, the construction of a pipe line from Norman Wells to White Horse and the erection of a refinery. It became evident later that less costly alternative means of meeting the need had not been considered by the War Department. Though there was little evidence that strategic necessity for the project had been coldly considered, a central coordinating agency was in a weak position to substitute its judgment for that of the War Department on the question of whether the probability of Japanese movement across our Alaskan communication lines warranted the outlay of resources necessary to develop a local supply of petroleum rather than their use in some other way. This case is, of course, only a single illustration of the type of problem which continually faces a central coordinating authority. It must weigh its judgment, which is based on a view of all war needs, against the judgment of officials charged with responsibility for results in certain sectors of the war program.[2]

The War Production Board also checked carefully the estimates of the military agencies of the materials and components which would be required to meet their needs. This review, however, was no different from that applied to the programs of the nonmilitary agencies of the Government. These estimates usually were inflated, although one should not underrate the technical difficulties of computing, for instance, what quantities of alloy steel had to be put into proper production channels during a particular three-month period if one were to have a specified number of tanks on hand at a given time in the future. Nevertheless, in the review of requirements it was often possible to reduce requests for steel, for example, without actually affecting the scheduled output of tanks or airplane motors.

---

[2] See Senate Report No. 10, pt. 14, 78th Cong., 1st sess. (Jan. 8, 1944);

If the power of the Chairman of the War Production Board had been carried to the limits expected by those seeking one-man control, he also would have been vested, in effect, with power to determine our economic foreign policy. He could have determined the magnitude of our lend-lease assistance to various of our allies and associates and the nature of our program of economic warfare.

The War Production Board was handicapped in its developmental stages by defects in administrative technique. It was naive to suppose that the Chairman of a War Production Board could sit at a table with the top officials of other agencies and determine the strategy for utilization of our economic resources. That job required the collaboration of literally thousands of men. The fundamental problem of technique was that of making sure that the broad decisions allocating large slices of our resources for various purposes were made effective through mechanisms for the detailed control of the flow of resources through the economic system and for the distribution of its products among different purposes. In this, the experience of the first World War was practically useless since the priorities procedures of that day were primitive in contrast with the refined techniques eventually developed by the War Production Board. By the end of 1942 there evolved the controlled-materials plan which was an effective method of executing broad allocation decisions in detail and of maintaining an effective control over the operations of each of the agencies of Government authorized to draw upon our resources.

The upshot of the evolution of the War Production Board was that it became not so much a center of leadership and policy initiative in the Government as a point at which total resources could be determined and the limitations on what could be done defined. Within the boundaries fixed by analyses by the War Production Board it was possible for decisions to be made by the President, by the Joint Chiefs of Staff, and by negotiation among the agencies of Government. The coordinating procedures of the Board would show when it was impossible to carry out all proposed programs. Some programs had to yield and in some instances WPB determined which was to yield. In other instances the decision was made at a higher level.

Managing the Anti-Inflation Program

The chain of events leading to the formation of the War Production Board and the experience with the operations of the Board thoroughly demonstrated that management of the home front could not be pivoted solely on the control of industrial production. No one foresaw the kinds of broad administrative problems which would arise in the application of a determined policy of economic stabilization. This in part was attributable to the fact that in World War I no real program of economic stabilization had been executed. Prices generally were allowed to rise without effective restraint. In World War II a radically different policy was followed and it eventually became necessary to establish a system for the overhead control of the agencies of Government concerned with maintenance of a stable price level.

The separate network of supervisory control over stabilization agencies resulted in part from the policy of withholding power to control prices from agencies concerned with production. This policy was based on the fact that agencies of Government tend to represent the interests of a constituency rather than to speak for the general welfare. The industry divisions of the War Production Board, for example, ordinarily were closely attached to the interests of the industries with which they were concerned. The Department of Agriculture has won no reputation for restraint in the advocacy of the interests of the farm population. It was believed that vesting control over prices in agencies closely affiliated with groups which desired price adjustments might result in an "easy" price policy. The strategy in the creation of an Office of Price Administration was to avoid these risks and to establish an administrative structure consisting of persons with an institutional interest in price stabilization.

The denial of the power of price control to agencies with a marked orientation toward an important clientele was criticized by both Congress and the public. It was urged persistently in Congress that the power of fixing prices of agricultural commodities should be placed in the Department of Agriculture and organizations of farmers were favorable to the vesting of this authority in the Secretary of Agriculture. The Price Control Act, adopted in January 1942, provided that no prices might be fixed "with respect to any agricultural commodities without the prior approval of the Secretary of Agriculture." This legislative provision immediately created a problem of coordinating the activities of the Office of Price Administration and the Department of Agriculture.

The case for separation of price control and production control was not one-sided. Under normal circumstances, price is the principal means for guiding production and even in a war economy prices and wage rates may have an important influence on what is produced. Nevertheless, in an economy controlled for war upward adjustments of prices generally result not in increased production but in higher prices for the same amount of production. Thus, if a factory is assigned a quota of 25,000 pressure cookers which it cannot exceed, the stimulant of a price increase will not boost production above that level. Or, if a factory is allotted 10,000 pounds of aluminum with which to manufacture kitchen utensils, the output is not likely to be raised significantly by a price increase. Price incentive was thought to be more important in the production of military goods and the procurement agencies were, for all practical purposes, free to offer what was necessary to induce production. In some fields, price adjustment did have some utility in causing minor adjustments in output by preventing the drift of workers, for example, from low-wage industries whose output was essential. In agriculture, price management is much more important in the manipulation of production than in manufacturing. These and other considerations stimulated a drive in 1942 by production agencies to acquire powers of price fixing over commodities in which they were interested.

Generally the adjustment of prices to meet the needs of the production agencies was handled by negotiation between the agency concerned and the Office of Price Administration. In a few situations, however, formalized arrangements for consultation existed. Thus, the Premium Price Quota Plan Committee was a joint WPB–OPA group which determined what increases in production of copper, lead and zinc by individual mines would be necessary in order to qualify for premium price payments by the Metals Reserve Company. By this sort of subsidy, increased output of particular commodities might be stimulated without raising their prices generally and by such administrative arrangement the views of both the production planning and price control agencies might be blended. Often, however, interagency agreement could not be reached by negotiation and it was necessary for differences to be settled by the President or by some person acting for him. Furthermore, the maintenance of a general stabilization policy required some means for controlling wage policy and for managing tax and borrowing policy in harmony with price-control policy.

The execution of a broad program of economic stabilization necessitated extensive coordination by the President or by some person acting on his behalf because a great many agencies of the Government possessed powers which had to be used properly if economic stabilization were to be assured. The Office of Price Administration had acquired price-fixing authority over most industrial products and over agricultural commodities with the concurrence of the Secretary of Agriculture. The Treasury, with responsibility for formulating administration policy on taxation and on borrowing, possessed powers of first-rate importance in the promotion of economic stabilization. The Reconstruction Finance Corporation, through its various subsidiaries, subsidized certain types of production and distribution to prevent upward price movements in some sectors of the economy. The War Labor Board, with its responsibility for wage policy, had to make decisions profoundly affecting price levels. It gradually became clear that the operations of all of these and other agencies had to be subjected to some central direction 'if their efforts were to contribute effectively to the prevention of excessive price rises.

Earlier authority having been inadequate, the President in September 1942, demanded the enactment of legislation to enable him to prevent a rise in the cost of living. A bill approved October 2 authorized the President "on or before November 1, 1942, to issue a general order stabilizing prices, wages, and salaries affecting the cost of living; and, except as otherwise provided in this act, such stabilization shall insofar as practicable be on the basis of the levels which existed on September 15, 1942." In executing this act, the President had the alternative of supervising the Government agencies concerned himself or of creating a special assistant to act on his behalf. He chose the second alternative and on October 3, 1942, established in the Executive Office of the President an Office of Economic Stabilization headed by a Director of Economic Stabilization. The Director was instructed to advise with an Economic Stabilization Board consisting of the Secretaries of the Treasury, Agriculture, Commerce, and Labor, the Chairman of the Board of Governors of the Federal Reserve System, the Director of the Bureau of the Budget, the Price Administrator, the Chairman of the National War Labor Board, and two representatives each of labor, management and farmers. To give effect to the policy of economic stabilization he was empowered to issue directives on policy to the Federal departments and agencies concerned.

The Executive order also contained specific provisions relating to significant types of coordination which had to be effected if the actions of the individual agencies were to fit together. For example, if the War Labor Board or the Price Administrator believed that a proposed wage increase might require a change in the price ceilings of the commodity or service involved, the proposed increase would become effective only if approved by the Director of Economic Stabilization. Disagreements between the Secretary of Agriculture and the Price Administrator over agricultural prices were to be settled by the Director. The Reconstruction Finance Corporation, the Commodity Credit Corporation and other governmental agencies were made subject to instructions by the Director with respect to the subsidization of any commodity to insure maximum necessary production or to prevent price rises.

In operation the Office of Economic Stabilization consisted of the Director and only a handful of assistants. Its physical location in the White House had the effect of giving notice to the agencies and departments that its operations were supported by the President.

Although the Office had been instructed in its Executive order to formulate and develop "a comprehensive national economic policy relating to the control of civilian purchasing power, prices, rents, wages, salaries, profits, rationing, subsidies, and all related matters," it actually operated more after the fashion of a court of appeal. It waited for conflicts to develop between agencies and then, on the basis of such information as it could accumulate, made a decision.

Events in late 1942 and the first half of 1943 placed a great strain on the price ceiling and illustrated the role of central machinery in leading the fight for economic stabilization. Operations under the order of October 1942, did not stop the rise in the cost of living. By April 1943, it had risen approximately 6.2 percent above the level of September 1942, at which Congress had said prices and wages should be stabilized. Food prices generally were up 13 percent and the retail prices of fresh fruits and vegetables were 58 percent above the levels of September 1942. Farmers and the Department of Agriculture were dissatisfied with prices for agricultural commodities. Labor unions sought wage increases to meet rising costs of living. The situation was made more complex by congressional intervention and threatened intervention and by difficulties within the administrative agencies. A high order of politico-administrative tightrope walking was required to maintain a political and economic equilibrium.

CHART 46. *Coordinating the Fight Against Inflation.*

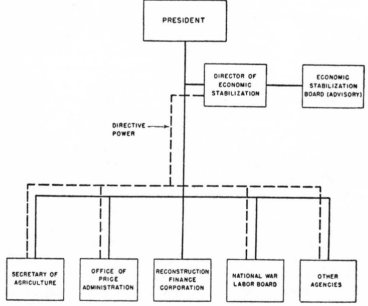

Source: Bureau of the Budget.

The Office of Price Administration, which had primary responsibility for holding down prices, at times seemed to be on the verge of collapse. Leon Henderson resigned as Price Administrator on December 18, 1942, amid charges that the OPA had been responsible for Democratic losses in the 1942 congressional elections. Former Senator Prentiss M. Brown was sworn in as Price Administrator on January 18 and, in accordance with the President's instruction, began a campaign to bring OPA through congressional investigations with an appropriation sufficient to finance the price-control job.

During the next three months OPA was deluged with appeals for price increases from businesses which interpreted Henderson's resignation as a sign that price controls were to be relaxed. Dozens of appeals were made by Congressmen on behalf of their constituents. Staff of the OPA, brought into the agency by Senator Brown, carried on a running fight in the press against other officials of the agency. Observers of the OPA reported: "It takes longer than ever before to act on important questions of policy . . . OPA is in danger of being discredited with the trade for its toughness, discredited with labor and the consumer for its softness, and discredited with its own personnel for the absence of direction and the vacillation in vital matters."

Meanwhile, pressure groups were making a strong drive for higher farm prices. Before adjournment of Congress in December, the House of Representatives, without a negative vote, passed a bill to require inclusion of farm labor costs in the computation of parity prices. This measure revived the issue which had threatened to prevent passage of the October 1942 Stabilization Act. Soon after the new Congress met in January, the House Committee on Agriculture again approved unanimously a bill to revise the parity formula by including farm labor costs and on March 19, 1943, the bill passed the House of Representatives.[3]

While the farm labor cost bill was being considered, the Senate approved the Bankhead bill which prohibited the deduction of subsidies paid to farmers in the computation of parity prices. The objective of this bill was to override a provision of the Economic Stabilization Order of October 3, 1942, which stated: "appropriate deductions shall be made from parity price or comparable price for payments under the Soil Conservation and Domestic Allotment Act, as amended, parity payments under the Agricultural Adjustment Act of 1938, as amended, and governmental subsidies."[4] Application of this policy in setting ceiling prices on potatoes and flour had provoked a storm of protests from Congress. The Bankhead bill was passed on February 25 by a vote of 78 to 2; the House approved a

³ *Congressional Record*, vol. 89, pt. 2, p. 2272.
⁴ Executive Order No. 9250, title IV, section 2, Oct. 3, 1942, 7 *Federal Register* 7871;

similar measure on March 24 by 149 to 40; and on March 31 the bill was sent to the President for his signature.[5]

On April 2 the President vetoed the Bankhead bill. He pointed out that under the bill the price of sugar could rise a cent and a half a pound, the price of bread might go up a cent a loaf, and the price of corn could rise almost 10 percent, which would "certainly call forth a demand for higher prices for hogs, and livestock, poultry, eggs, milk and other dairy products." Although "farmers generally are encountering increasing difficulty in securing necessary farm labor, farm equipment, and fertilizer . . . higher prices cannot, when steel is scarce, create new machinery; higher prices cannot, when manpower is short, create additional workers. In fact, higher prices for crops like wheat and corn might actually divert labor and machinery away from the production of other essential crops, such as soybeans, flax, grain sorghum, beans, and potatoes." [6]

As the cost of living increased and farm pressure groups marshaled their strength in Congress, a wage crisis developed in the demands of the United Mine Workers of America for higher wages to offset the rising cost of living. With price and wage controls threatened, the President on April 8, 1943, issued his "Hold-the-line" order which provided for better coordination of wage and price controls and also set forth more definite policies to guide the War Food Administration, Office of Price Administration, and War Labor Board.

Machinery for coordination was strengthened by delegation to the Director of Economic Stabilization of all powers and duties conferred upon the President by the Stabilization Act of October 3, 1942. The Director of Economic Stabilization was authorized and directed to take such action as he deemed necessary "to stabilize the national economy, to maintain and increase production and to aid in the effective prosecution of the war."

The order directed: (1) the Price Administrator and the Food Administrator "to place ceilings on all commodities affecting the cost of living . . . to reduce prices which were excessively high, unfair, or inequitable," and in the future to grant price increases only to the "minimum extent required by law"; and (2) the National War Labor Board and the Commissioner of Internal Revenue to "authorize no further increases in wages or salaries except such as are clearly necessary to correct substandards of living" or to compensate "for the rise in the cost of living between January 1, 1941, and May 1, 1942."

To reduce labor turn-over and to strengthen wage controls, the Chairman of the War Manpower Commission was authorized "to forbid the employment by any employer of any new employee or the

[5] *Congressional Record*, vol. 89, pt. 2, pp. 571, 632, 1308, 2438, 2826.

[6] *Congressional Record*, vol. 89, pt 2, pp. 2828–30.

acceptance of employment by a new employee except as authorized in accordance with regulations" issued by the Chairman of the War Manpower Commission with the approval of the Economic Stabilization Director, "for the purpose of preventing such employment at a wage or salary higher than that received by such new employee in his last employment unless the change of employment would aid in the effective prosecution of the war."

Meanwhile, Congress held the vetoed Bankhead bill in committee as a threat to the stabilization program. Action by Congress assuring higher food prices would have been an open invitation to the United Mine Workers to press their wage demands to the utmost. The contract between the union and the bituminous mine operators expired on March 31, and the union demanded a new contract which would provide a basic wage increase of $2 per day, an increased vacation bonus, portal-to-portal pay, and a 6-day-week guaranty. These demands were clearly in conflict with the stabilization program and the "Hold-the-line" order. Negotiations between the union and the mine operators, in which conciliators of the Department of Labor participated, broke down and the dispute was certified to the War Labor Board. The union refused to send representatives to a preliminary hearing called by the Board on April 24 and it seemed that the Board might not be able to survive the labor dispute. The President appealed to the miners to stay on the job; and the War Labor Board ordered the striking miners to return to work. But by May 1 approximately 400,000 miners were out on strike and mining operations had virtually stopped.

On May 1, 1943, the President directed the Secretary of the Interior to take over and operate the coal mines in the name of the United States Government and shortly thereafter some 3,400 bituminous mines were under Government operation. On June 23, union officials instructed workers to return to the mines and, contingent upon continued Government operation, to remain at work until October 31, 1943. By October 12, however, it was possible to return to private operation all the seized mines.

In May, the Administration launched a program "to roll back the cost of living and then to hold it," with the Office of Price Administration taking the lead. Price Administrator Brown announced a four-point program to achieve this objective. The program was: (1) "to extend price control across the board, to every important commodity," (2) "to roll back those prices which have got out of hand. The prices of meats, fresh and canned vegetables, coffee, among others, will be rolled back," (3) "to establish specific dollars-and-cents prices for foods," (4) "to bring the chiseler, the racketeer, the black market operator to justice." The Price Administrator pointed out that he had opposed passage of bills to increase farm prices. "Today we are faced with a crisis on the wage front . . . I am compelled to point out that if this wage increase [to the mine workers] is granted, increases cannot be denied to workers in other industries and increased prices cannot be denied to farmers. These increases in wages and in farm prices can only mean further rises in the cost of living. What will it profit workers to have more dollars in their pay envelopes if it takes all these extra dollars, and perhaps more, to feed and clothe their families?"

During May and June, OPA moved on each of these fronts. By the end of June, dollars-and-cents maximum prices, covering, on the average, about 1,000 grocery items, had been established in approximately 200 major cities. Ceiling prices were placed on 22 commodities and on food and beverages sold in restaurants. Prices of 39 commodities were "rolled back."[7] A survey was conducted by 200 investigators in 250 coal mining communities to determine the extent of violation of OPA price regulations.

The most sweeping action was announced on May 7—a reduction of about 10 percent in retail prices for beef, veal, pork, lamb, mutton,

CHART 47. *Food Subsidy Payments.*

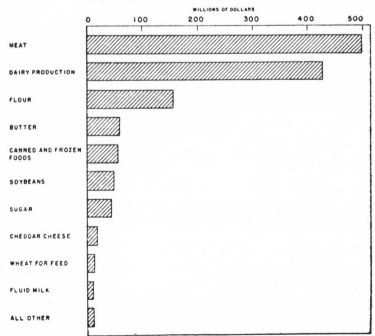

Source: Reconstruction Finance Corporation and Commodity Credit Corporation.

[7] Office of Price Administration. *Sixth Quarterly Report.*

coffee, and butter. The Price Administrator announced that, to prevent these reductions from affecting production adversely, "he was recommending to the Secretary of Commerce that subsidy payments be made to processors of the commodities involved." Economic Stabilization Director Byrnes stated that the program had his "full approval and that he was asking the Secretary of Commerce to take the necessary steps to carry it into effect." [8] The "roll back" subsidies were to go into effect on June 1 and the total cost of the program was estimated at $400 million.

Opposition to the "roll back" program developed quickly. Representatives of retail distributors predicted "complete demoralization if not annihilation." [9] The House of Representatives voted 160 to 106 to terminate the roll back subsidy program on July 1 and to prohibit future use of subsidies for the purpose of holding down consumer prices.[10] Price Administrator Brown informed a skeptical Senate Banking and Currency Committee that it would be impossible for the Office of Price Administration to "implement the mandates of the Price Stabilization Act without using Federal subsidies to 'roll back' agricultural prices." He pointed out that the Stabilization Act specified September 15 levels for retail prices, required fair and equitable margins for processors and distributors, and fixed parity as a minimum below which prices could not be set.

Toward More Inclusive Overhead Management

The very existence of a top policy office like the Office of Economic Stabilization, closely connected with the President, attracted to it for decision interagency issues not strictly within the sphere of stabilization. Thus, a train of events was set in motion which was to bring about an enlargement of the machinery to assist the President in the management of the Government as a whole. In fact, the Executive order establishing OES gave to it power to make policy decisions on rationing, a matter certainly not unconnected with stabilization but which theretofore had been considered in a different administrative context. The general theory had been that when the analysis of potential requirements and supply indicated a possible shortage of an item of essential and universal civilian need, the allocating authority would order that item to be rationed for civilian consumers. Since the allocating agencies, however, were not disposed to make timely rationing determinations, OPA, which had established a Nation-wide system of local rationing boards, acquired a keen interest in rationing policy. It was concerned lest it be directed to initiate rationing pro-

[8] OPA Press Release No. 2466, May 7, 1943.
[9] *New York Times*, May 19, 1943, p. 1, col. 3.
[10] *Congressional Record*, vol. 89, pt. 5, p. 6124.

grams without adequate time to act before shortages became serious. It became involved in disputes with the War Production Board, the Petroleum Administration for War, and the War Food Administration over such questions.

The inadequate appreciation by the allocating agencies of the problems of rationing came in part from a lack of knowledge of the technical problems of rationing, from a lack of concern for the interest of the consumer, and from fear that rationing might result in the disturbance of preexisting patterns of distribution within the industry. The Office of Petroleum Coordinator, for example, in 1942 fought the introduction of gasoline rationing,,in part because it failed to see the need for rationing, and in part because of its desire to maintain the existing allocation of business among distributors. The potential effect of the desire of OPC to maintain the pattern of distribution was demonstrated by the temporary rationing measures undertaken in 1942 which allocated to filling stations a uniform percentage of their earlier intake. The consequence was that some stations had more gasoline than they could sell and others had a totally inadequate supply. OPA contended that rationing programs should assure a distribution of the rationed commodity in accordance with consumer needs as shown by the use of ration coupons. The existence of such issues between OPA and the allocating agencies created a need for a common superior to settle them. With the creation of OES such a superior at a subpresidential level came into existence.

OES was given further powers by the Executive order of December 1942, vesting control over food in the Secretary of Agriculture. That order attempted to divide the priority power between WPB and the Secretary of Agriculture. It was impossible, however, for both the Chairman of WPB and the Secretary of Agriculture to determine the allocation of steel and other products between agricultural and other uses. Under this order, the Secretary of Agriculture might come into conflict with the Chairman of WPB in several areas. For example, the Chairman of WPB might not grant enough farm equipment to meet the requirements of the food program as seen by the Secretary of Agriculture. The two officials might not agree on the division of import space between foods and nonfood commodities. The order provided that disagreements between the Secretary of Agriculture and the Chairman of WPB would be settled by a person designated by the President, who named the Director of Economic Stabilization.

Soon after the establishment of the Office of Economic Stabilization, the problems of relations between WPB and other agencies in allocating economic resources were brought toward a solution. Under the controlled materials plan the requirements of governmental agencies could be considered as a whole and delegations made by

WPB to other agencies to deal with many detailed questions. PAW, for example, by the Executive order of December 2, 1942, was given broader authority over the petroleum industry. It became a claimant agency before WPB for the material and equipment necessary to maintain the petroleum industry. That is, PAW estimated the quantities of machinery, piping, and other supplies necessary to produce the required quantities of petroleum. These estimates were justified by the presentation of data showing what would be done with the requested equipment and material. The request of PAW was placed by WPB alongside the requests of all other agencies and appropriate adjustments made to bring total demands into balance with anticipated supply. Necessarily, this meant that WPB could decide the level of operation of the petroleum industry by determining the materials and equipment to be available for its operations. Further, insofar as allocation of the products of the petroleum industry was necessary, procedures were devised by which WPB would intervene only when necessary to bring PAW actions into accord with the general war program.

Similarly, the Department of Agriculture prepared estimates and justifications for farm equipment. The Office of Defense Transportation prepared estimates of needed transportation equipment and justified them by relating them to anticipated transportation requirements. The National Housing Agency, although not formally designated as a claimant agency, made studies of the need for housing in war production centers and presented to WPB estimates of what it would take to meet these requirements. Once the broad decisions were made by WPB, NHA through its subsidiaries was permitted to make the detailed decisions about what type of housing should be constructed and who should build them.

These arrangements brought to a central point the broad issues which had to be decided to limit the total demands on the economy to out total resources. Such a limitation of demand insured a higher degree of order in the operation of the entire industrial system. Yet, these developments also made the position of the Chairman of WPB more difficult. The civilian, no less than the military officers of government, chafed under the restraints which were necessarily imposed on their operations by WPB. Under the best of conditions, the decisions about the quantity of farm or petroleum equipment to be made available were questions of the utmost gravity and difficulty. The heads of agencies outside WPB did not discourage the bringing of pressure against WPB through Congress, through the press, and through other channels. Nor were they always disposed to try to get along with the least practicable quantity of new material and equipment in order to permit the maximum diversion of resources to the direct military effort. These agencies were disposed to advocate what their constituencies desired. All of these things conspired to make the position of the WPB Chairman extremely difficult and pointed toward the need for some official at a higher level who might be able to settle these disputes, if not to the satisfaction of the advocates of particular causes, at least in a manner so authoritative that they would keep quiet.

The Chairman of the War Production Board was in the unhappy position of not being able to satisfy everybody. He was battered, abused, and cajoled by other agencies of the Government. Instead of being an official of infinite wisdom and endless knowledge surveying the national scene from an Olympian vantage point and assigning our economic strength where it would do the most good—as envisaged by some of the speculators on industrial mobilization—he became the much-abused referee of a free-for-all fight among agency heads who knew no rules and were not above loading their gloves with Congressional blocs, pressure groups, and an occasional chit initialed by the President at their urging.

The tendency to place greater authority in commodity czars stimulated a move for another type of overhead coordination. This was an effort to establish an independent agency concerned with civilian supply. It originated with the Office of Civilian Supply of the War Production Board. This office was the lineal descendant of the Office of Price Administration and Civilian Supply whose civilian supply functions were inherited by the Division of Civilian Supply of the Office of Production Management and eventually by the Office of Civilian Supply of the War Production Board. Its functions were to estimate the needs of the civilian population and to advocate them before the allocating committees within the War Production Board. In the early stages of the life of the War Production Board, the Office of Civilian Supply operated principally as a gadfly to expedite the conversion of industry to war production. At the outset, it was not a defender of the civilian interest except in the sense that the acceleration of war production coincided with the national interest.

The OCS functions as a defender of the civilian interest were at first as broad as the jurisdiction of the War Production Board. Before the transfer of the food priority power to the Secretary of Agriculture, the Office of Civilian Supply could estimate the needs of the civilian population for food and advocate them in competition with military and export requirements before the Food Requirements Committee. It could formulate programs for farm machinery and equipment and make claims before the Requirements Committee for the supplies which it deemed necessary. It could estimate needs for tires, transportation, consumer durable goods, and all sorts of goods and services and make efforts to obtain allocations in accordance with its judgment of civilian needs. It was thus vested with the extremely important function of studying what was required to maintain the home front and of attempting to see that military and export demands were not carried so far as to impinge on the domestic production system.

With the rise of the czars and the evolution of the controlled materials plan with its system of claimants, the Office of Civilian Supply became the advocate only for certain residual civilian needs, i. e., supplies not within the jurisdiction of some other agency. The Office of Defense Transportation estimated transportation needs of the civilian population and sought to obtain the materials and equipment and manpower necessary to maintain that level of transportation. A subdivision of the Department of Agriculture estimated the needs of the civilian population for food and presented those claims in competition with military and export claims. The Petroleum Administration for War determined the quantities of fuel which were made available to the civilian population. The War Manpower Commission, as far as it had power to allocate the labor force, determined how manpower would be employed in the production of goods and services for the civilian population.

The Director of the WPB's Office of Civilian Supply in December 1942, informally proposed an Executive order to establish under the Office of Economic Stabilization an "Office of Civilian Supply for representation of the civilian economy in the war administration." This office would have estimated requirements for maintenance of the civilian economy and it would have been empowered, through the Economic Stabilization Director, to issue directives to all agencies of the Government concerned with allocation of resources to civilian uses. The scheme was posited on the assumption that the prospects for goods for civilian use in the coming months were dark and drastic steps were necessary to assure a proper minimum.

The proposed Executive order was not issued but its general idea found acceptance in Congress. A bill passed by the Senate early in May 1943, embodied, with considerable modification, the fundamental idea of the proposal made by the Director of the Office of Civilian Supply. The proposed Executive order and the bill which was passed by the Senate ignored the extreme difficulty of segregating that part of the economy which produced goods for civilian use and of providing special administrative arrangements to guide the operation of that part of the economy. Nevertheless, its passage was symptomatic both of a need for more effective general direction of the agencies of Government and of a state of mind in Congress and the country. The bill died in the House after the Chairman of the War Production Board changed personnel in the Office of Civilian

Supply and elevated its chief to the position of Vice Chairman for Civilian Requirements.

This agitation for greater control over the civilian economy did result in a specialized form of Nation-wide control. On the home front, the effects of rationing, production control, price fixing, construction of essential public works, and other activities all eventually made themselves felt in individual communities. It was extremely difficult to foresee from Washington all the things that needed to be done in a particular community in order that its contribution to the promotion of the war might be most effective. Problems arose especially in areas which had become congested as a result of expansion of war production or other war-connected activities. The Secretary of the Navy became concerned about conditions around port areas such as Portland, Maine; Newport, R. I.; Hampton Roads, Va.; San Diego and San Francisco. On the basis of surveys made for him, the Secretary of the Navy recommended to the President that he establish a coordinating committee with power to bring about the necessary coordination of Federal agencies in congested areas and to stimulate concerted work of Federal and local agencies.

On April 7, 1943, the President set up the Committee for Congested Production Areas consisting of the Director of the Bureau of the Budget as Chairman and one member from each of the following agencies: War Department, Navy Department, War Production Board, Federal Works Agency, National Housing Agency, War Manpower Commission. The Committee through its director designated an area director for each area which was found to be congested. The area director observed the progress of all Federal agencies in his area, and, through local channels or through the Washington office of the Committee, stimulated actions needed to cope with pressing problems in the locality. Through the members of the Committee it was possible to bring to the attention of high level officials in Washington matters within the jurisdiction of their agencies which had been neglected or which required more expeditious action than had been obtained.

Paralleling developments and discussion within the Administration of the problem of overhead management of the Executive Branch, there had been extensive agitation in Congress for establishment of an Office of War Mobilization. As early as December 1941, a House committee had proposed that there be created a single agency of the Federal Government with complete control over production and procurement. Other Congressional committees and subcommittees from time to time recommended reorganization of the machinery for top direction of the war agencies. In May 1943 the Subcommittee on War Mobilization of the Senate Military Affairs Committee reported on an inquiry into the overhead direction of the war effort. It concluded that questions of economic stabilization, production strategy, and manpower policy were being settled in separate compartments by the Office of Economic Stabilization, the War Production Board, and the War Manpower Commission. It observed that the Office of Economic Stabilization limited itself "to curative rather than preventive action." It recommended that there be established a War Mobilization Board which would formulate and submit to the President for his approval a comprehensive program for "mobilization and maximum utilization of the Nation's resources for the supply of military forces and essential civilian need." The Chairman of the Board would have been empowered, with the approval of a majority of the Board, to issue instructions and orders to the Executive departments and agencies. This report of the committee and other contemporary discussions were stimulated in part by extensive disputes among the various production czars in the early months of 1943 over the relative urgency of production programs in which they were interested.

The Office of War Mobilization

All the forces that have been detailed—the recurring difficulties in policing the battle of resources, the problems of economic stabilization which interlocked with production issues, and the clamor of public and Congress—pointed toward the development of additional top-level administrative machinery. In addition, the preparatory stages of the war were coming to a close, and major military and political decisions would require more attention of the Commander in Chief. In May, a meeting in Washington, the Trident Conference, of the President, the Prime Minister, and the Combined Chiefs of Staff, resulted in firm commitments on major lines of strategy. After the adjournment of the conference, the President by Executive Order of May 27, 1943, established the Office of War Mobilization in the Executive Office of the President. It was headed by a director who was to be advised by a War Mobilization Committee consisting of himself, the Secretary of War, the Secretary of the Navy, the Chairman of the Munitions Assignment Board, the Chairman of WPB, and the Director of Economic Stabilization. Subject to the direction of the President, it was made the function of the Office of War Mobilization—

(a) To develop unified programs and to establish policies for the maximum use of the Nation's natural and industrial resources for military and civilian needs, for the effective use of the national manpower not in the armed forces, for the maintenance and stabilization of the civilian economy, and for the adjustment of such economy to war needs and conditions.

(b) To unify the activities of Federal agencies and departments engaged in or concerned with production, procurement distribution or transportation

CHART 48. *Coordination of the War Agencies.*

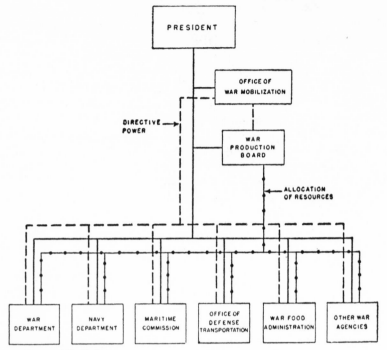

Source: Bureau of the Budget.

of military or civilian supplies, materials, and products and to, resolve and determine controversies between such agencies or departments, except those to be resolved by the Director of Economic Stabilization under section 3, title IV, of Executive Order No. 9250; and

(c) To issue such derectives on policy or operations to the Federal agencies and departments as may be necessary to carry out the programs developed, the policies established, and the decisions made under this order. It shall be the duty of all such agencies and departments to execute these directives, and to make to the Office of War Mobilization such progress reports as may be required.

The Director of Economic Stabilization, James F. Byrnes, was elevated to the position of Director of War Mobilization. His duties did not change markedly except that some of the purely stabilization matters continued to be handled by the Director of Economic Stabilization while the flow of more general questions to him increased in volume since his authority to deal with them had been formalized by the Executive order. The War Mobilization Committee did not constitute an effective instrument for consideration of questions. It was found more effective to bring together from time to time representatives of agencies interested in particular questions to consult with the staff of the Office.

Establishment of the Office of War Mobilization under an "assistant

President" with the job of coordinating home-front activities did not immediately dampen the enthusiasm of Congress for a "food czar" clothed with power over price, labor, production—with, in effect, an overriding priority over the interests of all other agencies and classes of people. Mr. Alfred M. Landon in June attributed the "food crisis" to the weather and the "confusion and inability of those in charge of production and distribution to arrive at a common understanding of the problem. We have a host of agencies working on the problem of farm labor and farm machinery, building materials, processing facilities, etc. But any worthwhile decisions have always been too late . . . The duplication of time and effort should be eliminated and all the different agencies dealing with the food requirements of the American people coordinated." [11]

Chester C. Davis, the Food Administrator, also believed that the various agencies responsible for parts of the food program should be pulled together. He was especially perturbed by the way in which food price and rationing policies were worked out by staffs of the Office of Price Administration and the Office of Economic Stabilization. Mr. Davis had been assured by the President that he would have authority commensurate with his responsibilities as Food Administrator and that he would report to the President. Instead, he found that food price and rationing authority was exercised by OPA and that he was responsible to the Director of Economic Stabilization. The roll-back subsidy program had been worked out by the staff of OPA and OES without consultation with the Food Administrator's staff. Mr. Davis, through an oversight, was not informed of the decisions that had been made, learned of the subsidy program through a radio announcement.

The President took notice of the criticisms of the roll-back program and the proposals to "put all controls over food under one man." A delegation of Congressmen visited the President on June 15 to "urge that one man be given authority over the production, distribution, prices and transportation of food." At a press conference which followed, the President was reported to have called the "suggestion that one man be given all food authority absurd." Someone had remarked that a food czar would "order a car of perishable foodstuffs transported ahead of everything else." But, the President pointed out, "this might conflict with needs for the shipment of airplanes and munitions needed on the fighting fronts." The President said that he had established the Office of War Mobilization to coordinate and control the agencies dealing with food.[12]

The drive for a food czar continued. On June 24 the House Com-

---

[11] *New York Times*, June 17, 1943, p. 10, column 3. Copyright article by Alfred M. Landon.
[12] *New York Times*, June 16, 1943, p. 1, column 2. Report on June 15 White House press conference.

mittee on Agriculture voted 18 to 8 to report out the Fulmer bill to give the Food Administrator authority over the Nation's food program, including the "production, processing, distribution, rationing, procurement, requisitioning rationing, allocation of priorities, storage, exportation and importation of, provisions of labor and facilities for, and the establishment, maintenance and adjustment of prices for, food and food facilities." The food industry gave its support to the proposal to coordinate authority over all phases of the food industry and to the Food Administrator as the recipient of authority.[13]

On June 28 the resignation of Chester Davis as Food Administrator and the appointment of Marvin Jones as his successor were announced. The announcement came about 10 days after a conference between the Director of Economic Stabilization, the Director of War Mobilization, the Price Administrator, and the Food Administrator over the way in which food policies were being determined. Mr. Davis protested that he had been given responsibility for the food program, but that others had authority and exercised it without consulting him. Byrnes and Brown both agreed with Davis' opposition to the general subsidy program which the President had announced. But the general discussion was unsatisfactory and Davis expressed a desire to see the President to "talk things over." Byrnes discussed the situation with the President and Davis' resignation was accepted. Davis was not given an opportunity to talk with the President.

One of the first major questions with which the Office of War Mobilization dealt was the problem of gearing together the activities of WPB and WMC. It has been noted that, under the general theory of WPB, it would have been able to indicate to WMC the order of priorities which should be followed in referral of available manpower to civilian employment, and, likewise to indicate to Selective Service considerations of labor supply for its guidance in the withdrawal of manpower from the labor market for the Armed Forces. WPB attempted to work out a relationship of this sort with WMC but encountered difficulties. The Executive order establishing WMC, in fact, empowered the Commission to "estimate the requirements of manpower for industry; review all other estimates of needs for military, agriculture, and civilian manpower; and direct the several departments and agencies of the Government as to the proper allocation of available manpower." On the basis of its Executive order, WMC questioned the authority of WPB to instruct it with respect to labor priorities.

As the position of WPB was weakened late in 1942 by the creation of czars it became less and less able to take an over-all view of manpower requirements and supply. The War and Navy Departments

---

[13] *New York Times*, June 25, 1943, p. 10, column 4. Views of the Chairman of the Food Industries War Committee and President of the General Foods Corp.

were claiming authority to establish unilaterally the drafts which they would make on the total manpower supply. The Selective Service Administration, which was the only agency with authority actually to control the use of manpower, was not disposed to discourage the congressional point of view that it should operate autonomously. Congress itself entered the field of manpower allocation by enactment of special measures to maintain the existing labor force in agriculture. All in all the mechanisms and procedures for assuring that manpower was assigned to the places where it was most needed were quite inadequate and poorly coordinated. Early in September 1943, OWM issued a directive which provided for the establishment of special machinery and procedures for assignment of manpower in certain congested areas of the West Coast. The procedure, eventually was extended to other areas as is described in Chapter 14.

13

Reorganizing the International Agencies

IN TIME of peace long debate and comparatively careful deliberation usually precede the undertaking of new governmental activity. Responsible officials have time to select and train a departmental staff with care, and policies, procedures, and organization may be planned in relative leisure. The organization evolves and proliferates over a period of many years. New conditions develop gradually. New organizational arrangements become necessary, but they are usually made after extended debate and consideration. In war, the tempo of events is more rapid. Organizational changes must be made quickly and the situation may soon change fundamentally again with a consequent need for further organizational adjustment. The persons building an organization do not hope for permanence; they can only hope to bring together in a semblance of order a staff adequate to meet the current crisis. By the time the organization functions smoothly, new problems emerge and the direction of movement must be altered again. The process of making such adjustments is invariably slowed by the inertia of existing arrangements, and by the difficulties in reassigning personnel without irretrievably damaging morale. It is also complicated by human limitations in perceiving the precise nature of forthcoming tasks whose outlines often become clear only in retrospect. These limitations often compel adoption of stop-gap and half-way measures as steps toward more complete reform.

The necessity for continual and rapid adjustment in war administration is illustrated by the crises that our agencies concerned with various aspects of our economic and political foreign relations faced in the summer of 1943. The machinery which had been erected to deal with wartime questions of foreign affairs during a period in which we were building up our military strength for offense showed defects as we began to move into territory previously held by the enemy and to look forward to the problems of relief and rehabilitation sure to exist in the wake of the advancing armies.

In keeping with the experience of World War I and with that of other countries, the facilities of our Department of State had been supplemented in various ways to cope with the problem of wartime foreign relations. The Office of Lend-Lease Administration had been created as an independent agency reporting directly to the President. It had remained under relatively close White House policy supervision because of the close connection between lend-lease transactions and high political and military commitments. Its close alliance with the White House had enabled it to engage successfully in the inevitable battle against departments naturally unfavorably disposed toward using resources to aid our Allies rather than for the immediate strengthening of our own forces. Lend-lease aid was proving its worth; in the summer of 1943 the German offensive in the east was soon checked and late in August the Russians recaptured Kharkov.

The Board of Economic Warfare (formerly the Economic Defense Board) had been established to control exports both positively and negatively, to see that friendly countries received from us goods essential for the maintenance of their economies and to see that goods from the United States and other sources subject to our control or influence did not reach the enemy. The Board also had a mandate to see that essential materials were bought abroad to meet our own needs and to prevent their falling into the hands of the enemy. In these activities it operated through subsidiaries of the Reconstruction Finance Corporation, a peacetime agency which it had been found expedient to retain and adapt to meet wartime needs. The Office of War Information had been established to undertake the dissemination of information abroad, information that would cement our friends more firmly to us and information that would put fear and doubt into the hearts of the enemy.

This diffusion of responsibility for foreign economic matters worked not perfectly but well enough, as long as we were preparing for offense. Lend-Lease and BEW were both concerned with exports but the logic of an independent Lend-Lease Administration limited the work of BEW in this field in the main to Latin-American countries. A rough geographical separation of the jurisdictions of OLLA and BEW was feasible. When we occupied North Africa, however, the multiplicity of agencies concerned with foreign economic affairs became embarrassing. Lend-Lease, BEW, the Department of State, the military, and other agencies of Government were all interested in the same area at the same time. Simplification of the administrative machinery was clearly indicated. The North African experience also stimulated speculations about the nature of the problems with which we would be faced as we moved into other enemy-occupied areas and about the type of preparations which should be made to meet them as they arose.

At about the time the moral of the North African experience was being recognized, a weakness long latent in the machinery for the conduct of foreign economic affairs produced a crisis. The Board of Economic Warfare was responsible for policy decisions in Government purchases abroad either to meet essential needs or to prevent goods reaching the enemy. Preclusive buying had to be carried on in such countries as Spain without much regard to fair price. A high price for a critical metal which might be sold to the Nazis might be a cheap price to pay for military safety. Subsidiaries of the Reconstruction Finance Corporation, however, had the job of actually buying and paying for goods in accordance with BEW directives. The RFC had been manned by reputedly careful and shrewd traders, anxious to maintain a good financial record. Friction between the two organizations was inevitable; the boiling point was reached in the summer of 1943 with an unseemly display of accusations and recriminations by the heads of the two agencies.

As military operations proceeded, it also became necessary to knit together more tightly the operations of different Governmental agencies. For example, when politico-military negotiations were under way which might lead to surrender, foreign propaganda needed to be most closely integrated with these negotiations. Illustrative was the furor raised by the use of the phrase "moronic little King" in reference to the King of Italy by the OWI in a broadcast late in July 1943. In discussion of the ousting of Mussolini, the OWI quoted this phrase from a column by Samuel Grafton. It acted in accordance with policy directives of its Overseas Planning Board, consisting of representatives of the OWI, State, War, and Navy Departments, and the Joint Chiefs of Staff, which permitted the identification of the King of Italy and Badoglio with Fascism. At the moment delicate negotiations were under way with the King and Badoglio which were to lead to unconditional surrender by Italy. It seemed clear that the State Department had not communicated fully to the OWI important changes in its plans and that the working staff of the OWI had dealt with an unexpected break in the news without adequate consultation.

As these developments were occurring, extensive public discussion questioned whether we were pursuing policies that would "win the peace" and whether we were adequately equipped administratively to meet the necessities of our postwar foreign policy. Considerations relating to the immediate necessities for the prosecution of the war, to the problem of arrangements for postwar relief and rehabilitation, and to the longer-term problem of machinery for the conduct of foreign relations combined to force action.

War and the Traditional Machinery of Foreign Relations

Eighteenth-, nineteenth-, and, to a lesser extent, twentieth-century practice had been for peaceful international relationships to be handled through foreign offices. It has been the established practice of our Government that foreign governments could deal with the United States only through the Department of State and that American private and public bodies could deal with foreign governments only if authorized to do so by the Department.

This traditional monopoly of foreign contacts was broken during the first World War when the necessities for speed and close collaboration brought the development of direct relationships between many governmental agencies other than foreign offices. The interwar period saw the development of many direct contacts between agencies of different governments concerned with technical and nonpolitical activities. With the outbreak of World War II, a continuation of this trend was inevitable. It also seemed inevitable, considering the habits of the Department of State, that its control over these relationships would be circumscribed. Questions on how these contacts were to be made and on the degree to which the Department of State should and could control such relationships arose early in the war.

Between the first and second World Wars, several civilian departments had found foreign representation of their interests essential to successful operation, notably the Treasury, Agriculture, and Commerce Departments. In 1939 their representatives were placed, as attachés, under the direction of the Department of State. In general, the Department viewed with alarm the development of independent international contacts by agencies other than itself. In part, this was a defense reaction against younger and more vigorous agencies. Consistently the Department had sought to maintain its position as the sole agency in foreign contacts, to require representatives of other agencies to act abroad only under its authority and to report to and through it, and to supervise the activities of American technical representation at international conferences. The central question of the degree of control to be exercised by the Department of State in international dealings was unsettled at the opening of World War II. Consequently, the relations between the Department of

State and other governmental agencies remained unsettled, undefined, and often strained. Correspondingly, our relationships with foreign governments and international organizations were often confused and ineffective.

This basic administrative problem was seen when the first defense agencies dealing with international affairs were established. In reviewing the budget requests for the Department of State in October 1941, the Bureau of the Budget recognized the possible points of conflict inherent in establishment of agencies in this field independent of the Department of State. At this time, at least four emergency agencies were concerned with problems falling within the scope of international affairs: (1) the Coordinator of Information; (2) the Economic Defense Board; (3) the Coordinator of Inter-American Affairs; and (4) the Office of Production Management. The problems involved were pointed out in the following language:

> The [Economic Defense] Board does not intend to supplant the Department [of State] in terms of staff or policy, but it will be necessary that the Department supply the Board with full information on its activities in . . . the field of economic warfare and postwar international economics as well as full response from its field missions.

Even at this early date, there was some criticism of the Department, including charges that it refused to supply some of the new defense agencies with the reports which they required. The departmental practice of paraphrasing messages (to protect its codes) before transmitting them to the interested agencies led to the charge of misrepresentation and of incomplete reporting.

Long-standing difficulties on these points had been experienced in the relationships between the Department of State and the Departments of Commerce, Treasury, and Agriculture. And they gave warning of the difficulties likely to be encountered by new agencies entering the foreign field. Several proposals for the consolidation of such activities, both within and without the Department of State, were put forward. It was not, however, until the explosive airing of differences between Henry Wallace and Jesse Jones that a degree of consolidation was achieved. Why were the new agencies created, allowed to grow, and given an opportunity to take on institutional habits and interests outside of the department normally responsible for handling foreign relations? In view of the difficulties encountered, why was the consolidation so long delayed?

The inability of the Department of State to deal vigorously and aggressively with the economic and cultural problems of foreign affairs in total war contributed to the creation of special emergency agencies to deal with some aspects of foreign relations. This inability of the Department was due largely to the dominance of the foreig ı·

service tradition, procedure, and tempo. The Department was not equipped with the technical personnel, or with the experience necessary for the day-by-day activities in such fields as export control, preclusive buying, the business details of lend-lease, and the conduct of psychological warfare. For these and other reasons, the emergency agencies sought to operate directly with only the unavoidable minimum of control by the Department of State.

The direct relationships between departments of the governments of allied nations sometimes were institutionalized in forms that omitted the foreign offices completely. The Combined Chiefs of Staff furnishes an illustration both of these combined agencies and of the forces that break the monopoly of external affairs held by foreign offices. Anglo-British military collaboration would have been difficult had the United States military leaders dealt with our State Department, which in turn communicated with the British Foreign Office, which consulted with the British military, and then eventually relayed the reply through channels to the military officials of the United States. Circumlocution of this sort could have lost the war; it was more sensible and more convenient for British and American military leaders to sit at the same table and negotiate directly with each other. Somewhat similar considerations led to the erection of other combined boards: the Combined Food Board, the Combined Raw Materials Board, the Combined Production and Resources Board, and the Combined Shipping Board.

Traditionally, the definition and announcement of our foreign policy was the responsibility of the Department of State. Strong considerations urged a degree of coordination of the many agencies where operations impinged on our foreign policy. The organizational problem, therefore, became that of finding means of coordinating the functions of the several agencies within the framework of policy decisions established by the Department and the President. Difficulties encountered in drawing the line between policy determinations and daily operations were present in the foreign and domestic activities in all fields. Despite many operational difficulties, however, the principle was consistently maintained that all of the agencies operating in the field of foreign relations did so under policies developed or approved by the Department of State.

At times, the assignment of functions under this principle seemed to imply direct and intimate control by the Department of State; at other times the assignment seemed to leave the emergency agencies free, for all practical purposes, from any direction on the part of the Department. Furthermore, it seems from the evidence available that the Department never clearly understood its role as coordinator and policy guide. This fact gave rise to many administrative difficulties during the summer months of 1943, and illustrated a number of basic administrative problems.

Establishment of OFRRO

Negotiations regarding the establishment of an international agency designed to aid in the prompt relief and rehabilitation of eligible nations got under way in 1942 and 1943. The landing of Allied troops in Africa intensified these negotiations and, in order to prepare our Government for participation in such a program, the President appointed Governor Herbert H. Lehman Director of the Office of Foreign Relief and Rehabilitation Operations. Mr. Lehman resigned as Governor of the State of New York on December 2 and was sworn into his new office on December 4, 1942.[1] The new Director was given the job of mobilizing our resources for the enormous humanitarian job ahead. While the Office was established within the Department of State, almost complete freedom of action was apparently contemplated, the Department was only a convenient place in which to place OFRRO pending the creation of an organization of nations to deal with relief and rehabilitation.

As soon as OFRRO was established, however, a host of jurisdictional and operating problems beset it both in Washington and in the area of its foreign missions. Some of this confusion seems clearly traceable to the fact that no formal Executive order had been issued and partly to the hasty or casual way in which the Department of State established the Office. The new Director relied upon his recollection of oral commitments as to the scope of his authority rather than upon more formal or written statements. Some of the difficulty is also traceable to the fact that both coordinating and operating functions seem to have been lodged within the agency. Relative to other Governmental agencies, OFRRO found itself in the position of both advocate and judge. Under such conditions critical disagreements and jurisdictional conflicts were inevitable, even with the best of good will. To these factors must be added the usual growing pains of a new agency.

For a period of 3 months, the new Director was concerned with the selection of his principal officials and with the manifold problems of interagency relationships. Jurisdictional problems seemed to be solved by a Presidential letter addressed to the Director on March 19, 1943. "You are authorized," wrote the President—

to plan, coordinate, and arrange for the administration of this Government's activities for the relief of victims of war in areas liberated from Axis control

---

[1] State Department, Departmental Order No. 1114, Dec. 4, 1942; White House Press Release of Nov. 21, 1942.

through the provision of food, fuel, clothing, and other basic necessities, housing facilities, medical and other essential services; and to facilitate in areas receiving relief the production and transportation of these articles and the furnishing of these services.

In planning, coordinating, and arranging for the administration of the above mentioned work, you may utilize the facilities of the various Government departments, agencies, and officials which are equipped to assist in this field and you may issue to them such directives as you deem necessary to achieve consistency in policy and coordination in administration . . .

Your operations in any specific area abroad will, of course, be subject to the approval of the U. S. military commander in that area so long as military occupation continues, and in matters of general foreign policy you will be guided by the directives of the Secretary of State . . .[2]

Shortly after this letter, the Director left for London to discuss the pressing problems of relief and rehabilitation with the American and Allied military and civilian personnel. Upon his return to this country, Mr. Lehman determined upon a vigorous program. He had received very fine cooperation from all parties in London and felt that vigorous action was imperative to the successful execution of the program entrusted to him by the President. He therefore prepared and sent on May 8 to all the Government agencies concerned, both military and civilian, a memorandum entitled "Statement of Policy for Relief and Rehabilitation in Future Liberated Areas."

This memorandum was based squarely upon the Presidential grant of authority to issue "directives . . . to achieve consistency in policy and coordination in administration." It recognized the full authority of the military commander in liberated areas and the power of the Secretary of State in "matters of general foreign policy." Realistically, the existing operational arrangements in North Africa were left undisturbed. Fully cognizant of the interagency impact, the Director defined relief in liberated areas, a function clearly assigned · to OFRRO, in the following terms:

Relief consists of furnishing the essential goods, facilities and services required by civilian populations, irrespective of the mode of distribution, whether by gift, sale, or barter.

The reason for this definition was clearly stated:

Relief cannot be limited to free distribution if we are adequately to utilize resources in liberated areas and to avoid the necessity for and the waste of a double supply line.

Furthermore, OFRRO was to be the "single agency" responsible for relief and rehabilitation, "and civilian supply related thereto" during the period of liberation in order to simplify the "problem of the Army by assuring the existence of a single civilian supply line and administration." A further reason for this concentration of authority was

---

[2] Department of State *Bulletin*, Mar. 27, 1943, vol. VIII, No. 196, p. 256.

to "make easier the transition to any United Nations relief organization that might hereafter be established." Once the responsibility for administration of relief and rehabilitation passed from military to civilian hands, Mr. Lehman stated that it was his responsibility "to control . . . the entire civilian supply for the particular liberated area." It would thus be necessary for OFRRO to formulate requirements for submission to the Lend-Lease Administration "and to the appropriate commodity control agencies," such as WPB and War Food Administration. He also reserved to OFRRO "direction of the distribution of all civilian goods imported into the liberated areas."

Under the policies established by this memorandum, financial and currency control remained with the Treasury Department and the Department of State subject only to coordination by OFRRO. The development and procurement of strategic and critical materials and the gathering of economic intelligence remained with the Board of Economic Warfare. In the tenor of this memorandum is to be found the full impact of the "coordinating" powers of the agency as they were viewed by OFRRO:

> With respect to operations in the field, the Office of Foreign Relief and Rehabilitation Operations must and does assume responsibility for the selection and direction of the Chief and members of the relief and rehabilitation mission in each liberated area. The mission chief will be answerable to me, as Director of the Office of Relief and Rehabilitation Operations, and his charter of operations will come from me.

Coordination by the Department of State

While OFRRO was working to establish its role as the coordinating and operating agency in the field of relief and rehabilitation, steps had been taken to strengthen the coordinating function in the Department of State. On May 8, the day on which Director Lehman issued his statement of policy, the President signed a letter requesting the Secretary of State to establish coordinating machinery, within the Department, covering the general field of foreign economic activity, including foreign relief and rehabilitation. During the ensuing month, discussions and conferences were held in order to reconcile the differences of opinion and program between the proposal of May 8 and the statement of policy as announced by Director Lehman. As a result, a new draft of the letter to the Secretary of State was developed and sent to him on June 3, 1943. The letter vested in the Department of State full responsibility for coordinating the economic operations of civilian agencies in areas liberated from enemy control. The President emphasized the necessity for cooperative action among all civilian and military organizations in liberated areas. Furthermore, he defined the functional assignments already granted to the civilian agencies.

CHART 49. *Lend-Lease and Reverse Lend-Lease Aid.*

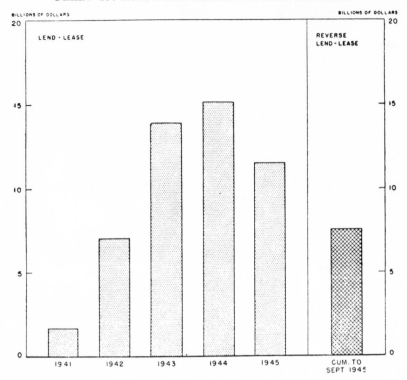

Source: Department of State.

In addition to the Department of State, those agencies concerned were the Office of Foreign Relief and Rehabilitation Operations, Office of Lend-Lease Administration, Board of Economic Warfare, and Department of the Treasury. The War Department and the Navy Department also were concerned because both had been insisting for some time that they deal only with a single responsible civilian agency in place of a number of independent civilian agencies and programs.

There were two areas in which clarification was needed in order to avoid possible disagreement and to achieve smooth interagency relationships and operations. Both of these dealt with relations between the Office of Foreign Relief and Rehabilitation Operations and the Lend-Lease Administration. These issues related to: (1) control of distribution in relief areas of free goods and those bartered or sold; and (2) the question of which agency should act as claimant for relief areas before the various allocating boards, such as the War Production Board.

Lend-Lease—Office of Foreign Economic Coordination

Lend-lease officials urged that control of all but "charity" materials should be delegated to the Office of Lend-Lease Administration. Director Lehman, as might be expected from his statement of policy, argued that to split such responsibility in distribution would result only in serious confusion and waste of effort. Distribution, in his opinion, was not in any way divisible—if an effective job were to be done.

The administrative soundness of the Director's position was commended to the President by the Director of the Bureau of the Budget. In his letter to the Secretary of State, the President designated the Office of Foreign Relief and Rehabilitation Operations as the agency responsible for distribution of all relief goods whether sold, bartered, or distributed free. To that office also was given the authority to distribute goods which would facilitate the production of basic civilian necessities. The President, however, reserved to himself the right to designate the specific liberated areas in which these functions would be exercised. It was also indicated that in certain other unnamed areas, civilian supplies, by arrangements with our allies, would be supplied by lend-lease. This arrangement left it possible for the properly constituted local government to indicate whether it wished to secure goods from Lend-Lease or from the Office of Foreign Relief and Rehabilitation Operations.

Lend-Lease officials preferred that allotments by American allocating authorities for OFRRO be included in the lump allocations to Lend-Lease. Thus Lend-Lease would appear before the War Production Board, for example, as the sole claimant for goods for relief areas. Lend-Lease then would parcel out parts of the goods allotted to it to OFRRO. The question at issue was whether Lend-Lease should be allowed to retain such control over the activities of OFRRO. Governor Lehman felt that vesting such control in the hands of Lend-Lease, or any other agency, would throw a large degree of uncertainty into the programs of OFRRO. He argued that unless his organization could appear as its own claimant, the program and plans of OFRRO could be vetoed by Lend-Lease. The President's letter provided that as long as Lend-Lease funds were to be used for relief and rehabilitatiion programs, Lend-Lease should act as the claimant agency. In presentation of requirements to the various allocating boards, however, joint action on the part of Lend-Lease and OFRRO was to be the rule. Furthermore, no change with regard to shifts in the accounts themselves could be made by Lend-Lease without approval of the allocating boards. Thus, OFRRO would have

CHART 50. *U. S. Exports by Type.*

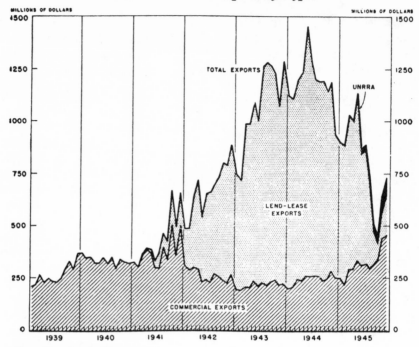

Source: Department of Commerce.

an opportunity to present its case on any shifts which might be recommended by Lend-Lease.

The Presidential letter also took cognizance of the fact that the appearance of a United Nations relief organization would necessitate a redefinition of this interagency relationship. Thus, there continued to be a large measure of uncertainty and interagency conflict was not settled.

The Office of Foreign Relief and Rehabilitation Operations was specifically granted the responsibility for the provision of technical advice and services for relief operations, plus the facilitation of agriculture, housing, and transportation in relief areas. The Board of Economic Warfare already possessed authority in the field of agricultural rehabilitation and had undertaken certain construction programs. It was pointed out by the President that OFRRO would be expected to take full advantage of this going service. The Board of Economic Warfare was also expected to continue its activities in the procurement and development of critical materials, in compilation of economic intelligence, and in other activities of economic warfare. It would also act as a consultant on all related technical matters.

No serious matters seemed to be involved regarding the sphere of responsibility delegated to the Treasury Department. It was to, continue its activities in the fields of fiscal control, exchange rates, and so on.

OFEC Organization

To perform its function of coordinating the foreign economic activities of the Government, the Presidential letter of June 3 suggested organizational changes within the Department of State, the chief of which was the establishment of an Office of Foreign Economic Coordination. The general plan had been developed by the Bureau of the Budget and was presented to the Secretaries of State, Treasury, War, and Navy, to the Directors of the Office of Foreign Relief and Rehabilitation Operations and the Office of Lend-Lease Administration, and to the Chairman of the Board of Economic Warfare. It provided for the establishment of an interdepartmental coordinating mechanism under the direction and leadership of an Assistant Secretary of State. The major objective of this interdepartmental machinery was to relate directly civilian economic plans and operations to those officials responsible for our foreign political policies. Further coordination of such plans and programs with those of the armed services and the United Nations was also envisaged by this arrangement. To this end, the plan provided that the Army and Navy would not withhold any information or guidance essential to the effective planning and operation of the civilian agencies concerned.[3]

There was general approval of the purpose and plan of the new organization. Detailed discussion among the agencies concerned brought substantial agreement on the operational feasability of the proposal and on June 24 the Secretary of State signed an order creating the Office of Foreign Economic Coordination within the Department. This new office was placed under the direction of Dean Acheson, Assistant Secretary of State. Soon thereafter Thomas K. Finletter was appointed executive director and he began to recruit personnel. During the following 2 months, there were many discussions and conferences, and there seemed to be an improvement in interagency relationships. Surface indications, however, were deceiving, as events during July and August were to show.

On August 18, the Bureau of the Budget reported to the Director of the Office of War Mobilization, James F. Byrnes, that at least four

---

[3] The selection of this type of organization was based upon the recognition that (1) there must be one central point in Washington for the coordination of interrelated activities abroad, (2) there must be a similar point in each liberated area, (3) interdepartmental machinery is the technique best adapted for close and continuous working relations as well as unified policy decisions among related agencies, and (4) such coordination within the Department of State did not remove the authority of individual operating agencies as already provided by statute, Executive orders, and so forth.

major problems remained unsolved—any one of which might well be crucial to the successful operation of the plan of June 3.

The President has not yet indicated . . . whether OFRRO or OLLA will be responsible for the distribution of civilian supply in liberated areas. Until this is done, it will be impossible for OLLA, OFRRO, and indirectly OFEC, to recruit their personnel and lay their plans for those areas . . .

The extent of the coordinating authority of the State Department is still very much in dispute. The State Department maintains that it must have enough power—in respect to personnel, the clearance of communications, etc.—to properly coordinate the activities of the operating agencies. Some of the agencies, however, insist that the State Department plans to operate as well as coordinate . . .

The Secretariat . . . and the central organization for OFEC, have not yet been established, and little or no progress has been made in recruiting the staff . . .

No agreement has so far been reached between the military and civilian agencies with respect to supply during and following military occupation. Without knowledge of the military procurement progress, the civilian agencies are completely unable to make plans and begin procurement.

Operation vs. Coordination

During the interim between the Presidential letter and the report of the Bureau of the Budget, a number of detailed problems developed. Precisely how was the State Department to coordinate the operations of other agencies? Action by the Department of State made it appear to the war agencies that the Department was extending its jurisdiction by a very broad interpretation of the meaning of "coordination." All sides admitted that the line between "operation" and "coordination" was an extremely difficult one to draw; the various agencies concerned, however, were made specifically responsible, by statute and by Executive orders, for operations in various segments of our total foreign economic activities. All the agencies agreed upon the need for a unified foreign economic program; they would not agree on how to attain it.

The State Department favored the establishment of a policy committee entitled an "Interdepartmental Committee for Economic Policy in Liberated Areas." Membership was to be composed of the top military and civilian administrators, or their immediate deputies. Its function was to establish over-all policy and programs of interagency concern. The chairman was to be the Assistant Secretary of State in charge of OFEC. Under this committee there was to be established a coordinating committee of members from the various agencies concerned, which was to review, coordinate, and adjust policy and area plans and operations to changing military and allied needs, its chairman to be the Assistant Secretary of State. Provision was made for reference of all unresolved decisions to the Policy Committee. It was also proposed that a series of "area" committees be established, each committee to have the responsibility for developing plans and programs to guide agency operations in the various liberated areas. These committees were to be interagency in composition, were to report to the Executive Director of the Office of Foreign Economic Coordination, and were to provide the channel through which the regular machinery of the Department of State would be meshed with the activities of our civilian and military agencies and allies.

The field organization prepared by the State Department provided for the selection of an area director for each of the liberated areas. This director was to be subject to the orders of the military com- mander but was to act within the policies established by the policy committee in Washington. He also would be specifically responsible for keeping the State Department fully informed of all activities in his area. The area director was to be the major channel of contact, in the field, between the civilian and military agencies of this Govern- ment. The plan also contemplated the speedy despatch of both communication and personnel to and from the liberated areas.

Secretariat

Prior to the issuance of the formal State Department order creating the Office of Foreign Economic Coordination, the department re- quested the aid of the Bureau of the Budget in making adjustments necessary to carry out the coordinating duties imposed by the Presi- dential letter of June 3. Plans presented by the Department for a rather large staff were discouraged on the grounds that a large staff invited almost certain duplication of personnel and that operation rather than coordination would become inevitable in such a situation. It was emphasized that coordination was the function assigned to the Department and that this might be accomplished best by the establishment of a suitable secretariat. Such a secretariat, designed to service the several committees, was viewed as the strongest coordi- nating device possible under the circumstances. This position was in line with the Presidential intention, as expressed in the letter of June 3, to emphasize the coordinating function of the Department of State and to leave the day-by-day job to the various agencies con- cerned. The Department accepted this point of view, but, as has been pointed out, nearly 2 months elapsed before even .a skeleton organization had been established. This lack of a Secretariat made the coordinating function a difficult one to establish.

The reorganization necessary, within the Department of State, to integrate the departmental machinery with OFEC was time-consum- ing. Reorganization on a fairly large scale seemed to be essential and such action was necessarily slow. Various interagency committees established by BEW, OLLA, OFRRO, and other agencies concerned with our foreign economic activities, had to be surveyed. These committees had been established in order to accomplish, on a more limited scale, coordination of our foreign economic activities. The dissolution of these committees and the consolidation of some of them with the new coordinating mechanism of the Department of State took considerable time.

OFEC—Operations

While these organizational problems were being reviewed and their solutions sought, the Executive Director of OFEC was carrying on discussions with military officials to determine the number of area committees needed and to develop operating procedures satisfactory to both military and civilian agencies. At the first meeting of the Policy Committee, held on June 17, the Assistant Secretary of State presented an outline of the ground rules and plans for activities as approved by the appropriate military officials. It was agreed that there should be an "area committee" for each of 12 areas designated by the Army and in subsequent meetings the procedures to be used in operating in each area were considered.

The area committee was designed as the point at which all proposals, policies, and studies from the various agencies could be brought together to develop a single coordinated foreign economic policy and plan of action. Such a unified program could then be fitted into the military and diplomatic picture as it changed from day to day. The agencies, however, seemed to view these committees as the place where most of the detailed planning was to be done. The Executive Director of OFEC did not believe that either policies or plans could be made in committee. In his opinion, the best device was the use of a standard operating procedure, which he had developed in consultation with the military officials. The failure to consult also with civilian agencies contributed to subsequent friction. The struggle over the proper demarcation between coordination and operation again provoked vigorous discussion. The standard operating procedure for supply, as presented by the Executive Director of the Office of Foreign Economic Coordination, appeared to place OFEC in the position of the procuring agency as well as the advocate before the various allocating boards. Strong objections were voiced to this position as being in direct conflict with the intention if not the letter of the presidential delegation of authority to the Department of State.

On July 1, representatives of the Board of Economic Warfare, the Treasury Department, the Office of Foreign Relief and Rehabilitation

Operations, the Office of Lend-Lease Administration, and the Office of Foreign Economic Coordination met for the purpose of discussing a revision of the standard operating procedure. At this time, two drafts were considered: one, pertaining only to the War and Navy Departments, and previously approved by the Civil Affairs Division of the War Department, provoked no comment; the other, dealing with civilian supply arrangements, was vigorously opposed by the Office of Foreign Relief and Rehabilitation Operations. The Director of that office maintained that draft sections as presented, providing for the transportation and distribution of supplies, made the Department of State the operator and left OFRRO in a purely "planning" position. The Executive Director of OFEC avowed that the intent of the document had been misunderstood, that the OFEC had no desire to undertake any operating responsibilities, and that such responsibilities were the specific duty of OFRRO. Counter-proposals were prepared and presented by BEW, OFRRO, and Treasury Department. A meeting of minds seemed increasingly difficult to accomplish. Out of these events the impression emerged that the Department of State, if left to its own inclinations would not utilize the interdepartmental machinery in the fashion intended under the original plan. The impression also remained that a large staff necessarily would be developed under the standard operating procedure. Difficulties seemed so formidable that plans for the consolidation of the agencies acting in the international field into a single agency outside the Department of State were revived and reviewed.

Relationships between OFRRO and the Department of State reached an apparent impasse by the end of August. On August 30, 1943, the Director of OFRRO sent a letter to the President raising at some length certain major policy questions affecting the Administration's plans for liberated areas. This direct appeal to the President can be understood only in light of the fact that the original delegation of authority to Mr. Lehman had been very wide. He had accepted, in the interests of interagency harmony, a greatly diminished definition of his responsibilities under the letter of June 3. The developments taking place under that delegation of authority to the Department of State seemed, to Mr. Lehman and his staff, to place OFRRO in the position of being unable to execute any action program.[4] He therefore requested the President to return to the original plan and to make the relief and rehabilitation of all liberated areas a "single,

---

[4] It is instructive to note that the OFRRO-State Department struggle under the June 3 letter was similar in many respects to the OFRRO-Lend-Lease struggle under the March 19 letter. In the first instance, the State Department was coordinating; in the second, OFRRO. In both instances, the coordinating agency was placed in the difficult position of being called upon to do an impartial coordinating job when at the same time they had an agency interest at stake. Under the March 19 letter, OFRRO was given "directive" power; State was not given such power. It subsequently requested it but such authority was not granted.

unitary job". Mr. Lehman argued further that with this function centered in OFRRO, the transition to a United Nations Relief and Rehabilitation Administration would be much smoother than if the functions were dispersed in a number of agencies. More specifically, the Governor recommended that—

1. A statement be issued reaffirming the authority of OFRRO in respect to the total relief and rehabilitation job.

.2. OFRRO should be free to prepare relief and rehabilitation plans without interference except for necessary coordination with the programs of other agencies.

3. Adequate supply reserves should be guaranteed for OFRRO.

4. Ample funds should be set aside for OFRRO's use.

5. OFRRO's freedom to operate should be subject only to the policy controls of the Secretary of State and the military, and the coordination of the area director.

On September 4, the Secretary of State forwarded a memorandum to the President setting forth the position and recommendations of the Department. Secretary Hull pointed out that relief and rehabilitation represented but one segment of our total foreign policy and that responsibility for total coordination was, in his opinion, properly placed in the Department of State by the Presidential action of June 3. He regretted exceedingly that the relationship between the Department and OFRRO had not been as cordial as those between the Department and other agencies but was convinced that the proposal he was presenting to the President was administratively sound and workable. He was certain, however, that the experience of three months indicated a need for "clarifying the authority of the State Department" in its role as coordinator.

It is accordingly recommended, for the President's consideration, that he authorize the Department of State, in any instance where there shall be a conflict of view between two or more interested agencies, or where in the Department's opinion an element of foreign policy is involved, or where some procedure must be established among our own agencies or with our allies, to make the necessary decision and to cause it to be carried into effect.

The Secretary of State and the Director of OFRRO met in the Secretary's office on Monday, September 6, to discuss the problem they had presented to the President. At the request of the Secretary of State for a "bill of particulars," the Director forwarded to him a lengthy memorandum on September 9, which discussed the problems of coordination in foreign missions, the line of command, the appointment of personnel, the clearance of communications, and other difficult administrative problems. The substance of his position was that OFRRO had to have direct control over its personnel and communications or it could not be held responsible for the effective execution of its mandate. He was of the opinion that the coordinating function of the Department of State had been used to control OFRRO's activities to the detriment of effective operations. The clash seems to have been administrative rather than personal; Director Lehman wrote in his covering letter to Secretary Hull:

I should like you to know that I left your Office deeply impressed at your earnest desire that the civilian agencies have authority to fulfill their responsibilities and that the activities of OFEC be confined in fact as well as in word to the coordinating function, which, we all agree, is necessary for consistence in American foreign policy in liberated areas.

The solution to this problem came from quite a different source, partially domestic and partially international.

Friction between BEW and RFC

Even before the State Department and OFRRO became involved and bogged down in the process of devising machinery to coordinate our foreign economic policy, relations between two other agencies—the Board of Economic Warfare and the Reconstruction Finance Corporation under the supervision of the Secretary of Commerce—had been simmering. At the end of June 1943 they reached the boiling point. On June 29, the Vice President, as Chairman of the BEW, released to the press a series of charges against the Secretary of Commerce. This was followed, 6 days later, by the reciprocal charges of the Secretary of Commerce. In order to secure an understanding of the forces behind this public display of differences, it is necessary to review briefly the administrative background of the conflict.

Executive Order No. 9128, April 13, 1942, vested in the Board of Economic Warfare complete control of all public purchase import operations. The language follows:

The Board of Economic Warfare is authorized and directed to—

(a) Receive and be responsible for executing directives from the Chairman of the War Production Board as to quantities, specifications, delivery time schedules, and priorities of materials and commodities . . . required to be imported for the war production effort and the civilian economy; and determine the policies, plans, procedures, and methods of the several Federal departments, establishments, and agencies with respect to the procurement and production of such materials and commodities, including the financing thereof; and issue directives, or initiate such proposals in respect thereto as it may deem necessary.[1]

The order also gave to the Board of Economic Warfare, subject to the approval of the President, the authority to direct the establishment of financial corporations to obtain "from foreign sources such materials, supplies, and commodities . . . as are necessary for the successful prosecution of the war. . . ." This power was made subject to the provisions of the act creating the Reconstruction Finance Corporation. Thus, BEW was not given its own funds and RFC retained its position as banker for the foreign economic activities

---

[1] Executive Order No. 9128, Apr. 13, 1942, 7 *Federal Register* 2809.

of BEW. Furthermore, BEW was given the authority to advise the State Department with respect to the forms and conditions to be included in the lend-lease "master agreements." The Board of Economic Warfare would thus act on directives from the War Production Board, issue directives to the Reconstruction Finance Corporation and advise the State Department in the field of international economic relations. The Board of Economic Warfare, however, was granted the authority to send technical, engineering, and economic representatives into foreign countries. Such appointments were made subject to the approval of the Department of State.

This Executive order provoked considerable protest. The protests were due to conflicting convictions regarding the proper role of economic warfare in the field of foreign affairs. In the view of the Department of State, economic warfare was a tool of diplomacy. The point was made that at the heart of our foreign policy was the question of what would we ask in return for lend-lease. Preclusive buying, supplying goods and commodities for rehabilitation purposes, export control—these and other actions were, in the opinion of the Department, devices for strengthening our bargaining position in foreign affairs.

The Reconstruction Finance Corporation had been established for the purposes of strengthening the business community of the Nation. It was inclined to view foreign purchases and foreign financial commitments from the point of view of accepted business practices. As Mr. Jones stated in his reply to the charges made by Mr. Wallace: "The Reconstruction Finance Corporation does not pay \$2 for something it can buy for \$1." [6] In the opinion of the Chairman of the Board of Economic Warfare, this was good business but hardly economic warfare. The Board was concerned solely with the basic problems of securing adequate goods and materials in the shortest possible time and keeping all such goods out of the hands of the enemy. Costs, protocol, and postwar diplomatic relations were secondary to the task assigned to the Board of Economic Warfare.

Executive Order No. 9128 did not reconcile these conflicting points of view. It simply placed the Board of Economic Warfare in a better position to define its responsibilities. Export control (with the exception of lend-lease), import control (under directives from the War Production Board), and the sending of economic missions abroad (upon the approval of the Department of State) were the functions of the Board of Economic Warfare.

In defining these responsibilities, two actions of significance were taken by the Board. The Department of State was requested to turn over to the Board of Economic Warfare all papers relating

---

[6] *Congressional Record*, vol. 89, pt. 5, p. 7260.

to pending or completed negotiations concerning production and procurement. Furthermore, the Board of Economic Warfare also requested the Department of State not to undertake any new negotiations regarding production and procurement abroad. This action stimulated sharp protest by the Department of State. The parties were temporarily pacified by a clarification and interpretation of Executive Order No. 9128 issued by the President on May 20, 1942:

> In the making of decisions, the Board and its officers will continue to recognize the primary responsibility and position, under the President, of the Secretary of State in the formulation and conduct of our foreign policy and our relations with foreign nations. In matters of business judgment concerned with providing for the production and procurement of materials to be imported into this country for the war effort, including civilian supply, the Department will recognize the primary responsibility and position of the Board. In many cases a decision may involve both matters of foreign policy and business judgment in varying degrees. No clear-cut separation is here possible. Accordingly, if occasions arise in which proposed action of the Board or its officers is thought by officials of the State Department to be at variance with essential considerations of foreign policy, the Secretary of State and the Chairman of the Board will discuss such matters and reach a joint decision, in matters of sufficient importance obtaining direction from the President.[7]

The "clarification" made operations somewhat simpler, but conflict at subordinate levels continued. The conflict was sharp largely because of the differences in psychology and structure of the war emergency agency and the long established permanent department. Neither the Executive order nor the "explanation and clarification" of it settled this basic difference of outlook and procedure. This conflict remained and was a factor in the final organizational consolidation some eighteen months later.[8]

Following the issuance of Executive Order No. 9128, relationships between the Board of Economic Warfare and the Reconstruction Finance Corporation and its subsidiaries improved considerably. In 8 months only three occasions found Mr. Jones and Mr. Wallace at basic variance regarding policies to be pursued. Two of these disagreements, thoroughly aired in the press, related to the rubber program. The appointment of the Rubber Director, with his authority to issue directives to both the Board of Economic Warfare and the Reconstruction Finance Corporation, resulted in an outcome favorable to the spirit of urgency prevalent in the Board of Economic Warfare and a consequent speeding up of the rubber program. It should be emphasized, however, that literally hundreds of individual transac-

---

[7] Clarification and Interpretation of Executive Order No. 9128 of Apr. 13, 1942, in respect to Certain Functions of the Department of State and the Board of Economic Warfare, May 20, 1942. 7 *Federal Register* 3843.

[8] It is important to note that the BEW-State Department relationship involved approximately the same problems as those encountered in the OFRRO-State Department relationships in the spring and summer of the following year. These relationships have already been recounted.

tions were peaceably and amicably consummated by the two organizations during these months.   Unfortunately for the speedy prosecution of the foreign procurement program, the periods of peaceful relations between the Board of Economic Warfare and the Reconstruction Finance Corporation were of short duration.   It could hardly be otherwise with the separation of financial control from operational and policy control and with the fundamental difference in point of view between the personnel of the two organizations.

On December 22, 1942, the President issued a memorandum addressed to all departments and agencies requesting that immediate steps be taken to eliminate any duplication or overlapping of functions between the various Government agencies.   Acting upon this memorandum, the Vice President, in his capacity as Chairman of the Board of Economic Warfare, issued Order No. 5.   This order provided that in foreign procurement, the negotiation, contract preparation, and the supervision and administration of contracts would be executed by employees of the Board of Economic Warfare while the corporate execution of contracts, disbursement of funds, accounting, and the acceptance and delivery of commodities and materials would be handled by the financing subsidiaries of the Reconstruction Finance Corporation.[9]

The reaction of Mr. Jones to this step can best be stated in his own words:

The President's Executive Order No. 9128 gave (the) Bureau [sic] of Economic Warfare authority to issue directives to the Reconstruction Finance Corporation with respect to foreign purchases.   That Mr. Wallace's own Order No. 5, issued while the President was in Casablanca, has equal force is open to serious question.

Under Mr. Wallace's Order No. 5, officials of the Reconstruction Finance Corporation are allegedly given no choice but to sign, without question or inquiry, any contract to make any commitments which the Board of Economic Warfare negotiates and prepares and gives a directive for, regardless of the terms and conditions of the contract or the extent of the Government obligations assumed . . .

Their duties and responsibilities (those of the Reconstruction Finance Corporation) cannot be properly discharged by signing blank checks or executing without careful examination contracts that commit the Government for hundreds of millions of dollars.[10]

By the 29th of May, Mr. Jones and Mr. Wallace seemed to have reached an understanding regarding the transfer of the United States Commercial Company to the Board of Economic Warfare.   Certain of the functions of USCC pertaining to the procurement of strategic and critical materials abroad were to remain with the Reconstruction Finance Corporation.   The Board of Economic Warfare, however, could utilize certain of the facilities of the Corporation, independently,

---

9 8 *Federal Register* 908-909.
10 *Congressional Record*, vol. 89, pt. 5, p. 7260.   Letter of Mr. Jesse Jones to Senator Carter Glass, July 5, 1943.

for the purpose of preclusive buying. The understanding, however, came to naught because of Mr. Jones's objections to the clearance of the arrangement in the customary manner through the Bureau of the Budget.

Reorganization

The public controversy between the Chairman of the Board of Economic Warfare and the Secretary of Commerce furnished the occasion for initiating steps leading to a greater degree of organizational consolidation of foreign-affairs functions carried on by agencies outside the State Department. After the two officials carried their cases to the press, the President, in line with a policy announced during the heat of the rubber controversy in the fall of the previous year, solved the immediate problem by removing Mr. Wallace and Mr. Jones from their respective posts as Chairmen of the Board of Economic Warfare and Director of the RFC subsidiaries in the field of foreign procurement. This announcement was made on July 15, 1943.

At the same time, the President abolished the Board of Economic Warfare and transferred its functions to a newly created Office of Economic Warfare. The USCC, the Rubber Development Corporation, the Petroleum Reserve Corporation, the Export-Import Bank of Washington, "and all other subsidiaries of the Reconstruction Finance Corporation which are now engaged in financing foreign purchases and imports, are transferred from the Department of Commerce and from the Reconstruction Finance Corporation to the new Office of Economic Warfare".[11] The general principle sought by the Board of Economic Warfare thus was established.

The new Office of Economic Warfare was to administer the foreign purchase program and to carry on the functions of BEW. Authority to unify and coordinate "the policies and programs of the agencies engaged in foreign economic matters in conformity with the foreign policy of the United States as determined by the State Department" was placed in the hands of the Director of the Office of War Mobilization.[12] This shifted to Mr. Byrnes the problem of unifying the activities of OFRRO, OLLA, OEW, and the State Department.

At the time of its issuance, the Executive order was regarded as a temporary step in the direction of final consolidation of the agencies into a single organization charged with foreign economic matters. Plans for the consolidation of these agencies had been under careful consideration for some time. The Bureau of the Budget had consistently urged such a consolidation and had repeatedly called the

---

[11] Executive Order No. 9361, July 15, 1943, 8 *Federal Register* 9861.
[12] Ibid.

attention of the President to the need for such action. The Wallace-Jones dispute provided the final argument. The creation of OEW was the first step. But nearly 3 months elapsed before the final action, the creation of the Foreign Economic Administration, was taken.

While the Jones-Wallace argument was being headlined in the press, the Office of Foreign Economic Coordination was struggling to establish itself as the coordinating mechanism of the Department of State. The administrative difficulties it faced have been recounted. The final decision regarding the proper relation between OFRRO and OFEC awaited the completion of negotiations with other United Nations on the establishment of a United Nations Relief and Rehabilitation Administration. With a date established for the organizational meeting of UNRRA, it was possible to reassess the problem of purely domestic Governmental machinery in the field of relief and rehabilitation. Likewise, by the end of the summer of 1943, considerations which made it desirable to maintain a separate organization to administer the lend-lease program had become less compelling. Furthermore, as described above, the State Department found it extremely difficult to exercise a coordinating function through OFEC. By the middle of September, it was clear that final consolidation of our foreign economic activities would have to be made outside of the Department of State.

Executive Order No. 9380, of September 25, 1943, provided for the establishment of the Foreign Economic Administration. This agency was to be composed of:

> The Office of Lend-Lease Administration, the Office of Foreign Relief and Rehabilitation Operations, the Office of Economic Warfare (together with the corporations, agencies, and functions transferred thereto by Executive Order No. 9361 as of July 15, 1943), the Office of Foreign Economic Coordination (except such functions and personnel thereof as the Director of the Bureau of the Budget shall determine are not concerned with foreign economic operations) and their respective functions, powers, and duties . . .[13]

At the same time, the President announced the appointment of Mr. Lehman as special assistant to the President. He was assigned the responsibility of preparing for the participation of the United States in a meeting of the United Nations to be held to create the United Nations Relief and Rehabilitation Administration. Mr. Lehman subsequently was elected Director General of that organization. The resignation of Under Secretary of State Welles and the appointment of Lend-Lease Administrator Stettinius to that post was announced by the White House at the time the Executive Order creating the Foreign Economic Administration was made public.[14]

---

[13] Executive Order No. 9380, Sept. 25, 1943, 8 *Federal Register* 13081.
[14] White House Press Release, Sept. 25, 1943; Department of State *Bulletin*, Sept. 25, 1943.

On October 6, the final consolidation of foreign economic functions took place under the authority of Executive Order No. 9385. The functions of the War Food Administration and of the Commodity Credit Corporation with respect to the procurement of food, food machinery, and other food facilities, in foreign countries, were transferred to and consolidated with the Foreign Economic Administration. An exception to this consolidation was made in the case of sugar produced in the Caribbean Area and food purchased in Canada, both of which remained with the War Food Administration.

A press release issued by the new Administrator, Leo T. Crowley, on October 6, 1943, announced the complete unification of the foreign economic operations formerly carried on by more than a dozen agencies and offices.[15]

On November 6, 1943, the Department of State abolished the Office of Foreign Economic Coordination and announced the appointment of four groups of advisers to be "concerned respectively with the foreign aspects of matters relating to the allocation of supplies, of wartime economic activities in liberated areas, of wartime economic activities in eastern hemisphere countries other than liberated areas, and of wartime economic activities in the other American republics".[16] Five days later the Department of State and the Foreign Economic Administration reached an agreement concerning the proper role of each agency in the conduct of foreign economic programs. This agreement covered the entire range of problems which had perplexed both the Department and the several operating agencies for more than 18 months. Important among its provisions was one providing for a method of settling differences or disagreements which might arise in the field or in Washington.

Thus, there was established, outside the Department of State, a single agency responsible for export control, foreign procurement, lend-lease, reverse lend-lease, American participation in foreign relief and rehabilitation, and economic warfare (including foreign economic intelligence). All of these activities were to be carried on under the administration of a single individual and in conformity with the established foreign policy of the Government of the United States as determined by the Department of State. While the consolidation as not perfect and some international economic activities remained

[15] The agencies and activities consolidated were: Board of Economic Warfare, Office of Lend-Lease Administration, Office of Foreign Relief and Rehabilitation Operations, Reconstruction Finance Corporation, Commodity Credit Corporation, United States Commercial Company, Export-Import Bank of Washington, Rubber Development Corporation, Petroleum Reserve Corporation, Cargoes Inc., Office of Foreign Economic Coordination, Metals Reserve Corporation, Defense Supplies Corporation, and Defense Plant Corporation. In the case of the RFC and its subsidiaries and the CCC, only those functions pertaining to foreign purchasing were transferred to FEA; in the case of OFEC, only those operating functions and personnel determined to be such by the Director of the Bureau of the Budget, were transferred; in the other cases, the transfers were of entire organizations.

[16] State Department, Departmental Order No. 1210, Nov. 6, 1943.

outside of the consolidation, points of friction had been reduced in number and a far-reaching administrative reorganization had been accomplished.

A merger of operating agencies such as those concerned with foreign economic relations produces friction and confusion, and for a time delays effective action till the inertia of established working habits and habitual procedures is overcome. This inertia is the more severe when one of the organizations in a merger is part of an established department with a long tradition of procedure. It therefore took time for the Foreign Economic Administration to become an effective instrument, but once it had settled down into an assumption of its new duties, it conducted foreign economic affairs without any further major change during the war. It handled the continuing burden of lend-lease exports, which reached their peak in 1944, the programming and licensing of exports to friendly nations, and other matters of economic warfare. Its responsibilities increased toward the end of the war. It determined questions of American economic policy for the areas that were liberated as the armies advanced, administered the reverse lend-lease transactions that became more important the longer our armies were abroad, and directed the search for German assets concealed outside Germany. Investigations by the FEA preceded later diplomatic action against those sources of Nazi strength based on assets concealed in safe havens outside the Reich.

The struggle that preceded the final organization of the Foreign Economic Administration, the hesitations and delays, were not exceptional in the Government during wartime, but they were not so inefficient as they looked. Government experience during the war strongly suggested that preparations for administration must remain flexible and adapted to change, even when changes may mean temporary dislocation of function. The real threat to efficiency was careful blueprinting for a rigid organizational structure which would make change to meet new crises almost impossible. The complexity of modern society and government forbids any accurate foresight of what may come and a rigid system of organization sacrifices future gain to an immediate ease of operation.

Allocating Labor Supply

BY THE fall of 1943, the structure of wartime administration had assumed virtually its final form. On the domestic front, the War Production Board had refined its techniques for allocating scarce materials and guiding the flow of components. The challenge to the general form of organization of war activities by the proponents of the czar system of commodity organization had been met. The progress of military operations furnished additional stimulus to efforts to refurnish the organization for the conduct of foreign economic affairs, and responsibility for these matters had been concentrated in the Foreign Economic Administration. In addition, the superstructure of war organization had been rounded out by the creation of the Office of War Mobilization to aid the President in coordinating the activities of the various war agencies.

Production requirements were still rising. The rapid progress in the Mediterranean theatre leading to the surrender of Italy in September prevented any reduction of needs. As preparations went forward for new invasions in Europe and the Pacific, the demand for munitions and troops mounted steadily. In the earlier stages of the war, production had been limited primarily by shortages of raw materials and fabricating capacity. But now labor supply began to act as the ultimate limit on production. Foundries, textile mills, lumber camps, and other industries offering relatively low wages or characterized by poor working conditions were unable to hold enough labor to attain desired production levels. Some areas, notably those on the Pacific oast, began to experience a shortage of male workers in almost all industries. In these areas it became increasingly important that workers be directed to the most essential jobs and kept on those jobs. It also became desirable to relieve the pressure on some areas by reducing future production schedules and placing the work elsewhere. A general scarcity of labor had been predicted by many people since early in 1942. Yet when it actually came to be, no operating procedures were in effect to meet it. This failure was due partly to the large number of agencies involved in the problem. The pattern of demand for labor was determined largely by the actions of the numerous procurement services while a considerable part of the labor supply was provided as an incidental effect of WPB limitation orders prohibiting or placing ceilings on production for civilian use. Thus, the most important actions influencing the use of manpower were not under the control of the War Manpower Commission, and its efforts to influence production and procurement policies were not markedly successful.

The slowness of the emergence of labor shortages, however, was probably the greatest preventive of comprehensive and timely action. Steps which, if taken during 1941 and 1942, would have reduced the scarcity of labor in later years, were not taken because labor shortages had not yet appeared. Thus it was not possible in 1941 and 1942 to get serious consideration of national service legislation, use of occupation rather than dependency status as the major criterion in selective service policy, or placement of procurement contracts and new production facilities in areas of relatively plentiful labor supply.[1] But by the time labor shortages actually became important, it was difficult to get action in these directions because of a widespread feeling that the most critical phase of the war was past and because administrative policies and procedures had solidified into rather firm patterns.

When spot shortages of labor did develop during 1943 and 1944, they were met mainly by improvisations by Selective Service, the Army, Navy, WMC, and WPB, which enabled us to get by with little loss of war production. The principal devices used were special deferment treatment by Selective Service, emergency recruitment campaigns by the Employment Service to man particular plants or industries, approval of higher wage rates by the War Labor Board to stimulate recruitment, furlough of trained workers by the Army for service in particular industries, and shifting of war contracts from points of acute labor shortage to other areas. The way in which these devices were combined varied from one situation to the next. In some cases, notably the textile industry, no effective action was ever devised and the industry continued to lose labor until the end of the war. In the textile case, however, the burden of reduced pro-

---

[1] The statement that these things were not done does not necessarily constitute a judgment that they should have been done. Each involves considerations other than mere production efficiency.

duction fell almost entirely on civilian consumption and did not interfere very much with military procurement.

While this was the over-all picture, a rudimentary system for allocating labor supplies, involving local cooperation among WMC, WPB, and the procurement services, was developed in a number of areas where scarcity of labor was particularly pressing—notably on the Pacific coast. The labor controls established during the winter of 1943–44 were much looser than the controls over critical materials, but the machinery created at this time could probably have been tightened up to handle more critical labor shortages had they developed. Because of its potential significance, the emergence of this system will be traced in some detail.

Emergence of a Labor Allocation System

The period from the summer of 1940 to the summer of 1943 was one of large-scale manpower mobilization. The unemployed were put to work, some 7 million new workers entered the labor market, other millions transferred from peacetime to wartime jobs, and geographic movement of workers and their families assumed unprecedented proportions. This vast movement did not result to any important extent from direct solicitation by the Employment Service, the Civil Service Commission, or other Government recruiting agencies. It represented the response of millions of individuals to a variety of economic and noneconomic pressures. Movement of workers from nonwar to war jobs was stimulated by the much higher average earnings in war industries and, in the case of men 18 to 38, by Selective Service pressures. New workers, primarily women, were attracted into the labor force by the ease of securing jobs, high wage rates, the opening to women of many new job opportunities, and the disruption of family life due to military mobilization.

By the fall of 1943 the labor reserves with which the United States had entered the war had been fully mobilized. Unemployment, which stood at about 9 million in July 1940, fell to 780,000 in September 1943, about the irreducible minimum. The number of women in the labor force, estimated at 13.8 million in July 1940, reached a peak of 18.7 million in July 1943, and then leveled off.[2] The number of young people under 18 in the labor force had also increased markedly. By the fall of 1943 everybody who would willingly take a job already had a job, and door-to-door recruiting campaigns conducted by the Civil Service Commission and the War Manpower Commission yielded negligible results. The work week in manufacturing had been increased by about 8 hours over prewar

---

[2] U. S. War Manpower Commission. *Manpower Statistics*, May 1945, No. 18, pp. 1–4.

levels,[3] and had reached what both employers and Government agencies considered to be the maximum for efficient production. Nor could war production centers any longer rely on the strong inflow of workers from farms and small towns which had prevailed throughout 1941 and 1942. The Italian surrender and the progress of the Russian armies during the fall of 1943 caused many to anticipate a speedy conclusion of the war; a marked outflow of workers from war production centers set in. By late 1943, many cities were experiencing a net loss of labor.

A stationary total labor supply meant a shrinking civilian labor force, for Selective Service inductions were still running at about 400,000 per month. At the same time the demand of war industries for labor was increasing. Munitions production was rising at a rate of about 4 percent per month,[4] and this called for some expansion of employment in war industries though not nearly so large an expansion as was indicated by some current estimates.[5] Turn-over also continued at a high rate. In September, 1943 the monthly quit rate reached a peak of 6.29, while total separations were 8.16—a rate of almost 100 percent per year. The case of the Boeing plant in Seattle, which had employed 250,000 people since June, 1940 but had only 39,000 employees in June 1943, was by no means unusual.

At this time, as throughout the war, the labor supply situation was very uneven in different parts of the country. Labor scarcity was greatest in a few areas—chiefly on the Pacific coast and in the northeastern States—into which facilities and contracts had been crowded and which had become congested with war workers and military personnel until no more could be absorbed. Several steps might have been taken to make certain that the labor needs of war plants in such areas would be met. The demand for labor could be reduced by inducing the procurement services not to place contracts in the area or to withdraw contracts already placed, and by curtailing nonessential civilian production in the area. While labor supplies could

---

[3] Average weekly hours in manufacturing increased from 37.3 in May 1940 to 45.3 in May 1943 (*Manpower Statistics*, Sept. 1943, p. 47). This represents a general increase from a scheduled work-week of 40 hours in 1940 to 48 hours in 1943. In shipbuilding and certain other war industries, however, a scheduled work-week of 60 hours or more was not uncommon at this time.

[4] The War Production Board's index of total munitions production rose from 97 in June 1943 to 117 (which proved to be the peak) in November 1943.

[5] It was estimated in July 1943 that employment in munitions and munitions materials industries would have to increase 1,700,000 by January 1944, to meet production programs (WMC, *Manpower Statistics*, September 1943 p. 1). As matters actually developed, employment in munitions industries reached a peak in November which was only 300,000 above the July level, and employment in January 1944 was exactly the same as in July 1943. This discrepancy between forecast and event probably arose in part from contract cut-backs not foreseen in July, from increased output per manhour as hoarded labor was put to work and more efficient methods were developed, and from the consistent tendency of employers to overstate their labor requirements (on which WMC estimates were based). This frequent forecasting on the basis of imperfect statistics of an impending "manpower crisis" which later failed to develop was an important factor tending to discredit WMC in the eyes of WPB and the military. WMC cried "wolf" so often that other agencies were skeptical even when shortages actually appeared.

CHART 51. *Munitions Production and Employment.*

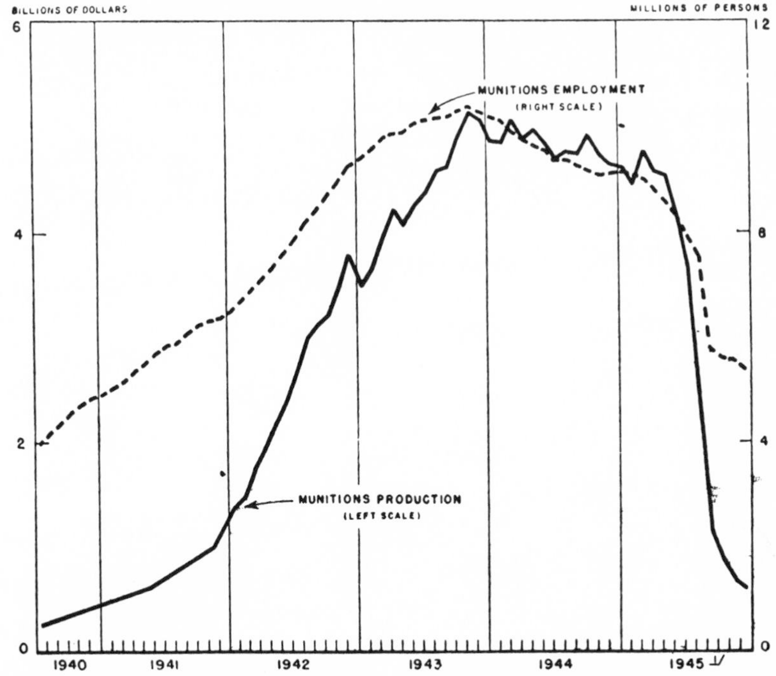

¹ Munitions production data for October, November, and December are estimated.
Source: Department of Labor, and Civilian Production Administration (formerly War Production Board).

not be increased, labor becoming available through turnover could at least be funneled into the local office of the United States Employment Service and directed, through a system of priorities or allocations, to the points of greatest need.

Previous efforts to reduce the demand for labor in areas of shortage had met with only limited success. In October 1942 the War Production Board, by its Directive No. 2, instructed the procurement services to consider the adequacy of labor supply in particular areas as a factor in contract placement; this directive was amended and strengthened in the fall of 1943. The impact of this directive on actual procurement practice, however, was not large. Among the reasons where the traditional independence of the procurement services, preoccupation with price and delivery considerations, reluctance to give up customary sources of supply, reluctance to give up a facility which may then be taken over by a competing procurement branch, and the absence of any continuous policing by Army Service Forces headquarters of compliance by contracting officers with Directive 2.

Some consideration was also given during 1942 to curtailment of

CHART 52. *Civilian Employment by the Federal Government.*

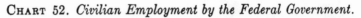
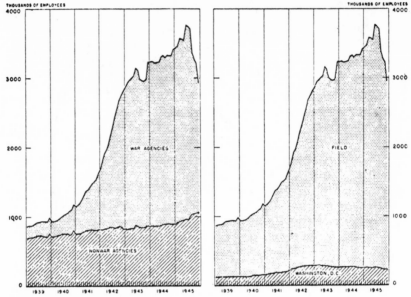

Source: Civil Service Commission.

certain lines of civilian production in tight labor markets through use
of WPB's controls over materials. Both WMC officials and the
Planning Division of WPB urged that WPB adopt a program of
"concentrating" specific civilian industries in areas of adequate labor
supply, on the lines of the concentration program already adopted in
Great Britain. Great opposition was encountered, however, not only
from industrialists and Congressmen in the areas where curtailment
was proposed, but also from WPB industry divisions. After two or
three relatively minor concentration orders had been issued, the
program was abandoned and was never revived.[6]

In the areas of greatest labor scarcity, then, it was not possible
either to increase labor supplies or appreciably to reduce the demand
for labor. Nor was it possible without national service legislation to
compel workers, except able-bodied men of draft age, to transfer from
nonwar to war work. There remained the possibility of inducing

---

[6] The orders issued covered production of farm machinery, kitchen stoves and typewriters. WPB also
ordered the closing of all gold mines in the North Central and Mountain States in order to release miners for
nonferrous metal mining. The "West coast program" announced in September 1943, details of which are
discussed below, contained a statement that WPB would consider steps to release labor by curtailing civilian
production on the west coast. Congressmen from the coast were at once flooded with inquiries and protests from businessmen. Within a few days Senator Downey called WMC and WPB officials before a subcommittee of the Senate Military Affairs Committee and pressed them for assurances that nothing would
be done on this point. Mr. Wilson of WPB assured him that his agency had no plans of this sort, and nothing further was ever heard of the matter. (U. S. Congress. Senate. Committee on Military Affairs.
Labor Shortages in the Pacific Coast and Rocky Mountain States, 78th Cong., 1st sess., Hearings on
S. Res. 88 and S. Res. 113, Sept. 9–10, 1943.)

CHART 53. *Average Hours of Work in Manufacturing Industries.*

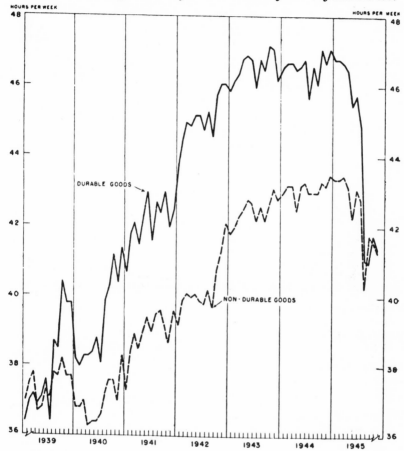

Source: Department of Labor.

workers already in essential war work to stay on their jobs, and directing to war work any people coming voluntarily into the labor market from the home, from other areas, from nonwar work, or (since turnover of war workers could not be entirely prevented) from other war jobs.

Before the end of 1942, the War Manpower Commission had begun trying to keep war workers on their jobs through local employment stabilization plans, under which employers in essential industries undertook not to hire a worker previously employed in an essential industry unless he presented a certificate of availability from his previous employer or from the Employment Service. Plans of this type were announced in Baltimore in August 1942, in Buffalo on October 15, 1942, in Louisville on November 9, 1942, and in Detroit

CHART 54. *Non-Agricultural Placements by U. S. Employment Service.*

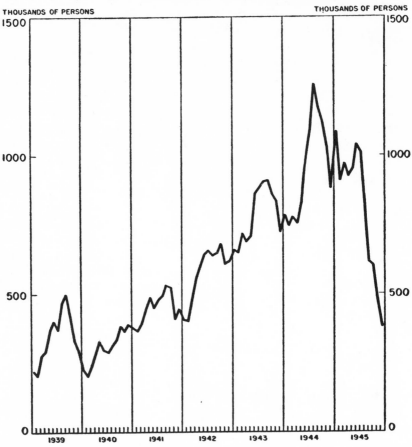

THOUSANDS OF PERSONS   THOUSANDS OF PERSONS

on December 10, 1942. As WMC appointed more and more area directors, employment stabilization plans were established in most of the important industrial areas of the country.[7] In addition to these area plans, the 12 regional directors had, by June 1943, established regional stabilization programs which—on paper, at least—covered all essential industries outside established manpower areas.

These plans do not appear to have been very effective in reducing turn-over in war industries. They depended entirely on voluntary compliance by employers. Nor were the controls over workers very stringent. A worker who was denied a certificate of availability by his employer could get himself fired or could apply to the Employ-

[7] By March 15, 101 area directors had been appointed and 44 employment stabilization plans were in operation.

ment Service for a certificate which might be granted on a variety of grounds. It is doubtful, therefore, that many workers who really wanted to change jobs were deterred from doing so by these plans. The plans did have the effect, however, of funneling more workers through the Employment Service,[8] and thus made it possible theoretically to apply a system of labor priorities.

The idea of labor priorities had been familiar to planning officers of the Employment Service since at least 1939. Their thinking was incorporated in an early directive[9] of the War Manpower Commission which instructed the Employment Service to give placement priority to essential plants in order of their importance, and in a number of field instructions to the Employment Service on this subject. As a result of these instructions many local employment offices adopted an informal priority system during 1942 and early 1943.

Operation of an effective labor priorities system, however, required authoritative determination of the relative importance of particular products and particular plants in the total war program. Neither local employment offices nor WMC headquarters could make such a determination. It was apparent fairly early, therefore, that determination of labor priorities would require some sort of cooperative action between WMC and the War Production Board. Negotiations to this end were carried on intermittently between the two agencies from mid-1942 to mid-1943 with very little visible result. This was due partly to differences of opinion concerning the relative roles of the two agencies in a joint program. Many people in WPB thought that the Board was in the best position to determine labor requirements and priorities, and that the role of WMC should be restricted to recruiting and supplying workers in the numbers and at the places specified by WPB. This was also the general view of the procurement agencies. WMC officials, on the other hand, insisted that the fact that a plant is making an important product or even that it is behind schedule does not necessarily indicate that it needs labor. Determination of the plant's need for labor requires information on labor utilization and other matters which WMC considered to be within its jurisdiction. WMC therefore argued that WPB should confine itself to furnishing a list of end-products arranged in order of urgency, and that from there on all work on labor requirements and priorities should be carried out by WMC.[10]

Perhaps more important than these differences of opinion was the fact that WMC had during 1942 no operating program to which infor-

---

[8] USES nonagricultural placements were 640,000 in August 1942, and 1,259,000 in August 1943.

[9] War Manpower Commission Directive No. III, June 22, 1942, 7 *Federal Register* 4748.

[10] Directive II of the War Manpower Commission, issued on June 22, 1942 (7 *Federal Register* 4748–9) instructed WPB to supply WMC with information on the relative importance of critical war products. Because of the difference of viewpoint just described, however, no action developed from this directive.

CHART 55. *Labor Turn-over in Manufacturing Industries.*

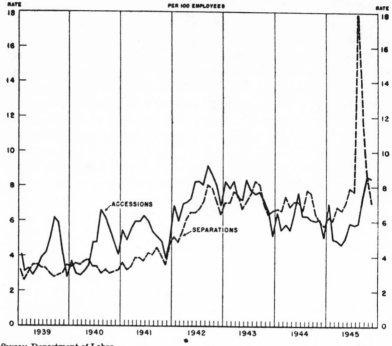

Source: Department of Labor.

mation obtained from WPB could be applied. A system of labor priorities had necessarily to be applied on a local basis, and could not develop until WMC area operations were firmly established.

A first step toward relating production programs and manpower requirements on a local basis was taken in June 1943, when Mrs. Anna Rosenberg, Director of WMC Region II, announced a revision of the Buffalo employment stabilization program. All male workers in the area were to be hired henceforth only through the Employment Service or other approved hiring channels. Although compliance with the program was voluntary, employers hiring outside the approved channels could be denied the facilities of the Employment Service. A labor priorities committee was created including representatives of WMC, WPB, and the procurement agencies. Taking into account the relative urgency of various end-products and the actual needs of individual plants for male workers, plants were placed on one of four lists: A priority, B priority, other essential plants, and other plants. All workers possessing the necessary skills were to be referred first to plants on the A priority list. The installation and initial success of this program led to intensified discussion at WMC headquarters of the possibility of extending labor priorities to other areas.

In the meantime a critical manpower situation had been developing on the Pacific coast. This region had undergone since 1940 a very great expansion of shipbuilding, aircraft and other production facilities, which were now striving to reach full production. Many military establishments requiring a large number of civilian maintenance and service workers had also been constructed on the coast. Immigration of workers from other states called for increased employment in trade, services, and other supporting activities, which, however, found it impossible to compete with the wage scales of war industries and tended instead to lose labor. Many war plant workers, dissatisfied with inadequate housing and community services, left their jobs after a short time. In the summer of 1943, the Pacific coast faced a situation in which labor demands were still being aggravated by placement of new contracts and facilities, turn-over was high and rising, there was heavy migration in both directions along the coast and from the coast to other areas, and no substantial reserves of labor existed.[11] Although all of the industrial areas had employment stabilization plans, certificates of availability were being issued very freely by the Employment Service, and did not constitute an effective control over the movement of labor.

The program developed to meet the situation on the West coast will be discussed in some detail, since it was subsequently extended to other areas and in fact constituted the main operating program of WMC for the remainder of the war. Early in August the Under Secretary of War informed James F. Byrnes, Director of OWM, that airplane production on the Pacific coast was seriously behind schedule because of labor shortages. Mr. Byrnes asked Bernard Baruch, who was at that time serving as an adviser to OWM, to investigate the situation and prepare proposals for action. After discussions with the interested agencies, Mr. Baruch and Mr. Hancock, his assistant, presented on August 19 a proposal for a "labor budget plan," involving adjustment of production programs on the west coast to available labor supplies and controlled referral of workers to plants on a priority basis. A detailed plan to accomplish these objectives was drafted by the War Manpower Commission. After further discussions among WMC, WPB, the War Department, and the Navy, the program was approved by Mr. Byrnes and released to the press on September 4. Its main provisions were:

1. In each critical area there was to be appointed an Area Production Urgency Committee representing all the procurement agencies under WPB chairmanship. The chairman of each committee was to determine the relative urgency of production programs in the area

[11] U. S. Congress. Senate. Committee on Military Affairs. Labor shortages in the Pacific coast and Rocky Mountain States, 78th Cong., 1st sess., Hearings on S. Res. 88 and S. Res. 113, Sept. 9–10, 1943.

and advise WMC of such determination, review proposals for any
new supply contracts and facilities in the area which would require
additional labor and recommend to WPB their approval or disapproval,
develop programs for balancing labor supply and requirements by
redistributing production from one area to another where necessary,
and recommend to WPB any adjustments in civilian production
necessary to bring labor requirements within the bounds of available
supplies.

2. In each area an Area Manpower Priorities Committee was to be
established, with substantially the same membership as the APUC,
but sitting under a chairman appointed by WMC. The Area Manpower Director, with the advice of the Area Manpower Priorities
Committee and using the information on production urgency provided by the APUC, was to list establishments according to the
urgency of their need for labor, set employment ceilings for individual
plants, and refer workers to jobs on the basis of these determinations.

3. The procurement agencies were instructed to present to the
appropriate APUC for review any contract involving an increase in
employment in the area, to give special consideration to the west
coast in making production cut-backs, to redirect existing production
from the west coast to other areas wherever feasible, and to encourage
their contractors to subcontract as much work as possible to producers outside the west coast region.

4. Selective Service was to give special consideration for deferment
to workers in critical occupations in high priority establishments.
Registrants qualified for critical occupations but not employed in
high priority plants were to be referred to the Employment Service
for placment in such plants.

5. At the request of a plant management or WPB, WMC was to
undertake studies of labor utilization in particular plants and make
recommendations for better utilization of labor; it was to make full
use, however, of the facilities and resources of all other Government
agencies—which meant principally the procurement agencies. WPB
and the procurement agencies were to cooperate in such surveys and
to use their influence to secure the execution of approved recommendations.

Announcement of the program aroused alarm and opposition on the
coast, which had received its first information concerning it from a
leak to the press on August 31. About 2 months' time was required
to allay this opposition and to develop the local administrative
machinery required to operate the program. By November 15,
however, production urgency and manpower priorities committees
were established in the five key areas of San Diego, Los Angeles,

San Francisco, Portland and Seattle.[12] Controlled referral was applied to all males in Los Angeles; to all males and all women in essential activity in Portland, San Francisco, and San Diego; and to all workers in Seattle.[13] Production urgency lists, manpower priorities lists, and employment ceilings were established for each area, and workers were referred to jobs in accordance with these priorities. The Selective Service System also took immediate steps, noted more fully below, to postpone the induction of necessary workers in west coast aircraft plants.

Certain parts of the program were never given much operating effect. The section calling for labor utilization studies, for example, was merely one more round in a long and unsuccessful struggle by WMC to acquire functions in this field. The Executive order establishing WMC had authorized it to develop programs to secure the maximum mobilization and utilization of the Nation's manpower. WMC had from the first interested itself in in-plant utilization of labor and had frequently attempted to assert its right to make plant inspections and to withhold labor from employers who were hoarding or otherwise misusing it. This conception, however, was vigorously resisted both by private management and by the procurement agencies. The management viewpoint was well presented in the discussions of the WMC Management-Labor Committee. Management members of the committee stated emphatically that the WMC labor utilization consultants, whose very title was indicative of their lack of status, should perform purely service functions for employers; they might make recommendations if the employer asked them to do so, but any action on these recommendations was a function of management. Labor members believed that utilization of labor was a proper subject for union-management discussion but tacitly agreed with industry that it was no affair of government.[14]

The procurement agencies took the view that labor utilization was a concern, first of management and second of the contracting officer in the plant. If a contractor was not using labor effectively, this was a matter between him and the contracting officer into which an "outside" agency such as WMC should not intrude. This was a tenable position provided the procurement agencies had themselves pressed employers to use labor effectively. But they were not staffed

---

[12] Although the plan was termed a "west coast" plan, it was in fact confined to these areas. Other parts of the three Pacific Coast States continued to be covered by the simpler employment stabilization programs.

[13] "Controlled referral" did not mean exclusive hiring through the Employment Service; company personnel offices and trade-union offices were named as authorized hiring agencies in many cases. In San Diego, for example, 146 unions were authorized to act in this capacity. While spot checks indicated that authorized hiring agencies were operating in general accordance with priorities rules, the controls were inevitably looser than they would have been had hiring been completely centralized.

[14] War Manpower Commission, Management-Labor Policy Committee, *Minutes*, Jan. 22, 23, 1943, pp. 7-11.

to do this and, with the exception of occasional flagrant cases, did not do it. Their activity was primarily directed to insisting that WMC meet at once the alleged manpower needs of any contractor. Their position, in other words, was that WMC was purely a labor recruiting and supplying agency which must accept at face value the labor requirements stated by employers.

The labor utilization section of the west coast program was another attempt by WMC to circumvent this attitude of the procurement agencies, and was no more successful than earlier efforts had been. WMC utilization consultants were not able even to gain admission to west coast plants working for the Maritime Commission and the Army Air Forces—and this included the largest plants in the region— and did not have much better success elsewhere.

The provisions of the west coast program which called for adjustment of labor requirements to available supplies on an area basis also proved to have little effect. Procurement agencies were required to submit to the Area Production Urgency Committee for review only those contracts which in their judgment, i. e., usually in the judgment of the contractor himself, would require the employment of additional labor. Even when contracts were presented for review, powerful community pressures worked against disapproval, and the volume of disapprovals recommended by area production urgency committees was negligible. The plan established no control over the letting of subcontracts to west coast firms. It did instruct the procurement agencies to induce prime contractors in the region to subcontract more work outside the region; whether any important results were achieved in this direction cannot be determined from the available data.

WPB took no action on the section of the program which authorized curtailment of less essential activities in order to release labor for war work. Action on this front would have been highly unpopular on the west coast. Yet so long as it was not taken, the procurement agencies were in an impregnable position in contending that their own activities should not be curtailed. Data on over-all labor requirements and supplies were so unsatisfactory that it was impossible to convince a procurement official that programs in which he was interested could not be carried out. In the absence of any genuine control over either aggregate labor demands or supplies, in the absence even of any reliable estimates on these matters, the "balancing of the labor budget" on an area basis which Baruch had recommended was bound to remain an unrealized objective.

The west coast program did not succeed either in reducing turn-over, though it may have prevented it from rising still higher. After a normal seasonal decline in the latter part of 1943, turn-over rose again to about the level at which it had been before the plan was announced. There was indeed no reason to expect a reduction of turn-over; the only restriction on quits was the certificate of availability, and certificates continued to be dispensed as readily after the plan was established as before. In November 1943 the percentage of requests for statements of availability which were denied was 4.6 in San Diego, 2.3 in San Francisco Bay, 8.3 in Los Angeles. These percentages were roughly the same as in September.

The program did, however, have at least four significant results. First, it eased the labor recruitment problem of high-priority plants by exposing a larger number of workers to jobs in these plants. Controlled referral channeled a larger proportion of the manpower flow through the Employment Service, and the priority system directed this flow to the points of greatest estimated need.

Second, the process of setting employment ceilings appears to have called forth a more realistic appraisal of labor requirements from employers and procurement officials. The apparent "tightness" of labor markets on the west coast, as elsewhere, was partly a statistical illusion resulting from highly inflated requirements and correspondingly alarming labor "deficits." When the fact of limited total supplies was impressed on everyone by an allocation procedure, some of these stated requirements were drastically reduced. The possibility that contracts might be withdrawn was also an inducement to employers to reduce the "tightness" of the area by cutting their requirements.

Third, adoption of the west coast program caused procurement officials in Washington to give increased attention to labor supply in placing contracts. While work already under way was not removed from the coast, a good deal of future work was canceled and many contracts which would otherwise have been crammed into the area were placed elsewhere. This did not effect a systematic balancing of labor supplies and requirements in each area but it did ease pressure on the west coast as a whole, and was doubtless the most important effect of the program.

Fourth, the west coast directive provided for the first time a program and an administrative framework within which the efforts of procurement, production, and manpower agencies could be organized to meet manpower shortages at the local level. This was an important achievement even though the stated objectives of the program were for the most part not achieved. The limited results of the program were due partly to the fact that the manpower situation did not deteriorate further but tended if anything to improve during 1944 as Selective Service withdrawals slackened, production cut-backs were made, and industrial efficiency increased. The pressure of acute scarcity necessary to overcome political and administrative resistances was not present. Had the manpower situation become really alarming during 1944, it would have been possible, by tightening up the machinery and enforcing the controls provided in the west coast program, to achieve additional improvements in the use of manpower.

Certain features of the west coast program were adopted in many other critical areas during the winter of 1943–44. This was done largely at the instance of State and area WMC directors. Because of the strength of management-labor opposition to "compulsion," which varied from area to area, WMC headquarters considered it unwise to order the establishment of any uniform pattern of controls throughout the country. Area directors, however, were often willing to add new controls after some other areas had tried it and "gotten away with it." Employment stabilization plans had spread in this way during the first half of 1943. Once the west coast program had demonstrated its ability to survive, certain of its provisions also tended to spread "on the grapevine" to other areas. By May 15, 1944, ten areas outside the west coast had the full equipment of manpower priorities, employment ceilings, and controlled referral.[15] While the results of these programs have not been appraised, the comments made above on the results of the west coast plan would probably be applicable rather generally.

On June 1, 1944, WMC instructed its regional directors to take action by July 1 to establish manpower priorities committees and controlled referral of male workers in all manpower areas, and employment ceilings in all shortage (group I and II) areas. This action rounded out a substantially uniform national pattern of manpower control on the lines of the west coast program. Only two additional "gadgets" were added to the program during the war: (1) In some areas especially critical plants were manned by limiting all referrals to them for a certain period; in other areas, however, employment service interviewers were merely instructed to "sell" jobs in high priority plants and exclusive referral was not used. (2) Beginning in January 1945, an effort was made to compel limited numbers of workers to transfer to essential work by reducing employment ceilings in less essential plants.

Selective Service Policy and National Service

The problem of industrial labor supply was part of the larger problem of obtaining a balanced allocation of manpower among industry, agriculture, and the Armed Forces. The creation of WMC, and the transfer of Selective Service to it in December 1942, had been

---

[15] U. S. War Manpower Commission. Bureau of Placement. *Report on the Manpower Program,* May 25, 1945, Table II "Areas with Manpower Programs Extending Beyond the Minimun Required by Regulation (7)." (Mimeo.)

steps in the direction of over-all manpower allocation. Progress in this direction was reversed, however, when Congress intervened, first to secure special Selective Service consideration for farmers, second to secure special consideration for fathers, and third—in December 1943—to remove the Selective Service System from the War Manpower Commission. The selection of men for military service was never part of a long-range and comprehensive manpower program. It was done by some 6,500 autonomous local boards, somewhat influenced by shifting policies hammered out at national headquarters under the immediate pressure of next month's draft call.

From 1940 until February 1943, more than 80 percent of the men inducted into the armed forces were single men under 30.[16] By the spring of 1943, however, the supply of such men was virtually exhausted. Draft calls were still running at a rate of about 400,000 per month. These calls could be met only by drafting men hitherto deferred because of their occupation or their dependency status. But which group should be called first? Should occupation or dependency constitute the primary basis of deferment? Should fathers be drafted while men without dependents remained deferred on occupational grounds?

The Selective Service System's freedom of choice in this respect had been somewhat limited in November 1942 by a Congressional requirement that agricultural workers be given special consideration for occupational deferment. Section 4 (K) of Public Law 772 (77th Cong., 2d sess., ch. 638, H. R. 7528)—the so-called "Tydings amendment"—required that local boards defer any worker "necessary to and regularly engaged in an agricultural occupation or endeavor essential to the war effort . . . so long as he remains so engaged and until such time as a satisfactory replacement can be obtained." While this simply repeated language already contained in Selective Service instructions to local boards on occupational deferment, it was a clear expression of congressional intent that farm workers be given special treatment and they were in fact given virtually a blanket exemption from this time on. By September 1, 1943, some 2,095,788 agricultural workers had been given occupational deferment, compared with 1,527,382 in all other industries. Agricultural deferments amounted to 47 percent of the number of men aged 18 to 44 who were in the agricultural labor force in 1940. Occupational deferments of other workers at this time amounted to only 7 percent of the 1940 male labor force aged 18 to 44.

WMC officials, preoccupied with the manpower needs of war in-

---

[16] Most of the remainder were under 38. Men 38 through 44 were accepted for service until Dec. 5, 1942, but only a small percentage of the men in this age bracket were able to meet the physical standards of the services.

dustry, wished to eliminate the dependency criterion as rapidly as possible and to base deferment primarily on the individual's productive contribution. Selective Service officials, on the other hand, were skeptical of alleged occupational indispensability, and were inclined to delay the drafting of men with dependents even if this meant cutting heavily into the occupationally deferred group. This feeling was particularly strong in the local boards, some of whom refused to draft fathers even after they had been instructed to do so by Selective Service headquarters. Whatever the merits of the matter, the Selective Service viewpoint was probably a more accurate reflection of congressional and public opinion than the WMC position.

A convenient way out of the difficulty might have been found if all men with dependents could have been induced to take necessary jobs in essential activities and then deferred on that ground. A step in this direction was taken on February 1, 1943, when the Selective Service System issued a list of "nondeferrable occupations." Local boards were instructed that men of draft age who did not leave these occupations—which were largely in the luxury manufacturing and service industries—by April 1 were to be classified as available for induction regardless of dependency status. The intention was to add occupations to this list from time to time and thus force more and more men with dependents into essential work. Because of the strong congressional criticism evoked by the order and for other reasons, however, this was never done.

This order was a major factor in the introduction by Senator Wheeler of the "father draft bill"—S. 763, Seventy-eighth Congress, introduced February 25, 1943—which would have exempted men with dependent children from induction regardless of their occupation. The order was rescinded on December 5, 1943, after passage by Congress of a revised version of the Wheeler bill, which is discussed below.

While discussion of alternative policies was proceeding, the pressure of high draft quotas continued inexorably. On April 12, Selective Service ordered that men with collateral dependents or with wives only were to be reclassified into I–A, leaving in III–A only "pre-Pearl Harbor fathers." By July it was apparent that fathers would have to be taken in the fairly near future. On July 31, the local boards were instructed to begin reclassifying fathers into I–A, though fathers were not to be inducted before October 1. Administrative procedures were set up to ensure that nonfathers would be called before fathers, and that fathers would be called from all local boards at about the same time. In public statements which were headlined in the press, WMC Chairman McNutt and Selective Service Director

Hershey announced that about 500,000 fathers would have to be inducted between October 1 and January 1.

As matters actually developed, however, only about 100,000 fathers were inducted during this period. Despite headquarters instructions, the local boards avoided drafting fathers by inducting the occupationally deferred at a much more rapid rate and by underfilling their quotas by about 30 percent during these months. This attitude was perhaps not unconnected with the fact that Congress began consideration of the Wheeler "father draft bill" on September 15; many boards hoped that if they held back on inductions of fathers and if the Wheeler bill passed they might never have to take this unpleasant step.

As finally enacted [17] by Congress on December 5, the Wheeler bill provided merely that fathers should be called after all available non-fathers, which was substantially what Selective Service was already trying to do. The act also contained a provision which reestablished the Selective Service System as an independent organization outside the War Manpower Commission. [18] The transfer of Selective Service to WMC in December 1942 had actually had very little effect on Selective Service operations. It had, however, displeased Selective Service officials and they were glad of an opportunity to secure a reversal of the President's decision from a Congress critical of WMC and easily disposed to blame it for the father draft problem.

Before large-scale induction of fathers got under way, the entire draft situation was changed by the Army's decision in early 1944 that its prospective needs were mainly for combat replacements and that these should be as young as possible. This pointed toward the induction of more young men who had until this time had occupational deferments. There were on February 1 some 998,400 men under 26 in the occupationally deferred classes (II–A, II–B, II–C and III–C), and of these 910,000 were nonfathers.[19]

In February the War and Navy Departments informed the President that the lag in inductions noted above was endangering the fulfilment of strategic plans. On February 26 the President sent a memorandum to Mr. McNutt and General Hershey calling for a review of all occupational deferments, particularly for men under 26. This memorandum was immediately wired to all State Selective

---

[17] 57 *Stat.* 596 (Public Law No. 197)

[18] Public Law No. 197 provided that the powers delegated to the President under the Selective Service Act could be delegated by him only to the Director of Selective Service. This was implemented by Executive Orders No. 9409 and 9410, Dec. 23, 1943, (8 *Federal Register* 17319) which respectively made the Director of Selective Service a member of WMC and delegated to him (rather than to the Chairman of WMC) the President's powers under the Selective Service Act.

[19] U. S. Congress. House. Committee on Military Affairs. Investigations of the National War Effort. Hearings before the Special Committee on Draft Deferment . . . 78th Cong., 2d sess., pursuant to H. Res. 30, March 15–31, 1944, p. 3. Of these 910,000, however, 562,400 were engaged in agriculture and were difficult to induct because of Congressional feeling that agriculture should be given special consideration.

Service directors with instructions to order such a review in their States.

This step completed a trend which had been evident for several months toward selection of men for military service on an age basis. On January 6, 1944, local boards had been instructed not to grant occupational deferments to men 18 to 21 except on certification by the State director.[20] This intensive scrutiny of occupational deferments was now extended to men 22 to 25. Selection policy had shifted definitely toward emphasis on age categories, 18 to 21, 22 to 25, 26 to 29, 30 to 33, 34 to 37—with the occupational deferment policy becoming progressively more liberal as one proceeded up the age scale. This was to remain the basic approach of Selective Service for the remainder of the war.

The new policy raised once more the problem of occupational deferment. Some local boards set about combing out all men under 26 with vigor and enthusiasm. The War Production Board was soon flooded with protests from employers and contracting officers that key men were being drafted and that production would be impaired. This problem had arisen earlier with respect to the west coast aircraft plants and a procedure had been developed under which an employer's request for deferment could be certified by the contracting officer in the plant and would then be given special consideration by local boards.[21] After discussions between the President, Mr. McNutt, Mr. Nelson, General Hershey, and the armed services, a similar procedure was developed for key men under 26. Men in this age group could be deferred by local boards only on receipt of a certification from the State director. Certain Government agencies—the War Department, Navy Department, Maritime Commission, War Production Board, Office of Defense Transportation, War Food Administration, Petroleum Administrator for War, Solid Fuels

---

[20] Local Board Memorandum 115, Mar. 16, 1942, amended Jan. 6, 1944 (mimeo.). Two steps in this direction had been taken even earlier. On June 4, 1943, at the same time that local boards were instructed not to induct fathers before Oct. 1, the State directors were told informally that all men under 25 appearing on plant replacement schedules should be scheduled out during the next 6 months. On Sept. 1, 1943, the local boards were instructed to reexamine all occupational deferments of men 18 to 25 (Local Board Memorandum 115–B). These instructions were not as compelling, however, as those issued in 1944.

[21] In August 1942 the War Department requested that no men regularly engaged in aircraft production on the west coast should be inducted for a 6-months' period. On August 2 the Director of Selective Service authorized the State directors in Washington and California to postpone the induction of such registrants even if they appeared on replacement schedules and even if their home boards were located outside these States. Between August 2 and September 4 some 1,045 men were given an emergency stay of induction. On Sept. 1, this authorization was extended for another 60 days. This procedure was subsequently extended to a number of plants not on the west coast which were making components for B–29 bombers (State Director Advice 254–A, Dec. 31, 1943). A special arrangement was also made with the War Shipping Administration for certification of merchant seamen (Local Board Memorandum 115–H, June 2, 1944, amended Oct. 28, 1944).

Administration, Rubber Director, and War Shipping Administration—were authorized to advise the State directors on the need for deferment of individuals in establishments under their jurisdiction. While their advice was not binding on the State directors, it would presumably be given heavy weight in their decisions on certification.[22]

It was obviously necessary that the agencies involved hold their requests for deferments within limits and that machinery be set up to establish a quota of deferments for each agency. The military agencies contended that this should be handled by the Production Executive Committee of WPB, on which they were heavily represented. Mr. McNutt, however, developed a plan for a new interagency committee under WMC auspices and secured a favorable vote on it in the Commission. In the end this plan was adopted, an interagency committee on occupational deferments was created in late March with Mr. McNutt as chairman, and agency quotas were set up totaling 40 thousand. The function of this committee, however, was merely to present recommendations to the Director of Selective Service, who retained the right to designate the establishment which would be permitted to operate under the plan.

The shift of Selective Service to an age basis was due to the demand of the armed services in 1944 for young men and to community pressure for drafting of occupationally deferred single men before fathers. Under the new policy, occupational deferment for men under 26 ceased to exist except for a limited number of men whose irreplaceability was certified by the employer, the responsible procurement agency, and the State Director of Selective Service. When the continuation of the war into 1945 forced a combing out of men aged 26 to 29,[23] the existing interagency committee established new deferment quotas for this group. The great majority of men over 30 continued for the remainder of the war in deferred classes—nominally on the basis of occupational essentiality, rather liberally interpreted, but actually on the basis of age and family status. The Selective Service System nevertheless followed a policy of "keeping the heat on" these men in various ways to ensure that as many as possible of them would remain in essential work.

In default of a general national service act, Selective Service applied sanctions as best it could to able-bodied men of draft age. The most important order issued for this purpose was the so-called "job-jumping" regulation (Local Board Memorandum 115–I, December 12, 1944) which provided that any occupationally deferred man who left

[22] State Director Advice 255-C, 255-D, Mar. 3, 1944; 255-E, Apr. 1, 1944. Washington, D. C.: Government Printing Office, 1944.

[23] Selective Service Regulations, Amendments No. 284 (10 *Federal Register* 2171-72) and No. 286 (10 *Federal Register* 2172-73).

his job without prior consent of his local board might be reclassified
into a class immediately available for service. The War Manpower
Commission opposed this order during discussions conducted by the
Director of OWMR, but finally agreed reluctantly when a clause was
added providing that USES referral cards should be given "serious
consideration" as evidence that a man was justified in leaving his
previous job. As its part of the arrangement, the War Department
agreed to accept "job-jumpers" for induction even if they did not
meet Army physical standards. Through June 1945 some 70,000 men
were given preinduction physical examinations and about 45,000
were inducted under this arrangement. The normal procedure with
respect to these men was to put them in Army camps and then after
a short time offer them a chance to return to their previous jobs as
members of the enlisted reserve—an opportunity which few men
declined.

Early 1944 also saw a revival of the national service issue, the
origins of which were discussed in chapter 7. A national service bill
drafted by Mr. Grenville Clark and others had been introduced by
Senator Austin and Representative Wadsworth in February 1943.[24]
Supported by the War and Navy Departments but solidly opposed
by labor, industry, and agriculture, the bill was not reported out of
committee. In December 1943, however, the War and Navy Departments convinced the President that the manpower situation was
sufficiently serious to require statutory controls. The President's
January message on the state of the union recommended the passage
of "a national service law—which, for the duration of the war, will
prevent strikes, and, with certain appropriate exceptions, will make
available for war production or for any other essential services every
able-bodied adult in this Nation." This recommendation was part
of a larger legislative program including heavier taxation, extension
of the price stabilization act, and use of subsidies to hold down the
price of food. The section of the message calling for a national service
act was inserted without consultation with the Chairman of the War
Manpower Commission.[25]

On January 11, 1944, Senator Austin and Representative Wadsworth introduced an amended version of their 1943 bill. The
amended bill declared that all men 18–65 and all women 18–50 were
obligated to perform personal services in support of the war effort.
A Director of National Service was to determine the number and
qualifications of workers needed in war industry, agriculture, and other

---

[24] S. 666 and H. R. 1742, 78th Cong., 1st sess., Feb. 8, 1943.
[25] U. S. Congress. House. Committee on Military Affairs. Investigations of the National War Effort.
Hearing before the Special Committee on Draft Deferment . . . 78th Cong., 2d sess., pursuant to H. Res.
30, March 15–31, 1944, p. 112.

essential activities. Responsibility for registering, classifying, and selecting workers, and for directing them to stay on their present jobs or assigning them to new jobs, was vested in the Selective Service System. Appeals could be taken from decisions of local boards through the regular machinery of Selective Service.

Hearings on the bill were begun in the Senate on January 12 and continued off and on until March 2.[26] Testimony in support of the bill was presented by Secretary Stimson and Under Secretary Patterson of the War Department, Secretary Knox of the Navy Department, and Admiral Land of the Maritime Commission. The main arguments advanced for the bill were that it would reduce strikes and labor turn-over, raise the morale of the armed forces, and impose equality of sacrifice on the entire pupulation. Mr. McNutt publicly announced his support of the President's request for a national service law; but the Austin-Wadsworth bill which gave administrative responsibility to the Selective Service System was disliked by WMC and no one from the Commission testified on it. William Green expressed the opposition of the AFL to the measure, and it was well known that other labor and management groups held similar views. The committee was obviously reluctant to proceed in the face of this opposition, and the bill was never reported.

After the Austin-Wadsworth bill bogged down, consideration was given to a more limited measure which would have empowered local Selective Service boards to assign IV–F's to essential work under penalty of induction into Army labor units.[27] This proposal was supported by the War Department, the Navy Department, and the Selective Service System, and was even given general approval by the War Production Board. The War Manpower Commission, industry, and labor opposed it. The fact that nothing came of the proposal was due partly to a sudden easing of the draft situation. In early April, the Army discovered that it had erred to the extent of several hundred thousand men in its figures of Army strength, and that it was already beyond the strength authorized for July 1. As a result of this, draft calls for subsequent months were considerably reduced and pressure for legislation subsided.

The controls exercised by WMC continued to the end to rest upon

---

[26] U. S. Congress. Senate. Committee on Military Affairs. National War Service Bill. Hearings on . . . S. 666, 78th Cong., 2d sess., Jan. 12–Mar. 2, 1944.

[27] U. S. Congress. House. Committee on Military Affairs. Investigations of the National War Effort. Hearings before the Special Committee on Draft Deferment . . . 78th Cong., 2d sess., pursuant to H. Res. 30, March 15–31, 1944. U. S. Congress. Senate. Committee on Military Affairs. Manpower for war production. Hearings . . . 78th Congress, 2d sess. on S.1864, May 4–29, 1944. A number of earlier "IV–F bills" had been introduced in both houses from the summer of 1942 on. See, for example, H. R. 3556 and 4329, 78th Cong., introduced by Mrs. Luce; H. R. 5615, 78th Cong., introduced by Mr. Case; S. 1702, 78th Cong., introduced by Mr. Brewster.

voluntary compliance by employers and workers, supplemented by
such influence as contracting officers chose to exert over the personnel
practices of their contractors. A comprehensive national service
system supported by penal sanctions, which might possibly have been
enacted immediately after Pearl Harbor, failed of Congressional
acceptance after that time.²⁸ Leaders of labor and management were
sincerely convinced that national service meant "regimentation" and
"forced labor," and steps to dispel their impression were not taken early
enough to be successful. Congress was extremely reluctant to touch
legislation opposed unanimously by labor, industry, and agriculture.
High officials of the Administration were aligned against each other
in shifting combinations on the question whether national service
legislation should be passed and whether, if passed, it should be
administered by WMC or Selective Service. Perhaps most important,
however, was the fact noted above that labor shortages never retarded
production sufficiently to compel action. The very great labor
reserves with which the United States entered the defense period
enabled the country to mount a very large military and production
effort without an effective manpower program. If the Nation had
been called on for a maximum effort—if the war had been longer,
military casualties heavier, the production program larger—the
absence of a tight manpower program would have had most serious
consequences.

After the spring of 1944, labor shortages were not a major problem,
though anxiety on this score was revived for a short time by the
German counteroffensive of December 1944. Military contracts,
which had been cut back considerably during the summer and fall of
1944 when the end of the European war appeared imminent, were
sharply increased after the counteroffensive began. Many plants
which had laid off workers were faced with a difficult problem of
rebuilding their labor force. At the same time, an atmosphere of
crisis was created by statements of military officials that the troops at
the front were short of ammunition and supplies, that production
programs were lagging, and that labor shortages constituted the most
serious production problem.

At the instance of the War and Navy Departments, and with the

---

²⁸ Curiously enough, no comprehensive national service law in the British sense was ever presented to
Congress for action. Drafts of such a law abounded in the War Manpower Commission, but the steadfast
opposition of the Management-Labor Policy Committee prevented their presentation. The bills which
were introduced in Congress, and which found support in Selective Service and the War and Navy Departments, were rather primitive "labor draft" laws to be administered by Selective Service and in some cases
applying to only men of military age. These bills were abhorrent not only to labor and industry but to
most Government officials experienced in dealing with labor matters. WMC, logically the proponent and
administrator of national service, thus found itself in the position of opposing all legislation on the subject
and of fighting continual rear-guard actions with the military agencies.

support of OWMR, the President included in his message on the state of the union (Jan. 6, 1945) a request for the passage of a national service act.[29] Pending action on such an act, the President recommended "that the Congress immediately enact legislation which will be effective in using the services of the 4,000,000 men now classified as IV–F in whatever capacity is best for the war effort." On the same day Representative May introduced a bill, H. R. 1752, which provided for "freezing" in their jobs of all draft registrants already engaged in essential work, and assignment of other draft registrants—principally IV–F's—to essential work through the Selective Service System. This bill strongly resembled proposals advanced in 1944 by Colonel Keesling of Selective Service and Mr. Patterson, the Under Secretary of War. The original draft of the bill provided that violators should be inducted into a special work corps under military supervision and at Army rates of pay. After testimony by the War Department that this provision might be burdensome to them, this clause was replaced by the regular criminal penalties of the Selective Service Act.

In hearings before the House Military Affairs Committee, H. R. 1752 was supported by the Selective Service System, the War and Navy Departments, the War Production Board, and the Farm Bureau Federation. Representatives of the AFL, CIO, railroad unions, Chamber of Commerce, and National Association of Manufacturers opposed the bill. The Deputy Chairman of the War Manpower Commission, testifying in the absence of the Chairman, made his lack of enthusiasm for the bill reasonably clear despite the limitations imposed on him by the official Administration position. The bill was reported favorably by the Committee on January 24 and was passed by the House on February 1 with only brief discussion.

By the time the May bill reached the Senate Military Affairs Committee, WMC had prepared a counteroffensive. First, it secured an agreement through Judge Byrnes' office that all the interested agencies would recommend to the Senate committee that administration of the measure be vested in OWMR; it was hoped that OWMR would then delegate its power under the Act to WMC rather than to Selective Service. Second, WMC prepared a substitute bill giving statutory support to existing WMC regulations and secured the consideration of this bill by the Committee. Third, the groups represented on the WMC Labor-Management Committee were induced to testify in favor of the substitute proposal in the hope of heading off

---

[29] The ability of the military agencies to press for manpower legislation was strengthened at this time by the presence of General Clay (formerly head of the Army Service Forces' Production Division) as Deputy Director of OWMR, while the position of the War Manpower Commission was weakened by the absence of its Chairman on a European trip.

passage of the May bill. This was the first occasion on which the major labor and management groups had supported any legislative proposal in this field.

The bill reported by the Senate committee on February 22 was substantially the WMC substitute bill. It authorized continuation of existing WMC hiring regulations under the general supervision of OWMR; penalties were imposed on employers for violation of these regulations, but there was no provision for penalties on employees. It thus differed radically in conception from the bill passed by the House, which was essentially a "labor draft" law applying to men of military age.

The bill reported by the Senate committee was passed by the Senate and the two bills sent to conference. The bill recommended by the conference committee on March 26 was in general the Senate bill with the addition of provisions for "freezing" labor in designated areas or activities and imposing penalties on workers who violated such orders. This bill was considered by supporters of the May bill to be too weak to meet the problem. The conference report was rejected by the House and the bill sent back to conference, where it remained until the rapidly approaching end of the European war removed the pressure for action. Had the war lasted another 3 months, legislation along the general lines of the Senate bill would probably have passed.

While discussion of legislation was proceeding, the War Manpower Commission was attempting to demonstrate that essential labor requirements could be met through an extension of its existing area programs. In several critical areas an attempt was made during February and March 1945 to compel transference of workers from less essential to more essential plants by reducing the employment ceilings of less essential employers. A basic difficulty was that wages and conditions in the plants to which workers were to be transferred were not sufficiently attractive to make transference palatable to the workers, and the War Manpower Commission had no power to change this situation. Moreover, with the end of the war obviously near, workers were unwilling to move from permanent to temporary jobs. Employers and unions were at best critical of compulsory transference and in some cases strongly opposed the program. In New Bedford, which soon came to be regarded as a test case, the program broke down entirely. In the other areas relatively few workers were transferred. Thus the program, which was intended to show that essential plants could be manned without legislation by an appeal to workers, unions, and employers in each area, ended by demonstrating the opposite. It proved impossible to compel workers to change jobs without a statute providing authority over employers as well as workers and including some guarantee to the transferred workers of reemployment in their previous jobs.

As the end of the European war approached, production schedules were once more reduced. Complaints of unemployment were heard for the first time in 3 years. The question of how men laid off from war jobs could most readily be reabsorbed into peacetime industry received increased attention. This was part of the larger problem of planning for the economic transition from war to peace, which came increasingly to the fore during 1945.

POSTLUDE TO WAR

Postlude to War

THE preceding pages have surveyed, in necessarily broad terms, the reorganization of the Nation's economy and government for the tasks imposed by war. The major changes necessary in government and in the economy to effectuate this purpose had largely been made by the end of 1943 or early in 1944. From the point of view of the prosecution of the war, the period from the spring of 1944 until the end of German and Japanese resistance was largely one of successful operation of the machinery previously erected for the task.

Were we to adopt a narrow definition of our subject matter this volume might end here. But the task of winning the war was not limited to a mobilization adequate to the military defeat of our enemies nor is the significance of the war experience to be summed up in the word "victory."

Our policies on postwar international relationships, our peace terms to our enemies and our plans for assuring the perpetuation of peace were developing significantly long before VE- and VJ-days. Almost at the same time that our production of munitions was reaching its peak late in 1943, and as victory seemed near, administrative preparations had to be undertaken to deal with such domestic matters as the settlement of war contract claims, the reconversion of industry, the reemployment of demobilized military personnel and war-industry workers, and the disposition of surplus war property. The nature of these problems, the goals to be achieved, and the methods by which they might be best attained were the subjects of that same process of free and thorough discussion by which the problems of defense and war had been thrashed out. From such public examination of problems and alternative courses of action came that reconciliation of divergent points of view which permitted the establishment of policies and administrative machinery which were to guide the Nation through the difficult days of postwar readjustment. The following chapter treats of these developments.

The events described in the first fifteen chapters of this volume culminated in victory and therein had their justification. A principal objective of this analysis, however, has been to ascertain what might be learned about our system of government from the process by which we went about securing victory. A volume such as this should properly end with a careful and considered appraisal of the significance of the events discussed.

The war years represent too profound an experience in the history of American democr cy to permit an evaluation by any single group of observers which will supply an adequate appreciation of its full meaning. Some appraisal of our war experience is possible, however, if we seek perspective by contrasting our methods with those of our major enemies, Germany nd Japan. Such comparison, undertaken briefly in chapter 16, reveals a vigor in American democracy which its citizens, who participate in its day-to-day operations, may not always appreciate and which neither the Germans nor the Japanese understood. War is a cruel test of the soundness of a nation's political and economic structure. Our political system, while retaining the important elements of individual freedom, succeeded in applying the Nation's resources to a national task in a manner which by comparison with that of Japan and Germany was highly efficient.

CHAPTER

15

Preparing for Peace

VICTORY over Germany came in May 1945 and was received with quiet elation. The death of Franklin Delano Roosevelt a few weeks earlier, and the realization of the magnitude of the task that lay ahead dampened public jubilation. But the opportunity for vociferous celebration was not to be long delayed. Less than 4 months after the remnants of the Nazi armies had signed terms of unconditional surrender, the Emperor of Japan requested an armistice. The formal surrender on September 1 on the battleship *Missouri* in Tokyo harbor was almost an anticlimax.

The task of organizing the Nation's energies and resources so as to focus upon the enemy all possible pressure had now been completed. Victory had been earned at an incalculable cost. Two hundred and ninety-six thousand American lives had been lost; many of the 680,000 wounded suffered permanent physical handicaps. The Nation had supplied its armies and those of her Allies with vast amounts of supplies and equipment; its natural resources had been heavily drawn upon in their production. The Nation would not soon be able to forget the national debt of $278 billion accumulated during these years.

The United States now turned from the bloody and destructive business of war to the task of rebuilding the lives of peoples and nations. The scars of war were deep and many unhealed wounds remained, not only in the bombed cities and villages of Europe and Asia and in the wrecked lives of those who had lived in them, but also in the economic, the political, and the social fabric of this unbombed Nation. For the United States had not been able to avoid some curtailment of cherished rights and privileges in the task of proving itself truly the arsenal of democracy. Victory held for us the hope

461

that it might be possible to return to the peacetime ways of life with the added knowledge gained during the war. Such desirable objectives were not to be taken for granted. The obstacles were many, bearing such names as demobilization, reconversion, decontrol, rehabilitation, inflation, surpluses, and shortages. There were few who looked upon the period in which such problems had to be solved as an easy one.

The measure of the task might be read in the magnitude of the mobilization which had been accomplished. At its peak the armed forces totaled 12.3 million men and women who had been taken from their normal occupations and trained to military duties. From the beginning of Selective Service to VJ-day, more than 15,000,000 individuals had experienced military service. Industry and agriculture had applied themselves to satisfying an insatiable demand by turning out an unparalleled volume of products. The quarterly rate of the Nation's output of goods and services had risen from $34 billion in the last quarter of 1941 to a peak of $52 billion (current prices) in the second quarter of 1945. The annual output rose from $96 billion in 1939 to in excess of $197 billion in 1944 and 1945. The total for the war period approximated $687 billion of which $273 billion was devoted to war purposes.

To achieve this tremendous expansion of production, not only was the use of available productive resources greatly intensified, but the supply of labor and of facilities was also greatly augmented. To replace the men drawn into the armed forces and to meet the labor needs of the war program, women had left their homes and youths their schools to enter industry. As a result, the total labor force was expanded from 54.5 million in 1940 to 64.6 million in 1945. Employment in the munitions industries had expanded 240 percent since 1939, and the manufacturing industries in 1945 accounted for 24 percent of all nonagricultural employment as compared with 12 percent in 1939. This augmented labor force helped to man $16 billion in new facilities built by the Government. Marked changes had occurred in the character of productive activities. Industries which had been insignificant parts of the economy in the days of peace became giant employers. The aircraft, shipbuilding, and ammunition industries occupied 5.6 million workers at their peak; only 0.7 million in 1939.

The Nation's production record was not accomplished without sweeping changes in its economic structure. Over the war period, governmental regulations and restrictions invaded one area of economic life after another and with constantly increasing stringency. Freedom to operate manufacturing facilities and to use raw materials and fabricated items was severely restricted under the orders of the War Production Board; freedom to buy was sharply curtailed under the priority regulations of the War Production Board, the ration restrictions of the Office of Price Administration, and the set-aside orders of the War Food Administration. Much of the seller's freedom to ask and the buyer's freedom to offer a price vanished under the sweeping price ceilings and regulations issued by OPA. The freedom to trade with foreign countries was hemmed in by regulations on all sides. Civilian use of the transportation system was subject to the priority of military travel and transport needs. Choice of occupation and the right to change jobs suffered curtailment by action of the Selective Service System and the War Manpower Commission. The National War Labor Board intervened in the free bargaining between employers and employees whenever disputes arose or wage increases were a part of the bargain.

With the coming of peace, the Nation turned to the task of dismantling the war-born governmental and economic structure. Members of the armed forces were to be discharged and absorbed into the civilian labor force, employment for all in peacetime pursuits must be provided, the distorted industrial structure had to be converted to producing the needs of a peacetime population, and many other problems raised by the transition to peace had to be solved. The nature of the problems involved and the means of their solution had long been the subject of study both within and outside the Government. The success of the reconversion period in attaining a healthy economy lay in large part in the nature of the preparations that had been made.

Early Planning

Concern over the effects of the war upon the United States began with the outbreak of hostilities on the European continent. Even before Pearl Harbor, Federal agencies were studying the effects upon the Nation of its defense activities and endeavoring to determine its probable role in international affairs once peace had been regained. After Pearl Harbor, it was clear that the character and the magnitude of mobilization would determine the nature of postwar problems and planning necessarily waited upon the full development of governmental policy, the attainment of its objectives, and the course of the war. Moreover, there were those who feared that attention to postwar problems was interfering with the complete devotion of the Nation's energies to the prosecution of the war. Among such opponents of planning were high Government officials, particularly in the military services.

Despite such difficulties and opposition, analysis of the impact of war began early and was carried on without interruption by a number of agencies. Among the most aggressive of Federal agencies in this field was the National Resources Planning Board. The work of this organization came to an end when the agency was terminated by Congress in August 1943. Nevertheless, postwar problems received much attention from the Nation's legislators. Before the end of 1942, the Congress on the President's recommendation had taken action to ease the adjustments of agriculture in the postwar period by authorizing the Commodity Credit Corporation to make loans at 90 percent of parity on basic crops for two full years after the formal termination of hostilities.[1] While the measure was designed to induce maximum agricultural production for war needs, it was also the earliest significant action dealing with reconversion taken by the Government. Congress continued in the months that followed to give attention to the problems of peace. Indeed, there were few organizations, Government or private, which did not find it possible and desirable to assign small staffs to work unobtrusively on such problems.[2]

The invasion of Italy in the fall of 1943, the satisfactory progress of the war in Russia, and indications of the mounting volume of the preparations for invasion of Northwestern Europe aroused increasing expression of the public interest in the problems of reconversion. Official governmental recognition was also forthcoming. The President had already in July requested of Congress demobilization legislation which would define the Federal Government's responsibilities in the task of readjustment to civil life of the members of the armed forces. In November, the Senate established a Special Committee on Post-War Economic Policy and Planning, under the chairmanship of Senator Walter F. George,[3] which began hearings on war contract cancellations, disposition of surplus property, and industrial demobilization and reconversion. The Chairman of the War Production Board, Mr. Nelson, testified before one of these hearings that WPB had begun planning for reconversion.[4] The Truman Committee likewise undertook investigations in these fields.[5] With the announcement by Justice Byrnes of the appointment of Bernard Baruch to study the problems of reconversion as head of a unit in his Office of War Mobilization, that office assumed leadership among Government agencies in planning for the transition period. All of these actions

---

[1] 56 *Stat.* 765.

[2] Galloway, George B., *Post-War Planning in the United States.* New York: Twentieth Century Fund, 1942; also Senate Document No. 106, 78th Cong., 1st sess., *Post-War Economic Policy and Planning;* and Lorwin, L. L., *Post-War Plans of the United Nations.* New York: Twentieth Century Fund, 1943, pp. 42–72.

[3] The House established a similar committee in the spring of 1944 under the chairmanship of Congressman William F. Colmer.

[4] U. S. Congress. Senate. Committee on Post-War Economic Policy and Planning. Hearings. 78th Cong., 1st sess., p. 410.

[5] U. S. Congress. Senate. Special Committee Investigating the National Defense Program. Hearings, 78th Cong., pursuant to S. Res. 6, p. 8613 et seq.

reflected a feeling of a need for haste in preparing a reconversion program. The announcement in December 1943, of the first cut-back of materials in the war program—the closing down of four aluminum pot lines—suggested that these moves were not premature.

By this time also, public thinking had reached one firm determination on postwar reconstruction. Reconversion of the Nation to a peacetime basis could not mean a return to the economic conditions of 1935–39. Rather, the postwar economy, toward which reconversion policy would be guided, would be one which would reflect as closely as possible the wartime intensity of resource utilization. How this was to be accomplished and what it meant were matters not easily definable in generally accepted terms. High level production, full employment, gross national product of 160 to 180 billion dollars, "close to 60 million jobs," were some of the forms in which these desires were given expression.

The President, in his annual budget message in January 1944, approached the problems of reconversion in some detail, indicating that the period of offensive war—the fourth and final stage of the war—was beginning. Pointing out that "demobilization begins long before hostilities end," the President outlined the objective to be reached in the postwar period as a "permanently high level of income and a correspondingly high standard of living." To achieve this end, the President said that "there must be concerted efforts by industry, labor, and Government and a well-planned demobilization program. As more and more materials are released from war service and production, such resources must be channeled to civilian production, consumption, and employment. The soldier, the worker, the businessman, and the farmer, must have assurance against economic chaos."[6] He proposed as a major aim of reconversion policy the stimulation of private investment and employment. In this message the President discussed "certain aspects" of the reconversion program under four principal headings:

1. *Contract termination, disposal of surplus property, and industrial reconversion.*—The President suggested that the policies followed would be of major significance in determining the speed and effectiveness of reconversion and, that a unified program was needed. He further stated that recommendations were in preparation by Mr. Baruch and the Joint Contract Termination Board in the Office of War Mobilization.

2. *Manpower demobilization and reemployment.*—The President urged that care be taken to prevent the weakening of existing job

---

[6] *The Budget of the U. S. Government for the fiscal year ending June 30, 1945,* Presidential Message Transmitting the Budget, p. x.

placement machinery and that a unified national employment and counselling organization supplemented by adequate job retraining, education, and rehabilitation services was essential.

3. *Public works planning.*—The President gave as his opinion that public works might be needed but that planning for such works should be closely coordinated and adapted to the broad economic situation. The Bureau of the Budget was assigned the task of coordinating various phases of a shelf of emergency public works and improvement programs. (The President, a few days later sent to the Congress a recommendation for a Federal highway program involving the postwar reconstruction, in cooperation with the States, of some 35,000 miles of needed highways.)

4. *Veterans legislation and social security.*—The President called attention to his recommendations of the preceding July for a military personnel demobilization program including mustering-out pay and educational benefits. He also recommended extension of social security coverage and an expansion and liberalization of unemployment compensation.

The President's statement was followed within a few weeks by a report of Messrs. Baruch and Hancock on reconversion.[7] Reconversion had now become a problem of official concern. The fact that the Baruch report was quickly followed by three Executive orders providing for the execution of many of its recommendations gave it the weight of official policy. The report was frequently used in the months ahead as justification for taking action on postwar problems. Although concerned largely with the financial aspects of industrial reconversion, with only relatively brief references to the human side of demobilization and the relaxation of Government controls, the report formed the core about which detailed policy development and administrative planning were to develop.

In establishing the Baruch unit to study reconversion, the Office of War Mobilization had taken leadership in the Government's planning and preparation for reconversion. This function, it and its successor agency continued throughout the war and in the reconversion period. The President, acting on the Baruch recommendations, assigned to OWM the policy-making responsibilities in the fields of surplus property disposal, contract termination, and reemployment. The administrative structure, including the constituent agencies which thus developed, were transferred by Executive order into the legislative organization established by Congress with the passage of the War Mobilization Act of 1944 in October of that year.[8] The Office of War Mobilization and Reconversion therein

---

[7] Senate Document No. 154, 78th Cong., 2d sess.: Baruch, Bernard M., and Hancock, John M., *Report on War and Post-War Adjustment Policy.*
[8] 58 Stat. 785.

provided for was given specific responsibilities for most phases of reconversion. Its jurisdiction was much broader than that of the Office of War Mobilization set up by the President's Executive order. Among other functions with which it was charged by Congress was "to promote and assist in the development of demobilization and reconversion plans by Executive agencies . . . and settling controversies between Executive agencies in the development and administration of such."

From this point on, preparation for peace was largely initiated and guided by the new agency. Its requests to the interested Government organizations involved for statements of their plans for reconversion stimulated such preparations; its actions in resolving stalemates between agencies were important steps in furthering action on matters relating to the coming era of peace. In its formal quarterly reports to Congress and in the frequent statements by its Director before congressional committees, are described the preparations made for the period of transition between victory over Germany and final victory over Japan as well as for the larger task of postwar reconstruction. These things the Office accomplished in a variety of ways. It established a Reconversion Planning Committee representing 28 agencies for the purposes of interchange and coordination of plans. A Deputy Director for Production was appointed to expedite plant reconversion and to review cutbacks to assure termination of unnecessary work. OWMR also established a Construction Coordinator who, working with WPB, OPA, and the National Housing Agency, sought to facilitate postwar construction programs. In addition, the OWMR developed staff which worked closely with the War Production Board, the Office of Price Administration, and other agencies in the development of reconversion planning within the sphere of responsibility of those agencies.

Planning World Peace

While this volume is largely concerned with the impact of the war upon the Nation's domestic organization and activities, the extremely important developments during the war period looking towards the Nation's participation in world affairs when peace came demand brief attention.

The effect upon public opinion of the international events of the war period is graphically shown in chart 56. Indications of the direction in which public leadership was moving came in September 1943 when the Mackinac conference of Republican Governors and Congressmen adopted a declaration favoring United States participation in international efforts to preserve the peace. Within a month both the House of Representatives and the Senate had endorsed American participation in international cooperation and organization to maintain the peace.[9]

Meanwhile the Executive branch of the Government was taking action expressive of the public's attitude. Progress on the crucial task of assuring peace in the postwar era began when the four major powers at the Moscow Conference of Foreign Ministers in 1943 pledged themselves to unity and cooperation in keeping the peace and in seeking peaceful means for settlement of international problems.

CHART 56. *Public Opinion on Membership in World Peace Organization.*
The question asked was: "Do you think the U. S. should join a world organization with police power to maintain world peace?"

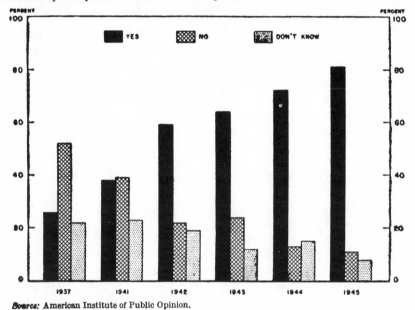

Source: American Institute of Public Opinion.

These four powers met again at Dumbarton Oaks in Washington, and in October 1944, announced proposals for a United Nations Security Organization. At the Yalta Conference between Britain, Russia, and the United States, agreement was reached for a conference to draft a charter for a world security organization. Fifty nations participated at the San Francisco Conference in the early summer of 1945 and formulated the United Nations Charter. The charter was ratified by the United States Senate in July 1945, and the United Nations Organization began functioning late that year.

Among other international problems those relating to food and to

---

[9] Fulbright Resolution (H. Con. Res. 25, 78th Cong., 1st sess., agreed to Sept. 21, 1943); and Connally Resolution (S. Res. 192, 78th Congress, 1st sess., agreed to Nov. 5, 1943.)

international financial matters were of particular importance. The United Nations Relief and Rehabilitation Conference met in 1943 to lay plans for the relief of war devastated countries. UNRRA was established as a result and participation by the United States was approved by Congress in November 1943. Some 7 months later a United Nations Conference on Food and Agriculture was held which resulted in recommendations that a permanent international commission on basic food supplies be established to assure more reasonable and adequate controls. Congress accepted the recommendations in the summer of 1945.

The need for developing adequate machinery to provide financial credits for postwar reconstruction and resource development led to discussions between Great Britain and the United States on the problem of exchange stabilization and international investment. These problems were the subject of the Monetary and Financial Conference at Bretton Woods in the summer of 1944. Agreement was there reached upon plans for the establishment of an International Bank for reconstruction and also upon an International Monetary Fund. Both received the approval of Congress in 1945, which also extended for 3 years the Reciprocal Trade Agreements Act.

In these actions and others the Nation had by VJ-day laid the ground-work toward American participation in world affairs and the maintenance of world peace.

Demobilization—the Human Side

At the peak of our war effort, some 45 percent of the Nation's labor force was enrolled in the military services or engaged in war production.[10] Mobilization had vastly disrupted the peacetime distribution of occupations and greatly expanded the number of individuals gainfully employed. The coming of peace would mean for many millions of people the cessation of their wartime employment and the need to find new sources of livelihood. The speed of industrial reconversion would determine in large part the degree to which war mobilization would result in unemployment but even with high levels of economic activity the readjustment of these millions of persons to peacetime pursuits was a task of great magnitude.

The Federal government already possessed the basic administrative machinery to carry out its responsibilities in facilitating demobilization. Demobilized soldiers and sailors would turn to the Veterans' Administration; unemployed civilians would seek help from the Unemployment Compensation System of the Social Security Board; both would expect guidance from the Employment Service in securing new

---

[10] *Survey of Current Business*, August 1944, p. 6.

employment. In addition, the veteran could turn to his local Selective Service Board for assistance in securing reemployment in his old job, a task with which Congress had charged it.[11]

To handle the task of planning human demobilization and reemployment and to coordinate the various agencies involved in such a program the President adopted the suggestion of Baruch and Hancock and established an Administrator of Reemployment and Retraining in the Office of War Mobilization. The Director of this organization was charged with the responsibility of developing programs for the absorption into the peacetime economy of persons discharged or released from the armed forces and from war work, and for the adequate care of disabled members of the armed forces.

The first action of General Hines, the Director, was to establish in each State a Veterans' Service Committee, composed of representatives of the Selective Service System, War Manpower Commission, and the Veterans' Administration to secure the establishment of veterans' information service centers.[12] The State and local communities were eager to cooperate in the establishment of coordinated and integrated activities in behalf of veterans. Ultimately more than 2,700 veterans' information service centers were established.

Aside from this activity, the Office accomplished little. The planning function delegated to the Administration was of such far-reaching character, as General Hines recognized,[13] as to be carried on largely elsewhere within OWM and other agencies better equipped for the task.

Meanwhile, the Administration had moved to strengthen both of the agencies which would play key roles in demobilization—the Veterans' Administration and the United States Employment Service. General Omar Bradley was named Veterans' Administrator on August 15, 1945, and inaugurated both a sweeping reorganization as well as an expansion of the agency's program and staff.

The USES was well equipped as a result of its wartime experience to handle the share of the task of peacetime adjustments which would fall to it. The chief danger to its effective operations was seen in the probable disappearance of its integrated and coordinated activities with the return of the services to State control. While the Congress refused to acquiesce in the President's request for the retention of the employment offices under Federal control during the reconversion period, his pocket veto of the First Supplemental Surplus Appropriation Recision Act 1946, continued Federal direction for an indefinite

---

[11] 54 *Stat.* 890. The responsibilities of Selective Service System under the act are interpreted in *Selective Service*, vol. 4, No. 4, Apr. 1945.

[12] 9 *Federal Register* 5391.

[13] U. S. Congress. House. Special Committee on Post-War Economic Policy and Planning. **Hearings** on H. Res. 408, 78th Cong., 2d sess. Exhibit No. 9, General Hines' Testimony, pp. 467-473.

time. In addition to such actions by the Executive branch, it was necessary that Congress determine the policies to be followed. In particular, it was essential that Congress determine the provisions it wished to make in assistance of the veterans of World War II, and that it review the adequacy of the unemployment compensation programs established in peacetime for the far heavier, war-created burdens that might be thrown upon it.

The President in October 1943, had urged upon Congress the need for legislation to facilitate the return of veterans to civilian life and the Congress responded to the suggestion with alacrity. In November, it passed legislation providing mustering-out pay for the Armed Services, and the following June it provided in the G. I. Bill of Rights[14] support for veterans in every phase of readjustment to civilian life.

The President also urged upon the Congress on a number of occasions the necessity for reviewing the adequacy of the existing unemployment compensation system to meet the problems of reconversion unemployment. A number of large groups who might be expected to suffer from reconversion unemployment, particularly maritime workers and Government employees, were not covered by existing legislation. Moreover, although the State unemployment compensation reserves had accumulated large resources during the war, there was grave danger that a substantial portion of these funds would be unavailable to meet reconversion needs because of limitations in State laws. Such laws restricted both maximum weekly unemployment compensation payments as well as the maximum number of weeks for which such payments could be made. These provisions had been subject to much criticism as inadequate to the needs of the unemployed and well below the capacity of the State funds to pay.

The battle in Congress on the reconversion bills in which these recommendations were incorporated was fought out in terms of the ability of the States to measure the needs of their unemployed and to administer their own programs. In the end all legislative proposals were defeated and no changes designed to broaden aid to the unemployed were made.

With the approach of victory in Europe, the armed forces announced their plans for demobilization on the basis of individual point scores computed on service experience.[15] After VJ-day, demobilization proceeded with phenomenal speed (chart 57), although never fast enough to satisfy the public. With the war over, the essentially nonprofessional character of the nation's armed forces once again

---

[14] 58 *Stat.* 284. This was followed within a few days by the Veterans Preference Act of 1944 (58 *Stat.* 387) giving veterans preferred status in employment in the Federal Civil Service. Liberalization of some of the provisions of the Servicemen's Readjustment Act were provided for by Congress in December 1945.

[15] Statement by Maj. Gen. Walter F. Tompkins, May 10, 1945. The Army had announced an earlier discharge plan on Sept. 6, 1944. The Navy announced its plan July 20, 1945.

CHART 57. *Mobilization and Demobilization of the Armed Forces.*

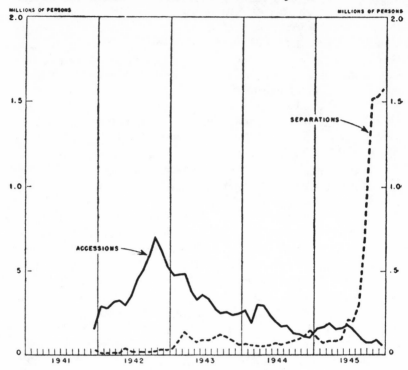

Source: War and Navy Departments.

became apparent. The men in the services wanted discharge without regard to the possible continuing needs of the Nation for military strength. Such wishes found strong support from their families at home. As a consequence of these demands, expressed in the press and through the Congress, demobilization proceeded at a pace far above that anticipated by military leaders and, in fact, limited only by the capacity of available transportation. Although the method remained that of the point system, with critical scores progressively liberalized,[16] the plans of the military to maintain a substantial prepared military force with newly trained draftees available in adequate numbers proved in fact unfeasible.

The demobilization of the war industries was likewise rapid. Over 2.5 million workers were released from war jobs in the month following the Japanese surrender. Employment in the aircraft, ammunition, and shipbuilding industries in August 1945, had fallen almost 50 percent below the May level, 1.2 million individuals losing their jobs

---

[16] By the Army Sept. 3 and 20, 1944, and Nov. 16, 1945; by the Navy Sept. 10, 1945, Oct. 24, Nov. 21, and Dec. 4, 1945.

in these industries. Employment in industries which could quickly reconvert to civilian production declined little, on the other hand.

Demobilization—the Financial Responsibility of Government

In the process of harnessing the nation's productive capacity to the requirements of war, the Government had become the purchaser of almost half of the products of industry; the owner of an unparalleled quantity of fabricated goods and raw materials, and an important group of manufacturing facilities. The attainment of victory would wipe out all but a minute fraction of the demands of government for industry's products and would make much of the Government's accumulated inventories unnecessary for war purposes. The policies which the Government might follow in settling its terminated contracts with industry would go far in determining industry's ability to turn speedily to producing for the civilain market. There was no more certain way of assuring abundant employment opportunities than to make possible a prompt conversion of industry to the production of the goods so much in demand on the civilian markets. On the other hand, the character of that market in many areas would be strongly influenced by the Government's policy in disposing of its surpluses.

In carrying out the war program, the Government's procurement agencies dealt with the Nation's business firms on a contractual basis. Over the war period more than 350,000 contracts were made between the Government and some 40,000 prime contractors. In addition, many times that number of contracts were made between these prime contractors and their suppliers or subcontractors.

A substantial part of the liquid capital as well as of the credit of the Nation's industrial firms was tied up by war contracts in purchases of raw materials and components and in fabricated parts.[17] Payments for delivered goods were made expeditiously but when contracts were canceled, payments waited upon the determination of the exact amount of the Government's obligations. Moreover, even if a firm possessed adequate liquid assets, it would in many cases find its plants clogged with Government-owned machinery, semifabricated equipment, and material. Until these were either purchased by the operator of the plant, or removed by the Government, resumption of the plant's normal production would be difficult and in many cases impos-

---

[17] Assistant Secretary of the Navy James V. Forrestal pointed out in 1943 that "American industry cannot stand a prolonged delay in settling its war contracts. Five automobile companies, which in 1939 had $3.30 of current assets for every dollar of current liabilities, had by the end of 1942 only $1.96 of current assets for every dollar of current liabilities. The manufacturing companies in the electrical, steel, rubber, and other industries, with $4.26 of current assets for every dollar of current liabilities in 1939, now have only $1.86. Industry has insufficient fat on which to live during a prolonged thawing out of frozen war contracts." Navy Department Press Release, Nov. 23, 1943, of Mr. Forrestal's address at the Wharton School of Finance and Commerce.

sible. Machinery was therefore necessary which would expeditiously and with uniform fairness settle terminated contracts so that funds would be quickly available for normal operations.

The experience in the International Harvester cut-back made in April 1943 greatly stimulated public interest in the problem.[18] Congress conducted several investigations and numerous bills were proposed.[19] The War Department had already developed detailed regulations which covered the subject which were used by all its various branches.[20] The Navy was similarly developing its own policies as were the other agencies.

Business interests, however, had in numerous ways expressed concern over the diversity of practices and policies that existed or were coming into being. The War Production Board's Procurement Policy Board had for some time been attempting to develop coordinated policies acceptable to all the procurement agencies. In spite of this effort, the War Department proposed in October 1943, the establishment of a contract termination board composed of representatives from the principal procurement agencies which had the function of determining policies of general applicablity. Such a board, with broad representation of Government agencies, was established in November 1943, by the Director of War Mobilization under the title of the Joint Contract Termination Board.

The preliminary conclusions of this Board's deliberations were largely incorporated in specific and detailed fashion in the Baruch-Hancock report. Among its recommendations was the settlement of terminated contracts by the contracting agencies through direct negotiations by trained termination settlement teams. These should operate on the principles of speed, finality, and protection of the Government. Policies should be developed by the Joint Contract Termination Board so that auditing would not "cripple the Nation into a panic." The Comptroller General's function should be limited to a simple mathematical check with the right to reopen settlement for fraud reserved.

These recommendations gave assurance to industry that much of its working capital would be quickly freed for reconversion. Working capital supplies were supplemented by interim financing arrangements provided for by private banks and the Reconstruction Finance Corporation. The report further recommended that the Government

---

[18] This cancellation of a $217 million contract involving 11 plants of the company, 438 principal subcontractors, and perhaps a thousand other subcontractors and suppliers required 16 months to settle.

[19] Senate Report No. 537, pt. 1, 78th Cong., 1st sess. House Report No. 809, 78th Cong., 1st sess. House Report No. 1268, 78th Cong., 1st sess. U. S. Congress. Senate. Committee on Military Affairs. Preliminary Report on Contract Termination (of the War Contract Subcommittee), 78th Cong., 1st sess., Subcommittee Print No. 1, Dec. 23, 1943.

[20] U. S. Army Service Forces. Procurement Regulations, No. 15, Aug. 14, 1943, War Department Basic Policy Statement

remove its property from private plants within 60 days after the receipt of the contractor's inventory.

A number of the Baruch-Hancock recommendations had been placed into effect some days before the appearance of the report when OWM approved a uniform termination article for fixed supply contracts.[21] Legislative action was needed to meet other important problems encountered by the Joint Contract Termination Board. This was supplied by the passage in July of the Contract Settlement Act of 1944, which established an Office of Contract Settlement as a part of OWMR. Broad principles were laid down in the statute under which its director and his advisory board were to operate. These were by and large similar to the policies which had already been developed by the Joint Contract Termination Board. The act, however, settled the controversy over the functions of the Comptroller General by limiting his function to a post audit review for fraud. The act also authorized provision of interim financing by the procurement agencies, either by advance payments on the claim filed by the contractor, or through direct or guaranteed loans. Also of significance were the provisions for permissive company-wide settlement and for settlements with subcontractors. The act established an appeal board to which a contractor might take complaints after having exhausted the appeals machinery provided by the procurement agencies. To meet the impact of an increasing volume of contract cancellations, the Office of Contract Settlement undertook extensive training programs both of governmental as well as industrial personnel.

The test of these preparations came with VJ-day. The flow of contract cancelations began some days before the Japanese surrender. During August the War Department canceled 70,848 contracts. By the end of 1945, of the wartime total of 303,000 canceled contracts, all but 52,000 had been settled although the number remaining included a large proportion of the more difficult cases (chart 58). These contracts represented claims of $64 billion. Almost half of that sum had been settled. While the face value of the claims remaining to be settled was very large, available evidence suggests that the machinery to finance a contractor in the period between the filing of his claim and its final settlement operated smoothly in reconversion. Partial payments on filed claims and guaranteed termination loans (T-loans) proved more than adequate to meet business needs. The advances made, including partial payments, termination loans, Government guaranteed production loans, and others, at the end of 1945 totaled $2.5 billion. In view of the magnitude of the Government's contractual obligations, this was a small sum.

---

[21] 9 *Federal Register* 478–80.

CHART 58. *War Contract Terminations and Settlements.*

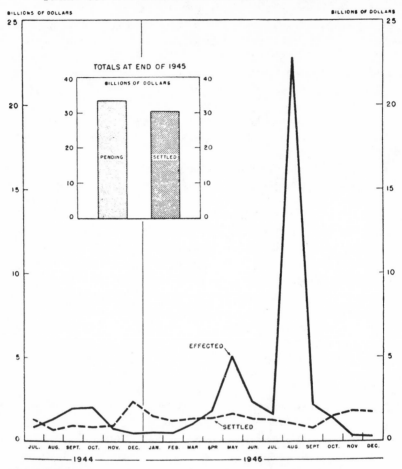

Source: Office of Contract Settlement.

Also of great importance to business was the work of the Office of Contract Settlement in supervising plant clearance of Government equipment. Congress had concurred with Messrs. Baruch and Hancock in recognizing the need to clear plants quickly of Government-owned equipment and material by requiring the removal of such property within 60 days after the operator filed an inventory. Administration of this policy required cooperation with RFC for storage space¹ with the Surplus Property Board in acceptance of surplus property, as well as with the procurement agencies who were owners of the property. This coordination was accomplished by an inter-agency committee. Although the volume of plant clearance rose very sharply after VJ-day, the work was, in fact, expedited and less than 6 percent of industry requests required more than 60 days to complete. The difficulties which had been anticipated in securing adequate storage space did not materialize.

The success achieved in the handling of terminated contracts was not duplicated, up to the end of 1945, in the handling of surplus goods. The problems faced were, of course, far more difficult; there was not the same clear-cut objective which commanded universal agreement; conflicting interests were more numerous and powerful. Moreover, the problem of the proper organization and administrative machinery for surplus disposal was not fully solved but continually plagued the Government.

The task of disposing of surplus property was extraordinarily difficult. Ascertainment of what there was to be sold, involving detailed inventories by the owning agencies, was in itself a gigantic task with hundreds of thousands of different types of goods scattered virtually all over the globe to be located and described, their condition determined, and their marketability decided. The establishment of sale policies in the face of the pressures and conflicting interests was also a task of great difficulty. Prices to be asked for the property and the timing of the sales were particularly vexatious problems.

As in the case of the administration of contract termination problems, the initial Government action was based on the recommendations of the Baruch-Hancock report. In accordance with that report, the President established by Executive order [22] a Surplus War Property Administration within the OWM which vested in an Administrator, assisted by a Policy Board, the general supervision and direction of the disposal of surplus property. The order further followed the Baruch-Hancock recommendation closely by assigning the disposal of surplus goods among four agencies according to the type of commodity involved. Mr. Will Clayton was appointed Administrator.

The President acted in the face of the fact that Congress had had surplus property legislation under consideration for more than a year. Surplus property disposal was becoming an acute problem and performance of the duties delegated to the SWPA was urgently needed. Moreover, it was indicated in the Executive order that no substitute for legislation was intended, but that congressional action was essential. Such legislation was not forthcoming for another 7 months.

The first problem demanding action by SWPA was that of expediting sales of contract termination inventories delayed largely because of the absence of authority or policy on which to act. A policy statement by SWPA served to clear the road.[23] Thereafter SWPA

[22] Executive Order No. 9425, Feb. 19, 1944, 9 *Federal Register* 2071.

[23] Surplus War Property Administration Statement of Policies to be Followed by Government Agencies in the Sale of Contract Termination Inventories, Apr. 21, 1944, 9 *Federal Register* 4559.

proceeded to establish its basic surplus disposal system, reviewing with the affected agencies the method of reporting surpluses and disposals, the control of inventories, the selection of trade channels and price policies.[24] Consumer goods were sold to the channels of trade normal for the item involved "in lot sizes which have been established for small business by trade custom."[25] Prices at which goods were actually sold were to be established through sealed bids, negotiations, and rarely through auctions. Resale by the private purchaser of such goods was under OPA regulation.[26]

In May, SWPA had been requested to prepare for the consideration of Congress necessary legislation on surplus property. An interagency committee was formed which prepared a draft bill, although Mr. Clayton took the position that immediate legislative action was not necessary and that it was desirable to gather experience before Congress should act.[27]

Acting on the Surplus War Property Administration proposal and its own intensive investigation, Congress in November passed the Surplus Property Act. The act earmarked the proceeds for the retirement of the national debt and while it generally affirmed the policies laid down by the SWPA, made significant administrative and policy changes.

A three-man Surplus Property Board was established replacing the single Administrator designated in the Executive order, the arrangement being a compromise between the Senate's desire for a five- or eight-man board and that of the House for a single administrator. The Surplus Property Administrator, Mr. Will Clayton, protested that the arrangement would be unworkable and announced his resignation effective whenever the new Board had been appointed.[28]

The act laid down a number of policies different from those developed by SWPA. In general, these were designed to recognize the claims of various groups to preferential treatment and to assure that surpluses be dispersed in accordance with the established antimonopoly policy. In establishing these criteria, Congress greatly accentuated the difficulties in disposing of surplus property.

The act established a mandatory system of priority rights to purchase of surplus property by (1) Federal agencies, (2) State governments and their subdivisions, tax supported and nonprofit

---

[24] Surplus War Property Administration. *Report to the Director of War Mobilization as to Activities under Executive Order No. 9425*, Oct. 31, 1944.

[25] SWPA Regulation No. 1, 9 *Federal Register* 5096, 9182, 12069.

[26] U. S. Office of Price Administration. *11th Quarterly Report*, pp. 7-8; *14th Quarterly Report*, pp. 4-6.

[27] U. S. Congress. Senate. Committee on Military Affairs. Summary of Recommendations Submitted on Surplus Property Legislation. Report . . . pursuant to S. Res. 198, 78th Cong., 2d sess., Subcommittee Print No. 5, June 5, 1944, pp. 146-48.

[28] U. S. Congress. House. Committee on Expenditures in the Executive Departments. Surplus Property Act of 1944. Hearings . . . on H. R. 5125, Aug. 8, 1944. The Director of OWMR, Mr. Byrnes, also expressed opposition to a board.

institutions, and (3) veterans, farmers, and small business, in that order. In the case of the 5,000,000 acres of surplus lands, it was required that priority to purchase be given in order to: (*a*) Federal agencies, (*b*) State governments and their subdivisions, (*c*) original owner, wife, or heirs, (*d*) original tenant, and (*e*) veterans. Congress sought to guard against monopolistic practices in the sale of surplus war plants by requiring the Attorney General's approval of the sale of plants valued at over $10,000,000. It furthermore required a detailed report to Congress on the contemplated sale of plants costing $5,000,000 or more. Leases of plants costing $5,000,000 or more were limited to 5 years, a short time in view of the frequently high reconversion costs.

The Board acted first to reorganize its disposal machinery. The Treasury's function in handling the disposal of consumers' goods was transferred to the Department of Commerce. Disposition of property in foreign countries except for ships and aircraft was left to the Army and Navy, the owning agencies. The designated disposal agencies were then:

Consumer goods—Department of Commerce.

Aircraft, plants, capital, and producers' goods—Reconstruction Finance Corporation.

Ships and maritime property—Maritime Commission.

Agricultural commodities and goods—War Food Administration.

Housing—National Housing Agency.

Real Property—Department of Agriculture, Interior, Reconstruction Finance Corporation, Maritime Commission, National Housing Agency, and Federal Works Agency.

Surplus goods in territories and possessions except for aircraft, ships, and agricultural commodities—Department of Interior.

Aircraft in foreign countries—Foreign Economic Administration.

All other property in foreign countries to the owning agencies.

Several important changes were made in the organization of surplus disposal before the end of the year. The three-man board provided by the Surplus Property Act proved administratively unsatisfactory. Disagreements obstructed and delayed necessary action on policies to guide the disposal agencies, a fact which Mr. Clayton had predicted in his testimony protesting such action by Congress. Its chairman, Senator Guy M. Gillette, upon his resignation after a 6-month period, recommended a single administrator. In July 1945, President Truman requested Congress to substitute a single administrator for the three-man Board. Congress acquiesced and passed the necessary legislation on July 17, 1945.

A second important change in disposal organization was made when, in November 1945, the disposal of consumer goods was transferred from the Department of Commerce to the Reconstruction Finance Corporation.[29] The RFC then consolidated all of its disposal activities into one organization, the War Assets Corporation. Some 90 percent of all surplus disposal was thus brought within the jurisdiction of one agency.

The surplus goods held abroad, a large part of the total, presented special problems. Most of these were owned by the Army and Navy, a small portion by FEA. The War and Navy Departments under the authorization of the Surplus War Property Board early in 1945 set

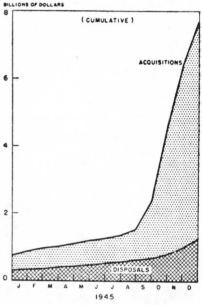

CHART 59. *The Surplus Property Problem.*

Source: Surplus Property Administration.

up an Army Navy Liquidation Commissioner to which was delegated the responsibility of disposal of overseas surpluses.

There were numerous problems peculiar to overseas sales which involved not only the Nation's interests in securing the highest possible net return but also its foreign policy. In meeting these problems, it was determined that sales were to be for American dollars and that care was to be taken not to sell in quantities beyond rehabilitation needs in order to protect future foreign export markets. Surplus property was also to be used to settle claims of foreign govern-

---

[29] Executive Order No. 9643, Oct. 19, 1945, 10 *Federal Register* 13039.

ments and nationals against the United States. To sell at all in a foreign country, it was necessary that agreements be reached with the foreign government. For these reasons it was necessary for the Army Navy Liquidation Commission to work closely with the Treasury and State Departments. Because the task was so intricately interwoven with the Nation's relations with foreign countries, this organization was abolished in late 1945 and the function transferred to an Office of Foreign Liquidation Commissioner, which was made a part of the State Department.[30]

The task of fitting the purchase priority scale established by the act into the sales machinery was a difficult one. To overcome the delays that might arise from the requirements of offering goods to a number of groups in sequence, the Board established a procedure which placed upon the interested Government agencies the necessity for taking initiative in expressing interests in merchandise and giving them limited periods within which to act. The Board sought to expedite sales to private priority groups by setting aside merchandise in what is believed to be adequate quantities.

At the end of 1945, some $12.9 billion of property had been acquired as surplus for disposal, of which $2.9 billion had been sold (chart 59). It was estimated that an additional quantity of goods valued at $33 billion would be declared surplus in 1946 with a substantially smaller quantity in 1947. Of the $10 billion surplus inventory at the end of 1945, about a third represented unsalable aircraft whereas only 10 percent of the surplus expected in 1946 was anticipated to be in that category. Quite clearly only a very small part of the surplus disposal job had been completed.

The experiences of 1945 brought about marked changes in organization. Responsibility for actual sale in the domestic market was highly centralized in the War Assets Corporation. With both food and housing in short supply as the year ended, the tasks of the National Housing Agency and the Department of Agriculture presented no serious difficulties. The disposal of ships by the Maritime Commission awaited the development of a national maritime policy. The disposal of property located on foreign soil was guided very largely by the political considerations which were the province of the State Department. Except for the latter, the problems associated with surplus property disposal were almost entirely in the hands of the War Assets Corporation. Now that there was no longer a reason for the separation of the policy-making function in the hands of the Surplus Property Administration from the selling function of the War Assets Corporation, further consolidation was in prospect.

---

[30] Executive Order No. 9689, Jan. 31, 1946, 11 *Federal Register* 1265-7.

Planning the Reconversion of Industry

As has been described in chapter 10, the War Production Board had developed over the war period an interlocking system of controls over the use of materials and the disposition of finished products which effectively channeled manufacturing activity into those uses which were determined as most necessary to victory. At the same time, these regulations operated to prevent manufacturers from producing for the civilian market. Wholesale removal or amendment of controls was necessary whenever any significant expansion in the supply of civilian products was to be permitted.

The Chairman of the War Production Board, Donald M. Nelson, early in 1943 had expressed his concern over the solution to these problems and the need for preparing to meet them.[31] In April of that year, Ernest Kanzler prepared for the WPB an intensive study of the reconversion problem. From that time on, the problem was under almost constant discussion and analysis within the agency and policies slowly came to be formulated. Originally the WPB's interest covered all matters relating to the termination of the wartime organization of industry, including contract termination and surplus property. As these and similar problems were assigned elsewhere, the WPB interest became increasingly focused on the utilization for the civilian economy of freed facilities and materials.

As with other aspects of reconversion, the Baruch-Hancock report called the problems to the public's attention, formed a foundation for much of the work that was to be done, and supplied essential support in the controversies that were to come.[32]

The basic point made by Messrs. Baruch and Hancock was that war contracts should be canceled as quickly as needs permitted, and that such cancellations should be coordinated with the planned expansion of civilian production. They recommended that the War Production Board was the appropriate agency to control the resumption of civilian production, since the unwinding of the economy could best be carried out by the same agencies which had mobilized the nation's resources. In the performance of this task, the report suggested that the War Production Board, as well as the armed services, prepare "X-day" plans which would show what production would be canceled and what plants released at the end of the European war.

---

[31] U. S. Congress. House. Committee on Appropriations. National War Agencies Appropriation Bill for 1944. Hearings. . . 78th Cong., 1st sess., May 27, 1943, p. 1083.

[32] It should be noted that Messrs. Baruch and Hancock drew heavily upon WPB thought in the preparation of their report. Mr. Nelson in response to a request from Mr. Baruch submitted to him some 47 WPB studies within the field, including a study of basic importance by its Planning Division. U. S. War Production Board, Policy Analysis and Records Branch, Report No. 15, *Development of the Reconversion Policies of the War Production Board*, p. 27.

They further recommended that retooling of plants for civilian production be permitted before war production was terminated.

The Baruch-Hancock recommendations reflected the view of most qualified civilian observers. There was at no time any significant controversy over the degree of decontrol of production once both Japan and Germany had been defeated. It would be sweeping in character. The problems in decontrol lay in the degree and character of the resumption of civilian production while the war still continued. It was argued that a decline in industrial activity would probably appear even before the victory had been achieved on either front. The pipe lines would be filled, inventories built up, facilities completed, and production of certain matériel reduced. Such slack presented both opportunity and need for resuming civilian production. An even greater opportunity for an orderly, partial transition of industrial activity from war to peace would arise with victory on one of the fronts. If this first victory should come in Europe, as was generally assumed, military requirements for continuance of the war in Asia could be met with a substantially reduced volume of war production, a reduction variously estimated at the time at from 10 to 40 or 50 percent with 35 percent the most generally used figure. This period between victories was viewed in many quarters as a challenge to the Government so to plan its controls as to assure a shift from the high levels of war production to comparably high levels of peacetime economic activity as quickly as possible and with a minimum of unemployment and lost production. The decline in economic activity which would follow from military cut-backs would be cushioned for a time by the continuance of large Federal expenditures. If civilian goods began to flow in volume from released industrial facilities with sufficient speed, it was believed possible to avoid the first serious threat to postwar economic prosperity—a sharp decline in economic activity during the prolonged reconversion period. Such action was deemed essential if there was to be reasonable assurance that the goal of high level production which the Nation had set itself was to be attained. Without challenging the merits of these arguments, there was nevertheless strong opposition, particularly from the military procurement agencies, to any action on them. In fact, the military services consistently expressed disapproval of public discussion of reconversion planning [33] and while not objecting to reconversion preparations by

---

[33] For example, in a public address in April 1944, Under Secretary of War Robert H. Patterson stated that "there has been far too large a crop of postwar planning; far too much thought given to proposals for making money after the war . . ." In October, the War and Navy Departments sent a telegram to the General Electric Co., protesting its plan to hold a meeting with business executives to discuss postwar planning. The telegram stated:

" The General Electric Co. has a splendid record for war production on an all-out basis. We know that you intend to keep the needs of the armed forces first and foremost as long as those needs continue. We are receiving urgent appeals for war supplies on an increased scale from the commanders of the fighting forces

Government agencies, vigorously opposed until after VE-Day all plans to take action on such programs.

Such opposition was founded on the ground that until victory was certain, no use of industrial facilities should be permitted which would interfere with their quick return to war production or which would in any way interfere with the attainment of scheduled war production. The fact that monthly munitions production until March 1945, never met scheduled production, provided the military with a very strong argument against reconversion. When driven from that position by the evidence that supplies were never inadequate,[34] they could argue that the existence of critical programs which lagged behind schedules were evidence enough against any action on reconversion and that attainment of such scheduled production would be even more difficult if manpower should be attracted to reconverting plants.

There was also the question of the administrative feasibility of attaining a degree of industrial reconversion before final victory had been secured. The task of translating the recommendations of the Baruch-Hancock Report and the views of the staff of WPB, the Military Services, industry, and the Congress into administratively feasible plans for reconversion was one of great difficulty. Essential to the problem was precise information on the magnitude of the continuing needs for military supplies. To control and guide cutbacks, the chief procurement agencies, at the request of OWM, had appointed in 1943 committees to review the procurement programs. A short time later, the Joint Chiefs of Staff established a Joint Production Survey Committee to review the actions of the procurement agencies in the curtailment of the procurement program. From this committee estimates were available as to the volume of military procurement. The availability of such data was, however, merely the first step in the process.

The key to the resumption of civilian production simultaneously with a continued program of war production lay in the specific incidence of the cutbacks to be made. Thus, even large cutbacks might have no effect on the opportunity to produce civilian goods if they were concentrated in Government owned and operated plants. On the other hand, in the spring of 1944 relatively small cutbacks in the

---

overseas. These demands make it plain that production of war materials must be increased rather than reduced. In view of these facts, it seems to us that any meeting of your executives at this time to consider postwar planning might be misunderstood and taken to mean that the needs of production are declining." See also U. S. War Production Board, *Development of the Reconversion Policies of the War Production Board*, Report No. 15, pp. 43-48, 92-102. Also, U. S. Congress. Senate. Special Committee to Investigate the National Defense, *Third Annual Report*. See statement of Maj. Gen. Lucius D. Clay, *ibid.*, p. 209-10.

[34] General Somervell testified in December 1944, that at no time had our Armed Forces suffered from a lack of supplies. U. S. Congress. Senate. Special Committee Investigating the National Defense Program, Hearings . . . pt. 26, p. 11990, December 4, 1944.

war programs, were it possible to locate them properly, could have released all consumer durable goods industries from war contracts.[35]

There was inherent in much of the thinking about reconversion, as in the Baruch-Hancock report, the idea that contract cancellation could easily be carried out so as to release facilities important to civilian production, retaining in war production those that were of less immediate significance. At the same time, however, conflicting concepts as to the policies to be followed in contract cancellation found considerable support. There were suggestions that preferential treatment in the resumption of civilian production be given to prewar companies over firms established during the war, to small business,[36] to specific industries, to certain geographical areas.[37] Among these proposals, only that of giving small business some advantage in reconversion was adopted as official policy, although for a time some preference was given to prewar companies over new firms.

The actual task of canceling contracts was in the hands of the procurement agencies who were strongly inclined when faced with diminished needs for specific items to follow basic financial considerations and to cancel first the contracts of the higher cost or least satisfactory producers. Any other cancellation policy would necessarily have to be imposed upon the procurement agencies by higher authority.

The establishment of a pattern of contract cancellation for the interim period based on the desirability of securing production of civilian goods rather than on a strict financial basis was fraught with difficulties. Policy decisions were required relative to—

1. Establishment of a system of priorities for civilian products.

2. Assurance that contract cancellations would single out appropriate facilities retaining in war production plants less adaptable to civilian production.

3. Assurance to the civilian industries of adequate supplies of raw materials and component parts. This involved the release from war production of adequate capacity to produce the supplies of components and parts needed for the civilian product.

4. Establishment of a policy on the treatment of competitive firms within the same industry if all could not be released from war production simultaneously and/or if materials were inadequate for capacity operation by the entire industry.

[35] *Survey of Current Business*, June 1945, p. 10–16.

[36] A view championed by the chairman of the Smaller War Plants Corporation, Mr. Maury Maverick, as well as by the Senate Small Business Committee.

[37] The Special Committee to Investigate the Centralization of Heavy Industry in the United States, of which Senator McCarran was Chairman, suggested freezing of new war plants and facilities in the 11 eastern states. (U. S. Cong. Senate. Special Committee to Investigate the Centralization of Heavy Industry in the United States, Hearings . . . pursuant to S. Res. 190, 78th Cong., 2d sess.)

5. Assurance that manpower would be available without interfering with war production.

During the summer of 1944, public optimism over an early end of the war in Europe was very great, an attitude supported by the quick success of the landings on the continent and the capture of Paris. The feeling was general that the war-planning job had been completed before D-day; the number of resignations at the War Production Board of men returning to their private occupations was very large. Demands that reconversion planning be hastened came from all elements; industrialists, labor leaders, members of Congress, and high Government officials. Congress was besieged for legislation covering surplus property, contract termination, and human demobilization; OPA for a price policy covering civilian products; and most particularly, WPB for detailed X-day planning. In May the demands upon WPB were given emphasis by the Baruch and Hancock criticism of delays and by the Brewster cutback incident.[38] Caught between these demands on the one hand and the firm opposition of the military on the other, the position of the War Production Board's Chairman was an unhappy one, accentuated by continued disputes between factions of his own staff.

Nevertheless, while warning that the first task of war production continued to be a military one, Mr. Nelson moved steadily toward establishment of a policy. Thus, in March he revealed, in reply to questions from Senator Maloney, the following WPB plans:

1. While the services have in the past consulted with WPB on cutbacks to only a limited extent, from now on the military services, when they have determined that a cutback is necessary, will collaborate with the War Production Board in determining where the cutback is made.

2. Manpower is the most critical determining factor in war production today. So far as possible, we attempt to guide the cutbacks in the critical labor areas, in order to ease the manpower situation in these areas.

3. The availability of manpower, materials, and component parts determines the extent to which civilian production has been cut back. The military services also are concerned over possible adverse effects of an expansion of civilian production at this time on morale both at home and among the fighting men abroad. With these factors in mind, our policy is to expand civilian production as it becomes possible to do so without interference with the over-all war program, and particularly in concerns whose war orders have been cut back. The Office of Civilain Requirements has prepared a number of programs for expanded production of civilian items and has listed their relative order of importance to the economy. It is our purpose to put these programs into effect whatever the military outlook, and the situation with respect to manpower, materials, and parts indicates the advisability of such action.

---

[38] U. S. Congress. House. Committee on Naval Affairs. Investigation of the War Effort. Report of subcommittee appointed to investigate the causes of failure of production of Brewster Aeronautical Corp. under its contracts with the Navy. Hearings . . . 78th Cong., 1st sess., pursuant to H. Res. 30. Also, U. S. Congress. Senate. Committee on Military Affairs. Mobilization and Demobilization Problems. Hearings . . . 78th Cong., 2d sess., p. 519 et seq.

4. While the idea of withholding conversion of a plant until an entire industry can be reconverted is fair and convenient, it is a physical impossibility. The entrance of new firms into an old industry cannot be restrained since it "has been my objective from the very start to confine detailed economic planning to wartime production of military and civilian essentials," and "it is all-important to maintain a competitive economy." [39]

The policies so stated formed the basis upon which the War Production Board program was to be developed. The details were worked out but slowly, shifting with the changes in the military situation and the consequent changes in estimated future requirements. Their implementation likewise expanded and contracted with the rate of military progress, beset with criticism as to timing from the military agencies.

Machinery to assure the attainment of the first point was created in June by the establishment of the Production Executive Committee Staff under Wilson, including on its membership the procurement agencies and the War Manpower Commission as well as WPB. This group had the function of inquiring into any feature of production, including scheduling, and to clear all cutbacks and terminations proposed by the procurement agencies. Its unanimous recommendations regarding such changes were binding on the procurement agencies; when opinion was divided, the PEC rendered the binding decision.

In June 1944 Mr. Nelson announced his reconversion program, which embodied the following provisions:

1. Restrictive orders covering aluminum and magnesium were to be removed to permit the use of these metals in fabricating essential products when manpower was available.

2. Manufacturers were to be authorized to acquire materials and components to build one working model of any product planned for postwar production.

3. Manufacturers were to be allowed to purchase machine tools and dies for civilian production, out of surplus stocks or, if necessary, through orders validated by the War Production Board for manufacture when war demands permitted.

4. Production of civilian items from available materials was to be permitted on the basis of individual authorizations made by the regional offices of the War Production Board in consultation with local representatives of the War Manpower Commission. This was the "Spot Authorization Plan."

In timing this announcement, Mr. Nelson recognized the demands of the public and of Congress for such action and had the support of an analysis by his staff which indicated that the Army's supply situa-

---

[39] *Congressional Record*, Vol. 90, pt. 2, pp. 2402–04. Mr Nelson restated his view that the War Production Board's scheduling of production was restricted to war and that such action during reconversion would be of "great violence to our system of free enterprise."

tion was satisfactory. The announcement, however, brought the conflict between Nelson and the Armed Services to the surface. Appealing to higher authority, the Army took its objections to the Director of War Mobilization, who ordered the effective date postponed pending his review. Justice Byrnes approved Nelson's proposal except that the effective date of the spot authorization was moved ahead to August 15 and that applications were made subject to the review of the local Production Urgency Committee who would give manpower problems strong consideration. The WMC became the key agency in industrial reconversion since its certificate that labor was available was required before the PUC's would approve a spot authorization application.

Although Mr. Nelson's action received wide public support, including that of Senator James M. Mead, chairman of the Senate War Investigating Committee, it was opposed by WPB Vice Chairman Wilson and the military. The latter carried their objections to the President with a demand for Nelson's removal. Meanwhile, Mr. Nelson had agreed to the President's request that he undertake a special mission to China. Shortly thereafter, Vice Chairman Wilson's resignation was also accepted and Julius A. Krug became Acting Chairman of the WPB.

The change in leadership resulted in no change in WPB's announced reconversion program. Indeed, for a short time reconversion planning and discussion moved at an accelerated pace. Mr. Krug told a Senate Committee that he was "in complete accord with" Mr. Nelson's plans for a gradual reconversion, and a few weeks later laid before that Committee detailed and integrated plans for industrial reconversion, for application after the fall of Germany and after the defeat of Japan. Early in September the War Production Board announced the first instances of resumed civilian production under the Spot Authorization Plan. Meanwhile, a committee to review the demobilization of controls was established in September. The following month it made a detailed report on the WPB controls which should be dropped and those which should be retained or modified for a one-front war.

The slowing of the war in Europe with the approach of the winter of 1944–45, the German counterattack and the resulting Battle of the Bulge set back the military schedule and forced an upward revision of military requirements. Discussion of reconversion disappeared amidst general recognition that the anxiety of the previous summer had been premature. Meanwhile, the war in the Pacific was moving rapidly, well ahead of schedule, with a consequent intensification of demands of equipment. The result was that while the munitions program had declined month by month during the first three quarters of 1944, it rose significantly in November over October and again in December. Faced with these rising schedules and an increasing number of critical programs, the Chairman of the War Production Board announced that from now on "we are assuming that the war will go on indefinitely." The War Production Board, War Manpower Commission, War and Navy Departments issued a joint statement reemphasizing the precedence to be given to the war programs.[40]

Reconversion progress under the spot authorization plan meanwhile had been very slow. Although Krug had in November rejected a demand from the Services that the spot authorization program be suspended for 3 months, the program was virtually inoperative in the following month in all labor markets. Reconversion planning in the War Production Board, as elsewhere, was driven underground by these events but continued to be the subject of careful and detailed examination. Such planning was necessarily a continuing operation because of the shifting nature of the demands of the military upon the economy and the changing significance of military operations to the time period for which planning was being carried out.

The rapid improvement of the military situation in Europe in the early spring of 1945 brought renewed public interest in reconversion and expression of anxiety over the plans made to meet declining war production. To these queries, Mr. Krug could reply that WPB had been working on, if not talking about, reconversion. In fact, a Committee on the Demobilization of Controls after VE-day had dealt with that problem during the winter. As a result of a request from OWMR Director Byrnes, asking WPB to formulate plans, the problem received intensified attention from a newly established Committee on Period One (the interval between VE- and VJ-days). Preliminary data on the requirements of the Services for the one-front war were made available in March and thereafter a succession of plans was prepared, based on the action that would be possible under various assumptions. By the middle of April, WPB had reviewed virtually all procurement cut-back proposals effective before the termination of the war against Germany.

In April, the European war was near its climax. Reconversion discussion was openly sanctioned by WPB without protest from the military and the Spot Authorization Plan was revitalized at approximately the same time that the first major cut-back—in aircraft—was announced, foreshadowing victory over Germany. WPB had prepared some months earlier for the increased load by establishing a Production Readjustment Committee to give its full attention to guiding the impact of cut-backs with the work of actually cutting

---

[40] War Production Board Press Release WPB-6922, December 1, 1944.

and guiding the facilities into new uses in the hands of the Field Termination Committees.

VE-day—May 6—brought no sudden change in industrial controls. Reconversion had, in fact, begun weeks earlier in the revitalization of the Spot Authorization Plan, and in the occasional liberalization of restrictive orders. A few days after VE-day, producers of civilian goods were given permission to place orders for steel, copper, and aluminum for delivery after July 1, and rating floors were removed to permit placing unrated orders if they did not interfere with war needs. Limitation orders on some 73 types of products were removed, and restrictions of this nature continued to be lifted almost daily during the interim period. Such actions were in the nature of granting hunting licenses for raw materials and meant civilian products only if the decline in the war program permitted.

WPB's inclinations toward a hurried removal of controls, a policy which had been formulated in the fall of 1943 by Chairman Nelson and Vice Chairman Batcheller, was opposed by other war agencies; by OPA and WMC who felt that production controls were necessary to the success of their operations; and by the military who sought maximum protection for their continuing production requirements. Of great importance was the fact that WPB was faced also with demands from civilian businesses for priorities for civilian production since materials continued in extremely tight supply. While the War Production Board recognized that the retention of certain controls, particularly on construction, were desirable, Mr. Krug's position was that WPB's jurisdiction was limited to war production and that such control should be exercised by some other agency. The Mead committee expressed itself in agreement with Mr. Krug's observation that a little competition was a good thing. Thus, the agency continued to move in the direction of an early complete disappearance of WPB and its controls over production.

Less than 4 months separated victory over Germany from the defeat of Japan. Scheduled production which controlled material availability for August was in May planned for at a rate only 15 percent below that in May.[41] While certain materials became fairly abundant, others remained tight, and important commonly used components remained difficult to secure.

The results of liberalized materials control between the abandonment of spot authorization and the end of the war are not susceptible

[41] Munitions production scheduled as of May 1, 1945, and that actually achieved was (in millions of dollars):

	Scheduled	Actual
May	$4,616	$4,542
June	4,373	4,153
July	4,086	3,661
August	3,924	2,448

to statistical measurement. In general, the result of the interim reconversion plans of WPB in terms of increased flow of finished products to consumers was very small. It is nevertheless true that the steps taken were of undoubted assistance in expediting the reconversion of industry when the end of the war came.

Lifting Controls

The central issue in the preparations made for peace was the disposition of the numerous controls that over the war period had been extended to virtually all phases of economic life. The public had accepted such restrictions as one of the prices to be paid for victory but, at the same time, from the time of their imposition and consistently thereafter had demanded assurances that they would be eliminated at the earliest possible time. The Nation's wartime production achievement had apparently served· to strengthen the public's faith in the values of freedom of economic action. It was recognized that some controls could not be removed as quickly as others. Military demobilization necessitated an adequate supply of transportation facilities. Assurances were needed that the armies of occupation receive adequate supplies. But for the rest the weight of opinion was heavily against the continuation of controls that had not existed in peacetime.

On the other hand, those who were most directly concerned with the many problems that would have to be solved in the immediate postwar period were concerned over the premature dropping of controls and in some cases advocated the retention of a substantial number of such administrative devices. Their point of view was that an orderly transition to a peacetime economy at the. highest possible level of activity and with the great possible speed was attainable only by continued controls over allocation of materials, rationing of certain products, and continued control over prices. To permit unfettered competition for the short supplies that would exist in many materials during the reconversion period was to jeopardize a smooth transition.

The policy of the Administration on this matter was enunciated by the President when at the end of the war he instructed the Federal agencies "to move as rapidly as possible without endangering the stability of the economy toward the removal of price, wage, production, and other controls and toward the restoration of collective bargaining and the free market".[42] Many of the war agencies already had plans consistent with the President's policy and many had previously publicly announced their intentions. In fact, in most agencies, such plans had been held in readiness since the fall of 1944.

---

[42] Executive Order No. 9599, Aug. 18, 1945, 10 *Federal Register* 10155-58.

In accordance with the Administration's policy, victory over Japan was celebrated with a very substantial restoration of economic freedom. On August 16, the day following the announcement of the surrender of Japan, all controls over manpower were dropped by the War Manpower Commission and the OPA removed ration restrictions on gasoline, fuel oil, processed foods, and heating stoves. Other ration orders were lifted during the rest of the year so that by the end of 1945 only sugar continued under rationing control.[43] Several hundred items were removed from price control within the first hundred days after VJ-day. By the end of August, the War Production Board had abolished most priority controls, the Controlled Materials Plan and with it all control over metals except tin, lead, and antimony, eased industrial construction restrictions, and revoked several hundred control orders. The Office of Defense Transportation had lifted several thousand controls on commercial motor-vehicle traffic and eased the ban on conventions. Early in September a large portion of controls over exports was lifted and coastal and intercoastal shipping was resumed.

The Fight Against Inflation

During the war, consumers' incomes had risen sharply, whereas the supply of goods available for purchase had increased much less rapidly: the supply of many consumer durables either declined or ceased altogether to be available. While increased tax payments, bond purchase campaigns, and voluntary savings served to absorb a substantial portion of the expansion in consumer incomes, imbalance between purchasing power and the supply of goods was sufficiently great to create dangerous inflationary possibilities.

Prior to the end of the war, there was no unanimity of agreement that such inflationary pressures would continue long beyond the attainment of victory. Some observers felt that the very sharp drop in Federal expenditures to be expected after VJ-day would result in serious deflation and that as a consequence unemployment would be the Nation's major problem. Others, recalling that during World War I price inflation had been far more severe after the end of hostilities than during the war, argued that consumers' purchasing power would for some time exceed the supply of available goods and that the danger of inflation would continue for an extended period.

The Government, in view of these two possibilities, prepared to combat both deflation and inflation. Plans for public works and the maintenance of consumer purchasing power were discussed. Chief

---

[43] Not all of these orders were actually operative. They included: men's rubber boots and rubber work shoes, Sept. 5; new adult bicycles, Sept. 23; coffee, Sept. 21; passenger automobiles, Oct. 29; firewood (Pacific Northwest only), Aug. 21; shoes; Oct. 30; meats, fats, canned fish, and cheese, Nov. 23; tires, Dec. 26, 1945.

emphasis was placed, however, on ways and means of combating inflation. The Baruch-Hancock Report had suggested that the problem would be one of controlling prices and President Roosevelt in his Budget message in January 1945 had said:

> When war production is extensively reduced some of the controls which were needed in an all-out war economy can be relaxed, although other controls must be continued to assure necessary war production and orderly reconversion. For example, we must avoid speculation in inventories such as contributed to the inflation after the last war. The fact that many businesses and individuals have ample funds for a buying spree necessitates caution in relaxing controls. The balance between incomes, savings and expenditures will still be precarious during the reconversion period. It will therefore be necessary to retain the machinery for allocation and price controls as long as certain materials and finished goods are in short supply."[44]

The situation after VJ-day was one of high-wage levels though somewhat reduced from wartime peaks, combined with favorable employment conditions, continuing large Federal expenditures, vast pent-up demands for many classes of goods, and very large liquid savings in the hands of individuals as well as business corporations. In view of the long time lag before the desired goods could appear on the markets in significant volume, the danger of an upward spiral of prices was very real. The Office of Price Administration had prepared to handle these problems well before VJ-day. Price control during the reconversion period, and until the Price Control Act came before Congress for renewal, was to be within the framework of administration and policy developed during the war.

Among the demands made by business groups in 1944 and early 1945 for adequate Government preparation for reconversion, requests for enunciation of a price control policy were frequent and insistent. The task was essentially that of reviewing and making the necessary adjustments in the price ceilings of products which were on the market in 1941–42 but which were not being manufactured for some time before the end of the war. It was necessary also to determine price ceilings for new products, a more difficult task but one with which OPA had acquired considerable experience. It was essential that the pricing program be developed so that these commodities would flow into the civilian market in maximum volume as quickly as possible after the end of war production. While the administrative burden was heavy, the number of commodities involved in the reconversion pricing program was relatively small and their production was highly concentrated in a small group of large firms.

The Office of Price Administration had given some attention to the problem of reconversion pricing since the last half of 1943; intensively so in the middle of 1944 when partial reconversion seemed

---

[44] *The Budget of the U. S. Government, Fiscal Year ending June 30, 1946*, p. xxiii.

probable.[45] The specific policy to be followed was, however, not announced until May 1945. Under the program, prices on reconversion products were set at 1941–42 levels with adjustments for legitimate increase in costs to be made upon application. Such adjustments would cover increased costs by the use of industry-wide formulae or in the case of smaller firms, on an individual basis.[46] There were, however, larger issues involving the entire framework of economic stabilization which required administrative action.

The problem of controlling prices after VJ-day differed sharply from the task in the war period. On the one hand, the decision to eliminate a maximum number of controls over production meant that price stabilization could find only limited support in that direction. On the other hand, President Truman had early indicated his agreement with the popular desire to return to free collective bargaining in labor relations at the earliest possible opportunity. If such release of controls was to mean a sharp rise in hourly wage levels, as did prove to be the case, inflationary pressures would be expanded. Such increase would be reflected in higher costs to consumers, increasing the cost of living. The task was thus one of reconciling the objective of continuing price control with the desire to eliminate or the impracticability of continuing other controls which over the war period had proven essential supports of the anti-inflationary effort.

On August 18, the President issued an Executive order "providing for assistance to expand production and continued stabilization of the national economy during the transition from war to peace, and for the orderly modification of wartime controls over prices, wages, materials, and facilities".[47]

By this order the whole process of decontrol—of removing wartime restrictions—became subject to the requirements of the stabilization program. The objectives of the Government were stated as the removal of price, wage, production, and other controls, and the restoration of collective bargaining and the free market. These were to be accomplished "without endangering the stability of the economy."

The Price Administrator was specifically instructed to "take all necessary steps to assure that the cost of living and the general level of prices shall not rise". Such price increases as might be approved for designated reasons were not to cause increases at later levels of production or distribution. Wage increases might be made by industry without approval of NWLB or the Director of the Economic Stabilization if such increases were not to be used to seek an increase

---

[45] Office of Price Administration. *11th Quarterly Report*, pp. 5–7.
[46] Office of Price Administration. *14th Quarterly Report*, pp. 2–4; *15th Quarterly Report*, p. 5.
[47] Executive Order No. 9599, Aug. 18, 1945, 10 *Federal Register* 10155.

in price ceilings or to increase the cost to the Government of products produced under Government contract. Wage increases to correct maladjustments and inequities might be approved by NWLB when such "interfered with the effective transition to a peacetime economy" but such increases when involving a change in a price ceiling were subject to the approval of the Director of Economic Stabilization.

This policy was clarified and strengthened October 30 by the President in an address to the Nation and with the simultaneous release of an Executive order.[48] By this order wage increases were to be approved by the Stabilization Administrator when NWLB found: (a) that total wage increases since January 1941 were not equal to the percentage increase in the cost of living from that date to September 1945; (b) where such increases were required to correct industry or area inequities; (c) and where such increases were found "necessary to insure full production in an industry, designated by the Stabilization Administrator, which is essential to reconversion and in which existing rates or salaries are inadequate to the recruitment of needed manpower."

In support of this stabilization program, certain controls over production were necessary. While an early complete disappearance of WPB's controls over industry had been anticipated, the importance to the price control program of an adequate supply of low price consumer goods forced reconsideration of the Government's postwar role in allocating scarce materials to such essential civilian items. With WPB's Chairman convinced that such a function was beyond WPB's powers, the issue was taken by the Director of OWMR to the President for settlement. In a letter to Krug, the President, while agreeing on the desirability of a quick removal of controls, urged the temporary retention of such controls as were needed to prevent or break bottlenecks in the production of low-priced goods. In consequence, when an effective date was set for the termination of the War Production Board, the creation of the Civilian Production Administration was also announced,[49] that new organization to take over the administration of some 60 orders in such fields as textiles and construction.

The task of reconciling labor's demands for higher wages with the economic stabilization program presented many great difficulties. Wage stabilization was essential to the program since it was to be expected that most employers would demand increases in price ceilings adequate to cover any production costs arising from increased wages. Although the Administration at various times suggested the feasibility and desirability of raising wages out of anticipated profits, strenuous

---

[48] Executive Order No. 9651, Oct. 30, 1945, 10 *Federal Register* 13487.
[49] Executive Order No. 9638, Oct. 4, 1945, 10 *Federal Register* 12591.

employer resistance was met. The resultant labor-management conflicts, when expressed as work stoppages, were a stumbling block to smooth and expeditious reconversion.

The problem presented serious administrative difficulties. During the war period NWLB had administered the wage stabilization program with marked success. Its accomplishment had rested very largely upon labor's adherence to the no-strike pledge at the beginning of the war and continued for the duration. It had consequently expired on VJ-day and the Board was in no position to take on new cases after that date. Although President Roosevelt in his Budget message in January 1945, had said, "We must also see to it that our administrative machinery for the adjustment of labor disputes is ready for the strains of the reconversion period" and urged that wartime lessons be applied in working out a long-range labor policy, nothing had been accomplished.[50]

President Truman made some effort to continue NWLB as an effective wage control organization. He requested labor to accept NWLB's jurisdiction and decisions and to continue the no-strike pledge until a labor-management conference could be convened to develop new machinery for maintaining industrial peace. In his Executive order of August 18, he directed that "disputes which would interrupt work contributing to the production of military supplies or interfere with effective transition to a peacetime economy are disputes which interrupt work contributing to the effective prosecution of the war." These efforts were not rewarded with success.

Organized labor had during the war years to a substantial degree, sacrificed the peculiarly favorable opportunities to obtain large wage increases which were inherent in the tight labor market situation. The sacrifice was not an easy one to make and labor had grown restive over the war period, resentful of the wartime restraints of the no strike pledge and the little steel formula, fearful of reduced weekly earnings as a result of the loss of overtime pay. In consequence, VJ-day was followed by an upsurge of work stoppages and strikes, despite the fact that public opinion strongly disapproved of such interferences with the progress of reconversion.

The lack of preparations which might have made of NWLB a useful postwar device to meet these problems was the result of labor's desire to escape all the wartime restrictions of Government intervention in collective bargaining, a desire with which industry appeared to be in substantial sympathy and which had previously been shared by Government officials including the members of NWLB. Thus, NWLB had not concerned itself with preparing for a role in the tran-

---

[50] *The Budget of the U. S. Government, Fiscal Year ending June 30, 1946*, pp. xx-xxi.

sition period but solely with making plans for finishing its backlog of work and then liquidating. By the time the threat of labor stoppages to reconversion had become clear, these steps had so weakened NWLB that its members felt it necessary to advise the President that it could not function effectively to handle the crisis. Without the no-strike pledge or some similar agreement on the part of labor to abide by NWLB rulings, the Government had only the device of plant seizure under the Smith-Connally Act with which to meet work stoppages. Consequently, NWLB proceeded with its plans to liqui-date, announcing in October that it intended to dissolve at the end of the year. The President, meanwhile, had requested that the Board set up a successor organization for the purpose of administering the wage stabilization program. The National Wage Stabilization Board, organized similarly to the National War Labor Board, was formed to begin operations the following year.[51]

Though it then had the administrative machinery to approve wage increases, the Administration was faced with the necessity of develop-ing quickly new policy with which to meet the threat of labor strikes in cases where labor-management disagreements could not be settled by collective bargaining. Such policy and accompanying machinery was hoped for as a product of the National Labor-Management Con-ference which the President called early in November. No formula or agreement whereby industrial disputes might be settled within the framework of announced economic stabilization policy was forth-coming, however.

Meanwhile, as a stop-gap device the President set up fact-finding boards to handle the most pressing of the industrial disputes, at the same time requesting of Congress action to bestow on such boards legislative sanction and authority. These boards had, in fact, no authority save only agreement by the two parties to accept them as arbitrators. Their awards did, however, carry the prestige of coming from a Presidential board and consequently carried with them con-siderable pressure for acceptance on both parties. In any case, the issue was what action OPA would take to cover the increased labor costs which might result from awards of increased wages. That agency attempted insofar as possible to obtain the absorption of such cost increases by the intermediary stages in the flow of products to ultimate consumers and thus prevent or at least reduce the impact upon the cost of living. This absorption policy met strenuous opposi-tion on the part of the affected industries, particularly wholesale and retail merchants, and became a basic issue in the controversy over the extension of the Price Control Act.

---

[51] Executive Order No. 9672, Dec. 31, 1945, 11 *Federal Register* 221–4.

Reconversion and Demobilization of the Executive Establishment

The needs of war required substantial expansion of many of the Government's normal functions and the addition of many activities unknown in peacetime. To carry on these operations, new agencies had been created; many old agencies had found it necessary to expand their staffs substantially and numerous shifts in functions and responsibilities among the agencies had been made.

As in the case of the other aspects of reconversion, the Government early began consideration of its demobilization problem and made preparations to reorganize the Government for the tasks of reconversion and peacetime. Continuous checking on the necessity of the operations of the Government's agencies and the need for staff were, in fact, part of the normal budgeting review operations of the Bureau of the Budget. Along with its assistance in establishing new agencies, the Bureau had from time to time throughout the war made recommendations that staff be reduced, agencies abolished, or functions transferred wherever such action was in the public interest. Thus, such agencies as the Office of Civilian Defense and the President's Committee on Congested Production Areas were terminated well before the end of the war when it was apparent that there was no longer any need for their functioning.

Such activities of the Bureau received a considerable impetus when on September 18, 1944, the President wrote the Director of the Bureau of the Budget stating:

> Upon the termination of hostilities, we must proceed with equal vigor to liquidate war agencies and reconvert the Government to peace. Some steps along these lines may be taken when the fighting ends in Europe. The transition from war to peace should be carried forward rapidly, but with a minimum of disorder and disruption. Only careful planning can achieve this goal.
>
> This is the time to do the planning, although the war—even in Europe—is not over. Most of the planning will probably have to wait for execution until the Japs have surrendered—and there is no way of telling when that will happen. But the plans should be ready.

The letter further requested that the Bureau reexamine the programs, organization, and staffs of Government agencies and prepare recommendations for "the liquidation of war agencies and the reassignment of such permanent or continuing functions as they possess; the reduction of Government personnel to a peace footing; and the simplification and adaptation of the administrative structure to peacetime requirements."

The Bureau promptly began its study, supplementing its own examination with a request to the head of each agency for a statement on program readjustment that might be made immediately and those which could be made following VE-day.

Congress meanwhile had inserted in the War Mobilization Act of 1944 instruction that the Director of OWMR study and determine the need for:—

simplification, consolidation, or elimination of such executive agencies as have been established for the purpose of the war emergency, for the termination, or establishment by statute, of executive agencies which exist under Executive order only.

While this was clearly a duplication of jurisdiction, the Administration refrained from any effort to secure a change in the legislation. Instead, Mr. Byrnes in a letter of November 29 requested that the Bureau of the Budget undertake the necessary study and thus avoided any conflict of jurisdiction.

The delay in achieving victory over Germany resulted, as elsewhere, in a reduced emphasis on this phase of demobilization. The Bureau of the Budget nevertheless continued to study the problem. One of the results was the view that little change in the Federal Government was to be expected until the war had been ended on both fronts. Thus, the Director of the Bureau of the Budget wrote the Director of War Mobilization in March 1945, that:—

Generally speaking, the war organization of the Government has been stabilized for some time, and will require but little adjustment except in consequence of material change in the programs of agencies. Contraction in the size of agencies may be expected in many instances, but wholesale reshaping of the war organization is not, in my opinion, in prospect until there is a substantial shift in production from war materials to civilian goods.

Meanwhile, the Bureau intensified its studies of demobilization and prepared detailed analyses of the programs of the Federal agencies. By VJ-day, it was well prepared with recommendations. Some of the agencies had also prepared plans for their liquidation soon after the end of the war.

A few days after the Japanese surrender, President Truman appointed a committee composed of the Director of OWMR, the Director of the Bureau of the Budget, and Judge Samuel I. Rosenman to make recommendations "on the proper disposition of the various war agencies." The recommendations of this committee were followed by quick action by the President. Thus, before the end of the year, the following were among the major agencies that had been formally terminated:

Agency terminated	Effective date	Action
Office of Civilian Defense	June 4, 1945	Executive Order No. 9562.
Central Administrative Services	Aug. 25, 1944	Executive Order No. 9471.
Office of War Information	Aug. 31, 1945	Executive Order No. 9608.
War-Refugee Board	Sept. 14, 1945	Executive Order No. 9614.
War Manpower Commission	Sept. 20, 1945	Executive Order No. 9617.
Office of Economic Stabilization	____do____	Executive Order No. 9620.
Office of Strategic Services	Oct. 1, 1945	Executive Order No. 9621.
Foreign Economic Administration	Sept. 27, 1945	Executive Order No. 9630.
Office of Army-Navy Liquidation Commissioner	____do____	Do.
Surplus War Property Administration to Reconstruction Finance Corporation.	Oct. 19, 1945	Executive Order No. 9643.
Office of Censorship (Censorship Policy Board)	Nov. 15, 1945	Executive Order No. 9631.
Munitions Assignment Board	Nov. 8, 1945	By action of Joint Chiefs of Staff, approved by President Truman and Prime Minister Attlee.
War Production Board	Nov. 3, 1945	Executive Order No. 9638.
Smaller War Plants Corporation	Dec. 27, 1945	Executive Order No. 9665.
National War Labor Board	Dec. 31, 1945	Executive Order No. 9672.
War Food Administration	June 29, 1945	Executive Order No. 9577.
Combined Production and Resources Board	Dec. 10, 1945	By agreement of President Truman with Prime Minister Attlee and Prime Minister King.
Combined Raw Materials Board	____do____	

The functions of some agencies came to an end with their dissolution; in others, functions were transferred to other agencies with the result that a considerable consolidation of Government activities was attained. The most striking example was that in the labor field. The Department of Labor was strengthened by receiving control of the United States Employment Service, the National War Labor Board, the National Roster of Scientific and Specialized Personnel, and the Reemployment and Retraining Administration. The Government's activities in international affairs were again concentrated in the State Department which received jurisdiction over some of the former functions of the Office of Strategic Services, the Office of War Information, and the Foreign Economic Administration, and would logically receive also the functions of the Office of Inter-American Affairs. Commerce strengthened its position by securing the functions of the Smaller War Plants Corporation as well as some of those of the Foreign Economic Administration.

Of special importance to the reconversion period was the consolidation of reconversion activities within OWMR. With the abolition of OES, stabilization coordinating functions were transferred to OWMR. Likewise, when WPB was abolished, the continuing priorities functions were vested in CPA which was instructed to report to OWMR. The President furthermore made OWMR responsible for the furtherance of his legislative program of September 6 requesting that agency reports on the status of the various elements of the program be made to him through OWMR. Thus, the guidance of the reconversion program was more highly centralized than the war program had been at any time during the period of hostilities.

*   *   *   *   *

Though the war with Japan ended far more quickly than was generally anticipated on the basis of military advice, the ease with which the Nation's economy entered the reconversion period paid tribute to 2 years of the preparations which had been made for it. World War I had served as an example of what not to do, and the Nation had profited from that experience.

The plans made were the product of no one group but in a real sense embodied the opinions and interests of a broad cross-section of the Nation. President Roosevelt performed an invaluable service in early calling attention to the importance of the problem, and the close association of President Truman as Senator and Chairman of the Senate War Investigating Committee with the problems involved meant a continuity of policy development of the utmost importance. Thereafter, initiative and over-all guidance was to a large degree supplied by OWM and its successor OWMR. Public expression of its interests were made not only through the Congress but more directly through the industry and labor advisory committees of WPB and OPA. By and large, the preparations reflected the Nation's wishes; the difficulties that were encountered were to be ascribed more to the public's clearly expressed desire for maximum economic freedom as quickly as possible than to misjudgments or miscalculations on the part of those responsible.

Though the reconversion period would merge into the post-war era without clear-cut indications to mark the transition, it was apparent that at the end of the year the process of readjustment from war to peace was still far more complete. The effectiveness of the preparations that have been described in this chapter are thus not within the purview of this book. It was clear, however, that the Nation was enjoying high levels of prosperity, that unemployment was far less serious than had been anticipated, that inflation was as much a threat as it had been at any time during the war period. The dangers of economic ills, of deflation and depression and heavy unemployment had been pushed well into the future. The degree to which that was true spelled the success of wartime planning for peace. The economic problems that lay in the future were to be met by actions which were not a part of the preparations for the conversion to peace but a part of the larger postwar era ahead.

CHAPTER

16

Assaying the Record

THE principal purpose of this account has been to report on the nation's experience in World War II from the point of view of the Government's discharge of its administrative and managerial responsibilities. The American nation faced its greatest challenge; those who were selected to manage and administer its affairs faced a most severe test. The fighting men we trained, the goods we produced, the battles we won, measure the magnitude of the problems that were faced and the degree of success attained.

This volume has dealt with only a small part of the whole field of our wartime experience [1] and cannot speak conclusively even on that portion. Like any attempt to capture the facts on a period of highly complex, swiftly moving events, immediately after their occurrence, this volume must suffer from a lack of perspective. Nor is it possible here to probe deeply into the meaning and significance of the many aspects of our war years. Constructive evaluation of our management of the war, like evaluation of the effects of war in the physical science as of the atomic bomb, in industrial technology, international relationships and social and economic changes, must await the factual and analytical contributions of many observers with widely divergent points of view enjoying the advantages of the perspective that time alone can give. It is hoped that this volume will stimulate numerous analysts to explore both more deeply and more broadly the many aspects of our society at war.

Even if evaluation of the events described in the preceding chapters is premature, it is nevertheless desirable to highlight certain aspects

---

[1] The Committee on Records of War Administration has actively encouraged the agencies of the executive branch of the Federal Government to prepare historical and analytical accounts of their war experience. A majority of these agencies now have such histories in preparation and they will constitute an important contribution to this field.

of our war administration. A particularly interesting method of doing this is by comparing the United States experience with the methods employed and the successes attained by our two major enemies, Germany and Japan. While much work remains to be done before the full story of the war activities of Germany and Japan will be available, sufficient information has already become accessible to permit the development of some highly important contrasts. The following discussion is based largely on the results of the expert examination of the German and Japanese war efforts by the United States Strategic Bombing Survey.[2]

The friends of authoritarian government (i.e., government without a broad base of public participation) have in the past made much of its supposed administrative efficiency in arriving at decisions and in executing them without the hurdles that a democratic system faces in operating through the unregimented processes of public discussion and consent. Such apologists have urged that the exposure of governmental problems to public analysis and decision is a source of delay and weakness and that dictatorship over governmental administration eliminates problems such as this country faced in the planning and coordination of its war effort. These considerations were sufficiently influential in the minds of the leaders of the Nazis and the Japanese expansionists to lead them to the conclusion that democracies could not successfully thwart their designs. It was a fundamental assumption in their plans that the democracies would be so immobilized as to be unable even to accept the challenge in meaningful fashion.

The speed with which the democracies did accept the challenge and the manner in which they overwhelmed those who sought gain through war suggests that there is need to reexamine the claims to administrative superiority of authoritarian governments. In making these comparisons, it must be noted that it is somewhat easier to analyze the factors that contributed to defeat than it is to ferret out the failures and weaknesses of the victor. Careful technical analysis may well indicate that both of our enemies programmed and executed in certain areas in a manner superior to ours. This may, for example, prove to be the case in certain phases of the German tank production program and in Japanese production of aircraft. Though we won the war, we cannot afford to close our eyes to the possible lessons we may learn from the experience of our enemy. This is a highly important task that technicians and scholars must perform if the full significance of the war experience is to be exploited.

---

[2] *The Effects of Strategic Bombing on the German War Economy*, Government Printing Office, 1945; and *The Effects of Strategic Bombing on Japan's War Economy*, Government Printing Office, 1946.

In many ways our task was far greater—from the administrative point of view—than that of either of our enemies. With a long antimilitaristic tradition, we were suddenly faced in late 1941 with war against the two most militaristic nations on earth. Both enjoyed the advantage of long preliminary planning and preparations. We faced the task of preparing simultaneously for two wars—one largely a land-air operation with naval support; the other primarily a naval-air operation with land support. In both cases the battlefronts were several thousands of miles distant imposing severe logistical problems. A third task was also thrust upon us: that of producing the supplies needed by our Allies and building a fleet of ships to carry these products to our Allies. The support of our Allies was invaluable to us but their pressing needs meant that we could not take time for long preparations since delay might deprive us of their support. Time, moreover, permitted our enemies to gain further strength from the exploitation of their conquests. To carry out simultaneously such complicated operations and to devote to each the proper proportion of our resources while avoiding the deadening effects of conflicts between those interested in one or another of these programs was an administrative achievement not to be disparaged.

The German leaders knew well that her productive potential was no match for a group of opponents which included the United States, and the Japanese were not unaware of the very great inferiority of their productive capacity. Both relied upon what they believed to be the "decadence" of our way of life and government to assure them that our superior resources would not be adequately employed to prevent the success of their challenge. Both relied further upon the strengthening of their economic potential by exploiting the resources of conquered territories. By the time we entered the war, Germany had brought all Western Europe into her economic orbit and Japan was in the process of vastly expanding the territory which she controlled in Asia. Both probably underestimated the time required to overcome the difficulties of such exploitation. While such conquests strengthened the German economy in certain critical areas, the aggregate contribution they made to her fighting potential was not great (see chart 60). The Japanese were probably even less successful.

Our possession of vast resources would have meant little or nothing if the administrative abilities of this Nation had not been equal to the task of converting those resources into an adequate supply of the things needed by our Armed Forces and our Allies. Military victory was possible for the United States because of our resources; it was achieved because our political structure and our administrative capacities were such that we obtained a speedy mobilization adequate to the tasks of war imposed upon us.

The Nation's management of its war tasks was not, as the preceding pages have shown, a smooth, uninterrupted, undeviating progress toward unchanging objectives. Our ultimate goal—of forcing the unconditional surrender of those who had declared war on us—was clear. Likewise, there was little uncertainty about the program in its broadest view.

The intermediate objectives were, however, highly flexible and the execution of the program was changeable, at times hesitant and uncertain. This had to be. The tasks were unique, the problems not well understood, the resources not well inventoried, the necessary objectives not always clearly visualized, the methods to attain them untried. The whole intricate machinery had to be modified as goals were approached in one area, as problems appeared in another, or as military requirements shifted. All of these problems had to be met and solved through the democratic processes of government: the democratic tradition of free discussion, Congressional control of major policy, party government, and the continued recognition of the basic rights and status of the individual.

It is useful for this purpose to divide our observations into those relating to the three major administrative aspects of war administration: the development of over-all war policy; the determination of a program adequate to secure victory, once war has been declared; and the execution of the program with maximum effectiveness.

Development of Policy

On the matter of policy toward war, it need be said only that a truly democratic government, with an intelligent well-informed electorate free to express its views is surely the best guarantee against aggressive military action. Certainly no one can read the first part of this volume and fail to be impressed by the reluctance of this nation to think of the possibility of armed conflict. The manner in which Germany and Japan went to war was possible only in governments in which such fundamental decisions were in the hands of a very few individuals who, controlling a propaganda machine, could cloak their decisions in plausibility and could impress their will upon an impotent public.

With war thrust upon us our reaction was to determine a program adequate to bring to a speedy conclusion the complete defeat of those who attacked us. The Government's executive branch established goals measured in such terms as scores of trained divisions, hundreds of ships, thousands of aircraft, thousands of tons of supplies to our Allies, objectives with which the legislative branch concurred and

CHART 60. *Combat Munitions Production of Major Belligerents.*

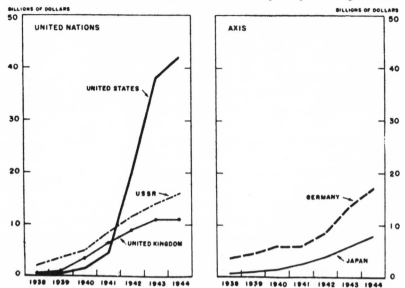

Source: Dr. Raymond W. Goldsmith, "The Power of Victory, Munitions Output in World War II,' *Military Affairs*, Spring, 1946.

to which it gave full support. Military operations were planned by military men, the needed supplies were provided by free men and women working in independent industries guided and coordinated to a common end by a vast system of nonmilitary controls. Though there were times when we seemed to move at a snail's pace, our performance does not suffer from comparison with that of the Axis.

It is now perfectly clear that the Axis countries had not planned adequately beyond their initial aggressive thrusts. Their objectives in beginning wars on either side of the world were limited; the German attacks on Austria, then Czechoslovakia, then Poland were limited, distinct actions, as were those of Japan in her attacks first on Manchuria, then on China. Their decisions to undertake aggressive military actions were arrived at without the careful weighing of possible reprisals or of alternative courses of action that free debate, both within the Government and among a freely speaking public, would certainly have prompted. Had such possibilities been carefully considered, had the decision been for war even after their publics had the opportunity to express their views, it is highly probable that all-out munitions production would have been immediately planned to take care of any eventuality that might arise. German war production in 1939, 1940, and 1941 was surprisingly low as measured not only by later achievements but also as compared with that of her principal opponents, Great Gritain and Russia (chart 61). Japanese production was likewise low. In both countries the limiting factor was not potential but the estimates of the war leaders as to what was required to accomplish the immediate aims. In both countries the planners of war assumed that short, quick military campaigns would accomplish their objectives. They moved in a series of separate thrusts at nations even less prepared than they. No prolonged war against superior resources effectively mobilized was contemplated. The superior economic potentials of the countries attacked were not considered significant factors. Victory was to be won by strategic moves based on accumulated munition stocks, executed with a speed which would throw the democracies completely off balance.

The Czechoslovakian settlement at Munich seemed to confirm Germany's analysis of the decadence, blindness, and inertia of the democracies; the Polish, French, and Norwegian campaigns strengthened her confidence in the blitzkrieg. Germany achieved control of the Western European continent with an expenditure of armaments that only slightly exceeded current production. Her stocks were not significantly depleted.

The failure of England to capitulate after the fall of France forced Hitler to consider invasion. Nazi strategy and possibly her planning and programming also failed for the first time. Though her armament production was fast approaching that of Germany, England was not considered an immediate threat. Hitler turned upon Russia as a more promising victim for his military strategy. The attack began in the confident expectation that the experience of earlier campaigns was to be repeated; Russia was to be completely subjugated in 3 or 4 months.

No plans appear to have been made to cover the possibility that Russia's preparedness had been underestimated. Moreover, the strength that was to destroy Russian resistance was little more than that which had been thrown against France. Application against Russia of the strategy that had been employed against France would have required preparations on a far greater scale since Russian space, war potential, and armed strength was far greater. In the 9 months that elapsed from the time the decision was made to invade Russia to the actual beginning of the campaign, such preparations could probably have been made in large measure. They were not. Instead, the munitions production program was cut back in the fall of 1940. The German leaders were apparently blind to the possibility that the Russian venture would produce anything but another battle of France.

The defeat at Moscow brought Germany to the realization that she was involved in a long war against formidable opposition which

CHART 61. *Gross National Product of the United States, Germany, and Japan.*

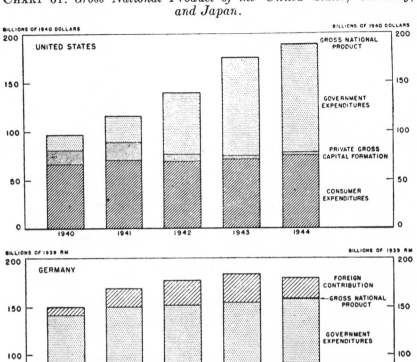

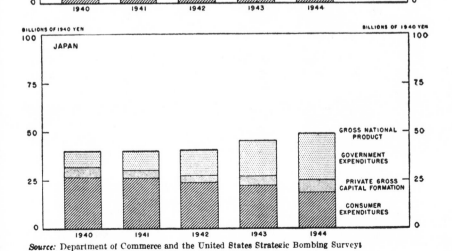

Source: Department of Commerce and the United States Strategic Bombing Survey‡

was gaining time to mobilize its strength. Even so, Germany did not yet take extreme measures to concentrate its strength. Germany prepared a second blitzkrieg. Only after it had burned itself out at Stalingrad did Nazism begin to plan in terms which called for full mobilization.

Japan came to war seeking to extricate herself from entanglements from which she had gained no significant success. Her attempt to secure economic domination of China was frustrated, yet her ruling cliques were politically unable to approve of withdrawal. Japanese expansionists were thus driven to seek a solution to their dilemma in the muddy back waters of the European conflict. Such a solution called for expansion southward which was in any case part of the aims of the more extreme influences in her government. The sharp American reaction to the invasion of Indo-China—the embargoes clamped on capital and certain raw materials—was unexpected. In the ensuing crisis in her domestic political affairs, no compromise could be reached between the various groups who shared political power. As a result, the extremists who considered Germany's victory a certainty came into power determined to secure their share of the spoils. The strategy they envisioned assumed that Britain and Russia would be defeated, that one or two blows could crush American power in the Pacific; that a defense line could then be established which would be held against American attacks. These, it was assumed, would come slowly and in little strength. The Japanese assumed that after such attacks had been repulsed, the United States would be willing to negotiate peace.

The first step in this strategy, the attack on Pearl Harbor, was spectacularly successful. It immobilized the American naval power to a degree that could hardly have been planned upon. The Japanese had won what should have been adequate time to conquer and exploit the southern seas if administrative insight and capacity had been adequate. Conquer she did, probably more than she had originally planned. But once her initial conquests were completed, Japan failed to correctly analyze the problems she faced, found herself unable or unprepared to consolidate her position, to exploit her new resources to the strengthening of her military position, or to ward off attack. She met disaster at Midway but it was the defeat at Guadalcanal in late 1942 that brought to the Japanese a realization of the bankruptcy of their strategy, less than a year after Pearl Harbor.

The parallel between the two aggressor nations continued. Both found themselves in late 1942 and 1943 with the task of recasting their strategy, building new administrative machinery, and beginning a thorough mobilization.

Programming for War

If the popular concept of autocratic governments had been correct we would have expected to find that after such a government had decided upon conquest, it would have laid down a precise program for achieving its objectives, a program that would comprise evaluations of all the requisites for certain success in definite terms, and at something more than minimum levels. We would have expected that adequate governmental machinery would be established or at least provided for to guarantee the required mobilization of the nation's resources to the assumed task.

In the case of the democratic United States, once a definite goal was laid before us in December 1941, the programming of mobilization went forward steadily, and by contrast with Japan and Germany, rapidly. Steps were taken to lay the foundations for the necessary administrative and economic organization. Our program and our organization remained flexible, changing as circumstances demanded. But the story of the preceding chapters is one of movement—sometimes hesitant and uncertain but from the long point of view, definitely, constantly, and successfully—towards fuller and fuller devotion to our military objectives. We did not know how much victory might require; we found it difficult to learn to think in the magnitudes involved, but over the long run as a Nation we were not inclined to underestimate.

Long before they entered the war, both Germany and Japan had developed administrative machinery designed to expand their economic capacity, particularly that which was useful in war. Such machinery was established within the framework of sharply limited objectives as well as available resources. In the case of Germany, it is clear that the organizational and administrative problems of war were underestimated. No thought was given to the possibility that the existing machinery might prove inadequate. As the requirements of the war mounted beyond the ability of the established governmental machinery to handle, it displayed marked inflexibility and resistance to change —the typical marks of senile bureaucracy. The situation in Japan was perhaps even worse. The task of war preparations was thrown upon the existing administrative establishment, only very slightly modified to meet new demands. The Japanese government found it even more difficult to secure the adaptability of administrative arrangements and policies required by war. Both nations entered upon war with the United States with few adjustments in administrative organization. When military reverses forced upon them consideration of tighter mobilization, both were forced to improvisation.

They experienced sharp internecine conflicts from which they suffered damaging delays.

Within a matter of months after Pearl Harbor, a civilian administrative branch of the American Government was charged with the responsibility of coordinating the demands of the military branches, Lend-Lease, and the civilian economy upon the Nation's industrial capacity. Its progress in securing such coordination was slow, hesitant and beset with obstacles. But the problem to be solved had been foreseen and the preliminary steps in developing a program that was to prove adequate had been taken with speed and dispatch. The difficulties and delays that were overcome, and the methods of executing the program and the results attained have been described in preceding chapters.

Prior to February 1942, Germany had no similar organization. Each of the three military branches was independently pressing its claims upon the nation's productive resources; protection of the civilian economy was a function of a fourth agency. The result was overlapping of orders, constant shifting of emphasis from one item to another, leakage of scarce materials into less essential uses, lack of interchangeability of products between the services, an inability to assure the production of most needed commodities first. These were wastes and inefficiencies that could not be tolerated when absolute capacity production became essential to the continued existence of the regime.

To correct such difficulties and to secure maximum volume of output of munitions finally seen as urgently needed, an Armaments Ministry was established early in 1943. Under the direction of Albert Speer, munitions output was substantially increased in 1943 and 1944. Since many segments of German industry were backward in the art of mass production, technical rationalization, such as simplication of design and standardization of products, was the source of much of the increase. Speer's method was that of expediting now one and then another program; now tanks, then aircraft, and at another time, artillery. The total gain was thus concentrated in particular items. No over-all or comprehensive program was ever developed. In fact not until 1944 was aircraft, the largest single segment of the German munitions program, brought under the control of the Armaments Ministry. In consequence, component shortages and imbalance in supplies continually plagued the Nazi war effort.

The failure to prepare military clothing supplies against the possibility of delay in the timetable in Russia in 1940 is well known. Such failures plagued the Nazis throughout the war. Thus, a very large tank program undertaken in 1943 failed of its objective because of the failure to synchronize it with the over-all program and the consequent lack of components. There was persistent confusion as to the relative needs for fighter as compared with bomber aircraft. The lack of programming became clearly evident in the middle of 1944 when substantial resources continued to go into aircraft production despite the rapidly increasing shortage in petroleum fuels. Among other failures in programming were those in ammunition which after the battle of Moscow were in the aggregate very short.

The expansion of armaments production which followed from the efforts of the Armaments Ministry after 1942 were very largely a measure of the previously relatively low level of production of individual industries rather than a measure of the nation's fully mobilized industrial potential. Aside from the lack of foresight and the programming defects, two of the more important causes for the failure of German production to reach higher levels may be cited. Long after it was apparent that steel supplies were short relative to the total need for munitions, the Government failed adequately to allocate this basic material. Until late 1942, steel allocation machinery was very primitive and it never was sufficiently well developed to prevent steel from going into less essential items or to restrict the accumulation of large inventories in the hands of private industrial firms. Of the same nature was the failure of the Nazis efficiently to utilize manpower. Labor and production controls were never integrated in the German war economy. There was at no time a synchronization of the activities of the three principal claimants on the available labor— the military, the munitions industries, and the civilian industries. The indiscriminate drafting of skilled and specialized labor into the armed services was a particularly damaging factor.

In the case of Japan, the measures that had been employed to make Pearl Harbor and the South Pacific conquests possible were relied upon until the end of 1942. During this time there was no expansion in the scale of economic planning and no significant shift in administrative organization. War responsibilities were exercised by the individual ministries of the Government, particularly by the Army and the Navy Ministries. No adequate coordinating function was performed, either within the Cabinet or elsewhere. The execution of production programs was the responsibility of the Industry Control Association which was headed by the executives of the great Japanese monopolies and cartels. The looseness of this orgnization and its inability to direct full efforts to the expanded war needs was recognized in late 1942. Almost a year passed, however, before Japan succeeded in establishing administrative machinery intended to coordinate demands and to secure full mobilization. But the great monopolies retained their positions, the Army and Navy remained to a large degree independent, and no single effective authority controlling the allocation of materials was ever established.

The programming deficiencies were equally, if not even more, striking. The economic life of the home islands of Japan was entirely dependent upon shipping not only for supplies of industrial raw materials but also for a significant portion of the nation's food supplies. Any benefit the expansionists could hope to derive from conquest, especially in strengthening her war potential, depended upon adequate shipping. Control of the seas was the cornerstone of her policies and programs. Even before the war, Japan did not possess under her own flag an adequate merchant fleet. Despite this obvious vulnerability, no adequate shipbuilding program was prepared. Although shipbuilding was on a relatively large scale during the latter thirties, new tonnage in 1941 was lower than in any year since 1935 while in 1942 it was well below 1940. Though the Japanese Navy was utterly dependent upon overseas sources of oil and though the nation was particularly deficient in tankers, there was no tanker-building program prior to 1943.

Other areas of deficient programming may be mentioned, particularly the failure—in what was otherwise an elaborate stockpiling program—to accumulate certain raw materials. It proved necessary in 1944 to reserve rubber for aircraft use while steel alloy metals were in·inadequate supply. The failure of Japan to develop a synthetic oil industry or an aluminum-shale industry was not a deficiency in her programming as much as it was evidence of the fact that she staked everything on her control of overseas resources and that she was unable to provide reserve sources of supply.

These broad illustrations, which can be multiplied in detail, suggest a fundamental generalization: that programming in a democracy such as that of the United States, while it may seem slower and more argumentative, results in a sounder course of action. There was within the Axis countries no effective public check on the soundness of the analysis of the problems that were faced or the programs that were required. The principle of dictatorial or oligarchical rule provided no legitimate opportunity to attain the ultimate advantages that come from a thorough thrashing out of problems. In the United States the resistance of self-interested groups to the sacrifices entailed in war mobilization could be fairly quickly broken down by publicity. There was constant, step-by-step discussion of programs and their execution. In this continuing examination, Congress and the public as well as administrative officials participated. While errors were made, they were neither so numerous nor so long maintained, and hence, not as serious, as the errors made by the Axis Governments.

Execution of the Program

If programming must be balanced, flexible, effective, adequate, and coordinated, execution must be equally so. In an operation as complicated as modern war, the whole business breaks down if an important element in plan, program, or execution fails of proper performance.

No direct comparison between the execution of our mobilization program and that of Germany or Japan is possible. Germany failed to see the necessity of maximum mobilization until early in 1943. When she did undertake to secure all-out production, her plans were inadequate, and bomb damage proved a major handicap in carrying out her program. Like Germany, Japan saw no need for full mobilization until late—until after Gaudalcanal in late 1942. Guadalcanal meant that her outer defensive zone had been penetrated and from that time on our submarine and aircraft attacks on her shipping were so successful as seriously to interfere with her efforts to expand production. It is nevertheless possible to point out some significant Axis shortcomings.

When in late 1942 and early 1943 the Axis countries were forced to a realization of their needs, they programmed sharp increases in production and sought administrative reorganization and economic tightening to attain it. Both countries pushed production upwards to reach peaks in 1944, peaks which were about three times their 1941 rate of output. In the case of the United States, we programmed production to the maximum possible beginning early in 1942. We achieved a fourfold increase in 1942 and reached in 1944 a peak ten times our 1941 level. The significant comparison is not so much the higher level reached by the United States, but the sustained speed with which we moved to it. We could have programmed for even higher levels in succeeding years had there been the need.

There is no support in such data for any argument for the superiority of autocratic methods of programming or executing a war plan. What military superiority the Axis possessed lay in their established semi-mobilized organizations and in their stocks. It was a superiority as limited as those inventories. Their production record clearly reflects the delay in their analysis of their needs; examination of their programming and execution will suggest that they were far from full efficiency in such matters also.

Once a program was established; the task of execution was that of maximizing a balanced flow of military products by efficient utilization of all available capital equipment, manpower, and raw materials. It is important to remember that the relative utilization of resources which obtains in the normal production of civilian-type commodities does not necessarily apply to the production of military necessities. A brief examination of comparative experiences with these factors is of interest.

Germany apparently enjoyed a general abundance of capital facilities, and suffered no stringency in this respect. There were a few notable exceptions to the generally easy situation, particularly in the synthetic oil and chemical industries, which were bottlenecks from the beginning, and the electric power system which was strained throughout most of the war. The German munitions industries generally, however, worked on a single shift throughout the war even after the all-out drive for production began in 1943. This compared with the United States where double- and triple-shift operations of facilities were very common. The German aircraft engine industry worked double shifts though the airframe capacity was sufficiently large to permit one-shift operation.

In the case of manpower, it is of interest to note that women were not mobilized, domestic service was reduced but slightly, and employment in civilian industries was largely maintained until late in the war. In each case the opposite was true in the United States. Hours worked per day were little greater than in this country. German civilian employment actually declined by 3.5 million, the result of withdrawals into the armed forces not sufficiently offset by the introduction of 7 million foreign laborers and prisoners of war.

The German situation was somewhat tighter in the case of raw materials. From their own point of view, steel supplies formed the basis for all war programming and were believed to be the limiting factor in their armament program. The fact was, however, that even in the peak production year of 1944 the steel supply was entirely adequate. This resulted, however, from the lack of a comprehensive over-all production program and also from a loose allocation system and not from an abundance of steel or lack of demand. By way of contrast, steel supply in the United States was always tight. Though large quantities of steel found their way to the civilian economy in Germany, the quantity available to the American civilian economy was throughout the war period at bed-rock minimum figures.

The German situation in other commodities was generally favorable, partly as a result of captured stocks and sources of supply, partly because of excellent execution of her conservation program. Her most vulnerable spot, as has been noted, lay in her supplies of liquid fuels. But her military strategy was adjusted to the available supply and these plans worked well until the debacle at Moscow.

The relatively easy situation of the German economy indicates that the Government failed in its efforts to achieve a balanced maximum mobilization either in plan or in execution. Many factors contributed to this result. Fundamental was the analysis of the needs of the military ventures. The inadequacy of those plans was reflected also in a lack of concern with the necessity of securing all possible production from the economy and this in turn led to an unwillingness of special groups to relinquish advantageous positions to the common good. In consequence of the absence of over-all programming, execution of the German war program followed the method of expediting now one item, then another. The situation was one of constant imbalance and hence of a smaller total then might have proven possible.

The Japanese situation is not easily subjected to evaluation in this manner. The nation had not had before the war any extensive volume of excess or underutilized capacity, and a large volume of new facility construction was undertaken. Yet while facilities in some areas remained inadequate, stocks of scarce materials were wasted expanding industries in which there was already excess capacity. Even after aircraft production was ostensibly unified under the Munitions Ministry in 1943, the controls were ineffective and branches of the Army and Navy continued to requisition materials, tools, and plants from manufacturers to whom they had been assigned. Accounting practices were so poor that control agencies were never able properly to regulate the distribution of materials. Scarce commodities leaked into the black market throughout the war.

Materials were sometimes channeled into low priority industries because the only way to keep peace between the Army and Navy was to give each half of available supplies; real power rested in the hands of committees which seldom agreed to take definite action. The fact that Japan from an early date was forced to resort to conscription to staff her munitions industries indicates that she suffered from a labor shortage which was particularly acute in the case of skilled labor. Here again, the lack of planning was costly and the training program which was undertaken began at too late a date to constitute an important contribution. But it was the narrow raw material base upon which the Japanese economy was built that was the crucial element. Efforts to broaden that base by the development of synthetic processes and the exploitation of low-grade resources were considered but not pushed. The Japanese economy in preparing for war could not afford to develop either the synthetic production of petroleum or the exploitation of low-grade sources of aluminum. In view of this fact, the failure to protect adequately overseas sources of supply, to secure maximum production of such material and maximum movement to the home islands were the key factors in Japanese failure. Perhaps nothing is more illustrative of the Japanese approach to the war than the fact that the manufacture of submarine locating devices was given only a very low production priority in 1941 and 1942; not until 1943 was their importance recognized. The Japanese war production peak in 1944 was attained by severe curtailment of the already low civilian standard of living, by the elimination of virtually all plant maintenance, and was well beyond the level which the raw material base could continue to supply.

One thing that a dictatorial government should be able to do better than a democracy—and this theory stimulated considerable demand in this country for a production or war czar—is to eliminate the pressures from different parts of the Government or the Nation for special advantages for their interests. Here again the theory failed to work. Nazi Germany constantly suffered from internal conflicts. Among these may be mentioned the unwillingness of the German Air Forces to accept an over-all, integrated production program, the conflicts over manpower, and then over production of civilian goods. In Japan the conflict between the Army and Navy over resources, and the failure of these two organizations to share stocks or facilities were serious deterrents to maximum effort. In both countries, the governments were unable to secure the full subservience of business efforts to their war efforts. Both were forced to work through and compromise with the great business cartels. These organizations remained special interest groups, never wholeheartedly devoted to the war effort but always concerned with maintaining relative advantage.

*   *   *   *   *

These comparisons are obviously not complete or conclusive. They cannot be. Even this evidence shows, however, how the organization and leadership of a free people operated in comparison with that of the dictatorships. The record dispels the notion that government in a time of stress is best conducted by autocrats. Our superiority in resources would have been of little significance without a parallel superiority in the ability to organize our efforts for the exploitation of these resources. Administrative personnel brought to the war agencies from business, from the colleges and universities, and from the permanent civil service demonstrated the existence of a reservoir of organizing talent superior to that of the dictatorships.

In the determination of our goals, free discussion occasionally brought delays—even dangerous delays—yet open debate operated to bring error into the open where it could be seen and corrected. The continuation in time of war of the politics of democracy occasionally enabled the advocates of private group advantage to threaten the general good, yet the give-and-take of the democratic process provided ways in which these tensions could be resolved before the war effort was seriously crippled. Our reluctance to establish even the semblance of autocratic rule may have been partly responsible for our constant struggle to coordinate or harmonize a mobilization effort made up of many separately operating parts, but problems of coordination do not disappear even in an autocratic administration and we developed methods that produced effective end results. Finally, freedom of expression and the absence of severe restraints on civil liberties aided mightily in enlisting the energies and loyalties of the people in the creation and supplying of a great war machine.

The record is one in which the American people can take pride. It was not without error, and while it contains much experience in administration that can profitably be studied, it does not contain a finished blueprint for governmental arrangements for future crises. It suggests, primarily, the strength of a free people, able and disposed to adjust their institutions and methods quickly to meet threats to their security.

Appendix I

The War Agencies of the Executive Branch of the Federal Government

[Status as of Dec. 31, 1945]

ADVISORY BOARD ON JUST COMPENSATION (WSA)

Established by Executive Order No. 9387 of October 15, 1943. Reestablished for 60 days by Executive Order No. 9611 of September 10, 1945, and extended by Executive Order No. 9627 of September 24, 1945, to run for 60 days.

ALASKA WAR COUNCIL

Established by Executive Order No. 9181 of June 11, 1942. The Executive Order provides for its continuance as long as title I of the First War Powers Act remains in force.

AMERICAN COMMISSION FOR THE PROTECTION AND SALVAGE OF ARTISTIC AND HISTORIC MONUMENTS IN WAR AREAS

Established June 23, 1943, by the Secretary of State with the President's approval. The 1946 appropriation for this agency requires the completion of its work by the close of the fiscal year 1946.

ANGLO-AMERICAN CARIBBEAN COMMISSION

Established March 2, 1942, by joint action of the United States and Great Britain and supported from State Department funds.

ARMY SPECIALIST CORPS

Established by Executive Order No. 9078 of February 26, 1942. Abolished as separate organization on October 31, 1942, and merged into a central Officer Procurement Service.

BOARD OF ECONOMIC WARFARE

Established as Economic Defense Board by Executive Order No. 8839 of July 30, 1941. Name changed to Board of Economic Warfare by Executive Order No. 8982 of December 17, 1941. Terminated by Executive Order No. 9361 of July 15, 1943, and functions transferred to Office of Economic Warfare.

BOARD OF WAR COMMUNICATIONS

Established as the Defense Communications Board by Executive Order No. 8546 of September 24, 1940. Name changed to Board of War Communications by Executive Order No. 9183 of June 15, 1942.

BRITISH-AMERICAN JOINT PATENT INTERCHANGE COMMITTEE

Established pursuant to article XIII of the Executive Agreement Series 268 (British-American Patent Interchange Agreement) as a result of an interchange of notes between the two governments. The agreement was effective as of January 1, 1942.

CARGOES, INC. (FEA)

Organized October 30, 1941, under Stock Corporation Law of the State of New York, originally named Ships, Inc. Placed under jurisdiction of Office of Lend-Lease Administration, June 17, 1942, and later placed under jurisdiction of Foreign Economic Administration by Executive Order 9380 of September 25, 1943. Has been dissolved.

CENSORSHIP POLICY BOARD

Established by Executive Order No. 8985, of December 19, 1941. Terminated by Executive Order No. 9631 of September 28, 1945.

CENTRAL ADMINISTRATIVE SERVICES (OEM)

Established in Offices for Emergency Management pursuant to a letter of the President dated February 28, 1941. Terminated by Executive Order No. 9471 of August 25, 1944. Functions transferred to various agencies; the residual fiscal functions transferred to Treasury Department for liquidation.

CIVIL AIR PATROL (OCD)

Established in Office of Civilian Defense under authority of Exccutive Order No. 8757, May 20, 1941, as amended by Executive Order No. 9134, April 15, 1942. Transferred to War Department to be administered under direction of the Secretary by Executive Order No. 9339, April 29, 1943.

CIVILIAN PRODUCTION ADMINISTRATION

Established by Executive Order No. 9638 of October 4, 1945, to succeed the War Production Board.

COAL MINES ADMINISTRATION (INTERIOR)

Established July 27, 1943, by Administrative Order No. 1847 issued by the Secretary of the Interior under authority of Executive Order No. 9340 of May 1, 1943. Terminated by Administrative Orders Nos. 1977 and 1982 of the Secretary of the Interior which transferred functions to the Solid Fuels Administration for War effective September 15, 1944.

COLONIAL MICA CORPORATION

Incorporated April 17, 1942, acting as an agent of the Reconstruction Finance Corporation.

COMBINED CHIEFS OF STAFF—UNITED STATES AND GREAT BRITAIN

Established as a result of discussions starting on December 23, 1941, between the Prime Minister of Great Britain and the President of the United States. Organization announced by the War Department on February 6, 1942.

COMBINED FOOD BOARD

Established June 9, 1942, by authority of the President and the Prime Minister of Great Britain. Termination effective June 30, 1946, by joint statement of December 10, 1945, by the President and Prime Minister.

COMBINED PRODUCTION AND RESOURCES BOARD

Established June 9, 1942, by the President and the Prime Minister of Great Britain. Terminated effective December 31, 1945, by a joint statement of December 10, 1945, by the President and the Prime Minister.

COMBINED RAW MATERIALS BOARD

Established January 26, 1942, by the President and the Prime Minister of Great Britain. Terminated effective December 31, 1945, by a joint statement of December 10, 1945, by the President and the Prime Minister.

COMBINED SHIPPING ADJUSTMENT BOARD

Established January 26, 1942, by the President and the Prime Minister of Great Britain. This agency became the United Maritime Authority in August 1944, and extended membership to other maritime countries.

COMMITTEE FOR CONGESTED PRODUCTION AREAS

Established by Executive Order No. 9327 of April 7, 1943. Liquidation provided for by Congress under Act of June 28, 1944 (58 Stat. 535). Termination effective December 31, 1944.

COMMITTEE ON FAIR EMPLOYMENT PRACTICE

Established by Executive Order No. 8802 of June 25, 1941, as amended by Executive Order No. 9346, May 27, 1943.

COMMITTEE ON PHYSICAL FITNESS (FSA)

Established in the Office of Civilian Defense early in 1942 and later transferred to the Office of Defense Health and Welfare Services on April 15, 1942, as authorized by the President on February 26, 1944. This agency was terminated on June 30, 1945, because of failure to receive appropriations beyond that date.

COMMITTEE ON RECORDS OF WAR ADMINISTRATION

Established by the Director of the Bureau of the Budget in March 1942, at the suggestion of the President.

COORDINATOR OF GOVERNMENT FILMS

Established December 18, 1941, by Presidential letter of that date which ordered Director of Office of Government Reports to act as Coordinator of Government Films. Transferred to Office of War Information by Executive Order No. 9182, June 13, 1942.

COORDINATOR OF INFORMATION

Established by Presidential order of July 11, 1941. Functions divided between the Office of Strategic Services and Office of War Information on June 13, 1942, by Military order and Executive Order No. 9182 of same date.

COPPER RECOVERY CORPORATION (RFC—METALS RESERVE)

Incorporated at the request of Metals Reserve Company on April 21, 1942, under the laws of the State of Delaware to act as agent of Metals Reserve Company. This corporation has been liquidated.

DEFENSE COMMUNICATIONS BOARD

Established by Executive Order No. 8546 of September 24, 1940. Name changed to Board of War Communications by Executive Order No. 9183 of June 15, 1942.

DEFENSE HOMES CORPORATION (NHA)

Incorporated pursuant to letter of the President to the Secretary of the Treasury on October 18, 1940. Transferred to the Federal Public Housing Authority by Executive Order No. 9070 of February 24, 1942. This corporation was in liquidation as of the end of 1945.

DEFENSE HOUSING COORDINATOR (NDAC)

Established by the National Defense Advisory Commission July 21, 1940. Transferred to Division of Defense Housing Coordination by Executive Order No. 8632 of January 11, 1941.

DEFENSE PLANT CORPORATION (RFC)

Incorporated August 22, 1940. Dissolved July 1, 1945, by Public Law 109, Seventy-ninth Congress.

DEFENSE RESOURCES COMMITTEE

Established June 15, 1940, by the Secretary of Interior, Administrative Order No. 1497. Replaced by the War Resources Council by Administrative Order No. 1636, January 14, 1942.

DEFENSE SUPPLIES CORPORATION (RFC)

Incorporated August 29, 1940. Dissolved July 1, 1945, by Public Law 109, Seventy-ninth Congress.

DIVISION OF DEFENSE AID REPORTS (OEM)

Established by Executive Order No. 8751 of May 2, 1941. Abolished by Executive Order No. 8926 of October 28, 1941, which created the Office of Lend-Lease Administration.

DIVISION OF DEFENSE HOUSING COORDINATION (OEM)

Established by Executive Order No. 8632 of January 11, 1941. Functions transferred to National Housing Agency by Executive Order No. 9070 of February 24, 1942.

DIVISION OF INFORMATION (OEM)

Established by Presidential letter February 28, 1941. Abolished by Executive Order No. 9182, June 13, 1942, and functions transferred to OWI.

ECONOMIC DEFENSE BOARD

See Board of Economic Warfare

FOOD DISTRIBUTION ADMINISTRATION (AGRICULTURE)

Established by Executive Order No. 9280 of December 5, 1942. Consolidated with other agencies into Administration of Food Production and Distribution by Executive Order No. 9322 of March 26, 1943. Consolidated into War Food Administration by Executive Order No. 9334 of April 19, 1943.

FOOD PRODUCTION ADMINISTRATION (AGRICULTURE)

Established by Executive Order No. 9280 of December 5, 1942. Consolidated with other agencies into Administration of Food Production and Distribution by Executive Order No. 9322 of March 26, 1943. Consolidated into War Food Administration by Executive Order No. 9334 of April 19, 1943.

FOREIGN BROADCAST INTELLIGENCE SERVICE (FCC)

Established February 19, 1941, in the Federal Communications Commission. Public Law 49, Seventy-ninth Congress terminated this activity in the FCC 60 days after the Japanese armistice. The activity was temporarily taken up by the War Department, however, which took over facilities and personnel formerly with FCC.

FOREIGN ECONOMIC ADMINISTRATION (OEM)

Established by Executive Order No. 9380 of September 25, 1943. Executive Order No. 9630 of September 27, 1945, terminated the agency and transferred its functions as follows:

(a) To State Department—the activities relating to lend lease, United Nations relief and rehabilitation, liberated areas supply and procurement, planning for control of occupied territories, and foreign economic and commercial reporting.

(b) To RFC—United States Commercial Company, Rubber Development Corporation, and Petroleum Reserves Corporation.

(c) To Agriculture—the Office of Foreign Food Programs and all other food activities.

(d) To Commerce—all other activities of the agency.

FOREIGN FUNDS CONTROL (TREASURY)·

Established by the Treasury Department, September 22, 1942, to carry out the provisions of Executive Orders Nos. 8389 and 9095.

GOVERNMENT INFORMATION SERVICE (BUDGET)

Established as the Office of Government Reports on July 1, 1939, to perform functions formerly exercised by the National Emergency Council. Its functions were transferred and consolidated into the Office of War Information by Executive Order No. 9182 of June 13, 1942. Subsequently they were transferred under the name, Government Information Service, to the Bureau of the Budget by Executive Order No. 9608, effective August 31, 1945.

INSTITUTE OF INTER-AMERICAN AFFAIRS (OIAA)

See OIAA.

INSTITUTE OF INTER-AMERICAN TRANSPORTATION (OIAA)

See OIAA.

INTER-AMERICAN DEFENSE BOARD

Established in accordance with Resolution XXXXIX of the meeting of the Foreign Ministers at Rio de Janeiro in January 1942. Resolution IV adopted by all American Republics at the Inter-American Conference on Problems of War and Peace, Mexico City, February 1945, states that the Inter-American Defense Board would be continued until the establishment of a permanent body created for the study and solution of problems affecting the western hemisphere.

INTER-AMERICAN EDUCATIONAL FOUNDATION, INC. (OIAA)

See OIAA.

INTER-AMERICAN FINANCIAL AND ECONOMIC ADVISORY COMMITTEE

Established on November 15, 1939.

INTER-AMERICAN NAVIGATION CORPORATION (OIAA)

See OIAA.

INTERDEPARTMENTAL COMMITTEE FOR COORDINATION OF FOREIGN AND DOMESTIC MILITARY PURCHASES

Established by Presidential letter of December 6, 1939. Dissolved by Presidential letter of April 14, 1941, upon establishment of Division of Defense Aid Reports.

INTERDEPARTMENTAL COMMITTEE TO CONSIDER CASES OF SUBVERSIVE ACTIVITIES ON THE PART OF FEDERAL EMPLOYEES

Established February 5, 1943, by Executive Order No. 9300.

INTERDEPARTMENTAL COMMITTEE FOR THE VOLUNTARY PAY-ROLL SAVINGS PLAN FOR THE PURCHASE OF WAR BONDS

Established by Executive Order No. 9135, April 16, 1942.

INTERIM INTERNATIONAL INFORMATION SERVÍCE (STATE)

Established by Executive Order No. 9608 of August 31, 1945. Abolished December 31, 1945, under section 3 (a) of Executive Order No. 9608.

INTERIM RESEARCH AND INTELLIGENCE SERVICE (STATE)

Established by Executive Crder No. 9621 of September 20, 1945. Abolished December 31, 1945, under section 2 of Executive Order No. 9621.

JOINT AIRCRAFT COMMITTEE

Established September 13, 1940, for the purpose of scheduling the delivery of and allocating the capacity for aircraft and aircraft components of all customers: Army, Navy, British, etc. It was dissolved October 1, 1945.

JOINT BRAZIL-UNITED STATES DEFENSE COMMISSION

Established in August 1942.

JOINT CHIEFS OF STAFF

Established December 1941 by instructions from the President.

JOINT CONTRACT TERMINATION BOARD

OWMR established this Board by memorandum on November 12, 1943. It was dissolved and superseded by the Contract Settlement Advisory Board which was established by the Contract Settlement Act of 1944.

JOINT ECONOMIC COMMITTEES—UNITED STATES AND CANADA

Established by the United States and Canada on June 17, 1941, to assist in the collaboration of the two countries in the utilization of their combined resources for the requirements of the war. Dissolved by agreement of the two governments as announced by the State Department on March 14, 1944.

JOINT MEXICAN-UNITED STATES DEFENSE COMMISSION

Established February 27, 1942, by authority of Executive Order No. 9080.

JOINT WAR PRODUCTION COMMITTEE—UNITED STATES AND CANADA

Established on November 5, 1941, as the Joint Defense Production Committee, and the name was later changed to the Joint War Production Committee.

MANAGEMENT LABOR POLICY COMMITTEE (LABOR)

Established by Executive Order No. 9279, December 5, 1942.

MATERIAL COORDINATING COMMITTEE—UNITED STATES AND CANADA

Established on May 14, 1941. Terminated early in 1946.

MEDAL FOR MERIT BOARD

Established by Executive Order No. 9331, April 19, 1943, and reconstituted by Executive Order No. 9637, October 3, 1945.

METALS RESERVE COMPANY (RFC)

Incorporated June 28, 1940. Dissolved July 1, 1945, by Public Law 109, Seventy-ninth Congress.

MUNITIONS ASSIGNMENT BOARD

Established January 26, 1942, by the President and Prime Minister of Great Britain. Terminated by the Combined Chiefs of Staff (CCS 19/3), November 8, 1945, with the approval of the President and the Prime Minister.

NATIONAL DEFENSE ADVISORY COMMISSION

Established on May 29, 1940, by Presidential approval of a regulation of the Council of National Defense pursuant to Section 2 of the Act of August 29, 1916 (39 Stat. 649). The following divisions were established in NDAC. Each division under the cognizance of an Adviser.

(a) Industrial Production Division—transferred to OPM and subsequently to WPB.

(b) Industrial Materials Division—transferred to OPM and subsequently to WPB.

(c) Employment Division—transferred to OPM, then to WPB, and finally to WMC.

(d) Farm Products Division—transferred to Office of Agricultural Defense Relations, later to Office for Agricultural War Relations.

(e) Price Stabilization Division—transferred to Office of Price Administration and Civilian Supply, later OPA.

(f) Transportation Division—transferred to ODT.

(g) Consumer Division—transferred to OPACS, later WPB.

(h) Division of State and Local Cooperation transferred to Office of Civilian Defense when that agency was established.

NATIONAL DEFENSE MEDIATION BOARD

Established by Executive Order No. 8716 of March 19, 1941. Ceased to exist upon creation of National War Labor Board created by Executive Order No. 9017, of January 12, 1942.

NATIONAL HOUSING AGENCY (OEM)

Established by Executive Order No. 9070, February 24, 1942.

NATIONAL INVENTOR'S COUNCIL

Established in August 1940, by the Secretary of Commerce with the concurrence of the President.

NATIONAL MUNITIONS CONTROL BOARD

Established pursuant to the Neutrality Acts of 1935 and 1939 (54 Stat. 10, 11, 12; 22 USC 452).

NATIONAL PATENT PLANNING COMMISSION (COMMERCE)

Established by Executive Order No. 8977, of December 12, 1941.

NATIONAL RAILWAY LABOR PANEL (NATIONAL MEDIATION BOARD)

Established by Executive Order No. 9172, of May 22, 1942.

NATIONAL ROSTER OF SCIENTIFIC AND SPECIALIZED PERSONNEL (LABOR)

Established on June 28, 1940, by a letter of authorization from the President to the National Resources Planning Board. Organizationally and administratively the Roster was at that time made a part of the United States Civil Service Commission by cooperative agreement between the Commission and the National Resources Planning Board. By Executive Order No. 9139, dated April 18, 1942, the Roster and its functions were transferred to the War Manpower Commission and by Executive Order No. 9617, September 19, 1945, transferred to the Department of Labor where it now operates as a Division of the United States Employment Service.

NATIONAL WAGE STABILIZATION BOARD (LABOR)

Established by Executive Order No. 9672, of December 31, 1945, to continue wage stabilization functions of the National War Labor Board.

NATIONAL WAR LABOR BOARD

Established by Executive Order No. 9017, of January 12, 1942. Abolished by Executive Order No. 9672, December 31, 1945, which established the National Wage Stabilization Board.

OFFICE FOR AGRICULTURAL WAR RELATIONS

See Office of Agricultural Defense Relations below.

OFFICE FOR COORDINATION OF NATIONAL DEFENSE PURCHASES (NDAC)

Established by order of Council of National Defense, June 27, 1940. Terminated January 7, 1941.

OFFICE FOR EMERGENCY MANAGEMENT

Established on May 25, 1940, by administrative order of the President, pursuant to Executive Order No. 8248, dated September 8, 1939.

OFFICE OF AGRICULTURAL DEFENSE RELATIONS

Established May 17, 1941, by Secretary of Agriculture Memorandum No. 905, issued pursuant to a letter from the President to the Secretary of Agriculture dated May 5, 1941. The name was changed to Office of Agriculture War Relations, it being thus referred to in the First Supplemental National Defense Act, 1943, approved July 25, 1942. The OAWR was abolished by consolidation into the Food Distribution Administration pursuant to Executive Order No. 9280, dated December 5, 1942.

OFFICE OF ALIEN PROPERTY CUSTODIAN (OEM)

Established by Executive Order No. 9095 of March 11, 1942.

OFFICE OF ARMY-NAVY LIQUIDATON COMMISSIONER

Established pursuant to War Department Memorandum No. 850–45, dated January 27, 1945, and the letter of the Secretary of the Navy, dated February 1, 1945. It was abolished by Executive Order No. 9630, September 27, 1945, and its remaining functions were transferred to the Department of State.

OFFICE OF CENSORSHIP

Established by Executive Order No. 8985, of December 19, 1941. Terminated by Executive Order No. 9631, of September 28, 1945, effective November 15, 1945.

OFFICE OF CIVILIAN DEFENSE (OEM)

Established by Executive Order No. 8757, of May 20, 1941. Terminated by Executive Order No. 9562, of June 4, 1945.

OFFICE OF COMMUNITY WAR SERVICES (FSA)

Established by Executive Order No. 9338, of April 29, 1943.

OFFICE OF CONTRACT SETTLEMENT (OWMR)

Established by the Contract Settlement Act of 1944.

OFFICE OF COORDINATOR OF INTER-AMERICAN AFFAIRS (OEM)

Originally established on August 16, 1940, by NDAC as the Office of Coordination of Commercial and Cultural Relations between the American Republics. This Office was transferred to the Office of the Coordinator of Inter-American Affairs when it was established by Executive Order No. 8840 of July 30, 1941. Name changed to Office of Inter-American Affairs by Executive Order No. 9532, March 23, 1945.

OFFICE OF DEFENSE HEALTH AND WELFARE SERVICE

Established by Executive Order No. 8890, of September 3, 1941. Abolished by Executive Order No. 9338, of April 23, 1943. Functions transferred to Office of Community War Services.

OFFICE OF DEFENSE TRANSPORTATION (OEM)

Established by Executive Order No. 8989, of December 18, 1941.

OFFICE OF ECONOMIC STABILIZATION

Established by Executive Order No. 9250, of October 3, 1942. Abolished by Executive Order No. 9620, of September 20, 1945; the functions were transferred to the Office of Stabilization Administration of the Office of War Mobilization and Reconversion.

OFFICE OF ECONOMIC WARFARE (OEM)

Established by Executive Order No. 9361, of July 15, 1943. Consolidated with Foreign Economic Administration by Executive Order No. 9380, of September 25, 1943.

OFFICE OF EXPORT CONTROL

Established July 2, 1940, by Presidential Proclamation No. 2413 pursuant to Public Law 703, Seventy-sixth Congress. Executive Order No. 8900, September 15, 1941, transferred functions to the Economic Defense Board.

OFFICE OF FACTS AND FIGURES

Established by Executive Order No. 8922, of October 24, 1941. Transferred and consolidated into Office of War Information by Executive Order No. 9182, of June 13, 1942.

OFFICE OF FISHERY COORDINATION (INTERIOR)

Established by Executive Order No. 9204, of July 21, 1942. Terminated by Executive Order No. 9649, of October 29, 1945.

OFFICE OF GOVERNMENT REPORTS

See Government Information Service

OFFICE OF INTER-AMERICAN AFFAIRS

Established by Executive Order No. 9532, of March 23, 1945. Some functions were transferred to State by Executive Order No. 9608, August 31, 1945.

OFFICE OF LEND-LEASE ADMINISTRATION (OEM)

Established by Executive Order No. 8926 of October 28, 1941, Consolidated into Foreign Economic Administration by Executive Order No. 9380, of September 25, 1943.

OFFICE OF MERCHANT SHIP CONTROL (COAST GUARD)

Established on June 28, 1940, by regulations issued by the Secretary of the Treasury to carry out the provisions of a Presidential proclamation, dated June 27, 1940. The Office was abolished on January 20, 1942, by order of the Commandant of the Coast Guard.

OFFICE OF PETROLEUM COORDINATOR FOR NATIONAL DEFENSE

Established by Presidential letter of May 28, 1941. Terminated on the establishment of the Petroleum Administration for War.

OFFICE OF PRICE ADMINISTRATION

Established as Office of Price Administration and Civilian Supply (OEM) by Executive Order No. 8734, April 11, 1941. Name and functions changed to Office of Price Administration by Executive Order No. 8875, August 28, 1941. The Emergency Price Control Act of 1942, January 30, 1942, established OPA as an independent agency.

OFFICE OF PRICE ADMINISTRATION AND CIVILIAN SUPPLY (OEM)

Established by Executive Order No. 8734, of April 11, 1941. Name changed to Office of Price Administration by Executive Order No. 8875, August 28, 1941. Civilian Supply functions were transferred to OPM.

OFFICE OF PRODUCTION MANAGEMENT (OEM)

Established by Executive Order No. 8629 of January 7, 1941. Abolished by Executive Order No. 9040 of January 24, 1942. Functions, personnel, etc. transferred to War Production Board.

OFFICE OF PRODUCTION RESEARCH AND DEVELOPMENT (WPB)

Established as a constitutent agency of WPB by its General Administrative Order, 2–66, effective November 23, 1942.

OFFICE OF SCIENTIFIC RESEARCH AND DEVELOPMENT (OEM)

Established by Executive Order No. 8807, of June 28, 1941.

OFFICE OF SOLID FUELS COORDINATOR FOR NATIONAL DEFENSE

Established by Presidential letter November 5, 1941. Terminated on establishment of SFAW.

OFFICE OF STABILIZATION ADMINISTRATION (OWMR)

Established pursuant to Executive Order No. 9620, dated September 20, 1945, which terminated the Office of Economic Stabilization created by Executive Order 9250. October 3, 1942.

OFFICE OF STRATEGIC SERVICES

Established by Military Order of June 13, 1942. Terminated by Executive Order No. 9621, effective October 1, 1945. Functions divided between State and War Departments. State created the position of Special Assistant to the Secretary of State, the Office of Research and Intelligence, and the Office of Intelligence Collection and Dissemination which on December 31 took over those parts of the former OSS program that are to be included in the permanent intelligence program. Similarly, War created the Strategic Services Unit in the Office of the Assistant Secretary of War.

OFFICE OF SURPLUS PROPERTY (COMMERCE)

Established on October 16, 1942, in the Procurement Division of the Treasury Department as the Federal Property Utilization Branch. On August 11, 1944, name changed to Office of Surplus Property. Transferred to Department of Commerce effective May 1, 1945, by Executive Order No. 9541, of April 19, 1945. Transferred to Reconstruction Finance Corporation by Executive Order No. 9643, effective November 5, 1945.

OFFICE OF WAR INFORMATION (OEM)

Established by Executive Order No. 9182, of June 13, 1942. Its liquidation was provided for by Executive Order No. 9608, August 31, 1945, which transferred the foreign information functions to State Department and certain domestic functions to the Bureau of the Budget. The State Department created the Office of International Information and Cultural Affairs, which on December 31 took over those OWI and OIAA informational activities that are to be included in the permanent foreign informational program.

OFFICE OF WAR MOBILIZATION

Established by Executive Order No. 9347, of May 27, 1943. Functions, personnel, funds, and property transferred to Office of War Mobilization and Reconversion (which was established by Congress under Act of October 3, 1944, 58 Stat. 785) by Executive Order No. 9488, of October 3, 1944.

OFFICE OF WAR MOBILIZATION AND RECONVERSION

Established by the War Mobilization Act of 1944 (50 USC A 1651).

PACIFIC WAR COUNCIL

Established March 30, 1942, by Presidential action. The records of this Council were disposed of in September 1945.

PETROLEUM ADMINISTRATION FOR WAR

Established by Executive Order No. 9276, of December 2, 1942.

PETROLEUM RESERVES CORPORATION (RFC)

Established on June 30, 1943, by RFC. Successively transferred to Office of Economic Warfare, Foreign Economic Administration, and finally to RFC again. Renamed War Assets Corporation effective November 15, 1945.

PRENCINRADIO, INC. (OIAA)

See OIAA.

PRESIDENT'S COMMITTEE ON DEFERMENT OF FEDERAL EMPLOYEES

Established by Executive Order No. 9309, of March 6, 1943. Public Law 23, 78th Congress, provided that no deferment should be granted employees of the Executive Branch of the Federal Government unless they be in accordance with this Executive Order.

PRESIDENT'S COMMITTEE ON WAR RELIEF AGENCIES

See President's War Relief Control Board.

PRESIDENT'S SOVIET PROTOCOL COMMITTEE

Established by the President on October 30, 1942, by a memorandum to the heads of agencies concerned. Terminated on October 1, 1945.

PRESIDENT'S WAR RELIEF CONTROL BOARD

Established by Executive Order No. 9205, of July 25, 1942, taking over the functions of the President's Committee on War Relief Agencies.

PRIORITIES BOARD (NDAC)

Established by order of the Council of National Defense, October 18, 1940. Terminated January 7, 1941.

PUBLICATIONS BOARD (OWMR)

Established in OWMR by Executive Order No. 9568, of June 8, 1945.

RECONSTRUCTION FINANCE CORPORATION

Defense Plant Corporation.
Defense Supplies Corporation.
Metals Reserve Company.
Rubber Reserve Company.

Public Law 109, Seventy-ninth Congress, dissolved these four subsidiary corporations of RFC on July 1, 1945. The liquidation of the affairs of these corporations will be continued by the RFC through the agency of the Offices of Defense Plants, Defense Supplies, Metals Reserve, and Rubber Reserve.

RETRAINING AND REEMPLOYMENT ADMINISTRATION (LABOR)

An agency known as the Retraining and Reemployment Administration was established by Executive Order No. 9427, dated February 24, 1944, in the Office of War Mobilization. All records, property, funds, and personnel of this agency were transferred to the Retraining and Reemployment Administration established by the War Mobilization and Reconversion Act of 1944 by Executive Order No. 9488, October 3, 1944. The agency was transferred to the Department of Labor by Executive Order No. 9617, September 19, 1945.

RUBBER DEVELOPMENT CORPORATION

Chartered November 1940, and commenced operations February 23, 1943.

RUBBER RESERVE COMPANY (RFC)

Incorporated June 28, 1940. Dissolved July 1, 1945, by Public Law 109, Seventy-ninth Congress.

SALARY STABILIZATION UNIT (TREASURY)

Established in the Bureau of Internal Revenue by Treasury Decision 5167, October 29, 1942, to administer the provisions of regulations prescribed by the Economic Stabilization Director.

SELECTIVE SERVICE SYSTEM

Established pursuant to the Selective Training and Service Act of 1940. Originally a separate agency, it was placed under the War Manpower Commission by Executive Order No. 9279, of December 5, 1942, as the Bureau of Selective Service. Reestablished as a separate agency by Executive Order No. 9410, December 23, 1942.

SHIPS, INC.

See Cargoes, Inc.

SHIPBUILDING STABILIZATION COMMITTEE (LABOR)

A constituent agency of the War Production Board which was transferred from its successor agency, Civilian Production Administration, to the Department of Labor by Executive Order No. 9656 of November 15, 1945.

SMALLER WAR PLANTS CORPORATION

Established by Act of Congress June 11, 1942 (56 Stat. 353; 50 USC 1104). The functions of the Smaller War Plants Corporation were divided between the Department of Commerce and the Reconstruction Finance Corporation by Executive Order No. 9665, December 27, 1945. The legislation authorizing this corporation provides that the corporation shall not have succession beyond December 31, 1946.

SOLID FUELS ADMINISTRATION FOR WAR (INTERIOR)

Established by Executive Order No. 9332 of April 19, 1943.

SOUTHWESTERN POWER ADMINISTRATION (INTERIOR)

Established by order of the Secretary of the Interior on September 1, 1943, to implement Executive Order No. 9366, July 30, 1943, and Executive Order No. 9373, August 30, 1943.

STEEL RECOVERY CORPORATION (RFC—METALS RESERVE)

Incorporated at the request of Metals Reserve Company on July 18, 1942, under the laws of the State of Delaware for the purpose of acting as agent of Metals Reserve Company. This corporation has been liquidated.

SUPPLY PRIORITIES AND ALLOCATIONS BOARD (OEM)

Established by Executive Order No. 8875 of August 28, 1941. Abolished by Executive Order No. 9024 of January 16, 1942, and functions transferred to the WPB.

SURPLUS PROPERTY ADMINISTRATION (OWMR)

Established by Public Law 181, Seventy-ninth Congress, September 18 1945, which abolished the Surplus Property Board.

SURPLUS PROPERTY BOARD (OWMR)

Established by Surplus Property Act of 1944, approved October 3, 1944 (58 Stat. 768). Terminated by Public Law 181, Seventy-ninth Congress, September 18, 1945 (59 Stat. 533) and all functions transferred to Surplus Property Administration.

SURPLUS WAR PROPERTY ADMINISTRATION (OWM)

Established by Executive Order No. 9425 of February 19, 1944. Functions, property, and personnel transferred to Surplus Property Board by Executive Order No. 9488 of October 3, 1944.

UNITED STATES COMMERCIAL COMPANY (RFC)

Incorporated March 26, 1942, by the RFC. Transferred to OEW by Executive Order No. 9361, July 15, 1943, and subsequently to FEA by Executive Order No. 9380, September 25, 1943. Returned to RFC by Executive Order No. 9630, September 27, 1945.

UNITED STATES EMERGENCY COURT OF APPEALS

Established by the Emergency Price Control Act of 1944, with jurisdiction over actions arising as the results of the administration of the Price Control Act of 1942, as amended.

UNITED STATES OF AMERICA TYPHUS COMMISSION

Established by Executive Order No. 9285 of December 24, 1942.

WAGE ADJUSTMENT BOARD FOR THE CONSTRUCTION INDUSTRY (LABOR)

Established by the Labor Department on May 29, 1942, by direction of the President.

WAR ASSETS CORPORATION (RFC)

Incorporated originally as the Petroleum Reserves Corporation by RFC on June 30, 1943. The name of the corporation was changed to War Assets Corporation on November 9, 1945, effective November 15, 1945.

WAR BALLOTS COMMISSION

Established by Public Law 277, Seventy-eighth Congress (58 Stat. 140) on April 1, 1944, to serve for the duration of the war and six months thereafter.

WAR CONTRACTS PRICE ADJUSTMENT BOARD.

Established by the Renegotiation Act of 1943 (58 Stat. 85; 50 USC 1191).

WAR DAMAGE CORPORATION (RFC)

Established December 13, 1941, by RFC Charter.

WAR EMERGENCY PIPE LINES, INC. (RFC)

Incorporated September 8, 1941, to act as the agency of the Defense Plant Corporation in the construction industry and as agent of the Defense Supplies Corporation in the operation. of pipe lines.

WAR FOOD ADMINISTRATION (AGRICULTURE)

Established by Executive Order No. 9334 of April 19, 1943. Terminated by Executive Order No. 9577 of June 29, 1945, and function transferred to Department of Agriculture.

WAR FORWARDING CORPORATION (WSA)

Incorporated by War Shipping Administration to assist in forwarding and classifying Lend-Lease shipments.

WAR HEMP INDUSTRIES, INC. (AGRICULTURE)

Chartered on February 1, 1943, and now in the process of liquidation.

WAR INSURANCE CORPORATION (RFC)

Name later changed to War Damage Corporation, q. v.

WAR MANPOWER COMMISSION (OEM)

Established by Executive Order No. 9139 of April 18, 1942. Terminated by Executive Order No. 9617 of September 19, 1945, and functions transferred to Department of Labor.

WAR MATERIALS, INC. (RFC)

Incorporated at the request of Metals Reserve Company on August 24, 1942, under the laws of the State of Delaware, for the purpose of acting as agent of Metals Reserve Company. This corporation is in liquidation.

WAR PRODUCTION BOARD (OEM)

Established by Executive Order No. 9024 of January 16, 1942. Terminated by Executive Order No. 9638, October 4, 1945, and functions transferred to Civilian Production Administration. Important constituent agencies included:

Aircraft Production Board
Aircraft Resources Control Office
Office of Civilian Supply
Office of Production Research and Development
Office of Rubber Director
Office of War Utilities
Procurement Policy Board
Production Executive Committee
Requirements Committee
Resources Protection Board

WAR REFUGEE BOARD

Established by Executive Order No. 9417 of January 22, 1944. Terminated by Executive Order No. 9614 of September 14, 1945.

WAR RELOCATION AUTHORITY (INTERIOR)

Established by Executive Order No. 9102 of March 18, 1942. Transferred to the Department of Interior by Executive Order No. 9423 of February 16, 1944.

WAR RESOURCES BOARD (ANMB)

Established August 1939, as a Civilian Advisory Board to ANMB. Dissolved by the President November 24, 1939.

WAR RESOURCES COUNCIL (INTERIOR)

Established by Interior Departmental Order 1636, January 14, 1942, supplemented by Departmental Order 1652, February 23, 1942, and 1687, May 1, 1942. Abolished by Departmental Order 2148, December 20, 1945.

WAR SHIPPING ADMINISTRATION (OEM)

Established by Executive Order No. 9054 of February 7, 1942.

Appendix II

List of Charts

Appendix III

List of Abbreviations

AAA	Agricultural Adjustment Agency.
ANMB	Joint Army and Navy Munitions Board.
APUC	Area Production Urgency Committee.
ASF	Army Service Forces
BEW	Board of Economic Warfare.
CCC	Commodity Credit Corporation.
CIAA	Coordinator of Inter-American Affairs.
CIO	Congress of Industrial Organization.
CMP	Controlled Materials Plan.
COI	Coordinator of Information.
CPA	Civilian Production Administration.
CSP	Controlled Scheduling Plan.
EDB	Economic Defense Board.
EPCA	Emergency Price Control Act.
FDA	Food Distribution Administration.
FEA	Foreign Economic Administration.
FEPC	Committee on Fair Employment Practice.
FPA	Food Production Administration.
FSA	Federal Security Agency.
GMPR	General Maximum Price Regulation.
ICC	Interstate Commerce Commission.
IMP	Industrial Mobilization Plan.
JCS˙	Joint Chiefs of Staff.
NDAC	National Defense Advisory Commission.
NDMB	National Defense Mediation Board.
NHA	National Housing Agency.
NWLB	National War Labor Board.
OADR	Office of Agricultural Defense Relations.
OCD	Office of Civilian Defense.
ODT	Office of Defense Transportation.
OEM	Office for Emergency Management.
OES	Office of Economic Stabilization.
OFEC	Office of Foreign Economic Coordination.
OFF	Office of Facts and Figures.
OFRRO	Office of Foreign Relief and Rehabilitation Operations.
OGR	Office of Government Reports.
OLLA	Office of Lend-Lease Administration.
OPA	Office of Price Administration.
OPACS	Office of Price Administration and Civilian Supply.
OPC	Office of Petroleum Coordinator for National Defense (War).
OPM	Office for Production Management.
ORD	Office of Rubber Director.
OWI	Office of War Information.
OWM	Office of War Mobilization.
OWMR	Office of War Mobilization and Reconversion.

PAW   Petroleum Administrator for War.
PRP   Production Requirements Plan.
PUC   Production Urgency Committee.
RFC   Reconstruction Finance Corporation.
SOS   Services of Supply.
SPAB   Supply Priorities and Allocation Board.
SWPA   Surplus War Property Administration.
SWPC   Smaller War Plants Corporation.
UNRRA   United Nations Relief and Rehabilitation Administration
USCC   United States Commercial Company (RFC).
USES   United States Employment Service.
WLB   War Labor Board.
WMC   War Manpower Commission.
WSA   War Shipping Administration.

Index